RUSSIA IN THE AGE OF REACTION AND REFORM
1801–1881

LONGMAN HISTORY OF RUSSIA
General Editor: Harold Shukman

Kievan Russia 850–1240
Simon Franklin and Jonathan Shepard

*The Crisis of Medieval Russia
1200–1304
John Fennell

*The Formation of Muscovy
1304–1613
Robert O. Crummey

*The Making of Russian Absolutism 1613–1801
(Second Edition)
Paul Dukes

*Russia in the Age of Reaction and Reform
1801–1881
David Saunders

*Russia in the Age of Modernisation
and Revolution 1881–1917
Hans Rogger

The Russian Revolution 1917
Steve Smith

*The Soviet Union since 1917
Martin McCauley

*already published

LONGMAN HISTORY OF RUSSIA

Russia in the Age of Reaction and Reform 1801–1881

DAVID SAUNDERS

LONGMAN
London and New York

Longman Group UK Limited
Longman House, Burnt Mill,
Harlow, Essex CM20 2JE, England
and Associated Companies throughout the world.

*Published in the United States of America
by Longman Publishing, New York*

© Longman Group UK Limited 1992

First published 1992

ISBN 0 582 48977 6 CSD
ISBN 0 582 48978 4 PPR

British Library Cataloguing-in-Publication Data

A catalogue record for this book is
available from the British Library

Library of Congress Cataloging in Publication Data

Saunders, David, 1951–
Russia in the age of reaction and reform 1801–1881 / David Saunders
    p.   cm. -- (Longman history of Russia)
Includes bibliographical references and index.
ISBN 0-582-48977-6 (csd). -- ISBN 0-582-48978-4 (ppr)
1. Soviet Union--History--Alexander I, 1801–1825. 2. Soviet
Union--History--Nicholas I, 1825–1855. 3. Soviet Union--History-
-Alexander II, 1855–1881. I. Title. II. Series.
    DK191.S27 1993   92-7477
        947'.07--dc20   CIP

Set 7A in Garamond 10/13
Produced by Longman Singapore Publishers (Pte) Ltd.
Printed in Singapore

Contents

CONTENTS

List of abbreviations

LIST OF ABBREVIATIONS

SS	*Soviet Studies*
TRHS	*Transactions of the Royal Historical Society*
VI	*Voprosy istorii*
VPR	*Vneshniaia politika Rossii XIX i nachala XX veka: Dokumenty rossiiskogo ministerstva inostrannykh del,* ed. A. L. Narochnitskii et al. (Moscow, 1960–)

List of tables and maps

Preface

The Russian Empire in the nineteenth century was a land of extremes – extreme poverty and extreme wealth, extreme ignorance and extreme sophistication, extreme size and extreme parochialism, extreme arrogance and extreme deference, extreme administrative uniformity and extreme cultural diversity, extreme might and extreme frailty. The extremes were too great to be reconciled. The last sentence of this book accuses populist revolutionaries of making compromise impossible, but the book as a whole spends most of its time trying to explain why compromise was difficult. The reasons included the personal failings of tsars; the regime's unjustifiable emphasis on maintaining its international standing; the reluctance of nobles to accept the loss of control over the countryside or the transformation of their sources of income; the consolidation of a bureaucracy which thought it knew better than the people for whom it was responsible; the desire to educate people without permitting the educated to express their views; the obsession of the educated with the values and material achievements of western Europe; the multiplicity of non-Russian cultures; and above all, the lack of resources to support innovation. Faced with these sources of combustion, tsars often gave the impression that strong-arm tactics were the only way forward. The terrorists of the late 1870s appeared to agree. Subsequent developments revealed that violence solved nothing, but it is still unclear whether Russians can accept the notion that politics is the art of the possible. In a part of the world where absolutes have attracted so many for so long, the temptation to run before walking remains powerful.

If it had been less of a mouthful I would have added a word to the title: not 'Russia in the Age of Reaction and Reform', but 'Russia in the Age of *Reform*, Reaction and Reform'. The unwieldy longer title would have emphasized my view that the keynote of the years 1801–1881 is swings of the pendulum. Perhaps the absence of a linear theme ('the making of Russian absolutism', for example, or 'modernization and revolution') explains why the first eighty years of the nineteenth century have been less attractive to historians than earlier and later periods of Russian history. There may, however, be other reasons. In the Soviet Union, scholars were permanently discouraged from considering whether the Romanovs ever had with practical ideas for solving their problems. Western scholars, meanwhile, have often had difficulty categorizing nineteenth-century Russia because it was out of step with the rest of the European continent. The Romanovs of the period 1801–1881 were still trying to answer a question which other European rulers had stopped asking themselves after the coming of the French Revolution. 'Can an absolute ruler promote enlightenment without reaping the whirlwind?' In central and western Europe kings and bureaucrats knew that the answer was 'No'. They responded to their knowledge by becoming die-hards or accepting that change was inevitable. In Russia, tsars havered. The key point is their indecision. It is not true to say that some of them were reformers and some of them reactionaries. All of them doubted. The doubts gave rise to 'stop-go' policies which create the impression of reform, reaction and reform. Whether the cycle should be seen as an ascending or a descending spiral depends on the view one takes of the 1917 revolutions, but 1917, I am pleased to say, is not my subject.

My greatest debt in writing this book has been to the dedicatees, but I am also extremely grateful to the following: Tony and Ruth Badger (for friendship), Professor J. L. Black (for assistance with Karamzin), Mark Evans and Michael Holmes (for getting the show on the road), John Gooding (for assistance with Speranskii), Julian Graffy (for kindnesses too many and various to relate), John Klier (for sending me his work on Russian Jews), Andrew MacLennan of Longman (for enthusiasm, patience and extremely constructive criticism), David Moon (for insisting on the intelligence of Russian peasants), Professor Marc Raeff (for reading and commenting on four chapters at a rate I found inconceivable), Patrick Salmon (for guidance in respect of international relations and reminders that the Baltic provinces of the empire were a place apart), Harold Shukman (for knowing how to temper the wind to the shorn lamb), the Small Grants Committee of the University of Newcastle upon Tyne (for money), Vladimir Somov (for proof that moderate intellectuals may occasionally be found in St Petersburg), the Study Group on Eighteenth-Century Russia (for allowing me to read a number of papers), Evgeniia Taratuta (for drawing my attention to the work of N. V. Minaeva) and Julian Walker (for hospitality). None of these bears any responsibility for my mistakes.

Except in respect of tsars, one or two other well-known individuals and a few geographical phenomena, I have transliterated Russian proper names and references to Russian sources in accordance with the system employed by the Library of Congress. Owing to the difference between the Julian and Gregorian calendars, dates in the nineteenth-century Russian Empire were twelve days behind dates in the west. I give Russian dates throughout, but add the western date in sections which deal with international relations.

DAVID SAUNDERS
March 1992

To my mother and father

CHAPTER ONE

The Enigmatic Tsar, his Friends and his Inheritance

WERE RUSSIA'S RULERS THEIR OWN WORST ENEMIES?

'Every state or civil society', wrote the Slavophile Aleksei Khomiakov towards the middle of the nineteenth century, 'is made up of two elements: the living historical element, which embodies all the society's vitality, and the rational or speculative element, which can achieve nothing by itself, but gradually imparts order to the fundamental or living element, sometimes pushing it aside and sometimes developing it'.[1] Not many Russian tsars would have understood abstractions of this kind, but even the intellectuals among them would have rejected the idea that the 'rational or speculative' part of Russian society – the government, the bureaucracy, the educated section of the community – could 'achieve nothing by itself'. Some tsars believed that they could radically transform their realm. Some were so far divorced from reality that they expected to reproduce in the Russian Empire the administrative successes of the countries which served them as models. Others sensed the near-impossibility of solving the problems which confronted them, but felt they must act dramatically if they were to make any progress at all. Others again, disdaining the idea of improvement, attempted to stop Russian society in its tracks. None could resign himself to the thought that life went on more or less irrespective of the government's decrees. None was prepared to have it said of him, as Sir Lewis Namier said of Metternich, that 'He annotated the margins of the great book of human insufficiency and inertia'.[2] None could have accepted with equanimity Sir Donald Mackenzie Wallace's observation, made after six years in Russia in the 1870s, that 'In spite of the systematic and persistent efforts of the centralised bureaucracy to regulate minutely all the departments of national life, the rural Communes, which contain about five-sixths of the population, remain in many respects entirely beyond its influence, and even beyond its sphere of vision'.[3] Because even the most conservative tsars took a highly interventionist view of their responsibilities, the country seemed to be constantly in the throes of 'reaction' or 'reform'. The tsars' temperamental and ideological differences only height-

1

ened the impact of their interventionism. The number of their edicts, most of which sank like stones, kept the surface of society in constant motion. In the quest for the philosopher's stone which would enable them to grasp and clear up the problems which faced them, the Russian Empire's rulers tried solution after solution, launching themselves into new projects, trying to batten down the hatches, raising and dashing expectations – and turning, usually, into muddled obscurantists. The description 'Russia in the Age of Reaction and Reform' could be applied not just to the years between 1801 and 1881, but to almost any eighty-year period of tsarist history.

Yet the greatest of Russia's historians, Vasilii Kliuchevskii, thought that the disjointed character of the Russian government's nineteenth-century performance was sufficiently pronounced to be worthy of special note. In a mordant diary entry written on the day after Nicholas II promulgated the Fundamental State Laws of 1906 – yet another governmental change of tack – he deplored the authorities' lack of constancy in the preceding hundred years and ascribed their volatility to malice aforethought. In doing so he composed an indictment of Russia's nineteenth-century rulers which is all the more striking for having come from the pen of a moderate. 'In the entire course of the nineteenth century,' Kliuchevskii wrote,

from the accession to the throne of Alexander I in 1801, the Russian government engaged in purely provocative activity: it would give society just as much freedom as was necessary to evoke in it a first response, and then collar and punish the simpletons who responded incautiously. Under Alexander I the policy worked like this: by virtue of his constitutional projects Speranskii became an involuntary provocateur, bringing the Decembrists out into the open and then having the misfortune, as a member of the investigative commission, to weep at the interrogation of his cornered political disciples. Under Emperor Nicholas I governmental provocation shifted its ground. If the period of the brazen Arakcheev (which had succeeded that of the bashful, conscientious Speranskii) had been dedicated to turning a plot into an armed rebellion, Nicholas I tried, by treacherously facilitating the activities of Benckendorff, to convert social discontent into plotting. The successful consequences of experimenting with this stratagem, manifested in the case of the Poles, long paralysed the strength of Russia's conspirators, fragmenting them into powerless circles, and the Petrashevskii affair starkly illuminated their powerlessness. Malcontents remained – Herzen, Granovskii, Belinskii – but they posed no threat, and the shameful reign of Emperor Nicholas I was successfully brought to a close by the Sevastopol' defeat and the Peace of Paris. It was the government of Emperor Alexander II which really fostered conspiracy in Russia. All its great reforms, unforgivably delayed, were nobly conceived, speedily elaborated, and dishonestly executed (apart from the judicial and military reforms). The monarch disposed wisely, the coadjutors whom he summoned (Samarin, the Miliutin brothers) self-denyingly drew up plans, but ministers of the camarilla (Lanskoi, Tolstoi, Valuev, Timashev) employed circulars to turn plans which had been approved on high into a mockery of the people's expectations. The tsar-reformer was threatened with playing the part of autocratic provocateur: Alexander II was going the same way as the first Alexander. With one hand he was granting reforms which excited the highest expectations in society, but with the other he was promoting and supporting agents who were dashing them. Not satisfied with tracking down illegal behaviour, and sensing a groundswell of discontent, the police sought to read men's hearts and minds by using denunciations and official searches. By enforcing retirements, by arrests and despatch into exile, they punished the schemes and designs which were afoot and transformed themselves imperceptibly from guardians of public order into an organized governmental conspiracy against society. Count Tolstoi and Katkov created an entire system of police academy classicism with the aim of turning students into models of uniformed official thinking, morally and intellectually castrated servants of the tsar and the fatherland. These deeply considered steps gave society, especially the younger generation, excellent lessons in conspiring against the government. The inclination to conspire grew fruitfully and quickly on the soil of public embitterment which the government had cultivated. Assassination attempts grew in frequency and culminated in the affair of 1 March.[4]

Kliuchevskii continued his account beyond the murder of Alexander II, and was no doubt wondering whether the concessions granted by Nicholas II in 1905–6 would prove any more lasting than those of his predecessors. From the standpoint of April 1906 his indictment was understandable, but this book will argue that it was blinkered. When Kliuchevskii pinned the misfortunes of early-twentieth-century Russia on her nineteenth-century rulers, he took the easy way out. Initiating and drawing back from change had been features of Russian governmental behaviour long before 1801, and were to be features of it long after Kliuchevskii's death. Nineteenth-century Russian tsars were no more interventionist, no more 'provocative', than their predecessors or successors. The personalities and policies of Alexander I, Nicholas I and Alexander II had less to do with the country's problems than the size of the problems themselves.

THE CHARACTER OF ALEXANDER I

The personality of Alexander I, however, with whose accession this book opens, has engaged historians to such an extent that it seems to be the key feature of Russia's history in the first quarter of the nineteenth century. In some presentations, Alexander does indeed look like a 'provocateur' in Kliuchevskii's sense of the term. On the other hand, his genes, his upbringing, his friends, and the manner of his accession gave him good reason to appear in many guises. Christened 'the enigmatic tsar' by one of his biographers, 'the sphinx of the north' by another, a 'paternalistic reformer' by a third, and 'the Russian Trajan' by his former tutor,[5] he justified all four titles at different points in his reign. As the grandson of Catherine the Great, 'the only articulate ideologist to rule Russia between Ivan IV and Lenin',[6] and the son of Paul I, a militaristic admirer of Frederick the Great whom 'Potsdam, Sans Souci, and Berlin pursued ... like a wild dream',[7] he was introduced at an early age to the conflicting environments of the schoolroom and the parade ground. Born in 1777, he was taken from his parents in the 1780s and exposed by his grandmother to the ministrations of a Swiss republican, Frédéric-César de La Harpe, who attempted to instil in him the ideals of the European Enlightenment. La Harpe's educational endeavours succeeded only up to a point, for by the time Catherine died, in November 1796, Alexander had found an antidote to the intellectual stringency of St Petersburg in the war games of his father's nearby estate at Gatchina. In 1793 and subsequently Catherine had considered bypassing Paul and making Alexander her heir, but her grandson would have no truck with the idea. He already sensed the enormity of the tasks that would confront him when he eventually succeeded to the throne. In May 1796 he wrote to his friend Viktor Kochubei of the 'incredible disorder' which permeated the administration of the empire, and expressed the view that ruling the country was beyond the powers of a genius, let alone of a moderately gifted fellow like himself. He envisaged abdicating, settling on the banks of the Rhine, and leading the peaceful life of a private individual who derived his happiness from the company of friends and the study of nature.[8] This vision captivated (or dogged) him to the end of his life, and played a part in the legend that, far from dying of typhus, he retired to Siberia and became a monk whose memory was still honoured in Tomsk in the 1930s.[9] Alexander was a dreamer. He was lazy, suggestible and given to sudden enthusiasms. But he also had a stubborn streak. Even in his celebrated letter of May 1796 he refrained from saying precisely when he would withdraw from public life; within a year of Paul's accession he had begun taking a more dynamic view of the way in which he would deal with the problems of the Russian Empire. Circumstances, not his kaleidoscopic character, were to be the main reason why he achieved few of the goals he set himself. He was less remarkable for changing his mind than for constantly returning to ideas of which he ought to have been disabused. He was defeated by the context in which he found himself, not by personal inadequacy.

ALEXANDER AND PAUL (1796–9)

It is usually said that Alexander was broadly loyal to Paul during the latter's short reign, and joined in the conspiracy against him only at the end and after much soul-searching. This is the view, for example, of Alan Palmer, but Natan Eidel'man has made a powerful counter-case.[10] It is true that, as heir to the throne, Alexander only once committed himself to a written indictment of his father. In a letter to La Harpe of September 1797 he reported that Paul had conceived the idea of imposing himself decisively on the state of affairs left by Catherine. Paul had started well, Alexander wrote, but had flattered to deceive. The disorder which already prevailed had merely been intensified. Soldiers wasted their time on parades, orders were issued and rescinded within a month, the regime as a whole was characterized by 'severity without justice, too much partiality, and the maximum inexperience in the handling of business'. The heir to the throne was obliged to spend all his time on the trivia of military service and had no chance of devoting himself to study, which he claimed was his favourite pastime. 'I have become the most unhappy of men'.[11]

Since Alexander never again spoke so strongly of his dissatisfaction with Paul, his discontent is supposed to have been transient. It is more likely, however, that he simply stopped expressing his sentiments in letters. He may even have stopped writing because he was beginning to take action. By 1797 he had discovered some like-minded near contemporaries with whom he could speak freely, all of them outsiders in the context of Russian high politics. Kochubei, to whom Alexander wrote the much-quoted letter of 1796, was a triply peripheral figure. He spent the greater part of the 1790s as ambassador in Constantinople and complained constantly of being out of touch with affairs in St Petersburg; he belonged to a Ukrainian coterie whose members looked like parvenus to the Russians with whom they competed for office; and according to one contemporary he was anti-social, a man of 'few words and murderous cold'.[12] Alexander had met the Pole Adam Czartoryski before the death of Catherine, and through him Pavel Stroganov and Nikolai Novosil'tsev. All of these had reasons for being discontented with their lot. Czartoryski had been brought to St Petersburg after the collapse of Poland in 1795 and focused the remainder of his long life on the cause of Polish rebirth. Stroganov had been tutored by the French revolutionary Gilbert Romme and was a radical. Captivated by the changes in France, he had to be brought back from Paris almost by force in 1791. Novosil'tsev took him in hand on that occasion, but Novosil'tsev had his own reasons for being dissatisfied. He was Stroganov's bastard cousin, 'brought up by his generous uncle like a poor relation'. Olga Narkiewicz describes him as 'a man of poor education, but devouring ambition; one who felt slighted by Russian society, but yet desired to belong to it'.[13]

These young men, all of them slightly older than Alexander, had been working closely with the Grand Duke before he wrote his letter of complaint to La Harpe. Czartoryski had been almost overwhelmed by the liberalism which Alexander expressed in a three-hour private conversation at the Tauride Palace in 1796. In April of the following year, Alexander was displeased by the events which surrounded Paul's coronation in Moscow. Quite apart from substituting one political clan for another in his affections, Paul distributed large numbers of state-owned peasants as gifts, flaunted his domination of the ecclesiastical hierarchy, and downgraded Catherine's Charter to the Nobility by declaring that nobles were to lose their immunity from corporal punishment. Alexander asked Czartoryski to prepare a draft manifesto for use in the event of his own eventual accession. In doing so,

Czartoryski spoke of the merits of freedom and justice and of Alexander's intention, after he had made a start on reform, to divest himself of power in order that someone more worthy might take over from him. Much later, Czartoryski claimed that he was well aware of Alexander's naivety, but it is likely that hindsight made him more perspicacious than he had been in the 1790s and that the draft manifesto which he drew up for Alexander embodied a firmer intention than he was prepared to admit. In the indictment of Paul which Alexander addressed to La Harpe, the heir to the throne spoke more precisely of the 'revolution' which he had in mind for his country. 'It would be the best sort of revolution,' he said, 'as it would be undertaken by a legal authority which would cease to exist as soon as the constitution was finished and the nation had chosen its representatives'. Alexander had in mind change from the top down, no doubt by way of staving off the sort of change from the bottom up which had been taking place in contemporary Europe.

At the time of the coronation festivities in Moscow, Novosil'tsev produced a sort of programmatic introduction to the constitutional innovations which Alexander was considering. It has not survived, but seems to have turned on the need to educate that part of the Russian public which would one day constitute the nation's representatives. In his letter to La Harpe, Alexander spoke of his circle's intention to commission the translation into Russian of 'as many useful books as possible' – the texts which underlay contemporary developments in France. Alexander did not envisage being able to distribute many such translations on the open market, but must have contemplated circulating them in manuscript and increasing the small number of those sympathetic to his intentions. In fact he managed a little more than this, by way of a periodical entitled *The St Petersburg Journal* which appeared in 1798. While Novosil'tsev, Stroganov and Czartoryski all contributed items for publication, Alexander provided the funds. The journal's editors were important figures in the early history of attempts at reforming imperial Russia. One of them, Ivan Pnin, played a key role in 'filling the gap between Radishchev and the Decembrists',[14] that gap which extended from Aleksandr Radishchev's arrest in 1790 for publishing his inflammatory *Journey from St Petersburg to Moscow* to the rising of the Decembrists in 1825. *The St Petersburg Journal* did much to perpetuate the idea of reform when Paul was doing his best to suppress it. It did not aim to topple the existing order, but to make use of it for the ends which Alexander had in view. The translations with which it abounded, from Montesquieu, Holbach and perhaps especially Antoine-Léonard Thomas, whose 'Epistle to the People' of 1760 spoke sharply of the need to pay the peasantry due respect for their contribution to the life of the community, accorded well with Alexander's mood in the first half of his father's reign.

Paul clearly sensed Alexander's hopes for the future, and attempted to break up his circle by sending Novosil'tsev to England. Czartoryski and Stroganov remained, however, and in 1798 Paul unwittingly strengthened Alexander's resolve by recalling Kochubei from the embassy in Constantinople. Paul showered Kochubei with honours and may have hoped he would modify Alexander's opinions, for he was a nephew of Aleksandr Bezborodko, the highly trusted Chancellor of the Empire. If this was indeed the tsar's idea it misfired, for Kochubei took Alexander's side and added weight to the Grand Duke's circle. He had more experience of affairs, greater authority, and more powerful connections than Alexander's other associates. He persuaded Bezborodko to write Alexander a 'Memorandum Concerning the Needs of the Russian Empire', which conceded that 'the condition of the peasants is such as to require improvement' and advocated an increased role for the Senate in the administration of the country.[15] Through Kochubei Alexander became acquainted not only with Bezborodko, but also with a second member of the generation which had grown up under Catherine. Dmitrii Troshchinskii, whom Bezborodko brought to St Petersburg in the 1780s and who had been a state secretary since 1793, acted as Kochubei's business agent throughout the ten-year period of the latter's absence in western Europe and Constantinople. He revelled in the success of his coterie during Paul's early years on the throne, but sensed, towards the end of the 1790s, that the political order from which he had profited was being subjected to intolerable strain. To judge by his behaviour on the night of Paul's assassination, he was familiar with Alexander's aspirations long before they had a chance to bear fruit.

Yet Alexander and his closest friends were not responsible for the tsar's murder. Alexander was prepared to consider what he would do when he became tsar, but not to take the initiative in hastening that time. He was much less rebellious than heirs to the throne tended to be in eighteenth-century Britain or Prussia. When Bezborodko died in April 1799 he lost a main prop in the edifice of his political relationships. As one of Bezborodko's clique put it, 'When an oak tree falls, the mushrooms get squashed'.[16] Kochubei married and went abroad; Troshchinskii left St Petersburg temporarily to undertake an official inspection of the provinces surrounding Moscow; Czartoryski had already been despatched, as Russian ambassador, to the Kingdom of Sardinia; Alexander's wife was in disgrace with the tsar for having borne Czartoryski's child; and Russian troops in Italy and Switzerland were under orders to capture La Harpe and convey him to St Petersburg. Even if Alexander had been prepared to plot against his father, he seemed to have little prospect of finding assistants who were free from suspicion.

The heir to the throne, however, was only one of Paul's many opponents. In the autumn of 1799 Nikita Petrovich Panin succeeded Kochubei as Vice-President of the College of Foreign Affairs. Nephew of Nikita Ivanovich Panin, an earlier advocate of reformist ideas, he remained broadly true to the dissentient tradition in which he had been reared. In foreign affairs he was pro-English, which explained why two of his closer associates were Lord Whitworth, British ambassador to St Petersburg, and Semen Vorontsov, the Russian ambassador in London. Whitworth's mistress was a sister of Catherine the Great's last favourite and connected Panin with a clique which had lost favour on the empress's death. More important than any of these was Peter von der Pahlen, Governor-General of St Petersburg. Panin and Pahlen apprised the Grand Duke Alexander of their intention to take action against Paul and gained his tacit sympathy.

THE COUP OF 1801

As 1800 progressed, Paul gave ever more grounds for dissatisfaction with his behaviour. After Bonaparte's coup of November 1799 in France, he felt able to break with Britain and adopt a pro-French orientation in foreign affairs. In May 1800 he exceeded even his own customary standards of brutality by ordering an army officer to receive a thousand blows of the knout for criticizing a recently introduced order of knighthood which the tsar had named after his mistress. In the same month, the population of St Petersburg openly lamented the death of Field-Marshal Suvorov. Suvorov's recent military successes in north Italy had incurred the tsar's envy, but imperial disfavour could not deter the inhabitants of St Petersburg from showing where their affections lay. Perhaps for the first time in Russia, public obsequies turned into a demonstration of dissatisfaction with the government.

Panin and Pahlen continued their machinations. The former, perhaps mindful of the events of 1788–9 in England, seems to have contemplated deposing Paul on the grounds of madness and installing Alexander as regent. The legal convolutions of such a course of action would have enabled him to effect the kind of limitations on the sovereign's power which his family had long stood for. Pahlen, less subtle but more vigorous, probably realized from the outset that the tsar would have to be murdered. The two men had to act quickly, for Paul, ever watchful and by now almost certainly paranoid, might have dismissed them at any time. Pahlen, indeed, lost his position as Governor-General of St Petersburg, only to be quickly reinstated. On 1 November 1800 Paul made a mistake. To mark the fourth anniversary of his accession, he issued decrees allowing military and civilian officials who had retired or been dismissed since November 1796 to return to St Petersburg and seek re-employment. The three Zubov brothers all benefited from this amnesty, as did another key figure in the events of March 1801, General L. L. Bennigsen, who had thought his career was over and was vegetating on his Lithuanian estates. Later in November, veering from one extreme to the other, Paul dismissed Panin. This apparently major blow ought significantly to have damaged the movement against him, but paradoxically it strengthened it. The disappearance from St Petersburg of the leading civilian opponent of the tsar gave the military the opportunity to pursue their more dramatic approach to the problems he posed.

By March 1801 Paul had given further striking signs of his unpredictability. He had set in train a movement of troops from Orenburg which was intended, eventually, to threaten Britain's possessions in India. He had proclaimed the annexation of Georgia from the Persians, which also seemed to signal large-scale ambitions in the east. His pro-French leanings had provoked British naval action in the Baltic which soon gave rise to the first battle of Copenhagen. In St Petersburg, a more than usually large number of gentry families were announcing their departure from Russia. A rumour began to circulate that Paul was planning to marry off his daughter Catherine to her cousin, Prince Eugen of Württemberg, and to make Prince Eugen his heir. Then it became apparent that Paul knew he was in danger. On 9 March 1801 he told Pahlen that he suspected there were plans afoot to repeat the events of 1762 (when Peter III had been deposed by Catherine the Great). Pahlen boldly admitted that a plot existed, but claimed that he was working to subvert it from within. He realized, however, that he would have to act quickly. He needed to secure the Grand Duke Alexander's final sanction for his plans. The two met on 9 March, but what they agreed is uncertain. Alexander seems to have been responsible for putting back the date of the proposed coup from 10 to 11 March, on the grounds that his own Semenovskii regiment would then be on guard duty at the palace where Paul had recently taken up residence; but whether he envisaged his father's murder, or merely his abdication and detention, is unknown. In view of the opinions Alexander held in the first three years of Paul's reign, he can hardly have been averse to his removal; but in view of his reaction to the events of 11–12 March, he did not wholly agree with the manner in which it was undertaken.

Like Chesterton's Prince of Heiligwaldenstein, but much more directly, Paul was killed by his sash. Led by Platon Zubov and Bennigsen (Pahlen, judiciously, bringing up the rear), a band of drunken Guards officers penetrated the ultra-secure Mikhailovskii Palace, discovered the tsar in his bedchamber hiding behind a fire-screen, and after a brief exchange of words and a blow from a snuff-box strangled him with one of his own insignia. The leading conspirators probably did not intend the tsar to die on the spot, for on the night of the murder Dmitrii Troshchinskii had been summoned by the Zubovs to prepare what seems to have been an abdication decree. Later the same night Troshchinskii was called upon again, this time to draw up Alexander's accession manifesto. The contradiction between these events seems to indicate that the murder took place in the heat of the moment. It certainly horrified its prime beneficiary. According to Adam Czartoryski, writing much later, 'This ineffaceable stain ... settled like a vulture on [Alexander's] conscience, paralysed his best faculties at the commencement of his reign, and plunged him into a mysticism sometimes degenerating into superstition at its close'.[17] If Czartoryski's interpretation holds water – and he was not alone in his view – Alexander displayed remarkable simplemindedness in March 1801. When Catherine the Great deposed Peter III in 1762, she accepted the inevitability of his subsequent

9

murder and kept faith with those who brought her to the throne. Alexander, apparently overwhelmed by the crime committed on his behalf, broke with its perpetrators and effected their rapid withdrawal from St Petersburg. Yet since he did so with impunity, and did not immediately abandon the principles to which he gave voice in the early part of Paul's reign, it may be that he achieved precisely what he wanted in 1801: an end to Paul's unpredictability and cruelty, a chance to put into practice his own plans for the empire's future, and the dismissal of men who might have had some hold over him. Alexander could certainly be duplicitous, and was just as likely to have been pretending when he displayed contrition about Paul's death as when he attempted to alter the course of Russia's development. The relatively small number of his concrete achievements on the throne did not necessarily mean that he was reluctant to do more. His limited success as a reformer derived from the intractability of his inheritance as well as from the extent of his commitment to change.

FOREIGN ENEMIES AND DOMESTIC MINORITIES

The Russian Empire in 1801 posed daunting problems. An early-twentieth-century historian considered that the country was at a crossroads at the moment the new tsar ascended the throne and that his 'contradictions' and 'hesitations' were 'the living reflection of hesitations and contradictions evoked by the struggle between the fundamental currents of his time'.[18] This approach has a good deal to recommend it. Superficially, Russia's eighteenth-century progress had been startling. The empire had greatly increased in size. Its population rose from about 15.5 million in 1719 to more than 42.5 million in 1811. In terms of both area and number of inhabitants it was the largest state in Europe. Its seventeenth-century adversaries, Sweden, Poland and Turkey, had all been put in their place. In the Great Northern War of 1700–21 Peter the Great had overtaken Sweden and established Russia's control of the eastern end of the Baltic. He had founded St Petersburg in 1703 and made it the capital of the empire in 1712. Poland, having been a Russian client-state for much of the century, disappeared from the map in 1795 after a series of partitions in which Russia colluded with Prussia and Austria. Turkey had given ground to Russia in the wars of 1736–9, 1768–74 and 1787–91, and had lost its vassal, the Crimea, in the Russian annexation of 1783. The Black Sea was beginning to look like a Russian lake. The town which became Odessa had only ten inhabitants in 1793, but by 1863 had become the fourth city of the empire. In 1796 Catherine the Great had initiated a Caucasian campaign against Persia, while Paul, as we have seen, had annexed Georgia and conceived of sending troops via central Asia to India. Russian forces had entered Berlin in 1760.

Russian ships had circumnavigated Europe and defeated the Turks off Asia Minor in 1770. Catherine the Great had mediated between Austria and Prussia during the War of Bavarian Succession at the end of the 1770s. Britain had suffered from the 'Armed Neutrality' which Russia set up in the Baltic in 1780 and which, despite its name, challenged British control of northern waters. In the Ochakov affair of 1791, Britain had proved unable to stem Russia's southward advance. With Bonaparte marooned in Egypt, Suvorov experienced triumph after triumph in northern Italy in 1799. Paul might have seemed to be endangering the empire's security by his complex diplomatic manoeuvres of 1800–1, but he clearly felt that he was negotiating from a position of strength. Russia's eighteenth-century dealings with the outside world seemed to justify his attitude.

Even in foreign affairs, however, the empire was not as well placed as it seemed to be. The elimination of Poland gave Russia common frontiers with Austria and Prussia which necessitated the constant monitoring of their ambitions. Even before Poland's disappearance, Russia had been obliged to form an alliance with Prussia to prevent her forming a liaison with the Turks. This alliance – Frederick the Great's 'greatest diplomatic triumph'[19] – was indicative of the balancing act in which Russia had to engage from the moment she became a full member of the European states system. She bypassed the Prussian alliance in 1781 and went into alliance with Austria, but in the nineteenth century the Habsburgs became increasingly reluctant to accept the prospect of Russian penetration of the Balkans. Their neutrality during the Crimean War reflected growing distrust of the tsars and marked a stage on the road to the Austro-German alliance of 1879, which lay at the root of Russia's fatal drubbing in the First World War. Even Britain, far to the west, sensed by the end of the eighteenth century that she could not allow Russian aggrandizement to proceed unchallenged. She failed to compel Russia to abandon Ochakov in 1791, but the shadowy part played by Lord Whitworth in the machinations which led to Paul's assassination reflected continuing British mistrust of Russia's intentions in the Baltic. In the 1850s Britain was to fight on Russian soil and in 1878 she contributed, at the Congress of Berlin, to the modification of Russian plans for the Balkans.

Despite having become a Great Power, Russia could not afford to discount her traditional enemies. After the war of 1788–90 she fought Sweden only once more (in 1808), but Turkey and Poland remained troublesome. Events of 1798–9 in the reign of Paul seemed to augur well for the future of Russo-Turkish relations, in that a Russian fleet took the Ionian Islands from the French and set up a Turkish protectorate over them. But this proved to be the only time in history that Russia and Turkey acted jointly in a military endeavour. The years 1806, 1828, 1853 and 1877 witnessed the outbreak of further wars between them. Russia had the whip hand in all four, at least initially, but western powers tended to come to Turkey's aid and prevent the tsar's forces from making the most of their superiority. Poland, meanwhile, refused to lie down. Poles agitated for the rebirth of their state in risings against the tsar of November 1830 and January 1863 and in constant attempts to engage the sympathy of western intellectuals and governments. One of their greatest spokesmen, Adam Mickiewicz, declared at the Collège de France in 1844 that France, who had given birth to the Grand Duchy of Warsaw in the course of the Napoleonic Wars, could not draw in her horns and concentrate wholly on domestic affairs. 'Having long stood at the head of the Christian nations,' Mickiewicz said, 'France cannot abandon them in the midst of moral ruin!'[20] His words may have had some effect, for when a Parisian crowd invaded the Second Republic's Chamber of Deputies in May 1848, one of its rallying cries turned on the need to do something about Poland. Poles did not benefit materially, but remained an irritant in Russia's dealings with the outside world.

They were a domestic problem, furthermore, even when they seemed to be causing no trouble, for their presence within the frontiers of the Russian Empire made it difficult for imperial administrators to frame universally applicable statutes. Because many more Poles than Russians belonged to the gentry estate (Poles constituted more than 50 per cent of the total number of nobles within the Russian Empire in the 1850s)[21], the Russian government had to modify its inclination to favour the nobility. The fact that more Poles than Russians tended to be avid for education came to affect the composition and political outlook of the empire's student body.[22] Educated Catholic Poles constituted a bridge between the cultures of eastern and western Europe, infecting the one with the other and preventing the Russian Empire from presenting a single face to the world.

Growing diversity of internal culture was a central consequence of Russia's eighteenth-century expansion. Poles were only the noisiest cuckoo in the nest. Edward Thaden concluded a book on the peripheries of European Russia in the eighteenth and nineteenth centuries by saying that 'in 1870 there was, in certain important respects, more diversity than there had been 160 years before'.[23] Before Poland was partitioned, Baltic and Ukrainian gentry spoke up for their local privileges at Catherine the Great's Legislative Commission of 1767–8. The Baltic Germans tended to be the most loyal of the tsars' non-Russian subjects, but only because making common cause with the Russians was a lesser evil than showing sympathy for the Latvian and Estonian peasants who constituted the bulk of the population in the north-western part of the empire. German communities on the Volga and in the southern part of the Ukraine – mostly immigrants who had been attracted to eastern Europe by the generous inducements offered by Catherine the Great – usually proved model farmers, but in doing so highlighted the contrast between native and foreign levels of agricultural expertise. As the Westphalian analyst of Russian agriculture, August von Haxthausen, said of the Mennonite colonies north of the Sea of Azov in the 1840s, 'In all of Russia there is no region where, on the whole, there exists such a uniformly high level of agricultural and social development as here'.[24] Ukrainians had a less clearly defined sense of their identity than Russia's German subjects, but could not be called surrogate Russians.

Despite losing their autonomous political institutions in the second half of the eighteenth century and tending to migrate from their heartland – the Ukraine east of the river Dnieper was the one part of the empire to experience a decline in population in the 1780s and 1790s[25] – they began developing the use of their language for literary purposes and never quite lost the feeling that they were culturally distinct from their masters. By the mid-nineteenth century the aspirations of a few of their number had begun to alarm the imperial government. Much more strikingly non-Russian were the Jews whom Russia acquired by partitioning Poland. Before 1772 Jewish subjects of the tsar were virtually non-existent. After 1795 they numbered something like half a million, and did not readily fit any of the social categories into which the government divided its population. Catherine the Great intended no hostility towards them, and can even be said to have treated them more generously than certain other elements in the population by granting them limited rights of movement; but the 'Pale of Settlement', however large, was to become an obstacle to Jewish development, and the concentration of Jews in one region of the empire made them seem a peculiarly striking excrescence on the landscape when doctrines of national identity took hold in Russia in the first half of the nineteenth century.[26]

RUSSIAN BACKWARDNESS

Defining the legal status of Jews was only one of the many difficulties experienced by eighteenth-century tsars in the realm of the law. Laws were their prime weapon in confronting their problems at home. No tsar envisaged limiting himself by admitting the existence of an authority higher than his own, but all of them had an interest in reducing the unpredictability of Russian society and fostering its potential for self-advancement. Promulgating laws seemed to be the best way of achieving these objectives. The notion of 'the well-ordered police state' penetrated Russia from central Europe at the turn of the seventeenth and eighteenth centuries and informed much of the Russian government's behaviour for 150 years.[27] If the empire could be placed on a uniform footing, it might be able to advance on a broad front. Laws could dovetail outlying regions with the central provinces; delineate social groups in such a way that every inhabitant of the empire knew his obligations and prospects; and facilitate the evolution of a governmental engine to power the redesigned machinery of society. Superficially, the Russian authorities made some progress in these directions in the eighteenth century. A number of distinguished provincial governors did something to carry the gospel of centralism to the remoter parts of the empire; gentry and peasantry received new or additional definitions of their standing (respectively beneficial and detrimental to their interests, but both clearer); and a bureaucracy began to emerge which could consolidate and extend the links between ruler and ruled. Catherine the Great can be praised for her 'attempt to construct a constitution intended to protect the subject as much from the unregulated self-seeking of his peers as from the arbitrary application of governmental authority'.[28] She can be applauded for the information-gathering which underpinned all her work (the three reassessments of the size of the tax-paying population, the General Land Survey ordered in 1766, the many 'topographical descriptions' of life in individual provinces). Her most famous statutes – on provincial administration, the police, the government of towns, the corporate identity of the gentry and the foundation of schools – look like a well-integrated answer to Russian lawlessness, rendered incomplete only by the absence of statutes on the central administration and the clerical and peasant estates. Had she been spared, Catherine could have moved into these areas. Had her successors matched her in sophistication, they could have completed the building she started. Had France not upset the European order, the Russian Empire could have become the jewel in its crown. Perhaps Catherine had lit upon the means of modernizing the tsarist regime.

Perhaps; but in Russia the gap between publishing decrees and making sure that they took effect was immense. Most of the passages in this book which treat the grassroots of Russian society are to be found in Chapters Five, Eight, Nine and Eleven, but the chasm which divided the country's lawmakers from Russian reality has to be kept in mind constantly. As Catherine admitted when she appointed Petr Rumiantsev Governor of the Ukraine in 1764, the province had hitherto been part of the empire only in name, despite the fact that it had been under the Russian crown for more than a century.[29] The phenomenal list of instructions with which the empress furnished her new Ukrainian governor touched on everything from the establishment of good border relations with Poland and Turkey and the intensification of land use to the improvement of roads, the planting of trees, the drying out of bogs and the introduction of vets. Needless to say, Rumiantsev fulfilled only some of his orders. Given its tradition of autonomy the Ukraine was always going to be a tough nut to crack, but even in areas closer to the heartland of the empire provincial governors faced an uphill struggle. In answer to the question how Russia's provincial bureaucracy 'managed to govern so many people and so much territory', Robert Jones, in a study centred on eighteenth-century Novgorod, declared that 'The simple answer is that for the most part it could not and did not govern them'.[30] Legislation of 1763 provided for about 16,500 paid civil servants. Contemporary Prussia had about the same number, but for 80 per cent fewer people and a much smaller area. In the mid-nineteenth century Russia still had only about a quarter as many civil servants per head of the population as contemporary Britain and France.[31] It was one thing to conceive of a 'well-ordered police state', but another to bring it into being. Dmitrii Troshchinskii, the civil servant who drafted Alexander I's accession manifesto, pointed out in a long memorandum written during his tenure of the Ministry of Justice (1814–17) that 'in the great majority of cases, at all times and throughout the empire, the well-being, tranquillity, property, honour and even life of the greater part of the population of the state depend almost exclusively on local institutions'.[32] Yet at the beginning of the reign of Catherine the Great nearly half of Russia's relatively small number of civil servants were to be found in St Petersburg and Moscow. The ratio between rulers and ruled got much smaller between the mid-eighteenth and the mid-nineteenth centuries,[33] but never reached the point where the central authorities could be sure that their policies would be put into effect.

To increase the potential number and the effectiveness of their servants, tsars needed to improve the empire's educational facilities. Before Peter the Great these had been negligible, and in reality, if not on paper, they remained poor at the end of the eighteenth century. Peter introduced 'cypher schools', Elizabeth founded Moscow University, and Catherine the Great set up a network of primary schools, but none of these was very substantial. There were about 20,000 pupils in Catherine's primary schools in 1800. Education was also to be had in certain other places, notably in establishments run by the armed forces and the church's seminaries, but even the most generous estimate of the number of pupils receiving instruction in 1800 goes no higher than 70,000.[34] Since the children of the better-off gentry were educated privately they did not appear in the school enrolments, but their number was too small to increase the total substantially. By the contentious method of retrospective forecasting Boris Mironov has claimed that perhaps 6.9 per cent of the inhabitants of European Russia aged ten and over were literate in 1797, that in towns the proportion may have been 21 per cent, and that among town males it may have reached 28.6 per cent.[35] He admits, however, that these estimates have to be reduced dramatically if one takes into account that literacy, once acquired, can be lost, and even his optimum figures fail to give the impression that eighteenth-century Russia was well placed to develop its internal resources, administer its new territories effectively, or compete on equal terms with its great power rivals. As Walter Pintner remarks, 'In 1755 the low level, indeed the general lack, of formal education among officials is startling even to one familiar with the limited development of Russian education'.[36] The situation did not change significantly until the first half of the nineteenth century.

Education suffered no less than other spheres of governmental activity from the empire's fundamental difficulty, shortage of funds. Responsibility for founding secular schools rested initially on the Boards of Social Welfare set up under Catherine the Great's provincial reform of 1775, but they were allocated a mere 10,000 rubles each for the provision of schools, hospitals, almshouses and asylums. The Commission on Popular Schools created in 1782 had a budget of only 30,000 rubles. Military schools and St Petersburg's Smol'nyi Institute for daughters of the gentry were relatively well endowed, but a much more substantial total outlay would have been needed to render the prospects of the empire's educational network anything other than bleak. The imperial administration could not find the cash. The state's outgoings exceeded its revenue by an average of one-third in the first ten years of the nineteenth century.[37] For much of that decade the empire was at war, but its budgetary deficits were not really transient. Russia had gone to war so often in the eighteenth century that she had to see military expenditure as a regular rather than an extraordinary outgoing. The state's need for money arose not only out of its constant involvement in fighting, but also out of its determination to systematize and intensify the administration of the territories it had acquired. In a way, it became a victim of its own success. It had found the resources to put Russia on a par with her neighbours, but it had to find more to stay in the race. Given the backwardness of the Russian economy and the nature of the taxation system, it was bound to be hard pressed. The gentry, potentially the most fruitful source of revenue, were exempt from personal taxation. Only the non-privileged orders paid the poll tax, and in view of their poverty the rate at which taxes could be increased was limited. The state's vodka monopoly constituted another of its prime sources of income, but developing the fiscal potential of vodka sales had the counter-productive effect, still noted by Russian governments, of impairing the labour force's application to duty. When, to cover its deficits, the government debased the coinage and started issuing paper money, the result was rampant inflation.

The root of Russia's economic problems lay in the relative infertility of her soil, her hostile climate and the strait-jacketed character of social relations in the countryside. Only just over 1 per cent of the population were nobles at the end of the eighteenth century.[38] The vast majority of the remainder were peasants, rather more than half of them belonging to the nobles (the serfs properly so called), about 40 per cent belonging to the state (the 'state peasants') and something under 10 per cent belonging to the church and the imperial family. Even at the best of times, the unprivileged majority of the empire's population had difficulty making ends meet. The soil which the peasants worked is usually said to have been much less fertile than agricultural land elsewhere in Europe. Steven Hoch has recently taken a contrary view, but his arguments await further empirical confirmation.[39] Neither Hoch nor any other authority attempts to deny that peasants were at the mercy of Russia's inclement weather. Broadly speaking, the picture of late-eighteenth-century rural conditions painted by the nineteenth-century historian Vasilii Semevskii has remained in place.[40] Though not entirely monochrome, it was unappealing. In the far north of the country there were relatively few serfs (6 per cent of the village population in Olonets in the 1780s), because in that part of the world the climate militated against intensive agriculture and the state was free from the possibility of enemy attack (which absolved the government from introducing gentry as frontiersmen and serfs as the reward for their pains). South and west of Olonets, serfs grew in number. In the province of Novgorod they constituted 50 per cent of the peasant population, in Smolensk 80 per cent, in the provinces of the 'golden ring' (around Moscow) more than 70 per cent. Serfs paid their dues to the landlord either in the form of *obrok* or quit-rent (in cash or kind), or in the form of *barshchina* (labour services). The former was infinitely preferable to the latter. It increased in the course of the eighteenth century, but still left the serf greater freedom of action. The fictional portrayal of the difference between a serf on *obrok* and a serf on *barshchina* which Turgenev conveyed in 'Khor' and Kalinych', a short story of 1847, was as true for the preceding fifty years as it was for the date of its publication. Quitrent prevailed over labour services only in the non-black soil area of the central part of the empire. In the black soil area, where the land was fertile and serf-owners aimed to cultivate it intensively, three-quarters of the serfs paid their dues in the form of labour services. Often they were working virtually full-time for their landlords. In a decree promulgated at his coronation in 1797, Paul attempted to prevent peasants from being obliged to work on Sundays and saints' days and suggested that landlords oblige them to work the demesne for no more than three days a week; but the second part of this edict was honoured in the breach. Landlords' control over serfs did not stop at being able to make them work the land. Indeed, the serfs who suffered most were probably the landless who worked in their owner's household (as craftsmen, clerks and domestic servants) and those who laboured, usually under some sort of lease, in factories or mines. By the end of Catherine the Great's reign, landlords had virtually unlimited rights to sell their serfs, to subject them to corporal punishment, to send them to Siberia and to encroach on their property. From 1767 serfs were denied the right to petition the authorities concerning malfeasance on the part of their owners. Inevitably, in the light of their circumstances, serfs resorted to violence. Thirty nobles were murdered in Moscow province in the space of six years in the 1760s. Serfs in the iron mines of the Urals flocked to Pugachev's banner in the 1770s. M. D. Kurmacheva has devoted a book to those serfs who, despite their origins, formed a sort of 'serf intelligentsia' in the second half of the eighteenth and the beginning of the nineteenth centuries by becoming artists, musicians or writers, but she admits that they represented only a small proportion of the total number.[41] Isabel de Madariaga has contested Semevskii's view that Catherine the Great intensified serfdom in depth and in extent, and even in the Soviet Union it became fashionable to dispute the claim that the serf population was growing at a slower rate than the population of other social groups because of the hardship which serfs had to endure and their consequently low birth rate and high mortality;[42] but these arguments become too rarefied when they lose sight of the fact that, without social reconstruction, the Russian economy was incapable of the quantum leap it had to make if the empire was to retain its newly acquired Great Power status.

The one social group which appeared to profit from the Russian Empire's eighteenth-century experience was the nobility. Having been obliged to serve the state by Peter the Great, nobles gradually escaped the obligation until, in 1785, they received a charter which spelt out their rights and formalized their identity as an estate. Since, ten years previously, the provincial reform had brought into being many elective offices which fell into their hands, it might be imagined that they were growing in confidence and that the crown had decided to rely on them for the future development of the country. These contentions underlie John P. LeDonne's study of Russian government under Catherine the Great,[43] but they are open to serious doubt. Eighty per cent of nobles possessed fewer than the hundred serfs which might have enabled them to disregard the benefits of employment by the state. Whether or not the crown obliged them to serve, they were likely to do so. Telling them they did not have to enter the government's employ improved their political status, but challenged their economic interests. Wealthy nobles, seduced by the prospect of turning themselves into aristocrats on the western European model, needed cash for the consumer goods which would turn the prospect into a reality. Their wealth, however, did not derive from a money-orientated economy, and they lacked the entrepreneurial skills to think of turning from production for subsistence to production for sale. The government began to make it possible for nobles to obtain loans on the security of their estates, but even these injections seem to have gone on consumption rather than investment. When Pavel Stroganov claimed, at a meeting between Alexander I and his closest friends in November 1801, that Russian nobles were decadent and much less likely to threaten the throne than their serfs, he spoke no more than the truth.[44] A few nobles had attempted to limit the power of the Empress Anna on her accession in 1730; a few more had been affronted by the extent to which Peter III had circumvented their prime political institution, the Senate, in 1762; and one or two, notably Pahlen and Panin, probably wanted to impose controls on Alexander I after the murder of his father. But in the long run the problems posed by nobles arose not out of their political recalcitrance but out of the increasing divergence between their interests and those of the state. The rapid growth of the civil service, a feature, above all, of the first half of the nineteenth century, rendered the government less dependent on the nobility than it had been in the past. Admittedly, civil servants were often of noble provenance, and even if they were not they could advance far enough in their careers to enter the noble estate; but they differed from nobles outside the service. They tended not to have served in the army; they tended not to own serfs; and they had received a much higher degree of formal education than nobles who did not spend their lives in government offices. Whatever the legal similarities, nobles inside and outside the service were becoming different social groups. Those who were less than wholly committed to a life of official duties were becoming 'superfluous men', epitomized in nineteenth-century Russian literature by Pushkin's Evgenii Onegin, Lermontov's Pechorin, Herzen's Bel'tov and Goncharov's Oblomov. A Russian tsar could not expect to transform his lands by relying on traditional elites.

THE REFORMS OF 1801–4

So Alexander I was faced, at his accession, by problems well-nigh insurmountable in their range and complexity. Before ridding himself of Pahlen in June 1801 he gave certain hostages to fortune. In his accession manifesto he declared himself anxious to return to the ways of Catherine II. Since he never praised her again, it is unlikely that this statement of intent came from the heart. Gustav Rozenkampf, a Baltic German who played a significant part in the discussions of reform with which the early part of Alexander's reign was replete, subsequently wrote that 'Those who hoped Emperor Alexander I would return to the great Empress's system of government and law-giving were cruelly mistaken'.[45] Yet a number of measures sanctioned by Alexander during his first few months on the throne tended to strengthen the impression that he was anxious to revive the style of his grandmother. He confirmed the charter which she had issued to the nobility in 1785; he set up a legal commission to continue the work left unfinished by Catherine's commission of 1767–8; and on 5 June 1801 he called upon the Senate to investigate its rights and duties and explain why its authority had diminished. All these steps implied a return to the supposedly halcyon period which had ended with Catherine's death; but none of them embodied what Alexander really hoped to do.

At Paul's death only one of Alexander's closest associates was in St Petersburg – Pavel Stroganov. The other three – Kochubei, Novosil'tsev and Czartoryski – quickly returned, and two days after Czartoryski's arrival Pahlen was banished. A week later, on 24 June, Alexander conferred with his four friends in the first session of what became known as the Unofficial or Secret Committee. At a series of meetings over the next two years, the tsar and his confederates discussed most aspects of Russia's internal and external affairs. The tsar's former tutor, La Harpe, became a sort of peripheral member of the confederacy during his residence in St Petersburg between August 1801 and May 1802. Alexander now had the prospect of acting upon the ideas he had expressed in 1797. At their first session, the members of the Unofficial Committee decided to draw up a picture of the current state of the empire. Novosil'tsev proposed dividing the labour into three stages: a review of the present situation (subdivided to include consideration of the empire's defence capabilities, its relations with foreign powers, and the condition of the economy and the administration); the reform of specific departments; and the preparation of a constitution to crown the transformed governmental edifice. The tsar and his friends began work immediately on the navy, but 'His Majesty manifested his anxiety to make passing on to the third stage of the labour possible'.[46] The members of the committee therefore turned their attention to the question of reforming the Senate, and Alexander voiced doubts about the step he had taken in this direction less than three weeks previously.

Because Alexander and his closest advisers sought an institutional break

19

with the past, Senate reform bedevilled the first two years of the reign. In view of the complete unpredictability of governmental behaviour in the reign of Paul, giving the Senate political clout seemed to mark a step in the direction of constitutional advance; but enhancing the status of a body which had already existed for ninety years could also be interpreted as retrogressive. In a memorandum of August 1801 Nikolai Novosil'tsev committed himself to the second of these points of view. 'The restoration of the Senate to the position it occupied at its foundation', he argued, 'is an issue which has no real connection with the job of establishing an institution or institutions defending ... the Natural Rights, the Lawful Freedom and the security of each member of society'.[47] Novosil'tsev implied that, even in its pristine form, the Senate was incapable of pursuing the goals which Alexander had in mind. His opinion was technically correct, in that originally the Senate had been designed merely to keep track of domestic affairs when the tsar was away on campaign. When the tsar was at the centre of affairs, senators belonged to the dignified rather than the efficient part of the constitution. It was true that their judicial functions were considerable, but in the course of the eighteenth century they had acquired an exaggerated sense of their importance. In 1801 some of them believed that their institution could become the focus of a new constitutional order. Writing much later, Adam Czartoryski was loud in his assertion that no real advance could ever have been achieved under the Senate's auspices, as senators 'were for the most part incapable and without energy, selected for their insignificance'.[48]

The description did not apply to Aleksandr Vorontsov, who, despite being a generation older than the tsar's immediate entourage and in some ways typical of the eighteenth-century upper nobility, sponsored the drafting of a coronation charter which would have opened the door to a radical transformation of Russian society. While confirming the rights of the Russian nobility, it acknowledged that noblemen who failed to enter the state's employ could not 'enjoy the advantages and privileges acquired by dint of service'. It looked forward to the preparation of a new law code; it laid emphasis on developing the economic resources of the empire; it stressed the importance of property rights and the right to personal security; it acknowledged the principles of habeas corpus and freedom of expression; and without referring to the possibility of new relations between master and man, it insisted that 'no agricultural implements and no things appertaining to his calling' should be taken from a peasant in the event of a claim being made against the land which he worked.[49]

These were all goals of which the tsar's friends approved. They probably participated in the drawing-up of Vorontsov's charter and they certainly discussed it in sessions of the Unofficial Committee. A recent student of the matter claims that the document came to nothing because the tsar himself opposed it.[50] The real reason for its demise, however, probably lay in the fact that, whether by accident or design, it would have enhanced the power of the country's existing elite. Since it posed no threat to the system

20

of estates, those who were already privileged were likely to be the principal beneficiaries of its provisions; and since it gave the Senate responsibility for adjusting existing laws while a new law code was being prepared, it promised to benefit a body which the Unofficial Committee wanted to weaken. Aleksandr Vorontsov and his collaborators probably saw their proposals as no more than a stage on a road. Anxious not to appear too radical, they advocated the adoption of new juridical principles without challenging the country's social or institutional order. The tsar thought that they were trying to turn the imperial system further to their own advantage. In his view, the existing political system could not be allowed to pursue new objectives. Mindful of the way in which he had come to power, and of the fact that he had felt obliged to dismiss Pahlen only three months after ascending the throne, he was extremely mistrustful of over-mighty subjects and the political order from which, in his view, they had sprung. Those who sought to gain his confidence had to do more than propose ideas which were dear to his heart; they had to propose means of implementing them which did not advance their own interests.

Of Alexander's closest advisers, La Harpe stood to gain least from proposing ideas to the emperor. A foreigner who intended to return home, he could afford to be altruistic. His letters to Alexander included long disquisitions on Swiss affairs, but so far as the Russian domestic scene was concerned his motives were pure. He found the idea of devolving power on the Senate ridiculous. In the Russian context he thought it counter-productive to devolve power at all. Despite his republicanism, he repeatedly urged Alexander to make full use of his autocratic authority. He was more interested in the achievement of specific ends than in the means by which they were arrived at. After Alexander had reorganized the empire's administration, abolished the Table of Ranks, founded a ministry of education, drawn up a law code, restructured the judicial system, colonized the south, improved communications, extended protection to industry and commerce, and above all facilitated the advance of the country's lowest social orders ('et surtout la restauration du tiers état') – then, and only then, in La Harpe's opinion, could the tsar proceed to the promulgation of a constitutional charter. 'To occupy oneself with such a charter today would be to abandon reality for the sake of pursuing a dangerous chimera'.[51] La Harpe wanted Alexander to 'hurry slowly', not to engage in the sort of grand gesture embodied in Aleksandr Vorontsov's proposal for a charter, not to insist on the sort of immediate 'revolution from above' which he seemed to contemplate as heir to the throne, but to work towards the introduction of regularity and reliability in the conduct of affairs and to instil in his subjects a sense that their government could be trusted.

This was sound advice, but it required of Alexander an interest in fine tuning which was not one of his gifts. It smacked of the schoolroom and offered few opportunities for cutting a dash. Alexander was not content to be the beagle that sat by the fire while the hounds were out in the fields. If he could enact a constitution, or spend his time thinking about one, do-

21

mestic affairs were of interest to him. If he had to bury his head in the wel-
ter of advice issuing from La Harpe, let alone attend to the many other projects which came up for consideration at meetings of the Unofficial
Committee, his spirits tended to flag. Because Alexander was unwilling to
attend to detail, only two of the spheres which La Harpe considered to be
of primary importance significantly changed their shape in the early years
of the reign. Central government underwent an overhaul in edicts of September 1802. The Senate, whose place in the country's administrative structure had occasioned so much discussion, was granted the right to object to
government edicts which it considered improper, and a network of ministries came into being which on paper marked a sharp break with the collegiate system of government established by Peter the Great. In education,
statutes of 1803 and 1804 introduced a four-tier system which looked considerably more sophisticated than that created by Catherine the Great's
Statute on Popular Schools of 1786. The empire had hitherto been acquiring a somewhat random network of low-level and underfunded educational establishments, but now received an educational ladder, the rungs of
which ascended from the parish via the district to provincial gymnasia and
universities. A degree of administrative devolution made possible the more
effective supervision of local educational developments. The empire was
divided into six educational districts (St Petersburg, Moscow, Vil'na, Dorpat, Khar'kov and Kazan'), each headed by a Curator and each containing
(or set to contain) a university, which was to be responsible for the three
other sorts of school in the district.

These improvements suffered from considerable deficiencies. The Senate's 'right of remonstrance' was soon shown not be worth very much.
When Seweryn Potocki complained that an edict of December 1802 which
obliged nobles below officer rank to serve twelve years in the army con-
flicted with the Charter of Nobility of 1785, the tsar responded by withdrawing permission for senators to voice their objections. Perhaps the
withdrawal of a fairly minor concession did not matter very much, but the
introduction of ministries, a much more far-reaching affair, was handled almost equally badly. The difference between collegiate and ministerial approaches to government was considerable. Colleges were headed by
committees, ministries by individuals, with the result that ministries were
more likely than colleges to despatch business rapidly. After Catherine the
Great's provincial reform of 1775 transferred many areas of government activity to the regions, the majority of the central colleges had either been
abolished or fallen into abeyance. Alexander I had at least two good reasons, therefore, for proceeding quickly to the introduction of ministries:
they were conducive to greater efficiency, and there was not much standing in their way. A ministry of crown properties had been established by
Paul, and the authority of the Procurator-General (head of the Senate) had
been waxing as the importance of the eighteenth-century colleges waned.
Since individuals were already prevailing over committees in certain fields
of government activity, turning a practice into a principle seemed sensible.

It would have speeded the enactment of any other reforms Alexander was contemplating. Yet he botched the job, by setting up ministries without finally abolishing the colleges. He subordinated the latter to the former, but made it hard for ministers to cut through the red tape beloved of their subordinates. It was not until 1811 that the ministries were put on a sounder footing, and even so, as an expert on imperial Russian administration points out, the last vestige of the eighteenth-century collegiate system did not disappear until 1863.[52] Had Alexander encouraged his new ministers to work together, he might have minimized the other flaws in his revision of the central administration; but although he set up a Committee of Ministers, he did not intend or allow it to turn into a cabinet.

Gaps and contradictions were similarly manifest in the reforms of education. The changes in this field looked far-reaching, but they flattered to deceive. Schools run by the army and the church remained outside the orbit of the new Ministry of Education (technically the 'Ministry of Public Enlightenment'). The gentry for some decades continued to educate their children at home or in private noble pensions. The new educational system was supposed to be classless, but without concurrent changes in policy towards the peasantry few serfs were likely to benefit from it. The government failed to decide at the outset how many students the universities might expect to enrol. It also failed to provide teachers quickly enough to staff the new schools and left to the regions the task of finding most of the money necessary to set the new institutions on their feet. The minister who was given charge of the educational system, Petr Zavadovskii, exemplified the government's lack of commitment to reform. He had handled Russian education more or less continuously since being made head of Catherine the Great's Schools Commission in 1782, but at the beginning of the reign of Alexander I he was over sixty and, by the admission of the tsar, 'a real sheep'; a mordant French resident in St Petersburg called him a 'pedant and sophist' who had 'a self-satisfied air and trifling capacities'.[53]

Alexander's larger ambitions, to transform Russian law and improve the prospects of the peasantry, made little progress in the early years of the reign. Admittedly, the legal commission set up in August 1801 to continue the many eighteenth-century attempts at codification included on its staff Aleksandr Radishchev, the radical thinker who had been sent to Siberia ten years earlier for publishing *A Journey from St Petersburg to Moscow*. Radishchev's reappearance in the capital for the first time in a decade (he had been allowed to return to his estates under Paul) seemed to be a mark of the seriousness of the government's attachment to change. Radishchev and Aleksandr Vorontsov were close, and the former probably played an important part in the preparation of the latter's coronation charter; but neither this nor the radical's writings for the legal commission bore fruit. Zavadovskii, Radishchev's superior at the legal commission, showed no more drive in respect of the law than he did at the Ministry of Education, and drove his subordinate to despair by asking him, with reference to his continuing radicalism, whether he had not had enough of Siberia already. In September 1802, the month when ministries were created and Alexander's reforms seemed to be getting somewhere, Radishchev committed suicide. In July 1803 the tsar was still speaking of a desire to confer civil rights on the nation,[54] but he was foolish to suppose that a general codex could be drawn up before the laws which were currently in force had been thoroughly studied; in this respect, as in so many others, he showed a naive inclination to run before he could walk.

Solving the problems posed by the peasantry was even more difficult than reforming the administration, the education system and the law. Alexander claimed in 1801 that he wanted to abolish serfdom and that, 'if education were on a higher level', he would risk his life to do so;[55] but he came up against a plethora of suggestions which buried him in detail. His friends differed considerably from each other in their views on the peasant question. Pavel Stroganov felt that the government ought to range itself on the side of the lower orders, Czartoryski and Kochubei occupied a sort of middle ground, and Novosil'tsev tended to relegate social reform to a back seat. Alexander achieved a little. He decided to abandon his father's and grandmother's practice of giving away large numbers of state-owned peasants to the nobility, and sanctioned an edict of December 1801 which entitled certain non-noble groups to purchase unpopulated land; but instead of giving away state peasants he tended to transfer them on lease (which amounted to the same thing), and he failed to act on the suggestion that the government should ameliorate the condition of landless household serfs by buying them from their owners and settling them on state-owned land. It was a measure of his confusion that, towards the end of his reign, he seemed to feel that he had abolished the practice of selling serfs independently of the land which they worked, whereas in fact he had merely abolished the right to advertise such sales in the official press.[56]

The one potentially important serf measure to reach the statute books in the early years of Alexander's reign was the Free Agriculturalists Law of February 1803, which allowed serfs to buy freedom and land by agreement with their owners. The initiative for this measure came from Sergei Rumiantsev, however, not from a central member of the administration, and Viktor Kochubei pointed out in a contemporary letter that it was to be interpreted extremely conservatively.[57] As a means of achieving substantial change, the law was seriously flawed. Landlords and serfs were unlikely to agree terms with ease, credit facilities available to serfs were few, and no upper limit was set to the amount landlords could ask for their serfs' freedom. Since only about 47,000 male serfs benefited from the new law in Alexander's reign, most of them in a small number of large-scale agreements, the countryside was hardly transformed.

CONCLUSION

Nevertheless, the Free Agriculturalists Law says something about Alexander's first years on the throne which is worth underlining. All the discussions which took place between 1801 and late 1804 (when the tsar began devoting almost all his attention to foreign affairs) turned on the need to elaborate guiding principles. Not many principles were actually enunciated – not, at least, with any great clarity – but once the hunt for them had begun it could not easily be arrested. The Free Agriculturalists Law foreshadowed the adoption of the principle that, if serfs were to be emancipated, they had to receive not only personal freedom but also enough land to maintain their independence. The counter-principle – that serfs be freed without land and thereby greatly impoverished – was also in the air and was to be enshrined in the emancipation of the Baltic peasantry (which took place in the second decade of the reign). Before the second and harsher principle received legislative sanction, a precedent had been set for taking a generous view of the way in which social relations should develop. Alexander had set other influential precedents by 1804. He had given a fillip to the notion of an autocracy based on law rather than whim. He had established that creating a smoother governmental machine was a praiseworthy objective. He had rendered classless education less than a fantasy. The complexity of the problems facing him had prevented him from turning his youthful idealism into a multiplicity of tangible improvements, but he had created an atmosphere in which principles could be canvassed and he had allowed discussions to take place whose effects could not easily be calculated. He promised more than he performed, but others, inside and outside the government, were to try turning his promises into reality. They might have been successful if the empire had not proceeded to spend a decade at war.

NOTES

1. A. S. Khomiakov, 'O sel'skoi obshchine', PSS (4th edn, 8 vols, Moscow, 1911–14), iii. 461.
2. L. Namier, *Vanished Supremacies* (Harmondsworth, 1962), p. 26.
3. D. Mackenzie Wallace, *Russia* (2 vols, London, 1905), i. 160.
4. V. O. Kliuchevskii, *Pis'ma, dnevniki, aforizmy i mysli ob istorii* (Moscow, 1968), pp. 298–9.
5. M. Paléologue, *The Enigmatic Czar* (London, 1938); H. Troyat, *Alexandre Ier: Le Sphinx du Nord* (Paris, 1980); A. McConnell, *Tsar Alexander I: Paternalistic Reformer* (New York, 1970); J. C. Biaudet and F. Nicod, eds, *Correspondance de Frédéric-César de La Harpe et Alexandre Ier* (3 vols, Neuchâtel, 1978–80), i. 613.

6. James Billington, *The Icon and the Axe* (New York, 1966), p. 217.
7. Anon (N. A. Sablukov), 'Reminiscences of the Court and Times of the Emperor, Paul I of Russia', *Fraser's Magazine*, vol. 72, no. 428 (August 1865), p. 224.
8. N. K. Shil'der, *Imperator Aleksandr I* (4 vols, St Petersburg, 1897–8), i. 276.
9. Galina von Meck, *As I Remember Them* (London, 1973), p. 393.
10. Alan Palmer, *Alexander I: Tsar of War and Peace* (London, 1974), p. 40; N. Ia. Eidel'man, *Gran' vekov: Politicheskaia bor'ba v Rossii: Konets XVIII – nachalo XIX stoletiia* (Moscow, 1982), passim.
11. Shil'der, *Aleksandr I* (above, n. 8), i. 280–2.
12. F. F. Vigel', *Zapiski*, ed. S. Ia. Shtraikh (2 vols, Moscow, 1928), i. 306.
13. O. A. Narkiewicz, 'Alexander I and the Senate Reform', SEER 47 (1969), 118, 120.
14. Marc Raeff, 'Filling the Gap between Radishchev and the Decembrists', SR 26 (1967), 396–9.
15. Marc Raeff, *Plans for Political Reform in Russia, 1730–1905* (Englewood Cliffs, NJ, 1966), pp. 69–74.
16. P. V. Zavadovskii, 'Pis'ma k brat'iam grafam Vorontsovym', in P. Bartenev, ed., *Arkhiv kniazia Vorontsova* (40 vols, Moscow, 1870–95), xii. 214.
17. A. Gielgud, ed., *Memoirs of Prince Adam Czartoryski and His Correspondence with Alexander I* (2 vols, London, 1888), i. 231–2.
18. A. E. Presniakov, *Aleksandr I* (St Petersburg, 1924), pp. 5–7.
19. H. M. Scott, 'Frederick II, the Ottoman Empire and the Origins of the Russo-Prussian Alliance of April 1764', ESR 7 (1977), 153.
20. A. Mickiewicz, *Les Slaves* (5 vols, Paris, 1849), v. 271.
21. A. P. Korelin, *Dvorianstvo v poreformennoi Rossii 1861–1904gg.: Sostav, chislennost', korporativnaia organizatsiia* (Moscow, 1979), pp. 292–303.
22. See, for example, J. Tabiś, *Polacy na uniwersytecie Kijowskim 1834–1863* (Cracow, 1974).
23. E. C. Thaden, *Russia's Western Borderlands, 1710–1870* (Princeton, NJ, 1984), p. 242.
24. August von Haxthausen, *Studies on the Interior of Russia,* ed. S. Frederick Starr (Chicago and London, 1972), pp. 172–3.
25. V. M. Kabuzan, *Izmeneniia v razmeshchenii naseleniia Rossii v XVIII – pervoi polovine XIX v. (Po materialam revizii)* (Moscow, 1971), p. 54.
26. Richard Pipes, 'Catherine II and the Jews: The Origins of the Pale of Settlement', in Pipes, *Russia Observed: Collected Essays on Russian and Soviet History* (Boulder, Colo., 1989), pp. 59–82; John Doyle Klier, *Russia Gathers her Jews: The Origins of the 'Jewish Question' in Russia, 1772–1825* (DeKalb, Ill., 1986).
27. Marc Raeff, *The Well-Ordered Police State: Social and Institutional Change through Law in the Germanies and Russia, 1600–1800* (New Haven, Conn. and London, 1983).
28. D. M. Griffiths, 'Catherine II: The Republican Empress', JFGO 21 (1973), 326.
29. Catherine II, 'Nastavlenie, dannoe grafu Petru Rumiantsovu, pri naznachenii ego malorossiiskim general-gubernatorom', SIRIO 7 (1871), 382.
30. Robert E. Jones, *Provincial Development in Russia: Catherine II and Jakob Sievers* (New Brunswick, NJ, 1984), p. 14.
31. S. Frederick Starr, *Decentralization and Self-Government in Russia, 1830–1870* (Princeton, NJ, 1972), p. 48.
32. D. P. Troshchinskii, 'O neudobstvakh, proiskhodiashchikh ot gosudarstvennogo upravleniia po forme edinolichnoi', SIRIO 3 (1868), 98.

33. Walter M. Pintner, 'The Evolution of Civil Officialdom, 1755–1855', in Walter M. Pintner and Don Karl Rowney, eds, *Russian Officialdom: The Bureaucratization of Russian Society from the Seventeenth to the Twentieth Century* (Chapel Hill, NC, 1980), p. 192.
34. K. I. Arsen'ev, 'Istoriko-statisticheskii ocherk narodnoi obrazovannosti v Rossii', *Uchenye zapiski vtorogo otdeleniia imperatorskoi Akademii nauk,* bk 1 (1854), section 2, p. 26; M. T. Beliavskii, 'Shkola i sistema obrazovaniia v Rossii v kontse XVIII v.', *Vestnik moskovskogo universiteta, Istoriko-filologicheskaia seriia,* 1959 no. 2, p. 110.
35. B. N. Mironov, 'Gramotnost' v Rossii 1797–1917 godov: Poluchenie novoi istoricheskoi informatsii s pomoshch'iu metodov retrospektivnogo prognozirovaniia', *Istorii SSSR,* 1985 no. 4, p. 149. As late as 1851 the urban population of the empire constituted only 7.8 per cent of the total: Jerome Blum, *Lord and Peasant in Russia from the Ninth to the Nineteenth Century* (Princeton, NJ, 1961), p. 281.
36. Pintner, 'Evolution of Civil Officialdom' (above, n. 33), p. 215.
37. A. Pogrebinskii, *Ocherki istorii finansov dorevoliutsionnoi Rossii* (Moscow, 1954), p. 19.
38. Walter Leitsch, 'The Russian Nobility in the Eighteenth Century', *East European Quarterly* 11 (1977), 317.
39. Steven L. Hoch, *Serfdom and Social Control in Russia: Petrovskoe, a Village in Tambov* (Chicago and London, 1986), pp. 28–36.
40. V. I. Semevskii, *Krest'iane v tsarstvovanie Ekateriny II* (2 vols, St Petersburg, 1881–1901), and Semevskii, *Krest'ianskii vopros v Rossii v XVIII i pervoi polovine XIX veka* (2 vols, St Petersburg, 1888).
41. M. D. Kurmacheva, *Krepostnaia intelligentsiia Rossii: Vtoraia polovina XVIII – nachalo XIX veka* (Moscow, 1983), p. 139.
42. I. de Madariaga, 'Catherine II and the Serfs: A Reconsideration of Some Problems', SEER 52 (1974), 34–62; P. G. Ryndziunskii, 'K izucheniiu dinamiki chislennosti krepostnogo naseleniia v doreformennoi Rossii', *Istoriia SSSR,* 1983 no. 1, pp. 209–12.
43. J. P. LeDonne, *Ruling Russia: Politics and Administration in the Age of Absolutism 1762–1796* (Princeton, NJ, 1984).
44. Grand Duke Nikolai Mikhailovich, *Graf P. A. Stroganov* (3 vols, St Petersburg, 1903), ii. 110–15.
45. P. Maikov, 'Baron Gustav Andreevich Rozenkampf', RS 120 (1904), 164.
46. Nikolai Mikhailovich, *Stroganov* (above, n. 44), ii. 63.
47. David Christian, 'The Political Views of the Unofficial Committtee in 1801: Some New Evidence', CASS 12 (1978), 259.
48. Gielgud, *Memoirs of Prince Adam Czartoryski* (above, n. 17), i. 291.
49. Raeff, *Plans for Political Reform* (above, n. 15), pp. 76– 84.
50. N. V. Minaeva, *Pravitel'stvennyi konstitutionalizm i peredovoe obshchestvennoe mnenie Rossii v nachale XIX veka* (Saratov, 1982), p. 82.
51. Biaudet and Nicod, *Correspondance de La Harpe* (above, n. 5), i. 533–55, esp. pp. 548–9.
52. N. P. Eroshkin, *Krepostnicheskoe samoderzhavie i ego politicheskie instituty (Pervaia polovina XIX veka)* (Moscow, 1981), p. 216.
53. Grand Duke Nikolai Mikhailovich, *Imperator Aleksandr I* (2 vols, St Petersburg, 1912), i. 359; P. Sadikov, ed., 'Frantsuzskii agent o russkom pravitel'stve v 1802–1803gg.', KA 20 (1927), 234.
54. Maikov, 'Rozenkampf' (above, n. 45), pp. 169–70.

55. I. M. Kataev, 'Zakonodatel'stvo o krest'ianakh pri imperatorakh Pavle I i Aleksandre I', in A. K. Dzhivelegov, S. P. Mel'gunov and V. I. Picheta, eds, *Velikaia reforma: Russkoe obshchestvo i krest'ianskii vopros v proshlom i nastoiashchem* (6 vols, Moscow, 1911), ii. 78.
56. A. N. Dolgikh, 'Krest'ianskii vopros v politike Aleksandra I v 1820 g. (o prodazhe krest'ian bez zemli)', *Vestnik moskovskogo universiteta, Seriia 8: Istoriia,* 1984 no 2, esp. p. 62.
57. V. P. Kochubei, 'Pis'mo k chernigovskomu gubernatoru Frensdorfu', RA, 1886 vol 2, pp. 163–4.

CHAPTER TWO

Russia and the Napoleonic Wars

INTRODUCTION

The way Russia got into the Napoleonic Wars was not of her own making, but the way she came out of them was. In the first years of his reign Alexander I chose to be at peace but was forced into war. After 1812, he might have had peace but chose to go on fighting. His decision to go on to the offensive at the end of 1812 can be explained by pointing to the events of the previous seven years, the competition between the pacific and the aggressive aspects of his personality, and the long-term ambivalence of Russia's attitude towards foreign involvements, but it proved to be unfortunate. By choosing aggression and sending his troops across Russia's frontiers Alexander greatly enlarged the tasks which his regime had to cope with. By making himself the arbiter of Europe, he reduced the likelihood that he would succeed in consolidating the ramshackle polity he governed.

In terms of square miles, the Russian Empire's eighteenth-century expansion had been less remarkable than it seemed to most contemporaries. 'The sea! The sea!' was an exciting theme, but getting to the Gulf of Finland and the Crimea actually marked a diminution of the rate at which the empire was pushing out its frontiers. Between 1550 and 1700 Moscow had been making much larger strides into the eastern and south-eastern interior. Tsars, however, did not measure their gains in square miles. They sought respect from their equals. Only the rulers of western Europe could confirm them in their self-esteem. Making western monarchs take note of them required the subordination of Sweden, Poland and the Ottoman Empire, the states that cut them off from the European heartland. This task occupied the greater part of the eighteenth century, and was still under way when the French Revolution broke out. By then Russia had done enough to make the west take notice, but at least four problems had emerged in the wake of her success. The tsars had gone beyond their original, already ambitious objectives; they found that pursuing even the original objectives placed enormous strains on their resources; they encountered severe criticism of their behaviour from various members of the small Russian elite; and they failed to provide for the possibility that changes in the west might alter the basis on which their foreign policy was conducted.

The second half of the reign of Catherine the Great epitomized all these difficulties. Not content with consolidating her uncertain position on the throne, coming out on top in her first war with the Turks, taking Belorussia from Poland, suppressing a far-reaching peasant rebellion and enacting a radical revision of Russia's civil administration, Catherine looked for foreign fields to conquer. The west was already fearful of Russian intentions. Around 1760 France had come into possession of a document purporting to be the 'Testament' of Peter the Great, which mapped out a scheme for the subjugation of Europe.[1] It was a forgery, a sort of rococo equivalent of the Protocols of the Elders of Zion, but enough of its details rang true to make the French wary. When Russia joined Prussia and Austria in annexing parts of Poland in 1772, western alarm intensified. At the far end of the continent Edmund Burke expressed the view that 'These powers will continue armed. Their armies must have employment. Poland was but a breakfast, and there are not many Polands to be found. Where will they dine?'[2] His anxiety attested to the fact that Russia was already receiving the respect she considered her due. But the Russian empress would not leave well alone.

After signing her first treaty with the Turks, the Treaty of Kuchuk-Kainardji of 1774, Catherine seemed to throw caution to the winds. Up to that point in her reign she can be absolved from the charge of wanton aggression. In a way, her first Turkish war resulted from complicated events in Poland which necessitated Russian violation of Ottoman territory. Arguably, the first partition of Poland resulted from the determination of Prussia to take advantage of Russia's engagement in the south. But after 1775 Catherine became more rapacious. What made Kuchuk-Kainardji hard for the Turks to swallow was the bestowal of independence on the Crimea, which foreshadowed Russia's annexation of the peninsula nine years later. Catherine, however, read much more than this into her triumph. When she informed her subjects of the peace treaty in 1775, she claimed that it gave her a protectorate over all the Christian inhabitants of the Ottoman Empire. For international consumption, she issued a French text of the agreement which tended to support her interpretation. The interpretation was unsound (the treaty actually obliged the sultan, not the tsar, to protect Turkey's Christian subjects), but 'The hoax was successfully foisted on Europe'.[3] Claiming a protectorate over Balkan Christians appeared greatly to enhance Russia's prestige, which now became Catherine's overriding concern. In 1779 she made two new forward moves. By joining France as a guarantor of the Treaty of Teschen between Austria and Prussia (which ended the War of the Bavarian Succession), she showed a readiness to extend Russia's diplomatic responsibilities into central Europe. By christening the future Alexander I's younger brother Konstantin (Constantine), she symbolized her interest in Russia's eventual acquisition of Constantinople.

Signs of the empress's commitment to southward expansion multiplied in the next decade. In 1780 she met Joseph II of Austria for the first time and began the process of abandoning her alliance with Prussia. While Maria Theresa lived, Austrian interest in an aggressive attitude towards the Ottoman Empire was limited to snapping up unconsidered trifles like the Bukovina in 1774–5, but her death in November 1780 freed the hands of her son. In 1781 Joseph and Catherine concluded a secret alliance which strengthened Catherine's position in the south. In 1782 Catherine put various proposals to Joseph for the further subversion of Turkey, the most ambitious of which envisaged replacing the sultan's regime with a Greek Orthodox empire under her younger grandson. The extent of Catherine's commitment to this far-reaching 'Greek Project' has been the subject of much debate among historians, but Hugh Ragsdale has recently produced new evidence to show that she was still very attracted by the idea when her second war with Turkey broke out in 1787.[4] Had that war gone well, Catherine's enthusiasm for expansion might have known no bounds.

The war went badly, however, and Catherine had to think again. Potemkin moved slowly in the field, Austria deserted her ally, Sweden attacked in the north, and Britain began a diplomatic shouting match. The Treaty of Jassy which concluded hostilities in late December 1791 gave Catherine only two strips of land for her pains, one to the west of the river Bug, the other to the east of the Sea of Azov. Poland, meanwhile, was showing distinct signs of recovering from the shock of the first partition. The 'Republic of Nobles' adopted a new constitution in May 1791 and threatened to escape the eye of the basilisk. Catherine dithered. The death of Potemkin in October 1791 and the absence at the Jassy negotiations of Aleksandr Bezborodko, Russia's principal expert on foreign affairs, allowed the empress's lover, Platon Zubov, to get the upper hand at court and persuade her to send troops into Poland.

By then, the spring of 1792, developments in western Europe were beginning to overtake events in the east. Revolutionary France had declared a 'war of peoples against kings' and begun to call in question the way in which foreign policies were traditionally conducted. Catherine inveighed against the revolutionaries and broke off diplomatic relations with France after the execution of Louis XVI in 1793, but she had to complete her unfinished business in eastern Europe before turning to the west. As a result, she looked on helplessly while the French shifted the international goalposts. 'Of all the great powers, Russia was the most strident in condemning the French Revolution' but 'the last to go to war against it'.[5] Completing the dismemberment of Poland occupied the years 1792 to 1795 and left Catherine with little time, energy or money for engagements in the west. She made deals with Austria and Prussia to effect the second and third Polish partitions in 1793 and 1795, but could not join them in taking on the French. By the time Poland had been erased from the map Prussia had withdrawn from the war with France and deprived Russia's troops of their quickest route across the continent. Catherine mustered her forces for intervention against the French Republic, but died before committing them to the fray.

Doing so would not have increased her popularity in the eyes of Russia's elite. Even her successes on battlefields close to home won her few plaudits from the native gentry. On the whole, eighteenth-century Russian society was sufficiently deferential to let monarchs get away with treating foreign affairs as a royal peculiar, but even autocrats discovered that they sometimes needed a little more than grudging acquiescence in the way they handled international relations. Peter III learned the hard way in 1762. Catherine II met opposition when she deviated from the peace policy with which she began her reign. Count N. I. Panin's 'northern system' in foreign affairs, which emphasized consolidating the territorial gains made by Peter the Great, received its first blow in the outbreak of war with Turkey in 1768 and was a dead letter by the early 1780s. Its demise, however, did not go unremarked. Robert Jones has made clear that, while historians have usually 'begun and ended with the assumption that the central points of controversy between Catherine's government and its critics were the issues of autocracy and serfdom', in fact Catherine's critics were mainly opposed to her foreign wars rather than the principles underlying the empire's political and social structure.[6] Opposition to war was no doubt to be expected from scions of the old nobility like Prince Mikhail Shcherbatov, to whom the entire course of eighteenth-century Russian history was uncongenial, but it also came from more forward-looking members of the gentry estate like the Vorontsov family, Governor Sievers of Novgorod, and the celebrated author of *A Journey from St Petersburg to Moscow*, Aleksandr Radishchev. War disturbed the patterns of Russian trade, opened the way for plague to penetrate Russia from the south, denuded Russian estates of the manpower essential to their profitability and made enlisted serfs miserable. Radishchev's indictment of the serfs' lot gained in pungency from being published in the summer of 1790 when war with both Swedes and Turks was at its height.

As heir to the throne, Catherine's son Paul found in her wars a good way of opposing her. By ranging himself with the 'pacifists' he gave the opposition hope. On succeeding his mother he did a few things to live up to the hope he inspired, releasing Radishchev from Siberian exile, treating the defeated Poles with a degree of magnanimity, not pressing ahead with the development of the empire's southern infrastructure and recalling Sievers to a prominent place in government. But he could not escape the fact that developments under Catherine had given the empire new interests and responsibilities. Although he probably did not intend to increase Russia's foreign policy commitments, and although, for the first year and a half of his reign, he succeeded in keeping them within bounds, he had to react to the fact that France was beginning to make her presence felt in the Mediterranean. Before Catherine's Turkish wars Russia could have viewed this development with equanimity, but once the Greek project was afoot Europe's southern sea became part of the Russian field of vision. Under the

Franco-Austrian Treaty of Campoformio, signed in October 1797, France set up a client republic in north Italy and took the Ionian islands from the defunct Venetian Republic. These intimations of French interest in the Mediterranean were soon to multiply. The French government was contemplating an invasion of England, but Bonaparte, its principal general, was not keen on the idea. He gave France's shortage of sea power as the main reason for his lack of enthusiasm, but proposed an alternative which also depended on ships. In May 1798 he embarked for Egypt. When the French fleet took Malta the following month, Paul felt obliged to act. He had been romantically attracted to the Knights of Malta from his youth, and had established a Russian Grand Priory of the Order soon after his accession to the throne. His personal concern for the Knights, the strategic importance of their island, and Bonaparte's obvious determination to press on to the east decided Paul to send Russian ships southward.

Once he had committed himself, complications ensued which he was unable to resolve. Ironically, Nelson's destruction of Bonaparte's fleet at Aboukir Bay in Egypt in August 1798 removed the French threat to the east almost as soon as it had been posed, but by this time Paul had already taken his decision to involve Russia in pan-European affairs. To get his ships to the Ionian Islands (where the French hold was tenuous), he had to go into alliance with Catherine the Great's principal adversary, Turkey. To challenge France on land, he had to work closely with Austria, which he found well-nigh impossible. To maintain good relations with the British he had to give them carte blanche in the management of neutral shipping, which militated against his own economic interests. The successes of Admiral Ushakov in the Mediterranean and General Suvorov in north Italy were not enough to compensate for these disadvantages. By 1799 Paul had realized that participating in a coalition against the French created more problems than it solved. He found it difficult, however, to retreat, because proposals for new courses of action rained down on him from all sides. Having escaped from Egypt, Bonaparte toppled the French government in November 1799 and began making up for lost time. In June 1800 he smashed the Austrians at Marengo in north Italy and extended the hand of friendship to the Russians. Paul was glad that the Austrians had been put in their place, but was not yet ready to make common cause with the enemy. Alternatives presented themselves. Prussia suddenly realized that her international interests were not best served by the inertia which had characterized her foreign policy for the previous five years. The peace which France was going to impose on Austria would significantly change the shape of central Europe. To upset it, Prussia informed Paul that she was prepared to join the Russians in a return to the battlefield. In northern Europe, meanwhile, Denmark and Sweden were feeling the effects on their trade of Britain's control of the sea. They were neutral in the conflict between France and her enemies, but tended towards the French side because of the economic consequences of the alternative. They needed Russian assistance to further their interests, and urged Paul to revert to a 'northern system' and proclaim the 'armed neutrality' of the Baltic countries.

In the summer of 1800, therefore, Russia faced a bewildering range of options. Accepting the French olive-branch meant dropping the Turkish alliance and taking on the aggressive role in the orient which Bonaparte had originally intended for himself; making common cause with the Prussians meant protracted campaigning in the European heartland; armed neutrality in the north meant incurring the wrath of the British. Paul tried the third course of action first, but found that, while it did indeed alienate the British, it did not strengthen his negotiating position *vis-à-vis* the French. At the end of 1800 he seems to have combined the northern policy with accepting the French olive branch. Making an ally of France, however, proved to be more than his domestic opponents could stomach.

Paul may not have intended a permanent Franco-Russian rapprochement. The latest students of his foreign policy agree in finding it rational (if tortuous), but disagree as to the tsar's long-term objective.[7] Paul did not live long enough to make his intentions clear. Russians who thought about foreign policy in early 1801 could not understand an approach which included friendly relations with an old enemy (Turkey), negotiating with the root cause of the continent's ills (France), and alienating Russia's principal trading partner (the British, who were about to defeat the Danish fleet at Copenhagen and sail up the Baltic). As Hugh Seton-Watson says, Russia's situation was 'extraordinary';[8] the new tsar had to unpick the twisted threads.

THE DESCENT INTO WAR (1801–5)

Like his grandmother and father, Alexander I began with a peace policy. It was becoming a convention for new Russian rulers to withdraw from the entanglements of their predecessors and devote their first years to domestic improvements. The new tsar's advisers, however, differed from each other in their understanding of the way in which peace was to be secured. Alexander's first foreign minister, Nikita Petrovich Panin, nephew of Catherine's adviser of the 1760s and one of those who had been prominent in the early days of the conspiracy against Paul, rested his policy on the traditional concept of the balance of power. At the beginning of a paper written at the start of the new reign he seemed to be arguing for a complete withdrawal from European affairs. 'It is on her own soil', he wrote, 'that Russia must make conquests'. But Panin did not believe that Russia could close her eyes to developments abroad. To be assured of a free hand at home, she had to be certain that Turkey remained backward, Sweden insignificant, and Austria and Prussia so well matched that they cancelled each other out. If these preconditions of peace were threatened, Russia had to be prepared to fight for their re-establishment. Ongoing alliances were the best means of ensuring that the preconditions remained in place. It was unwise to start contemplating alliances only when danger threatened, for, as Suvorov put it, 'a minute decides a battle, an hour decides a campaign, a day determines the fate of a kingdom'. If Russia abandoned the principle of making alliances, Panin argued, her former allies would seek them elsewhere. Austria, for example, would throw herself into the arms of France. Even republican Rome at the height of its glory had not fought shy of alliances. Russia's natural ally was Britain. She was standing up to France more or less single-handedly. Her pre-eminence in trade posed no threat to Russia so long as the Russians remained a non-trading nation. Rather than draw in her horns, therefore, Russia should work for peace by judiciously involving herself in the outside world.[9]

Not everyone in the upper reaches of Russian government agreed with Panin on the need for improving relations with Britain. Although Alexander recalled the 20,000 Cossacks whom Paul had despatched in the direction of India and ordered the Russian ambassador in London to work for the restoration of Anglo-Russian harmony, there were limits to his Anglophilia. In his early dealings with London he drove a hard bargain, insisting, for example, on the maritime rights of the neutral Baltic countries with whom Russia was closely associated. His preference was for a foreign policy which left his hands completely free. He made his position clear at a session of the Unofficial Committee in July 1801,[10] and at the end of September he made peace with France. Although he probably did not share the view of his former tutor La Harpe that a day might come when Russia and France could enjoy 'more intimate relations',[11] neither was he prepared to join Britain in devising new ways of putting the French in their place. His inclinations were shared in part by the friends of his own age group who made up the Unofficial Committee, and to a much greater extent by men of the older generation who thought that Russia had taken on too much in the reign of Catherine the Great. N. P. Panin belonged to the older generation but was prepared to contemplate alliances. Other members of the old guard – Nikolai Rumiantsev, Nikolai Mordvinov, Aleksandr Kurakin – advocated clear-cut withdrawal from the European scene. Rumiantsev, for example, on being appointed Minister of Commerce in 1802, initiated a Russian circumnavigation of the globe whose primary object was to improve Russia's economic prospects in the Far East.[12] Since by then Britain and France had made peace at Amiens, it looked as if a policy of standing aside from Europe was going to be sustainable.

Bonaparte, however, injected new life into the alternative policy of alliances. The peace treaty he signed with Britain at Amiens in March 1802 never looked likely to last. Its imminence persuaded the Turks that they too had to make peace with him, but Bonaparte thought of peace in the orient as a prelude to a new set of eastern adventures. Under France's agreement with Russia the Ionian Islands were supposed to be demilitarized, and according to the Treaty of Amiens Britain was supposed to withdraw from Malta, but neither Britain nor Russia took these provisions seriously. Before the end of 1801 even the pacific Viktor Kochubei was urging Alexander to despatch fresh troops to Corfu.[13] Having entered the Mediterranean at the end of the eighteenth century, Russia was not prepared to abandon it. Nor could she assume that normal relations would obtain for long in the European heartland. The multilateral peacemaking of 1801–2 offered no more than an opportunity for strategic reappraisal. Alexander made the point well in instructions he gave to his new ambassador at The Hague in May 1802. The extension of French power, he said, might cease to be alarming if France decided to enter upon a period of consolidation, but she was unlikely to do so. For the time being Russia had to pursue a peace policy, since neither she nor the other European powers were in a position to challenge French dominance. By 'good administration', however, Russia would once more be able to assume the influential role which belonged to her. The tsar strongly implied that his pursuit of peace was to be temporary.[14]

For about two years the pursuit of peace loomed larger in Russian policy than the subliminal recognition that peace was a daydream. From the second half of 1803, however, it became increasingly difficult to sustain the view that Russia could avoid returning to the fray. France had been interfering openly in the affairs of northern Italy, Switzerland and the Netherlands, and had presided over changes in the Holy Roman Empire which undermined the position of the Habsburgs without enhancing the role of Prussia. One way or another, most of the European land mass seemed to be in French hands. Aleksandr Vorontsov, by now the foreign minister, abandoned his commitment to peace. In an important memorandum of November 1803 he focused on the threat to Russian interests which was posed by French activity in north Germany. The French entry into Hanover, which had taken place in May, seemed likely to be followed by threats to Mecklenburg, the free cities of Hamburg and Lübeck, and even the duchy of Holstein. Since Russia's eighteenth-century foreign policy had assumed that the northern shores of mainland Europe were part of her sphere of influence, she could not allow French inroads to go any further. If the French compelled Denmark to close the mouth of the Baltic to British ships, Russia's entire trade would be brought to a halt for an indefinite period and inestimable domestic harm might ensue. In southern Europe, meanwhile, the French were marshalling their troops in Otranto and preparing to transport them from Italy to the Balkans. The Montenegrins could be expected to slow them down, but not to prevent an eventual French occupation of the Peloponnese and Rumelia. The Russian-backed regime on the Ionian Islands would fall and a 'democratic republic' might emerge in place of the Ottoman Empire. Russia had to be ready for war. Vorontsov proposed the creation of armies in the Russian Baltic provinces (to assist the Danes in a Holstein campaign), at Brest-Litovsk (to assist the Austrians in the conduct of central European affairs), and in the south (to enter Moldavia in the event of a threat to the Ottoman Empire). Russia's frontline troops were to be backed by a reserve army equal in numbers to their combined strength (deployed along the whole length of Russia's western frontier), and by naval squadrons in the Baltic and the Black Sea. The foreign minister's memorandum was an open confession that Russia had to abandon her short-lived concentration on domestic affairs and accept the implications of France's forward moves.[15]

It was some months before Vorontsov's insistence on the need to fight gained general acceptance, and a year after that before Russia sent her troops into battle. The tsar's continuing reluctance to grasp the nettle, Vorontsov's declining health, and the emergence of a crucial 'third force' in the management of Russian foreign affairs all played their part in delaying the empire's re-entry into the war with Napoleon. In accordance with the first of Vorontsov's proposals, Russia entered into detailed negotiations with Denmark with a view to the likelihood of joint action in north Germany. Agreement was eventually reached in May 1804, but progress was slow on the rest of the foreign minister's agenda. The tsar moved extremely cautiously. As Vorontsov's deputy put it in a letter of February 1804 to the Russian ambassador in London (Vorontsov's brother), 'The emperor is ready to enter the lists as soon as events require him to do so; but although he is not afraid of being forced into war by his enemies, he would not wish to be drawn into it by steps he has taken himself or by those of his friends'.[16] Vorontsov lacked the energy to force Alexander's hand. Although he remained foreign minister until his death in 1805, his involvement in affairs was minimal after the beginning of 1804. From 1803 the rather different ideas of his deputy became increasingly influential.

As we saw in the last chapter, Adam Czartoryski was one of the tsar's closest friends. As the first flush of enthusiasm for domestic reform receded, he started giving his undivided attention to the work of the foreign ministry (of which he had been second-in-command since its foundation in 1802). As a Pole, he knew what Great Powers could do to the impotent. He had two long-term objectives: the re-creation of Poland and the establishment of a European order in which Poland's existence would not seem anomalous. But he was far too clever to state his aims bluntly. In memoranda of 1803–5 he addressed himself to the entire range of European affairs. He made Vorontsov's wide-ranging paper of November 1803 look limited. He wanted Russia to act out of altruism as well as self-interest. His philosophizing fascinated the idealistic tsar, but probably also had the effect of confusing him. The fact that Alexander needed time to understand his ideas further postponed the re-entry of Russia into pan-European affairs. Although in retrospect Czartoryski can be seen to have had 'a more important role in initiating and carrying out a major policy than any of Alexander's other foreign ministers',[17] the policy took a year and a half to leave the drawing board. It was present, in embryo, in Czartoryski's paper of 1803 'On the Political System which Russia Ought to Follow'. This began by making the case for basing foreign policy on long-term principles and went on to address itself to Russia's current situation. Where others tended to emphasize the jeopardy in which all European countries found themselves as a result of the behaviour of Bonaparte, Czartoryski emphasized Russia's strength. He did not deduce from this that she could choose to be supine. She had a duty to the outside world. 'All the powers look towards her, consult her, address themselves to her, and however passive she wants to be, instances crop up every day in which it is necessary that she say yes or no'.[18] Russia should base her policy on courting England and spurning France. She should not look to Austria and Prussia for help. The former sought compensation for her recent reverses, the latter was a naturally acquisitive power. Russia should avoid provoking either of them, but should try to prevent them making common cause with one another. The best way to prevent them becoming a threat was to reconstitute Poland. The tsar's brother and heir, Konstantin, could be given the Polish throne, which would remove him from the Russian succession and prevent him bringing his despotic tendencies to bear on the country of his birth. In southern Europe Russia should contemplate the break-up of the Ottoman Empire, the creation of an independent Greece with control over the western side of the entrance to the Black Sea, the possible inclusion of the Balkan peoples in the Kingdom of Hungary, and the emergence of an independent republic in northern Italy which the rest of the peninsula would look to for inspiration. In central Europe Russia should work for a strong German federation from which Austria and Prussia were excluded. Throughout the continent she should aim at the establishment of regimes which neither attempted to inflame public opinion nor sought to suppress it. In conclusion, Czartoryski returned to his central point: that Russia could not afford to stand aside from Europe, but had to take action.

Only part of Czartoryski's grand design became official policy, but a large enough part to engender the War of the Third Coalition. Czartoryski was well aware that Alexander was unlikely to accept his proposals in their entirety. In some of his memoranda he moderated his aggressive inclinations. In February 1804, for example, he spoke less decisively about the attitude Russia should adopt towards the Ottoman Empire.[19] A month earlier the Serbs had risen against their Ottoman masters, and Russia had to consider whether she should intervene to support them. St Petersburg was not ready. Partly because Russia hesitated (at least in the early stages of the rebellion), this first Serbian uprising lasted nine years and achieved relatively little. But if the tsar was reluctant to adopt a forward policy in the Balkans, he was more easily persuaded of the need to respond to events in central Europe. Chance played a significant part in his decision, but an unexpected event in the West moved him more than the unexpected rising in the Balkans. In March 1804 Napoleon ordered the abduction of the Duc d'Enghien from Baden and his execution at Vincennes. Alexander was triply mortified. Enghien was a royal prince, Baden was the territory of the tsar's father-in-law, and the German principalities were part of the Holy Roman Empire of which Russia was a guarantor. Czartoryski seized the opportunity to call for war with France. In a fulminating speech at the Russian State Council in April 1804 he argued that the latest French outrage warranted the wrath of the entire continent, and if other countries were too frightened to act Russia should give them a lead. It was true, he said, that Russia would have been better off waiting a little before breaking with France, but the Enghien affair could not be allowed to pass. Other members of the Council were more cautious than the assistant foreign minister, and Nikolai Rumiantsev remained anxious to avoid war at almost any cost; but it was evident from now on that Russia would eventually return to the battlefield.[20]

Perhaps the principal effect of the State Council discussion was to ensure that Russia did not attempt too much on her own. In 1803 Czartoryski had had little time for European countries other than Britain. In the course of 1804, many states found themselves drawn into Russia's plans. Agreements were drawn up with Austria, Prussia, Denmark and Sweden which were to come into force if Napoleon activated them. Dealings with Britain, meanwhile, were designed to bring about an offensive. Alexander sent Nikolai Novosil'tsev to London with instructions drawn up by Czartoryski. In April 1805 Britain and Russia agreed to attack Napoleon without waiting for fresh provocations and to persuade other countries to adhere to their alliance. Apart from listing various specific objectives (such as obliging the French to withdraw from north Germany), the two sides committed themselves to 'The establishment of a European order which effectively guarantees the safety and independence of the different States and constitutes a firm barrier against future encroachments'.[21] Alexander could now start planning for war. To stand a chance of beating Napoleon on land, he needed additional troops and easy access to central Europe. He therefore approached the Austrians, who in August 1805 accepted the objectives of the Anglo-Russian alliance and acceded to the military proposals which Alexander had put forward in May. Prussia at first seemed less malleable, but in November signed a convention which marked her near-total acceptance of Russia's aims. Six weeks before squaring Prussia the tsar had agreed a defensive alliance with Turkey which ensured that he would have no difficulty on his southern borders while his troops were campaigning in the west. It looked as if a coalition was coming into being which might stand a chance of putting the French in their place. Although Czartoryski's ambitious foreign policy proposals of 1803 had been watered down, the assistant foreign minister had succeeded in persuading the tsar to end Russia's policy of non-interference in west European affairs. He had had to abandon the idea of resurrecting Poland, but he had probably exercised greater sway over a Russian ruler than any earlier or later head of the Russian foreign ministry.

THE WAR OF THE THIRD COALITION (1805–7)

The new war with France went badly. Only Britain benefited, and only up to a point. Two weeks after Austria adhered to the anti-French coalition, Napoleon gave up hope of getting his troops across the English Channel and despatched them eastwards to the Danube. Freed from the prospect of invasion, Britain went on to destroy the ships that were to have made the invasion possible. Nelson had been chasing the French Admiral Villeneuve for the greater part of 1805, and caught him off south-west Spain on 21 October. This victory, Trafalgar, gave Britain long-term control of the seas, prevented the French from reviving their Mediterranean ambitions of 1798, and facilitated an eventual British return to the war on land (by making possible Wellington's campaigns in Portugal and Spain). In 1805, however, Britain had no thought of sending armies into battle, and Napoleon was able to deal quickly with the troops of the other coalition partners. Austria and Russia failed to coordinate their military operations. The Habsburg Emperor moved both carelessly and too quickly. By sending his principal armies to northern Italy and the Tyrol, he left himself open to a direct French onslaught in the west. Kutuzov, the Russian general, had been urging a concentration of Russian and Austrian forces and a single large engagement. His plan was rejected and he was ordered to fall in with the dispositions of the Austrians. He could not get to western Europe quickly enough. Only Prussia could have reached the Austrians in time to render them effective assistance, but Prussia, at this time, was dithering so much that she would not even let Russian troops cross her territory, let alone take action herself. General Mack, the Austrian commander at Ulm, hesitated to retreat in the face of the French advance. Napoleon encouraged him not to do so by insinuating through an agent that Paris had risen and the British were landing on the French coast. Eventually Mack's position was so invidious that a single French bombardment was enough to shake his nerve. After his capitulation, on 5/17 October, Napoleon disparagingly remarked that he had won a battle 'simply by marching'. Kutuzov, now Vienna's only defence, had vastly fewer men than the enemy. He sought to avoid engagements but was overruled by his political masters. For the first time since Peter the Great, a Russian tsar had put himself at the head of his troops. Alexander's unhealthy respect for Germanic military planning led him to defer to Austria and accept the prospect of battle. On 20 November / 2 December 1805 Kutuzov and such Austrian forces as remained in the field were defeated at Austerlitz in Bohemia. On hearing the news, the dying British Prime Minister William Pitt remarked that the map of Europe could be put away for ten years. On 14/26 December Austria made peace at Pressburg (Bratislava), giving the French new possessions in the Adriatic which endangered Russia's forward position on the Ionian Islands and opened the Balkans to French influence. Because of Trafalgar France was unable to get to the eastern Mediterranean by sea, but she now looked capable of getting there by land.

The disastrous outcome of the 1805 campaign threw Russia's leading political figures into confusion. Czartoryski was strongly critical of the Prussians for their belated support of the anti-Napoleonic coalition. Despite Austria's defeat, he thought the war could be kept going if Russia maintained her alliance with Britain and somehow managed to stiffen Prussia's resolve. The second of these objectives, however, looked unattainable, for Prussia had come to terms with Napoleon within two weeks of Austerlitz (though the terms of the agreement remained fluid for nearly two months). When the tsar realized that, for the time being at least, he could expect no help from Berlin, he had to abandon all thought of attack and wait for more propitious circumstances. Even waiting was risky, as Prince Aleksandr Kurakin implied when he advocated negotiating with the French. A Russian emissary was sent to Paris, but the treaty which he concluded in July 1806 did not find favour in St Petersburg. It required the Russians to pull Admiral Seniavin out of the Adriatic and expose the Balkans to French influence, which ran counter to everything Russia had fought for in the Mediterranean since 1798. The tsar might have been more amenable to French wishes if Napoleon had been proposing to make concessions in central Europe, but Napoleon had no such intention. Indeed, at the very time he was negotiating with the Russian representative he was redrawing the map of Germany. The Holy Roman Empire gave way in the west to the French-backed Confederation of the Rhine. The French emperor was poised to attack his remaining opponents. Even timid Prussia saw the writing on the wall, and thought twice about her pro-French orientation. Without abandoning it altogether, she added a Russian alliance to her armoury. It did her no good. Napoleon violated her territory, forced her into war before the Russians could come to her assistance, and destroyed her armies at Jena and Auerstadt on 2/14 October 1806. France was picking off her opponents one by one. Austria and Prussia had fallen; only Russia, of the continental powers, remained.

By this time Czartoryski had resigned from the Russian foreign ministry. The tsar's cautious diplomacy of 1806 ran counter to his belief in the need for continuing firmness. Alexander had come to doubt all three aspects of Czartoryski's foreign policy – maintaining the English alliance, not relying on Prussia, and engaging in forward moves in the Balkans to divert France's attention from central Europe. As a foreigner, Czartoryski never succeeded in winning the trust of Russian bureaucrats. Once the tsar disagreed with him, his position became untenable. But the aftermath of Jena showed that his views had much to recommend them. Napoleon did not intend to stop at Berlin. A month after Jena he issued a decree from the Prussian capital which marked the beginning of his 'continental system', a device aimed at conquering the British by preventing them from trading with mainland Europe. The device would bite only if Napoleon could control the traffic of all Europe's ports, including those of Russia. Securing Russian adherence to the system necessitated bringing further pressure to bear on the tsar, perhaps by turning the Poles against him, certainly by persuading the Turks to abandon their Russian alliance and work for the French. If Alexander had not faltered in his Anglophilia, if he had given clear signs of preferring Poles to Prussians, and if he had shown the Turks who was master by acting more vigorously in the Balkans, Napoleon might have thought twice about pressing forward. As things stood, the French emperor felt able to continue his advance.

Only East Prussia and Poland stood between Napoleon and the Russian border. In November 1806 Czartoryski, Novosil'tsev and Pavel Stroganov wrote the tsar a joint letter urging specific, drastic action.[22] He responded with a controversial move, creating, for the first time in imperial Russian history, a militia to back up the army. The 612,000 irregulars whom he proposed to recruit looked capable of causing as many problems as they solved. As the ultra-conservative Fedor Rostopchin put it in a letter to the tsar, the usefulness of such a force would evaporate overnight if the recruits took it into their heads to turn on the gentry. According to Rostopchin, 'the influence of Frenchmen resident in Russia is already having a disastrous effect on the servant class, which already awaits Bonaparte in order to be free'.[23] Rostopchin belonged to Muscovite high society, which was beginning to take a dim view of the policies of St Petersburg; but in the capital, too, the militia question gave cause for concern. Viktor Kochubei, quondam reformer, Minister of Internal Affairs, and the only member of the Unofficial Committee still in office, instructed provincial governors to go about raising the new troops with extreme caution. Peasants were to be taken from their everyday duties for no longer than was strictly necessary; they were to be given arms only for the period of their training; and they were to receive only the most elementary instruction in warfare.[24] It was difficult, however, for the government to prevent popular volatility from surfacing. The regime needed mass support and had to take risks to get it. It enlisted the assistance of the church, promulgating via the Holy Synod an edict which called Napoleon 'Antichrist' and a 'false messiah'. The effect of such language was hard to judge. In autumn 1805 Alexander had set up a committee to safeguard domestic order while he was away on campaign. Still-born, it was replaced in January 1807 by a 'Committee of General Safety' with much the same brief. Again the body did little, but such escapades as it managed to uncover seemed to support the view that peasants were beginning to call for their freedom. The Russian government could and did employ literary devices to counteract French propaganda. It backed a new periodical, the *Journal du Nord*, to rebut the French press, and distributed flysheets behind the French lines to persuade enemy soldiers that they were fighting only for Napoleon, not for France. Techniques of this kind were irrelevant, however, to the maintenance of order among Russia's masses. Well might the young civil servant Aleksandr Turgenev confide to his diary, 'I imagine sans-culottes galloping and running down the long Moscow streets'.[25] He could have meant both French 'peasants in uniform' and Russian peasants in caftans.

Success on the battlefield or the reawakening of previously defeated powers might have saved the Russians from having to decide between retreating in the face of an invasion and negotiating with the enemy, but at the turn of 1806–7 neither possibility looked likely to become a reality. Napoleon had fewer troops at his disposal than he was to have when he invaded Russia in 1812, but he had more than his opponents and the morale of his men was high. At first, however, Russia performed well. Her soldiers finally crossed the frontier into East Prussia three weeks after the Prussian débâcle, early in November 1806. The following month, under Bennigsen, they won a small victory at Pultusk to the north of Warsaw, after which they withdrew to the north and based themselves at Königsberg. By early February 1807 Napoleon had regrouped and the second battle of the winter ensued, at Preussisch-Eylau to the south of the Russian headquarters. Napoleon failed in a concerted attempt to encircle the Russians and instead suffered considerable difficulties of his own. Because the Russians quit the field Eylau was technically a French victory, but both sides lost more than 20,000 killed and wounded. Had Alexander thrown caution to the winds and brought up more troops from Russia – including, perhaps, his new militia – he might have pressed the enemy to the limits. He feared an invasion of the empire, however, and had to keep a weather eye on his southern frontier, where the Ottomans had declared war on him and he was engaged in complicated negotiations with Persia. He felt able to do no more than restate his diplomatic objectives in Europe and encourage other countries to join him in pursuing them. At Bartenstein in April 1807 he and Frederick William III of Prussia signed a convention declaring that they could not accept either the continuing existence of the French-backed Confederation of the Rhine or France's military occupation of German territory. They did not wish to return to the status quo in Germany, but Prussia had to regain the territory she had lost as a result of her recent defeats and a 'constitutional federation' had to be set up in Germany which would be able to defend itself against future threats from the west bank of the Rhine. Since Prussia was by this time attenuated to the point of non-existence and could do little to give effect to the Bartenstein policy, only the adherence of Austria to the convention would have converted it into something more than a pious statement of intent. Austria, however, remembered Austerlitz, and quietly welcomed the thought that Europe's second German power was performing no better than General Mack in 1805.

Events in East Prussia now moved rapidly to their conclusion. After a two-month siege Napoleon captured Danzig and drove the combined Prussian and Russian garrison eastwards towards Königsberg. He planned to sever Bennigsen's lines of communication with the East Prussian capital and throw the Russians back across the river Niemen. Bennigsen moved on to the offensive, but changed his mind repeatedly about the best way to prevent the French marshalling their forces. In mid-June the Russians were cornered near Friedland. Their backs to the river Alle, their lines interrupted by lakes, they went down to the decisive defeat of the 1807 campaign and had to pull back to Tilsit and the east side of the Niemen. In less than two years the French had defeated Austria, Prussia and the forces of the tsar. The participants in the Third Coalition had failed to coordinate their actions and had added central and much of eastern Europe to the lands at Napoleon's disposal.

Alexander did not rush to make peace after his troops had crossed the Niemen. He had a line which could be defended against the enemy and he could afford a little time for reflection. Britain, the linchpin of Czartoryski's hopes, was still in the war. Russia's Anglophiles, however, had experienced a sharp deterioration in their position in the eighteen months since Trafalgar. The English were important to the Russians mainly as a source of funds, but they had not been very forthcoming. Twice in 1806 Alexander had had to order his finance minister to issue an additional 10 million paper rubles. At the end of 1806 his new foreign minister, Andrei Budberg, began negotiating with Britain for a long-term loan to cover Russia's budgetary deficit, but the negotiations had not been concluded by the time of Friedland. Nor had Britain been paying all the subsidies to which she committed herself when the Third Coalition was constructed in 1805. She seemed to want evidence of her partners' ability to win victories before transferring significant sums of money. Since, in 1805 and 1806, Britain had been irritated by Prussia's brief acquisition of Hanover, and since the Russian Minister of Commerce, Nikolai Rumiantsev, feared undue dependence on British ships in the conduct of Russian trade, there were reasons on both sides for thinking of Anglo-Russian relations as a mixed blessing. On meeting the hastily despatched British special representative, Lord Granville Leveson-Gower, a day or two before Friedland, the tsar 'kept up a running attack upon the conduct and disposition' of his ally.[26] The battle only intensified his feeling of betrayal.

Since Prussia's reawakening at Bartenstein in April 1807 had had disastrous consequences, and since Alexander was not tempted to return to the Anglophilia of his first years on the throne, Russia was obliged to make peace. She was probably not obliged, however, to make an alliance with France, and she almost certainly did not think of the alliance which materialized as the abject surrender which it has sometimes been made out to be. Napoleon, too, needed peace. He had insufficient troops for an invasion of Russia, he was worried about developments in Turkey (where Selim III had been deposed at the end of May), and he could not be certain that Britain would do nothing to counter his triumph at Friedland. It was he who initiated negotiations for a truce, and in moving towards a peace treaty he made no territorial demands on the Russian Empire. He was prepared to contemplate giving back Prussia some of her possessions in return for Russian withdrawals from the Ionian Islands and the European provinces of the Ottoman Empire. He clearly did not have in mind the exploitative treaties he had imposed on Austria after the battles of Marengo in 1800 and Austerlitz in 1805.

After a truce had been agreed on 21 June 1807, the rival emperors were keen to meet. It is probably wrong to say that the tsar surrendered to Napoleon's charms at their celebrated encounter on the raft in the river Niemen, for diplomats spent the next ten days in detailed exchanges at Tilsit. V. G. Sirotkin, the Soviet expert on the subject, claims that 'Russian diplomacy ... fought for each item of the agreements. The question of an alliance evoked the sharpest disagreements'.[27] In Sirotkin's view, Alexander realized after his midstream encounter with Napoleon that he had to tread carefully. If he went into the meeting expecting merely to expedite a peace treaty, he came away from it aware that the French wanted more. His response was to add Prince Aleksandr Kurakin to his negotiating team. When Kurakin had canvassed the possibility of a French alliance eighteen months previously (after Austerlitz), he had seen it not as a derogation from Russia's dignity but as a means of achieving specific objectives. This may have been Russia's attitude to the prospect of an alliance in mid-1807. Since most of the exchanges at Tilsit were oral, the documentary legacy of the negotiations is scanty, but Russian documents published in the 1960s indicate a remarkable consonance between the goals Alexander set himself in the build-up to the alliance and the content of the alliance itself.[28] In other words, the tsar may have been the victor rather than the vanquished at Tilsit. He may have had a better understanding of what he was doing than either most contemporaries or many historians.

France and Russia signed two documents, a peace treaty and an offensive–defensive alliance. The first was a relatively innocuous affair. Russia lost her toe-hold in the Adriatic and her interest in the Ionian Islands, and promised to withdraw her troops from the Ottoman provinces of Moldavia and Wallachia. She accepted French mediation in her quest for peace with the Ottoman Empire, and promised her own mediation in Napoleon's war with Britain. Prussia was reconstituted, but lost her Polish possessions to a 'Grand Duchy of Warsaw' set up under the French-backed King of Saxony. The second document, the alliance, was more far-reaching in its implications. In the event of Britain's refusal to accept Russian mediation in her war with France, Russia was to break off diplomatic relations with her and make common cause with the French. At that point, Denmark, Sweden and Portugal were to be invited to close their ports to the British and declare war. If they refused, they were to be treated as enemies. Austria was to be forced to join the coalition. If the Ottoman Empire refused the mediation of the French, it was to be exposed to Franco-Russian action and to lose almost all of its lands in Europe.

At first sight, the Tilsit alliance seemed to give Napoleon everything he wanted. By virtue of the fact that the lesser European powers were about to adhere to the 'continental blockade' which France had set in train at the end of the previous year, Britain was to be subjected to enormous pressure. But Alexander and his negotiators (above all Prince Kurakin) may have been subtler than they seemed. Although the tsar went into the negotiations naively hoping to restore Franco-Russian relations to the friendly footing of 1801, he manoeuvred shrewdly when he found that this goal was unattainable. Tilsit made plain that the lesser European powers were to be obliged to close their ports to the British if the latter refused Russian mediation, but it did not state unequivocally that St Petersburg had to close the ports of the Russian Empire. One of the Russian background documents, furthermore, made the point that if Denmark and Sweden did indeed join the French, Russia could afford to close her ports to Britain's ships because the British would be unable to penetrate the Baltic and punish her. And so long as trade could continue in neutral vessels, to which, again, the treaty of alliance made no reference, Russia's economic prospects were better than they appeared to be. Finally, Alexander had a few months to prepare Russian society for the implications of his about-face, since the deadlines referred to in the alliance did not require Russia to take obviously aggressive action until the end of 1807. Alexander went too far when he claimed in a letter to his mother, in 1808, that he had acceded to the Tilsit alliance only to give himself a breathing space;[29] but some of his entourage seem to have been thinking of the alliance in that way in 1807, and scrutiny of the alliance document lends credence to the proposition. Alexander's three principal officials in the period of the Tilsit alliance, Prince Kurakin (who was appointed Russian Ambassador in Paris in 1808), Count Nikolai Rumiantsev (who became foreign minister the same year) and State Secretary Mikhail Speranskii (whose main concern was domestic affairs), have all been described as wholehearted enthusiasts for France. Patricia Kennedy Grimsted calls Rumiantsev, for example, 'a perfect figurehead for the policy of peace'.[30] All three, however, adopted the French orientation with their eyes open. Kurakin thought it was Russia's only option and, at Tilsit and subsequently, did what he could to modify its implications. Rumiantsev, who remained Minister of Commerce when he was put in charge of foreign affairs, was anti-British rather than pro-French and believed that the French alliance would be an effective way of ending Britain's domination of Russia's trade. In a note to the tsar of November 1807 he admitted that breaking with Britain would put Russia's seaborne trade in difficulties, but claimed that increased trade across the land frontier would remedy the shortfall.[31] Speranskii wanted peace for the sake of introducing changes at home, but knew that the alliance would break down eventually. Reflecting on Franco-Russian relations four years after Tilsit, he argued that the alliance could be maintained but that Russia still had to prepare for war.[32]

ALLIANCE WITH FRANCE (1807–12)

It may be that Pieter Geyl was right, therefore, to propose that 'Since the Russian archives have been opened ... nothing remains of [the] theory of the innocent Tsar and the wicked Napoleon'.[33] Some of Alexander's advisers, and perhaps the tsar himself, thought Tilsit could be made to serve Russia's purposes. Very few Russians, however, shared their opinion. The tsar was violently criticized for what looked like abject surrender. It was not surprising that he felt obliged to defend himself when writing to his mother, for the Dowager Empress was one of his most outspoken opponents. His sister, the Grand Duchess Catherine, was another. Catherine quickly became a focus for wider discontent. Three months after Tilsit, the Swedish ambassador to St Petersburg reported that dissatisfaction with the tsar was growing; people were saying that the entire Romanov male line ought to be removed from power and Catherine elevated to the throne. At the end of 1810 Catherine commissioned the conservative ideologue Nikolai Karamzin, the empire's 'Official Historiographer', to write a paper describing the country's misfortunes. After Austerlitz and Friedland, Karamzin wrote, 'we should have forgotten Europe, ... and turned all thoughts to Russia, in order to safeguard her internal welfare. ... We could have rejected Europe without suffering disgrace, but we could not maintain our honor by transforming ourselves into an instrument of Napoleon in Europe after we had pledged ourselves to rescue it from his tyranny'.[34] Karamzin spoke for many. A letter urging Alexander not to give ground to foreigners had circulated widely in Russia in 1807.[35] Czartoryski, Novosil'tsev and Stroganov, the Anglophile former members of the Unofficial Committee, thought the French orientation disastrous. At the other end of the political spectrum, the Moscow conservative Fedor Rostopchin worked hard to confirm the Grand Duchess Catherine in her opposition to the tsar.

Alexander's critics had the better of the argument. The tsar and his advisers may have convinced themselves that alliance with France was the lesser of two evils, but it turned out to be evil enough. If Alexander had seriously expected Britain to accept Russian mediation, he was quickly disappointed. The British signalled their determination to prevent the Baltic countries uniting against them by bombarding Copenhagen in September 1807 and capturing the Danish fleet. The tsar broke off diplomatic relations with London early in November 1807 and placed an embargo on British ships in Russian ports. For a while he fought shy of full participation in Napoleon's blockade of the British, but a series of measures between late 1807 and August 1808 effectively made him part of it. The consequences for the Russian economy were damaging. Russia's trade balance remained favourable, but the volume of her trade declined steeply. British ships had carried 63 per cent of the goods exported from St Petersburg in 1804. Without their involvement as carriers, Russia could neither buy nor sell to the extent that she wanted. In the early days of the Tilsit alliance trade in neutral ships was permitted, but apart from those of the United States and the Hanseatic ports there were few such ships on the seas. The turnover of Russian maritime trade declined in value by two-thirds between 1807 and 1808. Because British loans and subsidies no longer backed the paper ruble, its rate against silver sank even more rapidly than it was sinking already. Since Russian defence expenditure actually increased during the period of the French alliance (because policy-makers knew that the alliance was a temporary expedient), Alexander had to put additional quantities of paper into circulation. France was in no position to replace Britain as Russia's main trading partner. She could not supply the goods Russia needed (even supposing the Russians had been able to pay for them); she had no use for many of the staple Russian exports, the most important of which went into shipbuilding; and she could not trade by sea, which alone would have made goods cheap enough to be worth exchanging. Without British goods and British ships, the Russian economy became ever more parochial. It had been parochial enough before 1807, but the tsars had been trying to increase the international element. Alexander's frustration mounted as France provided additional proof that her 'continental system' was intended to benefit only the French. Since, like Russia, France could not do without British goods, in 1809 Napoleon began issuing licences which permitted French vessels to carry them. Then in August 1810 he dealt a blow to neutral trade by promulgating the 'Trianon tariff', which increased duties payable on non-European goods from any country, neutral or not. By incorporating the whole of the north European coastline into France in mid-December 1810, he extended the area to which the Trianon tariff applied and effectively closed down the Hanseatic ports of Bremen, Hamburg and Lübeck. By this time Alexander was beginning to feel he had had enough. At the very end of 1810 he promulgated a highly protectionist statute which lowered a sort of economic 'iron curtain' between Russia and the rest of the continent. He claimed that it did not conflict with Napoleon's ordinances, but this was only technically true. He was really admitting what his critics had been telling him for a long time, that the implications of Tilsit were highly detrimental to Russia's economic interests.

It took more than trade, however, to cause Alexander to lose faith in the alliance altogether. No Russian tsar thought mainly in terms of economics. Alexander would probably have been happy enough with Tilsit if it had facilitated a few territorial acquisitions and generally improved the stability of his borders. He would then have had something to show for his pains. Unfortunately, the years after Tilsit demonstrated that the alliance was not going to serve this purpose. It could even be argued that Russia's main eighteenth-century adversaries, Turkey, Poland and Sweden, posed her just as many problems when she had France as an ally as they posed when Russia dealt with them on her own. Napoleon managed these countries in the light of his policies as a whole, whereas Alexander approached them with narrower ends in view. The frustration which arose out of irreconcilable objectives led to endless confusion.

Oriental questions were the first to expose differences between the allies. In the instructions to his negotiators at Tilsit Alexander made plain that he had no interest in a root-and-branch partition of the Ottoman Empire. 'Russia', he said, 'will never have a less dangerous neighbour' on her southern frontier, 'and consequently any change which leads to the destruction of this empire would be disadvantageous' to St Petersburg.[36] While he was keen on 'reorganizing the government' of the Ottoman provinces which most concerned him (Moldavia, Wallachia, Serbia), and while he conceded that Napoleon would want to do the same in the western Balkans, his ambitions were limited. In the event, the agreements signed at Tilsit threatened to require more of him than he wanted to undertake. If Constantinople refused to accept French mediation in the Russo-Turkish war, he was virtually committed to far-reaching action. He really wanted no more than to extend Russia's frontier to the Danube, but Napoleon was trying to use him for a much larger purpose. Paradoxically, France was reluctant to let Alexander make small gains but anxious to let him make big ones. She knew that Britain might allow Russia to get away with small boundary adjustments and administrative improvements on the western shores of the Black Sea, but she felt certain that the British would have to take steps if the Ottoman Empire looked likely to collapse. If Britain became extensively embroiled in the east she would be poorly placed to handle new French moves in the European heartland. In other words, Napoleon sought to employ Russia in a large-scale diversion which served nobody's purpose but his own. The extent and the point of the diversion became clear in his celebrated letter to the tsar of February 1808, in which he proposed sending a Franco-Russian army via Constantinople into Asia. It 'would no sooner appear on the Euphrates, than it would put England into a panic, and make her beg for mercy from the continental powers'.[37] Alexander did not fall for the proposal, but as a result he did not get his own way either. The Russo-Turkish War which Tilsit was supposed to bring to an end dragged on until 1812, at which point Russia had to abandon the prospect of getting Moldavia and Wallachia and settle for the small province of Bessarabia.

The one good thing to come out of Napoleon's attempt to persuade Alexander of the merits of an aggressive southern policy was a significant Russian territorial advance in the north. Having learned the extent of France's ambitions in the south, Alexander moved cautiously in the north, attaining his own objectives without significantly furthering those of his ally. France and Russia agreed at Tilsit to oblige Sweden to join the Continental Blockade, but after Britain captured the Danish fleet at Copenhagen in September 1807 only Russia was in a position to pressurize Sweden effectively. Whereas the French could not easily get across the Baltic, Russia could move into Swedish-controlled Finland. In the Balkans Napoleon could participate in events from the eastern coastline of the Adriatic, but in northern Europe his options were limited. In a conversation of 1 March 1808, Napoleon's ambassador to St Petersburg pressed the tsar to march on Stockholm as quickly as he could. Russian troops had crossed into Finland a week before and were to make rapid progress in the first two months of their advance, but they then got bogged down. Since Napoleon was in no position to cajole them, they concentrated on consolidating their initial successes before moving against Sweden proper. By the time they attacked the Swedish mainland across the ice of the Gulf of Bothnia in March 1809, Russian policy was to do no more than make sure of the annexation of Finland. If in 1807 Alexander had intended to fulfil his obligations under the Tilsit alliance and bring Sweden into the French orbit, in 1809 he no longer felt strongly on the subject. Even so his actions produced the downfall of the Swedish king, the emergence of a pro-French party at the Swedish court, and the fear that Napoleon, having attained his original objective, would try to restore Finland to Swedish rule. Speranskii advised the tsar to resist any such attempt on the part of the French. He realized Napoleon would not welcome Russian aggrandizement, but he felt that in northern Europe Alexander could defend his gains.[38] He was right, and for once Alexander had the better of a scheme promoted by Napoleon. He did not even lose Swedish friendship, for by 1812 Russia and Sweden were allies again.

The acquisition of Finland, however, was a relatively small gain to set against the unproductive war against the Turks. It looked even smaller alongside the dilemma posed by Poland. After French troops entered Warsaw in November 1806 Napoleon wrote home: 'It is difficult to convey a proper idea of the national movement in this country. ... Priests, nobles, peasants – they are all of one mind'.[39] His creation of the Grand Duchy of Warsaw under the Tilsit peace treaty established French credentials with the Poles and deeply troubled the east European autocracies. At first the Grand Duchy consisted of Polish territory taken only from Prussia, but after defeating Austria again in 1809 Napoleon enlarged it by adding lands which had been ruled from Vienna. The new Polish unit had many faults in the eyes of Polish patriots, but it possessed a constitution and an army and it abolished Polish serfdom. Its emergence and expansion were the price Alexander paid for rejecting a pro-Polish policy in 1805. The tsar floundered in his quest for an appropriate response. Polish patriotism was so intense, the former Polish frontiers so extensive, that it was impossible to predict what the new Poland might become. In 1808 and 1809 Alexander and his advisers saw Franco-Polish plots everywhere. Rumiantsev reported a French plan for a rising in Galicia, Kurakin a French scheme to push Russia's frontiers back to the Western Dvina and the Dnieper.[40] Until about 1810 Alexander did no more than indicate his antipathy to the Poles' revival by acquiring little tracts of Polish territory for himself. At Tilsit he secured the Bialystok district, after Austria's defeat in 1809 a portion of eastern Galicia. Then it occurred to him that the Poles might be finding Napoleon oppressive. They had fought hard for the French in 1809 but had secured only part of the additional territory they were hoping for. Through Czartoryski, Alexander attempted to elicit Polish opinion. From December 1810 the former director of Russia's foreign affairs began to come back into favour. By April 1812 Alexander was prepared to consider not only trying to transfer Poland from French suzerainty to Russian, but also adding to it the lands ruled from St Petersburg which had formerly belonged to the Polish Commonwealth.[41] It was a measure of his desperation that he thought of promising so much, for as the British Prime Minister Lord Liverpool was to put it in 1814, 'If [the tsar] detaches the Polish provinces incorporated with Russia ... for the purpose of forming a Polish kingdom, he will never be forgiven by the Russians'.[42] Trapped by the conflicting demands of Polish and Russian opinion, Alexander was not to succeed in resolving the post-Tilsit form of the Polish question; but his anxiety to do so played no small part in his readiness to accept war in 1812.

The Tilsit alliance, therefore, beset Alexander with problems. Whether or not he originally thought that it could be turned to Russia's advantage, he discovered that in the event it could not. But it hardly suited Napoleon either. Indeed, from Napoleon's point of view the balance sheet of the alliance looked almost as unhealthy as it did to Alexander. The fact that the Russians were gaining territory without involving themselves wholeheartedly in the Continental Blockade inclined the French to question the wisdom of maintaining close relations with them. What felt like frustration from the point of view of Alexander looked like profiteering from the point of view of Napoleon. The two emperors were already moving apart from one another by the time of their second meeting, at Erfurt in central Germany in October 1808. They agreed then to meet a third time, but no more summits materialized. When Alexander more or less withdrew from the continental system at the end of 1810, renewed Franco-Russian hostilities were only a matter of time. If the French had not been preoccupied in Spain, the alliance would probably have fallen apart sooner than it did. Aleksandr Kurakin, Russia's principal negotiator at Tilsit, insisted in a despatch from Paris of August 1811 that France was trying to roll Russia back – 'in a word, to make her a purely Asiatic power'.[43] If one of the chief proponents of the French alliance now saw the writing on the wall, it was time to beat ploughshares into swords. A flurry of diplomatic activity in the first half of 1812 enabled the Russians to settle their differences with Turkey and Sweden and the French to force Austria and Prussia into backing their plans for the march on Moscow. Not only diplomats felt a sense of urgency. At Tula, centre of the Russian armaments industry, the gunsmiths voted in May 1812 to give up their free time in order to produce an extra thousand rifles a month.[44] In June Napoleon crossed the Niemen and entered Vil'na, expecting, so he said, to be in Moscow in a month.

DEFEATING NAPOLEON (1812–14)

Napoleon hoped for a decisive battle, like the one at Friedland which had brought the Russians to the conference table in 1807. He nearly had his way, for Alexander's principal military adviser, General von Phull, advocated making a stand at Drissa. The two Russian armies, however, under

Barclay de Tolly and Bagration, were too far apart to join forces. If they had been close enough to effect a conjunction, 'the temptation and the clamour to give battle would have been irresistibly overwhelming'.[45] It was fortunate for the Russians that a confrontation was out of the question, for they were heavily outnumbered and needed to wear Napoleon down. It was also fortunate for them that Barclay, their commander-in-chief, differed from von Phull. In 1807 he had evolved a strategy of withdrawal which now proved its worth. By the time he joined forces with Bagration at Smolensk at the beginning of August, Napoleon's army had already dwindled from about half a million to under 200,000 men. Most Russians thought Barclay pusillanimous, but the strategy which saved them was his. After abandoning Smolensk he lost the overall command to Kutuzov, who was supposed to be made of sterner stuff; but this ageing disciple of Suvorov was far too shrewd to make many alterations in a policy which was working. As the French pressed on, Kutuzov began to sense victory. When he eventually gave battle at Borodino on 26 August / 7 September, he lost far fewer men than the enemy. On the grounds that Napoleon's reserves were nearer than his own and that the shame of losing Moscow had to be weighed against 'the whole of Russia, the salvation of St Petersburg, and the freedom of Europe',[46] he went on retreating. Napoleon entered Moscow a week after Borodino but quickly discovered that he had won a Pyrrhic victory. The city's governor, Fedor Rostopchin, pointed out that if 'The emperor of Russia will always be formidable in Moscow,' he was 'terrible in Kazan, and invincible in Tobol'sk'.[47] In other words, the possible extent of Russian withdrawal was virtually limitless. Since Alexander refused to negotiate, the French had to turn back. They certainly could not stay in Moscow after fire razed much of it to the ground. Their lines of supply were overstretched and they ran the risk of being cut off. Russian guerrilla activity along the road between Smolensk and Moscow was intensifying. As Kutuzov said to the French diplomat Lauriston at the beginning of October (when the French were putting out peace feelers), the ordinary Russian equated the French with the Mongols and could not be prevented from treating them as such.[48] After thirty-three days in the old Russian capital, Napoleon struck camp.

While the Emperor of the French had been wondering what to do next, Kutuzov had altered the direction of his march. French scouts at first thought he was still heading east, but he moved clockwise and encamped at Tarutino to the south, cutting Napoleon off from food and the ironworks of Tula. Russia's forces grew in number as the militia came on stream. Kutuzov organized flying squadrons to monitor surreptitious French movements. He delivered a sharp rebuff to the French cavalry under Murat on the day before Napoleon began the general retreat from Moscow. On 11/23 October Russian troops moved into the abandoned city. Napoleon had not quite given up, for at first he moved south-west towards Kaluga rather than back the way he had come, but despite mauling General Dokhturov at Maloiaroslavets on 12/24 October he felt unable to risk another full-scale engagement. Far to the west, Polotsk had fallen to the Russians. If the French did not hurry, few of them would escape. Few of them did. By the time Napoleon reached the river Berezina to the west of Smolensk at the end of November, he was under pressure not only from Kutuzov but also from Russian armies converging on him from north and south. Nothing became Alexander's six-year war with Turkey like the leaving of it. Withdrawal from the south enabled Chichagov to bring back his soldiers just in time for the last significant encounter of the year. Napoleon was caught in a vice – Kutuzov behind him, Chichagov on the west bank of the Berezina, the troops who had taken Polotsk pressing down from the north. The onset of winter had prompted the French to burn their pontoons for the sake of unencumbered movement, but an untimely thaw meant that they needed them again. Only about 20,000 effectives crossed the river. Napoleon forsook them a week later, and around 1,000 were left when Marshal Ney completed the Grand Army's departure from the Russian Empire in the middle of December.

The next three years (from Napoleon's expulsion to the signature of the second Peace of Paris on 20 November 1815) marked the slow working-out of the implications of France's defeat in Russia. At the end of 1812 the Russians debated whether to cross their own frontier and take the war across Europe. They were wary of fighting alone and not certain of finding allies. Austria and Prussia, too weak to sever their ties with Napoleon unilaterally, feared that unpleasant consequences might flow from turning to the tsar for assistance. None of the earlier coalitions against Napoleon had succeeded in pitting the four principal European powers against the French at the same time, and the coalition which took shape in 1813 only gradually looked likely to do so. Rumiantsev, Alexander's foreign minister, believed that fighting in Europe might serve the purposes of Britain rather than Russia. The conservatives Rostopchin (Governor of Moscow) and Aleksandr Shishkov (who had succeeded Speranskii as State Secretary) held that stepping westward would excite unwelcome popular enthusiasm for a radical reconstruction of the continent. December 1812 saw resistance on the part of peasants in the province of Penza to the prospect of being sent abroad in the militia. 'Many nobles feared domestic complications in the wake of the mass arming of the peasants and a large-scale popular war'.[49] Kutuzov wanted to rest and regroup his forces. When Karl Nesselrode, Alexander's new foreign policy adviser, wrote to the Russian ambassador in Vienna that the troops had halted in Vil'na solely to recover their strength,[50] he was telling only part of the truth.

The tsar's more cautious advisers did not get the better of the argument, but they may have been more far-sighted than those who advocated continuing the chase. In view of the long-term effects of Russia's victory in the war with Napoleon, Alexander would probably have been well advised to stop the advance at the frontier. If Napoleon had been brought down without direct Russian involvement in the decisive battles, the tsar would not have felt responsible for the future security of western Europe. The policy of 'free hands' which a number of his ministers had urged on him in the first years of his reign might have become a practical possibility. He could have concentrated on domestic reform. Instead, he greatly increased the responsibilities of the Russian government and denied himself the chance of a vital period of retrenchment. The heat of the moment, however, was too great for sober counsels to prevail. After the Prussian General Yorck defected from the French camp with 20,000 troops on the penultimate day of 1812, a Russian refusal to continue the war would have looked extremely faint-hearted. Russia and Prussia formed an alliance at Kalisch at the end of February 1813, and under the Treaty of Reichenbach, at the end of June, Austria promised to join them unless Napoleon accepted terms within three weeks. This he had no intention of doing. He had demonstrated at Lützen and Bautzen in May that his skill as a general had been in no way impaired by the Russian débâcle, and at Dresden, in August, he threw back the combined forces of the new triple alliance. At Leipzig, however, two months later, he was defeated. Germany was liberated and France herself laid open to attack. By April 1814 Napoleon was forced to capitulate. The exciting postscript to his career, the hundred-day period in the spring of 1815 when he threatened to re-establish himself on the French throne, gave rise to the most famous of all his battles without altering the verdict of the previous year.

THE CONGRESS OF VIENNA

By the time of Waterloo the Congress of Vienna had completed its deliberations. The European powers had made peace with France after Napoleon's first abdication, but at that time they had postponed the settlement of non-French affairs. Allowing the postponement was probably Alexander's biggest mistake in the course of the peacemaking. When Napoleon's four principal opponents (Russia, Austria, Prussia, Britain) signed the Treaty of Chaumont in March 1814, his armies were riding the crest of a wave and his power was at its peak. The Russians' authority was so great that they could have imposed their blueprint for the post-war world on their allies. Instead, they accepted a bland statement of allied aims ('the re-establishment of equilibrium among the powers')[51] and a list of specific goals which did not include their own central objectives. Fourteen months later Alexander claimed in a circular letter to his diplomats that his behaviour at Chaumont was a proof of his moderation,[52] but it really showed his ineptitude. Czartoryski realized at once that omitting Poland from the list of specific problems to be solved was giving a hostage to fortune. Within days of Chaumont he wrote the tsar two letters urging upon him the need for a Polish policy.[53] By the time Alexander had come up with one, his stock was sinking. As usual at the end of wars, the victors disagreed about the division of the spoils. Success went to Alexander's head. In France and London in the summer of 1814 he alienated governments by standing on ceremony and flirting with domestic opposition groups. The Congress of Vienna, scheduled to begin on 1 October, had been conceived as a means of winding up problems which had been discussed in the months since the defeat of Napoleon. Because of the tsar's inconstancy, it opened with much remaining to be done.

At least Alexander had defined his policy fairly clearly by the time he actually arrived in Vienna. He wanted Poland, the Poland of the Grand Duchy of Warsaw, and he was prepared to see Austria compensated in north Italy and Prussia in Saxony for the loss of the Polish territory they had received as a result of the third Polish partition of 1795. Had Russia stuck to the pursuit of this objective, she might have achieved it without giving offence. In the terms of conventional power politics, she could legitimately claim some material reward for the part she had played in the campaigns of 1812–14. Alexander confused the Polish issue, however, by mysteriously and unnecessarily making it appear the prelude to future forward moves, and by pretending to bow in the direction of nationalism and liberalism when he was really doing no more than incorporating new territory into the Russian Empire. The other participants in the congress began to think that, after taking Poland, Alexander intended to turn on the Ottoman Empire. They also wanted to know what constitutional arrangements the Russians had in mind for the former Grand Duchy of Warsaw. The second of these issues was particularly troublesome. If, as seemed likely, the tsar conferred a liberal constitution on his new Polish subjects, he would encourage the few Poles who remained under Austrian and Prussian rule to demand equivalent concessions from their masters. If, on the other hand, Alexander extended Russian autocracy to the Poles, he would plant the traditional Russian menace deep in the heart of Europe. Either of these intentions might have been made acceptable to Alexander's fellow negotiators if it had been stated explicitly, but neither was. Russia left her allies in the dark, with the result that they conspired against her. Britain, Austria and a rehabilitated France formed an alliance on 3 January 1815 which threatened to put paid to the entire proceedings of the congress. Although Alexander compromised and eventually received almost as much Polish territory as he would have done anyway, he had succeeded in engendering an atmosphere of mistrust which augured ill for the future.

This mistrust undermined Alexander's chances of achieving his other great post-war objective, the creation of a collective security system. Although a collective security system of a sort came into being as a result of the powers' second peace treaty with France (that of November 1815), it did not embody what Alexander had in mind. It amounted, in effect, to the maintenance of the Chaumont alliance of March 1814, which in Alexander's view was unnecessarily anti-French in the context of late 1815. So far as Europe as a whole was concerned, the tsar was anxious, once Napoleon had been removed from the scene, to restore France to the international community and make her a counterweight to Austria and Prussia. Castlereagh, the British foreign minister, succeeded in gaining support for his rather different understanding of the requirements of the post-war period. Alexander objected, however, not merely to Castlereagh's view of the correct way to treat France, but to the whole principle of conducting international relations as if they depended solely on the power of the countries involved in them. Wanting to base inter-state dealings on abstract principles derived from religion, he proposed a new 'Holy Alliance' which 'differed, in orientation and in the nature of the obligations it envisaged, from the traditional treaties of alliance and agreements of the time'.[54] It was accepted by Austria and Prussia at the end of September 1815, and subsequently by all the states of Europe apart from Britain, the Papacy and the Ottoman Empire, but it is doubtful whether any of the adherents really understood what it was for. The text of the document described European countries as members of a single Christian family and spoke of the signatories' commitment to the pursuit of Christian principles both at home and abroad. It did not make clear what Christian principles meant in these contexts. Alexander himself probably did not know what he meant by them. His religiosity had been growing for some years and had reached a peak in June 1815 under the influence of a certain Baroness Krüdener, but in practice it did not seem to imply more than a vague beneficence. Since Russia had caused a near breakdown in international relations by the way in which she pursued her material goals at the Congress of Vienna, it was not surprising that her subsequent adoption of spiritual goals was received with great scepticism. In time, as Alexander's opinions moved to the right, the Holy Alliance proved to be a vehicle for his prejudices. As a device for altering the way in which the peace of Europe was ensured, it was still-born. Having covered themselves with glory at the end of the Napoleonic Wars, Russia's armies, and perhaps her population as a whole, could be forgiven for thinking that the peacemaking process had left them with a larger range of problems than they had faced when the wars began.

NOTES

1. Text in Hugh Ragsdale, *Détente in the Napoleonic Era: Bonaparte and the Russians* (Lawrence, Kan., 1980), pp. 14–15.
2. D. B. Horn, *British Public Opinion and the First Partition of Poland* (Edinburgh, 1945), p 13.
3. Roderic H. Davison, '"Russian Skill and Turkish Imbecility": The Treaty of Kuchuk Kainardji Reconsidered', SR 35 (1976), 476.
4. Hugh Ragsdale, 'Evaluating the Traditions of Russian Aggression: Catherine II and the Greek Project', SEER 66 (1988), 91–117.

5. T. C. W. Blanning, *The Origins of the French Revolutionary Wars* (London and New York, 1986), p. 185.
6. Robert E. Jones, 'Opposition to War and Expansion in Late Eighteenth Century Russia', JFGO 32 (1984), 34, 36.
7. Ragsdale, *Détente* (above, n. 1), passim; Ole Feldbaek, 'The Foreign Policy of Tsar Paul I, 1800–1801: An Interpretation', JFGO 30 (1982), 16–36.
8. Hugh Seton-Watson, *The Russian Empire 1801–1917* (Oxford, 1967), p. 67.
9. VPR , i. 62–7.
10. Ibid., i. 60.
11. Jean Charles Biaudet and Francoise Nicod, eds, *Correspondance de Frédéric-César de La Harpe et Alexandre Ier* (3 vols, Neuchâtel, 1978–80), i. 553.
12. V. G. Sirotkin, ed., 'Dokumenty o politike Rossii na dal'nem vostoke v nachale XIX v.', IA, 1962 no. 6, pp. 85– 99; E. V. Mezentsev, 'Iz predystorii organizatsii pervoi krugosvetnoi ekspeditsii russkogo flota v knotse XVIII – nachale XIX v.', *Sovetskie arkhivy*, 1987 no. 1, pp. 73–6.
13. VPR, i. 157–9.
14. Ibid., i. 207–8.
15. Ibid., i. 550–5.
16. Ibid., i. 638.
17. Patricia Kennedy Grimsted, *The Foreign Ministers of Alexander I: Political Attitudes and the Conduct of Russian Diplomacy, 1801–1825* (Berkeley and Los Angeles, Calif., 1969), p. 130.
18. Patricia Kennedy Grimsted, 'Czartoryski's System for Russian Foreign Policy, 1803: A Memorandum, Edited with Introduction and Analysis', *California Slavic Studies* 5 (1970), 52.
19. VPR, i. 619–24; M. S. Anderson, ed., *The Great Powers and the Near East 1774–1923* (London, 1970), pp. 23–5.
20. VPR, i. 686–92.
21. Ibid., ii. 356.
22. A. V. Predtechenskii, *Ocherki obshchestvenno-politicheskoi istorii Rossii v pervoi chetverti XIX veka* (Moscow and Leningrad, 1957), p. 223; VPR, iii. 374.
23. A. A. Kizevetter, 'F. V. Rostopchin', *Istoricheskie otkliki* (Moscow, 1915), p. 149.
24. VPR, iii. 442.
25. V. G. Sirotkin, *Duel' dvukh diplomatii: Rossiia i Frantsiia v 1801–1812 gg.* (Moscow, 1966), p. 49, n. 26.
26. H. Butterfield, *The Peace Tactics of Napoleon 1806–1808* (Cambridge, 1929), p. 199.
27. Sirotkin, *Duel'* (above, n. 25), p. 91.
28. VPR, iii. 754–60.
29. Ibid., iv. 330.
30. Grimsted, *Foreign Ministers* (above, n. 17), p. 187.
31. VPR, iv. 114–15.
32. Ibid., vi. 256, 724.
33. Pieter Geyl, *Napoleon For and Against* (Harmondsworth, 1965), p. 86.
34. Richard Pipes, *Karamzin's Memoir on Ancient and Modern Russia: A Translation and Analysis* (New York, 1966), p. 145.
35. Grand Duke Nikolai Mikhailovich, *Imperator Aleksandr I: Opyt istoricheskogo issledovaniia* (2 vols, St Petersburg, 1912), i. 576–80; Predtechenskii, *Ocherki* (above, n. 22), pp. 224–8.
36. VPR, iii. 758.

37. J. M. Thompson, ed., *Napoleon's Letters* (London and New York, 1954), p. 193.
38. VPR, vi. 8–10.
39. Thompson, *Napoleon's Letters* (above, n. 37), p. 157.
40. VPR, iv. 459, v. 23.
41. Ibid., vi. 351.
42. W. H. Zawadzki, 'Russia and the Re-opening of the Polish Question, 1801–1814', IHR 7 (1985), 42.
43. VPR, vi. 143,
44. V. N. Ashurkov, 'Tul'skie oruzheiniki v 1812 godu', VI, 1987 no. 11, p. 182.
45. Michael and Diana Josselson, *The Commander: A Life of Barclay de Tolly* (Oxford, 1980), p. 112.
46. L. G. Beskrovnyi, *Russkoe voennoe iskusstvo XIXv.* (Moscow, 1974), p. 111.
47. Michael T. Florinsky, *Russia: A History and an Interpretation* (2 vols, New York, 1947–53), ii. 675n.
48. VPR, vi. 576.
49. N. M. Druzhinin, 'Osvoboditel'naia voina 1813 g. i russkoe obshchestvo', in L. G. Beskrovnyi et al., eds, *Osvoboditel'naia voina 1813 goda protiv napoleonovskogo gospodstva* (Moscow, 1965), p. 57.
50. VPR, vii. 21.
51. Ibid., vii. 591.
52. N. K. Shil'der, *Imperator Aleksandr I* (4 vols, St Petersburg, 1897–8), iii. 540–8; VPR, viii. 347.
53. VPR, vii. 617–21.
54. Ibid., viii. 695, n. 276.

CHAPTER THREE

Constitutions, Congresses and Classes under Alexander I

THE NAPOLEONIC WARS AND RUSSIAN CONSTITUTIONALISM

Alexander did not abandon the idea of civil improvement while trying to cope with Napoleon. It is true that, having renounced secret police methods on ascending the throne, he appeared to go back to them as soon as hostilities broke out. The domestic surveillance committees of 1805 and 1807 (mentioned in Chapter Two) and the foundation of a Ministry of Police in 1811 gave the impression that the regime had turned from reform to reaction. In some ways, however, Russia's much greater involvement in European affairs intensified her interest in new approaches to government. Either because the tsar was determined not to lose sight of the liberal objectives to which he had committed himself on ascending the throne, or because he sensed that one of the best ways of defeating an enemy was to use the enemy's weapons, he went on expressing his sympathy for reform in the course of the war with the French. The Ministry of Police was only one of a number of Russian innovations which owed their origins to developments in the west. Others dovetailed less well with the traditional interests of the Russian autocracy.

When fighting or preparing to fight, Alexander indicated his liberal sympathies not at home but in two other ways: in his attitude towards the domestic affairs of foreign countries and in describing his reasons for standing up to Napoleon. In stating his views on these matters he never gave the impression that he wanted to turn his back on the world ushered in by the French Revolution. On the contrary, he seemed to welcome it and to believe that Napoleon was corrupting it. Hindered or interrupted in his attempts to make changes in Russia, he remained enthusiastic for non-autocratic systems elsewhere. It is doubtful whether, even in the early 1790s, the Russian government imagined that a return to pre-revolutionary principles would be possible. Although Catherine the Great had spoken of restoring the French king, she had also spoken of respecting the *cahiers de doléance* of 1789 and not cancelling the sale of the French church's property. Paul, for whatever reason, had been prepared to go into alliance with the French Republic. But Alexander went further than either of his predecessors in his readiness to adapt to the new European order.

The new tsar's foreign policy quickly made plain that he believed domestic political systems could no longer be derived from the world of the *ancien régime*. As we have seen, the Ionian Islands off the west coast of Greece were the part of Europe which first required him to take action. The action he took was not just military. Admiral Ushakov had drawn up a moderately representative constitution for the islands in 1799, but in 1801 it was supplanted by another which gave almost all authority to the local hereditary gentry. Alexander intervened, with the result that a third constitution 'broadened the basic structure of the government' in 1803.[1] Perhaps the Ionians were a special case, in that Alexander shared responsibility for them with the Turks and wanted to look more beneficent than his ally. His interest in Switzerland, however, derived solely from La Harpe's determination to bring it to his attention. The tsar expressed views which ought to have warmed the heart of his radical mentor. Alexander was appalled by the pressure to which France was subjecting the Swiss. 'In my judgment,' he wrote in 1802, 'every free country has the right to choose a form of government which suits its circumstances, its soil and the character of its inhabitants.'[2] If this was the doctrine which the tsar intended to apply to his own country, Russia would change dramatically once Europe was rid of Napoleon.

As he prepared for the war of 1805, Alexander put his name to liberal war aims. The instructions he gave to Nikolai Novosil'tsev on despatching him to London for negotiations in September 1804 marked his 'unequivocal recognition of the irreversibility of the changes which had taken place in Europe'.[3] The prospective allies, Alexander said, had to make plain that they were not fighting for the reintroduction of old abuses. They must affirm that their objective was to put liberty on a sound footing. Napoleon claimed that this was what his own policies were designed to achieve, but he was deceiving people. Since he was winning the public relations war, Britain and Russia could compete with him only by adopting an equally populist approach. The agreement which resulted from Novosil'tsev's journey embodied the tsar's philosophy. Britain and Russia declared that French proprietors and office-holders could count on retaining the benefits which they had derived from the Revolution. France could have any government 'compatible with public tranquillity' which the French 'national will' brought into being.[4] Russia's parallel agreement with Austria was even more explicit. The signatories did not consider that they had the right to prevent 'the free will of the French nation' from expressing itself. They were not trying to bring about a counter-revolution, but merely to save Europe from danger.[5]

It was likely, of course, that when Russia was about to return to the battlefield she would downplay the extent of her ambitions. It paid her to claim that her enemy was Napoleon rather than his subjects, for if the French could be persuaded to turn on their Emperor, the coalition partners would benefit inestimably. Alexander was consistent, however, in his view that the civil changes wrought by the French Revolution had come to stay. Just after the battle of Eylau, for example, when success in the 1807 campaign seemed a possibility, the Russian Foreign Minister spelt out a policy for the *émigré* Frenchmen who would return to power if Napoleon was defeated. It included confirming French people in the possession of acquisitions they had made since the Revolution, and spoke of 'forgetting the past entirely'.[6] The same policy informed the Russo-Prussian Bartenstein Convention of April 1807, in which the signatories declared that, while they felt bound to resist France's aggrandizement at the expense of other countries, 'They are not fighting for the abasement of France, nor to meddle in the concerns of its government or its internal affairs'.[7]

Whether the members of the Third Coalition were sincere in their attitude towards French domestic affairs was not put to the test. The five years of the Tilsit alliance, however, gave Alexander time for the domestic problems of countries closer to home. The first of these was Finland, which he invaded early in 1808 with the object of forcing Sweden to join Napoleon's Continental System. The military details of the invasion have been dealt with in Chapter Two, but the political implications require further discussion. Finland was the second non-Russian territory for which Alexander had to make political arrangements (the first being the Ionian Islands). He naturally began his invasion promising to confirm the various rights and privileges which Finnish leaders had extracted from the Swedes in the eighteenth century. When the early fighting went well, his promises took a back seat. When his troops got bogged down, the promises resurfaced. In March 1809 Alexander convened a Diet at Porvoo and promised to respect the Finns' 'constitution' and 'fundamental laws'. What he meant by these promises has been intensively debated. The fact that the Finnish Diet did not meet again until 1863 seems to show that Alexander did not intend to give more ground than he had to. Nevertheless, Finland occupied a place in the constitutional structure of the Russian Empire which was unique at the time of the union and was subsequently paralleled only by the position of Poland after 1815. The Finnish Grand Duchy had its own laws and its own customs dues. Finns were not enserfed, not recruited into the Russian army, and had dual citizenship (of the Duchy and the Empire). For at least a decade after their transfer from Swedish to Russian suzerainty they were treated attentively. In December 1811 they achieved one of their most important objectives, the transfer to the Grand Duchy of the Russian border province of Vyborg. David Kirby finds it 'unlikely that Alexander I or even his mentor Speransky, who played a vital role behind the scenes in 1809, ever considered using Finland for constitutionalist experimentation'. Perhaps not, but Edward Thaden and the most recent Soviet analysis present things slightly differently. Speranskii may not have wanted to use the Finns as guinea-pigs, but he certainly seems to have respected and learnt from them. Otherwise he would hardly have called Finland 'a state, and not a province'.[8]

THE PLANS OF MIKHAIL SPERANSKII

The fact that at first Russia treated Finland with respect suggests that Alexander I had enlightened plans for the other state whose domestic problems he had to deal with in the period of the Tilsit alliance. This was Russia itself. Whatever the tsar said and did about countries beyond his frontiers, the acid test of his reformism was whether he would let it inform his behaviour at home. Between 1807 and 1812 he had a chance to show whether he retained the enthusiasm for change which he had shown when he first ascended the throne. He rose to the challenge by promoting the unlikely figure of Mikhail Speranskii to the centre of affairs. His new chief adviser was highly untypical of Russia's elite. 'His life', says a recent Soviet analyst, 'is more of a subject for a novelist than material for the historian'.[9] Although the members of Alexander's Unofficial Committee differed significantly from the courtiers who surrounded them, at least they were gentry. Speranskii rose from the depths. His grandfather was a Ukrainian Cossack, his father a priest in the Russian province of Vladimir. He was not sure of the year of his birth. He acquired his surname at the Vladimir seminary, when his instructors, perceiving their pupil's ability, named him after the Latin for hope. Summoned to the Alexander Nevskii seminary in St Petersburg, he was on the staff there in the 1790s when Prince Aleksei Kurakin turned to the church authorities for a secretary. When Kurakin became Procurator-General under Paul, Speranskii transferred to the civil service. He stayed on after his patron lost office and soon reached the point on the Table of Ranks which entitled him to hereditary nobility. After the administrative reorganization of Alexander's first years he entered the Ministry of Internal Affairs and wrote papers which assisted the Unofficial Committee in its deliberations. After Tilsit he became Deputy Minister of Justice and State Secretary, and from late 1808 to early 1812 he wielded more authority than anyone below the throne.

Speranskii's success did not spring from personal charm. He made no attempt to adopt the mores of the aristocratic world which he entered. He married the daughter of an English governess and liked bread and butter and bacon and egg. He lived near the Tauride Gardens rather than on one of the fashionable streets of central St Petersburg. According to one hostile observer, he manifested 'complete indifference to everything other than himself and his constructs'. According to another, he thought he was 'in touch with superior beings' and 'initiated into the high purposes of a Providence created by his own egoism'. Even his sympathetic first biographer, Baron Korf, thought it unlikely that he had a single sincere friend or that there was a single person in the world whom he loved. Tolstoy painted a distinctly unflattering portrait of him in *War and Peace*. The most serious Soviet student of his career argues that 'Apparently it never even entered his head that it was necessary to explain to someone or other the need for producing the particular document on which he was working'.[10] His inability to ingratiate himself was to be part of his undoing, but his determination to confront the empire's problems enabled him to achieve a little and to perpetuate discussions which would otherwise have petered out.

Contemporaries misunderstood Speranskii's objectives and historians have only recently begun to present them convincingly. Baron Korf did no more than hint at the radical aspects of the State Secretary's thinking. Marc Raeff presented Speranskii as an open-minded conservative rather than an advocate of checks on the autocracy or an apostle of social movement. A new edition of Speranskii's writings in 1961 facilitated reconsideration of his career, but only a few scholars have engaged in it.[11] Yet Speranskii's desire to transform the Russian autocracy is undeniable. In one of his early papers he listed the characteristics of an ideal constitution. They included the participation of free social elements in the making of laws, the power of public opinion to prevent the law from being implemented perversely, the responsibility of the executive to 'an independent social layer', a system of civil and criminal law acceptable to the community, an independent judiciary, open government, the freedom of the press, 'an adequate level of education and an abundance of the means needed to execute the laws'.[12] If these were the objectives towards which Speranskii was striving, in the Russian context he was a red-hot radical. It was not his intention to put Russia's existing system of government on a sounder footing, but to re-place it with another. He called his goal 'true monarchical government' – the monarchy of Montesquieu rather than the monarchy of the tsars.

It is true that, even in his incisive early writings, Speranskii showed a certain ambivalence. Although his ideal Russia differed greatly from the visions of his contemporaries, whether he thought the ideal could be realized is debatable. He seems to have had alternative maximum and minimum programmes, the second of which he presented at greater length than the first because he believed it was more likely to be implemented. Several of the early papers stressed the need for gradualism and for acting in accordance with public opinion. Contrived improvement, Speranskii argued, would not last. Russia's 'best laws' often failed to take effect because they were out of step with the society at which they were aimed. Political freedom could not be introduced at the behest of a single sovereign, but had to be willed over many years. The population had to learn that the government's commitment to change was wholehearted. Speranskii pointed out that late-eighteenth-century Russian government had been un-predictable. Under Catherine the Great, he claimed, enlightened ideas had prevailed at the centre whilst despotism obtained in the provinces. Under

Paul, the reverse had been true: 'The provinces were ruled in a European manner but central government was completely Asiatic'.[13] The contrast enabled Speranskii to argue that Alexander I had to combine the virtues of the two previous administrations, which he could manage only by adhering to a single set of principles for several decades.

Unfortunately for Speranskii, the Tilsit alliance never looked as if it would give him long enough to put his ideas into action. He worked hard to give them a chance. In late 1809 he produced 'An Introduction to the Codification of State Laws' and a series of short memoranda which summarized the contents of the main work and proposed a time-scale for its implementation. The intention was to give the State Council oversight of the workings of the imperial administration, and beneath it to make clear distinctions between the legislative, executive and judicial arms of the government. The judicial and executive arms were to be headed by revamped versions of the Senate and the ministries, but the legislative arm was to consist of a four-tier system of representative assemblies stretching from the canton level at the bottom to a State Duma or parliament at the top.

At first sight Speranskii's proposals seem to deal with administration rather than social structure, and to aim at greater efficiency rather than a shift in focuses of authority. Even the proposed State Duma is normally said to have been conceived as a consultative body devoid of all power. Closer inspection, however, brings a different interpretation to the fore. The part of the 'Introduction' in which Speranskii laid bare the rationale for his proposals began where his early papers left off, by emphasizing the importance of introducing reforms only when circumstances were ready for them. But it soon forsook the idea of gradualism and argued that Russia was ready for change. The country, Speranskii said, had been striving for political freedom since the establishment of the autocracy in the sixteenth century. Many attempts to attain it had been ahead of their time, most strikingly Catherine the Great's Legislative Commission of 1767, but the end of the eighteenth and the beginning of the nineteenth centuries had witnessed considerable progress towards the coveted goal. Paul's introduction of a law to regulate the succession to the throne and his recommendation that serfs work no more than three days a week for their landlords had offered the prospect of order in two areas of perennial flux. Alexander I had gone further, by granting all free estates of the realm the right to own property, by creating the new social category of Free Agriculturalists, by establishing central government ministries and by introducing a statute to amend the condition of serfs in Livonia. In the light of these developments, Speranskii claimed that the time for Russia's political transformation had either arrived or could be made to arrive.

He adduced negative as well as positive reasons for taking far-reaching action. Government ranks and honours were falling into disrepute. Because contemporary thought patterns were completely out of step with the form of the government, the authority of the administration was declining. It was impossible to remedy the situation by making piecemeal changes.

Confused civil laws could not be disentangled from one another without 'firm state laws' to make clear the principles which were guiding the government's actions. Neither state finances nor education nor industrial enterprises could be put on a sound footing without a dramatic transformation of the context in which they were supposed to prosper. How did education, for example, benefit a slave? Only by making him better able to perceive the utter misery of his situation. The pervasive contemporary discontent, Speranskii argued, reflected a general alienation from the way in which Russia was conducting her affairs.

The urgency of Speranskii's language had less to do with his convictions than with the particularly testing circumstances in which the empire found itself in 1809. The unpopularity in Russia of Alexander I's alliance with Napoleon meant that the government was forced to put a brake on the precipitous decline in its credibility. When Speranskii compared the Russian popular mood in 1809 with the atmosphere which obtained in France on the eve of the Revolution he made clear that a note of panic had entered his thinking. In one of his shorter papers he suggested an extraordinarily brief timescale for the reforms he was proposing. He denied that external circumstances were the prime reason for moving quickly, but he was protesting too much. He was not above pressing for the rapid reformation of the State Council on the grounds that essential new taxation had to be newly legitimized.

Speranskii's objectives, however, remained as ambitious in 1809 as they had been in 1802. The 'Introduction' explained that the purpose of the projected transformation was 'to establish and consolidate the hitherto autocratic government on the basis of immutable law'.[14] The key word here was 'hitherto'. Marc Raeff's influential biography of Speranskii conveyed the impression that the reformer was not really trying to do anything other than make the Russian autocracy run more efficiently and predictably. David Christian, on the other hand, has emphasized that Speranskii envisaged replacing a 'hitherto autocratic' system with one which was not autocratic.[15] Speranskii argued that it was impossible to place administration on a legal footing if the sovereign made and executed laws on his own. 'For this reason,' he said, 'it is essential to allow the participation of the people in the making of law'.[16] Although this resounding remark was excised from the final version of the 'Introduction', it underpinned the entire document. Speranskii contemplated two different ways of altering the status quo: clothing the autocracy in 'all the external forms of law' while leaving its power substantially intact, and limiting it materially as well as on paper. These were his 'minimum' and 'maximum' programmes. Both involved reorganizing the legislative, executive and judicial arms of the government, but only the second meant giving the reconstituted bodies substantial authority. Speranskii admitted that even the minimum programme would serve the educational purpose of preparing public opinion for accepting changes, but his preference for the maximum programme was evident. He argued, incidentally, that changes akin to the minimum programme had been enacted in Napoleonic France, a point which would have been enough in itself to dissuade most Russians from adopting it.

The rest of the 'Introduction' and the shorter papers of 1809 fleshed out the governmental and social system implied by Speranskii's preliminary exposition. They said a great deal about checks and balances. The sovereign would propose the laws, but they would be discussed in the State Council and the central legislature. The tsar would promulgate the laws, but preface his edicts with the words 'Having hearkened to the opinion of the Council'. The legislature could initiate steps to offset actions of the government which threatened personal or political freedom. The sovereign was to be the head of the executive, but his ministers would be responsible to the legislature for their actions and could be indicted for failing to carry out their duties. The forms of judicial procedure would be laid down from above, but judges would be chosen by the citizenry.

All this seemed to leave the tsar considerable authority, but in a more detailed discussion of law-making Speranskii made plain that the central legislature would occupy an important place in the new governmental order. He aimed to give it charge of all measures which altered the relationship between the state and the individual and the relationship of individuals with each other. The resulting list of measures was a long one, and left the executive with exclusive control only in respect of war and peace, sudden crises, and the elaboration of details overlooked in existing legislation. The central legislature was not assigned much initiative, but was to be given a right of veto. Marc Raeff says otherwise, but John Gooding has proved him wrong by pointing to the passage in one of Speranskii's summary papers of 1809 where he wrote that 'A law held by majority vote to be inappropriate is not to take effect'.[17] The acceptance of this principle would have transformed Russian political life.

Russian social life, apparently, was to be altered less dramatically. 'The law defining personal freedom', Speranskii argued, 'cannot be the same for everyone'; 'no one ought to be deprived of it, but not everyone can have it in an equal degree'.[18] Access to high positions in the judiciary, the civil administration, and the army was to be restricted to those who possessed superior educational qualifications. The ownership of populated land was to be reserved for people sophisticated enough to manage it. Political rights were to be graduated in accordance with economic status. Only property-owners could vote, and only the better-off property-owners could stand for election. It was impossible, Speranskii argued, to avoid social differentiation in Russia. Peasants had to be tied to the land to make sure it was exploited economically and to facilitate government troop levies. Even so, Speranskii felt, Russian peasants were better off than the landless labourers of Britain, France and the United States.

Although these aspects of the 'Introduction' seem to indicate that it lacked a programme of social renewal, a number of commentators believe that it was an even more 'democratic' document than the memoranda of 1802. Their judgement can be supported. Although in 1809 Speranskii did not suggest, as he had once suggested, that it was necessary to abolish some of the existing social categories into which the population of the Russian Empire was divided, he emphasized the need for easy movement from one class to another. Peasants were to be allowed to acquire immovable property and to enter the 'middle estate'. Members of the latter were to be entitled to achieve personal nobility by service. Hereditary nobles were to lose their status if they refused to enter government service. Above all, Speranskii no longer advocated the principle of primogeniture. He had once seen it as the principal foundation of an aristocratic class whose function would be to mediate between the throne and the rest of the population. In 1809, however, he thought it a stumbling-block. He was no longer interested in perpetuating a particular social group, but rather in social fluidity. Different social categories would remain, but no one was to be protected from the consequences of his own lack of effort or prevented from bettering himself. Speranskii's blueprint admitted the possibility of making careers open to talents. When the reformer said that slaves had always existed but that it was not necessary to conclude that civil slavery was essential, he meant it. 'There is no justification for supposing', he wrote, 'that [civil slavery] cannot be abolished in Russia, provided effective measures are taken to this end'.[19]

SPERANSKII'S DOWNFALL

Not much of Speranskii's 'Introduction' was enacted. He hoped to give effect to all of it in time for the tenth anniversary of Alexander I's accession in March 1811, but by then he had realized the full enormity of the task he was facing. His concept of social fluidity went by the board virtually completely, as did the local assemblies and the central Duma or Parliament. Edicts of 1810 and 1812 threatened to end the nobility's longstanding immunity from taxation, and in May 1810 the government announced its intention of making state lands available for sale to all 'free classes' rather than just the traditional landowners; but although these steps implied a readiness to treat Russian society more even-handedly than in the past, they were almost certainly undertaken out of financial necessity rather than a desire for social equalization. The successful implementation of some of the purely administrative parts of Speranskii's plan served only to make the state machine more cumbrous. The reorganized State Council started functioning on 1 January 1810 and survived until the end of the empire, but without the rest of the plan it turned into a new focus of administrative confusion. Ivan Krylov, 'the Russian Aesop', satirized the chairmen of its four departments in a poem called 'The Quartet', in which a monkey, a donkey, a goat and a bear try to overcome their inability to make music together by repeatedly rearranging their chairs, until a nightingale tells them that what they lack is not organization but intelligence and sensitivity. Speranskii knew perfectly well that rearranging chairs was a poor answer to Russia's problems. Statutes of July 1810 and June 1811 clarified some of the demarcation lines within and between the ministries of 1802 (and set up the Ministry of Police), but they did not integrate the ministerial system or give rise to cabinet government. The Committee of Ministers which had been instituted in 1802 was put on a sounder footing just before Speranskii fell from power, but its activities threatened to duplicate those of the State Council. In 1811 Speranskii expended much energy on a scheme to divide the Senate into executive and judicial halves, only for the tsar to delay putting it into effect after accepting it over the heads of a majority in the State Council. The upshot of all these changes and attempted changes was to make confusion worse confounded. Without well-qualified staff existing institutions remained moribund and new institutions could not achieve the purposes for which they were designed. In August 1809, before completing his 'Introduction', Speranskii had secured the enactment of a law requiring upper-level civil servants to show evidence of significant educational attainment; but although it remained on the statute books until 1834, it was phenomenally unpopular and honoured as much in the breach as the observance. The Imperial Lycée founded at Tsarskoe Selo on Speranskii's suggestion in 1811 was to become one of the outstanding educational institutions of the tsarist empire, but even in the long term it was incapable of producing enough graduates to make a substantial dent in the prevailing obtuseness of the country's administrators. In the short term it could make no impression at all. For all Speranskii's efforts, his one-time superior, Viktor Kochubei, repeated in a memorandum of 1814 many of the strictures he had levelled at the Russian governmental system in a report of 1806.[20]

Speranskii did not abandon his objectives without a fight. In his annual report for 1810 he painted a dismal picture of his achievements so far. He could give up, he said, but he chose to go on. He asked only to be relieved of his ancillary duties in order to concentrate on codifying the law. While the faintest hope remained of achieving the original goals, 'no considerations, no unpleasantnesses will prevail over my desire to witness their realization'.[21] In December 1811 Speranskii read Alexander I a paper entitled 'On the Strength of the Government', in which he made even clearer his commitment to the principles which he had been advocating since 1802. By this time, however, his opponents were beginning to get the better of him. It was pointed out in the last chapter that at the end of 1810 the tsar's sister, the Grand Duchess Catherine, commissioned from Nikolai Karamzin an indictment of contemporary imperial policies. Karamzin read his analysis to the Grand Duchess at the very time Speranskii was presenting his report for 1810 to the tsar. In March 1811 Alexander himself received a copy.

Karamzin's *Memorandum on Ancient and Modern Russia* attacked not only Russia's alliance with France but also the whole range of governmental activity since 1801. The notion of subordinating the monarch to the law, it argued, would merely create antagonism between them: 'Two political authorities in one state are like two dreadful lions in one cage, ready to tear each other apart'.[22] New political institutions, Karamzin believed, complicated the form of the government without increasing its efficiency. Replacing colleges with ministries and subordinating the Senate to the State Council had been unnecessary. Machiavelli, Karamzin said, had advised retaining a body's name when changing its character; Russian reformers were doing the opposite, changing names without changing the essence. Founding universities before strengthening secondary education was putting the cart before the horse. Making experienced civil servants go back to school to qualify for promotion was a pointless irritation. The likely consequences of the abolition of serfdom were too frightening to contemplate. Radical steps to restore confidence in the empire's paper money were just as destabilizing as issuing too much paper money in the first place. The time was not ripe for the foreign notion of codifying the law. What the empire needed was not an abstract code but a collection of the laws in force. 'The main trouble with the legislators of the present reign is their excessive reverence for political forms'.[23] The government should be concentrating on finding good servants rather than pointlessly altering job descriptions. It should be looking, above all, to the gentry.

Karamzin's *Memorandum* was not the determining factor in Speranskii's fall, but it summarized the disquiet to which his measures gave rise. As relations with Napoleonic France deteriorated, official commitment to domestic reform gave way to military preparations. Ever torn between the classroom and the parade ground, Alexander I made another move from the one to the other. Since some of Speranskii's ideas owed their shape to French models (the reconstructed State Council, the Ministry of Police, a normative law code), anti-reformers could argue for his dismissal by insinuating he was on the side of the enemy. Uncertainty got the better of the tsar. 'You know the mistrustful character of the Emperor,' Speranskii is supposed to have said to the police minister, 'he does everything by halves ... he is too feeble to rule and too strong to be ruled'.[24] Alexander used the new police ministry to have his State Secretary watched, and in March 1812 he succumbed to the pressure for his dismissal. Speranskii was exiled. In letters from Nizhnii Novgorod and Perm' he argued that his reform plans were no more than 'a rational development' of everything to which the tsar had aspired since 1801. The validity of this argument did his conscience more good than his circumstances. Work continued on the law code to which he was so strongly attached, but in 1815, after vigorous objections from an old-fashioned Minister of Justice, it was shelved. The greatest of the would-be reformers of imperial Russia seemed to have sunk without trace.

ALEXANDER AND THE KINGDOM OF POLAND

Yet Alexander continued to show reformist sympathies. Within a few months of dismissing Speranskii he recognized the Spanish constitution of 1812, perhaps the most far-reaching of all attempts to check the pretensions of monarchs in the first part of the nineteenth century. The Spanish king, Ferdinand VII, accepted it only because he wanted to go home, but Alexander was less cynical. The tsar could not prevent Ferdinand from setting the constitution aside on his return to Madrid in May 1814, but he was well placed, by then, to urge moderation on the returning Louis XVIII of France. The Charter with which Louis endowed his subjects in June 1814 owed not a little to the advice of the tsar and the Russian Ambassador in Paris. 'The concessions it offered should not be underestimated.'[25] It was a delicate plant after Waterloo, and could have been undermined by statements from the victorious powers which placed too much emphasis on keeping France in her place. Alexander did not want to foster the recrudescence of the French right by appearing to treat France punitively. In his negotiations with Britain, Austria and Prussia, he therefore emphasized that adherence to the 1814 Charter was to be made a touchstone of French political behaviour. The Duke of Wellington was not so broadminded. The tsar went on monitoring the course of French political life after the second Peace of Paris, and expressed pleasure, for example, at the dissolution of the right-wing *Chambre introuvable* in September 1816.

Alexander did more than advocate moderation in western Europe. His conversion of Napoleon's Grand Duchy of Warsaw into a Russian-ruled Kingdom of Poland made him unpopular even with his own foreign policy advisers. Unlike Britain, France and Austria (who, as we saw in Chapter Two, contemplated going to war on the subject), the advisers did not object to Russian control of large tracts of Polish territory. Safeguarding the empire's western frontiers was a central concern of everyone involved in the making of Russian foreign policy. What Nesselrode, Capodistria and Pozzo di Borgo disapproved of was the type of regime Alexander sought to install. They doubted whether a distinction should be made between the administration of Poland and that of the rest of the empire. 'Pozzo seriously questioned whether Alexander could reign simultaneously as both an autocrat [in Russia] and a constitutional monarch [in Poland].'[26] Alexander, however, had been thinking about this question for more than a decade. Although he rejected the idea of allowing Russian-controlled Poland to have a ruler other than himself, he had been persuaded of the need for a separate Polish constitutional identity and he left open the possibility of enlarging Polish territory by adding to it parts of the Russian Empire which had formerly been ruled by Poles. In Novosil'tsev he found an agent capable of implementing his policy, but it was the tsar himself who took the crucial decisions. His 'central role in the establishment of the kingdom cannot ... be disputed; had he not fought so persistently for his prize, Poland

70

would have been dismembered yet again along the partition lines of 1795'.[27] In November 1815 Alexander promulgated Poland's new constitution. Despite leaving most authority in the hands of the sovereign or his viceroy, it created a political system as progressive as any on the European mainland. Parliaments were to meet every two years for a period of thirty days. More Poles were to have the vote than Frenchmen under the Charter of 1814. The inhabitants of the new kingdom acquired freedom of the press, habeas corpus, freedom of religion, and other civil rights.

Initially, furthermore, Alexander seemed anxious to make sure that the Polish constitution actually worked. His motive went beyond placating Poles. When he opened the first session of the Polish parliament in March 1818, he made plain that he saw the kingdom as a testing-ground. Poland, he said, was sufficiently advanced to receive the 'liberal institutions' which he hoped to extend to all the territories in his charge. Although he hinted that the first extension might come by way of attaching western provinces of the empire proper to the newly established kingdom, he clearly intended his speech to make waves in the Russian heartland as well as on the periphery. He achieved his objective, for within a week his words were echoed in St Petersburg by 'a lengthy discourse (immediately published) that still stands as perhaps the single most progressive document ever written by a ranking official of the autocratic government'.[28] Addressing the empire's Central Pedagogical Institute, the Curator of the St Petersburg educational district, S. S. Uvarov, spoke in Hegelian terms of 'the natural progress of political freedom'. Although Uvarov issued many caveats about the need for Russians to be patient while freedom flowered, his speech left auditors and readers in no doubt about the road the empire should be taking. The conservative Nikolai Karamzin contented himself, at first, with mockery. His initial response was to 'Let young people enthuse whilst we smile'. By August 1818 he had become more acerbic. 'To give Russia a constitution in the fashionable sense', he wrote, 'is to dress up an important person in the clothes of a buffoon'.[29] The following year, in a substantial memorandum on the Polish question, he deplored the idea of extending the kingdom's boundaries and lamented the unsettling effect on Russia of the developments which Alexander was contemplating. The preservation of the status quo remained his central concern. 'Let the Kingdom of Poland exist *as it is now*, but let Russia exist *as it is* also, as it was left to [Alexander] by Catherine!'[30]

Alexander, however, had not yet finished. Until 1820 constitutional reform was never very far from his mind. His next undertaking issued from the speech he had made in Warsaw. He commissioned Novosil'tsev, who had become the principal Russian civil servant in Poland, to prepare a constitutional charter for the empire as a whole. Who contributed to this document and how many drafts it went through have been subjects of much controversy. It was never enacted, and saw the light of day only in 1831 (when it was published by Polish rebels). There is no doubt, however, about its originality. Its key feature, decentralization, has rarely endeared itself to the rulers of Russia. 'It is one of the few instances in Russian administrative history of a proposal along genuinely federal lines.'[31] Apart from dividing the empire into vicegerencies, it also laid great emphasis on civil liberties and proposed the creation of elective assemblies at both the regional and the national level. Of its 191 clauses, 122 derived from the Polish constitution, but a modern investigator holds that it was also informed by 'unofficial' juridical proposals of the day (including the unpublished memoranda prepared by Speranskii before 1812).[32] Although the constitutional charter never reached the statute book, it was more than a pipedream. On a visit to Warsaw in October 1819 Alexander approved what may have been the final version. Early the following month he appointed A. D. Balashev (formerly Minister of Police) to the Governor-Generalship of a group of provinces south of Moscow. Provision had been made for the appointment of governors-general in Catherine the Great's Provincial Statute of 1775, but the practice of appointing them had fallen into disuse. Tsars had probably been afraid of creating over-mighty subjects. In giving the impression that he might move away from the 'divide and rule' principle of one governor per province, Alexander may have been taking a first tentative step in the direction of the constitutional charter's idea of vicegerencies. Balashev was in fact the second Governor-General appointed in 1819, for Speranskii, who was slowly coming back into favour, had been made Governor-General of Siberia in March. Siberia was so different from the Russian heartland that it was bound to be administered in its own way. Nevertheless, Speranskii was given an explicitly reformist brief. The appointment of Balashev, meanwhile, was a novelty that could hardly have been lost on perceptive contemporaries. No documentary link can be established between the Warsaw plans for a constitution and the simultaneous changes in Russian local government,[33] but the tsar may have covered his traces because he feared opposition. He was so successful in covering them that he was accused by Vasilii Karazin, a reform-minded Ukrainian, of refusing to give his own people what he had granted their Polish enemies.[34] That he was trying to confer on the empire as a whole what the Poles had already received would have been common knowledge if the tsar had also believed in glasnost.

THE ABANDONMENT OF REFORM

Between 1801 and the end of 1819, therefore, Alexander I gave repeated (if sometimes shadowy) indications of his desire to make far-reaching changes in the structure of the Russian polity. Nikolai Druzhinin, one of the two most imaginative Soviet historians of nineteenth-century Russia, concluded that between 1801 and 1820 'the Russian autocracy endeavoured to create a new form of monarchy, one which placed legal limits on absolutism whilst in practice maintaining the personal power of the emperor'.[35] This may not sound like much more than a cosmetic endeavour, but, as Druzhinin points out, Alexander's goals were certainly more wide-ranging than those of his supposedly 'enlightened' grandmother. Whereas Catherine the Great found the principle of popular representation abhorrent, Alexander espoused it. He may have thought of it as a means of improving the empire's line management, but after it had been introduced its effects would have been far-reaching.

Although, in August 1825, Alexander assured Karamzin that he still intended to give Russia 'fundamental laws',[36] he paid very little attention to the idea of systematic reform after shelving the idea of a federalist constitution in about 1820. One of the standard explanations of his change of course is that his commitment to political change was feeble in the first place, but the interest he showed in it for a period of some twenty years makes this view unsatisfactory. Three other possibilities must be brought into play. First, political change was only one of the many sorts of change in which Alexander was interested. Other sorts exercised an increasing hold over him in the second half of his reign and relegated constitution-making to a back seat. Second, by the end of the Napoleonic Wars Russia had become the principal authority in mainland Europe and could not avoid her responsibility for keeping the peace. Third, and most important, the social complexity of the Russian Empire became increasingly apparent after 1815. When the war was on, differences between social groups and between parts of the realm tended to be masked by the common desire to defeat the enemy. Thereafter, the centrifugal character of social and geographical relations tended to reassert itself. No reorganization of the governmental structure could solve the problems which the regime faced on the ground. Alexander discovered the difficulty inherent in approaching Russia's problems from the top down rather than the bottom up.

The concern for religion which marked Alexander's invention of the Holy Alliance in 1815 had already, by then, affected his priorities in domestic affairs. It played a large part in dissipating his political energies. Whereas the political doctrines with which the tsar engaged belonged to the eighteenth-century age of Enlightenment, his new religious interests owed their origins to Romanticism. They increased his sympathy for the mass of humanity, but reduced his capacity for attending to political details. Baroness Krüdener, perhaps the principal figure in Alexander's religious awakening, wanted to purge him of 'the life of Adam' in order to fill him with 'the life of Christ'.[37] The tsar was ill served by this encouragement to relax his hold on reality. Only a few public benefits derived from his intensified humanitarianism. He prohibited the slitting of nostrils in 1817, leaving the branding of criminal exiles as the only form of mutilation sanctioned by law. He encouraged an English Quaker to tour Russian schools and recommend the adoption, where appropriate, of the 'Lancastrian' method of teaching (in which the older pupils instructed the younger). On the recommendation of two other Englishmen, he sanctioned the foundation of a society for prison reform in 1819. Above all, he permitted the establishment of a Russian Bible Society in December 1812 and converted the Ministry of Education into a Ministry of 'Spiritual Affairs' and Education in October 1817. These bodies were conceived as improvements, but by about 1820 they were giving rise to more problems than they solved.

The Bible Society was an offshoot of the British and Foreign Bible Society which had been founded in London in 1804. Bestowed on Russia as a sort of votive offering (just at the point when the last French troops were leaving the empire), its standing was high. Its president, Prince Aleksandr Golitsyn, had been the secular head of the Russian Orthodox Church since 1803 (and was put in charge of the revamped Ministry of Education in 1817). Its vice-presidents included some of the most prominent officials of the day. It was non-denominational. At first it had the right to proselytize only among the non-Orthodox inhabitants of the empire, but it soon received permission to court the Orthodox too. Swimming with the tide, prominent Orthodox, Catholic and Protestant clergymen joined the board, and within a decade the Society had succeeded in establishing 55 principal and 177 secondary branches. Its fundamentalist outlook, however, was ill-suited to the country in which it was operating. Fostering literacy and encouraging people to read the scriptures for themselves was anathema to both Orthodox clergymen and traditionally minded laymen. When the Society produced the first translation of parts of the Bible into modern Russian, trouble began to brew. The antediluvian Admiral Shishkov 'suggested that Church-Slavonic was the original language of the Holy Writ'.[38] Orthodox clerics realized that 'Religions thrive on the ignorance of religion'.[39] Reports reached St Petersburg of a village in which the inhabitants had nominated an old man and a boy as God the Father and God the Son, and of a province in which the peasants were supposed to have adopted the principle of possessing their women in common.[40] Translating the Bible seemed to be subverting the social order. An Orthodox backlash set in. The enlarged Ministry of Education fell victim to a pair of careerists, Mikhail Magnitskii and Dmitrii Runich, who employed the specious charge of infection with western ideas to purge the faculties of Kazan' and St Petersburg universities in 1819 and 1821. The Jesuits, who had enjoyed the protection of the tsars throughout the forty years of their suppression by the Papacy, were expelled from the Russian Empire in 1820. In July 1822 Alexander ordered the withdrawal of Russian students from foreign universities. In August 1822, in a move aimed primarily at freemasons, he prohibited secret societies. In 1824, through the machinations of the visonary Archimandrite Photius, 'a ruthless bigot',[41] Golitsyn lost both his key offices. As head of the Bible Society he was replaced by Metropolitan Serafim of St Petersburg (who emasculated it) and as Minister of Education by Shishkov (who attempted to put back into the school syllabus a textbook of civic duties which had been drawn up in the reign of Catherine the Great). Having adopted a non-traditional view of religion with the intention of conferring additional blessings on his subjects, the tsar had not only lost the thread of political reform but also awoken the benighted Orthodox Church from its torpor and jeopardized the universities whose foundation was one of the principal achievements of his reign. In grasping at a shadow, he appeared to have lost the substance.

In fact, the period of the Bible Society's pre-eminence did not do lasting damage to the development of Russian education. Even the universities of Kazan' and St Petersburg came better out of the crisis than might have been expected. The central authorities refused to take up Magnitskii's suggestion that Kazan' be closed down, for 'Why destroy it', Alexander asked, 'when it can be improved?'[42] Within a few years the celebrated mathematician and local graduate Nikolai Lobachevskii had been appointed Rector. The professors dismissed from St Petersburg University quickly found positions elsewhere in the educational system and fulfilled their promise. The tsar's brother Nicholas asked ironically whether further dismissals were to be expected, as the effect of those which had taken place had been a blessing in disguise. It is true that Uvarov, the head of the St Petersburg educational district whose speech at the Pedagogical Institute in 1818 had echoed the liberal sentiments expressed by Alexander in Warsaw, resigned his post in 1821 because of the depredations of Runich. Having effected the conversion of the Pedagogical Institute into St Petersburg University in 1819, he was appalled to think that its statute would be finalized in the spirit of religious obscurantism. Although he lost his personal battle, however, he won the war, for St Petersburg did not acquire a uniquely repressive set of regulations; in 1824 it was simply made to adopt the university statute which obtained in Moscow. The country's other universities had never been so seriously threatened. Adam Czartoryski resigned as head of the Vil'na educational district in 1823, but not for reasons directly associated with the Ministry of Education's devotion to religion. The Baltic university, Dorpat, acquired a statute rather like the one for which Uvarov had struggled in vain in St Petersburg. The southern university, Khar'kov, experienced only two dismissals and was showing signs of becoming a focus of intellectual life in the Ukraine.

In many ways education boomed under Alexander I. Nicholas Hans pointed out long ago that 'the original [educational] programme was almost accomplished at the end of the reign'.[43] It had provided for six universities, three lyceums, 57 gymnasia and 511 district schools. Only the district schools were fewer than the designated number in 1825, and at 370 they were twice as numerous as the Catherinian 'minor schools' they replaced. Parochial and private schools, moreover, were flourishing, and the seminaries, transformed in legislation of 1808–14, were threatening to produce far more graduates than the ecclesiastical estate could employ. It is customary to say that the state educational system was underfunded and that the moneyed orders ignored it. Neither proposition is quite so valid for the end of Alexander's reign as it is for the beginning. The state certainly devoted too small a proportion of the educational budget to primary and secondary schools, but the public, through town councils and provincial Boards of Public Welfare, did a good deal to make up for governmental parsimony. 'Donations for the small district and parish schools ... were decisive in allowing elementary institutions to operate'.[44] After Speranskii's introduction of formal educational requirements for civil servants in 1809, the gentry were obliged, however reluctantly, to take state schooling more seriously. By the 1830s and 1840s the overwhelming majority of Russians who attended a university went to institutions within the empire rather than Leiden, Göttingen, Marburg and Halle.

Ultimately, therefore, the religious enthusiasm which overtook Alexander in the second half of his reign threatened his educational achievements without negating them. It had the unfortunate effect, however, of distracting the tsar's attention from his other grand designs. Alexander was easily distracted, for, like most Russian rulers, he lacked the ability to delegate. As the French ambassador put it in 1821, he was a person 'undoubtedly animated by the noblest sentiments and the purest intentions, but who gets lost in a plethora of detail because of his exaggerated fear of allowing himself to be influenced or dominated'.[45] The more interests Alexander acquired, the less likely he was to pursue any of them to a conclusion. Foreign affairs presented him with an almost inexhaustible supply. It is an overstatement to say that the idea of civil improvement lost its appeal for him from the moment he smelt his first whiff of grapeshot, but international relations were never far from his mind, often had the effect of driving out other considerations, and prevented the tsar from concentrating hard enough on the domestic schemes he might otherwise have brought to fruition. They also excited him. The journalist Nikolai Grech was probably not far wide of the mark when he claimed that, once peace had been concluded, Alexander found the world 'silent and gloomy'.[46] Great Power congresses offered relief from boredom. They were more fun than drawing up constitutions.

POST-WAR DIPLOMACY

For some time after the Congress of Vienna Alexander managed to reconcile his pursuit of reformist objectives at home with his involvement in the affairs of the continent. So long as Europe was quiet, the tsar could afford to abide by the liberal sentiments of his General Instruction to Diplomatic Missions of May 1815. In the Corfiote Greek John Capodistria Alexander had a foreign policy adviser who 'kept alive ... the hopes and prospects for reform which had long been a major attraction for him'.[47] The first post-war meeting of the victorious wartime powers, held at Aix-la-Chapelle (Aachen) between September and November 1818, was occasioned by the promise given to France in 1815 that she would be considered for international rehabilitation at the end of three years. Her readmission to the conference table, quickly agreed, dovetailed admirably with Russia's desire to broaden the basis on which international relations were conducted. Alexander still worried about the way in which Austria, Prussia and Britain had threatened to turn on him over the Polish question in 1815. France could be his means of forestalling them in the future. At this time Russia mistrusted Metternich's view that the four powers which had won the war against Napoleon ought to take upon themselves the preservation of order in Europe. The order which Metternich had in mind differed from the order which attracted Alexander. The tsar felt that his own device, the Holy Alliance, offered a better prospect of long-term peace. Most European countries were party to it, and in Alexander's opinion it represented the only legitimate means of resolving future difficulties. In a long 'position paper' drawn up before Aix-la-Chapelle, Capodistria pointed out that Russia 'had never admitted' that the terms of the Quadruple Alliance allowed the signatories to interfere in the affairs of non-signatories. This being the case, 'General alliance is preferable'.[48] The tsar's foreign policy adviser was arguing for a sort of international equivalent of the religious non-denominationalism which Alexander was trying to practise at home. Religious toleration surfaced explicitly at Aix, in a memorandum sponsored by Alexander on the question of granting civic and political equality to Europe's Jews. It did not attract support, but it showed that the tsar could be just as idealistic in foreign affairs as he was trying to be at home.

Very soon after the first post-war congress, Alexander's room for idealism diminished. He had given the impression of supposing that few dangers confronted Europe and that the time was ripe for moving on to a higher plane. 'Castlereagh and Metternich', writes Henry Kissinger, 'sought a world of intermediary nuance; Alexander one of immediate perfection'.[49] The tsar's naivety was soon exposed. German students had been troublesome since October 1817, when they held a large demonstration at the Wartburg Castle near Eisenach to mark the 300th anniversary of the Reformation. Alexander had been disturbed enough to circulate a pamphlet about the 'Wartburgfest' at the Aix congress, but he believed that censorship and strict control of the universities would keep the trouble within bounds. Metternich was less sanguine. When, in March 1819, the German student Karl Sand murdered the right-wing playwright August von Kotzebue at Mannheim, Austria's Chancellor decided on a crackdown. Alexander had good reason to go along with him, as Kotzebue received money from the Russians for providing them with information about intellectual currents in Germany. Nevertheless, Russia had doubts about Metternich's Karlsbad Decrees of August 1819, and especially about their ensuing imposition on the entire German Confederation. The next eighteen months witnessed furious international wrangling about the extent and nature of the Great Powers' responsibility for the European status quo. The question posed by the death of Kotzebue was restated in other parts of the continent. In February 1820 a member of the royal house was murdered in France. In March of that year the military rose against Ferdinand VII in Spain and revived the constitution of 1812. In July the Kingdom of the Two Sicilies fell apart. When the second meeting of Europe's leaders took place at Troppau and Laibach between October 1820 and February 1821, the problems confronting the sovereigns and diplomats were much larger than they had been at Aix.

Alexander, and especially Capodistria, attempted for a time to avoid lending Russian support to the principle of concerted military action. In October 1819 the tsar responded to an alarmist letter from the Emperor of Austria by speaking of his pride in the constitutional structure which was taking root in Poland. Six weeks later he expressed considerable reservations about Metternich's intimidation of the German Confederation. In February 1820 his ambassador in Paris wrote that equity in international relations had been severely threatened by the haste with which the Karlsbad Decrees had been promulgated. In a summary response to developments in Germany, France and Spain, Capodistria held that the Great Powers were showing insufficient 'wisdom' and 'moderation', and that it was unreasonable for them to expect tranquillity to be universal so soon after the end of the Napoleonic Wars. Even after the murder of the Duc de Berry, which must have reminded Alexander of the murder of the Duc d'Enghien in 1804, the tsar instructed a special emissary to caution the French against pursuing reactionary policies. Alexander still held that his Polish administration was a model worth copying. In view of the number of threats to which European peace was exposed, his attempt to hold the line did him credit.[50]

Soon after Europe's leaders foregathered in Troppau, however, Alexander received news from home which inclined him to think again about international affairs. The Semenovskii Guards regiment had mutinied in St Petersburg. The tsar played down the revolt in his press releases, but in private he ascribed it, quite mistakenly, to the machinations of secret societies. Although the regiment was quickly disbanded and re-formed, the mutiny both reduced the likelihood of political reform in Russia and diminished Alexander's capacity for resisting Metternich. With the tsar's blessing, Austrian troops crossed into Italy at the beginning of 1821. In 1822 the moderate Capodistria left his post. In 1823 Alexander waxed enthusiastic about French intervention in Spain. Russian foreign policy became almost wholly subordinate to that of Vienna. Alexander rediscovered his independence only at the very end of the reign. Having gone over to the side of reaction, he was in no position to respond as he might otherwise have done to the Greek revolt of 1821, the one European revolution with which he felt sympathy and from which he stood to gain. Between 1821 and 1825 he tried without success to find an internationally acceptable means of assisting the Greeks against the Turks. A few months before his death he gave up the unequal struggle and reverted to the foreign policy of the immediate post-war years. In August 1825 Nesselrode informed Russian ambassadors that the empire intended to stop negotiating with its allies on the question of doing something for Greece. Russia would again be guided by self-interest and the principle of maintaining the balance established by 'the great transactions of 1814, 1815, and 1818'.[51] She acknowledged, in other words, that her foreign policy since 1820 had been a mistake. Time that might have been spent on reorganizing the empire's political structure had been spent on an approach to foreign affairs whose benefits had been few.

THE PROBLEM OF DEMOBILIZATION

Whatever his foreign policy, Alexander chose not to reduce the size of his army, which had grown from three or four hundred thousand men at the end of the eighteenth century to a million by 1815. Alexander loved armies. John Keep says that his militarism was hardly less than that of Paul and Nicholas I, two of the most soldierly of all the Romanovs.[52] That apart, there were good practical reasons for retaining a high military capability after 1815. Whether maintaining the peace of Europe or preparing to assist the Greeks, Russia seemed to need troops in number. Her soldiers, furthermore, became free men when they enlisted. Suddenly returning large numbers of them to the villages might have excited social envy. Even in open societies demobilization is notorious for giving rise to social complications. If the British had to found a 'Society for the Suppression of Begging' in 1818, what sort of suppression might have been called for in Russia? Nevertheless, retaining a large army was not a decision to be taken lightly. On the negative side of the ledger, it placed an intolerable strain on the exchequer. In 1815 soldiers accounted for about one-third of the government's expenditure. The state treasurer, Baron Kampenhausen, had told Alexander in 1812 that, by comparison with the war against Napoleon, the wars of Catherine the Great had been 'a mere bagatelle (*igrushkoi*)'.[53] Alexander found paying off his international debts a perpetual irritation. In respect of the army, he was the victim of a sort of 'Catch-22'. On financial grounds his soldiers ought to have been disbanded, but for the sake of imperial security they had to be kept under arms. Alexander found an answer to the conundrum, but one which sharply illuminated the third and main reason why his reformist aspirations failed to bear fruit. It laid bare the intractable nature of Russian society. Whereas embracing religion and travelling to international congresses distracted the tsar's attention, Russian society stood in his way. It is doubtful whether he fully grasped the point, but equally doubtful whether he could have done much about it. Speranskii had seen the need for social reform but had been unable to achieve it. The second half of Alexander's reign made plain what the autocracy was up against.

Alexander lit upon his answer to the problem of maintaining a large peacetime army in 1810, in the period of his alliance with France. A visit to the model estate of his War Minister, Aleksei Arakcheev, showed him what could be done by applying military discipline to the organization of private land. The tsar decided to extend the idea to the lands of the state. By settling troops in the countryside and creating self-perpetuating 'military colonies' he could kill several birds with one stone: keep the army at full strength, enable it to support itself, eliminate the boredom of soldiers in peacetime, systematize farming, free the nobility from its obligation to part with serfs for the forces, and (by choosing locations carefully) strengthen the empire's border defences. The tsar's first experiments were interrupted by the Napoleonic invasion, but early in 1815 Arakcheev drew up plans for a massive campaign. By the end of 1825 a third of the army, over a third of a million men, had become military colonists. Counting women and children, the number of people in the colonies may have been 750,000. In ten years the tsar's scheme had changed the social complexion of Novgorod and St Petersburg provinces in the north, Mogilev in the west, and the southern and eastern Ukraine.

In theory, the colonies were a noble undertaking. Richard Pipes compares the idea behind them with the model communities advocated by Robert Owen and Charles Fourier in the west; 'in spirit and programme,' he says, 'the entire undertaking stood closer to the earlier, more idealistic part of Alexander's life than to the policy of repression usually identified with the second half of the reign'.[54] Unfortunately for Alexander's ideals, military colonies could not be created in isolation from the rest of Russian society. Since soldiers could not be expected to become farmers without practical advice, they were mixed with peasants owned by the state. Heads of state peasant households in the areas marked out for military colonization were transferred to the military estate and obliged to provide board, lodging and instruction for the soldiers who were billeted on them. Adult non-heads of household in the affected areas became soldiers themselves. Minors became 'military cantonists' (the term used for soldiers' children), and unless they were eldest sons entered reserve battalions at the age of eighteen. The government made a virtue out of this intermingling. Speranskii, for example, wrote in 1825 that the colonies' purpose was 'to constitute [a single whole] out of the two divergent elements, to put the first [the state peasants] on a military footing without disturbing their economic activities and their property, to turn the second [the soldiers] into settlers without disturbing their mode of service'.[55] Since state peasants who became colonists were exempt from state taxes and had access to the soldiers' labour, they might have been expected to welcome the change in their status. They did not. Their costs turned out to be four or five times greater than the taxes from which they had been exempted, and they usually had to hand over at least half their harvest to the battalion granary. Since they were also being turned into soldiers themselves, they were in effect having to provide labour services (from which, on state lands, they had been free).

Worst of all, state peasants were subject to the iron hand of Russian military discipline. Alexander may have intended his innovation to produce model villages, but he was not in charge of the detailed administration of his experiment. That task was the province of Arakcheev, whose severity filled the gap created by his lack of imagination. Arakcheev had become Alexander's right-hand man. The only thing he had in common with Speranskii, his predecessor, was a consciousness of his social inferiority. A squire among aristocrats, a Russian among Westernizers, a soldier among sophisticates, a favourite among seekers for favour, he was universally despised. The way in which he ran the military colonies typified his small-mindedness. Everyone wore uniforms. Buildings and plots of land were numbered and colonists were obliged to wear the numbers on their epaulettes. Set times were prescribed for rising, going to work, returning home and sleeping. Regulations laid down the streets along which settlers could drive their livestock to pasture and the way in which they were to feed them. Punishment for infractions was severe. 'The state peasant who became a military colonist could not organize his work, his time, his economic affairs, or even his children as he wished.'[56] Not surprisingly, colonists objected to the way they were treated. The first great revolt broke out at Chuguev in the south in 1819. Arakcheev's mistress was murdered in 1825 on the model estate which had given Alexander his inspiration. In 1826 a colonel was brave enough to tell Nicholas I that the colonies were a dangerous undertaking which ought to be disturbing the sleep of St Petersburg. In 1831 a massive revolt took place in the colonies of nearby Novgorod. In 1818 Alexander had announced that he intended, in time, to turn four-fifths of the state peasantry into military colonists, at which point the colonies would have contained more than a quarter of the empire's total population. A few foreign observers were impressed, but hardly anyone at home. Even Karamzin objected to the colonies in his last confabulation with the emperor. Nobles stood to profit if colonists' children freed them from having to provide serf recruits for the army, but they feared the compulsory purchase of private estates which stood in the way of the colonies' expansion and they suspected that the government was trying to create an enormous, free-standing military caste. Maintaining aristocratic pre-eminence was more important than the burden of supplying recruits.

SERFS, BUREAUCRATS AND MERCHANTS

Alexander's great social innovation, therefore, made state peasants furious and nobles suspicious. Privately owned peasants – serfs – were in ferment anyway. Admittedly, serfdom was no longer growing in extent. Alexander did not enserf Finns under the arrangements of 1809, did not extend serfdom to the south-western corner of the empire on acquiring Bessarabia from the Turks in 1812, and did not reintroduce serfdom for Poles after the collapse of the Grand Duchy of Warsaw. He sanctioned the modification of serf obligations in the Baltic province of Livonia in 1804, and between 1816 and 1819 went on to abolish serfdom both there and in the adjacent provinces of Estland and Kurland. Liberality towards the peripheries of the empire seemed to mark his attitude to serfdom no less than his attitude to constitutions. In the social sphere, however, the tsar did not seriously consider applying the experience of the border zones to the imperial heartland. Although in 1818 he instructed Arakcheev to draw up proposals for the general emancipation of the serfs, he required him to find a scheme which the nobility could accept. Having incensed the nobles by making them acquire new educational qualifications to get on in the civil service, and having given them the impression that, by means of the military colonies, he was greatly increasing the autocracy's potential for repression, Alexander apparently took the view that he would be unwise to attack the foundation of their economic well-being. It is true that contemporaries unsympathetic to serf reform worried about his intentions. When he convened the Senate unexpectedly in March 1820, rumour had it that he was going to announce the serfs' emancipation. He devoted the meeting, however, to the quite different matter of his brother's divorce; his plans for the serfs were far less advanced than conservatives imagined. Even his one concrete achievement, the abolition of serfdom in the Baltic provinces, flattered to deceive, for since it gave the serfs no land it consigned them to destitution.

To judge by the occasions on which serfs protested, their plight was getting worse. Of the 150 instances in which troops had to be called out against serfs in the reign of Alexander, 66 took place in the period 1816–20. Landlords who had suffered financially as a result of the Napoleonic Wars felt obliged to press their serfs harder, and peasants who had served in the militia or as partisans were reluctant to return to their former condition. Serf economic activity was becoming more variegated. Cottage industry had received a fillip from the loss of factories as a result of the French invasion. More peasants were engaging in trade. More of them took the technically illegal step of submitting petitions to the tsar, more were prepared to take up arms, and protests tended to be sustained for longer periods of time. Merely by standing still, the government was allowing the gap between the law and reality to widen. In 1820 the biggest disturbance of the reign came to a head on the river Don. After General Chernyshev put it down, Alexander closed the door on reform, informing provincial governors that 'instances of disobedience cannot be tolerated, whatever their source'.[57]

By this time Alexander was running out of social groups to depend on. His ecumenism had alienated the clergy, his military colonies the state peasants. He had fostered mistrust among the nobility and done little to diminish the recalcitrance of the serfs. Only bureaucrats and merchants were left. He appears to have cultivated them, but they were not strong enough to counterbalance the estates he had failed to please. The former were ascending, the latter descending. Whether Russian bureaucrats can legitimately be called a distinctive 'social group' in the early nineteenth century is a debatable question. They were becoming one, but the point at which trends gave rise to self-consciousness is uncertain. Russian civil servants of the mid-eighteenth and the mid-nineteenth centuries had much in common when judged by the criteria of social origin, ownership of serfs and nationality. When judged by three other criteria, however, bureaucrats of the mid-nineteenth century differed notably from their predecessors. They were much more numerous; many more of them spent their entire working lives as civil servants (instead of starting as soldiers); and they were much more highly educated. The second and third of these changes start showing up in the years between the death of Catherine the Great and the end of the Napoleonic Wars – the third, in large measure, because of Alexander's educational reforms of 1803–4 and the examination statute of 1809. It was some time, however, before entrants into the civil service who embodied the new characteristics could achieve positions of authority, and it is unlikely, therefore, that in the reign of Alexander I the outlook of bureaucrats differed much from the outlook of nobles. It would have been pointless for Alexander to think of relying on a bureaucratic *esprit de corps* for support against potential opponents.[58] Nor could he rely on the economic muscle of the trading and manufacturing community. The fortunes of the merchant estate fluctuated dramatically in the course of his reign. In the period of the Franco-Russian alliance merchants prospered, but in the second decade of the century (and especially after the Congress of Vienna) the adoption of free trade looked likely to cut them to ribbons. After returning to protectionism in 1819, in 1824 Alexander enacted a reform of the guilds which tried to safeguard Russia's merchants from the trading and manufacturing activities of non-merchants (by making it harder for people from other estates to engage in commercial activities without being taxed on them). The most recent Soviet and Western accounts of this measure agree that it flew in the face of reality. The Russian economy could no longer be sectionalized in the way that the guild reform envisaged. The government had to move in the direction of merging estates rather than stick to the policy of keeping them separate from each other. If merchants were going to rely on the defence of the law, their future was bleak. They were certainly in no position to offer the autocracy support against other sections of the community.[59]

Under-commitment to liberal objectives, religious fervour, and an obsession with foreign affairs are not enough on their own to explain why Alexander's long-term interest in political reform came to nothing. Without a reordering of Russian civil society, new governmental arrangements would not have meant very much; but reordering Russian society was much more difficult than rearranging governmental institutions. The sheer complexity of the social problems facing Alexander I goes a long way towards explaining why he failed to resolve them. In 1820 the French ambassador to St Petersburg spoke of the inhabitants of the Russian Empire as 'half-savage peoples' and of the empire as a place 'in which everything, so to speak, still has to be done'.[60] Alexander understood this subliminally, but responded to it intermittently and timorously. Speranskii, in the years before 1812, was more consistent and braver. Even he, however, was determined to keep the empire on its feet while trying to put it to rights. Some of the people who appear in the next chapter gave much less priority to the bureaucratic love of continuity.

NOTES

1. Norman E. Saul, *Russia and the Mediterranean 1797–1807* (Chicago and London, 1970), p. 169.
2. VPR, i. 327.
3. A. L. Narochnitskii, 'Rossiia i napoleonovskie voiny za gospodstvo nad Evropoi (Soprotivlenie i prisposoblenie)', in Narochnitskii, ed., *Problemy metodologii i istochnikovedeniia istorii vneshnei politiki Rossii: sbornik statei* (Moscow, 1986), p. 97.
4. VPR, ii. 366–7.
5. Ibid., ii. 177.
6. Ibid., iii. 519.
7. Ibid., p. 558.
8. D. G. Kirby, ed., *Finland and Russia 1808–1920: From Autonomy to Independence* (London and Basingstoke, 1975), p. 11; Edward C. Thaden, *Russia's Western Borderlands, 1710–1870* (Princeton, NJ, 1984), p. 86; VPR, iv. 587–9 (n. 105); M. M Speranskii, 'Otchet v delakh 1810 goda', SIRIO 21 (1877), 456.
9. V. A. Kaliagin, *Politicheskie vzgliady M. M. Speranskogo* (Saratov, 1973), p. 3.
10. F. F. Vigel', *Zapiski*, ed. S. Ia. Shtraikh (2 vols, Moscow, 1928), i. 154–7; M. Korf, *Zhizn' grafa Speranskogo* (2 vols, St Petersburg, 1861), ii. 40 (the opinion of Gustav Rozenkampf); A. V. Semenova, *Vremennoe revoliutsionnoe pravitel'stvo v planakh dekabristov* (Moscow, 1982), p. 60 (a judgement which Korf left out of his biography); L. N. Tolstoy, *War and Peace*, tr. Rosemary Edmonds (2 vols, Harmondsworth, 1957), i. 497–508, 543–7; A. V. Predtechenskii, *Ocherki obshchestvenno-politicheskoi istorii Rossii v pervoi chetverti XIX veka* (Moscow and Leningrad, 1957), p. 266.
11. Marc Raeff, *Michael Speransky: Statesman of Imperial Russia 1772–1839* (The Hague, 1957); M. M. Speranskii, *Proekty i zapiski*, ed. S. N. Valk (Moscow and Leningrad, 1961; hereafter cited as Valk).
12. Valk, p. 113, n. 99.
13. Ibid., p. 141.
14. Ibid., p. 164.
15. David Christian, 'The Political Ideals of Michael Speransky', SEER 54 (1976), 199.

16. Valk, p. 164, n. 189.
17. John Gooding, 'The Liberalism of Michael Speransky', SEER 64 (1986), 408; Valk, p. 227.
18. Valk, p. 181.
19. Ibid., p. 179.
20. See V. P. Kochubei, 'Zapiska ob uchrezhdenii ministerstv, marta 28 1806g.', SIRIO 90 (1894), 199–211, and Kochubei, 'Zapiska o polozhenii Imperii i o merakh k prekrashcheniiu besporiadkov i vvedenii luchshego ustroistva v raznye otrasli, pravitel'stvo sostavliaiushchie', ibid., pp. 5–26.
21. Speranskii, 'Otchet' (n. 8, above), p. 462.
22. Richard Pipes, Karamzin's Memoir on Ancient and Modern Russia: A Translation and Analysis (New York, 1966), p. 139.
23. Ibid., p. 192.
24. P. S. Squire, The Third Department: The Political Police in the Russia of Nicholas I (Cambridge, 1968), p. 35.
25. Alfred Cobban, A History of Modern France, vol. 2 (2nd edn, Harmondsworth, 1965), p. 73.
26. Frank W. Thackeray, Antecedents of Revolution: Alexander I and the Polish Kingdom, 1815–1825 (Boulder, Colo., 1980), p. 12.
27. W. H. Zawadzki, 'Russia and the Re-opening of the Polish Question, 1801–1814', IHR 7 (1985), 43.
28. Cynthia H. Whittaker, The Origins of Modern Russian Education: An Intellectual Biography of Count Sergei Uvarov, 1786–1855 (DeKalb, Ill., 1984), pp. 45–6.
29. V. I. Semevskii, Politicheskie i obshchestvennye idei dekabristov (St Petersburg, 1909), p. 267.
30. N. M. Karamzin, 'Opinion of a Russian Citizen', in J. L. Black, ed., Essays on Karamzin: Russian Man-of-Letters, Political Thinker, Historian, 1766–1826 (The Hague and Paris, 1975), p. 196 (italics in the original).
31. Marc Raeff, Plans for Political Reform in Imperial Russia, 1730–1905 (Englewood Cliffs, NJ, 1966), p. 110.
32. N. V. Minaeva, Pravitel'stvennyi konstitutsionalizm i peredovoe obshchestvennoe mnenie Rossii v nachale XIX veka (Saratov, 1982), p. 194.
33. Predtechenskii, Ocherki (n. 10, above), p. 393.
34. Grand Duke Nikolai Mikhailovich, Imperator Aleksandr I (2 vols, St Petersburg, 1912), ii. 351–2.
35. N. M. Druzhinin, 'Prosveshchennyi absoliutizm v Rossii', in Druzhinin, Izbrannye trudy: Sotsial'no-ekonomicheskaia istoriia Rossii (Moscow, 1987), p. 261. The other outstanding Soviet historian of nineteenth-century Russia was P. A. Zaionchkovskii.
36. N. M. Karamzin, 'Novoe pribavlenie', Starina i novizna, 1898 bk II, section 2, p. 19.
37. Nikolai Mikhailovich, Aleksandr I (above, n. 34), ii. 215.
38. Peter K. Christoff, The Third Heart: Some Intellectual-Ideological Currents and Cross Currents in Russia 1800–1830 (The Hague / Paris, 1970), pp. 72–3.
39. Stanislaus Joyce, My Brother's Keeper (London, 1958), p. 114.
40. Nikolai Mikhailovich, Aleksandr I (above, n. 34), ii. 359.
41. Joseph L. Wieczynski, 'Apostle of Obscurantism: the Archimandrite Photius of Russia (1792–1838)', J Eccl Hist 22 (1971), 319.
42. James T. Flynn, The University Reform of Tsar Alexander I 1802–1835 (Washington, DC, 1988), p. 97.

43. Nicholas Hans, *History of Russian Educational Policy 1701–1917* (London, 1931), p. 58.
44. Franklin A Walker, 'Popular Response to Public Education in the Reign of Tsar Alexander I (1801–1825)', *History of Education Quarterly* (Winter 1984), 531.
45. Nikolai Mikhailovich, *Aleksandr I* (above, n. 34), ii. 399.
46. N. I. Grech, *Zapiski o moei zhizni* (Moscow, 1990), p. 218.
47. Patricia Kennedy Grimsted, *The Foreign Ministers of Alexander I: Political Attitudes and the Conduct of Russian Diplomacy, 1801–1825* (Berkeley and Los Angeles, Calif., 1969), p. 241.
48. VPR, x. 415, 422.
49. Henry A. Kissinger, *A World Restored: Metternich, Castlereagh, and the Problems of Peace 1812–22* (London, 1957), p. 187.
50. VPR, xi. 134–5, 263, 337–40, 347.
51. Ibid., xiv. 234.
52. John Keep, 'The Military Style of the Romanov Rulers', *War and Society* 1 (1983), 61–84.
53. V. G. Sirotkin, 'Finansovo-ekonomicheskie posledstviia napoleonovskikh voin v 1814–24 gody', *Istoriia SSSR*, 1974 no. 4, p. 49.
54. Richard Pipes, 'The Russian Military Colonies, 1810–1831,' in Pipes, *Russia Observed: Collected Essays on Russian and Soviet History* (Boulder, Colo., 1989), p. 83.
55. L. P. Bogdanov, 'Voennye poseleniia', VI, 1980 no. 2, p. 180.
56. V. A Fedorov, 'Bor'ba krest'ian Rossii protiv voennykh poselenii (1810–1818)', VI, 1952 no. 11, p. 116.
57. I. Ignatovich, 'Krest'ianskie volneniia pervoi chetverti XIX veka', VI, 1950 no. 9, p. 67.
58. For statistics and most of the interpretation suggested here see Walter M. Pintner, 'The Evolution of Civil Officialdom, 1755–1855', in Walter McKenzie Pintner and Don Karl Rowney, eds, *Russian Officialdom: The Bureaucratization of Russian Society from the Seventeenth to the Twentieth Century* (Chapel Hill, NC, 1980), pp. 190–226.
59. Iu. Ia. Rybakov, *Promyshlennoe zakonodatel'stvo Rossii pervoi poloviny XIX veka* (Moscow, 1986), pp. 33–5; Wayne Dowler, 'Merchants and Politics in Russia: The Guild Reform of 1824', SEER 65 (1987), 38–52.
60. Nikolai Mikhailovich, *Aleksandr I* (above, n. 34), ii. 308–9.

CHAPTER FOUR

The Decembrist Movement

THE SUCCESSION CRISIS OF 1825

In two senses, one narrow, the other broad, Alexander I was to blame for the dramatic consequences of his death. Kliuchevskii's bitter reflections on the provocative character of the nineteenth-century Russian monarchy (quoted in the first section of Chapter One) find their strongest justification in the events of December 1825.

Ironically, the narrow sense in which the tsar was to blame for the crisis of 1825 turned on one of the few points of Russian law which seemed to be unambiguous. For most of the eighteenth century tsars had had the right to nominate their heirs, but in 1797 Paul had decreed that succession to the throne was to be hereditary in the male line. Since Alexander was childless, it was logical to suppose that he would be succeeded by the oldest of his three brothers, the Grand Duke Konstantin, Viceroy of Poland. In 1820, however, Konstantin had entered into a morganatic marriage with a Catholic Polish aristocrat, which in Alexander's view debarred him from inheriting the Russian throne. In 1822 the tsar obliged Konstantin to ask for release from the order of succession. The following year Alexander commissioned Metropolitan Filaret of Moscow to draw up a manifesto proclaiming the transfer of Konstantin's rights to their younger brother Nicholas. He then made the mistake of keeping what he had done secret. Although Filaret persuaded the tsar to lodge copies of the relevant documents with the Senate, the Synod and the State Council in St Petersburg, their contents remained secret until the death of the tsar. This took place unexpectedly on 19 November 1825 at Taganrog on the Sea of Azov. The news reached St Petersburg eight days later, whereupon Alexander's dispositions were revealed. They caused a storm. The Governor of St Petersburg, Mikhail Miloradovich, declared that an unpublished manifesto did not have the force of law, and that anyway it contravened Paul's statute of 1797. The Guards, he said, might treat the accession of Nicholas as usurpation. The younger brother could ascend the throne only if Konstantin renounced his claim in public.

In these unique circumstances an oath of loyalty was sworn to the Viceroy of Poland. Konstantin told his entourage in Warsaw that he would abide by the arrangements made in 1822–3, but he failed to put out an official statement. After about two weeks Nicholas could stand the tension no longer. Having learned that conspirators intended to take advantage of the interregnum to insist on changes in the constitution of the empire, he decided that, with or without a statement from his brother, he would have an oath of loyalty sworn to himself on 14 December. News of this development brought the conspirators whom he feared into the open. For the second time, 14 December was to mark a turning-point in the history of the tsarist regime. On 14 December 1766 Catherine the Great had summoned her Legislative Commission. What happened on 14 December 1825 can be seen as the start of the Russian revolutionary movement. By treating the empire as a private fief, the Romanovs demonstrated that they were very far from understanding the constitutionalism on which Alexander had spent so much of his time. If they could not obey laws they had made on their own, they were unlikely to obey laws framed with the assistance of others. Some people concluded that it was time to make sweeping changes in the political system.

These people, the 'Decembrists', were not a hot-house growth. Because the interregnum caught them unawares they were dealt with very quickly, but their movement had been taking shape for at least a decade. They owed their inspiration to the broadening of the country's horizons and the growth of Russian self-confidence in the first quarter of the nineteenth century. Alexander I had played a large part in the broadening and was therefore responsible in a general as well as a technical sense for what happened after his death. Nikolai Basargin, one of the lesser conspirators, thought the tsar failed to grasp what effect his behaviour might have. Writing in the 1850s, he found it strange 'that heads of government at that time ... did not foresee that their highly significant words would strike a chord not only with thinking people but even among the masses; that the hopes they inspired would give rise to expectations, demands, and disturbances'.[1] Basargin underestimated the tsar's perspicacity. Alexander I knew where his actions were leading, but drew back when the rate of change began to accelerate. He intended the changes he enacted in the first years of his reign, the infinitely greater involvement of Russia in European affairs, the promotion of Speranskii, the bestowal of constitutions on Finland and Poland, and the speech at the Warsaw Parliament of 1818 to create an atmosphere in which more Russians reflected on the future of their society. He admitted as much, rather ruefully, on receiving a report about European secret societies in 1821. 'I have shared and encouraged these illusions and these errors,' he said. 'It is not for me to be harsh'.[2] The diversity of his political interests, unrest in western Europe, and an increasing awareness of the complexity of Russian society persuaded Alexander to abandon the cause of reform in the last years of his life, but by then it was too late to put the genie back in the bottle. The tsar had been more succesful than he expected. All sections of the educated community had started responding to his aspirations. In the civil service, among poets and writers of fiction, in the academic community, among the spiritually inclined and in the army there were people who applauded their ruler's open-mindedness and wanted him to take his innovations further. Some of these free-thinkers took the opportunity of the 1825 interregnum to express the full extent of their radicalism.

THE ROOTS OF REVOLT: BUREAUCRATS, WRITERS, ACADEMICS, MASONS AND SOLDIERS

Some of the civil servants who were privy to Alexander's longstanding interest in reform regretted the fact that few of his ideas had reached the statute book. The conspirators who tried to take advantage of the confusion of December 1825 planned to set up an interim government consisting of people known to the inhabitants of the country who would bolster their authority while they organized elections. They believed that prominent officials would sympathize with them. A few civil servants had actually joined their ranks, and others were clearly anxious to press on with reforms if circumstances allowed them to do so. Prince Petr Viazemskii, for example, who served in the Russian administration of Poland, played a large part in drawing up the constitutional charter which Alexander contemplated between 1818 and 1820. Having realized, during the congresses of Troppau and Laibach, that it was going to be shelved, he expressed irritation at the way in which Alexander abandoned change at home for the sake of maintaining the status quo in Europe. 'Finish building your own house,' he wrote, 'before going to repair other people's'.[3] Speranskii was a much more obvious example of a bureaucrat who had every reason to become a radical. By 1825 he was back in St Petersburg, chastened by his long exclusion from the highest offices of state but no less reform-minded than previously. On the morning of 14 December he is supposed to have told one of the activists, 'Win first, then everyone will be on your side'.[4] Viazemskii and Speranskii might have come out against the regime if its authority had been subjected to a sustained challenge. One or two officials were actually prepared to play a part in mounting that challenge. When serving as Governor-General of Siberia, Speranskii had virtually adopted Gavrila Baten'kov, a former soldier and engineer who became his right-hand man and travelled with him to the capital at the end of his governorship. Like Speranskii, Baten'kov was a constitutional monarchist. Unlike him he was prepared to do more than wait for the conspirators' success. Having arrived in St Petersburg in the unfortunate last years of the reign, he was repelled by his work in the administration of the military colonies and convinced that the colonists could be persuaded to rise in revolt. He joined the regime's opponents in November 1825 and via Speranskii found out the date of the oath-taking to Nicholas, which enabled the conspirators to set in train their final preparations.

Baten'kov's contribution to Decembrism was dwarfed by that of Nikolai Turgenev. Of all Alexander I's administrators, Turgenev was probably the one whose devotion to radical change was the most deep-seated. Son of a man who had been closely associated with the eighteenth-century Russian radical Nikolai Novikov, he was educated at Moscow and Göttingen Universities and took up a post in the Commission on Legal Codification in 1812. In the latter years of the war he headed the Russian section of the central administrative department of the allied powers (under the Prussian reformer Baron Stein), and thereafter worked for the State Council and the Ministry of Finance. He had access to the papers impounded after the dismissal of Speranskii and was close to reform-minded members of the State Council like the Counts Seweryn Potocki and Nikolai Mordvinov. He did not fall victim to the bureaucrat's propensity for moderation. At Göttingen he had drafted an *Essay on the Theory of Taxation*. Since the Russian government's principal source of revenue was the poll tax, which was paid only by peasants, talking about taxes meant talking about social relations. These, for Turgenev, lay at the heart of Russia's difficulties. He was not really interested in constitution-making. In 1818 he published his *Essay*. Just before it appeared he confided to his diary: 'I hate all the infamy of slavery more than ever before now that I see closely what it leads people to and how it can exist. All the arguments and defence brought forward to excuse slavery are the emptiest rubbish'.[5] Turgenev emancipated his household serfs and urged his friends to emancipate theirs. He disseminated among people outside the civil service the plans for change which circulated within it. He played a considerable part in organizing the groups from which the uprising of December 1825 eventually emerged. Despite being out of the country when the tsar died he was found guilty of involvement in the conspiracy. He did not return to take his punishment. Twenty years after the coup's failure he published in Paris the first substantial intepretation of its genesis and significance, and went on to outline the course which Russia should pursue in the future. He welcomed the reforms of the 1860s with enormous relief. At his death in 1871 his relation, the novelist Ivan Turgenev, picked out singlemindedness as his great virtue. If the civil service of Alexander I could throw up such people, it was clear that reformist aspirations were not confined to the tsar and his immediate entourage.

The activities of writers showed that sympathy for change was to be found outside as well as inside the government. It is usual to trace the politicization of Russian literature to the 1830s, when the iron hand of Nicholas I made open expressions of political opinion impossible. Even under Alexander I, however, 'Russian literature was in the process of becoming the barometer of the nation's social and political development'.[6] Alexander Radishchev's subversive travellogue *A Journey from St Petersburg to Mos-*

cow looked like a voice crying in the wilderness when it appeared in 1790, but the severe punishment meted out to the author did not prevent others from expressing political opinions through poetry and prose. Alexander I espoused the technique personally when he provided financial support for the forward-looking *St Petersburg Journal* of 1798. One of its editors, Aleksandr Bestuzhev, fathered four Decembrists. The journals *Messenger of Europe*, founded in 1802, and *Son of the Fatherland*, founded in 1812, provided long-lasting outlets for writers with a social conscience. In the preface to the first number of the *Messenger*, Nikolai Karamzin wrote that literature might perform more valuable services in Russia than in other countries, since Russians were only just beginning to read and their responses might be fresher and more forthright. Later in the same year he enthused about the growth in the market for reading-matter. The *Messenger* had to double its print-run almost immediately after publication began.

Karamzin hardly envisaged using literature as a vehicle for radicalism, but progressives, too, saw that literature could be a valuable means of furthering their ideas. Aleksandr Pushkin, who was to become Russia's greatest poet, proved a nuisance to the authorities from the moment he left the lycée at Tsarskoe Selo in 1815. In 'Freedom: An Ode' (1817) he expressed the view that even tsars were subject to the law, that the assassination of Paul I had been justified, and that a regime based on punishments, rewards, dungeons and altars did not have a dependable future. In 'Fairy Tales' (1818) he called Alexander I a 'nomadic despot' whose promises would come to nothing. In 'The Dagger' (1821) he sang the praises of assassination. In 'Barren Sower of Freedom' (1823), which was occasioned by the French invasion of Spain, he lamented the international atmosphere of Alexander's last years on the throne. His play *Boris Godunov*, written at about the time of the abortive coup, implied a good deal about the proper relationship between tsars and their subjects. Because the government exiled Pushkin from St Petersburg in 1820 he played little part in the conspiracy which resulted in the uprising of 1825, but other writers were closer to the Decembrists. Fedor Glinka, an army officer who knew almost all of them, broadened the range of political discussion by publishing, in 1819, a historical novel on the seventeenth-century revolt of Ukrainian Cossacks against Poland. The moral for contemporaries was not hard to discern. Aleksandr Griboedov, whose play *Woe from Wit* circulated in thousands of manuscript copies after being banned by the censor in 1823, spent the first half of 1826 in jail on suspicion of direct complicity in the movement which produced the uprising. Five writers actually participated in the events of 14 December 1825 in St Petersburg. One of the principals in the abortive coup was Kondratii Ryleev, whose poems on Ukrainian themes breathed the spirit of Cossack freedom and whose almanac *The Polar Star* (1823–5) included much of the literary output of the generation to which the Decembrists belonged. 'I am not a poet,' wrote Ryleev, 'I am a citizen'.[7] His belief in the civic function of literature was shared by Wilhelm Küchelbecker, the brothers Nikolai and Aleksandr Bestuzhev, and Aleksandr Odoevskii, all of whom made their names as littérateurs before playing an active part in the St Petersburg uprising. Two Soviet critics hold that 'The Decembrists for the first time, and consciously, connected literary activity with revolutionary work'.[8]

Scholars parallelled writers by furthering progressive ideas in lectures and non-fictional literature. The most influential academic of his day was Aleksandr Kunitsyn. The son of a priest, he left the Tver' seminary for the St Petersburg Pedagogical Institute in 1803 and went on to Göttingen University in 1808, in a group of Russian students which included Nikolai Turgenev. Having formulated liberal views on social relations and economic productivity, Kunitsyn began to disseminate them in Russia after taking up a post at the Imperial Lycée in Tsarskoe Selo in 1811. Just before war broke out in 1812 he seemed to be calling for social revolution. 'An enslaved people', he declared in *Son of the Fatherland*, 'has the right to make war even in time of peace'.[9] Nearly all his students spoke well of him. Pushkin revered him. Aleksandr Gorchakov, who was to be Russia's foreign minister for a quarter of a century after the Crimean War, retained the notes he made on Kunitsyn's lectures to the end of his life. Encouraged by Alexander I's Warsaw speech of 1818, Kunitsyn declared that the time when tsars ruled entirely in their own interests had come to an end. In 1818 and 1820 he published the two volumes of his major work, *Natural Law*. He gave private classes to a number of future Decembrists and in 1819 collaborated with Nikolai Turgenev in an abortive scheme to found a new radical journal. He was not the only forward-looking teacher of the reign of Alexander I. In St Petersburg a second professor, Karl German, was hired by future Decembrists to instruct them in political economy. In Moscow Mikhail Pavlov introduced Küchelbecker and Odoevskii to German idealism. In Khar'kov the first stirrings of Ukrainian Romantic nationalism centred on the university. The tsar's expansion of the education system was increasing the rate at which ideas circulated.

As we have already seen, in the last part of his reign Alexander tried to use the education system to promote the idea of religion. In western Europe the religious revivals of the early-nineteenth-century tended to belong to the right of the political spectrum, but in Russia they could imply change as well as stability. By giving religion his imprimatur, the tsar let another cat out of the bag. Chapter Three gave examples of the way in which the activities of the Russian Bible Society unsettled the country's peasants. Religion also excited the minds of the educated. The Lutheran Pavel Pestel', the devoutly Orthodox Sergei Murav'ev-Apostol and the Catholic Mikhail Lunin were all prominent Decembrists who drew part of their enthusiasm for a new political order from the religious creeds to which they were committed. Freemasonry, meanwhile, which had first made significant strides in Russia in the eighteenth century, combined the appeal of spirituality with the principle of covert organization, a combination which was likely to prove attractive to potential conspirators. Nikolai Turgenev, Kondratii Ryleev and Pavel Pestel' all belonged to Masonic lodges at one time or another. Pierre Bezukhov's initiation as a Mason in *War and Peace* was not a figment of Tolstoi's imagination. In a poem to a liberal general and father of two Decembrists, Pushkin imagined him issuing a call for freedom to the sound of the Masonic gavel. The tsar tried to stop Masonry in its tracks by suppressing secret societies in 1822, but by then the semi-mystical rites of the craft had played some part in creating a movement which was not to be halted.

Thus the movement which culminated on 14 December 1825 drew part of its strength from frustrated bureaucrats, progressive writers, academics and Freemasons. Its heart, however, lay elsewhere. Although a few people in these categories desired change, in the main they took a dim view of their chances of getting it. Not many of them turned into revolutionaries. In a letter to Nicholas I written from the Peter and Paul fortress in St Petersburg in January 1826, Baron Shteingeil', one of the captured Decembrists, claimed that the new tsar could eradicate free-thinking only by eradicating 'an entire generation of people who were born and educated in the last reign'.[10] In a centenary sketch Prince Mirsky expressed the same opinion: 'the Decembrists were not a party, or a sect; they were a generation'.[11] These were gross exaggerations. Although most thoughtful Russians were revising their ideas in the early nineteenth century, very few of them considered turning words into action. Generalizing about the activists of December 1825 is dangerous. Most of the enthusiasts for change mentioned so far jibbed at the thought of conspiracy or the prospect of imminent violence. Civil servants, whatever their disillusionment, tended to keep their own counsel. Few of those who recognized that the tsar's generous impulses were diminishing were prepared to take the law into their own hands. Prince Viazemskii kept out of the movement which led to the upheaval of December 1825. Gavrila Baten'kov opted out of the coup on the day and Mikhail Speranskii closed his mind to it completely. Speranskii's remark about supporting the conspirators in the event of their success cannot be confirmed, and the investigation into the conspiracy found no evidence against the former State Secretary. Officials were not so alienated from the regime that they were ready to cut their moorings. Even Nikolai Turgenev, the civil servant who came closest to wholehearted adoption of Decembrism, seems to have distanced himself from the conspiratorial aspects of the movement. He certainly did so in everything he wrote after the conspirators had been captured.

Similar things can be said of the other groups mentioned above. Although it is tempting to suppose that early-nineteenth-century Russians saw literary activity as a way of preparing the ground for direct action, and that writers who involved themselves in the coup stood for writers in general, one must be careful about drawing these conclusions. Ryleev may have thought of *The Polar Star* as a contribution to the development of progressive attitudes, but Prince Evgenii Obolenskii, one of the most vigorous participants in the events of December 1825, spoke of it as an imaginative way of making money. The general politicization of Russian literature had not yet arrived. Forward-looking work did not necessarily imply an activist author. Fedor Glinka, a writer who was closely associated with the men of 1825 a few years before they took to the streets, whose credentials as a progressive were apparently impeccable, and whose military position would have enabled him to render material assistance to the conspirators, remained loyal to the government at the moment of crisis. A modern study has pointed out that his ideas did not differ as much they seemed to do from those of his much more conservative brother Sergei.[12] Neither of the two most famous writers of the reign of Alexander I were party to the events of December 1825, despite the fact that both were politically to the left of centre. No firm evidence linked Aleksandr Griboedov with the coup, and he was allowed to pick up the threads of his distinguished career in the Russian diplomatic service. Politically minded contemporaries took care to exclude Aleksandr Pushkin from their discussions. He was too lighthearted. He wrote many more love poems than tracts for the times. He dashed off 'Freedom: An Ode' at the suggestion of Nikolai Turgenev, and laughed as he wrote it. He reflected opinions without adopting a political position of his own. No doubt partly from self-interest, he condemned the Decembrists when their activities came to light. Writers, in other words, were by no means agreed that the authorities had to be opposed at all costs. They enlarged debates, but did not insist on the importance of turning words into deeds. The handful who became activists were late additions to a movement whose roots were non-literary.

The scholarly community produced even fewer activists than the writers. Certain professors may have reflected and broadened the Decembrists' outlook on life, but none played a part in the events of 1825. After the authorities dismissed Kunitsyn from his posts early in 1821 (and proscribed his magnum opus), he retreated from radicalism and thought mainly of working his way back into favour. Both he and Karl German, the other St Petersburg professor whom the Decembrists paid to instruct them, reacted to dismissal by seeking re-employment rather than contemplating revolution. Many Decembrists received higher education – thirty-seven attended Moscow University alone – but it was not their teachers who inspired them to action. Finally, the quasi-conspiratorial practices of Freemasons contributed less than is sometimes said to the genesis of political action. Future Decembrists disagreed about Masonry's usefulness. Pavel Pestel' found it congenial and attempted to make use of the Masonic style in promoting subversion, but Prince Sergei Trubetskoi thought this approach ill-judged. Most Russian Freemasons, moreover, were of a conservative rather than a radical disposition. The latest work on St Petersburg's Grand Lodge of Astraea holds that 'we need to modify' the traditional view that Russian Freemasonry 'was a liberal, even a potentially revolutionary phenomenon which provided a training ground for the radical Decembrist movement'.[13] Although the Grand Lodge grew rapidly between its foundation in 1815 and its suppression seven years later, it was dominated by traditionalists rather than innovators and, perhaps most remarkably, by Germans rather than Russians.

The traditionalism of Russia's Freemasons exemplified a broader feature of Alexander I's reign which militates against the notion that Decembrism sprang from some sort of mass alienation on the part of Russian civil society. The events of the reign may have intensified liberal sentiments, but they also produced, in some quarters, a greater degree of conservatism. The patriotism engendered by the war convinced some of the educated that further westernization of Russian culture was unwise. Nikolai Karamzin, for example, had been a progressive under Catherine the Great, but, as we have seen in Chapters Two and Three, became a major spokesman of the right under Alexander. His opposition to the Franco-Russian alliance, to the reform plans of Speranskii, and to treating Poland generously bespoke a man who felt that Russia was losing touch with her past. Nikolai Rumiantsev's change of direction was even sharper. As foreign minister at the time of the Tilsit alliance he had been one of the prime champions of working closely with France, but the shock of Napoleon's invasion brought his westernism to an end. In the last fourteen years of his life (between 1812 and 1826) he spent his income on the first circle of Russian scholars to devote itself exclusively to the history and culture of the Slavs. The publications which resulted were dry, but the sentiment which lay behind them was to be transformed by a later generation into the potent philosophy of Slavophilism, a doctrine which asserted Slavonic uniqueness and emphasized the danger of mingling the doctrines of east and west. Karamzin and the Rumiantsev circle were not alone. The playwrights Ozerov and Shakhovskoi brought quintessentially Russian subject-matter to the stage. Admiral Shishkov campaigned against neologisms in the Russian language. The Polish ethnographer Adam Czarnocki (Zorian Chodakowski) lauded the virtue of the Slavonic common man. The novelist Vasilii Narezhnyi set some of his work in the Ukrainian countryside. In a speech at the opening of the Imperial Public Library in St Petersburg in 1814, the poet Nikolai Gnedich deplored the effect on Russian literature of the educated classes' propensity for speaking French. These cultural manifestations showed that battle had been joined for the future of the Russian identity. Not everyone wanted the country to catch up with recent developments in western Europe. While conservatives shared with liberals a strong sense of Russia's historic mission, they disagreed with them about the direction, the pace and the means of change. They accepted that standing still was impossible, but felt that Russia had to turn back to her roots rather than ascend to a higher plane of political sophistication.

The major publishing event of the reign intensified disagreements between intellectuals on the right and the left. Karamzin had been working on a monumental *History of the Russian State* since 1803 and issued the first eight volumes in February 1818. After the turgid eighteenth-century histories of Tatishchev and Shcherbatov the book was a breath of fresh air. The print-run sold out in three weeks. The remaining four volumes appeared in the 1820s and the *History* went through at least ten editions between then and 1917. Between 1818 and 1830 at least 130 discussions of the work appeared in the Russian periodical press. Everyone admired its flair. Pushkin wrote that 'Ancient Russia seemed to have been discovered by Karamzin just as Columbus discovered America'; Prince Viazemskii that the *History* was 'an epoch-making event in the civil, philosophical, and literary history of our people'.[14] As a stylist, Karamzin was the Russian equivalent of David Hume or Thomas Babington Macaulay. In politics, however, he was more like the former than the latter, and his conservatism earned him abuse. The *History* started coming out a month before Alexander I's celebrated reformist speech to the Warsaw parliament. The two events highlighted the gap between right and left. Unlike Alexander, Karamzin did not believe that the Russian state was in need of transformation. He was prepared to criticize the behaviour of particular tsars (with the result that the Grand Duke Konstantin thought him a dangerous radical), but the preface expressed the hope 'that there may never be a change in the firm foundation of our greatness'.[15] The closing words of the dedication claimed that 'The history of the people belongs to the tsar'. Nikita Murav'ev, who was to be one of the leading figures in the rising of 1825, circulated a review which began by saying that, on the contrary, the history of the people belonged to the people. Despite enthusing about the *History* as a work of literature, Pushkin was not blind to its political orientation. Its 'elegance and simplicity', he commented sarcastically, showed 'the need for autocracy and the charms of the knout'.[16] Nikolai Turgenev may have been the author of an anonymous epigram of 1823 which vilified Karamzin for demonstrating that 'it is possible to think very badly and write very well'.[17]

What Karamzin and his critics disagreed about was the proper size of the political nation. Conservatives believed that, because the Russian polity had emerged triumphant from the strain of the Napoleonic Wars, it was not in need of revision. Reformers felt that Russia's triumph over Napoleon had been achieved in spite of the system rather than because of it, and that the community as a whole deserved a larger say in its fate. This disagreement about the size of the Russian political nation was part of a more involved discussion of what it meant to be Russian. In 1819 Viazemskii coined a new word, *narodnost'* (literally, 'people-ness'), to describe a social orientation whose pursuit would enable Russian intellectuals to distance themselves from the twin pillars of the Russian polity, the Orthodox Church and the autocratic state. Viazemskii lifted the idea from France via Poland, but in Russia it was new. It proved enormously attractive. *Mutatis mutandis*, the concept of *narodnost'* appeared as frequently in Russian intellectual debates of the 1820s as *glasnost'* did in those of the late 1980s. Unfortunately, *narodnost'* settled nothing. Having emerged as a reformist idea, it proved to have both left- and right-wing implications. Karamzin and his heirs could and did argue that Orthodoxy and the state had made the Russian people what they were. In the view of the right, Russian 'people-ness', or nationality, could not be defined without reference to these traditional characteristics. The left disagreed, and the debate, in one form or another, has continued ever since. It bred confusion as much as clarity, and hardly engendered the strength of purpose which the rebels of December 1825 displayed when they tried to take the politcal system into their hands.

Where then did Decembrism come from? Without commitment and muscle no attempt at toppling the autocracy stood a chance of success, yet potential dissidents in civil society were in a minority, intellectual currents were conservative as well as progressive, and the regime could probably handle almost any amount of free-thinking on the part of poets, journalists, professors, retired government ministers and middle-grade civil servants. Army officers, however, were a different story. Of the 289 men sentenced in the wake of the rising of 1825, 211 were serving as officers when it took place and 253 had been officers at one time or other. Many of those already mentioned in non-military connections – Baten'kov, Ryleev, Fedor Glinka, Pestel', Sergei Murav'ev-Apostol, Lunin, Obolenskii, Trubetskoi, Nikita Murav'ev – had had distinguished military careers during the war against Napoleon, and most of them were still in the army in 1825. Calling the Decembrists a military coterie is a good shorthand way of describing them. John Keep implies that it is more or less the only proper way to describe them. 'The abundant literature on the Decembrist movement', he writes, 'treats it almost wholly as a civilian phenomenon, which in our view has led to grave distortion'.[18] His social history of the Russian army treats the Decembrists as a 'military intelligentsia' whose members took 'the praetorian option'.[19] This approach has a lot to recommend it. Russia's soldiers had been making and unmaking tsars since the late seventeenth century. In the eighteenth century their confidence had been growing. The empire had won most of its battles and military commanders had played a large part in the administration of civil society. Outraged by Paul, the Guards had brought Alexander I to the throne. Defeated in the period of the Third Coalition, the troops had come well out of the victories of 1812–14. The officers' mess was a much more obvious unit of political organization than the Masonic lodge. By 1825 the idea of military intervention in politics came naturally. The army was unlikely to stand aside from the confusion which followed Alexander's death.

Professor Keep claims, however, that army officers intervened in politics in 1825 mainly for military reasons. While acknowledging that some soldiers were influenced by the changing intellectual currents of the day, he believes that, in the final analysis, 'Dissent grew out of the internal situation of the army itself'.[20] This is too narrow a view. Soldiers' interests were far more wide-ranging than those of the military conspirators who had overthrown tsars in the past. Service in the army was onerous, officers banded together for the discussion of matters of common interest, and some of the matters they discussed were military; but future Decembrists did not think only or even mainly about their military honour. Drawing a distinction between Russia's early-nineteenth-century 'military intelligentsia' and educated members of the contemporary gentry is as hard as distinguishing between the gentry and the bureaucracy. The groups were interrelated and shared much common ground. Soldiers were more likely to possess the courage of their convictions, but the free spirits among them did not draw a line between themselves and civilians. The people sentenced for their part in the 1825 conspiracy differed from their peers in the intensity rather than the nature of their aspirations. Soldiers who became Decembrists possessed a higher degree of education than many of their well-placed contemporaries.[21] They saw beyond the demands of their profession and thought they represented society as a whole. Aleksandr Bestuzhev spoke for many of them when he pointed out in evidence to the Investigating Commission of 1826 that although his profession obliged him to study 'military sciences', he studied literature for amusement and, 'in keeping with the spirit of the age' (*po naklonnosti veka*), applied himself in particular to the study of history and politics. The opinions he derived from studying developments in western Europe were shared, he believed, by around one-third of the Russian gentry. Many Russian noblemen kept out of the coup of 1825, he said, because they were more cautious than the activists, not because they disagreed with them.[22]

FIRST ATTEMPTS AT ORGANIZATION

The organizational pre-history of the rising of 1825 confirms the impression that Russian army officers took an interest in much more than soldiering. A 'Mathematical Society' set up by soldiers in the first decade of the nineteenth century became the basis of a 'School for Column-Leaders' and eventually proved to be the starting-point of the Russian Empire's General Staff Academy. Since it was sponsored by a Major-General, the authorities can hardly have expected it to encourage dissent. The Major-General, however, was Nikolai Nikolaevich Murav'ev, whose clan was to produce more Decembrists than any other. The Society and the School of Column-Leaders did not confine themselves to the pursuit of military efficiency. 'Independence of mind was not only not suppressed, but encouraged'.[23] Twenty-four future conspirators passed through the School in the seven years that Murav'ev was in charge of it. Nor was political reflection confined to periods of training. Soldiers with a taste for free-thinking cultivated it in their units through the medium of cooperatives. Ostensibly a means of saving money, these bodies served the larger purpose of facilitating discussion. Murav'ev's sons founded the 'Holy Artel'', a group of officers on the General Staff who combined affection for the Russian past with sympathy for the west European present. They foregathered at the sound of a bell which evoked the assembly of the medieval republic of Novgorod, and kept abreast of modernity by attending the lectures of Professors Kunitsyn and German. Only Russia's contemporary political arrangements seemed to be missing from their eclecticism.

Soldiers saw more of the world than their contemporaries. Ninety members of the secret societies which gave rise to the revolt of December 1825 fought in the wars of 1805–7 and 1812–14.[24] Many of them claimed that seeing western Europe had a profound effect on their political outlook. Ivan Iakushkin, one of the more radical Decembrists, wrote that 'Spending a whole year in Germany and then several months in Paris could not fail to change the views of young Russians who possessed even a small capacity for reflection'.[25] Some soldiers served in western Europe even after the war had come to an end, as members of the Russian army which was stationed in France to ensure that the French paid their indemnity. Baron Rozen, one of the conspirators, believed that the three-year occupation played a key part in the genesis of the Decembrist revolt. In his view, 'Young men who had spent the greater part of their lives in the monotony of Russian provincial towns or among the bacchanalia and revelries of the capitals suddenly saw on the flowering banks of the Loire and the Garonne a new and better world, to the charms of which they surrendered themselves with delight'; 'the flower of the Guards' officer corps', Rozen went on, 'returned home with the intention of transplanting France to Russia'.[26] Rozen exaggerated, but his argument ought not to be wholly discounted. Russia's soldiers in France were based at Maubeuge on the border with Belgium, less than fifty miles from the principal concentration of French republicans at Brussels. The border was barely controlled. Since correspondence was much less subject to scrutiny on the Belgian side, 'These three years witnessed a massive despatch of books and pamphlets to Russia'.[27] Radical French newspapers published in Belgium became the daily reading of the Maubeuge officers. Nikolai Turgenev's youngest brother, Sergei, founded a Masonic lodge in which the Russians in France could air their highmindedness. The general in charge of the occupying forces, Mikhail Vorontsov (nephew of the early-nineteenth-century Russian foreign minister), had the reputation of being one of the most liberal soldiers of his generation. In 1820 the French Ambassador in St Petersburg reported that almost all Russian Guards officers 'read and re-read the works of Benjamin Constant and believe they understand them'.[28] Residence in France played a part in their enthusiasm for the panjandrum of Western liberalism.

Officers who had seen the west, mixed with republicans, cultivated a high moral tone and read works of political philosophy were not likely to welcome the relative absence of changes at home. The sense of mission which had brought them through the war could not be suppressed in time of peace. They expected external victory to be followed by domestic reform. According to Aleksandr Bestuzhev, footsoldiers complained after returning to Russia that although they had 'delivered the country from a tyrant ... the lords are once again tyrannizing over us'.[29] Some officers shared the disgust of their men. One of the Murav'evs recalled in his memoirs that 'Poland received a constitution, but Russia in return for her heroic efforts in 1812 received – the military colonies!'[30] Other officers continued for a time to put their trust in the regime. Prince Trubetskoi, a moderate, felt that Decembrism originated in a desire on the part of 'certain young men' to support the tsar's natural reformist inclinations. 'Few in number, they were convinced that their circle would grow by the day, that others like them would not want to be limited to the glory of military achievements and would desire to manifest their enthusiasm and love for the fatherland ... by dedicating all their means and abilities to the furtherance of the general good in all its aspects'.[31] This moderate pursuit of the 'general good' marked the original impulse behind Decembrism. It was military only in form. In content, it represented an attempt to redesign Russia's political structure and relieve the frustrations of Russian civil society. These objectives were shared by the soldiers who took action in 1825 and the civil servants, writers, Masons and academics who went no further than discussing what action was necessary. The narrative of Decembrism, then, centres on soldiers, but the soldiers had more on their minds than the concerns of the army.

The determination of reform-minded officers to apply their wartime enthusiasm to civilian affairs is apparent from the moment conspiracy began in earnest in 1814. 'I believe I was the first person in Russia', claimed Major-General Count Mikhail Orlov, 'to think up a plan for a secret society'.[32] The idea came to him in western Europe, where he had played a significant part in the final defeat of Napoleon and been impressed by the conspiratorial Prussian *Tugendbund* (League of Virtue). After the tsar said in Paris that, having overcome his external enemies, he would take on his enemies at home, Orlov decided to leave the army and turn his hand to rooting out 'pocket Napoleons' in Russia. With Count Matvei Dmitriev-Mamonov he founded an 'Order of Russian Knights'. The founders' ideas were modest, perhaps not much more advanced than those of the upper echelons of the aristocracy which had tried to restrict the freedom of the Empress Anna in 1730. They wanted to make the tsar's right to promulgate laws, raise taxes and wage war dependent on the consent of the Senate, and to make the Senate more representative of the nation by enlarging its membership to 1,000, of whom 200 were to be hereditary peers, 400 representatives of the nobility, and 400 of the people at large. The plan was derived from the Senate-based French constitution of 1814, with the introduction of which Orlov had been associated. Orlov and Mamonov were only moderate political reformers – Orlov was strongly opposed to the constitution that Alexander I conferred on Poland – and they apparently had no programme for the reform of Russian society. Nikolai Turgenev, however, the civil servant whom they made privy to their plans, believed from the outset that the object of the circle's deliberations should be finding a way to abolish serfdom. His views were to acquire greater prominence in later stages of the Decembrist movement.

By 1817 the Order of Russian Knights had petered out. Mamonov left Russia to take medical treatment abroad and Orlov discovered that another secret society had come into being whose objectives appeared to be similar to his own. The continuous history of what subsequently became known as Decembrism began in 1816, when a small group of army officers set up a 'Union of Salvation'. The prime mover seems to have been Aleksandr Nikolaevich Murav'ev, oldest son of the director of the School of Column-Leaders. He persuaded Prince Trubetskoi and a relative, Nikita Mikhailovich Murav'ev, to join him, and at a meeting which took place in the barracks of the Semenovskii guards regiment in St Petersburg the three converted Ivan Iakushkin and the brothers Matvei and Sergei Murav'ev-Apostol. These six 'founding fathers' epitomized the diversity of the movement. Trubetskoi, as we have seen, was a moderate. In principle, he welcomed the tsar's two visible initiatives in post-war domestic policy (the emancipation of the serfs in the Baltic provinces and the introduction of the military colonies), and he believed that the prime duty of the Union of Salvation was to monitor their implementation and to promote sympathy for them among doubtful contemporaries. Iakushkin wanted more. He despised the bulk of the Russian gentry, thought serfdom depraved, and considered that the only way forward was to capture the minds of the young. He was rebuked by the other founders for bringing his commanding officer into the conspiracy without their permission. His uncle thought he had gone mad when he announced his determination to emancipate the serfs in his own possession. He was not alone, however, in his radicalism. Pavel Pestel', an early adherent of the organization, expressed the view that France had prospered under the Committee of Public Safety of 1793–4. He drew up a statute for the Union which would have obliged members to remain in state service (so that eventually they would occupy key positions) and not to swear an oath of allegiance to the next emperor unless he or the present tsar had accepted limitations on the autocracy.

Pestel''s draft proved unacceptable to a number of the conspirators. There were only about twenty or thirty of them, all Guards officers, but they never succeeded in agreeing on a policy document in the two years of the Union of Salvation's existence. The moderates lowered their sights and founded a legal 'Military Society' in 1817 whose object was simply to bring together like-minded soldiers. The Union then fell apart on a question which exposed the members' narrow-mindedness. Rumours surfaced in Moscow (where most of the conspirators were temporarily stationed) to the effect that the tsar was going to enlarge the Kingdom of Poland and announce (from Warsaw, if necessary) the emancipation of the serfs. There was some justification for believing the rumours to be true. Before making his celebrated liberal speech to the Polish Parliament in March 1818 Alexander had set up a Lithuanian corps which wore some of the insignia of the Polish army, and he was constantly toying with the peasant question. Members of the Union of Salvation might have been expected to like what they heard, since the Congress Kingdom of Poland had a representative system of government and improving the lot of the serfs was an objective to which they all paid lip-service. Their Russian patriotism, however, rendered them incapable of accepting the prospect of generosity to Poland. The Union of Salvation's alternative name was 'Union of True and Loyal

Sons of the Fatherland', and being a true son of the fatherland meant refusing to give ground to non-Russians. Iakushkin and Aleksandr Murav'ev responded to the rumours about concessions to Poles by advocating the assassination of the tsar. Their proposition was rejected after heated discussion, whereupon Iakushkin withdrew his support for the Union. The conspirators had to think again about the purpose of their organization.

For a time gradualists appeared to prevail over activists. In 1818 they renamed their association 'The League of Welfare', to make it sound less radical. Mikhail Murav'ev, Aleksandr's brother, had been reluctant to join the conspiracy while it preached violence, but from 1818 could participate with a clear conscience. The League of Welfare's constitution, the 'Green Book', stated that the conspirators had four concerns: philanthropy, education, justice and the economy. The most moderate of the Murav'ev family, Nikita, spelt out what these concerns meant in practice: 'the abolition of serfdom, equality of citizens before the law, glasnost in state affairs, glasnost in judicial procedure, the abolition of the liquor monopoly, the abolition of the military colonies', and various improvements in the organization of the army.[33] Since these objectives have been shared by most Russian reformers of the last 200 years, it is not surprising that Decembrism attracted more adherents in its middle phase than earlier or later. It had something to offer almost everyone. Some 200 people were associated with the movement in the years 1818 to 1821. Drawing up a new political framework for the empire took second place behind humanitarianism. The League encouraged relations with non-conspiratorial organizations like the Free Society of Lovers of Russian Literature. It had an elaborate administrative structure which was supposed to ensure cohesion, but many of the members pursued those parts of the programme which suited them without worrying about the need for concerted action. Some of the radicals deferred to the wishes of the majority. Iakushkin concentrated on educating the peasants on his estate near Smolensk. Aleksandr Murav'ev got married and left the movement. The prospects for steady progress looked good.

Not all the Decembrists, however, had reconciled themselves to the modification of their ambitions. According to M. V. Nechkina, very few of them had done so. The Green Book, she says, 'did not set out the full programme of the League of Welfare'.[34] In Nechkina's interpretation the surviving constitutional document of the League was an inducement to the uncommitted and a means of deceiving potential government informers. The conspirators' real goals remained the radical transformation of the empire's political system. This argument receives support from Mikhail Lunin's declaration to the Investigating Commission of 1826 that the League of Welfare 'had two goals: the declared one of extending enlightenment and beneficence; the covert one of introducing a constitution or a free government based on law'.[35] No unequivocal evidence can be adduced, however, to confirm the case for duplicity. It is likelier that the more radical Decembrists simply went on hoping that their views would eventually prevail.

This was certainly the attitude of Pavel Pestel', who ploughed his own furrow in the southern reaches of the empire while the northerners seemed to be moderating their enthusiasm.

Pestel' was the brightest of the Decembrists. Son of the reactionary governor of Siberia whom Speranskii replaced in 1819, he was top of the class at the Imperial Corps des Pages and reached the rank of colonel before he was thirty. Metternich and Alexander I both had occasion to express their approval of his official reports. He combined intellectual ability with more than a dash of his father's authoritarianism. According to Nikolai Basargin, 'he expressed his thoughts with such logic, such coherence, and such conviction that it was difficult to resist his influence'.[36] Ivan Iakushkin believed there were no limits to his enthusiasm for the cause. If the movement failed, Iakushkin wrote, Pestel' intended to divulge the names of the conspirators in order to maximize the number of martyrs; he would have been happy if the regime had hanged five hundred Decembrists rather than five. Military service kept Pestel' out of St Petersburg and spared him from having to compromise with the proponents of moderation. He was absent from the capital when the radical constitution he had drafted for the Union of Salvation was rendered superfluous by the creation of the League of Welfare. The Green Book did not please him. At Tul'chin in Podolia, headquarters of the Second Army, he found a congenial environment. His commanding officer, P. D. Kiselev, was probably even more sympathetic to the leanings of reform-minded officers than M. S. Vorontsov in France or A. P. Ermolov in the Caucasus. 'In Tul'chin, fearing no special surveillance, the members of the Secret Society communicated freely with each other almost every day, thereby strengthening each other's resolve'.[37] Ivan Burtsov led a moderate faction, but Burtsov could not stand up to Pestel'. Northern and southern Decembrists began to draw apart. In January 1820, at a meeting in Fedor Glinka's apartment in St Petersburg, Pestel' appeared to secure the northerners' commitment to republicanism, but after he returned to the south disagreements resurfaced. The movement seemed to be falling apart.

THE SCHISM OF 1821

At this point Ivan Iakushkin came out of retirement and attempted to put the conspirators back on course. He had spent most of 1818 and 1819 in the country, trying to find a way of emancipating his serfs. In 1820 he travelled to St Petersburg to discuss his plans with the relevant authorities. Realizing that the secret society had increased in size but lost its sense of direction, he organized a Moscow summit conference for the beginning of the following year. Before it convened he went south, to canvass opinion among the conspirators at Tul'chin and to extend an invitation to Mikhail

Orlov at Kishinev. For once, Pestel' missed a trick. He very much wanted to attend the Moscow meeting, but was dissuaded from doing so by the argument that, since he had no obvious reason for travelling there, his request for leave would be viewed with suspicion by the authorities. When the gathering took place, the moderate Ivan Burtsov represented the southerners, Nikolai Turgenev and Fedor Glinka the northerners. These principals gave the assembly a more pacific tone than that of the movement as a whole. Remarkably, Mikhail Orlov seemed to be the most radical of the delegates. Having been left behind after the demise of the Order of Russian Knights, he now proposed the establishment of an underground printing press and the circulation of counterfeit money. Some scholars have argued that he was deliberately courting expulsion from the movement, on the grounds that his prospective father-in-law had insisted he abandon his taste for conspiracy. This explanation, as we shall see, is ill-founded, but his proposals were rejected and his involvement in the conference came to an end. After three weeks' discussion, the moderates agreed to liquidate the League of Welfare. Nikolai Turgenev subsequently maintained that they took this decision with the best of intentions. He felt that the conspirators ought to concentrate on improving the lot of the peasantry, and that they could do so by freeing their serfs and setting an example to others. Activity of this kind could be undertaken in the open. The memoirs of Ivan Iakushkin, however, make plain that dissolving the League was a ploy. Turgenev's account was designed to clear his name after the Decembrist movement had run its course. In 1821, even the moderates did not want to bring their activities to an end; they merely wanted to increase their say in future developments. They planned to restart the secret society with a carefully selected new membership, and to this end drew up a revised statute which went beyond the Green Book and committed future conspirators to the explicit objective of imposing limitations on the autocracy. New members were to dedicate themselves to preparing the army for an uprising.

The key question was who to admit to the redesigned organization. Burtsov was anxious to bypass Pestel'. Although the Moscow meeting envisaged placing limitations on the autocracy, it did not restate the commitment to republicanism which had been adopted in 1820. Pestel' was not going to be pleased. Partly because he knew Pestel' would object, and partly for reasons of personal antipathy, Burtsov proposed returning to Tul'chin, reporting the demise of the League of Welfare, and subsequently re-enrolling all the southerners bar their leader. His plan came to nothing. On being told that the League of Welfare had been wound up, Pestel' declared that the Moscow conference had gone beyond its brief. The other southerners backed him, and Burtsov did not even have the nerve to tell them about the surreptitious continuation and the revised statute. 'Thus,' Pestel' said to the investigators of 1826, 'republican government continued to be the goal of those parts of the League of Welfare which did not acknowledge the dissolution'.[38] Burtsov was ostracized, and the effect of the Moscow conference of 1821 was to divide the Decembrist movement into

Northern and Southern Societies, the latter more radical than the former.

Tension within the movement derived only partly from personality clashes and abstract disagreements about long-term objectives. It was also occasioned by changes in the domestic atmosphere and developments in the outside world. The context in which the Decembrists made their plans was in flux. So long as the tsar appeared to be a 'Westernizer', the conspirators could pretend that the goals to which they aspired were also the goals of their masters. By the end of 1820, however, Alexander I's reformism had come to an end and advocates of change were bound to review their position. The diverse events which caused the tsar to adopt a bunker mentality had the opposite effect on his critics. The rising of military colonists at Chuguev in the eastern Ukraine in the summer of 1819 provoked a brutal response from the authorities, but eliminated from the minds of liberals any lingering doubts about the colonies' possible usefulness. The dissolution of the Semenovskii Guards regiment after the mutiny of its rank-and-file in St Petersburg in October 1820 enraged the high-minded army officers who were at the heart of the secret society. Although they had played no part in generating the mutiny (and Sergei Murav'ev-Apostol had done his best to bring it to an end), they had no time for the regimental commander who provoked it and they held that the punishment was at odds with the crime. The affair had a particular as well as a general effect, in that it resulted in the transfer of former members of the regiment to the south and enlarged the pool from which the Southern Society could draw its recruits. 'The Southern Society', says Joseph Wieczynski, 'was encouraged in its work of revolution by the spirit of the Semenovsky troops'.[39]

Events abroad, however, played a larger part than events at home in convincing radical Decembrists that they were right to press on. The murders of August von Kotzebue in 1819 and the Duc de Berry in 1820 revived their interest in assassination. Mikhail Orlov's extremism at the Moscow conference arose from his involvement in preparations for the Greek uprising of 1821. At Kishinev in Bessarabia he was in touch with Aleksandr Ipsilanti, the Greek leader in Russian service whose contribution to the revolt of his fellow-countrymen took the form of an attempt to move down on the Balkans from the north. Pestel', too, thought hard about Greece. He was ordered to Bessarabia three times in 1821, with instructions to report on Balkan affairs for his military superiors. According to O. V. Orlik his reports 'deliberately masked the revolutionary character of the Greek events'.[40] He was trying to kill two birds with one stone. If the tsar could have been persuaded to intervene on the Greeks' behalf (which was possible, in view of their Orthodoxy), progressive sentiments might have gained official sanction in Russia and Russian generals would have been too busy even to contemplate suppressing revolution in western Europe. This logic appealed to many contemporaries. 'The news of the Greek uprising', recalled one of the Decembrist rank-and-file, 'fired the young more than anything. Everyone was convinced that the tsar would extend the hand of friendship to our co-religionists and that our armies would be moved into Moldavia'.[41] Because Alexander I failed to act, however, the Spanish revolt of 1820 eventually turned out to influence future Decembrists more deeply than any of the other contemporary European upheavals. It taught Russia's potential rebels two things: the best way to effect change was through the army, and dealing harshly with the outgoing authorities was essential. Spanish army officers reinstated the liberal constitution of 1812 without inciting the masses, but then let the king slip through their fingers. The French subsequently intervened on his behalf and the soldiers' three-year endeavour came to nothing. Russian army officers concluded that by avoiding the Spaniards' mistake they could crown a similar manoeuvre with success. Two of the most prominent members of the Southern Society, Mikhail Bestuzhev-Riumin and Sergei Murav'ev-Apostol, drew much of their inspiration from the events of the early 1820s in Spain.

PESTEL' AND THE SOUTHERN SOCIETY

Pestel', meanwhile, was trying to decide what the Russian Empire would look like after the existing order had been overthrown. By outlining 'a structure based on precise and just laws and statutes',[42] his *Russian Justice* sought to prevent tsars from treating the empire as a privately owned fief. Many thinking Russians had this end in view in the early nineteenth century, but Pestel''s approach was his own. Unlike Alexander I, he had no sympathy for the idea of devolving power from the centre to the localities. After listing the problems to which weakening the centre gave rise, the first chapter of his programme concluded that federalism was 'utterly ruinous and wholly evil'.[43] Chapter Two acknowledged the racial diversity of the empire's inhabitants but argued that the same laws should apply to all national groups. Chapter Three dwelt on social levelling. Unlike Speranskii, Pestel' disapproved of demarcation lines between social estates. He accepted the need for gradation, but felt that distinctions ought to derive from people's jobs rather than their origins or their wealth. Nobles were to be levelled downwards. It was immoral for them to own serfs, to escape personal taxation, to be exempt from certain sorts of punishment, to be spared conscription, and to possess titles. The right to engage in trade was to be extended to all. The military colonies were to be brought to an end because they had already proved to be a disaster in practice and because they threatened to divorce the army from the community at large. Serfdom was to be gradually abolished.

These were the only sections of *Russian Justice* that Pestel' completed. He sketched out the fourth and fifth chapters (the first of which contained interesting proposals for redistributing the land), but since he planned another five chapters and worked on the document for almost ten years, he

can hardly be said to have consolidated his theoretical insights. It is probable that he dealt with his primary concern at the outset, when he insisted
on the need for a strong central authority. The republic he envisaged was
to be of the Spartan rather than the Athenian variety. Rather surprisingly,
Ivan Iakushkin wrote that all those who knew Pestel' and read *Russian Justice* agreed that the author's outlook was 'profoundly practical'.[44] It was not
practical in the sense of expressing opinions on which a consensus already
existed. Most contemporary reformers thought that the power of the government ought to be severely restricted, but Pestel' thought the reverse.
Even General Kiselev, commanding officer at Tul'chin, believed that his
young colonel wanted to give too much power to the executive. Kiselev
was not a conspirator and subsequently worked for change through the
medium of the tsarist state, but his enthusiasm for executive authority did
not persuade him that it ought to be significantly increased. Pestel' was
shrewd enough to realize, however, that a military coup was ill-suited to
the rapid introduction of representative democracy. If the League of Welfare had remained in place for decades, a large number of people might
eventually have been ready to participate in a post-tsarist government.
After the League's demise in 1821, opponents of the tsar had to accept that
they were going to remain relatively few in number for the foreseeable future. Their means of obtaining power were to be violent. They would
probably have to go on using force to impose their programme. It was
practical, therefore, to draw up a political blueprint which allowed them
freedom of action. The means, for once, justified the end.

The means of the Southern Society were both small and poorly coordinated. After 1821 the conspirators were not even concentrated at army
headquarters. Nechkina says that 'Tul'chin easily maintained its central
role',[45] but her magisterial study of the Decembrists constantly exaggerates
their cohesion and sense of direction. Pestel' was not just trying to cover
his back when he claimed in 1826 that the Tul'chin section recruited very
few new members in the last five years of its life. Part of the reason continued to be Pestel' himself. 'For all his intelligence and power of conviction
he lacked the gift of inducing loyalty, the openness essential to the enjoy-
ment of general confidence'.[46] Defeating Ivan Burtsov in 1821 had not been
enough to eliminate differences of temperament. The government, meanwhile, was beginning to make inroads into the conspirators' capacity for
action. Historians have dubbed Vladimir Raevskii 'the first Decembrist' by
virtue of his arrest at Kishinev in 1822. The following year Mikhail Orlov
was found guilty by association and deprived of his division. These blows
put paid to the Decembrists' most southerly outpost. The focus of the
Southern Society's activities shifted east and north of Tul'chin, to sections
established at Kamenka (near Chigirin) and Vasil'kov (south of Kiev). Theoretically these were subordinate to a central 'Directory' dominated by Pestel', but in practice they went their own way. Nechkina dwells on the
Southern Society's Kiev 'congresses', but they seem not to have solved very
much. The southerners were a motley crew. One of the principal figures at

Vasil'kov, Sergei Murav'ev-Apostol, had been radicalized by the dissolution of the Semenovskii regiment in 1820 and the initial success of the army officers' revolt in Spain (where his father had been Russian ambassador). The other, Mikhail Bestuzhev-Riumin, joined the section in 1823 and devoted himself to forging ties with outsiders. Having facilitated negotiations with the Polish Patriotic Society, he negotiated personally with the Society of United Slavs. The alliances which resulted had the effect of blurring the southerners' clarity of purpose. Pestel''s attitude towards Polish conspirators was ungenerous. In evidence to the Investigating Commission he claimed that the Southern Society had endeavoured to bend the Poles to its will and that the question of Polish independence had barely arisen. Bestuzhev-Riumin, however, had been prepared to make significant concessions to Polish opinion. The Borisov brothers, founders of the Society of United Slavs, had no social ties with the other Decembrists and only a vague idea of their own intentions. Their main objective, 'the liberation of all Slavic tribes from autocracy',[47] served only to muddy the ideological waters. By opening discussions with the Borisovs and inspiring a deal with the Poles, the Vasil'kov section weakened Pestel''s authority. When Nikolai Lorer joined the Southern Society in 1824 he had the impression that Vasil'kov was not part of it but equal to it. If the southerners could not agree among themselves, they were unlikely to persuade the northerners that their plans were worth imitating. The northerners, however, had to be persuaded, for the north contained the capital and the key to the empire's future.

DECEMBRISTS IN THE NORTH

Pestel' made clear in his depositions of 1826 that when the time came for revolution, he expected it to take place in St Petersburg. The provinces' role was to cooperate with a northern uprising which would be brought about 'by means of a rising of the Guards and the fleet, the despatch of members of the imperial family to foreign parts, ... the summoning of the Senate to announce the new order, the establishment of a Provisional Government to introduce it, or the summoning (via the Senate) of people's deputies to approve a constitution'.[48] After the Moscow discussions of 1821 there was no certainty that these northern developments would ever take place, let alone that they would produce the sort of society which Pestel' had in mind. When Prince Trubetskoi returned to St Petersburg early in 1822 after two years abroad, he found only four northerners who remained true to the objective of altering the empire's system of government. One of them, Nikolai Turgenev, may himself have been faltering. Another, Nikita Murav'ev, was drafting a political programme which differed significantly from that of Pestel. The various drafts of Murav'ev's constitutional projects contained high-sounding statements of principle ('Autocratic power is equally ruinous for both rulers and society'; 'The source of supreme power is the people'; 'All Russians are equal before the law')[49], but they also betrayed an author who became less radical with the passage of time and was always less radical in practice than in theory. Although Murav'ev wanted to abolish classes, titles, ranks and guilds, bring serfdom to an end, replace the police by elected officials and extend trial by jury, he also intended to retain the tsar, to base the franchise and the right to be elected on graduated property qualifications, to guarantee landlords the possession of their estates and to grant emancipated serfs only their houses, gardens, tools and livestock. The biggest difference between Murav'ev and Pestel' lay in their attitude towards centralization. Murav'ev was a federalist. The empire was to be divided into thirteen states, their assemblies overseen by a national two-chamber legislature.

The north, then, suffered from shortage of personnel and lack of revolutionary fervour. Unwittingly, the tsar contributed to the alleviation of the first of these difficulties. Increasingly mistrustful of the Guards, he despatched them to the western provinces to engage in military exercises and increased the likelihood that they would spend their evenings talking to each other. The many new members who were persuaded to join the secret society proceeded to recruit others after they got back to St Petersburg. In 1823 Ivan Pushchin enlisted the soldier-turned-civil-servant Kondratii Ryleev, whose energy did much to increase the Northern Society's enthusiasm.

Reconciling the political programmes of north and south, however, proved harder than finding new northern adherents. Pestel' had preserved the fiction that a single conspiracy was afoot by giving Murav'ev a place in his southern 'Directory', but relations between the Northern and Southern Societies tended to irritate both partners. In the spring of 1823 Pestel' sent two of his acolytes north to reproach the northerners for inactivity. A year later he went north himself with the object of bringing together the two halves of the movement and undertaking concerted action in 1826. His success was short-lived. In the main, those who fell prey to his influence returned to counsels of moderation after his departure. Pestel' took out an insurance policy by creating what amounted to a St Petersburg branch of the Southern Society. At the end of 1824 the moderate Prince Trubetskoi accepted a posting to Kiev in order to keep watch on the southerners. Internecine strife seemed to be growing rather than diminishing. The principles which divided north and south were too diverse to be dovetailed. Federalism and centralism, gradualism and violence, monarchism and republicanism, dictatorship and representative government were not the sort of opposites which attract. Pestel' acknowledged under interrogation that, so far as military plans were concerned, the Decembrists never succeeded in agreeing on a 'precise, detailed, positive, complete and binding proposition'.[50] He could have said as much about the conspirators' political ideas.

THE ABORTIVE RISING

The tsar's death revealed the movement's lack of readiness for the fray. Although members had grasped that the best moment to act was the point at which one reign gave way to another, and although they had considered bringing that point forward by assassinating Alexander I, they were caught unawares when Alexander died unexpectedly. Baron Rozen acknowledged that if the authorities had publicized Alexander's plans for the succession as soon as they learnt of his death, everyone would have sworn the oath to Nicholas and the transition to the new reign would have been smooth. The regime was weak, but the Decembrists were weaker. The conspirators' activities between the death of Alexander and the accession of Nicholas smacked of desperation rather than determination. Rozen believed that if he and about half a dozen others had been arrested, no rising would have taken place. As it became apparent that the oath of allegiance to Konstantin was to be superseded by an oath of allegiance to Nicholas, the northerners tried making plans. On 12 December 1825 a group of them met at Ryleev's apartment and agreed 'to gather on Senate Square on the day appointed for the new oath, bring as many troops there as possible on the pretext of supporting the rights of Konstantin, entrust command of the troops to Prince Trubetskoi, ... declare the abolition of the monarchy and speedily introduce a temporary government'.[51] As this scheme was emerging, one of the junior conspirators, Iakov Rostovtsev, was informing Nicholas that sedition was afoot. The plan, nevertheless, went ahead. If the leaders had been resolute their efforts might just have been crowned with success, for they managed to get 3,000 men on to Senate Square. Nicholas had three times as many but was reluctant to send them into action. If the rebels had seized the initiative, the government's forces might have changed sides. Onlookers might have been drawn into the struggle. The rebels, however, lost their nerve. Prince Trubetskoi took shelter in the Austrian Embassy. The ultra-radical Aleksandr Iakubovich explained that his long-held desire to assassinate the tsar applied only to Alexander I, not to his younger brother. Petr Kakhovskii inflamed matters by killing the popular General Miloradovich when he tried to negotiate on behalf of the authorities. Baron Rozen halted his troops on a bridge leading to Senate Square and awaited developments instead of trying to accelerate them. In the end Nicholas ordered his men to fire and his opponents were put to flight.

The southern conspirators fared even less well. Denounced in mid-1825 by Arkadii Maiboroda and the Englishman John Sherwood, they had little chance of making an effective stand. Pestel' was arrested on the day before the northern rising. Sergei Murav'ev-Apostol and Mikhail Bestuzhev-Riumin, who were arrested two weeks later, escaped from custody with the assistance of the Society of United Slavs and incited the Chernigov regiment to revolt, but this last throw came to nothing on 3 January 1826. The new tsar, Nicholas I, was untiring in the subsequent investigation: 579 individuals were questioned, 289 of them sentenced. In July 1826 Pestel', Sergei Murav'ev-Apostol, Mikhail Bestuzhev-Riumin, Ryleev and Kakhovskii were executed. Thirty-one Decembrists were exiled to Siberia for life and eighty-five for specific periods. Gavrila Baten'kov spent nearly twenty years in the Peter and Paul Fortress in St Petersburg. The clean-up seemed to be brutally effective, the possibility of revolutionary action eradicated for the foreseeable future.

CONCLUSION

It is easy to make light of the Decembrists. The ideas to which they subscribed and the action in which they engaged seem to have been backward-looking. Had Pestel' dominated a post-revolutionary government, he would presumably have run it like an eighteenth-century despot. Russian political activists had apparently not registered that the Enlightenment had given way to Romanticism. The St Petersburg uprising evoked memories of the king-making in which Russia's Guards regiments had engaged in 1740, 1762 and 1801. One of the standard works on Decembrism concludes: 'Thinking in terms of eighteenth-century palace revolutions which were chiefly maneuvered by the Guard, the [northern] Decembrists, as products of their time, endeavoured to transform the Senate Square into a *Place de la Révolution*, and their attempt was sadly inadequate. ... Even the more gallant stand taken by the Southern Society had to fail, partly for the same reasons'.[52]

The conspirators were few in number, and the activists among them even fewer. Potential Decembrists were much more numerous in 1820 than in 1825. Trubetskoi pointed out bitterly, naming names, that 'Many who had been enthusiastic members [of secret societies] in their youth became lukewarm with the passage of time'.[53] One of the Murav'evs changed tack altogether and eventually crowned his career by playing a vital part in the brutal suppression of the Polish rebellion of 1863. By then he was boasting of being 'the sort of Murav'ev who hangs, not the sort who gets hanged'.[54] Activists took to the streets in 1825 because of the interregnum, not because they had chosen their moment. In the absence of a succession crisis, they too would probably have forsaken radicalism. Those who survived the death of their hopes did not refer to themselves as members of a coherent party but as 'Siberian' or 'prison' comrades. The term 'Decembrist' became current only in the 1860s, when a later generation of radicals was trying to give itself a pedigree.

The leaders of the rebellion were able to make a showing only by employing a large number of recent converts. Of the fifty-one presumed members of the Northern Society condemned by the Investigative Com-

111

mission, more than thirty had been recruited in the year of the rising (most of them in November). Only four members of the League of Welfare were involved in the preparation of the St Petersburg coup. Some of the conspirators claimed that a significant proportion of the nobility shared their opinions, but they did not succeed in converting that sympathy into active support. When the crisis came, 'the whole of Russian society, with very few exceptions, turned away from them and manifested its legitimist stand and loyal attachment to the throne'.[55]

The Decembrists' attitude to commoners was patronizing. They failed to impart an understanding of their objectives even to the soldiers whom they commanded. When instructed to shout for 'Konstantin and a constitution', the rebel troops on Senate Square were said to believe that 'constitution' was the name of Konstantin's wife. One of the best recent analyses of the Decembrist revolt emphasizes that 'the actual undertaking was the work of a rather small group of revolutionaries who led into revolution men who often did not understand their aims and who sometimes did not even know what aims there were'.[56] There had been no conscious attempt on the part of the conspirators to reach people outside their class. Serfs were quite unaware of the Decembrists' enthusiasm for emancipation. Indeed, they seem to have credited the conspirators with a desire to oppress them. In July 1826 a police agent reported that the peasants approved of the punishments meted out to the Decembrists, and wished only that the entire nobility could be treated likewise. The tsar, they believed, was their only protector.[57]

In view of the longstanding Soviet determination to present the Decembrists as misguided but virtuous forerunners of more successful revolutionary movements, some debunking of their activities is salutary. The work of M. V. Nechkina needs to be taken with a large pinch of salt.[58] Hugh Seton-Watson was ill-advised to refer to the Decembrists as 'perhaps the noblest figures in the whole history of Russian revolutionary action'.[59] When Mikhail Lunin claimed, in Siberia, that Decembrism was to the history of Russia what Runnymede and Magna Carta were to the history of Great Britain, he showed only that the rebels were good at deluding themselves.

Criticism, however, should not be taken too far. Baron Rozen was right to point out that, as a result of the official investigation into the conspiracy, 'The new tsar got to know the entire condition of Russia better in a few months than his predecessors had managed to do in decades'.[60] Nicholas wanted the information partly in order to batten down the hatches, but his knowledge also inclined him to make a few concessions. One or two people with Decembrist connections achieved influential positions in public life. Not all of them copied the Murav'ev who became a hangman. Speranskii returned to the path of reform. Lev Perovskii, a one-time member of the League of Welfare, became Minister of the Interior in the 1840s and promoted civil servants who went on to play a key part in the emancipation of the serfs. P. D. Kiselev, the commanding officer and friend of most of the leaders of the Southern Society, became Minister of State Properties and an enthusiast for improving the condition of the state peasantry. These officials took a different route from the one chosen by the men of 1825, but they never entirely forsook the liberal sympathies of their youth. They were partly responsible for generating the atmosphere of the late 1850s in which the Decembrists were amnestied and the government abandoned its thirty-year struggle to hold the line. When the government finally accepted the need for radical change, Iakov Rostovtsev was able to make amends for denouncing the Northern Society by playing a crucial part in the emancipation of the serfs.

It is hard, however, to make a positive case for the Decembrists simply by pointing to their material legacy. Their main significance lies elsewhere. The methods and ideas with which they experimented and the example they set to the next generation of thinking Russians were new. The similarity between their uprising and the military upheavals of 1740, 1762 and 1801 was more apparent than real. Unlike earlier generations of the Guards, they acted, eventually, in the open. They evolved blueprints for the total transformation of the political and social structure of the country. It is true that some of the remedies they outlined would have had worse consequences than the diseases they were designed to cure, but their ideas were much more wide-ranging than any contemplated by earlier military conspirators or by the authorities. The regime was right, therefore, to be frightened of what the Decembrists stood for. They were not trying to amend the status quo, but to abolish it. When, in 1857, the government published a self-serving account of the rising, the *émigré* radical Alexander Herzen attacked it head-on. In Herzen's opinion, the tsarist regime ought not to pursue the material sinews of modernity without permitting greater fluidity in social relations. The authorities' blinkered attitude to reform would produce 'something like Chinghis-Khan with telegraphs, steamships, and railroads' – an even more oppressive version of the existing autocracy.[61] Herzen believed that the Decembrists had grasped the direction in which government policy was tending and had tried to do something about it. His goals were more ambitious than those of the Decembrists, but his defence of them rang true.

NOTES

1. N. V. Basargin, *Zapiski* (Krasnoiarsk, 1985), p. 10.
2. Hugh Seton-Watson, *The Russian Empire 1801–1917* (Oxford, 1967), p. 185.
3. VPR, xi. 793.
4. John Gooding, 'Speransky and Baten'kov', SEER 66 (1988), 413.
5. B. Hollingsworth, 'Nicholas Turgenev: His Life and Works', unpublished PhD dissertation, Cambridge University, 1965, p. 198.

6. Gordon Cook, 'Civic Criticism and Public Libraries in Early Nineteenth Century Russia: Interplay or Isolation?', *The Journal of Library History* 12 (1977), 27.
7. F. A. Walker, 'K. F. Ryleyev: A Self-Sacrifice for Revolution', SEER 47 (1969), 446.
8. S. I. Mashinskii et al., eds, *Pisateli-dekabristy v vospominaniiakh sovremennikov* (2 vols, Moscow, 1980), i. 5.
9. F. N. Smirnov, 'Kunitsyn i dekabristy', VI, 1967 no. 6, p. 216.
10. V. A. Fedorov, ed., *Memuary dekabristov: Severnoe obshchestvo* (Moscow, 1981), p. 250 (hereafter cited as Fedorov).
11. D. S. Mirsky, 'The Decembrists', *Slavonic Review* 4 (1925– 6), 400.
12. Franklin A. Walker, 'Reaction and Radicalism in the Russia of Alexander I: The Case of the Brothers Glinka', CSP 21 (1979), 489–502.
13. Lauren G. Leighton, 'Freemasonry in Russia: The Grand Lodge of Astraea (1815–1822)', SEER 60 (1982), 247.
14. A. S. Pushkin, 'Otryvki iz pisem, mysli i zamechaniia', PSS (17 vols, Moscow and Leningrad, 1937–59), xi. 57; V. I. Saitov and P. N. Sheffer, eds, *Ostaf'evskii arkhiv kniazei Viazemskikh* (5 vols, SPB, 1899–1913), i. 107.
15. Marc Raeff, *Russian Intellectual History: An Anthology* (New York, 1966), pp. 123–4.
16. B. V. Tomashevskii, 'Epigrammy Pushkina na Karamzina', in M. P. Alekseev, ed., *Pushkin: Issledovaniia i materialy,* vol. 1 (Moscow and Leningrad, 1956), p. 208.
17. L. N. Luzianina, 'Epigramma na Karamzina', in V. G. Bazanov and V. E. Vatsuro, eds, *Literaturnoe nasledie dekabristov* (Leningrad, 1975), pp. 260–5.
18. John L. H. Keep, 'The Russian Army's Response to the French Revolution', JFGO 28 (1980), 515.
19. John L. H. Keep, *Soldiers of the Tsar: Army and Society in Russia 1462–1874* (Oxford, 1985), chs 10–11.
20. John L. H. Keep, 'The Russian Army's Response' (above, n. 18), 520.
21. W. Bruce Lincoln, 'A Re-examination of Some Historical Stereotypes: An Analysis of the Career Patterns and Backgrounds of the Decembrists', JFGO 24 (1976), 359.
22. I. Ia. Shchipanov, ed., *Izbrannye sotsial'no- politicheskie i filosofskie proizvedeniia dekabristov* (3 vols, Moscow, 1951), i. 497–8 (hereafter cited as Shchipanov).
23. M. V. Nechkina, *Dvizhenie dekabristov* (2 vols, Moscow, 1955), i. 103 (hereafter cited as Nechkina).
24. See the biographical appendix in L. Ia. Pavlova, *Dekabristy-uchastniki voin 1805–1814 gg.* (Moscow, 1979), pp. 99–118.
25. Shchipanov, i. 98.
26. A. E. Rozen, *Zapiski dekabrista* (St Petersburg, 1907), p. 57.
27. Jean Breuillard, 'L'occupation russe en France, 1816–1818', in A. Bourmeyster, ed., *Le 14 Décembre 1825: Origine et Héritage du mouvement des Décembristes* (Paris, 1980), p. 37.
28. Grand Duke Nikolai Mikhailovich, *Imperator Aleksandr I* (2 vols, St Petersburg, 1912), ii. 309.
29. Nechkina, i. 110.
30. Fedorov, p. 124.
31. Ibid., p. 27.
32. Shchipanov, ii. 309.
33. Fedorov, p. 126 (and see p. 141 for the fact that this list should be attributed to Nikita rather than Aleksandr Mikhailovich Murav'ev).

34. Nechkina, i. 192.
35. S. B. Okun', *Dekabrist M. S. Lunin* (2nd edn, Leningrad, 1985), p. 36.
36. Basargin, *Zapiski* (above, n. 1), p. 9.
37. Shchipanov, i. 126 (from the memoirs of Ivan Iakushkin).
38. Ibid., ii. 170.
39. Joseph L. Wieczynski, 'The Mutiny of the Semenovsky Regiment in 1820', RR 29 (1970), 179.
40. O. V. Orlik, *Dekabristy i vneshniaia politika Rossii* (Moscow, 1984), p. 99.
41. N. I. Lorer, *Zapiski dekabrista* (Irkutsk, 1984), p. 60.
42. W. J. Leatherbarrow and D. C. Offord, eds, *A Documentary History of Russian Thought from the Enlightenment to Marxism* (Ann Arbor, Mich., 1987), p. 53.
43. Ibid., p. 55.
44. Fedorov, p. 142.
45. Nechkina, i. 347.
46. Basargin, *Zapiski* (above, n. 1), p. 20.
47. Marc Raeff, *The Decembrist Movement* (Englewood Cliffs, NJ, 1966), p. 160.
48. Shchipanov, ii. 171.
49. Leatherbarrow and Offord, *A Documentary History* (above, n. 42), pp. 42–4.
50. Shchipanov, ii. 174.
51. A. E. Rozen, *Zapiski dekabrista* (Irkutsk, 1984), pp. 122–3.
52. Anatole G. Mazour, *The First Russian Revolution, 1825* (Stanford, Calif., 1961), p. 264 (first published in 1937).
53. Fedorov, p. 40.
54. B. N. Chicherin, *Vospominaniia: Moskovskii universitet* (Moscow, 1929), p. 99.
55. Waclaw Lednicki, *Russia, Poland and the West* (London, 1954), p. 110.
56. Lincoln, 'A Re-examination' (above, n. 21), p. 362.
57. M. A. Rakhmatullin, 'Krepostnoe krest'ianstvo Rossii i dvizhenie dekabristov', *Istoriia SSSR*, 1977 no. 4, pp. 127–51.
58. On Nechkina's domination of the Soviet literature see John Gooding, 'The Decembrists in the Soviet Union', SS 40 (1988), 196–209.
59. Seton-Watson, *Russian Empire* (above, n. 2), p. 197.
60. Rozen, *Zapiski* (above, n. 51), pp. 137–8.
61. Iskander (Herzen), 'Pis'mo k imperatoru Aleksandru II (po povodu knigi barona Korfa)', *Kolokol*, 1 October 1857.

CHAPTER FIVE

The Administrative and Social Policy of Nicholas I

NICHOLAS I AS CONSERVATIVE

When, in 1857, Herzen spoke of 'Chinghis-Khan with telegraphs', he was not really thinking of the future of the Russian Empire but of its immediate past. It is hard to speak well of the thirty-year reign of Nicholas I. The most charitable thing to be said about it seems to be that since very few Russian 'telegraphs, steamships, and railroads' were actually constructed between 1825 and 1855, the tsar's despotism was tempered by inefficiency. Of Nicholas himself it might be admitted that his upbringing gave him little chance of being ready for the throne. Almost all Romanov princes found their greatest happiness among soldiers, but those born to be king were taught to accept that civil as well as military affairs had to be paid some attention. Not only Alexander but even Paul occasionally doubted whether militarism was the complete answer to Russia's problems. Nicholas, a younger son, had been allowed to take the academic part of his studies less seriously than the instruction in soldiering. 'At seven,' in 1803, he 'was learning how to make bombs out of wax and how to besiege a mock fortress'.[1] The classroom never rivalled the parade ground in his affections. His mother, the Dowager Empress Maria Fedorovna, had been prevented by Catherine the Great from playing much part in the early education of the Grand Dukes Alexander and Konstantin, but made up for lost time by cultivating in Nicholas and his younger brother Mikhail the memory of Paul. When the young Nicholas was asked to write an essay on the subject 'Military service is not the only kind for a nobleman', he refused. His civilian tutors, the jurist Mikhail Balugianskii and the economist Heinrich Storch, appear to have made a much smaller impression on him than the experience of joining Russia's forces in western Europe in 1814. Marriage to a daughter of the King of Prussia in 1817 brought him into close contact with the European dynasty whose military traditions approximated most closely to those of the Romanovs. In the crisis of December 1825 the new tsar made plain that he would be paying little attention to the empire's civilian chain of command. 'Today', he said to the State Council, 'I request

116

you; tomorrow I shall command you'.[2] Even an elderly nobleman who deplored the revolution of 1917 admitted that 'The Emperor Nicholas I ruled his country like a gamekeeper'.[3] Other commentators have been far more severe.

Nicholas made a resolution at the time of the Decembrist uprising from which he never departed. 'Revolution', he wrote to the Grand Duke Mikhail, 'is on Russia's doorstep, but I swear that it will not penetrate the country while there is breath in my body'.[4] The tsar played a central part in the first interrogation of the arrested conspirators. 'The evidence of the captives was so various, so extensive and complicated,' he said later, 'that one needed special mental firmness in order not to get lost in the chaos'.[5] He found the firmness he needed. While a predominantly military investigative commission spent six months collecting the Decembrists' detailed testimony, the tsar set about ensuring that dissent would never resurface. In June 1826 he promulgated a censorship statute which 'meant ... the virtual banishment of literature from the state'.[6] In July 1826 he founded a police agency, the 'Third Department', whose malevolence became legendary. By the time the Decembrists had been dealt with, Nicholas had apparently charted his course. Reluctant to be seen in a context which implied that his power was less than absolute, he put off being crowned King of Poland until 1829. By then he had twice sent his armies to war. At home, in 1828, he issued a decree on primary and secondary education whose preamble spoke not of the advancement of learning but of limiting schools to transmitting 'the knowledge most necessary for each class'. A revolution in France in July 1830, a rising in the Kingdom of Poland in November 1830, and disturbances in various parts of the empire in the wake of the cholera epidemic of 1830–1 confirmed the tsar in his belief that he had to be perennially on guard against disorder. S. S. Uvarov saved him the trouble of putting his policy into words. Having conducted an inspection of Moscow University as Deputy Minister of Education in 1832, Uvarov reported that education had to be combined with 'a sincere belief in the quintessentially Russian protective principles of Orthodoxy, Autocracy, and Nationality [*Narodnost'*], which constitute the last anchor of our salvation and the most dependable guarantee of the strength and greatness of the Fatherland'.[7] Early in 1833 Nicholas made Uvarov Minister of Education and allowed him to reiterate the principles of 'Orthodoxy, Autocracy, and Nationality' in his first ministerial circular.

Uvarov's three abstractions became bywords. In the 1870s the historian Aleksandr Pypin gave them the collective name 'Official Nationality', which has been the standard term for Nicholas's policy ever since. In Pypin's interpretation, the important word was 'Official'. Unofficial opinions were proscribed, and the public exchange of ideas which had been a feature of intellectual life under Alexander I came to an end. The conservatism of Nikolai Karamzin had apparently triumphed. When the Official Historiographer of the Empire inveighed against Speranskii in 1810 and the Poles in 1819, he seemed to be conducting a desperate rearguard action. After

1825, the rearguard became the vanguard. Nicholas's agents made a sorry crew. Servants of the crown included a police chief who sometimes forgot his own name and a Minister of Education (Uvarov's successor) who claimed to be 'merely a blind tool of the Emperor's will'.[8] Faddei Bulgarin and Nikolai Grech, journalistic exponents of 'Official Nationality', 'closed their minds to broader political questions in 1825'.[9] The university professors Mikhail Pogodin and Stepan Shevyrev were only a little more broad-minded. Nicholas found a remarkable number of ways to flesh out his philosophy. Promoting Orthodoxy led him to increase the printing budget of the Holy Synod from 2,000 silver rubles in 1825 to nearly 500,000 in 1849. Promoting autocracy meant not only supporting the police and the army but also stating explicitly that representative monarchy was 'the rule of lies, fraud and corruption'.[10] Promoting nationality meant emphasizing Russianness. Nicholas's 'Testament' of 1835 (drawn up at a time when the tsar feared attacks on his life) emphasized the importance of not allowing members of the imperial family to develop cosmopolitan sympathies. An 'Archaeographic Commission' set up in 1834 took over the private manu-script-gathering which had gone on in the late eighteenth and early nine-teenth centuries and made the state the prime mover in the delineation of Russia's historical identity. The creation of university professorships in Slavonic studies in 1835 implied an attempt to diminish Russia's cultural dependence on western Europe. A series of steps designed to depress the fortunes of the Polish gentry, promote those of their non-Polish serfs, and present the history of the 'western provinces' as if they were an age-old part of Russia made plain which of the Slavonic peoples, in the opinion of the regime, should prevail over the others. Twenty years of military conflict with the Muslim peoples of the Caucasus and the non-recognition of foreign laws in parts of the empire which had once belonged to other countries suggested that Russianness was to be not only cultivated, but also implanted. Calling Russian Jews 'aliens' in a collection of laws published in 1835 lent credibility to the notion that the regime was positively racist. Changing the tune of the national anthem because it came from England showed the lengths to which the tsar's patriotism could take him. Nicholas's enthusiasm for Glinka's *A Life for the Tsar* derived from the pleasure of knowing that his principles could be exemplified 'even in the opera house'.[11] The erection of the Alexander Column on Palace Square in St Petersburg, the construction of the General Staff Building and the near-completion of St Isaac's Cathedral seemed to exemplify in stone what Russianness meant to the tsar: commemorating triumphs, preparing for war, and thanking the Orthodox God.

Nicholas's contemporaries despised him, though most of those who were within his reach kept their thoughts to themselves. One who failed to do so, Petr Chaadaev, was condemned as a madman for publishing a despairing essay on Russia's backwardness. Wisely, Pushkin consigned to his desk drawer a poem which said that his verses dwarfed the Alexander Column. When the young historian Sergei Solov'ev was climbing the academic ladder in the 1840s and 1850s, no one knew that he thought Nicholas comparable with the mad Roman emperor Caligula. Later, Solov'ev wrote that the two rulers differed only in so far as Nicholas 'did not wish that the people had a single head which it would be possible to cut off with a single blow; he wanted ... the possibility of cutting off all heads which rose above the general level'.[12] Foreigners could afford to be bolder than the tsar's subjects. Hatred of Russia in Britain led the peculiar David Urquhart to prefer the Ottoman Empire. The Marquis de Custine admired the Russian Empire before visiting it in 1839, but in 1843 published one of the most withering of all indictments of the tsarist regime. The tsar encouraged a German to reply, but August von Haxthausen's *Studies on the Interior of Russia* were too judicious to be called an encomium. Russians who lived abroad were perhaps the most outspoken of those who combined first-hand knowledge of the empire with the freedom to publish. Ivan Golovin's *Russia under the Autocrat Nicholas I*, which was published in London in 1846, continued the long tradition of *émigré* attacks on Russia's rulers. Nikolai Turgenev's *Russia and the Russians*, which came out in Paris in 1847, combined a memoir of the Decembrist movement with analysis of Russia's difficulties and recommendations for their solution. By the end of Nicholas's reign Alexander Herzen was conceiving, in London, what became the most successful anti-tsarist campaign ever to be launched in the west. By then even Russians at home were taking up their pens, for the tsar had responded to the European revolutions of 1848 by dedicating himself unremittingly to the prevention of change. The young Boris Chicherin, who was not to prove a radical, began circulating subversive memoranda. Later, Chicherin recalled feeling that by the time of Nicholas's death 'The monarch's goal had been achieved; the ideal of eastern despotism had taken root on Russian soil'.[13] It was hardly surprising, therefore, that an influential twentieth-century historian, Aleksandr Presniakov, called his book on Nicholas's reign *The Apogee of Autocracy*.

NICHOLAS I AS REFORMER

Yet Nicholas was not a blind reactionary. Though hostile to dramatic change, he thought seriously about the country's administrative and social structure. The energy he displayed at the beginning of his reign was far from wholly destructive. The investigation of the Decembrist uprising had positive as well as negative ends in view. The secretary of the investigative commission, Aleksandr Borovkov, provided the new tsar with a clear-cut list of the steps he ought to take if he wanted to prevent discontent re-emerging. Nicholas had to:

grant laws, implant justice by establishing the fastest possible judicial procedures, raise the moral education of the priesthood, strengthen ... the nobility, issue firm regulations for the resurrection of trade and industry, provide young people with a different sort of education and one suitable for all classes, improve the circumstances of farmers, abolish the humiliating sale of human beings, revive the fleet, ... in short, remedy countless signs of disorder and wrongdoing.[14]

If Borovkov felt able to write so frankly, Nicholas had clearly not instilled in his minions the feeling that reform proposals were unwelcome. The informative early reports of the new police agency lend weight to the impression that, at the beginning of his reign, Nicholas wanted to know not just what to proscribe but what to set right. There are other indications that the tsar's early severity can be exaggerated. The iron censorship statute of 1826 was modified two years later. Even at the time of its enactment Nicholas showed that he could treat writers with generosity as well as contempt, for in September 1826 he gave the frustrated Aleksandr Pushkin permission to return to metropolitan life. Although the preamble of the education statute of 1828 took a narrow view of the advancement of learning, the body of the text did little to subvert the generous attitude to schooling which had been enshrined in the laws of 1803–4. Although Nicholas tried hard to get out of being crowned as a constitutional monarch in Poland, in the end he was unwilling to ride roughshod over the Polish Charter of 1815 and went through the motions of accepting its provisions. The early wars against Persia and the Ottoman Empire were not of the tsar's making and might have happened if his brother had still been on the throne. Even the promulgation of 'Orthodoxy, Autocracy, and Nationality' in the educational circular of 1833 may not have been as benighted in origin as it became in effect. Tsars had always expressed allegiance to 'Orthodoxy' and 'Autocracy', but 'At the start of the '30s nationality was not just a word'.[15] As we saw in Chapter Four, the word *narodnost'* – 'people-ness' or 'nationality' – originally represented an idea which appealed to the left of the political spectrum. After 1833 its conservative content began to prevail over its capacity for stimulating change, but when it was adopted by the regime its meaning was still ambivalent. Since Uvarov, its promoter, was more imaginative than the apologists with whom 'nationality' subsequently became identified, he may have been hoping to prevent the regime from cutting itself off completely from the reformist sentiments of the reign of Alexander I.

Thus even those aspects of the early part of Nicholas's reign which are most frequently cited in support of the view that the tsar was a reactionary may be interpreted in more ways than one. They should be seen, moreover, in the context of actions which make the tsar appear forward-looking. By dismissing Arakcheev within a few days of ascending the throne Nicholas distanced himself from the darker side of his brother's last years. When he created a new department to put order into the law in early 1826, he showed a willingness to take up the subject which reformist tsars had always placed at the centre of their attention. By entrusting the department to Balugianskii and Speranskii, furthermore, Nicholas demonstrated that one of his tutors had made a certain impression on him and that the most radical bureaucrat of the previous reign was no longer beyond the pale. The tsar's readiness to contemplate changes was not confined to the law. On 6 December 1826 he established a high-powered committee to work through the papers of Alexander I and report 'what was proposed, what the situation is currently, what would remain in place, what is good, what has to go, what will replace it, and what methods will be employed to achieve the desired results'.[16] This body sat 173 times in the five-year period of its existence and came up with many schemes for amending both the administrative and the social structure of the country. Borovkov's summary of the reasons for the Decembrist uprising found favour with the committee in February 1827. In mid-1828 the committee virtually ran the country when the tsar was away on campaign. Its breadth of vision and the trust Nicholas placed in it led one of the most authoritative modern scholars to say that, in his first years on the throne, the tsar's 'contemporaries formed the impression that an age of reforms had begun in Russia'.[17] Another scholar has written that the tsar was making 'a last feverish effort to strengthen the crumbling system of serf-based statehood by transforming it radically'.[18] Although both these scholars argue that Nicholas's reformist aspirations disappeared within a few years of his accession (and unlike those of Alexander I, never resurfaced), it may be worth dwelling a little longer on the notion of Nicholas I as reformer. It is already clear that Nicholas did not close his mind to change immediately after the Decembrist uprising. Why then should he have done so in the early 1830s, when no greater crisis affected him?

Instead of saying that Nicholas I battened down the hatches, whether in 1825 or 1831, it is truer to say that, in the wake of Decembrism, Russians inside and outside the political system both shifted their ground. Neither lost sight of the need for change, but both adopted new policies and neither understood the other. The new tsar differed from his predecessor in refusing to pay even lip-service to the thought of moving towards representative institutions. Non-governmental intellectuals had seen the futility of direct action and retreated into private discussion circles. Because the two sides had different views of the direction in which the country should go and different views of the tools they needed to change it, their sympathy for one another was vestigial. The government came to believe that people who thought for themselves were dangerous subversives, whereas people who thought for themselves believed that the government had become despotic. Both sides were mistaken. Both, in fact, were to play a part in facilitating the radical social and administrative changes which eventually took place in the next reign. Since Nicholas's contribution to those developments has rarely been acknowledged, it will occupy the rest of this chapter.

THE GOVERNMENTAL MACHINE

The tsar rejected the notion of representative institutions but did not abandon the idea of administrative innovation. By 1825 it was becoming a tradition for Russian rulers to bypass the creations of their predecessors. Peter the Great had replaced the chanceries of the seventeenth century with Colleges and the Senate; Catherine the Great had subordinated the Senate to the Procurator-General while decentralizing at the expense of the colleges; Alexander I had re-emphasized the importance of the centre by establishing Ministries, a Committee of Ministers and the State Council. In administrative matters Nicholas was at least as radical as his forebears. Divesting the State Council, the Committee of Ministers and the Senate of their more significant functions, he ruled through *ad hoc* committees and the vast expansion of his personal office. The committees gave the tsar a chance of seeing the wood for the trees. That of 6 December 1826 probably came up with as many good ideas in the course of its five-year existence as Alexander I had produced in the entire course of his reign. Nicholas rightly believed that special-purpose committees gave him a better chance of effecting changes than the organs of government which existed at his accession. He was reluctant to see the activities of the new committees impeded. When Prince I. V. Vasil'chikov asked him to put a committee proposal to the State Council – the body which remained, in theory, the linchpin of the government – he agreed only on condition that no 'superfluous opinions' were put forward to delay its enactment.[19]

The emperor's personal office or chancery exemplified his direct style of rule even better than the committees. Although it had had a number of unofficial seventeenth- and eighteenth-century precursors, 'His Majesty's Own Chancery' first acquired statutory legitimacy in 1812. Under Alexander I it had been the power-base of Arakcheev, but Nicholas took it into his own hands and rapidly turned it into the nerve-centre of the empire's administrative machine. By the early 1840s it had six departments. Under edicts of 1826 and 1827, the first of them was to receive frequent reports from almost all central government agencies. From 1832 even provincial governors had to report to it twice a year. From 1836 it became responsible for monitoring the service records of civil servants. When a Civil Service Inspectorate was set up in 1846, the head of the First Department was put in charge of it. 'I want to elevate the civil service', Nicholas said, 'as I have elevated service in the army. I want to know all my officials, as I know all the officers of my army'.[20] The Second and Third Departments were the bodies mentioned above which were given responsibility for law reform and police matters in 1826. The Fourth Department (charitable institutions) was set up in 1828, the Fifth (state peasants) in 1836, the Sixth (Caucasian affairs) in 1842. 'Each of these departments constituted an independent institution with a head, functions, budget, clerical work, and direct reports to the tsar'.[21]

It is usual to say of departments of the chancery other than the first that they had a short life, or that they were dedicated to rather specialized areas of governmental activity which could not easily be undertaken by the existing ministries, or that they were engaged in repressive rather than reformist undertakings. None of these criticisms is entirely valid. Only the Sixth Department had a short life. The Second Department's work on law reform was specialist, but its outcome affected all aspects of Russian administration and society. The Third Department became a byword for repression, but in its early days spoke frankly to the tsar about the need to make far-reaching changes. Some examples will serve to correct the impression that the Third Department's outlook was utterly unconstructive. In its report on developments in the year 1827 the department emphasized that the governmental machine was in disarray. Justice and industry were the keys to improvement. The situation was critical. Well-intentioned people were saying: 'If this tsar does not reform Russia, nothing will prevent its demise'. The following year the department spoke even more urgently. 'The bankruptcy of the nobility, the venality of justice, and serfdom', it reported, 'are the elements which Russian patriots feel able to make use of at the right time in order to incite agitation on behalf of a constitution'. The department implied that the tsar ought to remedy these deficiencies rather than allow the initiative to be taken from him. In 1829 the Third Department pointed out that the Ministry of Education, which a decade earlier had been accused of falling victim to mysticism, was now being accused of obscurantism. In 1830 it returned to the fundamental questions of injustice and venality, and added a remark about the 'despotism of ministers'. The circumstances which made governing Russia almost impossible in 1830 – cholera, a bad harvest, sluggish trade, revolution in France, revolt in Poland – were brought firmly to the tsar's attention.[22]

Ad hoc committees and the expansion of his personal office gave Nicholas the means of bypassing a central government structure whose arteries had hardened. Although the new organs of administration also increased his ability to monitor his subjects' activities, repression was by no means their sole function. The Buturlin censorship committee of 1848 became notorious for its part in creating the undoubtedly chilling atmosphere of the last years of the reign, but it should be set against the Committee of 6 December 1826, which tried hard to foster the regime's capacity for change. In the sense, furthermore, that in 1857 Alexander II began moving towards the emancipation of the serfs by establishing a 'Secret Committee on the Peasant Question', it could be said that Nicholas I bequeathed to his son the institutional device which enabled him to set about the biggest single alteration in the social structure of the nineteenth-century Russian Empire. The departments of the chancery, no less than the committees, need to be seen in the round. Calling the Third Department a force for good may be straining the evidence, but paying undue attention to the secret police obscures the achievements of the Second and Fifth Departments in the fields of the law and the state-owned peasantry, both of which will be dealt with below.

Nicholas was no less ready to contemplate changes in the sphere of local government than he was to revise institutional arrangements at the centre. Aleksandr Kizevetter's assertion that the tsar sowed 'the seeds of local self-government' goes too far,[23] but Nicholas certainly tried to inject life into the moribund administration of the Russian provinces and municipalities. The tsar's agents outside the highest echelons of government were of two kinds, bureaucrats and representatives of local social groups. Paradoxically, Nicholas's attitude towards bureaucrats in the provinces ran counter to the spirit of his institutional innovations in St Petersburg. At the centre, the use of committees and the expansion of the chancery had the effect of reducing the importance of the ministerial bureaucracies. In the provinces, the ministerial principle received a fillip. In 1827 Nicholas brought to an end the experiment with provincial 'vicegerencies' which had been running under A. D. Balashev since 1819, and in 1837 he abolished the office of Governor-General in all parts of the empire other than St Petersburg, Moscow and the borderlands. Because vicegerents and governors-general had direct access to the tsar, whereas governors were officials of the Ministry of Internal Affairs, the disappearance of the former (at least from the imperial heartland) increased the likelihood that decisions taken by the Ministry of Internal Affairs would have some effect in the localities. This likelihood became greater still with the strengthening of the governors' control over the people who were supposed to implement their instructions, a process which was completed in 1845 when agents who served on the governors' staff but owed their primary allegiance to local social groups were eliminated. Provincial governors were still constrained by the fact that the Ministry of Internal Affairs was not the only ministry with offices in the provinces, but the tsar had enhanced the governors' authority and clarified the way in which provinces were run. The introduction of official provincial newspapers in 1838 perhaps showed that he was interested in the development of local cultural identities as well as in the simplification of the provinces' administration.

Where towns rather than the countryside were concerned, Nicholas accepted a statute for St Petersburg in 1846 which was extended to Moscow in 1862 and Odessa in 1863 and became the starting-point for Alexander II's general municipal reform of 1870. This may have been the most imaginative of all Nicholas's institutional innovations. Kizevetter, a specialist on Russian municipal administration, called it 'the boldest step of the Nicholaevan government on the way to reform'.[24] A modern expert admits that 'for all the imperfections of the reform of 1846 it was a clear step forward'.[25] With the exception of a recent revisionist study which argues that, in the province of St Petersburg in the late eighteenth century, 'The problem of town government was not ... that it did not work, but that it worked too well',[26] all authorities agree that Catherine the Great's Charter to the Towns of 1785 failed to provide Russian towns with effective organs of administration. Catherine had hoped to persuade all non-tax-paying city-dwellers to play a part in the management of their affairs, but the urban gentry had not taken advantage of the opportunity and substantial merchants had been reluctant to spare time from the running of their businesses. A digest of the empire's laws published in 1842 implied that the government had come to accept gentry non-involvement, but in the same year Nicholas I created within the Ministry of Internal Affairs a 'Provisional Section for the Reorganization of Municipal Government and Economy'. Its head, Nikolai Miliutin, worked for the restoration of the principle of all-class involvement in the running of the empire's cities. Although, in the event, he preserved the principle of representation of the various groups in the community by estate rather than by head, and although he set a high property qualification for receipt of the vote and introduced bureaucrats alongside elected officials, St Petersburg's new municipal administration represented the community much more nearly than any of the other institutions which ran Nicholaevan Russia. Local government in the capital was no longer the exclusive preserve of merchants and had not simply been taken away from them and handed over to the gentry.

THE BUREAUCRACY

Thus Nicholas I was anything but inflexible in his attitude towards the structure of the empire's administration. In this regard, indeed, he should probably be criticized for displaying too much imagination rather than too little, for contradictory philosophies informed his treatment of the different arms of the state. A 'personal' principle lay behind the expansion of the tsar's chancery, the 'ministerial' principle of the previous reign explained the abolition of governors-general in the Russian heartland, and a 'representative' principle underpinned the reform of city government in St Petersburg. The different approaches threatened to increase the number of administrative crossed wires. Their profusion, however, was less detrimental to the prospects of domestic advance than the numerical and qualitative deficiencies of the bureaucracy. No amount of tinkering with the administration of the state could alter the fact that officials were more important than offices. Although 'the process of bureaucratization of the state apparatus accelerated sharply' in the first half of the nineteenth century, and although the ratio of officials to the total population of the empire increased from 1:2,250 in 1796 to 1:929 in 1851, the tsar still had many fewer bureaucrats at his disposal than, for example, Britain and France, where the ratio of civil servants to total population stood at 1:244 and 1:208 in 1851 and 1845 respectively.[27] Since, in the 1840s, 165,000 'sheets of official papers headed "urgent" were being prepared annually in the Ministry of the Interior alone', and since in 1851 1,351 separate documents were needed to notify all the relevant authorities of the sale of a piece of land,[28] bureaucrats were always likely to be behind with their work.

Their quality was almost as unsatisfactory as their quantity. The proportion of officials on the Table of Ranks who had received their education entirely at home went down from more than 30 per cent in the first decade of the century to 5 per cent by the 1830s, but the tsar's servants had a long way to go before their conception of public service matched their intellectual abilities. Venality prevailed at all levels of the administration. Nicholas I's bureaucracy was notably superior to that which had served the empire in the eighteenth century, but it was not improving rapidly enough to keep pace with the vastly increased range of its duties. Thoughtful contemporaries harped on its deficiencies rather than its merits. After assisting the Chairman of the State Council in a fruitless attempt to find someone fit for promotion to its ranks in 1838, the senior civil servant M. A. Korf recorded in his diary that 'The lack of personnel is fearsome – and not just at this highest level, but also in jobs of secondary importance'.[29] The head of the Third Department reported in the early 1830s that educated and established people were reluctant to become provincial governors because they knew the degree of responsibility which they would have to assume and how few were the resources on which provincial governors could rely. The outstanding prose-writer of the reign of Nicholas I, Nikolai Gogol, satirized the small-mindedness of city administrators in his play *The Government Inspector* of 1836.

Because bureaucrats' principal reward for serving the crown was the acquisition of personal or hereditary noble status (personal at rank fourteen on the Table of Ranks, hereditary at rank eight), increasing the supply of well-trained and public-spirited civil servants meant changing the character of the Russian nobility. The forebears of established nobles had themselves acquired nobility by serving the crown, but children and grandchildren tended to forget their families' indebtedness and to develop a sense of their independence. In the second quarter of the nineteenth century nobles of long standing believed that newly ennobled bureaucrats would threaten the values they held dear. In this they were probably correct, for Walter Pintner has shown on the basis of extensive statistical analysis that by 1850 'High officials were far more likely to be totally divorced from the land and entirely dependent on the state for their economic livelihood and social prestige than they had been fifty years earlier'.[30] In other words, nobles who were high officials differed greatly from nobles who were not. Not surprisingly, the latter sought to prevent the watering-down of their estate by non-landowners. According to a late-nineteenth-century Russian historian, 'The key feature of the history of our nobility, by comparison with the nobility of western Europe, consists of the fact that it has always been a political institution, existing and changing in accordance with the aims and requirements of the government'.[31] If this had been the case, Nicholas I would have had little difficulty in obliging non-service-orientated nobles to accept the replacement of their authority by that of civil servants. In fact, the tsar was in a cleft stick. On the one hand, he faced pressure from long-established nobles to prevent civil servants from joining them by working

126

their way up the Table of Ranks. On the other, he had to offer bureaucrats appropriate rewards for their labours. He needed both groups – the first to keep order in the countryside, the second to staff his burgeoning administration. Which of them to give precedence to was a dilemma he failed to resolve.

His failure to come down on one side or the other has usually been taken to be one of the best indicators of his inadequacy as a ruler, but he did not fail for lack of effort and, despite appearances to the contrary, he did not end by surrendering to nobles of long standing. On balance, indeed, Nicholas probably did more for bureaucrats than for aristocrats. In view of the murder of his father and the revolt of December 1825 the tsar had every reason to fear the noble estate, and at the beginning of his reign he seemed to defer to it. The Committee of 6 December 1826 devised a 'Supplementary Law on the Estates of the Realm' whose enactment would have enabled long-established nobles to pull up the ladder behind them by breaking the connection between service in the bureaucracy and the acquisition of noble status. All it offered bureaucrats was entry into a new social estate called the 'citizenry' (*grazhdanstvo*). The law, however, was never passed. In March 1830 the State Council approved it unanimously, but the tsar was shrewd enough to perceive that he might have difficulty recruiting bureaucrats if the possibility of eventual entry into the noble estate was taken from them. In May 1830 Nicholas's brother, the Grand Duke Konstantin, seems to have convinced him that the smooth running of the bureaucracy was more important than the goodwill of the existing nobility. The fall of Charles X in France in July 1830 may have confirmed the tsar in his view that a strongly pro-noble policy was ill advised. The tide of events in Europe seemed to be turning against aristocrats. Russia's nobles thus failed, in the early part of Nicholas's reign, to prevent the entry of non-nobles into their ranks. Rejection of the proposed Supplementary Law may even have derived from the fact that the tsar's interest in it sprang not from a desire to give nobles what they wanted, but from the possibility that creating a 'Citizenry' would facilitate the emergence of a Russian middle class. Nicholas may have dropped the law when he grasped that nobles were going to be the principal beneficiaries. He still introduced the social category of 'Honoured Citizen' (*pochetnyi grazhdanin*) in 1832, but without intending it to become a receptacle for upwardly mobile bureaucrats.

Meanwhile, the law of October 1827 which stated that people from taxable estates could not enter the civil service as chancery clerks was honoured in the breach. The 1833 summary of legislation on the civil service stated explicitly that no one could enter it who belonged to a taxable estate, but in practice it exempted individuals who had graduated from institutions of higher learning, many of which were open to all sections of the community. The abolition, in 1834, of the Act of 1809 which required civil servants to show proof of their educational achievements took place not because the state was giving education a lower priority, but because the Act had done its work. Without a significant degree of formal education, even a nobleman could no longer scale the civil service ladder. With it, even a non-nobleman was able to do so. Nicholas took a number of steps which militated directly against the interests of nobles: attempting to make them serve in the provinces before entering the central government ministries; forbidding noble youths under the age of eighteen from going abroad to finish their studies; putting a five-year (and subsequently a three-year) limit on nobles' passports for foreign travel; increasing the cost of such passports; and, as we shall see later, placing limits on their power over their serfs. Between 1836 and 1843, 7,200 people reached rank eight on the Table of Ranks, 4,700 of them from non-noble estates. In June 1845 Nicholas appeared to accede to noble interests by requiring civil servants to reach rank nine rather than rank fourteen on the Table of Ranks before receiving personal nobility, and rank five rather than rank eight before their noble status became hereditary. Even this, however, failed to stop civil servants of non-noble origin becoming nobles, for promotion through the ranks merely accelerated.

In the European crisis of 1848, Nicholas made an often-quoted speech to the St Petersburg nobility in which he asserted: 'Gentlemen! I have no police, I do not like them. You are my police. Each one of you is my steward'.[32] He seemed, at last, to be showing where his true allegiance lay. At a time of potential unrest, however, it was hardly surprising that he attempted to make amends for his longstanding reluctance to prevent the entry of parvenus into the nobles' ranks. The tsar was not a convert to the cause of social mobility, but he knew that nobles alone were incapable of running his administration. He could not afford to be wholly identified with noble conservatism, and consequently, almost in spite of himself, he promoted the empire's bureaucracy. Perhaps he sensed what effect his behaviour would have, for he chose many of his principal advisers from two groups whose characteristics marked them off from the rest of the aristocracy. Generals felt greater loyalty to the traditions of the army than to the aristocratic environment from which, in the main, they sprang. Baltic Germans felt few affinities either with their Russian peers or with the people who surrounded them in the Baltic countryside (who were neither Russian nor German). Both groups relied more heavily on the tsar than on the rest of the empire's nobility. The tsar could use them without fearing that they would try to subvert his domestic initiatives.

REFORMING THE LAW

Nicholas could take only a few initiatives, however, when the social basis of the regime was in flux. Far-reaching changes had to be left to the next generation. In the short term, the tsar had to confine innovations to fields in which his authority was untrammelled or which were non-controversial. He found one in reform of the law, and proved much more successful than his forebears in addressing an issue to which the rulers of the empire had been devoting their attention for more than a hundred years. Borovkov had pointed out in his summary of the problems exposed by the Decembrist revolt that 'We have one edict after another. One stops something, the next re-starts it, and for every phenomenon we have a multiplicity of mutually contradictory laws. As a result, the strong and slanderers profit whilst the poor and the innocent suffer'.[33] Putting order into the law not only was of value for its own sake, but also offered the further potential benefit of reducing calls for a constitution. If the government could claim that the existing administration was functioning smoothly, the need to alter it would seem less pressing.

The Second Department of the tsar's chancery addressed itself to the problem without delay. Balug'ianskii and Speranskii set out to publish a 'Complete Collection' of laws promulgated since the Law Code of 1649 and a 'Digest' containing the laws which were still in force. Speranskii wanted to go further and produce a normative law code, but the tsar set his face against generalities. Nicholas had no interest in legal abstractions. The first volume of the Digest, 'The Fundamental Laws of the Russian Empire', made few general statements beyond declaring that the monarchy was absolute and unlimited. Only its title implied that there were some laws to which even the sovereign had to defer. The Second Department was not engaged in 'codifying' Russian law, but rather in stripping out contradictions and rendering what was left accessible. These were nevertheless worthwhile objectives. Balug'ianskii made his main contribution in the first part of the work, Speranskii in the composition of the Digest. Progress was rapid. The Complete Collection, in forty-five chronologically arranged volumes, was printed between 26 May 1828 and 1 April 1830; the 'Digest', in fifteen volumes arranged thematically, was published in 1832, approved by the State Council in 1833, and came into effect on 1 January 1835.

Given the speed with which the enterprise had been undertaken, it was hardly surprising that the Complete Collecton turned out to be fairly ramshackle. It did not contain edicts which had been promulgated during the various constitutional crises of the period 1725–1825, because the regime had no intention of drawing attention to the points in its history when it had been less than secure. Nor did it include legislation on matters pertaining to the Church and the Court. The Digest, too, had weaknesses. When laws contradicted each other, it merely reprinted the most recent. No attempt was made to determine which laws were the best. Whatever the drawbacks, however, the Second Department of the Chancery accomplished in a few years what seventeen legal commissions had failed to achieve since the beginning of the eighteenth century. On paper, order had been put into the Russian law. Speranskii also made arrangements for a handful of gifted seminarians to undertake specialist legal training, with the object of employing them to educate the next generation of Russians in the importance of taking law seriously. When an Imperial School of Juris-prudence was established in 1835, it seemed possible that this dream might be realized. The Second Department moved on to collecting the laws of foreign origin which applied in non-Russian parts of the empire (though this part of its work bore little fruit). By the time Speranskii died in 1839, he had realized more of his youthful dreams than looked likely when he was dismissed from office in 1812. It was paradoxical that his greatest claim to fame rested on a task which Nicholas rather than Alexander made it possible for him to accomplish.

STATE PEASANTS

Law reform showed that the government could make changes to which powerful interest groups were indifferent (or which they welcomed), but in the contentious area of social policy the tsar came up against well-nigh insuperable barriers. He was not averse to social reform *per se*, however, for he acted energetically in respect of the one element within the com-munity which was more or less wholly within his charge. 'State peasants' – peasants owned by the state – constituted about half the empire's total number of rural workers and about 40 per cent of its total population. Ni-cholas showed an interest in them as soon as he came to the throne. In 1826 he ordered the creation of 'model administrations' for state-owned land in the provinces of St Petersburg and Pskov. Ten years later he acted with much greater vigour, opening a new department of his chancery (the fifth) specifically to consider transforming the lives of state peasants. General P. D. Kiselev, one-time friend of the Decembrists, was put in charge of the new office and ordered to investigate state-owned properties and prepare appropriate suggestions for their reorganization.

Kiselev's survey revealed a parlous state of affairs. State peasants were the responsibility of the Ministry of Finances, but the ministry had not thought of investing in them in order to improve their revenue-producing capacity. Surveyors, foresters and doctors were virtually absent from the state-owned countryside. Provincial offices of the Ministry of Finances had no money to spend even on investigating the peasants' lot, let alone trans-forming it. At lower levels of administration, the district and the canton, state peasants were the responsibility of police agencies. These were either gentry-dominated and unlikely to operate as a buffer between the peasants and the treasury, or concerned solely with the maintenance of order. The various local agencies often failed to prevent state peasants from moving il-legally from one place to another, or to notice that state peasants were fall-ing into the hands of private landlords. The government was losing large sums of money. Kiselev estimated, by way of example, that in the 1830s state-owned forests produced income of about 600,000 rubles a year while losing 900,000 to fire and illegal tree-felling. A comparison of tax arrears and government expenditure on famine relief with predicted revenue from the state peasants for the year 1833 produced an estimated loss to the centre of 26 per cent. Egor Kankrin, the Minister of Finances, freely admitted that he knew almost nothing about the state's rural resources. In response to one of Kiselev's investigators he wrote: 'Concerning the construction of houses, the number of souls engaged in agriculture, in trade, or not possessing a definite income derived from trade, the extent of sown land, and the quantity of productive livestock (horned or otherwise), the Department has absolutely no information'.[34]

The government was only the most obvious victim of Kankrin's ignorance. Kiselev rightly observed that 'the lack of organization and the absence of economic management were damaging, above all, to the well-being of the peasants'.[35] Their traditional institutions were in a state of apparently terminal decline. The centre had made no attempt to dovetail its requirements with the way in which they lived their lives. It had decided, for example, that units of 300 or 500 state peasants would be charged with paying taxes, units of 1,000 would provide recruits for the army, and units of an unspecified size would be responsible for the maintenance of roads and bridges. These units bore no relation to the groups in which peasants associated for the primary purpose of working the land. Peasant communes had been drastically weakened. State peasants had many rights – to leave the land, to enter educational institutions, to become civil servants, to acquire all sorts of property apart from populated estates, to enter into contractual agreements – but such rights were largely meaningless in the absence of effective barriers between peasants and the state. State peasants' landholdings were often too small to enable them to meet their obligations or to provide them with the necessities of life. They had to rent large quantities of land from the gentry. Inadequate harvests were frequent. Growing potatoes rather than grain was almost unheard-of except in the Baltic and western provinces of the empire. Putting the situation to rights was going to require strong medicine.

It took the form of a new ministry, the Ministry of State Properties, which came into being at the end of 1837. At the centre, the new body had a chancery and four departments – two with broad responsibilities for specific geographical areas (Russia proper and the outlying regions of the empire), two with narrowly focused special interests (forests and land use). The Ministry set up offices in the provinces to give it a chance of implementing its edicts on the ground. In the management of local economic affairs peasant communes were reallocated pride of place (though the size, frequency and juridical authority of their meetings were reduced). The legal rights of state peasants as laid down in volume IX of Speranskii's *Digest of the Laws* were confirmed, with the addition of enhanced power for parents in family disputes, new provisions for guardianship over children and wastrels, and the introduction of attorneys to act on behalf of peasants in the courts. Kiselev believed that these new arrangements would not only benefit St Petersburg but also bring about 'the economic and moral improvement of the twenty-million-strong estate of free peasants'.[36]

The Minister of State Properties seems to have been justified in his belief so far as the centre was concerned, for revenue from state properties went up from 280.5 million rubles in the period 1826–38 to 356.5 million in the period 1838–50. From the point of view of the inhabitants of state land, the benefits of the government's initiative were less clear cut. Although Kiselev claimed in 1850 that rural schooling, the layout of villages, fire-fighting, rural insurance, provision against bad harvests, medical facilities, the care of orphans, the allocation of labour duties, the system of selecting recruits for the army, the size of peasant holdings and peasants' farming practices had all changed for the better as a result of the new ministry's activities, he admitted that he had done no more than prepare the ground for future more substantial changes. The regime, he said, lacked the personnel to make rural progress easy. Nor was this its only difficulty. As the state derived greater profit from its peasants, so the private individuals who had been making illegal profits from them in the past felt that their interests had been attacked. As the state peasantry came to be administered on the basis of law, so private serf-owners began to fear that their own arbitrary behaviour in the countryside was about to be challenged. Kiselev warned that the advances which had taken place had been hard won, and could not easily be extended. State peasants were responsible for only one-sixth as many disturbances as privately owned peasants in the period between 1796 and 1856, but reports from provincial officials of the Ministry of State Properties in 1855 (the year of Nicholas I's death) confirmed that much remained to be done in the state-owned countryside. When, for example, some of the state peasants in Smolensk were offered the chance of resettlement in Siberia, they declared their willingness to go on the grounds that 'Here, nothing but death remains'.[37] The ministry's agent in Pskov lamented the local state peasants' incorrect use of their land, the poor quality of the local soil, the shortage of hayfields and livestock, the poor quality of seed, incorrect crop choices, the shortage of wood, and the absence of navigable rivers and of good communications in general. Other local officials made comparable remarks. One complained about the scattered nature of peasant landholdings, another about the fragmentation of peasant holdings which resulted from the practice of partible inheritance. Others called for irrigation schemes, canals to improve communications, agricultural education, and government-appointed agronomists. Kiselev may have achieved a good deal, but there were limits to what could be done with the unpromising resources of which he had charge.

SERFS

Despite the drawbacks of the state peasant reform, however, the energy with which the government pursued it showed that, when it had a free hand, it was prepared to introduce potentially far-reaching changes. In respect of the privately owned half of the peasantry – the serfs – Nicholas I is usually said to have done almost nothing. It is true that at the beginning of his reign he seemed to be interested only in keeping them in their place. In a major statement on rural matters of May 1826 he condemned rumours that emancipating serfs formed part of his agenda and enjoined provincial governors to bring rumour-mongers to book. When, in 1827, the tsar forbade serf entry into gymnasia and universities on the grounds that it had a deleterious effect on pupils from other social groups and gave the serfs ideas above their station, he seemed to be rejecting the idea of social mobility out of hand. Yet Nicholas also gave many signs that he thought serfdom had to be modified. In 1827–8 he placed constraints on the gentry's right to send serfs to Siberia. In 1829 he set up a committee to study (once more) the question of selling serfs without land. The reduction of military service from twenty-five years to fifteen in 1834 made one of the most hated of the serfs' obligations less objectionable and gave rise to fears among the gentry that an increasing number of demobilized soldiers would return to the countryside as freemen and pass on their experience in the handling of weapons. The committee of 1835–6 which set in train plans for improving the lot of the state peasants also considered a proposal from the Minister of Finances for the landless emancipation of the serfs. In 1841 gentry who did not own populated estates were forbidden to buy serfs without also buying the land to which they were attached. In 1842 gentry who had once been serfs were prevented from acquiring populated estates. In the same year a 'Law on Obligated Peasants' permitted landlords and serfs to put their relations on a more coherent footing. Landlords were to retain ownership of the land but to be able, if they chose, to give serfs the use of specific parts of it in return for agreed payment in labour, money or produce. The arbitrary nature of landlord power, in other words, could be limited by the drawing up of written contracts. A law of 1844 made it possible for household serfs (*dvorovye liudi*) to buy themselves out altogether. In 1845 the government collected detailed statements of the duties performed by serfs in the western provinces of the empire. Drawing up such 'inventories' was a longstanding practice of the predominantly Polish gentry in this part of St Petersburg's domains, but previously there had been no obligation upon them to submit the inventories to the Russian authorities. The Poles rightly took the view that St Petersburg's new-found interest presaged the reduction of their authority. In 1845–6 limits were set on the rights of the gentry to punish serfs physically. In March 1846 the tsar set up a committee under the future Alexander II to discuss 'On the Eradication of Serfdom in Russia', a paper by the Minister of Internal Affairs which proposed working towards emancipation by means of applying to landlord–peasant relations in general a procedure similar to that which had been inaugurated in the western provinces. In the wake of this committee Kiselev pressed for giving serfs the right to own immovable property, a right which they acquired in March 1848 on condition that their owners assented and that the land they acquired was unpopulated. In November 1847 the tsar accepted another committee's recommendation that serfs be permitted to buy their freedom if the estate on which they lived was being sold at auction. In 1853, finally, the leasehold ownership of populated estates was forbidden.

Put like this, Nicholas I's measures in respect of the serfs can be made to look respectable. Historians, however, have given them a very bad press. The late-nineteenth-century student of Russian serfdom, Vasilii Semevskii, called the government's use of inventories in the western provinces a measure which 'was not devoid of results which were to a certain extent beneficial',[38] but he thought the rest of Nicholas's steps insignificant. The tsar thought differently. Of the Law on Obligated Peasants of 1842 he said to his wife: 'I am on the point of undertaking the most significant act of my reign. I am putting to the State Council a plan which represents the first step towards the emancipation of the serfs'.[39] Nicholas introduced the plan in a speech which is usually cited as an example of his extreme pusilla-nimity, but it is not surprising that, in addressing the State Council, he tem-pered the wind to the shorn lamb. It may be that the later passages of the speech, in which the tsar spoke of the landowners' propensity to misuse their authority and said that 'it is clear to every right-minded observer that the present state of affairs cannot continue for ever' should be taken more seriously than the earlier part, in which he declared that he would never go so far as to give the serfs their freedom.[40] In drawing up the Law on Obli-gated Peasants Nicholas was influenced by the failure of Alexander I's Free Agriculturalists Law of 1803, a measure which had come to nothing be-cause it required the gentry to part with some of their land. Because the law of 1842 involved the regularization of landlord–serf relations rather than the alienation of immovable property, the tsar hoped that it would be received with greater warmth than its predecessor. If it was, he could go further in the direction of improving the lot of the serfs. At least one con-temporary came close to understanding the direction in which his thoughts were tending. The government censor Aleksandr Nikitenko, who had him-self been born a serf, confided to his diary that the Law on Obligated Peas-ants could not be 'a final measure; it's much too strange and contrary to our politics'. Either the regime intended to go further, or it had somehow ensured the acquiescence of the gentry by issuing 'supplementary direc-tives' which it was keeping to itself.[41] The evidence of the law of 1847, under which serfs could buy their freedom if the estate on which they lived was being sold at auction, supports the view that Nicholas intended to go further. This was the one serf measure of the reign which permitted serfs to take action without securing the compliance of their owners. Since many landowners were in debt and many estates were sold at auction, the law was potentially far-reaching in its implications. After twenty years on the throne, Nicholas had apparently decided to start overriding the interests of the gentry.

Unfortunately for the interests of serfs, landowners were equal to the government's admittedly tentative attack on their power. They took almost no notice of pro-serf legislation which required their cooperation. The liberally orientated soldier Mikhail Vorontsov was the only noble to respond immediately to the law of 1842, and by 1858 only five others had followed his example. The 1844 legislation on household serfs seems to have borne no fruit at all. Whatever the theoretical significance of the law of 1847, the government repealed it after landowners complained that it undermined their ability to secure loans and encouraged serfs to bankrupt themselves in the effort to raise money for the purchase of their freedom. The replacement law of 1849 brought serf 'buy-outs' into line with the other serf legislation of the reign, by making them dependent on landlord consent. Thus the regime's one positive attempt to increase serfs' freedom of action came to nothing, and its overall record of achievement on the peasant question was slight.

Nevertheless, the evidence for Nicholas I's longstanding interest in the amelioration of the peasants' condition is substantial, and the dramatic changes which took place in the next reign were facilitated, in part, by the information-gathering which took place in his time. Before his handling of rural matters is condemned, moreover, the context in which he was acting must be examined more closely. While there is evidence for the view that he did little to improve the lot of privately owned peasants because he was afraid of their owners, and while it was clearly the case that the gentry deplored measures which prevented them from exercising untrammelled authority over their labour force, the tsar may have had another reason for hurrying slowly. Paradoxical though it may seem, radical changes may not have been necessary. The fact that serfdom was abolished six years after Nicholas's death implies that there was a great deal wrong with it in his lifetime, but recent work has cast doubt on this view. Remarkably enough, the striking thing about Nicholas I's attitude towards the peasants may not be that he failed to make sweeping changes in their condition, but that he tried repeatedly to do so. He may actually have been more energetic than the situation required. This paradox breaks down into two more: the possibility that serfdom was less deplorable in the second quarter of the nineteenth century than it is usually made out to be, and the difficulty of explaining, if this was the case, why the tsar did anything about it at all.

At the end of what remains the most important study of landlord–peasant relations in pre-emancipation Russia, Jerome Blum discussed the five reasons most frequently given for the abolition of serfdom in 1861: its economic inefficiency, the threat posed by serf uprisings, a growing conviction that shackling the lower orders was immoral, the need to transform Russian society in the wake of defeat in the Crimean War, and the personal conviction of the 'tsar-liberator', Alexander II. Blum spent most of his time on proponents of the view that serfdom was a drag on the Russian economy. They claimed, he said, that 'The old system, because of its inefficiency, low productivity, and restrictions on free movement, was an obstacle to the growth of towns, commerce, and industry'; that 'Lack of capital, the low productivity of serf labor, and the nature of the structure of the entire "feudal" economy, blocked the introduction of technical improvements and efficient organization'; that attempts to modernize the Russian economy without abolishing serfdom produced 'violently fluctuating prices, an absolute decline in the number of serfs, increasing seignorial indebtedness, and a quickening in the tempo of peasant unrest'; and that by the middle of the nineteenth century Russian serf-owners had been convinced of the need to move from a servile to a free labour force, provided they did not have to grant land as well as freedom to their former serfs.[42]

All these claims may be doubted. Serfdom may not have been unduly damaging either to the fortunes of landlords, or to the development of new sorts of economic activity, or even to the serfs themselves. Serfdom seems to have remained profitable. The notion that the Russian gentry were mortgaged up to the hilt, for example, appears to have been greatly exaggerated. A recent essay puts serf-owners' debts in the 1850s at only 27 per cent of the value of their estates, which is much less than half the percentage which used to be given. By way of comparison, the authors of the new estimate point out that in 1980 'the ratio of all liabilities to all nonfinancial assets on American farms was 17.8 per cent'.[43] Russian landlords had certainly not been convinced by economic hardship that the legal relationship between master and man had to be transformed. They were not short of labour. Indeed, the fact that they were taking a much larger proportion of the land into their direct charge seems to indicate that they were confident of finding the labour to work it. Where their need for labour was greatest, in the central agricultural zone of the empire, serfs were thick on the ground. More than two-thirds of Russian serfs lived in fourteen provinces around Moscow. Whereas, at the end of the eighteenth century, serfs had farmed 82.3 per cent of privately owned land for their own purposes, in the 1850s they farmed only 34 per cent. Just before serfdom was abolished, in other words, about two-thirds of the Russian Empire's privately owned land was being exploited by the gentry in their own interest. Gentry who were farming additional land presumably did not feel that a serf-based society was unworkable. Nor did gentry whose property lay in parts of the country where serfs were a rare commodity. Because their land was rarely worth cultivating intensively, they were no more likely to advocate a free labour market than gentry for whom finding labour was easy. Neither serfs nor freemen would have enabled them to make profits out of agriculture.

Gentry who possessed few serfs of their own but needed labourers could probably have found them. All figures indicate a rapid increase in the size of the Russian hired labour force in the half-century before emancipation. Hired labourers, however, tended to be engaged in non-agricultural activities. If serfdom continued to facilitate the exploitation of the land, it also permitted economic diversification. Because only a relatively small fraction of the Russian Empire's territory was suitable for agricultural exploitation, landowners often permitted serfs to pay their dues in rent (*obrok*) rather than labour (*barshchina*). Serfs on *obrok* found the money they needed in many different ways. Some engaged in non-agricultural pursuits in the countryside; others left the land to find sources of revenue elsewhere. Far from objecting to these forms of employment, nobles promoted them. Some set up industrial enterprises on their property. An official report of 1813–14 showed that 64 per cent of mining manufactures, 78 per cent of woollen cloth and 60 per cent of paper production issued from gentry-owned enterprises. In the main, however, gentry who put their serfs on *obrok* left them to find their own means of paying their dues. Many went to the towns. Peasant migrants (*otkhodniki*) made up almost half the population of St Petersburg in 1840 (nearly a quarter of a million people). Industry benefited from arrangements which allowed serfs to leave their villages. In 1825 seven branches of factory production employed 31.7 per cent of the entire labour force of the empire. Thomas Esper has argued that 'serfdom in the Urals did not have any appreciable [negative] impact on the level of technological development or on the economic condition of the metallurgical industry'.[44] If Russian metal production was less sophisticated than metal production elsewhere, the reason was not to be found in the social status of the country's labour force. Far from blocking the development of Russian industry, the existence of serfdom may positively have encouraged it.

Richard L. Rudolph has claimed in an ambitious recent essay that the 'crisis of Russian serfdom' in the first half of the nineteenth century was not a crisis of decay but a crisis of transformation. In Rudolph's view, serfs were changing their forms of economic activity at such a rapid rate that the Russian Empire can be said to have been experiencing 'proto-industrialization'; 'the extent to which the peasantry provided the source for the development of mercantile and entrepreneurial activities', he claims, 'is probably unparalleled in Europe'.[45] The fact that more than 80 per cent of Russian nobles owned a hundred serfs or fewer creates the impression that the empire consisted almost entirely of small estates, but more than 80 per cent of serfs actually lived on estates of a hundred serfs or more. Concentrations of serfs were usually large enough, in other words, to make cottage industry viable. Both landlords and serfs seem to have been shrewd enough to recognize the fact. Even parts of the country where serfs continued to perform labour services can be integrated into the argument which presents the pre-emancipation Russian economy as 'proto-industrial'. Edgar Melton's study of the southern province of Kursk, a region in which *barshchina* predominated, points out, first, that Kursk peasants produced marketable woven fibre which gave them a cash income and so turned them into potential purchasers of proto-industrial goods produced elsewhere, and second, that peasants in Kursk supplied other peasants with food, thus freeing them for proto-industrial activities.[46] Analyses of Russian serfdom which highlight its inflexibility thus have to be reworked. Olga Crisp goes so far as to say that 'economic progress ... not only failed in Russia to sweep away serfdom, but indeed strengthened it and adapted it to manu-facturing'.[47]

Landlords may not have been the only beneficiaries of the changes which were taking place in the economy. Serfs were no doubt unsettled by having to engage in new forms of economic activity (often far from the es-tates on which they had been born), but their lives were not uniformly de-pressing. A few made a great deal of money. Nikolai Shipov showed such entrepreneurial skill that at one point, in the 1820s, he was being charged 5,000 rubles in *obrok*. The first Savva Morozov (1770–1860), founder of one of the greatest of the Russian Empire's industrial dynasties, raised 17,000 rubles to buy his freedom in 1820. These were not the only peasants who took goods to market. The authorities encouraged peasants to engage in trade by not requiring them to gain entry to the merchant estate in order to deal in their produce; between 1814 and 1883 no special documents were needed to participate in commercial activity at the empire's many fairs. Ex-perts on the development of the flow of goods in imperial Russia have esti-mated that in the 1850s between 11 and 17 per cent of peasant grain production was surplus to the peasants' basic requirements. They have also calculated that between 1767 and 1858 peasant consumption of manu-factured goods went up thirty-four times, and that between the mid-eight-eenth and the mid-nineteenth centuries the tax burdens on the peasantry rose less rapidly than the prices of farm produce, with the result that peas-ants were likely to have cash to spare.[48] Because speaking of the peasantry as a whole masks differences between the various parts of the country and between different categories of peasant, some peasants may have been doing very well while others slipped backwards; but a strong case can be made for the view that peasants were becoming more prosperous.

Serfs who worked in the Urals iron industry, therefore, may not have been alone in enjoying 'a level of material prosperity that compares quite favorably with contemporary conditions in western Europe and in Great Britain'.[49] The acid test of the serfs' well-being, however, is the condition of the majority who stayed on the land. Ultimately, arguments about their economic standing turn on the ratio of grain harvested to grain sown. If it was as low as 3:1, peasants must have spent the bulk of their time worrying about where the next meal was coming from. Although Jerome Blum re-jected the centrality of economic arguments in the explanation of the serfs' eventual emancipation, he still believed that grain yields in Russia in the first half of the nineteenth century were lower than anywhere else in Eu-rope and 'just about the same as they had been ... as far back as the six-teenth century'.[50] In Blum's view, Russian grain production increased only because new areas of land were brought under the plough. Increases, moreover, failed to keep pace with the growth of the population. Only limited economic advance was to be expected if the grain yield stood at

3:1. It may, however, have been much higher. Steven Hoch claims a ratio of 5:1 for the empire as a whole and 8.5:1 for the Tambov village of Petrovskoe on which he concentrated. The inhabitants of Petrovskoe, he says, 'were ... better nourished than their French or Belgian counterparts at the turn of the nineteenth century and certainly had a better diet than most persons living in developing countries today'.[51] Since a specialist on the province of Riazan' has further discerned a 'steady upward trend in the [peasants'] mean age at marriage',[52] it may be that serfs were producing not only more food but also fewer children. If so, the problem of food distribution was diminishing at the same time as the problem of food supply.

But the possibility that serfs were producing fewer children may indicate serfdom's degeneracy rather than its viability. The slaves of the American South are usually thought to be the only community of bondmen that continued to grow in size after enslavement came to an end. Since enserfment was rare in the Russian Empire after tsars stopped giving away state peasants to the gentry in 1801, serfs in the first half of the nineteenth century ought have been experiencing a demographic crisis. Whether they were is an issue that has generated intense controversy. Their numbers were declining both relatively and, to a lesser extent, absolutely, but the reasons for the decline are uncertain. In 1857 Nikolai Bunge, a professor at Kiev University, claimed serfs were fewer in number because their material circumstances were deteriorating. The government statistician Aleksandr Troinitskii accepted that the serfs' fertility and mortality were respectively lower and higher than those of other estates, but he nevertheless believed that the decline in their numbers was illusory. Because many serfs were being transferred into other legal categories (particularly by way of military recruitment and sale to the state), he held that the number of serfs at any one time was significantly smaller than the proportion of the population which had belonged to the serf estate at one time or another. Scholars have never agreed on the question whether the serfs' conditions prevented them from growing in number, but it is probably fair to say that the heirs of Troinitskii have made a better case for their point of view than the heirs of Bunge.[53]

If it is correct to argue that, from the point of view of the economic development of the Russian Empire, serfdom was much less damaging than it has been made out to be, why did Nicholas I feel the need to tinker with it? He made his most important remarks on the subject in his speech to the State Council of March 1842, in which he held, among other things, that 'The Pugachev rebellion showed what the masses' unpredictabilty can lead to'.[54] The reference to the Cossack-led rising of 1773 implied a fear of peasant violence. Perhaps Nicholas had been influenced by an alarmist report from the Third Department which had passed across his desk in 1839. 'In general,' the report declared, 'the entire mood of the people is orientated towards a single goal – emancipation'. According to the Third Department, Russian peasants could not understand why many of the empire's minorities were free when they were not, nor why some categories of peasant were treated more generously than others. They thought the gentry were preventing the tsar from freeing them. They envied soldiers on long leave from the army (who had been serfs before they were recruited). Since, in the Third Department's view, the huge number of civil servants who were landless nobles had nothing to lose from disorder in the countryside, pressure for the abolition of serfdom was likely to grow at the centre as well as on the ground. 'Overall,' said the police, 'serfdom is a powder cellar below the state'; 'It is necessary to start [on emancipation] sometime and with something, and it is better to start gradually, carefully, rather than wait until a start is made from the bottom, by the people'.[55]

Peasants appeared to be 'making a start' on emancipation at the very time of the Third Department report. Indeed, they seemed to be some way down the road. According to one set of data there were 148 peasant disturbances between 1826 and 1834, 216 between 1835 and 1844, and 348 between 1845 and 1854. Peasants killed 173 landlords and bailiffs between 1835 and 1854 and attempted to kill 75 more. 'Out of 261 risings between 1836 and 1854 for which the details of pacification are known, troops were used to quell 132'.[56] Disturbances peaked, moreover, in years of general political uncertainty. The high points between 1796 and 1856 were 1797, 1812, 1826 and 1848 – just after the death of Catherine the Great, at the time of the Napoleonic invasion, just after the Decembrist uprising, and at a time of pan-European revolution. According to Peter Kolchin, serfs 'demonstrated an impressive awareness ... of what was going on in the country'.[57] In the disturbances of 1848 they seemed even to demonstrate an awareness of what was going on abroad.

But despite the signs of growing peasant assertiveness, the Russia of Nicholas I did not experience anything on the scale of the Bolotnikov, Razin, Bulavin and Pugachev rebellions of the seventeenth and eighteenth centuries. The tsar admitted in his speech of 1842 that, since Pugachev, disturbances had 'always been successfully brought to an end'. At the end of the 1970s a group of Soviet scholars asked why, if the last 'peasant war' in Russia took place in the eighteenth century, the 'peasant movement' of the first half of the nineteenth century was still 'the most important factor in the abolition of serfdom'.[58] It may not have been. Although the total number of disturbances occasioned by serfs was growing, and although it seems that a desire for freedom rather than mere dissatisfaction played a growing part in serfs' outlook on life, in the first half of the nineteenth century individual manifestations of peasant discontent were small scale. At the turn of the eighteenth and nineteenth centuries private landowners had extended their holdings into the southern and south-eastern parts of the empire where the 'peasant wars' of the early modern period had taken place. Cossacks had been transformed from nomads into settlers and the imperial government had established effective control in areas where it had formerly been impotent. Upheavals were being dealt with before they had a chance to coalesce. Despite a certain amount of evidence to the contrary, serfs were probably no more outward-looking than they had been in the past. The latest work on the 'social mood of the serfs' in the reign of Nicholas I does not support the view that the imperial government was obliged to improve the lot of the serfs because of a rising tide of serf protest. On the contrary, it argues that serfs remained essentially deferential. The fears expressed by the Third Department in 1839 were exaggerated. Serfs expected the tsar to free them, but were prepared to wait until he did so. In so far as their political views can be ascertained, they were monarchists. The years 1797 and 1826 were highpoints of the 'peasant movement' because new monarchs had recently come to the throne and peasants were trying to encourage them to have the courage of their supposedly reformist convictions. Serfs got excited when new legislative acts inclined them to believe that, at last, the autocrat was about to take action. They seem not to have been motivated by hostility to exploitation *per se*, but rather by changes in their circumstances – even changes designed to make their lives bearable. They were agitated by the introduction of 'inventories' of their duties in the western Ukraine after 1845, despite the fact that the inventories were supposed to set limits to the landlords' power over them. They objected strongly to attempts to make them sow potatoes, despite the fact that the new crop offered them a better prospect of coming through times of dearth. Their political awareness led them to respond to events but not to take initiatives. It could be argued that the government was itself responsible for many of the serf disturbances it was apparently anxious to avoid. If it had done nothing, serfs might have been quieter than they were. In 1989 the major living Soviet historian of the emancipation of the serfs admitted that 'Soviet literature frequently exaggerates the part played by peasant movements in the build-up to the abolition of serfdom'.[59] Nicholas I and Alexander II were both prepared to raise the spectre of peasant violence, but not necessarily because they were afraid of it. They may have made use of it in order to advance their policies.[60]

The question, then, remains: if a serf-based economy was viable and peasant upheavals were manageable, why did the Russian government consider altering the relations between master and man?

There seem to be four possible answers. First, in line with his promotion of non-noble bureaucrats, the tsar may have wanted to chip away at the gentry's economic well-being. He needed nobles to keep order in the countryside and could not afford to attack them head on, but he was not averse to reminding them where ultimate authority resided.

Second, the tsar could not guess what historians were going to say about serfdom a century after its demise. There is a difference between views of serfdom drawn up after its disappearance and the view of people who lived with it in the first half of the nineteenth century. Not surprisingly, the former are more dispassionate than the latter. The fact that no major serf risings took place in the Russian Empire in the first half of the nineteenth century did not mean that Russians thought of them as a thing of the past. Reports drawn up by the Third Department implied that large-scale risings were possible. Whatever the truth of the matter, furthermore, mid-nineteenth-century Russians were unanimous in the view that free labour was more profitable than serf labour. 'The development of industry', wrote Kiselev's deputy at the Ministry of State Properties in 1841, 'requires not only protection of the individual and his property, but also freedom to organize one's time and labour and to choose one's place of residence. Naturally, therefore, the status of serf, which binds a man to the land, hinders the development of industry, even among peasants on *obrok*'.[61] Ivan Turgenev's short story 'Khor' and Kalinych' and Aleksandr Koshelev's essay *Enthusiasm Works Better than Constraint* (*Okhota pushche nevoli*), both of which appeared in 1847, left no doubt in the minds of their readers that serfs worked harder for themselves than they did for their landlords. Boris Chicherin's assertion in 1856 that only free labour could 'significantly promote industry' may have been false, but Chicherin spoke for all thinking contemporaries, including most people in authority.[62]

Third, apart from believing that serfdom was unprofitable, many contemporaries thought it immoral. 'There is no doubt', wrote Chicherin, 'that serfdom has greatly contributed to the complete disappearance amongst us of the feeling that men and citizens are morally valuable. Without this feeling a man neither aspires to the heights, nor acts vigorously and energetically, nor senses what is legal and just'.[63] 'Formerly,' wrote August von Haxthausen, 'serfdom was not an unnatural, pernicious, and unsuitable institution, and it may even have been necessary for Russia's political development. ... Today [it] has become an unnatural relationship, and it is becoming more and more evident that in time it will be impossible to maintain this institution in its present form'.[64] When even a well-informed observer who did not desire the collapse of the Romanov regime argued that serfdom had to be brought to an end, the tsarist authorities were unlikely to be able to put it from their minds.

Fourth, and probably most important, serfdom was being abolished everywhere else in Europe. Outside the Russian Empire, thirty-seven European states embarked on serf emancipation in the eighteenth and nineteenth centuries. Thirty-six of them took action before St Petersburg. So long as it retained a serf-based economy, the tsarist regime ran the risk of being unable to adjust to changing times as rapidly as the countries against which it measured its achievements. The degree of economic diversification which serfdom permitted was too small to prevent the empire's international authority from declining. The Russian government had to find ways of accelerating the entry of serfs into non-serf estates. It had to bring the empire's estates system into line with the way in which the social structure was actually developing. The Russian economy may have been further behind the rest of Europe in the first half of the nineteenth century than it was when serfdom was introduced. In 1860 fewer than 1 million of the empire's total population of about 74 million worked in factory industry. The empire contained 1 merchant for every 1,127 inhabitants in 1850, at a time when Prussia contained 1 merchant to 118. The ratio of townsmen to villagers was 1:17 in 1794 and 1:11.4 in 1840, whereas the rates for Britain and

France in 1840 were respectively 1:2 and 1:4.8. 'In [mid-nineteenth-century] England ... 50 per cent of the population lived in cities ... [in] Russia ... only 7.8 per cent'.[65] Russian communications were improving only gradually. The postal authorities gave the impression in a report of 1850 that the empire was much better integrated than it had been when Nicholas ascended the throne twenty-five years previously, but the improvement was from a very low starting-point. Russian rivers were often frozen, and anyway ran only north–south. 'By the 1860s, Russia could boast only 9000 versts (6000 miles) of macadam road'.[66] Russia lagged way behind Europe in the development of railways. An Austrian, Franz Anton von Gerstner, proposed constructing them in early 1835. He was backed by the Minister of Communications and got the go-ahead within six months, but the authorities were not really enthusiastic. Although Russia's first railway opened in 1838 and the line from St Petersburg to Moscow was completed in 1851, at Nicholas's death in 1855 only Italy and Spain, of European countries, had fewer miles of track. Whether or not economic advances took place in the last half-century of serfdom, much more rapid diversification was essential if the Russian Empire was to maintain, let alone increase, its influence in the world at large. The chances of increasing the rate of diversification were small when life in the countryside continued to be life at the margins. Even Steven Hoch does not claim that the lives of mid-nineteenth-century Russian serfs were idyllic. Rather, he believes that considerations other than those usually emphasized should be given pride of place in explaining their difficulties. 'In the small rural worlds of servile Russia,' he says, 'dearth and disease were far more potent forces than czar or landlord'.[67] From the point of view of the serf, the difference was not very great.

CONCLUSION

Thus Nicholas I may have believed that serfdom benefited the gentry rather than the state, that it was unlikely to be as profitable as free labour, that it was immoral, and that it prevented the Russian Empire from keeping up with its international competitors. A subliminal recognition of the force of these arguments probably gave rise to the changes which took place in the circumstances of the serfs in the 1830s and 1840s. Since mid-nineteenth-century Russian serfdom seems to have been economically viable, the tsar should be forgiven for not doing more.

Nicholas can be defended, therefore, from the charge that his regime was inert. In administrative matters he was imaginative and in social relations he was perhaps as progressive as the situation required. In what remains the outstanding analysis of his domestic policies, Aleksandr Kizevetter rejected the idea that the tsar engaged in 'the politics of stagnation' and asserted that, on the contrary, a major feature of his reign 'consisted ... of the self-confidence with which the ruling bureaucracy addressed itself to resolving broad and fundamental state tasks'. Why then has Nicholas been so vilified? Probably, as Kizevetter pointed out, because he was committed to 'the rejection of all kinds of social spontaneity and initiative'. The tsar knew that changes had to be undertaken, but was determined not to allow them to be promoted by any movement or group beyond the control of the government. He believed that reform could be achieved by the government acting alone. This shortsightedness ensured that his regime eventually became 'a victim of its own powerlessness'.[68] Refusing to involve the community at large in the pursuit of his objectives was Nicholas's greatest failing. Because educated people were not made privy to the government's ideas, they assumed that the regime had stopped thinking about the empire's problems. They therefore felt obliged to develop ideas of their own. How they were able to do so and what their ideas consisted of forms the subject-matter of the next chapter.

NOTES

1. John Keep, 'The Military Style of the Romanov Rulers', *War & Society* 1 (1983), 66.
2. W. Bruce Lincoln, 'The Composition of the Imperial Russian State Council under Nicholas I', CASS 10 (1976), 369.
3. N. Wrangel, *From Serfdom to Bolshevism: Memoirs* (New York, 1971 [1st edn 1927]), p. 14.
4. S. A. Artem'ev, 'Sledstvie i sud nad dekabristami', VI, 1970 no. 2, p. 115.
5. B. Syroechkovskii, ed., 'Iz zapisok Nikolaia I o 14 dekabria 1825 g.', KA 6 (1924), 226.
6. Neil Cornwell, *V. F. Odoyevsky: His Life, Times and Milieu* (London, 1986), p. 197.
7. N. Barsukov, *Zhizn' i trudy M. P.Pogodina* (22 vols, SPB, 1888–1910), iv. 83.
8. P. S. Squire, *The Third Department: The Establishment and Practices of the Political Police in the Russia of Nicholas I* (Cambridge, 1968), p. 125; Cynthia H. Whittaker, *The Origins of Modern Russian Education: An Intellectual Biography of Count Sergei Uvarov, 1786–1855* (DeKalb, Ill., 1984), p. 237.
9. Neil Malcolm, 'Ideology and Intrigue in Russian Journalism under Nicholas I: *Moskovskii telegraf* and *Severnaya pchela*', unpublished D.Phil. dissertation, Oxford University, 1974, p. 257.
10. Marquis de Custine, *Letters from Russia*, ed. and tr. Robin Buss (Harmondsworth, 1991), p. 87.
11. Jennifer Baker, 'Glinka's *A Life for the Tsar* and "Official Nationality"', *Renaissance and Modern Studies* 24 (1980), 94.
12. S. M. Solov'ev, *Izbrannye trudy; Zapiski* (Moscow, 1983), p. 309.
13. B. N. Chicherin, *Vospominaniia: Moskva sorokovykh godov* (Moscow, 1929), p. 158.

14. I. Ia. Shchipanov, ed., *Izbrannye sotsial'no- politicheskie i filosofskie proizvedeniia dekabristov* (3 vols, Moscow, 1951), i. 576.

15. V. V. Poznanskii, *Ocherk formirovaniia russkoi natsional'noi kul'tury: Pervaia polovina XIX veka* (Moscow, 1975), p. 144.

16. N. P. Eroshkin, *Krepostnicheskoe samoderzhavie i ego politicheskie instituty* (Moscow, 1981), p. 188.

17. P. A. Zaionchkovskii, *Pravitel'stvennyi apparat samoderzhavnoi Rossii v XIXv.* (Moscow, 1978), p. 109.

18. Eroshkin, *Krepostnicheskoe samoderzhavie* (above, n. 16), p. 190.

19. A. A. Kizevetter, 'Vnutrenniaia politika v tsarstvovanie imperatora imperatora Nikolaia Pavlovicha', in Kizevetter, *Istoricheskie ocherki* (Moscow, 1912), p. 452.

20. Eroshkin, *Krepostnicheskoe samoderzhavie* (above, n. 16), p. 141.

21. Ibid., p. 139.

22. A. Sergeev, ed., 'Gr. A. Kh. Benkendorf o Rossii v 1827– 1830 gg. (Ezhegodnye otchety III otdeleniia i korpusa zhandarmov)', KA 37 (1929), 138–74, and 38 (1930), 109–47 (quotations from pp. 153, 165, 126).

23. Kizevetter, 'Vnutrenniaia politika' (above, n. 19), p. 456.

24. Ibid., 460.

25. V. A. Nardova, *Gorodskoe samoupravlenie v Rossii v 60-kh – nachale 90–kh godov XIX v.: Pravitel'stvennaia politika* (Leningrad, 1984), p. 15.

26. Janet Hartley, 'Town government in Saint Petersburg Guberniya after the Charter to the towns of 1785', SEER 62 (1984), 84.

27. Quotation from N. P. Eroshkin, 'Chinovnichestvo v Rossii', in E. M. Zhukov et al., eds, *Sovetskaia istoricheskaia entsiklopediia* (16 vols, Moscow, 1961–76), xvi. 46; Russian ratios from Zaionchkovskii, *Pravitel'stvennyi apparat* (above, n. 17), p. 221; British and French ratios calculated from S. Frederick Starr, *Decentralization and Self-Government in Russia, 1830–1870* (Princeton, NJ, 1972), p. 48.

28. W. Bruce Lincoln, 'The Daily Life of St. Petersburg Officials in the Mid Nineteenth Century', OSP 8 (1975), 95, 92.

29. Zaionchkovskii, *Pravitel'stvennyi apparat* (above, n. 17), p. 115.

30. Walter M. Pintner, 'Civil Officialdom and the Nobility in the 1850s', in Walter McKenzie Pintner and Don Karl Rowney, eds, *Russian Officialdom: The Bureaucratization of Russian Society from the Seventeenth to the Twentieth Century* (Chapel Hill, NC, 1980), pp. 246–7.

31. A. Romanovich-Slavatinskii, *Dvorianstvo v Rossii ot nachala XVIII veka do otmeny krepostnogo prava* (St Petersburg, 1870), p. I.

32. V. A. Fedorov, *Sbornik dokumentov po istorii SSSR dlia seminarskikh i prakticheskikh zaniatii (period kapitalizma): Pervaia polovina XIX veka* (Moscow, 1974), p. 82.

33. Shchipanov, *Izbrannye proizvedeniia dekabristov* (above, n. 14), i. 568.

34. L. V. Vyskochkov, 'Nekotorye dannye dlia biudzhetov gosudarstvennykh krest'ian peterburgskoi gubernii pervoi poloviny XIX v.', in A. G. Man'kov et al., eds, *Gosudarstvennye uchrezhdeniia i klassovye otnosheniia v otechestvennoi istorii: sbornik statei* (2 vols, Moscow and Leningrad, 1980), ii. 186.

35. P. D. Kiselev, 'Obozrenie upravleniia Gosudarstvennykh Imushchestv za poslednie 25 let s 20 noiabria 1825 po 20 noiabria 1850 g.', SIRIO 98 (1896), 472.

36. Ibid., p. 476.

37. T. A. Koniukhova, ed., 'O khoziaistvennom polozhenii gosudarstvennykh krest'ian okrain Rossii (1855 g.)', IA, 1960 no. 4, p. 147.

38. V. I. Semevskii, *Krest'ianskii vopros v Rossii v XVIII i pervoi polovine XIX veka* (2 vols, SPB, 1888), ii. 535.

39. Zaionchkovskii, *Pravitel'stvennyi apparat* (above, n. 17), p. 109.

40. Fedorov, *Sbornik dokumentov* (above, n. 32), pp. 74–5.

41. Aleksandr Nikitenko, *The Diary of a Russian Censor*, abridged, ed. and tr. Helen Saltz Jacobson (Amherst, Mass., 1975), p. 86.

42. Jerome Blum, *Lord and Peasant in Russia from the Ninth to the Niineteenth Century* (Princeton, NJ, 1961), pp. 611–18, esp. 612–13.

43. Evsey D. Domar and Mark J. Machina, 'On the Profitability of Russian Serfdom', J Ec Hist 44 (1984), 949.

44. Thomas Esper, 'The Incomes of Russian Serf Ironworkers in the Nineteenth Century', P & P 93 (1981), p. 157.

45. Richard L. Rudolph, 'Agricultural Structure and Proto-Industrialization in Russia: Economic Development with Unfree Labor', J Ec Hist 45 (1985), 53.

46. Herman Edgar Melton, Jr, 'Serfdom and the Peasant Economy in Russia: 1780–1861', unpublished PhD dissertation, Columbia University, 1984, passim.

47. Olga Crisp, *Studies in the Russian Economy before 1914* (London, 1976), p. 59.

48. B. N. Mironov, *Vnutrennii rynok Rossii vo vtoroi polovine XVIII – pervoi polovine XIXv.* (Leningrad, 1981), pp. 113, 97, 114–15.

49. Thomas Esper, 'The Condition of the Serf Workers in Russia's Metallurgical Industry, 1800–1861', JMH 50 (1978), 663.

50. Blum, *Lord and Peasant* (above, n. 42), p. 330.

51. Steven L. Hoch, *Serfdom and Social Control in Russia: Petrovskoe, a Village in Tambov* (Chicago, 1986), pp. 30–6, 50.

52. Peter Czap, Jr, 'Marriage and the Peasant Joint Family in the Era of Serfdom', in David L. Ransel, ed., *The Family in Imperial Russia: New Lines of Historical Research* (Urbana, Ill., 1978), p. 122.

53. For a summary of the debate by one of the 'heirs of Troinitskii' see P. G. Ryndziunskii, 'Vymiralo li krepostnoe krest'ianstvo pered reformoi 1861 g.?', VI, 1967 no. 7, esp. p. 57; for the continuing vitality of the 'heirs of Bunge' see V. M. Kabuzan, 'Krepostnoe krest'ianstvo Rossii v XVIII – 50-kh godakh XIX veka: chislennost', sostav i razmeshchenie', Istoriia SSSR, 1982 no. 3, pp. 67–85.

54. Fedorov, *Sbornik dokumentov* (above, n. 32), p. 74.

55. A. V. Predtechenskii, ed., *Krest'ianskoe dvizhenie v Rossii v 1826–1849 gg.* (Moscow, 1961), pp. 343–5.

56. Blum, *Lord and Peasant* (above, n. 42), p. 558.

57. Peter Kolchin, *Unfree Labor: American Slavery and Russian Serfdom* (Cambridge, Mass., 1987), p. 326.

58. V. I. Buganov et al., 'Nekotorye problemy istorii krest'ianstva SSSR dooktiabr'skogo perioda', Istoriia SSSR, 1979 no. 3, pp. 66–7.

59. L. G. Zakharova, 'Samoderzhavie, biurokratiia i reformy 60–kh godov XIX v. v Rossii', VI, 1989 no. 10, p. 8.

60. Sophisticated recent work on the political outlook of the Russian peasantry in the last half-century of serfdom includes P. G. Ryndziunskii, 'Ideinaia storona krest'ianskikh dvizhenii 1770 – 1850-kh godov i metody ee izucheniia', VI, 1983 no. 5, pp. 4–16; David Moon, *Russian Peasants and Tsarist Legislation on the Eve of Reform: Interaction between Peasants and Officialdom, 1825–1855* (Basingstoke and London, 1992); and M. A. Rakhmatullin, *Krest'ianskoe dvizhenie v velikorusskikh guberniiakh v 1826–1857gg.* (Moscow, 1990).

61. Fedorov, *Sbornik dokumentov* (above, n. 32), p. 34.

62. Anon. (B. N. Chicherin), 'O krepostnom sostoianii', in A. I. Gertsen and N. P. Ogarev, eds, *Golosa iz Rossii* (9 vols, London, 1856–60), ii. 136.
63. Ibid., ii. 160.
64. August von Haxthausen, *Studies on the Interior of Russia*, ed. S. Frederick Starr (Chicago, 1972), p. 74.
65. Anne Lincoln Fitzpatrick, *The Great Russian Fair: Nizhnii Novgorod, 1840–90* (Basingstoke and London, 1990), p. 1.
66. Ibid., p. 44.
67. Hoch, *Serfdom and Social Control* (above, n. 51), p. 2.
68. Kizevetter, 'Vnutrenniaia politika' (above, n. 19), pp. 419–20, 502.

CHAPTER SIX

The Emergence of the Russian Intelligentsia

INTRODUCTION

Russians who thought for themselves despaired of the empire's future after the defeat of Decembrism. They seemed to be wholly out on a limb. 'The élite,' to which the conspirators belonged, 'had not yet overcome its isolation from the people, and now its ties to the state were cut too'.[1] Although, with benefit of hindsight, some of Nicholas I's policies look constructive, to people who had been conditioned by the events of December 1825 to think of the authorities as their enemy they looked benighted. The tsar turned to outright oppression only in the last years of his reign, but never moved forward quickly or openly enough to prevent a widening of the gap between the state and the educated public. The result was the emergence of what subsequently came to be known as the Russian intelligentsia.

The intelligentsia was not solely the product of aristocratic disillusionment, for Nicholas I's domestic critics came from both privileged and non-privileged parts of the community. The emergence of the 'post-Decembrist' generation of dissidents ought to be related to the phenomenon of social displacement in general, not to the changing fortunes of any one section of Russian society. Some nobles felt they were moving downwards, some non-nobles felt that they ought to be moving upwards. The former sensed that the regime was becoming less reliant on them, the latter believed that their new-found education ought to enable them to improve their fortunes. Both sorts of dissident, the former reluctantly, the latter voluntarily, were looking for ways to express themselves which differed from those of their fathers. Although not everyone whose social status had changed or was changing felt himself to be at odds with the government (one of the outstanding proponents of 'Official Nationality', the university historian Mikhail Pogodin, was born a serf), many of the people whose views differed from those of the authorities found difficulty in reconciling the aspirations which their background or education had given them with the circumstances in which they found themselves.

DISCONTENTED NOBLES

Although the intelligentsia was socially diverse, in numerical terms its ranks were dominated by nobles. Privileged members of Russian society had been freed from their obligation to serve the state in 1762 and appeared to have benefited from Catherine the Great's Charter to the Nobility of 1785, but in reality they were being elbowed aside by the bureaucracy, losing their dominant position in the Russian polity, and becoming surplus to the requirements of the regime. The failure of Decembrism confirmed the fact. In 1887 Vasilii Kliuchevskii described the effect of reading, as a young man, Pushkin's *Evgenii Onegin*.[2] Why, he asked himself, did the talented fictional aristocrat on whom the work centred not feel at home in the society to which he belonged? The answer, Kliuchevskii believed, lay in the western-orientated culture of the Russian Empire's eighteenth-century nobility, which had cut nobles off from the traditions of their homeland. The shock of the French Revolution and the Napoleonic Wars had led the 'Onegin' generation to attempt reintegration, but its members were too far removed from their roots to succeed in this last-ditch endeavour. Russian nobles seemed to dwell on the fringes of their society. In 1851 they acquired the name 'superfluous men' from the title of a story by Ivan Turgenev, but the phenomenon of superfluity existed before words were found to describe it. It was not confined to the lands of the tsar. Lenore O'Boyle speaks of 'an excess of educated men' in early-nineteenth-century western Europe: 'too many men were educated for a small number of important and prestigious jobs, so that some men had to be content either with under-employment or with positions they considered below their capacities. There was a disparity between an individual's estimate of his own worth and the rewards in money and status that his society accorded him'.[3] This was precisely the difficulty in which many Russian nobles found themselves.

They responded to their marginalization in different ways. The disaster of 1825 ruled out direct action, but discussion, in one form or another, continued. Some of the regime's noble opponents who remained at liberty or who came to maturity after 1825 espoused new ideological currents which penetrated the Russian Empire from western Europe; some looked back with affection on what they thought had been happier times; some simply floundered; and some, like Onegin, surrendered to pessimism. None felt at home in his native environment. The Decembrist Mikhail Orlov probably suffered more than most, despite escaping punishment in 1826 because his brother was a highly placed police official. Physically free, he was spiritually emasculated. Alexander Herzen called him 'a lion in a cage' in the 1830s, consumed by a thirst for activity but obliged to spend his time on the study of chemistry.[4] Pushkin, by contrast, may have succeeded in working off some of his frustration in verse. A few members of the Russian elite expressed their disillusionment unequivocally. Petr Chaadaev had been a distinguished young army officer when, in 1820, Alexander I's hard-line response to the mutiny of the Semenovskii regiment in St Petersburg convinced him that he had to abandon the pursuit of a military career. Thereafter he failed 'to establish any role which ... would return to him the sense of importance that as a younger man he had once enjoyed'.[5] As early as 1817 Pushkin had deplored the fact that the Russian Empire was failing to provide Chaadaev with an appropriate outlet for his talents. By the end of the 1820s the quondam soldier was elaborating what became one of the most celebrated expressions of Russian backwardness, claiming, in the first of a series of 'philosophical letters', that 'There are no delightful recollections or charming images in our national memory, no powerful lessons in our national tradition'. 'We have not added a single idea to the sum total of human ideas'; 'we have not contributed to the progress of the human spirit, and what we have borrowed of this progress we have distorted'. Chaadaev deplored the divergence of Russian culture from that of western Europe and considered the British constitution 'the most representative of the modern spirit'.[6] His tract gave the impression that only a radical realignment of Russian culture could save the country from continuing degeneration. Not surprisingly, its language was far too strident for the cautious regime of Nicholas I. As we saw in Chapter Five, the author was officially pronounced a madman when his essay appeared in print in 1836.

Chaadaev was not alone. Independently, Ivan Kireevskii voiced similar ideas in an essay of 1832 which compared the 'enlightenment' of western Europe with that of the Russian Empire. By the standards of the 'educated' countries of Europe, Russia was young. Such enlightenment as she had was not a natural growth but an implant, 'so that its external form is still at odds with the form of our national identity'. Russia was not backward by accident. The country had never been part of the classical ancient world and lacked a church strong enough to knit its people together. 'If we had inherited the remnants of the classical world, our religion would have had more political force, we would have commanded a higher degree of education and greater spiritual unity, and, consequently, our very fragmentation [in the middle ages] would not have had the barbaric character it did have nor such deleterious consequences'. Because, in Kireevskii's view, Peter the Great's transformation of Russia in the early eighteenth century had had only limited effects, the empire still had a great deal of ground to make up; the 'Chinese wall' which separated Russia from the west was still standing.[7]

Kireevskii was refused permission to publish the part of his essay which related to Russia (though the text circulated in manuscript). His journal, *The European*, was closed down after two issues, and his literary career appeared to have been brought to an end almost before it had begun. If disgruntled Russian nobles were alone in feeling that the country had to change course, their dissatisfaction did not look as if it was going to amount to very much. They faced the prospect of becoming as frustrated as the talented churchman, Metropolitan Filaret of Moscow. 'Born to be a minister, he became an archpriest. If he had become a Roman Catholic prelate, he would have found himself an outlet, but he became a Russian archpriest, in whom the government admired intellect and talent only to the extent that they were employed exclusively in governmental service'.[8] On Filaret no less than on Mikhail Orlov, Petr Chaadaev, and the young Ivan Kireevskii, the effects of the atmosphere of Nicholaevan Russia seemed to be wholly damaging. The empire's privileged orders appeared to have been silenced.

COMMONERS

Not all the creative minds of the time of Nicholas I, however, belonged to the socially well placed. Members of non-noble estates gave heart to the 'superfluous' privileged by injecting additional life into discussions of Russian culture. A scion of the Siberian merchantry, Nikolai Polevoi, taught himself French and German, moved to Moscow, and 'There, without collaborators, without connections, with no literary reputation, conceived the idea of editing a monthly journal'.[9] *Moscow Telegraph*, which lasted from 1825 to 1834, bridged the gap between the defeat of the Decembrists and the point at which new ideas began to offer thinking Russians a respite from despair. Polevoi was not enamoured, for example, of the conservative philosophy underlying Karamzin's *History of the Russian State*, and subjected the work to a hostile review when its twelfth and final volume was published in 1829. 'As a littérateur, philosopher, and historian,' he wrote, 'Karamzin belonged to the last century'.[10] According to Polevoi, Karamzin's magnum opus emphasized the importance of the state at the expense of the community at large and implied that Russians should acquiesce in the oppression to which they were subjected. The journalist's rival *History of the Russian People* (1829–33) lacked the artistry and learning of its predecessor and failed to attract as many readers, but his appraisal of Karamzin nevertheless constituted one of the major contributions to a wide-ranging contemporary debate about the historical legitimacy of tsarist absolutism. Hostility to Karamzin was only one of the many ways in which Polevoi irritated the authorities. Eventually, they closed down his journal for criticizing a historical drama which dealt sycophantically with the Romanovs' accession to power. By then Uvarov, the Minister of Education, was convinced that the editor of the journal was bent on subversion. 'The Decembrists were not destroyed,' he said, 'and Polevoi wanted to be their organ'.[11] The most sustained effort to keep freedom of thought alive in the first years of the reign of Nicholas I appeared to have come to nothing.

In the year Polevoi's luck ran out, however, a second non-noble intellectual emerged who proved, between 1834 and his death in 1848, to be the central figure in the reorientation of Russian culture under Nicholas I. Born the son of a poor country doctor in the province of Penza in 1811, Vissarion Belinskii had been expelled from Moscow University and was trying to make a living by his pen. He was a man of violent likes and dislikes. Herzen claimed that he 'palpitated with indignation and groaned with rage at the eternal spectacle of Russian absolutism'.[12] Another contemporary pointed out that 'The topic of his speech, in the main, was either the unsparing demolition or the joyous, sincere praise of a work of literature, a social fact, a littérateur or a social activist'.[13] 'Unsparing demolition' was the keynote of his first essay, a ten-part diatribe entitled 'Literary Musings' in which he claimed that Russia had no literature worthy of the name. What the empire needed, Belinskii concluded, was 'learning! learning! learning!'[14] The essay ended, however, on a note of optimism. Russian education, in Belinskii's view, was already making rapid strides. This observation touched upon one of the principal reasons why Nicholas I's efforts to suppress initiatives from below were bound, in the long run, to fail.

The fact that domestic critics of the Russian Empire under Nicholas I included not only disgruntled aristocrats like Chaadaev and Kireevskii but also members of non-noble estates such as Polevoi and Belinskii showed that the 'learning' by which Belinskii set so much store was no longer accessible only to the privileged. Neither Polevoi nor Belinskii had benefited much from official educational institutions – the former was self-educated and the latter had failed to complete his university course – but many of their contemporaries had done so and a 'market for ideas' was growing. According to Herzen, writing in 1850, 'The thirst for instruction is taking hold of the entire new generation'.[15] This was an exaggeration, but figures indicate that the schools and universities on which the regime had been placing great emphasis since the 1780s were beginning to make significant strides. Whereas there had been about 62,000 pupils in the schools set up by Catherine the Great at the end of the eighteenth century, official educational establishments contained about a quarter of a million pupils in the 1830s. By 1856, the year after Nicholas I's death, 450,000 pupils were being educated in more than 8,000 schools. Secondary schools doubled their intake in the first ten years of Nicholas's reign; universities doubled theirs between 1836 and 1848. By one reckoning, the number of people receiving education went up 74.6 per cent between 1808 and 1834 and a further 80 per cent between 1834 and 1856.[16] The empire was still educating only 1 out of 208 of its inhabitants in 1834 and 1 out of 143 in 1856, but the upward trend of the figures was evident.

The government would have preferred not to allow members of nonprivileged estates to profit unduly from the educational opportunities it was providing. When Nicholas published the sentences on the Decembrists in July 1826 he ascribed their misdemeanours, in part, to the false direction taken by the Russian educational system under his brother. His statutes of 1828 on primary and secondary education and 1835 on universities seemed to subject educational institutions to greater central control.

The historian Sergei Solov'ev, who grew up under Nicholas, wrote of his reign that 'enlightenment ceased to be meritorious and became a crime in the eyes of the government'.[17] This was certainly the view of Admiral Shishkov, the ultra-conservative Minister of Education of the mid-1820s who believed that 'Making the whole people or too large a proportion of them literate would do more harm than good'.[18] Nicholas's edict of 1827 forbidding secondary schools and universities to educate serfs showed that he agreed with his minister. Some of the tsar's educational initiatives – the foundation, for example, of the Imperial War Academy in 1832 and the Imperial School of Jurisprudence in 1835 – were designed solely for the benefit of the country's elite. The transfer of Alexander I's Imperial Lycée from Tsarskoe Selo to St Petersburg in the 1840s gave it a higher profile but did nothing to broaden its intake. Universities were growing in size not just because non-nobles were entering them, but because the tsar wanted nobles to complete their education at home rather than abroad.

Whatever the authorities' natural inclinations, however, they failed to draw fine lines between the parts of the community for which they thought education was worthwhile and the parts they wanted to keep in their place. Even ultra-conservatives seemed to realize that it was impossible to increase the size of the bureaucracy and the professions by relying entirely on people of noble origin. Some of the country's rulers, moreover, were less conservative than others. Uvarov, Nicholas's longest-serving Minister of Education, did much to preserve the universities' freedom of manoeuvre by omitting from the statute of 1835 general statements about the value of education and the social groups for which it was designed. His shrewdness maintained the principle of relatively wide access to education which had been enshrined in Alexander I's reforms of 1803–4. Herzen claimed in the 1850s that 'Until 1848 the structure of our universities was entirely democratic. Their doors were open to anyone who could pass the examination and was neither a serf nor a peasant without a passport from his commune'.[19] For long periods of his reign Nicholas appears not to have insisted on the strict application of his rules about access to education. The fact that in 1845 he asked Uvarov to consider whether it was possible to prevent non-nobles from gaining admission to secondary schools showed that, below the level of the university, social origin had not been preventing the unprivileged from getting a foot on the educational ladder. The best-known student of the social background of educated people in the Russian Empire calculates that in the 1840s the country's 'bourgeois [ie non-noble] intelligentsia' consisted of between 15,000 and 20,000 people.[20] The regime had educated them in order to staff its burgeoning administration, but could not easily prevent them from putting their education to uses other than those approved of by the state. An explicit attempt on the part of Sergei Stroganov to run Moscow University in the interests of the gentry had unexpected results. Solov'ev said that Stroganov wanted 'to give [the upper ranks of the gentry] the means of ... remaining the upper ranks for ever', and that he thought educating them as well as possible at Moscow University was the best means of achieving this end.[21] Stroganov succeeded in making the university 'the centre of all intellectual activity in Russia',[22] but in doing so increased its attraction for people other than those whom he sought to benefit. Public lectures given by Professor Timofei Granovskii in the winter of 1843–4 on the history of the Middle Ages marked 'the first attempt to bring academic questions out of tight-knit literary circles and make them the property of society as a whole'.[23] The lectures drew huge audiences and became the talk of the town. The following winter, Professor Shevyrev's disquisitions on medieval Russian literature went down less well but were attended by almost as many people. Stroganov was unable to broaden the appeal of the university without also broadening its narrow social orientation. In the period of his curatorship of the Moscow educational district commoners made up more than 50 per cent of the university's student body, whereas in the university system as a whole they constituted only 37 per cent.[24] This was a classic illustration of the way in which improving the empire's educational facilities created as many problems as it solved. When, in 1845, students demonstrated their support for Granovskii at the heated public examination of his master's dissertation, Stroganov realized that developing the university was having consequences other than those he intended. He acted, therefore, to make future such manifestations impossible.

OUTLETS FOR OPINION

The condemnation of Chaadaev, the closure of *The European*, and the suppression of Polevoi's *Moscow Telegraph* implied that people who thought for themselves under Nicholas I were likely to experience great difficulty in writing for the public. In fact, however, some of those who passed through Russian educational institutions in the second quarter of the nineteenth century refused to apply themselves to the administrative tasks for which the government thought it was training them and succeeded in making literary careers. Sometimes simple inefficiency on the part of the authorities came to their aid. The most famous example in Russian history of a mistake on the part of the censors belongs to the next reign (the stamp of approval given to Nikolai Chernyshevskii's subversive novel *What is to be Done?* in 1863), but if the censorship had been efficient under Nicholas, Chaadaev's 'First Philosophical Letter', the 'shot that rang out in the dark night',[25] would never have found its way into print. When promulgating the relatively liberal censorship statute of 1828 the tsar had taken the precaution of instructing the Third Department to act as a second, covert check on the press, which enabled him to indulge in post-publication as well as pre-publication censorship, but when writers expressed themselves subtly, or when it was not clear that their writings had political implications, the bodies which monitored their output tended to allow their work to appear. Thus Gogol was able to publish *The Government Inspector* in 1836 and *Dead Souls* in 1842, neither of which had purely recreational value. In the case of *Dead Souls*, the left hand of the administration did not know what the right was doing, for the book was rejected by the Moscow censor before being cleared in St Petersburg. It is probable, however, that on this occasion the regime's shortsightedness was fed by uncertainty, for the St Petersburg censor, Aleksandr Nikitenko, was not at all sure that suppressing thought-provoking literature was in the interests of his superiors. Nicholas may have had similar doubts, for if he had been determined to prevent unofficial opinions from seeing the light of day he could have given the censorship and the Third Department blanket instructions to this effect. Only three journals, however, were closed down in the course of the reign – those of Kireevskii and Polevoi, mentioned above, and *The Telescope* in 1836 for publishing Chaadaev. Literary figures were pursued by the authorities on other occasions (Lermontov for reflecting bitterly on Pushkin's pointless death in a duel in 1837, Turgenev for lamenting Gogol's death in 1852), and writers did not trouble the censors with manuscripts which they knew would get them into trouble; but authors came into conflict with the regime on surprisingly few occasions and did not escape prosecution simply because they censored their own work before trying to publish it.

In at least two respects, one practical, one ideological, the regime positively encouraged writers to write. First, Nicholas I passed a copyright law in 1828 which prevented piracy and 'helped cause a steady, profit-centred growth in the publishing industry'.[26] Second, the regime seems to have allowed writers a certain latitude because it believed that it could win ideological exchanges. By founding or supporting journals which expressed the government's point of view – the *Journal of the Ministry of Education* in 1834 (whose first issue contained Uvarov's proclamation of 'Orthodoxy, Autocracy, and Nationality'), the provincial gazettes of 1838, and especially *The Muscovite* of 1841 (which took on the task of responding to Belinskii's invective) – the authorities showed a readiness to use the tools of their critics. By doing so they actually encouraged an interplay of ideas which, in the long run, worked to their disadvantage. Sydney Monas goes so far as to say that the tsar 'felt it as part of the mission of enlightened absolutism, which he had taken upon himself, to encourage the flourishing of letters',[27] and argues that therefore there is no paradox in the fact that the age of 'Official Nationality' was also the 'Golden Age of Russian Literature'. Perhaps, when Nicholas acted as Pushkin's personal censor and partly funded the poet's journal (*The Contemporary*), he was trying not only to ensure that the output of the country's greatest writer contained no aspersions on the regime, but also to bask in the reflected glory of association with the principal literary figure of the day. This may be claiming too much, but although Nicholas probably felt less warmly towards Pushkin, Lermontov,

Gogol and the early works of Dostoevsky and Turgenev than he did towards more obsequious writers like Nestor Kukol'nik (the author of the play about the accession of the Romanovs which Polevoi was punished for criticizing), at least until 1848 he seems to have been only half-hearted in his hostility towards writers whose opinions differed from his own.

Slowly, more printed matter became available. One scholar claims that 'The quantity of literature published in Russia between 1801 and 1837 went up three times', though she also finds that the increase came to a halt between 1837 and 1850.[28] Whereas the record number of books published in a single year in the eighteenth-century Russian Empire was about 450, the average number of books published each year in the period 1844–54 was 944.[29] A student of history books published in the reigns of Alexander I and Nicholas I argues that they sold in relatively large editions relative to the size of the population, that they were bought by the non-privileged as well as the privileged, and that they were to be found in many parts of the country.[30] Not even Karamzin's *History of the Russian State* approached the popularity, at the other end of the continent, of Macaulay's *History of England* (the first two volumes of which sold 22,000 copies within a year of their publication in London in 1848); but the demand for works of history in Russia was far greater in the reign of Nicholas I than it had been in the eighteenth century.

Magazines, however, were the most successful form of publication. Whereas 129 were founded between 1801 and 1825, 224 came into being between 1826 and 1854.[31] The latter figure is larger than it would have been if the authorities had not created the forty-two provincial gazettes which began to appear in 1838, but even when the gazettes are discounted an average of more than fifty journals were appearing at any one time under Nicholas, which was nearly twice the average for the reign of Alexander I.[32] Although, after the suppression of *The European* in 1832, the tsar took it upon himself to consider personally all applications for permission to create new journals and on a number of occasions refused his assent, he did not attempt to reverse the upward trend but rather to slow it down. Between the foundation of *The Polar Star* by the Decembrists Ryleev and Bestuzhev in 1823 and the demise of *Northern Flowers* with the number for 1832, authors of fiction and poetry tended to publish their works in annuals or 'almanacs', but as the 1830s advanced the market proved able to sustain publications of a similar size at more frequent intervals. By the mid-1840s Osip Senkovskii's *Library for Reading* (founded in 1834), Pushkin's *The Contemporary* (1836), Kraevskii's *Notes of the Fatherland* (1839) and Pogodin's *The Muscovite* (1841) were all appearing monthly. Subscriptions to the press sometimes reached notable heights. The conservative daily newspaper *Northern Bee* had a circulation of 7,000 in the 1830s and 10,000 in the 1850s. *Library for Reading*, Russia's first 'thick' journal (rightly so called, since each number ran to about 300 pages) peaked at 7,000 subscribers in 1837. *The Muscovite* had only 300 subscribers in the mid-1840s and *The Contemporary* only 233 in 1846, but the latter's fortunes improved dramatically when it attracted Belinskii to its staff in 1847. The fact that *Notes of the Fatherland* retained its subscribers after Belinskii's departure showed that by the late 1840s two relatively high-circulation magazines could appear at the same time. The leading Russian journals were by this time selling as many copies as the *Westminster Review* in England and the *Revue des deux mondes* in France.[33] Belinskii's editor at *Notes of the Fatherland*, though not Belinskii himself, became a rich man. Belinskii complained in 1845 that 'In contemporary Russian literature the journal has completely killed the book' and Ivan Kireevskii asserted in the same year that 'journalistic literature has replaced artistic', but Herzen was probably right to see journals as 'the best means of spreading light in a vast country' and to claim that 'Their very periodicity had the advantage of waking up lazy readers'.[34] Gogol refused to allow *Dead Souls* to come out in instalments and was prepared, he said, to 'give away all [his] property for the sole purpose of not placing [his] works ahead of time',[35] but Pushkin, Lermontov, Dostoevsky and Turgenev all published major works in the periodical press of the 1830s and 1840s and gave it a new-found distinction.

Since Belinskii and other critics commented on all of the newly published literature, readers were now being offered both new texts and new interpretations. Censorship made open political discussion impossible, but writers often succeeded in implying what they were forbidden from making plain. Readers became skilful at discerning meanings in literature which differed from those perceived by officialdom. In a country where open political discussion was impossible, the likelihood that literature would be read closely was considerable. Without wholeheartedly accepting Leszek Kołakowski's claim that the Russian Empire was 'a country in which ... there was no clear-cut dividing line between literary criticism and assassination',[36] one can still see that, in the absence of other forums for debate, imaginative responses to literature might address themselves to the relationship between literature and reality. Because they tended to do so, Herzen was able to say in 1850 that 'Superficially Russia remained stationary' under Nicholas I, 'but deep down everything changed, questions became more complicated and solutions less simple'. Herzen went too far when he claimed that 'revolutionary ideas gained more ground in [the past] twenty-five years than in the entire century which preceded them', but his perception goes further to explain the rapidity of change in Russia after Nicholas's death than the idea that his reign was a cultural desert.[37]

In view of the fact, however, that intellectuals could never speak or write openly about politics in the reign of Nicholas I, they probably expressed their most important opinions to each other rather than to the public at large. Educational institutions and journals were becoming increasingly significant as forums for debate, but remained less important than the small private circles which, in retrospect, stand out as the key feature of the Russian intelligentsia's emergence. To a degree the distinction between public and private means of expression is an artificial one, since although some 400 private circles have been discerned between 1801 and

1855,[38] the most important of them in the 1830s were those centred on Alexander Herzen and Nikolai Stankevich, both of which originated at Moscow University when the members were students. Apart from Herzen and his closest friend, Nikolai Ogarev, no one in the Herzen circle subsequently made a name for himself, but almost everyone in the Stankevich circle did apart from Stankevich himself (who died at the age of twenty-seven). The love-child of an aristocrat, Herzen spent his first seventeen years in comfortable but frustrated isolation from the society which surrounded him. When he went to university in 1829 he found a group of like-minded contemporaries and began the long journey towards a Russian brand of socialism. The five years before he was exiled to Viatka in 1834, when he led his peers, applauded the French Revolution of July 1830, won a silver medal for his studies, and discovered the writings of the French socialist Saint-Simon, were probably the happiest of his life. The Stankevich circle, founded in 1831, remained a definable entity throughout the 1830s and included not only Belinskii and Granovskii but also future representatives of three of the most striking intellectual currents in later-nineteenth-century Russia: Mikhail Katkov (who became an extreme conservative), Mikhail Bakunin (who turned into an anarchist) and Konstantin Aksakov (whose views led him in the direction of panslavism). Neither the Herzen nor the Stankevich circle had rules or a plan of campaign. Unlike the army officers who constituted the backbone of Decembrism, neither considered drawing up political programmes for a redesigned empire. Edward Brown describes the Stankevich group as 'a casually organized body which met on Fridays ... to discuss philosophy, listen to music, and read romantic poetry'.[39] This makes the intellectual circles of the reign of Nicholas I seem a poor vehicle for the development of coherent opinions. Other criticisms could easily be added: that they were overwhelmingly aristocratic at a time when representatives of non-gentry estates were beginning to play a part in Russian intellectual life, and that they were to be found mainly in Moscow, when the only way to make changes in Russia was to infiltrate the centres of power in St Petersburg. It is true that some contemporaries thought circles a waste of time. 'A circle', wrote Ivan Turgenev in 1848, 'is a lazy and flabby kind of communal, side-by-side existence, to which people attribute the significance and appearance of an intelligent business'.[40] In 1850 Mikhail Zagoskin decried Moscow literary evenings on the grounds that they consisted of 'a whole crowd of deep thinkers who, having arrived at the age of twenty, had managed to experience everything, feel everything, and bore everyone'.[41] Reproaches like these, however, missed the point of the circles, which Boris Chicherin explained to Turgenev after reading his attack on them. 'The stuffy atmosphere of an exclusive circle', Chicherin said, 'undoubtedly has its drawbacks; but what is to be done, when people are not allowed out into the open air?'[42] The press was freer than it seemed, but the only place in which educated contemporaries could be absolutely frank with each other was the private drawing-room. Chicherin could have said more, for frankness in private was more than a transitory lifeline. In a few cases it forged bonds which laid the basis for future practical activities, but above all it facilitated deeper reflection on the country's future than would have occurred if intellectuals had been willing to enter the service of the regime. The circles of the 1830s and 1840s eventually had an importance disproportionate to their size and at odds with the abstract character of their discussions; they proved to be the bridge between the shattered hopes of the Decembrists and the reforms of the reign of Alexander II.

THE POLITICAL IMPLICATIONS OF LITERARY EXPRESSION

Views which made their way into print in the 1830s and 1840s were rarely as forthright as Polevoi's critique of Karamzin, Chaadaev's 'First Philosophical Letter' or Belinskii's 'Literary Musings'. Nevertheless, many publications either showed signs of a political orientation or allowed critics to pretend that they did. Pushkin's poem *The Upas Tree*, published at the end of 1831, portrayed a ruler who was prepared to sacrifice a subject in order to be able to poison his enemies. Reviewers of different persuasions took the Ukrainian setting of Gogol's short stories *Evenings on a Farmstead near Dikan'ka* (1831–2) to stand either for the virtue of tradition or for freedom from the strait-jacket of modern society.[43] Herzen wrote in 1850 that nothing indicated the psychological changes which were taking place among Russian intellectuals in the reign of Nicholas I more effectively than the difference between Pushkin and Lermontov. Whereas the former had been prepared to make peace with the regime, the latter, who was half a generation younger, was not. According to Herzen, Lermontov's novel *A Hero of Our Time* (1840) depicted the despair which life under Nicholas could induce.[44] Gogol's play *The Government Inspector*, first performed in April 1836, outraged proponents of 'Official Nationality' because it painted an extremely unflattering picture of life in the empire's backwoods. Prince Viazemskii defended Gogol from the charge that the play contained 'not a single honest or right-thinking individual' on the spurious grounds that the 'right-thinking individual' was the government which allowed the play to appear. Sensing the frailty of his argument, he subsequently claimed that contemporaries were wrong to think of the play as a veiled indictment of the authorities because Gogol did not intend political conclusions to be drawn from his work. This was true, but did not allow for the fact that audiences and readers were not privy to Gogol's intentions.[45] The literary work which gave rise to the greatest controversy in the reign of Nicholas I was probably Gogol's novel *Dead Souls*, which appeared in 1842. Nikolai Grech, one of the principal spokesmen for 'Official Nationality', saw in it 'a peculiar world of ne'er-do-wells which never existed and couldn't exist', but Pushkin's successor as editor of *The Contemporary*, P. A. Pletnev, believed that Gogol had met a fundamental requirement of contemporary literary criticism by producing a work of art which described the world around him.[46] The future panslavist Konstantin Aksakov lauded the novel on the grounds that it belonged to the universal tradition of the epic and could be compared with Homer, while Belinskii, despite being an even greater admirer, thought that universality was not at all the book's key feature and that, on the contrary, only Russians could understand it.[47] Herzen, who shared Belinskii's view that the novel's virtue lay in its depiction of Russian reality, claimed that *Dead Souls* 'shook the whole of Russia' because it represented a savage indictment of the empire's provincial nobility.[48]

In the mid-1840s literary politics intensified. Ivan Kireevskii revealed the extent to which he had moved to the right since the closure of *The European* in 1832 by editing three numbers of the conservative *Muscovite* in 1845. 'With his characteristic wit and humour, but also with his characteristic superficial sophistry, he inveighed against the whole of western philosophy ... and offered the prospect of salvation solely in the bosom of the Orthodox Church'.[49] When *The Contemporary* changed hands two years later, the first number put out by the new management constituted 'an embryo political demonstration' on behalf of the left. By publishing the first of Ivan Turgenev's *Sportsman's Sketches* ('Khor' and Kalinych') and Konstantin Kavelin's non-fictional 'Glance at the Juridical Life of Ancient Russia', the editors hinted strongly that individuality offered better prospects than Nicholaevan regimentation.[50] Just before his death in 1848 Belinskii published what was perhaps the most trenchant of all his published writings, 'A Survey of Russian Literature in 1847', in which, by concentrating on Herzen's novel *Who is to Blame?* and Ivan Goncharov's *An Ordinary Story*, he argued that a writer's primary duty was tȯ engage in pictorial representation of his environment. Since, by then, it was clear what the country's greatest critic thought of his environment, the subtext of the argument was not difficult to discern.

Literature printed under Nicholas I thus said a good deal about contemporary attitudes to the tsarist political and social system. It was only a pale reflection, however, of the range and profundity of contemporary intellectual developments. Out-and-out sympathizers with the regime – Nikolai Grech and Faddei Bulgarin at *The Northern Bee*, Osip Senkovskii in *Library for Reading* – could print more or less exactly what they meant, but others had to refrain from making public the depth of their feelings. A private exchange between Gogol and Belinskii illustrated the difference of degree between views which found their way into print and the views for which they stood proxy. In 1847 Gogol published *Selected Passages from Correspondence with Friends*, in which he made plain that he was much less critical of Russian reality than contemporaries had thought him to be on the basis of *The Government Inspector* and *Dead Souls*. Conservatives like

Bulgarin and Senkovskii were delighted. Belinskii, in a review published in the second number of the revamped *Contemporary*, objected. Gogol then attempted to justify his new book in a letter to Belinskii, who was receiving treatment for tuberculosis at Salzbrunn and was temporarily out of reach of the Russian censor. Belinskii's reply to Gogol's letter was vitriolic. 'Russia', he wrote, 'sees her salvation not in mysticism, asceticism, or pietism' – the remedies Gogol was proposing – 'but in the advances of civilization, enlightenment and humanism'. 'The most vital national problems in Russia today', he went on, 'are the abolition of serfdom, the repeal of corporal punishment, and the strictest possible implementation of at least those laws which do exist'. Yet at a time when the country's situation was desperate, 'a great writer whose wonderfully artistic and profoundly truthful works have so powerfully stimulated Russia's self-awareness and enabled her to see herself as if in a mirror, comes out with a book which in the name of Christ and the Church teaches the barbarian landowner to squeeze even more money out of his peasants, who are criticized for their *unwashed snouts!*'[51] In Belinskii's view, Gogol had abandoned the forces of light for the forces of darkness. The sense of betrayal and the sheer anger which characterized his letter clearly represented what he would have said in print if he had been able to do so. Whatever the extent to which literature published under Nicholas I reflected the ideological currents of the day, it did not allow the expression of feelings as strong as this.

Belinskii felt more deeply than his peers, but he was not alone in possessing views which, in the interests of self-preservation, he had to keep from the government. Even on the right of the political spectrum intellectual developments were occurring which their progenitors did well to pursue quietly. The conversion of Ivan Kireevskii from the man who enthused about western Europe in 1832 to the man who 'inveighed against the whole of western philosophy' in 1845 looked like a triumph for the regime, but in fact represented an attack on it from a novel perspective. Just after the closure of *The European* Kireevskii had begun spending a great deal of time with Aleksei Khomiakov, 'an extraordinarily consistent character' whose 'convictions were a deep devotion to the Orthodox Church and a Russian patriotism which ... contained from early on a definite hostility to the European Russia of Peter the Great'.[52] The two men and their coterie disagreed both with the regime and with modernizers like Belinskii. In 1839 they knocked their ideas into shape in two privately circulated essays. Khomiakov played devil's advocate. It was wrong, he felt, to believe that everything had been better in Russia before westernization began in the early eighteenth century. 'If neither the old ways nor the Church generated a tangible form in which the old Russia would have been encapsulated, ought we not to acknowledge that they lacked an element, or even several elements?' The question, however, was rhetorical. Khomiakov went on to claim that medieval Russia did indeed embody purity, simplicity and mutual love. Modern Russians had to understand 'that man achieves his moral fulfilment only in a society in which the strength of the individual belongs to everyone and the strength of everyone to the individual'. In Khomia-kov's view, medieval Russia was precisely such a society. Although mod-ern Russia could take advantage of 'chance discoveries' made in the West, she ought not to attach any great significance to them. 'Then ... ancient Russia will revive ... full of living, organic force, not hesitating endlessly be-tween life and death'.[53] Kireevskii continued the discussion.[54] The circle, he said, was trying to answer the question whether 'ancient Russia ... [was] better or worse than present-day Russia'. He realized that the western in-fluences which had penetrated modern Russia could not be expunged, but he considered western rationalism to be 'a one-sided, deceptive, corrupt-ing and treacherous principle'. Because, in medieval Russia, social relations depended on the church and the peasant communes, collectivism pre-vailed over individualism. 'Private and individual life, the very cornerstone of Western development, was as little known in Russia as political rule by the people'. Kireevskii believed that the traditions of medieval Russia had engendered consensus and harmony whereas those of the West depended on 'material force, physical superiority, the power of the multitude and compromise between differing views'. He was uncertain whether the clock could be turned back, but he ended ironically by saying that it would be possible to turn it back if a Frenchman or a German made the case, for Russians were more likely to believe foreigners than their own intellec-tuals.

At first sight it seems odd to say that Khomiakov and Kireevskii did well to develop their ideas in private. Far from threatening the regime, they ap-peared to have a lot in common with it. Their enthusiasm for the Orthodox Church dovetailed with Nicholas I's 'Official Nationality'. Their affection for the traditions of the countryside seemed to justify the government in adopting a tentative approach to the abolition of serfdom. These resem-blances, however, obscure the fact that Khomiakov and Kireevskii dis-agreed with the government almost as much as modernizers like Belinskii who wanted to bring the empire into line with the west. The circle which grew up around Khomiakov and Kireevskii advocated regression to an idyllic past. Modernizers sought the empire's salvation in movement to-wards a western-orientated future. What united the two groups was dissat-isfaction with the contemporary state of the country. Both were looking for a way out of what, to them, was a blind alley. 'Official Nationalists', mean-while, were willing to strengthen the regime's foundations and tinker with its superstructure, but rejected the idea of changing the direction in which the regime was moving and refused to quicken their step. In these circum-stances, Khomiakov and Kireevskii had to keep their heads down. Their essays of 1839 did not see the light of day until six years into the next reign, when both the authors were dead.

SLAVOPHILES

Exponents of the modernizing and backward-looking philosophies which took shape under Nicholas I came to be called Westernizers and Slavophiles, the former because they looked to the west for inspiration, the latter because they set great store by the indigenous culture of the Slavs. In everyday parlance the terms stand for 'progressives' and 'reactionaries', but since disillusionment with the regime was one of a number of things on which the two groups agreed, drawing sharp distinctions between them is difficult. Socially and intellectually, Westernizers and Slavophiles sprang from the same stock. Most members of both circles were noblemen, and most of them had been brought up on the principal west European philosophies of their day. Explaining why they fell out with each other is harder than it seems.

According to one expert, 'Slavophilism was the ideology of the hereditary Russian nobility who were reluctant to stand up on their own behalf as a privileged group defending its own selfish interests, and therefore attempted to sublimate and universalize traditional values and to create an ideological platform that would unite all classes and social strata representing "ancient Russia"'.[55] This definition makes the Slavophiles look more conservative than they were. At least two of them, Ivan Kireevskii and Ivan Aksakov, began their intellectual careers as Westernizers. Kireevskii 'even reached the point of rejecting the need for the existence of God'.[56] Neither these nor the other Slavophiles closed their eyes to the need for change. 'We were very far,' wrote Aleksandr Koshelev, 'from rejecting the great discoveries and improvements accomplished in the West'. 'We certainly did not want', he said, 'to resurrect ancient Russia'. Slavophiles, according to Koshelev, 'did not put the peasant on a pedestal, did not bow down before him and certainly did not envisage turning [them]selves and others into people like him'. Rather, they looked to the common man for what was quintessentially Russian and sought means of developing it. In Koshelev's view the circle was not hostile to progress, merely to types of progress which could not be transplanted to Russia.[57] This analysis of Slavophilism from the pen of a Slavophile is supported by the best retrospective study of the phenomenon, in which N. I. Tsimbaev controversially asserts that 'The liberalism of the Slavophiles is indubitable'.[58] Whatever the differences between members of the group, and whatever the twists and turns in their outlook as the movement changed over time, Slavophiles always believed in freedom of speech and the press, freedom of public opinion and freedom of conscience. One of their number, Iurii Samarin, was horrified by the peasant disturbances which took place after the emancipation of the serfs in 1861, but probably not because the authoritarianism of a nobleman inclined him to deny the lower orders a say in their own affairs. Rather, Slavophiles took exception to violence of all kinds, whether instigated by the population at large or by the authorities. Peter the Great's violent methods, rather than the goals he was pursuing, may have played the greater part in the Slavophiles' objection to his transformation of Russia. Nicholas I's strong-arm tactics were certainly anathema to them.

Slavophiles did not admire the pre-Petrine period for its own sake. The emphasis placed by Kireevskii and Khomiakov on the peasant commune did not derive solely from the fact that, in their view, it was the one Russian institution which had survived the Petrine storm. Rather, they believed that 'from its development an entire civic order might develop'.[59] Slavophiles did not spend much time writing history. They buttressed their arguments with historical references, but the arguments related to the present and the future. On the basis of a memorandum submitted by Konstantin Aksakov to Alexander II in 1855 it has often been argued that the Slavophiles were prepared to acquiesce in the tsar's untrammelled exercise of his powers. Aksakov began by saying that 'The Russian people are not political', which implied that the government could do what it wanted. In the course of the paper, however, he also sounded a warning note. By pointing out to the tsar that 'The people see a new act of oppression in every step taken by the government', he urged Alexander to abandon the autocratic predilection for ignoring the views of the populace. What Aksakov really wanted was the introduction of a clearer demarcation line between public and private spheres of activity and the significant enlargement of the citizen's freedom of action.[60]

Kireevskii's abandonment of the editorship of *The Muscovite* after only three numbers in 1845 showed that, whether or not he was a conservative, he was not as conservative as Mikhail Pogodin and Stepan Shevyrev, the 'Official Nationalists' who remained in ultimate charge of the journal. The arrest of Fedor Chizhov in 1847 and of both Iurii Samarin and Ivan Aksakov in 1849 showed that, whether or not contemporary non-Slavophile intellectuals thought of Slavophiles as conservatives, the authorities perceived them as a threat. The involvement of Samarin, Ivan Aksakov and Prince Vladimir Cherkasskii in the process of serf emancipation in the late 1850s showed that certain Slavophiles not only believed in change but also were prepared to work for it. It is true that some of the Slavophiles' beliefs were impenetrable, that the enthusiasm with which they adhered to them sometimes verged on bigotry, and that the importance they attached to the Orthodox Church tended to identify them with the regime, but the difference between them and the Westernizers turned on their manner as much as the content of their arguments. When one of the Slavophiles, Konstantin Aksakov, affected medieval dress, and another, Khomiakov, looked to Herzen like 'a hardened old duellist of dialectics' who 'turned everything in the world to use, from the casuistry of Byzantine theologians to the subtleties of a shifty lawyer',[61] it is easy to see why Slavophiles irritated their opponents. Yet even Khomiakov could be moderate among friends. At the end of a long exchange with Kireevskii in 1852 he conceded that the past had not been perfect and that humankind's development had to continue.

'The present age', he said, 'would not have been necessary, if former ages had accomplished everything of which human reason was capable; future ages would not be necessary if the present had reached the final goal'.[62] Above all, the Slavophiles were a broad church. Khomiakov and Konstantin Aksakov may have been intransigent by comparison with some of the other members of the circle, but since, as Ivan Kireevskii pointed out in 1847, Slavophiles did not agree on what they meant by calling themselves 'Slavs', on what they meant by the emphasis they placed on *narodnost'* ('nationality'), and on what their attitude should be towards state institutions,[63] they were unlikely to become an exclusive brotherhood. The balance between their conservative and liberal inclinations was constantly shifting; and as long as it went on doing so, they provided an example of intellectual fluidity which was worth more than the kaleidoscopic opinions of the group's individual members.

WESTERNIZERS

The Westernizers were a broad church too. In the opinion of Boris Chicherin it was they rather than the Slavophiles who were conspicuous for their variety. Whereas the Slavophiles were 'an out-and-out sect', the Westernizers 'possessed no common doctrine'. Westernizers, Chicherin said, included 'the devoutly Orthodox and the utterly irreligious, metaphysicians and empiricists, social-democrats and moderate liberals, statists and advocates of pure individualism'.[64] Individual Westernizers were no more consistent than the group as a whole. At the end of the 1830s Belinskii went through a period known as his 'reconciliation with reality', when he seemed, for a time, to be accepting the world as he found it. Alexander Herzen radically modified his political opinions after witnessing the failure of the west European revolutions of 1848 and was soon speaking with well-nigh Slavophile enthusiasm of the virtues of the Russian peasant commune.[65] If one accepts Nicholas Riasanovsky's view that 'the bureaucratic formalism and legalistic oppressiveness of the imperial system had never been attacked so powerfully and especially from such a strong theoretical base as they were ... by Khomiakov and his friends',[66] Westernizers can hardly be said to have been more hostile than Slavophiles to the tsarist regime. Nor were they more practical than their opponents, for (unlike the Decembrists) they took no interest in devising anti-autocratic constitutions. Edward Brown points out that calling the early Westernizer Nikolai Stankevich 'an enemy of the Czarist social order' is to strain the evidence.[67] Granovskii fell back on card-playing during Nicholas I's last years on the throne, but retained his professorship at Moscow University. Herzen's enthusiasm for the reform process inaugurated by Alexander II in the second half of the 1850s implied that he was prepared to back autocracy when it was put to good use. Sometimes it is hard to see why the Westernizers have gone down in history as radicals.

In the main, moreover, Westernizers and Slavophiles felt warmly towards each other. When, in the early 1840s, Franz Liszt was taking Moscow by storm, Khomiakov suggested to Herzen that they start an argument in the pianist's presence in order to demonstrate that not everyone was obsessed with the distinguished visitor. Ivan Kireevskii had to miss Granovskii's public lectures at Moscow University in the winter of 1843–4, but congratulated him on their success, deplored those who criticized him, asked for transcripts, and expressed the conviction that, whatever the differences between them, no historian combined 'so much spiritual warmth with such intellectual elegance and spiritual vitality'.[68] Passing Herzen in a Moscow street in 1844, Konstantin Aksakov got out of his sleigh to express regret for their differences. With benefit of hindsight Herzen was prepared to say openly that Westernizers and Slavophiles had had a lot in common: 'like Janus, or the two-headed eagle, they and we looked in different directions while one heart throbbed within us'.[69] Although the Westernizers' admiration for Peter the Great's innovations seemed to be wholly at odds with the Slavophiles' emphasis on the traditions of the church and the countryside, the two sides disagreed about means more than ends; both sought ways of changing the status quo.

It was the Official Nationalists and Belinskii who were primarily responsible for the acrimony between Westernizers and Slavophiles which undoubtedly existed for a few years in the mid-1840s. Stepan Shevyrev's attack on Belinskii in the first number of *The Muscovite* for 1842 prompted a stinging reply which affected not only Shevyrev himself and his associate Pogodin but also Khomiakov and the Kireevskii brothers. Unlike the Westernizers, the Slavophiles rarely had control over a journal and never included in their ranks a professor like Granovskii who could speak for them in the lecture rooms. In their search for outlets, they sometimes entered into uneasy dealings with apologists for the regime. Belinskii had no sympathy for their dilemma. The larger the number of those whom he could consider his enemies, the more his spirits rose. When Vasilii Botkin wrote to him in St Petersburg of the effect his indictment of Shevyrev was having in Moscow, he was delighted. Polemic, he said, was his lifeblood. Having come out of the 'Right Hegelianism' of his 'reconciliation with reality' period, Belinskii seemed determined to over-compensate for the interruption in his ideological development. When, later in 1842, *The Muscovite* published an attempt by Konstantin Aksakov to rebut the literary critic's interpretation of Gogol's *Dead Souls*, Belinskii felt confirmed in his natural inclination to treat the Slavophiles as if they were Official Nationalists. As late as 1842 the word 'Slavophile' could still refer to adherents of an early-nineteenth-century school of thought which sought to strip the Russian language of foreign accretions and return it to its Slavonic roots. Belinskii himself still employed the word in this sense, but as his wrath mounted he enlarged its meaning and made it a term of abuse. Khomiakov and Ivan Kireevskii were investing it with new meaning at the same time, but Belinskii did not trouble himself with the difference between the two reinterpretations. He needed opponents on whom to vent his spleen. Having found them, he lost interest in niceties. Granovskii's lectures of 1843–4 and Ivan Kireevskii's editorship of *The Muscovite* in 1845 would have highlighted the differences between Westernizers and Slavophiles whether Belinskii existed or not, but his intemperate language poured oil on the flames. Although Herzen and Granovskii maintained some sort of dealings with their adversaries even at the height of the quarrel between the two orientations, Belinskii called himself 'a Jew by nature' who would not 'eat at the same table with the Philistines'.[70] His explosive temperament not only injected life into Russian intellectual exchanges, but also involved opponents of the regime in spending time on mutual recriminations which would have been better spent on pooling their intellectual resources.

CONCLUSION

Perhaps the Russian intellectuals who emerged in the reign of Nicholas I ought not to be taken too seriously. They were relatively few in number, had few means of addressing themselves to large audiences, avoided, for the most part, the limelight of St Petersburg, devoted most of their time to discussing abstractions, never dreamed of running the risks taken by the Decembrists, and weakened themselves by internal dissension. Their commitment to ideas was intense, but 'A man who went for a walk in Sokolniki … in order to surrender himself to the pantheistic feeling of his identification with the cosmos' and 'ten-year-old boys' who spoke of 'concrete objectivity' were hardly likely to set the world on fire.[71] Comparing the fictional Khor' and Kalinych with Goethe and Schiller was a credit to the breadth of Ivan Turgenev's imagination, but rang hollow in a short story which readers thought of as an indictment of serfdom.[72] The very small number of intellectual circles which the government felt obliged to break up in the reign of Nicholas I (of which more in Chapter Seven) reflected not so much the authorities' kindheartedness as the fact that few if any of the circles generated anything other than literary criticism, novels and salon talk.

Attempts by Soviet scholars to speak of a 'liberation movement' or even a 'revolutionary movement' in the reign of Nicholas I thus seem to be special pleading.[73] Although, with benefit of hindsight, Westernizers and Slavophiles can be treated as the founders of continuous intellectual traditions which have been discernible in recent times in the views, for example, of Andrei Sakharov and Alexander Solzhenitsyn, resemblances between ear-

lier and later exponents of the two orientations may be entirely coinciden-
tal. It is not unusual, after all, for advocates of change to consist on the one
hand of people who look for inspiration beyond their country's frontiers
and on the other of people who dedicate themselves to the promotion of
native traditions. It may even be doubted whether the men of the 1830s
and 1840s deserve the high-sounding name 'intelligentsia', for although the
word is of Russian origin it entered the language only in the 1860s and
tended to mean a good deal more than 'people who dedicated themselves
to ideas'. In a celebrated essay of 1909 Peter Struve argued that membership of the intelligentsia implied either absolute or relative alienation from
the state. This conception, he said, had been 'ideologically prepared' in the
1840s, but the anarchists and social-democrats of his own time exemplified
it to a much higher degree than their literary precursors.[74] Most subsequent
students of the term have agreed with Struve in expecting a higher degree
of political oppositionism from members of an intelligentsia than was evident in the often comfortable lives of those who felt alienated by the
regime of Nicholas I.

Yet as early as 1840 the head of the Third Department reported to Nicholas I a statement he had received from one of his subordinates in Moscow: 'I do not know exactly, but something is wrong'. 'Of course,'
Benckendorff went on, 'nothing bad has as yet happened', but states of
mind were 'less propitious than at any time during the entire last fifteen
years'.[75] The authorities seem dimly to have suspected that philosophical
ideas had practical implications and that they could somehow pass from
the pages of journals, the lecture halls of universities, and the salons of the
Moscow gentry to places where action was initiated. Taken out of context,
the wrangling of Westernizers and Slavophiles often looked inconsequen-
tial, but the government's suspicions were not altogether without foundation. The major practical implication of the ideas which circulated in the
reign of Nicholas I derived from the fact that virtually all the intellectuals of
the reign were Hegelians. Even Khomiakov depicted the history of the
Church in terms of the principle of power, the principle of freedom and the
principle of love, a triad which, like all Hegelian triads, implied movement.
If the Hegelian idea of dialectical movement reached the chanceries of
government ministries, Nicholas I's piecemeal innovations would begin to
seem petty.

The idea, furthermore, was already within the walls. Boris Chicherin
could afford to deprecate service to the government on the grounds that it
consisted of 'playing up to the bosses, never giving voice to [your] convictions, and often undertaking what seemed to be positively wrong',[76] but
others either had to work for a living or felt that life without employment
was impossibly self-indulgent. Nikolai Miliutin, the author of the St Petersburg Municipal Reform Act of 1846, fell into the first of these categories;
Ivan Aksakov, with some hesitation, into the second. Their willingness to
enter official employment exemplified one of the main ways in which the
intellectual exchanges of the reign of Nicholas I made a mark on Russian

politics. In one of the most imaginative studies of any aspect of nineteenth-century Russian history, W. Bruce Lincoln has demonstrated that the 1830s and 1840s saw not only the entry into the empire of a new set of west European philosophies, but also the emergence in St Petersburg of a group of 'enlightened bureaucrats' who were to play a notable part in the reforms of the early 1860s.[77] Lincoln connects the two phenomena. Encouraged by P. D. Kiselev (the Minister of State Properties), Lev Perovskii (the Minister of Internal Affairs) and subsequently by the Grand Duke Konstantin Niko-laevich (Nicholas I's younger son) and the Grand Duchess Elena Pavlovna (his sister-in-law), products of the empire's higher education establishments began to occupy positions which gave them scope for collecting information on the true state of the country. Having been exposed as young men to the philosophies which gave rise to Westernizers and Slavophiles, they continued, after entering government service, to move in unofficial circles which encouraged them in their reformist inclinations. By combining their commitment to ideas with the knowledge they acquired in the course of their duties, they put themselves in a position to exercise an influence disproportionate to their numbers. Under the next tsar, they were to make their mark.

Most of the 'enlightened bureaucrats' were Westernizers, but a collateral descendant of Slavophilism was also to prove influential in the politics of the next reign. When, in the wake of the failure of the west European revolutions of 1848, Herzen proclaimed 'what a blessing it is for Russia that the rural commune has never been broken up',[78] he revealed a new-found sympathy for the ideas of Khomiakov and Kireevskii which led him to a Russian brand of socialism. His 'activist communalism' differed sharply from 'the socially passive, religious kind' invented by the Slavophiles,[79] but shared with it the principle of capitalizing on indigenous Russian culture. By combining the western idea of progress with the notion of Russian uniqueness, Herzen and other mid-nineteenth-century intellectuals converted the second generation of the Russian intelligentsia to populism, a dynamic creed which gave rise to action far more radical than that of the enlightened bureaucrats.

It might be argued, therefore, that the intellectuals of the 1830s and 1840s not only planted 'the seeds of much later political speculation',[80] but actually shaped the political history of the reign of Alexander II. While the ideas of the Westernizers penetrated the bureaucracy, those of the Slavophiles – reinterpreted – contributed to the country's first significant period of violent revolutionary activity since Decembrism. Before these developments could ensue, however, Nicholas I's style of rule had to be exposed as inadequate. Until the regime lost a war, it was unlikely to lose its grip.

NOTES

1. Marc Raeff, *Origins of the Russian Intelligentsia: The Eighteenth-Century Nobility* (New York, 1966), p. 170.
2. V. O. Kliuchevskii, 'Evgenii Onegin i ego predki', *Sochineniia* (8 vols, Moscow, 1956–9), vii. 403–22.
3. Lenore O'Boyle, 'The Problem of an Excess of Educated Men in Western Europe, 1800–1850', JMH 42 (1970), 471.
4. Alexander Herzen, *My Past and Thoughts*, tr. Constance Garnett (rev. edn, 4 vols, London, 1968), i. 164.
5. Gordon Cook, 'Petr Čaadaev: The Making of a Cultural Critic, 1826–8', JFGO 21 (1973), 561.
6. Marc Raeff, *Russian Intellectual History: An Anthology* (New York, 1966), pp. 163, 167, 171.
7. I. V. Kireevskii, *Izbrannye stat'i* (Moscow, 1984), pp. 70– 80.
8. S. M. Solov'ev, *Izbrannye trudy; Zapiski* (Moscow, 1983), p. 236.
9. A. I. Gertsen (Herzen), 'Du développement des idées révolutionnaires en Russie', *Sobranie sochinenii* (30 vols, Moscow, 1954–65), vii. 85.
10. N. A. and K. A. Polevoi, *Literaturnaia kritika: Stat'i i retsenzii 1825–1842* (Leningrad, 1990), p. 35.
11. Aleksandr Nikitenko, *The Diary of a Russian Censor*, abridged, ed. and tr. Helen Saltz Jacobson (Amherst, Mass., 1975), p. 48.
12. Gertsen, 'Du développement' (above, n. 9), p. 89.
13. V. A. Panaev, 'Iz "Vospominanii"', in D. V. Grigorovich, *Literaturnye vospominaniia* (Moscow, 1987), pp. 172–3.
14. V. G. Belinskii, 'Literaturnye mechtaniia (Elegiia v proze)', PSS (13 vols, Moscow, 1953–9), i. 102.
15. Gertsen, 'Du développement' (above, n. 9), p. 82.
16. R. G. Eimontova, 'Prosveshchenie v Rossii pervoi poloviny XIX veka', VI, 1986 no. 10, pp. 92–3.
17. Solov'ev, *Izbrannye trudy* (above, n. 8), p. 311.
18. Eimontova, 'Prosveshchenie' (above, n. 16), p. 79.
19. Gertsen, 'Byloe i dumy', *Sobranie sochinenii* (above, n. 9), viii. 107 (incorrectly translated in Herzen, *Past and Thoughts* [above, n. 4], i. 95).
20. V. R. Leikina-Svirskaia, 'Formirovanie raznochinskoi intelligentsii v Rossii v 40-kh godakh XIX v.', *Istoriia SSSR*, 1958 no. 1, p. 94.
21. Solov'ev, *Izbrannye trudy* (above, n. 8), p. 245.
22. B. N. Chicherin, *Vospominaniia: Moskva sorokovykh godov* (Moscow, 1929), p. 34.
23. Ibid., p. 7.
24. Philip Pomper, *The Russian Revolutionary Intelligentsia* (Arlington Heights, Ill., 1970), p. 33.
25. Herzen, *Past and Thoughts* (above, n. 4), ii. 516.
26. Charles A. Ruud, *Fighting Words: Imperial Censorship and the Russian Press, 1804–1906* (Toronto, 1982), p. 56.
27. Sidney Monas, *The Third Section: Police and Society in Russia under Nicholas I* (Cambridge, Mass., 1961), p. 292.
28. R. N. Kleimenova, 'Moskovskii universitet i izdatel'skoe delo v Moskve v pervoi polovine XIX v.', in A. A. Zaitseva et al., eds, *Kniga v Rossii XVI – seredina XIX v.: knigorasprostranenie, biblioteki, chitatel'* (Leningrad, 1987), p. 166.

29. Nicholas V. Riasanovsky, *A Parting of Ways: Government and the Educated Public in Russia 1801–1855* (Oxford, 1976), p. 282.

30. A. A. Formozov, 'Tirazhi istoricheskikh izdanii pervoi poloviny XIX v. v Rossii', VI, 1970 no. 2, pp. 192–6.

31. A. G. Dement'ev et al., eds, *Russkaia periodicheskaia pechat' (1702–1894): Spravochnik* (Moscow, 1959), pp. 102–89, 190–332.

32. Ruud, *Fighting Words* (above, n. 26), pp. 253–4 (tables 1 and 2).

33. Ibid., pp. 65, 74, 79, 94, 278; Dement'ev, *Russkaia periodicheskaia pechat'* (above, n. 31), pp. 297, 241.

34. V. G. Belinskii, 'Tarantas', PSS (above, n. 14), ix. 75; Kireevskii, *Izbrannye stat'i* (above, n. 7), p. 128; Gertsen, 'Du développement' (above, n. 9), p. 87.

35. N. V. Gogol, *Perepiska* (2 vols, Moscow, 1988), i. 387.

36. Leszek Kołakowski, *Main Currents of Marxism* (3 vols, Oxford, 1978), ii. 307.

37. Gertsen, 'Du développement' (above, n. 9), p. 79.

38. Riasanovsky, *A Parting of Ways* (above, n. 29), pp. 283–4.

39. Edward J. Brown, *Stankevich and his Moscow Circle 1830–1840* (Stanford, Calif., 1966), p. 9.

40. Ivan Turgenev, *Sketches from a Hunter's Album,* tr. Richard Freeborn (Harmondsworth, 1967), p. 196; and compare P. V. Annenkov, 'Molodost' I. S. Turgeneva 1840–1856', in Annenkov, *Literaturnye vospominaniia* (Moscow, 1983), p. 376.

41. M. N. Zagoskin, *Moskva i moskvichi: Zapiski Bogdana Il'icha Bel'skogo* (Moscow, 1988), p. 187.

42. Chicherin, *Moskva* (above, n. 22), p. 6.

43. D. B. Saunders, 'Contemporary Critics of Gogol's *Vechera* and the Debate about Russian *narodnost'* (1831–1832)', *Harvard Ukrainian Studies* 5 (1981), 70.

44. Gertsen, 'Du développement' (above, n. 9), pp. 93–4.

45. P. A. Viazemskii, *Estetika i literaturnaia kritika* (Moscow, 1984), pp. 153–4, 411–12.

46. P. A. Pletnev, *Stat'i, stikhotvoreniia, pis'ma* (Moscow, 1988), pp. 59, 362.

47. K. S. and I. S. Aksakov, *Literaturnaia kritika* (Moscow, 1981), pp. 141–50; V. G. Belinskii, review of K. S. Aksakov's *Neskol'ko slov o poeme Gogolia,* PSS (above, n. 14), vi. 253–60.

48. Gertsen, 'Du développement' (above, n. 9), p. 99.

49. Chicherin, *Moskva* (above, n. 22), p. 20.

50. Leonard Schapiro, *Turgenev: His Life and Times* (Oxford, 1978), pp. 53–4; Victor Ripp, *Turgenev's Russia: From 'Notes of a Hunter' to 'Fathers and Sons'* (Ithaca, NY, 1980), p. 44.

51. W. J. Leatherbarrow and D. C. Offord, eds, *A Documentary History of Russian Thought: From the Enlightenment to Marxism* (Ann Arbor, Mich., 1987), p. 131 (italics in the original).

52. Abbott Gleason, *European and Muscovite: Ivan Kireevskii and the Origins of Slavophilism* (Cambridge, Mass., 1972), p. 144.

53. A. S. Khomiakov, 'O starom i novom', PSS, 4th edn (8 vols, Moscow, 1911–14), i. 28–9.

54. Ivan Vasilevich Kireevsky, 'A Reply to A. S. Khomyakov', in Leatherbarrow and Offord, *A Documentary History* (above, n. 51), pp. 79–88.

55. Andrzej Walicki, *The Slavophile Controversy: History of a Conservative Utopia in Nineteenth-Century Russian Thought* (Oxford, 1975), pp. 177–8.

56. A. I. Koshelev, *Zapiski* (Berlin, 1884), p. 73.

57. Ibid., pp. 76–7.
58. N. I. Tsimbaev, *Slavianofil'stvo: Iz istorii russkoi obshchestvenno-politicheskoi mysli XIX veka* (Moscow, 1986), p. 232; for a historiographical article which sets this important work in context see V. A. Kitaev, 'Slavianofil'stvo i liberalizm', VI, 1989 no. 1, pp. 133–43.
59. Khomiakov, 'O sel'skoi obshchine', PSS (above, n. 53), iii. 462.
60. Konstantin Sergeevich Aksakov, 'Memorandum to Alexander II on the Internal State of Russia', in Leatherbarrow and Offord, *A Documentary History* (above, n. 51), pp. 95–107.
61. Herzen, *Past and Thoughts* (above, n. 4), ii.535.
62. Khomiakov, 'Po povodu stat'i I. V. Kireevskogo "O kharaktere prosveshcheniia Evropy i o ego otnoshenii k prosveshcheniiu Rossii"', PSS (above, n. 53), i. 258.
63. Kireevskii, *Izbrannye stat'i* (above, n. 7), pp. 322–3.
64. Chicherin, *Moskva* (above, n. 22), p. 223.
65. In 'The Russian People and Socialism' (1851): see Alexander Herzen, *From the Other Shore and The Russian People and Socialism*, tr. Moura Budberg and Richard Wollheim (Oxford, 1979), pp. 163–208.
66. Nicholas V. Riasanovsky, *The Image of Peter the Great in Russian History and Thought* (New York and Oxford, 1985), p. 149.
67. Brown, *Stankevich* (above, n. 39), p. 129.
68. Kireevskii, *Izbrannye stat'i* (above, n. 7), pp. 314–15.
69. Herzen, *Past and Thoughts* (above, n. 4), ii. 549.
70. Ibid., ii. 543.
71. These remarks of, respectively, Herzen and Ivan Kireevskii, are quoted in Isaiah Berlin, *Russian Thinkers* (London, 1978), p. 132, and Vladimir C. Nahirny, 'The Russian Intelligentsia: From Men of Ideas to Men of Convictions', CSSH 4 (1961–2), 411.
72. Annenkov, 'Molodost' I. S. Turgeneva' (above, n. 40), p. 381.
73. I. A. Fedosov, *Revoliutsionnoe dvizhenie v Rossi vo vtoroi chetverti XIX v. (revoliutsionnye organizatsii i kruzhki)* (Moscow, 1958); V. A. D'iakov, *Osvoboditel'noe dvizhenie v Rossii 1825–1861 gg.* (Moscow, 1979).
74. P. B. Struve, 'Intelligentsiia i revoliutsiia', in *Vekhi: Sbornik statei o russkoi intelligentsii*, 2nd edn (Moscow, 1909), pp. 158–60.
75. Riasanovsky, *A Parting of Ways* (above, n. 29), pp. 249–50.
76. Chicherin, *Moskva* (above, n. 22), p. 114.
77. W. Bruce Lincoln, *In the Vanguard of Reform: Russia's Enlightened Bureaucrats 1825–1861* (DeKalb, Ill., 1982).
78. Herzen, *From the Other Shore* (above, n. 65), p. 189.
79. Abbott Gleason, *Young Russia: The Genesis of Russian Radicalism in the 1860s* (Chicago, 1980), p. 52.
80. Leonard Schapiro, *Rationalism and Nationalism in Russian Nineteenth-Century Political Thought* (New Haven, Conn., 1967), p. 59.

CHAPTER SEVEN

The Russian Bear

WAR WITH THE OTTOMAN EMPIRE AND PERSIA

Nicholas's chances of losing a war were small, because although his out-look was militaristic, he did not really like fighting. What he liked was order, which armies embody in peacetime but abandon in the field. Since for most of his reign he avoided going to war, he hardly deserves the repu-tation for belligerence which contemporaries conferred on him. He ac-quired it partly by accident, for war was near when he ascended the throne. Alexander I had decided in the second half of 1825 that the interna-tional problems which derived from the conflict between Greeks and Turks could not be resolved by the Concert of Europe. His dealings with the other Great Powers had neither benefited his Mediterranean co-religionists nor furthered Russia's long-term policy of controlling the Ottoman Empire. The Turks had deployed Egyptian soldiers in the hope of suppressing the Greeks and were simultaneously ignoring Russian interests in the Yugoslav and Romanian parts of their territory. If he had lived, Alexander would have had to take action. Metternich, in Vienna, thought that the new tsar was even likelier to do so. During the interregnum which followed Alexan-der's death he hoped the Russian crown would go to the Grand Duke Kon-stantin, whom he considered a moderate. In January 1826 he sent an emissary to Warsaw to find out whether Konstantin would use his in-fluence to temper Nicholas's supposed enthusiasm for hostilities. Had he known what advice was reaching the tsar in St Petersburg, his anxiety would have been greater still. Just after his emissary met Konstantin, a for-mer Russian ambassador to Constantinople urged Nicholas to abandon the idea of international cooperation and present the Turks with an ultimatum. In February 1826 the usually cautious Russian foreign minister, Nesselrode, echoed the views of the ex-ambassador. According to Nesselrode, the em-pire had the right to use force and need not fear reprisals from other Euro-pean countries. The stage seemed set for battle.

Nicholas, however, proved to be significantly more cautious than the men around him. Nesselrode's hawkish memorandum had concluded by recommending that, before fighting, the tsar ought to provide 'irrefutable proof of his pacific intentions'.[1] This meant addressing various specific requests to the Turks, telling them what the consequences of refusal would be, and informing the major European courts that Russia was giving the Ottoman Empire a last chance. The tsar adopted these suggestions but reduced the number of specific requests. Pedantic or fearful, Nicholas was reluctant to do more than ask Turkey to abide by earlier Russo-Turkish agreements. Since these said little about Greece, the ultimatum which the Turks received dealt with their treatment of Romanians and Yugoslavs. Where Greece was concerned, Nicholas sought an international solution. Even Alexander, in October 1825, had gone back on his decision to deal with the Greek question unilaterally and had instigated talks on Greece with Britain. The Duke of Wellington came to St Petersburg early in the new reign, and on 23 March / 4 April 1826 Britain and Russia signed a 'Protocol'. Britain agreed to offer mediation between Greeks and Turks on the basis of Greek autonomy, thereby removing at least one of the reasons for Russian military intervention in the Balkans. Romanians and Yugoslavs, however, remained problematical. If the sultan rejected the tsar's ultimatum, war would break out in the Balkans despite the Anglo-Russian agreement. Fortunately, Mahmud II proved compliant. Turkish emissaries arrived in Akkerman on the river Dniester on 24 July / 5 August 1826, and after two months of intermittent wrangling the Russian and Ottoman Empires agreed a codicil to the 1812 Treaty of Bucharest. For the time being, differences over the 'Danubian Principalities' (the future Romania), Serbia (heartland of the future Yugoslavia) and Turkish forts in the western Caucasus were eliminated. Nicholas had shown a preparedness to use diplomatic means which was to be the main feature of his conduct of international relations.

For reasons beyond his control, the new tsar found himself at war with Persia just as he was coming to terms with the Turks. Russia's peaceful acquisition of Georgia in 1801 had given her a foothold south of the Caucasus mountains which seemed to threaten Persian and Turkish interests in the Middle East. To consolidate his hold on Georgia, Alexander had been moving east to the Persian-controlled shore of the south-western Caspian and west to the Turkish-controlled shore of the south-eastern Black Sea. The talks at Akkerman had apparently cleared up disagreements with the Turks, but the Shah, and particularly his son, believed that the Russian domestic crisis of December 1825 had created enough uncertainty in St Petersburg to justify a challenge to the Russo-Persian treaty of 1813. Nicholas sensed the danger and sent Prince Aleksandr Menshikov to Tehran for talks. Abbas Mirza, the heir to the Persian throne, was not to be dissuaded from aggression. Persian forces crossed the river Araxes in mid-July 1826 and forced Russia's frontier troops to fall back on the Georgian capital of Tiflis (Tbilisi). In September Nicholas responded with a formal declaration of war.

At first, from the Russian point of view, the fighting went badly. Nicholas despatched Denis Davydov and Ivan Paskevich to help Aleksei Ermolov, the local commander-in-chief, but Paskevich and Ermolov differed radically in character and fell out over tactics. Paskevich wanted to cross the Araxes without further ado and move on Tabriz and Tehran, whereas Ermolov believed that the fortress of Erevan had to be taken first. Because Ermolov had been commanding Russia's forces in the Caucasus for more than a decade (and because he was something of a maverick), Paskevich had more friends in St Petersburg. Ermolov was dismissed in March 1827, Paskevich took not only Erevan but also Echmiadzin, Nakhichevan and Tabriz, and by the time the Shah accepted terms at Turkmanchai in February 1828 Russian forces were moving in the direction of the Persian capital. The set-back of 1826 had been turned into a triumph. Persia paid a large indemnity and surrendered her Armenian provinces of Erevan and Nakhichevan, thus giving Russia a cushion against future threats from the south. Without having courted war, the new tsar had achieved one of the greatest Russian successes in the century-long history of Russo-Persian enmity.

Despite the negotiations at Akkerman, Nicholas soon had to fight the Turks. Because Istanbul showed no sign of accepting British mediation on the question of Greek autonomy, Britain and Russia, now joined by France, signed the Treaty of London in July 1827. Reiterating their support for Greek autonomy, they declared that, if the Turks did not accept international mediation within a month, they would enter into commercial relations with the Greeks and 'determine the ulterior measures to which it may become necessary to resort'.[2] This was not quite a final decision to go to war, but when allied ships under Admiral Codrington moved into Navarino Bay on the south-western edge of the Peloponnese in October 1827 and, without having set out to do so, destroyed the fleet of the Sultan's Egyptian forces, war became inevitable. After finishing his business with Persia, the tsar sent his troops into the Danubian Principalities in April 1828. Nicholas impeded his generals in the first campaigning season by taking the field personally, but in 1829 Ivan Dibich led the army deep into eastern Thrace while Paskevich, in the east, took Kars and Erzerum (a campaign immortalized in prose by Aleksandr Pushkin).

For someone whose nature was supposed to be grasping, Nicholas was remarkably generous to the Turks at the peacemaking. Each of the three most recent treaties between the Russian and Ottoman Empires (Kuchuk Kainardji in 1774, Jassy in 1791, Bucharest in 1812) had shifted the tsars' frontier to a new river on the north-western edge of the Black Sea (the Bug, the Dniester and the Pruth). The Treaty of Adrianople of September 1829 went only a little further, transferring the northern shore of the Danube to Russian control from the point where the Pruth flowed into it. 'The annexation of the Danube delta ... was no great acquisition'.[3] Apart from the delta, Turkey had to concede the right of merchant ships to pass through the Bosphorus and the Dardanelles (which was crucial from the point of view of Russian trade), and to surrender rather more significant territories in the eastern part of her empire (because Russia was determined to control the eastern shore of the Black Sea and to enlarge her buffer zone around Georgia). Russia's main concern in 1829, however, was to protect the interests of the sultan's Romanian subjects without enlarging the territory under direct Russian control. She achieved this end by establishing a temporary protectorate over the Danubian Principalities of Moldavia and Wallachia under P. D. Kiselev (the former friend of Decembrists and future Minister of State Properties). Over a five-year period Kiselev transformed the administration of the lands between the Pruth and the Danube to such an extent that it was to be hard, thereafter, for the sultan or outsiders to prevent the eventual emergence of an independent Romania. When Russian forces finally retreated from the Danubian Principalities in 1834, Nicholas seemed to have achieved the final stabilization of his southern frontier.

Peace rather than war had been his goal throughout. Just before St Petersburg learned that the sultan had accepted the Treaty of Adrianople, a conference of senior Russian ministers agreed 'That the advantages of maintaining the Ottoman Empire in Europe are greater than the difficulties which it presents'.[4] This belief underpinned Russian policy towards Turkey for the greater part of the reign. The major European states thought Russia intended to dismember the Ottoman Empire, but in fact she sought to keep it in being. A weak neighbour could be bullied; a power vacuum would attract the attention of Britain, France and Austria.

NICHOLAS I AND THE POLISH PROBLEM

The preservation of the status quo was also Nicholas's prime concern with regard to central and western Europe, though here, paradoxically, his policy should have involved much more fighting than it did. In July 1830 the French overthrew the main line of the Bourbon dynasty and replaced it with a cadet branch represented by King Louis Philippe. In August and September of the same year the Belgians rebelled against the Kingdom of the Netherlands and established an independent state. Since by this time various German principalities were also in ferment, the entire European settlement of 1815 appeared to be in jeopardy. Determined to keep it in place, Nicholas mobilized his troops. Soon, 'a confrontation between Russia and France seemed inevitable'.[5] For two reasons, however, no confrontation took place. First, Nicholas had no hope of undertaking a campaign at the opposite end of the continent without the assistance of Austria and Prussia – but Austria and Prussia were reluctant to join him. Second, Nicholas could hardly afford to send troops abroad unless he could be sure that all was well at home – but at the end of November 1830 a coup took place in Warsaw. Years later Nesselrode wrote that the European revolutions of

1830 'opened a new period' in Nicholas I's foreign policy, turning him into 'the representative of the monarchical idea, the bastion of principles of order and the impartial defender of European equilibrium'.[6] This may have been Nicholas's opinion of himself, but it did not affect many of his actions. As the events which followed the Warsaw coup illustrated, circumstances required 'the Russian bear' to spend more time mauling the non-Russian inhabitants of the Russian Empire than attacking non-Russians abroad. For most of the 1830s and 1840s Nicholas's policy towards non-Russians took the form of 'inter-national' rather than 'international' relations. Ethnicity, to use modern terminology, occupied more of the tsar's attention than diplomacy.

Many reasons may be adduced for the Polish uprising of November 1830: the Russians' two-year hunt for 'Polish Decembrists'; the tsar's reluctance to be separately crowned as King of Poland; the refusal of St Petersburg to attach to the 'Congress Kingdom' of Poland the provinces to the east which had once been part of the Polish-Lithuanian Commonwealth; the emergence of Polish literary figures who 'understood romanticism as embodying a patriotic call to restore the old republic within its old frontiers';[7] the decline of the Polish economy; the inspiration of the events of 1830 in France and Belgium; and the arrest, just before the rising, of a number of militant soldiers and students. In the light of this long list of grievances, it was remarkable how slowly the rising took hold. If the Viceroy, the Grand Duke Konstantin, had been firm, he could probably have prevented the Poles' discontent from escalating. He abandoned Warsaw to the rebels, however, whereupon they convened a Diet. Even the Diet did not immediately call for offensive action against Russia, but it decided to do so when the tsar refused to negotiate on the basis of anything less than abject Polish submission. On 13/25 January 1831 the Poles dethroned the Romanovs. Early the following month General Dibich led the Russian First Army into the Congress Kingdom.

Partly because the First Army had not seen service since 1814 (the Second Army having been responsible for the victories of 1828–9 in the Balkans), the Russian advance into Poland was hesitant. The Poles won two early victories before the tide began slowly to turn against them. The battle of Grochów in February 1831 'was ... counted as a Polish victory, [but] produced at the time a state of panic in Warsaw'.[8] Although Dibich failed to enter the Polish capital and the tsar became increasingly dissatisfied with him, three months after Grochów Russian troops established a decisive superiority at the battle of Ostrołęka on the River Narew. Even then Dibich's death from cholera on 29 May / 10 June 1831 slowed down the advance of the tsarist troops, but Paskevich had already been summoned from the Caucasus and eventual Russian victory was assured. On 27 August / 8 September the tsar's forces retook Warsaw.

Nicholas's suppression of the Polish rebellion outraged public opinion in western Europe and dealt his reputation a blow from which it never recovered. Having welcomed his accession in 1825, the British press came to treat him as 'the master of noble slaves, the ravisher of women, the destroyer of domestic happiness, the assassin of children ... [and] a monster in human form'.[9] Adam Czartoryski, who was forced into Parisian exile after having proved a less than satisfactory choice as head of the Polish insurgent government, found himself able, in the west, to create 'a diplomatic agency which was to influence, and at times even direct, the foreign policies of the great powers'.[10] In France, radicals who agreed on little else invaded the National Assembly in May 1848 with the object of goading it into action on the Polish question. Unabashed, Nicholas dedicated himself to purging the Congress Kingdom of dissent. According to Paskevich, whom he put in as Viceroy (the Grand Duke Konstantin having died, like Dibich, of cholera), 'The Poles ... experienced not vengeance and retribution but assistance and the consignment of their guilt to oblivion'.[11] The Poles themselves must have felt differently. The governmental, social, economic, military, legal, educational and ecclesiastical structures of the kingdom underwent dramatic changes. The Diet was abolished; a large number of hereditary Polish nobles deprived of noble status; the woollen industry destroyed; the separate army eliminated; the legal system Russianized; the University of Warsaw closed; and an Orthodox eparchy introduced to compete with the Roman Catholic Church. The Poles of the Congress Kingdom were not broken, for even Paskevich admitted in 1850 that the calm he had established merely reflected their 'awareness of their powerlessness and their conviction of the incontestable might of your Imperial Highness'.[12] The tsar, however, believed he had found a better way to knit his territories together than any conceived by his predecessors. Since the Congress Kingdom of Poland was only one of a number of outlying parts of the empire which required his attention, and since he could hardly afford a forward policy in western Europe or the Balkans until his own peripheries were fully integrated into the imperial structure, he spent more time in the 1830s and 1840s on his own non-Russian subjects than on dealings with foreigners.

Because Poles were the dominant national group not only in the Congress Kingdom but also in the region to the east of it which St Petersburg called the 'western provinces', the latter as well as the former became the subject of new policies after the Polish uprising of 1830. Few inhabitants of the western provinces were Russian. Apart from the Polish gentry, the main population groups were Lithuanian, Belorussian, Ukrainian and Jewish. As an experienced head of the educational system in Vitebsk pointed out in 1832, it was 'extremely difficult to persuade capable and reliable Russians to come here, even to take important posts'.[13] Nicholas engaged in a long-term programme of social engineering. By closing down Polish educational institutions (notably the university at Vil'na and the lycée at Krzemieniec), by suppressing the Uniate Church (in 1839), by abolishing Magdeburg Law in Kiev (in 1835) and the Lithuanian Statute throughout the region (in 1840), by promoting the publication of history books which argued that the western provinces had been Russian from time immemorial, by depriving many Poles of noble status, by promoting the interests of their Ukrainian and Belorussian serfs, and by insisting that local administration be conducted in Russian, he sought to make clear what he meant by allowing 'Nationality', *narodnost'*, to be attached to 'Orthodoxy' and 'Autocracy' in the celebrated circular of 1833. Nationality, for Nicholas, meant being or becoming Russian. His Minister of Education, Uvarov – the propagator of the doctrine – understood the tsar's position only too well. In a lengthy report on his first ten years in office he made much of the fact that, whereas 'Russian was scarcely to be heard' in the western provinces at the time of his appointment, it now had 'an indisputable primacy'.[14]

Nicholas and Uvarov flattered themselves, however, if they believed that the western provinces were becoming less intractable than the Congress Kingdom. The government's 'integrationist' policies merely scraped the surface of the problems they were supposed to resolve. Very few Russian nobles moved west, but 'in 1858 the majority of the nobles in the Russian Empire ... still lived in the nine western *gubernii* [provinces]'.[15] An enormous number of Polish nobles, therefore, had survived the government's attempts to relegate them to lesser estates. Nor had Polish nobles suffered unduly from the disappearance of Polish schools, for most of them received their education at home. Although those who studied at Kiev University (Vil'na's successor) had to know enough Russian to understand lectures, they constituted the majority of the new university's students for the first thirty years of its life and did not need Russian to consort with their peers. It is even possible that, far from weakening the Poles' sense of their national identity, Nicholas's educational endeavours gave it a fillip. 'One nationalism furthers other nationalisms'.[16] To judge by the number of Poles at Kiev University who joined a conspiratorial society organized throughout the western provinces by Szymon Konarski in 1838, exposure to Nicholas I's Russocentric educational system sometimes had consequences very different from those intended by the authorities in St Petersburg.

UKRAINIANS AND JEWS

The expansion of the Russian educational system also had unexpected effects on Ukrainians. After the Russians, these were the second most numerous ethnic group to be ruled from St Petersburg and occupied an area which, apart from the north-eastern corner of the Habsburg Empire, included the three southernmost of Russia's nine western provinces and an equally large region on the left or eastern bank of the river Dnieper. Ukrainians tended to be less troublesome than Poles because most of their gentry had been Polonized or Russified in the two centuries prior to 1800. St Petersburg called them 'Little Russians' and treated them like country cousins. Ukrainian peasants' sense of their ethnic identity was poorly developed. They described themselves as *rusyny*, a term which merely indicated descent from the inhabitants of the medieval principality of Rus'. The ethnic term 'Ukrainian', though not the geographical expression 'the Ukraine' (or 'Ukraine'), is a late-nineteenth-century invention which was adopted by most of the people to whom it applies only after 1917. After obliging the last autonomous ruler of the Ukrainian heartland to resign (in 1764) and breaking up the Ukrainian Cossacks (in 1775), Catherine the Great had subjected Ukrainians to the poll tax and extended to their territory her reform of Russian provincial administration. These measures occasioned little resistance. Whereas, at the beginning of the nineteenth century, Ukrainian subjects of the Habsburg Empire were beginning to think of themselves as a distinct ethnic group, Ukrainian subjects of the tsar appeared not to do so. Despite the fact that the southern Decembrists operated on Ukrainian soil, they attracted few Ukrainian collaborators or imitators. 'We cannot speak of "Ukrainian Decembrists", but ... only of Decembrists in the Ukraine'.[17]

After reaching a low point, however, the notion of a difference between Ukrainians and Russians began to gain ground. Despite adopting the Russian language, welcoming incorporation into the Russian gentry, and often abandoning the Ukraine for St Petersburg, well-placed Ukrainians tended to demonstrate a continuing affinity with the land of their birth. Meanwhile, the introduction of Russian educational institutions into the Ukraine proved to have centrifugal as well as centripetal implications. The opening of Khar'kov University in 1805 and of Kiev University in 1834 stimulated native interest in the parts of the Ukraine which they served. In the second and third decades of the nineteenth century the publication of locally orientated journals, the collection of Ukrainian folksongs, and attempts to use Ukrainian as a literary language marked the beginnings of divergence between the recently dovetailed northern and southern parts of the Russian Empire. At first, the imperial authorities saw no danger in a Ukrainian cultural awakening and even thought it might assist them in their conflicts with the Poles. In the 1840s, however, St Petersburg took fright. Three Ukrainians, Taras Shevchenko, Panteleimon Kulish and Mykola (or Nikolai) Kostomarov, 'combined the local Ukrainian historical and literary traditions with the nationalistic terminology emanating from St Petersburg to produce new syntheses in Ukrainian literature and history'.[18] When Kostomarov, probably in collaboration with kindred spirits, wrote an emotive tract which concluded by saying that 'Ukraine will become an independent People's State in a Slavonic union',[19] his cultural activities seemed to be taking on clear political overtones. Nicholas I's regime had no interest in federalism. After receiving information from an impoverished student at Kiev University, the authorities arrested ten Ukrainian activists in 1847 and subjected the best known of them, the poet and painter Taras Shevchenko, to military service with deprivation of writing and drawing materials.

The arrests of 1847 exposed an organization called the Kirillo-Methodian

Brotherhood, whose purpose, the regime believed, was to dismember the empire. The authorities' heavy-handed intervention showed just how sensitive they were to the question of the empire's internal diversity, for the Brotherhood's goals were in fact much less radical than St Petersburg supposed and Shevchenko and Kulish may not even have been members. Poles had proved in 1830–1 that they posed a genuine threat to the unity of the empire, but Ukrainians were not to constitute a significant danger for decades. Uvarov, however, went so far as to redefine 'Official Nationality' in the wake of the Brotherhood's demise. In effect, he made the interpretation of the word 'Nationality' (*narodnost*) even more dependent on the traditional notions of 'Orthodoxy' and 'Autocracy' than it had been when he promulgated Nicholas I's tripartite programme in 1833. 'Russian Slavdom', he wrote,

must in its pure form express unconditional allegiance to orthodoxy and autocracy; everything which passes beyond these bounds represents the admixture of alien concepts, the play of fantasy, or a mask behind which the ill-intentioned try to ensnare inexperience and entice dreamers.[20]

By occasioning the promulgation of this revised version of Official Nationality, the first generation of Ukrainian cultural activists acquired an importance far greater than their numbers warranted.

If a few Ukrainians suffered as individuals at the hands of the Nicholaevan regime, Jews, like Poles, suffered collectively. Whereas Catherine the Great had confined them to the western and southern borderlands of the empire and Alexander I had encouraged them to consider economic diversification and cultural assimilation, Nicholas intervened in their lives more dramatically. In 1827 he not only obliged them to start performing military service but also declared that Jewish recruits were to be enlisted at the age of twelve rather than twenty. Herzen came across even younger Jewish children on their way to the army in the first half of the 1830s. A Jewish Statute of 1835 which reiterated the pious sentiments of Alexander I's statute of 1804 proved to be more impressive on paper than in reality. The classification of Jews as 'aliens' in the 1835 digest of imperial legislation seemed to encapsulate the government's true attitude. At Nicholas's behest, P. D. Kiselev designed a series of measures in the 1840s whose aim was to quicken the rate at which Jews abandoned the traditions of their fathers. By abolishing their organs of self-government, attempting to enrol them in secular educational institutions, and trying much harder than earlier legislators to force them out of the countryside into the towns, the Minister of State Properties intensified the subversion of Jewish communal life which had begun when community leaders had to make invidious choices about recruits for the army. Not surprisingly, Nicholas I came to be 'almost universally reviled in Russian-Jewish historiography as the Russian Haman'.[21]

It is unlikely that the tsar felt more strongly about Jews than about other ethnic groups. He found them socially and administratively anomalous, but this was also his opinion of Poles. Nicholas believed that the best thing non-Russians could do was become Russian. Jews had a better chance of effecting the transition if, for example, they were recruited into the army as children. From the tsar's point of view, his handling of Jewish matters was progressive. Reform-minded Jews, furthermore, actually welcomed some of his innovations. Michael Stanislawski paints a grim picture of Jewish affairs under Nicholas I but admits that 'at no time in this period did policy toward the Jews depart from the framework and pattern of overall government activity'.[22] The tsar was trying to integrate his domains. Since Jews deviated further than most other groups from the blueprint he had in mind, he needed to take particularly strong measures to make them conform to it.

THE CAUCASUS, CENTRAL ASIA, SIBERIA, FINNS AND BALTS

Poles, Ukrainians and Jews were all to be found in the western, south-western and southern parts of the empire. Far to the south-east of St Petersburg, in the Caucasus, Nicholas fought the second of his two domestic wars. Suppressing the Poles had taken less than a year, but the pacification of Muslims in the mountainous region between the Black Sea and the Caspian was to continue beyond the end of the reign. Although Nicholas's victories over the Persians in 1828 and the Ottoman Empire in 1829 had made him temporarily safe from international complications in this area, they did little for the extension of Russian control over the peoples who lived to the north of Georgia. The imperial frontier had moved to the south, but pockets of unconquered territory remained in the rear. When congratulating Paskevich on the end of the war with the Turks in 1829, Nicholas told him that his next task was to be 'the permanent pacification of the mountain peoples or the extermination of the recalcitrant'.[23] In the tsar's view, the new assignment was much more important than the one Paskevich had just completed.

Aleksei Ermolov, the Russian commander in the Caucasus whom Paskevich replaced in 1827, had been pursuing a conciliatory or 'regionalist' policy for more than a decade. Between the late 1820s and the early 1840s, St Petersburg tried the opposite approach – imposing Russian practices on people to whom they were totally alien. Paskevich soon moved from the Caucasus to Warsaw, but other proconsuls continued his work. Even Georgia proved troublesome in 1832, when a small number of aristocrats tried unsuccessfully to reverse the annexation of 1801. Foreign rule, it seemed, had 'not only united a previously divided Georgian territory, but reactivated a sense of Georgian identity'.[24] Muslims, however, proved to be much more intractable than Christians. In the early stages of the war for the Caucasus the Russians concentrated their resources in the west. Having acquired the eastern coast of the Black Sea from the Turks, they found that forts were insufficient to protect it against raids from the interior. While they were working their way into the hinterland, various peoples of the eastern Caucasus adopted a militant version of Islam and found a leader in the legendary Shamil. By 1843 Dagestan, to the north-east of Georgia, was in uproar. Fifteen years of insisting on integration had borne little fruit. The tsar's attempts to dictate policy from St Petersburg had culminated, in 1842, in the creation of the Sixth Department of the Imperial Chancery, the only subdivision of that body to be charged with responsibility for a discrete geographical area.

Nicholas had begun to grasp, however, that even the most determined central intervention in Caucasian affairs was unlikely to further the cause of imperial unity. In 1844 he signalled a change of direction by appointing Mikhail Vorontsov to the new post of Caucasian Viceroy. Both the office and the office-holder were remarkable. By creating a Viceroyalty, the tsar went beyond the policy of devolution which had operated in the Caucasus under Ermolov. The new Viceroy was assigned greater authority than any other servant of the crown. Even Paskevich, in the Congress Kingdom of Poland, had to defer on occasion to the ministries of the central government. Vorontsov was an unlikely choice for the new position. Although he had had a distinguished military record as a young man, he was sixty-two and had been engaged in predominantly civil duties for the previous twenty years. It was doubtful whether he could take on mountain tribes. His reputation, moreover, was that of a liberal. Because he had been brought up in England (where his father was a long-serving Russian ambassador), his outlook was broader than that of the majority of Russian nobles. He had been the first serf-owner to take advantage of the reformist Law on Obligated Peasants. Although he had always worked hard to maintain good relations with the tsar and the central government, he was not a professional courtier. His great qualification for the new post lay in the fact that since 1823 he had been an outstandingly successful Governor of New Russia (the coastal part of the modern Ukraine). There, he had presided over a society only slightly less diverse than that of the Caucasus and had fostered its development without trespassing dangerously on local sensibilities. This experience gave him at least a chance of succeeding in the Caucasus.

After an abortive attempt to force Shamil into the open in 1845, Vorontsov combined a policy of gradually strangling the rebellious highlanders with an approach to civil administration which allowed natives a little room for manoeuvre. Opinions differ on the extent of his success. Recent scholars have pointed out that 'When Nicholas died in February 1855, the Caucasus remained unconquered' and that Vorontsov's 'undertakings were often limited and not as successful as he hoped'.[25] The region remained peaceful during the Crimean War, however, and Shamil's twenty-five-year career was brought to an end in 1859 (five years after Vorontsov retired). In the context of a general discussion of Nicholas I's attitude towards non-Russians (both inside and outside the empire), it is more important to note the sheer complexity of Caucasian affairs than to grade the first Viceroy's performance. So long as frontier zones of the empire remained insecure, the tsar had to eschew an ambitious foreign policy. He could make himself out to be the apostle of order in Europe, but he had to devote far more his attention to order at home. The Caucasus alone would have been enough to incline him to seek peace in external relations.

If the Caucasus had been easier to control or the Khan of Khiva less suspicious, the western shore of the Caspian might have become the embarkation point for central Asia. As early as 1819 Ermolov despatched Captain N. N. Murav'ev from Baku across Turkmenia into the territory of the Uzbeks. On reaching Khiva, however, he failed to convince the local khan that Uzbek goods ought to travel due west instead of north-west to Astrakhan. The central Asian khanates (Khiva, Bukhara and Kokand) did not trust the Russians enough to take their advice on trade routes. They were probably right to suspect that St Petersburg had begun to think of intervening in their affairs. The prominent politician Admiral Mordvinov had recommended the creation of a strong Russian colony at Krasnovodsk on the eastern Caspian in 1816. In 1819 the Ministry of Foreign Affairs acquired a permanent Asiatic desk, and in the same year Alexander I created an inter-ministerial body, the Asiatic Committee, to consider how Russia's trade with the Orient could best be maintained and improved. If central Asia could not be approached from the Caspian it had to be penetrated from the north, which meant bridging the gap between Russia's south-eastern military outpost at Orenburg and the Aral Sea. The nomads of Kazakhstan, in other words, had to be brought more firmly under Russian control.

In the reign of Nicholas I, 'The flow of Russian settlers into northern Kazakhstan increased sharply'.[26] When Khiva backed the Kazakhs in their resistance to Russian penetration, St Petersburg vacillated. It could either launch an offensive against Khiva or gradually pacify Kazakhstan by constructing forts and attempting to persuade Khiva that its behaviour was ill judged. The problem could not be ignored, for Britain was strengthening her hold on northern India, pushing into Afghanistan and despatching agents into the khanates from the south. The question of securing the central Asian trade began to look urgent. In 1839 advocates of direct action experienced a severe set-back when the governor of Orenburg led an expedition against Khiva which ended in disaster. Russia needed peace until the construction of forts in Kazakhstan had improved her lines of communication. Fortunately, from the point of view of the tsar, the Khan of Bukhara was pro-Russian and gave him the chance to threaten Khiva from the rear. A crisis, however, was in the offing. Although a survey of Russia's dealings with central Asia in the first half of the nineteenth century concludes that 'Bukhara, Khiva, and Kokand were not primary objects of interest', the work as a whole provides massive evidence for the view that only the problem of traversing Kazakhstan prevented the khanates from coming to the top of the imperial agenda.[27] When central Asia became a prime focus of tsarist policy in the next reign, Britain was sufficiently involved in the region to object. Thus the time spent on securing Kazakhstan turned what might have been a sideshow in central Asia into a major international issue.

Other non-Russian parts of the empire posed fewer problems in the reign of Nicholas I than the Polish west, the Ukrainian and Caucasian south, and the Turkic south-east. The native peoples of Siberia were allowed to go on benefiting from the reforms which Speranskii had introduced in 1822; in this area 'there was no sustained programme of enforced Russification or even christianisation'.[28] Although the exiled Decembrists worried local officials and prompted a Governor-General to recommend that they be sent elsewhere because they were 'gradually disseminating their ideas and ... might be harmful',[29] they were far less militant than exiled Poles, whose plans to take over Omsk in 1833 seem to have given the authorities their largest Siberian scare of the reign. Sensibly, from the point of view of the regime, Nicholas had taken the precaution of consigning the one prominent conspirator of 1825 who actually came from Siberia, Grigorii Baten'kov, to the Peter and Paul Fortress in St Petersburg. It was not until the last decade of Nicholas's reign that a Governor of Eastern Siberia began recommending a forward policy in northern China, and not until the accession of Alexander II that he gained the ear of the tsar. Whereas Kazakhstan was already thought to be a springboard for additional territorial acquisitions, Siberia, as yet, was not. Indeed, Russia seemed to be drawing in her horns on the eastern edge of her dominions. In 1821 Alexander I had tried to stop foreign powers fishing and whaling between the Sea of Okhotsk and Russian Alaska, but in 1824 he modified his policy in the light of the United States' promulgation of the Monroe Doctrine. In 1832 Nicholas made a trade agreement with Washington which lasted for the rest of the century. Since no more than 1,000 Russian citizens lived in Russian America at any one time in the history of the Russian-American Company, holding on to Alaska indefinitely was going to prove difficult. The sale of Fort Ross in California in 1841 marked a well-defined stage on the road to withdrawal.

Even Finns and the non-Russians on the southern coast of the Baltic Sea gave St Petersburg fewer headaches in the reign of Nicholas I than inhabitants of the western and southern parts of the empire. Finns, Estonians and Latvians all had grounds for complaint. Finland had been annexed only recently, and the impoverishment of the Baltic peasantry which resulted from their emancipation under Alexander I could have given rise to extensive social unrest. The government trod carefully, however, and the two regions remained at peace. Finns profited from the accident that their Governor-General, Aleksandr Menshikov, was one of Nicholas's most prominent, trusted, and above all busiest officials. Menshikov could not afford to devote much time to his Finnish duties, but 'identified Finland with his own authority'.[30] As a result, he was unlikely to initiate a Russianizing drive of his own but equally unlikely to let others begin one. So long as Finland remained tranquil, Menshikov was prepared to listen to advisers in the Grand Duchy who put the interests of the local population before those of Russia. Separate Finnish tariffs, the Finnish Lutheran Church and Finnish laws survived the reign unscathed. The Finnish language actually gained in status as a result of Elias Lönnrot's publication of Finnish folk poetry in the *Kalevala.*

In the Baltic provinces, meanwhile – modern Estonia and Latvia – the tsar considered the German nobles his friends. Russianization was pointless while they kept the lower orders in their place and went on providing generals for the Russian army. The tsar was prepared, on occasion, to reproach German nobles for allowing the condition of the Estonian and Latvian peasantry to deteriorate, and in educational and especially religious affairs he sanctioned attempts to bring the Baltic provinces into line with the rest of the empire. In 1845, however, he recognized the privileges of the German barons in a two-volume collection of local laws, and in 1849 he subjected the Slavophile, Iurii Samarin, to twelve days in the Peter and Paul Fortress and a personal interrogation for inveighing against the German hegemony in privately circulated 'Letters from Riga'. By comparison with his policies in the western provinces and the Caucasus, Nicholas's policy towards the non-Russians of the northern part of the empire was to leave well alone.

Despite the relative tranquillity of Siberia and the European north, coping with the frontier zones as a whole significantly reduced the imperial regime's capacity for taking decisive action in international affairs. Quite apart from the borders' incessant claims on the tsar's attention, they tied down his troops. In the late 1830s eighteen of the regime's twenty-three infantry divisions were stationed in Poland and the western provinces, two in the Caucasus, one in Finland, one in Siberia and one at Orenburg on the edge of Kazakhstan, a distribution which accurately reflected the importance of the various 'peripheral' difficulties. Western powers were wrong to believe that tsarist troops in Poland were aimed at the heart of Europe, for they were needed where they were. They were needed even in the heartland of the empire. In Nicholas's reign soldiers rarely had to deal with large-scale disturbances in the Russian part of the empire (apart from the rebellion of the Novgorod military colonists in 1831), but since the bureaucracy was small (relative to the size of the empire's population) they were constantly engaged in business which other societies left to civilians. 'One signal achievement of the French Revolution', writes John Keep, 'was to affirm the primacy of the civil power'. Owing to the shortage of suitable personnel, no such primacy existed in the mid-nineteenth-century Russian Empire. Military authorities often performed the duties of the judiciary: 'civilians found themselves facing court martial because they fell into one of the categories – 41 in all – which placed them within military jurisdiction'. Between 1827 and 1846, for example, some 3,400 people were sent to Siberia as a result of judicial procedures conducted by soldiers.[31]

Thus the fact that the tsar possessed a large army did not mean that he could risk significant external commitments. He needed it to keep himself afloat at home. Financial exigency as well as domestic security dictated a peace policy, for the second of the two early wars and the suppression of the Polish rebellion inflated the national debt from 652 million paper rubles in 1828 to 823 million in 1832. Financial considerations may have played as big a part as stupidity in explaining the military administration's failure to switch from smooth-bore to rifled muskets before the Crimean War. If they did, the tsar must have known that fighting a major European power was ill advised. Even if they did not, he had reason enough to stay his hand. When, therefore, Nesselrode said that the European revolutions of 1830 turned Nicholas into 'the impartial defender of European equilibrium', he did not mean that the tsar had decided to back his 'impartiality' with force. The memorandum gave that impression, but it was written in the light of developments occasioned by the European revolutions of 1848. For the greater part of the 1830s and 1840s Nicholas I dedicated himself to international peace.

THE TURKISH PROBLEM IN THE 1830S AND 1840S

Just after Nicholas had completed the subjugation of the Poles, the Ottoman Empire threatened him with the need for further military action. In 1831 the Sultan's Egyptian vassal, Mehemet Ali, launched an assault on Syria which challenged Constantinople's authority and endangered the strong position which Russia had acquired on her southern flank as a result of the Treaty of Adrianople. Egyptian forces captured Acre and Damascus in May and June 1832 and continued their march northward. In November 1832 Nicholas sent an emissary to Turkey and Egypt to stiffen the resistance of the former and confront the latter with the prospect of Russian intervention. In December Mehemet Ali's son overwhelmed the Turkish army at Konya in southern Asia Minor. Since France was pro-Egyptian and Britain's fleets were otherwise engaged, the Sultan had to ask Russia for more than diplomatic assistance. By invitation, some twenty Russian ships and 10,000 Russian soldiers arrived outside Constantinople in February and March 1833. The fundamentally cautious Mehemet Ali decided to withdraw from Asia Minor and content himself with Syria, but Nicholas realized that, to prevent a recurrence of the crisis, he had to find a way of institutionalizing his short-term assistance to the Ottomans. He was not confident of his ability to do so. In February he had told the Austrian Ambassador in St Petersburg, 'I lack the power to give life to a corpse, and the Turkish empire is dead'.[32] He was not prepared, however, to involve himself in the European war which would have resulted from a substantial direct intervention in Turkish affairs. Only one option remained: reverting to the policy of alliance with the Ottomans which his father, Paul, had adopted in 1798. In July 1833 Russian and Turkish representatives signed the Treaty of Unkiar-Skelessi, a defensive agreement under which St Petersburg promised to assist the Turks in times of crisis and Constantinople promised to prevent warships from passing through the Dardanelles.

Third parties believed that Unkiar-Skelessi marked a further stage in Russia's southward advance. It was unclear to them why St Petersburg should promise the Turks assistance in return for the closure of the Dardanelles, when closing the straits between the Aegean and the Black Sea was a longstanding Turkish principle. Nicholas appeared to have acted gratuitously. The British Foreign Secretary, Palmerston, wrote in a despatch of December 1833 that there could be 'No reasonable doubt ... [but] that the Russian Govt. is intently engaged in the prosecution of those schemes of aggrandizement toward the South which, ever since the Reign of Catherine, have formed a prominent feature of Russian policy'.[33] In reality, aggrandizement was very far from Russia's thoughts. The tsar had been slow to attack Turkey at the beginning of his reign, and had adopted an explicitly pro-Turkish policy afer winning the war of 1828–9. He wanted an assurance that the Dardanelles would remain closed to warships because he feared the possibility of a British or French attack on the southern part of the Russian Empire. He promised the Turks assistance not because he wished to establish a protectorate over them, but because he wanted their regime to survive and Britain had been unable to assist them. Two months after Unkiar-Skelessi, at Münchengrätz in Bohemia, he explained his Turkish policy to the Emperor of Austria and persuaded him to act as an additional guarantor of the integrity of the Ottoman lands. In 1834, as we have already seen, he brought to an end his six-year occupation of the Danubian Principalities. The flaw in his Near Eastern policy arose not from its objectives, which were peaceable, but from the secrecy with which all foreign policies were conducted in the nineteenth century and which often prevented the Great Powers from understanding each other.

When, in 1839, the Sultan made a disastrous attempt to recoup his losses of 1833, all the Great Powers saw the need for keeping the new conflict within bounds. Egyptian forces again proved militarily superior to the Turks; the Turkish fleet went over to the enemy; the Sultan died when hostilities were at their peak; and an Egyptian march on Constantinople seemed even likelier than at the end of 1832. True to the policy of backing the Constantinople regime, Nesselrode told the Russian ambassador in Paris that St Petersburg could not allow 'the Pasha of Egypt ... to place ... the existence of the Ottoman Empire in peril'.[34] Because, on this occasion, the other four Great Powers seemed to agree with the Russian Foreign Minister, the crisis promised to be short-lived. France, however, realized that her good relations with Egypt would suffer and her influence in the Levant diminish if she participated in an international move to force Mehemet Ali's withdrawal from Syria. The powers' united front broke down and the crisis lasted two years. Britain believed that she came out of it very well. Un-daunted by French bluster, she took Beirut and Acre in 1840 and played the major part in obliging the Egyptians to return home. She then deprived the tsar of the special status he had enjoyed at Constantinople since 1833. In 1841 all five Great Powers – France having returned to the fold – signed a 'Straits Convention' which internationalized the Treaty of Unkiar-Skelessi. Not just Russia, but all the major European countries, committed them-selves to banning non-Turkish warships from the Bosphorus and the Dar-danelles when the Ottoman Empire was at peace. Palmerston seemed to have defeated the tsar. Nesselrode, however, the tsar's foreign minister, had good reason for feeling satisfied with the course of the Near Eastern events. Since, whatever western countries believed, it was tsarist policy to keep the Ottoman Empire in being as long as possible, he welcomed foreign assistance in the pursuit of that objective. Having been unable to get it in 1833, he was glad that it was forthcoming in 1841. Unkiar-Skelessi had been due for renewal anyway. The enmity which arose between France and Britain in 1840 was a bonus, since it reduced the likelihood that the two countries would act jointly against Russia on a future occasion. Far from damaging Russian diplomatic interests, Nesselrode felt that the sec-ond crisis over Mehemet Ali had advanced them.

Unfortunately, Nicholas now proceeded to misunderstand British policy on the Near East as badly as Britain misunderstood the policy he was pur-suing himself. Long years of involvement in Turkish affairs had led him to believe that, whatever he did to prevent it, the Ottoman Empire was going to collapse sooner rather than later. Aggressively inclined courtiers like Prince Menshikov (who was much more militant as a diplomat and as Navy Minister than as Governor of Finland) were beginning to press for pre-emptive action. The tsar still shared Nesselrode's view that the Turkish regime should be kept alive as long as possible, but he was determined not to be caught napping if the health of the 'sick man of Europe' broke down irrevocably. The way in which the crisis of 1839–41 was resolved per-suaded him that Britain might welcome an exploration of the two coun-tries' thoughts on the future of the Near East. On a visit to London in 1844, the tsar expressed his conviction that the demise of the Ottoman Empire was inevitable. He affirmed that he would continue to work for the main-tenance of the status quo, but he felt that the Great Powers could no longer avoid discussing the international consequences which would ensue when Turkey fell. Nicholas took British acceptance of Nesselrode's subsequent summary of his London exchanges as tantamount to acquiescence in a pol-icy of bilateral action on Turkey. Since he also believed, after the meeting at Münchengrätz in 1833, that Austria would take a lead from Russia on Ot-toman affairs, he began to feel that he had a mandate for resolute action when the 'eastern question' next arose. In London, however, he had failed to broach a central issue. 'The precise point which was never treated in de-tail was the degree of imminence of the admittedly forthcoming dissolution of Turkey'.[35] Had she been asked, Britain would have said that she thought 'dissolution' was much further off than it was in the mind of the tsar. Whereas from Britain's point of view the London exchanges decided nothing, from the tsar's point of view they cleared the decks for international action. Seeds of non-comprehension had been sown which were to lead, within a decade, to major hostilities.

RUSSIA AND THE EUROPEAN REVOLUTIONS OF 1848

In the pan-European crisis of 1848, however, Nicholas made plain that where external relations were concerned he was still fundamentally timorous. The belief that his response to the fall of Louis Philippe was to say, 'Saddle your horses, gentlemen! A republic has been declared in France', is unfounded.[36] The multiple revolutions which took place in western and central Europe had a far greater effect on his domestic policies than on his readiness to engage in foreign adventures.

Admittedly, the tsar issued more threats and undertook more fighting in 1848 and 1849 than he had done when Europe last fell prey to upheavals in 1830. The meeting at Münchengrätz in 1833 had increased his confidence not only *vis-à-vis* the Ottoman Empire but also in respect of the West, for Austria and Russia (and subsequently Prussia) had agreed not only to maintain the integrity of the Sultan's possessions, but also to guarantee each other's Polish territories and to assist any established regime which found itself threatened by insurgents. The second of these three articles of agreement had given rise to tripartite action against a rising of west Galician Poles in 1846. In 1848, the third aspect of the arrangement looked ripe for activation. Two days after learning of the establishment of the French Second Republic, the tsar ordered a partial mobilization of the troops on his western borders. In a public statement of mid-March 1848 he proclaimed that he was 'ready to meet [his] enemies, wherever they may appear'.[37] Russian troops crossed the Pruth into Moldavia in June and in August moved on to Wallachia.

For once, the occupation of the Danubian Principalities had an object other than frightening the Turks. Constantinople took fright, but the tsar intended his troops to move west into Transylvania and attack the Austrian emperor's rebellious Hungarian subjects in the rear. Simultaneously, Croatian forces loyal to Vienna were to attack the Hungarians head-on. In November 1848, however, after the Hungarians had beaten off the Croatians, Nicholas ordered his soldiers not to cross the Austrian frontier. He returned to the offensive only when a Polish general in Hungarian service, Józef Bem, took most of Transylvania out of the hands of the local Austrian commanders. Nicholas pretended that Hungarian forces were being used in the Polish interest: 'both Austrians and Russians skilfully manoeuvred with the assertion that the Hungarian Revolution was not a Hungarian national movement, but a Polish plot against the Russian State'.[38] A small number of Russian troops crossed into Austrian territory in February 1849 at the invitation of the hard-pressed Austrian officer on the ground. Driven out in March, they returned in massive numbers in June, this time from the north as well as the east and after Nicholas had obliged the Austrian Emperor to beg for help in person. Under military pressure on all sides (in the main, as it turned out, from revivified Austrian forces under General Haynau), the Hungarians capitulated to the Russians on 13 August. Russia fell out with Turkey before the end of the month because the Sultan refused to extradite Polish and Hungarian refugees who had fled to his territory, but this negative consequence of the invasion seemed hardly to matter. The tsar could congratulate himself on Russia's first military triumph since the suppression of the Polish rebellion in 1831.

The Russian invasion of Hungary made Nicholas look like a firebrand, but it had not involved him in taking many risks. 'The tsar and his generals expected an easy campaign marked by heart-warming victories',[39] which was more or less what they got. Nicholas was far too worried about the possibility of domestic complications to contemplate foreign entanglements whose outcome was unpredictable. Even in connection with Hungary he moved slowly and undertook extremely thorough diplomatic preparations. He may really have believed that Poles were running the Hungarian rebellion and could carry disaffection north of the Carpathians. If he did, he was bound to conclude that his vital interests were at stake. The most wanton of his foreign exploits could thus be said to have been conceived, misguidedly, as an act of self-defence.

That Nicholas was far more concerned about the domestic than the international repercussions of the 1848 revolutions is evident from the much greater dynamism of his domestic behaviour. According to the Prussian ambassador to St Petersburg, he was relatively confident at the beginning of February 1848 that he could prevent the dissatisfaction which was mounting elsewhere in Europe from penetrating his domains. His complacency in domestic affairs disappeared overnight when the news arrived of the fall of the French monarchy. After receiving alarmist reports from the heads of both the Second and Third Departments, on 27 February / 11 March 1848 Nicholas set up a committee under Menshikov to recommend ways of limiting the circulation of unwelcome ideas. When news arrived that not only France but also the Habsburg Empire was tottering, he became yet more strongly inclined to batten down the hatches. The Prussian ambassador who had thought Nicholas sanguine about the stability of his regime in February found him anything but relaxed in March. The ambassador reported that 'The Emperor is monitoring the serious political illness which has gripped all countries, and believes his empire very far from being immune from infection'; Nicholas was now of the opinion that 'Highly reprehensible principles have been disseminated among young people who completed their university courses around three years ago, among people who have lived abroad for a long time, and also among teachers, professors, writers and journalists. The supervision of journalists, furthermore, has been too feeble'.[40] On 14/26 March 1848, two days after the Prussian ambassador despatched this report, Nicholas imposed strict limitations on the publication of news about foreign disturbances. The public declaration that he was 'ready to meet [his] enemies, wherever they may appear' was aimed not only at foreigners but also at his own subjects. Inflammatory proclamations had already been pasted on the cathedral in Riga. A manifesto printed in Germany had been circulating in the western Ukraine. When Vienna emancipated the serfs of Galicia in May 1848, the Governor-General of the Russian Empire's south-western provinces reported unrest among Ukrainians on the tsar's side of the Galician border. These events make it likely that the mobilization of troops on the western borders was designed to keep order among the empire's non-Russians rather than to prepare the ground for an invasion of central Europe. Nicholas instructed his foreign missions to issue no visas for entry into Russia without seeking St Petersburg's assent. Foreign merchants were still to be permitted to enter the country, but Russian subjects were not to be allowed to leave and Russians living abroad were summoned home. Early in April 1848 the committee which Nicholas had set up under Menshikov reported negatively on the two most popular journals of the day, *The Contemporary* and *Notes of the Fatherland*, and recommended the creation of a new body to supervise the activity of the regime's censors. Nicholas accepted the suggestion instantly and turned three members of Menshikov's team into what became known as 'The Buturlin Committee' (after the name of its chairman) or 'The Committee of 2 April 1848' (after the date of its foundation).

The Committee of 2 April 1848 remained in being until 1855 and became one of the most striking embodiments of the tsar's descent into obscurantism. Although intellectuals had always lived dangerously under Nicholas, they had never been silenced altogether. Now they were. In the atmosphere fostered by the Buturlin Committee even the work of academics became suspect. In September 1848 Moscow University's Society of Russian History and Antiquities published a translation of Giles Fletcher's *Of the Russe Commonwealth*, a description of Muscovy written in the late sixteenth century. Fletcher's book contained a 'devastating description of Russian manners and morals',[41] but was so antique that its scholarly translators must have thought themselves safe in making it accessible. By law they were free to publish any work which related to a period before the Romanov dynasty came to the throne. In late 1848, however, the law was no defence. The relevant issue of the Society's journal was recalled, the journal was temporarily closed, and the secretary of the Society, Professor Bodianskii, was banished to Kazan'. Fletcher's book was not to appear in Russian for another fifty-seven years.

Paradoxically, the Society of Russian History had felt the wrath of the Minister of Education, an official who was less benighted than some of his peers. Not long before *Of the Russe Commonwealth* was suppressed, Uvarov had dismissed Sergei Stroganov as Curator of Moscow University. To get his own back, Stroganov took advantage of the atmosphere of March 1848 to complain to the tsar of the Ministry of Education's 'liberalism'. Uvarov then attacked the Moscow University History Society because Stroganov remained its chairman. Aleksandr Nikitenko, the liberally inclined censor, confided to his diary that 'such incidents involving government officials only demonstrate the deep, pervasive immorality to which everyone is accustomed here'.[42] Uvarov's little victory was one of his last successes. The Committee of 2 April 1848 had been set up partly because his ministry was thought to be soft. The minister said that he felt as if he were being pursued by a wild animal and could only throw off his clothes to distract its attention. 'During the reaction of 1849 there was nothing left to throw off, and Uvarov retired'.[43] What finally undermined him was the arrest, in April 1849, of a group of St Petersburg intellectuals associated with Mikhail Petrashevskii.

Petrashevskii, the son of a St Petersburg doctor, had been eccentric even as a teenager at the Tsarskoe Selo lycée. He became a junior official in the Ministry of Foreign Affairs in 1840, but was never a promising candidate for promotion in the government service. A long black beard and a penchant for smoking cigars in the street were the outward signs of a nonconformity whose intellectual dimension consisted of enthusiasm for French utopian socialism. In the course of the 1840s the young radical put together an informal association of disaffected contemporaries whose ranks, at one time or another, included the novelist Dostoevsky, the satirist and future provincial governor Mikhail Saltykov-Shchedrin, the future panslav Nikolai Danilevskii, Vladimir Miliutin (a brother of the man who reformed St Petersburg's municipal administration in 1846), Valerian Maikov (brother of a distinguished lyric poet) and Nikolai Speshnev, who turned out to be the most extreme member of the company but was also 'the only one ... to lead the life of a leisured gentleman'.[44] Not many of Petrashevskii's friends were budding revolutionaries. When the friends met at his apartment on Fridays, 'no specific projects or plots were ever worked out, but criticisms of the existing order were voiced, as were gibes and regrets about our present condition'.[45] The group communicated their ideas to the public by collaborating on *A Pocket Dictionary of Foreign Words Which Have Entered the Vocabulary of the Russian Language,* a work whose purpose was to discuss not foreign words *per se* but rather the social and political phenomena to which many of them related. Maikov, prime mover in the relatively mild first volume, deplored chair-bound intellectuals in a discussion of the word 'Academic' and put forward a 'great man' view of history in the discussion of 'Authority'. In Volume Two, when Petrashevskii himself was in charge, 'the thought of socialist writers [was] presented with reckless enthusiasm'.[46]

Both volumes of the *Dictionary* passed the censorship (in 1845 and 1846 respectively), but Volume Two was proscribed a month after publication when the authorities grasped what the circle was up to. Unrepentant, the naive Petrashevskii proceeded in February 1848 to circulate a document which called for granting merchants the right to own populated estates on condition that they dealt with their serfs in accordance with the Law on Obligated Peasants of 1842. The timing could hardly have been worse. The Ministry of Internal Affairs placed the circle under surveillance and delayed making arrests only because it wanted to demonstrate, by compiling the fullest possible dossier, that its investigative abilities were superior to those of the Third Department. On reporting to the tsar in 1849, the Minister received the title of Count for providing Nicholas with more information about a group of dissidents than he had had since the exposure of the Decembrists. Of 252 people who were questioned, 51 were exiled and 21 condemned to death. The death sentences were commuted at the end of 1849, but only when the prisoners had arrived at the place of execution and been led to believe, as Dostoevsky put it, that they 'had no more than a minute left to live'.[47] Dostoevsky underwent a spiritual transformation in Siberia which turned him into the greatest of nineteenth-century writers, but Petrashevskii died there and was buried in unconsecrated ground in 1866.

With the exception of Speshnev's subsection, the 'Petrashevtsy' (as Petrashevskii's associates came to be known) were no more radical than others who dissented from the administrative and social practices of Nicholas I. The *Dictionary of Foreign Words* was one of a number of indirect criticisms of the regime to find its way into print in the 1840s. Petrashevskii's proposal that merchants be allowed to buy populated estates hardly bespoke a passion for social revolution. Dostoevsky's main offence seems to have been reading Belinskii's 'Letter to Gogol'. The main significance of the circle lay not in the views of its members but in the viciousness of the government's response to them. Apart from the Ukrainophile Kirillo-Methodian Society, which the regime thought particularly dangerous because of its obsessive concern for the unity of the empire, no circle of intellectuals was treated as harshly as the Petrashevtsy in the period between 1826 and 1848. After revolution had begun in Europe, Nicholas was less determined to send his troops abroad than to make clear that he would brook no dissent at home.

Education, in the tsar's view, lay at the heart of his domestic difficulties. On 30 April 1849, eight days after the Petrashevtsy were arrested, Nicholas reduced student enrolments to 300 per university, a cut of nearly two-thirds. Uvarov's position as education minister became untenable and he resigned six months later. What little sympathy the authorities had shown for the advance of enlightenment came to an end. Arts-based schools turned into technical colleges. The new education minister, Shirinskii-Shikhmatov, shared none of his predecessor's intellectual curiosity. On a visit to Moscow University he was appalled by the historian Sergei Solov'ev's observation that it was difficult to work out what precisely the medieval chronicler Nestor had contributed to the chronicle which went by his name. In the minister's opinion Nestor's chronicle was a treasure whose worth should not be questioned. Fortunately, from the point of view of Shirinskii-Shikhmatov, the newly appointed Curator of Moscow University was 'a typical Nicholaevan general, the limited and ignorant V. I. Nazimov', who took the view that students ought not to go into cafés to read papers and ought to do up their jackets and wear three-cornered hats and swords.[48] Nazimov's enthusiasm for discipline was applied by a new Governor-General to Moscow as a whole. Merchants were not famous for taking exception to the behaviour of government appointees, but one of them likened the new Moscow Governor, A. A. Zakrevskii, to an Asiatic khan or Chinese viceroy. Zakrevskii's political opinions were so far to the right that he thought the Moscow Slavophiles were dangerous subversives; his antipathy to modernization led him to deplore not only the construction of new factories in Moscow but also the expansion of old ones. The fate of the Russian educational system and of the inhabitants of Moscow was shared, between 1848 and 1855, by the country as a whole. Aleksandr Nikitenko spoke for many intellectuals when, in 1852, he privately advised people who thought for themselves 'to completely scorn this stupid nonsense, this contemporary life, while consoling yourself (if you can) with faith in a brighter future'.[49]

From the regime's point of view, however, the policy of responding cautiously to events outside the country while insisting remorselessly on conformity at home seemed to be an unqualified success. In the second half of 1848 the Prussian ambassador was reporting to Berlin that St Petersburg's main concerns were not revolution but a cholera epidemic, the expectation of a poor harvest and a shortage of cash. Life, in other words, had returned to normal. Summoning Russians back from abroad proved to be a mistake in view of the fact that the 80,000 'returnees' disseminated information about the startling developments in Paris, Berlin and Vienna, but the news was not enough to prevent the Russian Empire from remaining the one continental power to escape the consequences of the 'springtime of the nations'. Isaiah Berlin has argued that because educated Russians failed to stage a revolution in 1848 they were 'unbroken by the collapse of liberal hopes in Europe in 1849–51' and lived to fight another day.[50] This was true, but took some time to become clear. For the moment the tsar not only held all the cards at home but also was continuing to improve his position abroad. Prussia's attempt in 1850 to capitalize on Austrian weakness and turn herself into the pre-eminent power in Germany came to nothing when the Austrians made plain that they had recovered their nerve and were prepared to go to war on the matter. Russia backed Austria, only to make plain in 1851 that she was no more willing to contemplate Viennese domination of German affairs than she had been to back Prussian. In the wake of the 1848 revolutions St Petersburg appeared to have acquired a larger say in the affairs of central Europe than it had possessed for a generation. In 1850 Nesselrode expressed the view that 'Russia's position and that of her Sovereign has not been as attractive or as powerful since 1814'.[51] Nicholas had put down the Hungarians, rounded up dissidents, held the ring

between Austria and Prussia, re-advertised Russia's claim to be the strongest power on the European mainland, and given notice that he could keep
his regime in place for the foreseeable future. From the point of view of the
tsar, Russian skies seemed to be cloudless.

THE CRIMEAN WAR AND THE DEATH OF THE TSAR

Far to the west, however, a change had taken place which gave a new
twist to relations between the Great Powers. Habsburgs and Hohenzollerns
were back in their palaces, but France's king had gone for good. A nephew
of Napoleon I had been elected President of the French Second Republic
in December 1848 and was to become Emperor of the French in 1852. In
the period of his presidency Louis Napoleon's principal concern was to
maximize his domestic authority in order to prepare the ground for turning
himself into Napoleon III. When, in 1849, he despatched French troops to
reinstate the Pope in Rome, and when, the following year, he revived Catholic claims to control various Christian buildings in Jerusalem and Bethle-
hem, he was trying to convince Catholics at home of his piety. The second
move, however, had dangerous implications. Because the tsar could not
allow Catholics to challenge the standing of the Orthodox Church in the
Ottoman Empire, and because he could not overlook a renewal of French
interest in the Near East, he was bound to contest French claims to the
management of the 'Holy Places' of Palestine. What seemed to be a 'mere
church wardens' quarrel' turned into 'a question of power and influence'.[52]
In time, a cloud no bigger than a man's hand produced a thunderstorm.

France's leader understood what he was doing. Although at first he had
to consolidate his position at home, it was always his ambition to undermine the European order which had come into being after the defeat of his
uncle. Since, in 1850, the one bastion of that order which had escaped
major trouble in 1848 was the Russian Empire, it was likely that at some
point France would throw down the gauntlet to the tsar. By raising the
question of the Holy Places the French President not only gained ground at
home but also set in train a long-term policy.

Nicholas, on the other hand, was labouring under several misapprehen-
sions. He had probably become over-confident in his attitude to the outside world. In twenty-five years on the throne he had suffered no major
international reverses. It had become difficult for him to imagine anything
other than a successful outcome to his diplomatic and military operations.
He did not expect that he would have to go to war over the Holy Places,
but if he was called upon to do so, he thought that he could produce the
men, guns and money he would need for victory. He also believed, first,
that France was unlikely to be able to secure an alliance with Britain (be-

cause of the two countries' disagreement about the Near East in 1840); second, that Britain might support Russia in the event of a Russian attack on the Ottoman Empire (because of the Anglo-Russian discussions which had taken place in London in 1844); and third, that in any event he could count on the support of Austria (because of the assistance he had rendered Vienna in putting down the Hungarians in 1849). All these opinions turned out to be mistaken.

The Ottoman Empire, meanwhile, sensed the beginning of new friendships. When France asked the Sultan to make concessions to Catholics in the Holy Land, both parties knew that Russia would object. France, therefore, had to promise the Ottomans that she would come to their aid if complications arose. Since, in 1849, the British had encouraged Constantinople to reject Russian requests for the surrender of the Polish and Hungarian refugees who had fled to Ottoman territory after the failure of the Hungarian revolution, the Turks believed that Britain, as well as France, had their interests at heart. In other words, they felt more confident about their capacity to deal with the tsar than at any point since the end of the 1820s. In 1850 neither St Petersburg nor Constantinople nor the western powers realized that war was on the horizon, but with hindsight it is possible to see that the battle-lines were drawn.

In December 1852, after two and a half years of dithering, the Ottoman Empire acceded to French demands in respect of the Holy Places. Nicholas knew that he had to do something, but he was not sure what. In the first half of 1853 he initiated or sanctioned three responses: 'He appealed to Great Britain for support, and took out of the lumber room the forgotten agreement of 1844';[53] he sent an emissary to Constantinople for bilateral talks; and he began to make plans for fighting. All three approaches were highly speculative. The British Prime Minister, Lord Aberdeen, was inclined to be sympathetic to Russian entreaties, but his government was a coalition and some of his ministerial colleagues disagreed with him. The British ambassador at Constantinople, meanwhile, was pro-Turkish to the point of ignoring instructions from London which told him to advise the Turks to give ground to Russia.

The tsar's second response to the crisis of early 1853, sending an emissary to Constantinople, seemed to promise more immediate rewards than the first. His emissary, Menshikov, spent two and a half months at the Turkish capital and succeeded in reversing the Turks' decision on the Holy Places. Finesse, however, was not one of his most notable characteristics. Having scored a point, he made the mistake of trying to score another. Taking advantage of the discretionary powers granted him by the tsar, he asked for a treaty guaranteeing Russia's right to a protectorate over the Orthodox Christians of the Ottoman Empire. This was unacceptable to the Turks because it would have involved them in legitimizing Russia's long-standing and deliberate misinterpretation of the Treaty of Kuchuk-Kainardji of 1774. By pressing Russia's claims, Menshikov plucked defeat out of victory.

Russia's battle plans, meanwhile, were based on the apparently sound proposition that Austria would fight on her side. Austria not only had historical reasons for taking Russia's part, but also was at odds with the Turks over the principality of Montenegro in the western Balkans. It was hardly surprising, in these circumstances, that Nicholas abandoned a hair-brained scheme for launching a direct attack on Constantinople and replaced it with Paskevich's proposals for a Russian occupation of the Danubian Principalities, an Austrian occupation of Serbia and Herzegovina, a blockade of the Bosphorus, and an eventual Austro-Russian partition of the Ottoman Empire. Depending on Austrian cooperation was unwise, however, for Austria had more to lose from the Ottoman Empire's collapse than any of the Great Powers. It was not sensible for her to contemplate enlarging her domains. The year 1848 had demonstrated that she was unable to control the territory which was hers already. In the long run, collaboration with Russia would have turned her into Russia's vassal. The tsar was wrong to think that he could rely on payment for the help he had given Austria in 1849. 'Was not Schwarzenberg himself [the Austrian first minister who died in 1852] alleged to have declared that Austria would one day astound the world by the greatness of her ingratitude?'[54]

Nicholas certainly did not want to fight alone, and probably did not want to fight at all. Nesselrode, his foreign minister, remained pacific to the end. The crisis had been brewing for so long, however, that the tsar could not be bought off with a decision on the Holy Places. Only an agreed statement of his rights vis-à-vis the Christians of the Ottoman Empire would have convinced him that the game had been worth the candle. On 21 June / 3 July 1853, Russian troops again crossed the river Pruth. In August 1853 Britain, France, Austria and Prussia drew up a letter for despatch from the sultan to the tsar which gave Nicholas what he wanted. The sultan, however, refused to avail himself of this 'Vienna Note', on the grounds that it required him to make too many concessions. Nicholas rejected Constantinople's amendments to the note and on 22 September / 4 October 1853 the Ottoman Empire declared war. At the last, Britain's ambassador to Constantinople abandoned the encouragement he had been giving the Turks and advised them to go on negotiating, but by this time neither Britain nor France was in a position to withdraw the backing which they had been giving the sultan. Their fleets soon arrived at Constantinople and the war promised to be the most wide-ranging since the fall of the first Napoleon.

For nearly a year, not much happened. Russia destroyed the Turkish fleet in the southern Black Sea port of Sinope on 18/30 November 1853, but only after Turkish ships had provoked her into doing so by making sorties in the direction of the Crimea. Nicholas had no plans for a blitzkrieg. In a letter to Paskevich of 22 October / 3 November 1853 he envisaged crossing the Danube in the spring of 1854, declaring the independence of the Danubian Principalities and Serbia, capturing the important fortress of Vidin (in the future Bulgaria), pressing the Turks in eastern Anatolia, appealing for Orthodox Christians to rise against the sultan, and using the winter of 1854–5 to raise native militias. In early 1855 he intended to press on after assessing the degree of continuing Anglo-French hostility and the extent to which the Sultan's Christian subjects had rallied to his banner. These ideas failed to allow for Austrian objections to Russian gains in the Balkans and grossly exaggerated the inclination of the Balkan Slavs to fight for their freedom, but they had the virtue of giving the tsar time to negotiate.

Russia's opponents acted only a little more energetically. The Turkish manoeuvres which culminated in what seemed to be the disaster of Sinope had the object of making Nicholas look aggressive, but if the sultan hoped to increase the determination of Britain and France to put Russia in her place, he found that Britain, at least, dragged her feet. Even after Britain and France declared war on Russia in March 1854 (more than five months after the Turks had done so), the inclination to find a diplomatic solution to the crisis remained strong on the part of all interested parties other than the Turks and the French.

Austria considered herself directly affected when, at about the time of the Anglo-French declarations of war, Russian operations got under the way on the south side of the Danube. Increasingly aware that a successful Russian campaign would diminish her authority in the Balkans, Austria sought a statement of allied war aims. France prepared one, hoping that Russia would reject it and that the Habsburg Empire would join the western powers. Many members of the British cabinet were by this time reluctant to make peace on any terms short of a glorious victory, but after tortuous negotiations Austria, France and Britain agreed the 'Four Points' on 27 July / 8 August 1854. These envisaged peace on four conditions: if the Russian protectorate over the Danubian Principalities was replaced by a European guarantee; if Russian control of the mouth of the Danube came to an end; if the Straits Convention of 1841 was revised in the interests of the European balance of power; and if the protection of Ottoman Christians by Russia was replaced by the collective protection of Europe's five Great Powers. 'The Four Points were the most celebrated diplomatic achievement of the Crimean war',[55] but did not seem so at the time they were agreed because Nicholas had just begun withdrawing his forces from the Danubian Principalities. Austria, consequently, lost interest in pressurizing him, and Britain and France, for the moment, lost the chance of adding a third Great Power to the anti-Russian coalition.

Only now did war come to the Crimea. Anglo-French forces landed there in September 1854 and fought the battles of the Alma, Balaklava and Inkerman in the next two months. The object of the landing was to take Sevastopol', but Eduard Totleben was strengthening its defences. In the view of William Howard Russell, the first and greatest of war correspondents, the allies 'had run away with the notion that [Sevastopol'] was a kind of pasteboard city'.[56] They soon became irritated by their inability to capture it, and turned back to diplomacy. The Four Points came into their own. On 20 November / 2 December 1854 Austria, Britain and France signed a treaty on the basis of the Four Points which was designed to force Russia to the conference table by the end of the year. Nicholas was astonished by Austria's collusion with his enemies. In a reference to events of the late seventeenth century he asked, 'What are the names of the two most foolish kings of Poland? I will tell you: John Sobieski and myself; we both committed the supreme folly of saving Vienna from destruction'.[57] The good relations between Austria and Russia which had obtained more or less interruptedly since 1726 came to an end. Foundations were laid for a rivalry between the two countries which was to be one of the principal causes of the First World War.

In public, however, Nicholas reacted coolly. He accepted the Four Points and obliged his opponents to say precisely what they meant by them. Point Three was the stumbling block, for the only significant alternative to the equitable Straits Convention of 1841 was completely to eliminate Russian naval power in the Black Sea, which would have had the effect of handing control of the region to the British. Elucidating Point Three was probably going to have the effect of encouraging the tsar to continue the war, for if Point Three meant promoting British interests, it was probably also going to have the effect of inclining Austria not to enter the lists.

The outcome of the interested parties' diplomatic exchanges depended heavily on the course of the fighting. From Vienna, where negotiations were taking place, the Russian plenipotentiary Aleksandr Gorchakov wrote to Nesselrode on 23 January / 4 February 1855 that 'A brilliant success in the Crimea would have enormous significance'.[58] Because, on the day of Gorchakov's despatch, the British government fell and the jingoistic Palmerston became Prime Minister, the western allies would shortly be prosecuting the war with much greater vigour. The need for an immediate Russian success intensified, but an attack on the allied disembarkation point of Evpatoriia came to nothing. On Nicholas's behalf the heir to the throne dismissed Russia's Crimean commander (Menshikov again) in a letter of 15/27 February. The tsar's fortunes had reached their nadir. Not only had his troops let him down, but he was expecting Austria and probably the entire German Confederation to enter the war on the allied side. He had also been ignoring his health. His son had to dismiss the Crimean commander on his behalf because after catching a cold Nicholas had insisted on inspecting troops in twenty-three degrees of frost. The Russian winter, famous for defeating the country's enemies, this time put paid to a tsar. On 18 February / 2 March 1855 Nicholas died of pneumonia.

Despite the beliefs of foreigners, he had not really been a warmonger. By comparison with Alexander I and most eighteenth-century tsars he had been remarkably inactive beyond his frontiers. He knew only too well that keeping the peace at home required most of his attention. His mistakes in foreign affairs sprang not from expansionism or malevolence but from non-comprehension, shortsightedness and an undue sense of his own importance. 'It was one of the major tragedies of Nicholas I that his reign ended in a war over the Turkish problem which he had worked for so long to solve by peaceful and negotiated agreement'.[59] It was nevertheless the case that the Crimean War represented a far greater crisis than that with which the reign had begun. Unless Russia's military fortunes unexpectedly improved, dramatic changes lay ahead not only in international relations but in the domestic structure of the Russian polity. A regime that could not win a war on its own soil was ripe for reform. Nicholas's son had to decide whether and to what extent he was prepared to diverge from his father's methods.

NOTES

1. VPR, xiv. 399.
2. G. A. Kertesz, ed., *Documents in the Political History of the European Continent 1815–1939* (Oxford, 1968), p. 32.
3. V. Ia. Grosul, *Reformy v dunaiskikh kniazhestvakh i Rossiia (20–30 gody XIX veka)* (Moscow, 1966), p. 198.
4. M. S. Anderson, ed., *The Great Powers and the Near East 1774–1923* (London, 1970), p. 36.
5. Mark Brown, 'The Comité Franco-Polonais and the French Reaction to the Polish Uprising of November 1830', EHR 93 (1978), 775.
6. K. R. Nesselrode, 'Vsepoddaneishii otchet za 25 let tsarstvovaniia Imperatora Nikolaia I', SIRIO 98 (1896), 288.
7. Angela T. Pienkos, *The Imperfect Autocrat: Grand Duke Constantine Pavlovich and the Polish Congress Kingdom* (Boulder, Colo., 1987), p. 97.
8. R. F. Leslie, *Polish Politics and the Revolution of November 1830* (London, 1956), p. 166.
9. John Howes Gleason, *The Genesis of Russophobia in Great Britain: A Study of the Interaction of Policy and Opinion* (Cambridge, Mass., 1950), p. 134.
10. Robert A. Berry, 'Czartoryski's Hôtel Lambert and the Great Powers in the Balkans, 1832–1848', IHR 7 (1985), 66.
11. I. E. Paskevich, 'Raport namestnika Tsarstva Pol'skogo Ego Imperatorskomu Velichestvu', SIRIO 98 (1896), 597.
12. Ibid., 615.
13. Leningrad, Tsentral'nyi gosudarstvennyi istoricheskii arkhiv, fond 733, opis' 66, delo 47, list 2.
14. Sergei Uvarov, *Desiatiletie ministerstva narodnogo prosveshcheniia 1833–1843* (SPB, 1864), pp. 37, 46.
15. Edward C. Thaden, *Russia's Western Borderlands, 1710–1870* (Princeton, NJ, 1984), p. 124.
16. Ronald Grigor Suny, 'Georgia and Soviet Nationality Policy', in Stephen F. Cohen et al., eds, *The Soviet Union Since Stalin* (London and Basingstoke, 1980), p. 219.
17. Ivan Rybakov, '1825-i rik na Ukraini', *Ukraina*, 1925 no. 6, p. 16.
18. Orest Pelech, 'Towards a Historical Sociology of the Ukrainian Ideologues in the Russian Empire of the 1830's and 1840's', unpublished PhD dissertation, Princeton University, NJ, 1976, p. 261.

19. N. Kostomarov, *Knigi bytiia ukrainskogo naroda* (Woodridge, New York, 1977), p. 20.
20. P. Bartenev, ed., 'Ob ukrainsko-slavianskom obshchestve (iz bumag D. P. Golokhvastova)', RA, 1892 no. 7, p. 348.
21. John D. Klier, 'The Concept of "Jewish Emancipation" in a Russian Context', in Olga Crisp and Linda Edmondson, eds, *Civil Rights in Imperial Russia* (Oxford, 1989), p. 129.
22. Michael Stanislawski, *Tsar Nicholas I and the Jews: The Transformation of Jewish Society in Russia 1825–1855* (Philadelphia, Pa, 1983), p. 5.
23. M. M. Bliev, 'K voprosu o vremeni prisoedineniia narodov severnogo Kavkaza k Rossii', VI, 1970 no. 7, p. 54.
24. Stephen F. Jones, 'Russian Imperial Administration and the Georgian Nobility: The Georgian Conspiracy of 1832', SEER 65 (1987), 57.
25. E. Willis Brooks, 'Nicholas I as Reformer: Russian Attempts to Conquer the Caucasus, 1825–1855', in Ivo Banac et al., eds, *Nation and Ideology: Essays in Honor of Wayne S. Vucinich* (Boulder, Colo., 1981), p. 249; Anthony L. H. Rhinelander, *Prince Michael Vorontsov: Viceroy to the Tsar* (Montreal and Kingston, 1990), p. 178.
26. Alton Donnelly, 'The Mobile Steppe Frontier: The Russian Conquest and Colonization of Bashkiria and Kazakhstan to 1850', in Michael Rywkin, ed., *Russian Colonial Expansion to 1917* (London and New York, 1988), p. 205.
27. N. A. Khalfin, *Rossiia i khanstva srednei Azii (pervaia polovina XIX veka)* (Moscow, 1974), passim (quotation from p. 389).
28. Alan Wood, 'From Conquest to Revolution: The Historical Dimension', in Wood, ed., *Siberia: Problems and Prospects for Regional Development* (London, 1987), p. 46.
29. O. S. Tal'skaia, 'Bor'ba administratsii s vliianiem dekabristov v Zapadnoi Sibiri', in L. M. Goriushkin et al., eds, *Ssylka i katorga v Sibiri (XVIII – nachalo XX v.)* (Novosibirsk, 1975), p. 75.
30. Thaden, *Borderlands* (above, n. 15), p. 202.
31. John Keep, 'Justice for the Troops: A Comparative Study of Nicholas I's Russia and France under Louis-Philippe', CMRS 28 (1987), 33, 35.
32. G. H. Bolsover, 'Nicholas I and the Partition of Turkey', SEER 27 (1948–9), 116.
33. R. L. Baker, 'Palmerston on the Treaty of Unkiar Skelessi', EHR 43 (1928), 86.
34. Anderson, *Great Powers* (above, n. 4), p. 45.
35. Vernon John Puryear, *England, Russia, and the Straits Question 1844–1856* (Berkeley, Calif., 1931), p. 53.
36. For a debunking of this story see, for example, V. N. Vinogradov et al., *Mezhdunarodnye otnosheniia na Balkanakh 1830–1856 gg.* (Moscow, 1990), p. 193.
37. Michael Cherniavsky, '"Holy Russia": A Study in the History of an Idea', AHR 63 (1958), 625 n. 40.
38. Eugene Horváth, 'Russia and the Hungarian Revolution (1848–9)', *Slavonic Review* 12 (1933–4), 635.
39. Istvan Deak, *The Lawful Revolution: Louis Kossuth and the Hungarians, 1848–1849* (New York, 1979), p. 291.
40. Gerkhard Bekker, 'Oppozitsionnoe dvizhenie v Rossii v 1848 g. (Po doneseniiam prusskogo posol'stva v Sankt-Peterburge)', *Novaia i noveishaia istoriia*, 1968 no. 1, p. 71.
41. Richard Pipes, 'Introduction to Giles Fletcher's *Of the Russe Commonwealth (1591)*', in Pipes, *Russia Observed: Collected Essays on Russian and Soviet History* (Boulder, Colo., 1989), p. 26.

42. Aleksandr Nikitenko, *Diary of a Russian Censor*, abridged, ed., and tr. Helen Saltz Jacobson (Amherst, Mass., 1975), p. 118.

43. B. N. Chicherin, *Vospominaniia: Moskva sorokovykh godov* (Moscow, 1929, repr. Cambridge, 1973), p. 28.

44. J. H. Seddon, *The Petrashevtsy: A Study of the Russian Revolutionaries of 1848* (Manchester, 1985), p. 21.

45. D. D. Akhsharumov, 'Iz moikh vospominanii', in B. F. Egorov, ed., *Pervye russkie sotsialisty: Vospominaniia uchastnikov kruzhkov petrashevtsev v Peterburge* (Leningrad, 1984), p. 180.

46. F. M. Bartholomew, 'V. N. Maykov and the *Karmannyy slovar' inostrannykh slov*', SEER 62 (1984), 97.

47. Liza Knapp, ed. and trans., *Dostoevsky as Reformer: The Petrashevsky Case* (Ann Arbor, Mich., 1987), p. 109.

48. N. M. Druzhinin, *Izbrannye trudy: Vneshniaia politika Rossii, Istoriia Moskvy, Muzeinoe delo* (Moscow, 1988), p. 144; Chicherin, *Moskva* (above, n. 43), p. 81.

49. Nikitenko, *Diary* (above, n. 42), p. 130.

50. Isaiah Berlin, *Russian Thinkers* (London, 1978), p. 6.

51. Nesselrode, 'Vsepoddaneishii otchet' (above, n. 6), p. 296.

52. Norman Rich, *Why the Crimean War? A Cautionary Tale* (Hanover, NH, and London, 1985), p. 20.

53. David Wetzel, *The Crimean War: A Diplomatic History* (Boulder, Colo., 1985), p. 46.

54. W. E. Mosse, *The European Powers and the German Question 1848–71* (Cambridge, 1958), p. 47.

55. Wetzel, *The Crimean War* (above, n. 53), p. 115.

56. Nicolas Bentley, ed., *Russell's Despatches from the Crimea* (London, 1970), pp. 113–14.

57. Wetzel, *Crimean War* (above, n. 53), p. 127.

58. O. V. Marinin, 'Russko-angliiskie otnosheniia v pervoi polovine 1855 goda', *Istoriia SSSR*, 1986 no. 5, p. 151.

59. Bolsover, 'Nicholas I' (above, n. 32), p. 144.

CHAPTER EIGHT

The Politics of Emancipation

THE ACCESSION OF ALEXANDER II AND THE END OF HOSTILITIES

Making decisions was not one of the new tsar's greatest gifts. Indeed, an upbringing which gave Alexander II many qualifications for the tasks which confronted him failed to conceal the fact that he was not very gifted at all. Born in 1818, he had been educated under the supervision of the liberally inclined Romantic poet Vasilii Zhukovskii. Between 1835 and 1837 he heard lectures on Russian law from the reforming bureaucrat Mikhail Speranskii. After travelling extensively at home (and becoming the first Romanov to see Siberia), in 1838 and 1839 he toured Europe. Having married a princess of Hesse-Darmstadt in 1841 (by whom he rapidly had six children), he was gradually introduced to his future duties. Nicholas appointed him to the State Council and the Committee of Ministers and then made him chairman, in 1842, of the committee which supervised the construction of the railway between St Petersburg and Moscow. In 1846 he sat on one of the tsar's many secret committees on peasant affairs, in 1848 he chaired another, and in 1849 he succeeded his uncle, the Grand Duke Mikhail, as head of the empire's military schools. By 1855, as we have seen, he was sufficiently trusted to dismiss the Crimean commander on his father's behalf.

The historian and jurist Boris Chicherin, who was predisposed to like him, believed that Alexander had been denied 'an upbringing capable of providing him with guidelines in the precarious circumstances in which he found himself'.[1] Another contemporary, Sergei Solov'ev, made the same point more acerbically when he said that 'In the Roman Empire emperors ascended the throne from various callings', whereas 'in the Russian Empire Alexander II ascended the throne from the ranks of the heads of military-educational institutions'.[2] In some ways, however, Alexander was better prepared for the throne than either of his immediate predecessors. His educational opportunities had been considerable and he had seen a good deal of Russian government from the inside. His difficulties did not derive from the way he was reared. Nor, apparently, did they spring from his disposition, for his outlook was less severe than that of his father and he was quite devoid of that propensity for abstraction which had impaired the prospects of Alexander I. Although he liked parades and reviews, his inclinations were not really militaristic. The Marquis de Custine, who observed him at Ems in 1839, thought that he would 'command obedience by the inherent appeal of charm, rather than by fear'.[3] The British traveller and journalist, Sir Donald Mackenzie Wallace, believed Alexander 'had inherited from his father a strong dislike to sentimentalism and rhetoric of all kinds' and that 'This dislike, joined to a goodly portion of sober common-sense, a limited confidence in his own judgment, and a consciousness of enormous responsibility, prevented him from being carried away by the prevailing excitement' with which his reign began.[4] His background, therefore, and some aspects of his personality, seemed to fit him for government.

The tsar could be cold, however – 'he trusted neither himself nor others, and therefore lacked the ability to attach anyone to himself'[5] – and unsympathetic observers were less sure of his temperament than the indulgent Mackenzie Wallace. The 'anarchist Prince', Petr Kropotkin, who was a boy in the Corps des Pages in the late 1850s and a revolutionary in exile by the time the reign ended, thought Alexander suffered from a split personality: 'two different men lived in him, both strongly developed, struggling with each other. ... He could be charming in his behaviour, and the next moment display sheer brutality. He was possessed of a calm, reasoned courage in the face of a real danger, but he lived in constant fear of dangers which existed in his brain only'.[6] He was not very bright. Even a courtier admitted that although he was tactful and judicious he possessed less character, less resolution and less intelligence than his father.[7] 'When the emperor talks to an intellectual,' said the poet Fedor Tiutchev, 'he has the appearance of someone with rheumatism who is standing in a draught'.[8] He let Turgenev know that he had enjoyed his *Sportsman's Sketches*, but his interest in them probably derived from his love of hunting rather than from the fact that the stories cast aspersions on serfdom. If Alexander II had died before ascending the throne, it is hard to believe that some Russian Fortinbras would have said he was 'likely, had he been put on, to have proved most royal'.

It was to be many months before the new tsar accepted defeat in the Crimean War. At the end of 1854 Britain and France had received the promise of military assistance from the north Italian Kingdom of Piedmont, but on 29 January / 10 February 1855, less than three weeks before his death, Nicholas had provided for a much greater increase in the size of the Russian armed forces by ordering the creation of a pan-imperial militia. On 23 February / 7 March, five days after his accession, Alexander told the ambassadors of Austria and Prussia that in foreign affairs he would adhere to the late tsar's principles. 'These principles', he said, 'are those of the Holy Alliance. If this alliance no longer exists, it is certainly not the fault of my father'.[9] The talks which Nicholas had made possible by accepting the Four Points as a basis for negotiation opened in Vienna three weeks later. Even the relatively uncontroversial Points One and Two (the Danubian Principalities and control of the mouth of the Danube) occupied the negotiators' attention for some weeks. Point Three, revision of the Straits Convention, proved intractable. On 17/29 April 1855 Aleksandr Gorchakov, the Russian plenipotentiary, declared that St Petersburg was happy with the Straits Convention as it stood. He wanted to make concessions, but his masters at home were intransigent. The Russian government would accept no reduction in the size of the empire's Black Sea fleet. Austria tried to mediate between the belligerents, but her efforts came to nothing. When the Vienna conference ended on 4/16 June, Point Four (the Christian inhabitants of the Ottoman Empire) had not even been aired. The siege of Sevastopol' continued. The young soldier Lev Tolstoy made his literary debut by publishing the first of three *Sevastopol' Stories* in *The Contemporary* in June. After conveying much of the horror of the siege, Tolstoy concluded optimistically. 'The one central, reassuring conviction you have come away with', he wrote, 'is that it is quite impossible for Sevastopol' ever to be taken by the enemy'.[10] On 27 August / 8 September, Sevastopol' fell. The third of Tolstoy's *Sevastopol' Stories*, which appeared early in 1856, described the 'remorse, shame and violent hatred' with which the Russians evacuated the city.[11]

The tsar remained hopeful. He urged his new Crimean commander (another Gorchakov and a relative of the Russian negotiator in Vienna) to 'think of the year 1812 and trust in God. Sevastopol' is not Moscow, and the Crimea is not Russia. Two years after Moscow burned, our victorious army entered Paris. We are still the same Russians and God is with us'.[12] In a way Alexander was right to persist. Even at Sevastopol' the fighting continued. The Russians had withdrawn from the southern to the northern side of the harbour, but survived there until the end of the war. One scholar points out that, in a sense, the siege of the city lasted not 349 days but 533.[13] Although Britain and France had captured the main part of Sevastopol', their military prospects were unattractive. Britain had 50,000 troops and 10,000 horses in the Crimea, France 200,000 and 34,000, but penetrating the interior of the Russian Empire would prove much more difficult than winning victories in the Crimean peninsula. Even if the Russians could be dislodged from the north side of Sevastopol', the allies would soon reach the point where their ships were unable to help them. They would also have to undertake exceptional recruitment measures at home. The assistance which they continued to seek from Austria might not tip the scales in their favour. Indeed, Austrian entry into the war might provoke a crisis in the Habsburg Empire greater than that of 1848–9 and throw the whole of central Europe into the melting-pot. In the Caucasus, meanwhile, Russia was performing more successfully than in the Crimea. N. N. Murav'ev, Vorontsov's successor as Caucasian Viceroy, took Kars in eastern Anatolia on 14/26 November 1855 and looked able to threaten Constantinople. The

Russians now held more enemy territory than their opponents and could contemplate taking the war into a fourth year.

But Russia also suffered from severe disadvantages. Her Black Sea fleet had by this time been destroyed, the allies had landed not only in the Crimea but also at Nikolaev to the west and Novorossiisk to the east, and the Turks retained a position at Sukhumi which gave them the chance of counter-attacking in the direction of Tiflis. Away from the principal theatre of the war, the Russian Baltic fleet was blockaded at Sveaborg and Kronstadt, St Petersburg was under threat of attack, and the empire could do little to protect its Arctic and Pacific coastlines. At the beginning of the war Russia had felt able to commit no more than a quarter of her field army to the southern part of the empire, as she needed the other three-quarters on her western frontier to defuse possible threats from Austria, Prussia and Sweden. Troops had been withdrawn from the west, but not because the likelihood of attack in that quarter had diminished. When Austria finally despatched an ultimatum to St Petersburg on 16/28 December 1855, the need to make peace looked overwhelming.

On 3/15 January 1856 the tsar chaired a meeting at which various dignitaries argued that Russia would eventually lose the war anyway, that she was financially exhausted, and that the loyalty of the empire's national minorities could not be guaranteed. The Minister of War probably had the most influential voice, for one of his officials, Dmitrii Miliutin – older brother of Nikolai, the 'enlightened bureaucrat' who had redesigned St Petersburg's municipal administration in 1846 – had armed him with a wide-ranging and incisive brief entitled 'On the danger of continuing military action in 1856'. Numerically, Miliutin wrote, Russia's forces looked strong, but it was doubtful whether they could withstand the fresh and well-organized armies which the enemy would be putting into the field against them. Losses in the three campaigns which had already taken place meant that most of Russia's rank-and-file soldiers had been recruited recently and that there were not enough officers to train them. Even if the troops currently under arms could be knocked into shape, finding yet more reserves of manpower was going to be difficult. In theory 25 million men were subject to the draft, but 12 million were exempt on health grounds, 5 million for various technical reasons, and something over 6 million for the simple reason that the economy required their labour. By Miliutin's reckoning, no more than 1.8 million men could actually be enlisted, and 800,000 of these had been called to the colours already. When shortages of equipment, powder, bombs and food were set alongside the shortage of men, the prospect of eventual victory receded still further. Even if resources had been plentiful, Russia lacked the roads and railways she needed to get them to the front. In 1854–5 the state had spent the equivalent of three years' income on the war and had accelerated inflation by covering the deficit with paper money. Miliutin pointed out that, if the war ended badly, all Russia's sacrifices would represent no more than 'the futile exhaustion of [her] last resources'.[14]

The tsar sued for an armistice and in March 1856 accepted the Peace of Paris. The settlement turned on the Four Points of 1854. To meet the requirements of Point One, the treaty contained a series of clauses which accelerated the evolution of the Danubian Principalities into the independent kingdom of Romania. In the light of Point Two, Russia was deprived of the sliver of territory which gave her a toe-hold on the Danube. Point Three, the main bone of contention between the two sides, led to the total demilitarization of the Black Sea. In settlement of Point Four, the sultan expressed goodwill towards his Christian subjects in return for an acknowledgement, on the part of the Great Powers, that they had no right to interfere in the internal affairs of the Ottoman Empire. Russia's major loss was the right to a Black Sea fleet. When Peter the Great gave up the first Russian fleet in southern waters after being disastrously defeated by the Turks in 1711, he said that 'The Lord God drove me out of this place, like Adam out of paradise'.[15] Nearly a century and a half later Alexander II might have been forgiven for feeling an even greater degree of disappointment. His humiliation was smaller than that to which the country had been subjected on being invaded by Napoleon in 1812, but so was the likelihood that Russia would be able to reverse her defeat in the near future. Sergei Solov'ev was wrong, however, to accuse the tsar of conducting the war with a lack of resolution.[16] He had in fact conducted it with a somewhat surprising degree of determination. It had done him no good, but the same quality was to stand him in good stead when he turned away from international relations to the many domestic difficulties which the war had engendered or highlighted.

DOMESTIC UNREST

Dmitrii Miliutin was not the only tsarist official to speak frankly, in the later stages of the war, of the strain it was placing on the country's resources. Just after the meeting of 3/15 January 1856 A. F. Orlov, the head of the Third Department, put his views in writing. 'The war', he said, 'is extremely burdensome for Russia. The recruit drafts, the militia, the interruption to trade increase people's needs and poverty'; 'Russians are ready to surmount still more hardships, [but] if the government attained peace on honourable terms, maintaining its resolve and dignity, that would bring general joy to the empire'.[17] Lesser officials sensed that their superiors were prepared to entertain criticism of the conduct of the empire's affairs and submitted devastating analyses of the particular fields of administration for which they were responsible. In the Ministry of State Properties a long memorandum of October 1855 brought together information from the provinces concerning the abject condition of state-owned peasants.[18] An employee of the Ministry of Finances pointed out at the beginning of 1856 that Russia's lowest social groups were far more heavily taxed than their counterparts in other countries. Making fathers pay the poll tax for their under-age children, he said, hindered the growth of population, which had advanced less in the twenty years since the mid-1830s than it had in the twenty years before that. The Finance Ministry official concluded with an indictment of the entire governmental system of the empire. 'Nowhere', he wrote,

is there so much and at the same time so little centralization as there is in Russia. On the one hand the ministries have arrogated to themselves the virtually exclusive right to decide all matters, but at the same time there is not the slightest link between the separate ministries. ... Everyone's perpetual concern to safeguard himself against having to take legal responsibility necessitates a fearful expenditure of effort, paper, ink, and time, slows down the transaction of business, removes from the provincial and district agencies all feelings of independence, and teaches them to act surreptitiously if at all. It goes without saying that all this stops short at the people, who have been abandoned to the authorities' exploitation.[19]

Miliutin went on writing memoranda after the war had come to an end. His paper of January 1856 turned out to be only the beginning of a long argument about the need to abolish serfdom in order to put the Russian army on a sounder footing. On 29 March 1856 he wrote a wide-ranging paper on the disadvantages of Russia's current military organization and the means of eliminating them. The prime disadvantages, he believed, were two: 'Absence of a territorial military organization' and the 'need to maintain a large peacetime army at great expense due to the lack of a ... reserve'. In Miliutin's words, 'serfdom does not permit us either to reduce the term of service or to increase the number of unlimited leaves so as to diminish the present number of troops'.[20]

Disquiet among supporters of the regime was to be found not only in the St Petersburg ministries but also at the imperial court and in the provinces. The new tsar's aunt, the Grand Duchess Elena Pavlovna (liberal German widow of the reactionary Grand Duke Mikhail), expressed a commitment to reform on the day after Nicholas I's death. The tsar's brother, the Grand Duke Konstantin Nikolaevich, spoke of the desirability of emancipating the serfs as early as the spring of 1855.[21] In a paper of late August 1855 P. A. Valuev, Governor of the province of Kurland on the Baltic coast, deplored the conduct of the war, asked whether the present structure of Russian government facilitated the development of the country's strengths, lamented the paralysis of the empire's administration, and deplored the fact that Russian government and society seemed to be at odds with one another.[22] Since, when he became Minister of Internal Affairs in the 1860s, Valuev was not to be noted for liberalism, it appeared that the new reign and the effects of the war were creating enthusiasm for change in places where it tended, under normal circumstances, to be rare.

At a time when potential reformers included senior officials and members of the royal family, it was to be expected that educated people outside the government would emerge from the bunker to which they had been relegated in 1848. The Westernizers and Slavophiles who had hitherto been able to voice their opinions only with extreme caution embarked upon a deliberate policy of circulating handwritten memoranda. For the Westernizers the process was set in train by the young Boris Chicherin, who completed 'The Eastern Question from the Russian Point of View' in the month of Nicholas's death. Always an independent spirit, Chicherin had been particularly irritated in 1853 and 1854 by the fact that neither Moscow nor St Petersburg Universities would examine his Master's dissertation on the provincial institutions of seventeenth-century Muscovy. The Dean of his Faculty in Moscow informed him that his view of medieval Russian administration was too bleak. His response was to depict the contemporary Russian Empire in no less lurid a light. His first memorandum began by indicting the government's supposedly annexationist motives for going to war and went on to inveigh against the economic and cultural backwardness which the conflict had brought to light. In a second paper Chicherin advocated freedom of conscience, the end of serfdom, freedom of opinion and the press, freedom of instruction in the schools and universities, open governmental activity and open judicial proceedings. In a third he concentrated on serfdom. Without its abolition, he wrote, 'no questions can be decided, whether political, administrative, or social'.[23] In Chicherin's view, the emancipation of the serfs had to take place before the government could reconstruct its financial system, set military recruitment on a sound footing, introduce press freedom, reform the country's legal institutions, encourage the development of industry or promote the education of the masses. Although circumstances could be imagined in which serfdom might profit a state, Chicherin wrote, they no longer obtained in Russia. When the inhabitants of a country were nomadic they had to be tied down in order to ensure that the land was properly exploited, but because in Russia they were predominantly sedentary state institutions could monitor their activity. In other words, the fields would still be sown when the population was free. Chicherin believed not only that serfdom was immoral but also that it was acting as a brake on the economy, that it could not be justified as a bastion against pauperism, and finally – a somewhat unusual argument – that it entailed the improper transference to the gentry of responsibilities which ought to be exercised by the state. Because of the demoralizing effect of serfdom, Chicherin declared, Russians had completely lost their sense of the individual's personal worth. Tinkering with the institution was futile. It had to be abolished, for the peasants were resisting it with increasing militancy and a mass uprising was entirely conceivable.

The pressure for change to which intellectuals were subjecting the government was perhaps best illustrated by the fact that on the right of the political spectrum even Mikhail Pogodin, the philosopher of Official Nationality, fell out with the authorities in the course of the war. When hostilities began he merely wanted the regime to behave dynamically. The first of his 'Historico-Political Letters' (December 1853) urged Nicholas to abandon the policy of good relations with Austria in favour of fomenting rebellion in the Balkans. Letters of April and May 1854 urged the government 'to proclaim the independence of Poland and to create a mighty Slavonic alliance with Russia at its head and its capital in Constantinople'.[24] Because Nicholas himself had entertained such dreams in passing, Pogodin could be accused at this stage of nothing more than super-patriotism. In the autumn of 1854, however, after the allied landing in the Crimea, he began to dwell on the domestic hardships to which the war was giving rise. The Russian countryside, he observed, was dangerously volatile. Western republican ideals were unlikely to make much headway in Russia, but a peasant rebellion was feasible. Other right-wing intellectuals were making the same point. The Slavophile, Ivan Aksakov, believed that landlord–peasant relationships were deteriorating by the year and could be stabilized only if the government acted quickly. At the end of 1854 another Slavophile, Iurii Samarin, went so far as to speak up for peasants who murdered their landlords. When riot and murder were the peasants' only means of self-preservation, he argued, 'murder becomes an act of altruism'.[25] Pogodin addressed himself to the spectre of peasant unrest in April and May 1855 and called upon the government to allow freedom of expression. By January 1856 he was asking not only for the relaxation of censorship but also for a constitution, various political amnesties, the gradual emancipation of the serfs, non-interference in the domestic affairs of European nations and assistance for national-liberation movements. The spectacle of the principal apologist for Official Nationality biting the hand that fed him must have convinced many doubters that the regime which Alexander II had inherited was intolerable. If even Pogodin had become an advocate of reform, friends of the status quo were likely to be thin on the ground.

All the critics mentioned so far kept their criticism within certain limits. Government officials were not trying to subvert the tsarist system, but to modernize it. Right-wing intellectuals such as Pogodin, Ivan Aksakov and Iurii Samarin were disillusioned with Nicholas I but sympathized with tsarism in principle. Even Chicherin, the most vocal of the Westernizers, was less radical than he seemed. 'Active opposition,' he wrote, 'let alone revolutionary movements, are quite alien to our character'.[26] He hoped that the government would set an example to the nation by inaugurating a period of change, but he did not believe that the estates of the realm should be given extensive political rights or that the power of the tsar should be dramatically reduced. None of these intellectuals attacked the regime as unequivocally as Alexander Herzen, who practically danced in the streets of London when he heard of Nicholas's death. Herzen had founded a 'Free Russian Press' almost immediately after arriving in England in 1853, but the fifteen flysheets and brochures he published between then and 1855 did little more than lose him money. From the start of the new reign his publications prospered. A day or two after Nicholas's death he decided to found

211

a journal. The first number of *The Polar Star* (named after Ryleev's almanac of the 1820s) came out in the summer of 1855 and enjoyed a degree of success which encouraged Herzen to publish further volumes and to embark on *Voices from Russia* in 1856 and *The Bell* in 1857. Beyond the reach of the imperial censors, these publications were to play a significant part in the politics of the late 1850s. Citizens of the tsar read them and contributed to them. Although it became easier to speak freely at home, only Herzen's periodicals escaped the censor entirely. When he said 'Give us free speech' in the first number of *The Polar Star*,[27] he made plain one of the two main things which Russia lacked. When he asked the new tsar to give land to the peasants he made plain the other. Up to a point the tsarist police could control the activities of intellectuals within the confines of the empire, but silencing Herzen was beyond their powers.

Although much of the dissent of 1855 and early 1856 was to be found in obscure memoranda written by one bureaucrat for another, manuscripts circulated by hand among the intelligentsia, and a journal which came out in faraway London, the Russian government also had reason to worry about dissent with a high public profile. Moscow was the most unsettled of the empire's cities. When Nicholas allowed the university there to celebrate its centenary in mid-January 1855 he hoped that the occasion would provide a morale-boosting opportunity for lauding one of the regime's successes. Unfortunately, from his point of view, the celebrations turned into an open demonstration of the values which Russian intellectuals had been cultivating since the 1830s. Kindred spirits reaffirmed loyalties which the authorities had been trying to suppress. Slavophiles gathered at the house of Samarin, Westernizers at that of Granovskii. Konstantin Kavelin took the train from St Petersburg and persuaded Chicherin to write the first of his anti-governmental memoranda. 'A huge number of meetings with after-dinner speeches and greetings took place in Moscow's inns'.[28] In February 1855 Moscow's gentry assembly chose the retired liberal general, A. P. Ermolov (one-time ruler of the Caucasus), to raise the supplementary armed forces which Nicholas had called for at the end of the previous month. This provocative election showed that dissatisfaction with the government had spread from intellectuals to the privileged. When the oath of loyalty to Alexander II was administered in Moscow on 19 February 1855, a bell fell through three floors of a Kremlin church where the ceremony was taking place and prompted speculation on the part of the common people that the new tsar would be dogged by misfortune. Even Moscow's lower orders, it seemed, were beginning to voice their disquiet. Alexander tried to steady Muscovites by visiting the city in September 1855, but his visit was offset by the effect on public opinion of the Westernizers' laments for Granovskii, who died after a short illness on 4 October. Slavophiles spoke out in late November at festivities for Mikhail Shchepkin, the greatest Russian actor. Not surprisingly, Muscovites took little notice of the death among them of Uvarov, for in the atmosphere of late 1855 Granovskii and Shchepkin were dearer to their hearts than a former government minister.

Meanwhile, alarming developments were taking place in the country-side. Nicholas's call for an all-Russian militia provoked a token protest from Moscow's gentry but a wave of disorder among the peasantry. Although serfs became free only when they were recruited into the regular army, not when they enrolled in a militia, in the mid-1850s they chose to believe otherwise. In April 1854 Nicholas had ordered the recruitment of irregulars in four northern provinces for the purpose of strengthening Russia's naval defences on the Baltic. Rumours that he had granted peasants a chance of achieving their freedom spread far beyond the region to which his edict applied. 'Whole villages of the provinces of Moscow, Riazan, and Tambov left their work and flocked to Moscow to enroll'.[29] Despite these difficulties Nicholas was obliged to order the creation of a much larger militia in January 1855. Although the authorities proceeded cautiously (issuing the call to the colours at different times in different places and eventually pro-mulgating appeals in no more than about half the provinces of the Euro-pean part of the empire), trouble still ensued. Peasants may have been keen to enlist because they were genuinely patriotic, but their mood was invariably febrile when the throne changed hands. Since those who caused the most difficulty were Ukrainians in the provinces of Kiev and Voronezh, and since Ukrainians retained relatively recent memories of the days of Cossack freedom, it is likely that many of the rural dwellers who proved hard to handle were motivated by the belief that they could bring their emancipation nearer. This was certainly the conclusion of contemporary intellectuals, almost all of whom thought that the government's attempts to raise additional troops created more problems than they solved. Dmitrii Miliutin, at the War Ministry, was not alone in his view that creating a mili-tia was no answer to the army's manpower problem. Chicherin's discussion of the militia question ended with a rhetorical question: 'When the ele-ments of insurrection exist, who knows whether or not the age of Pu-gachev can recur?'[30]

Discontent seemed to be general. Bureaucrats, members of the royal family, intellectuals of various persuasions, city dwellers and the peasantry all seemed to be pressing for radical changes in the structure of the Russian polity. Tsars often ascended the throne in difficult circumstances, but the situation in which Alexander found himself was undoubtedly worse than that which confronted his father in 1825 or his uncle in 1801. Chicherin (with benefit of hindsight) described the challenges which lay ahead as follows:

[Alexander] was called upon to execute one of the hardest tasks which can con-front an autocratic ruler: to completely remodel the enormous state which had been entrusted to his care, to abolish an age-old order founded on slavery, to re-place it with civic decency and freedom, to establish justice in a country which had never known the meaning of legality, to redesign the entire administration, to intro-duce freedom of the press in the context of untrammelled authority, to call new forces to life at every turn and set them on firm legal foundations, to put a repressed and humiliated society on its feet and to give it the chance to flex its muscles.[31]

ALEXANDER'S CAUTION

It is tempting to explain the startling developments which duly took place in Russian domestic affairs in the second half of the 1850s and the first half of the 1860s by saying that the tsar recognized the extent of the difficulties which confronted him and applied himself to resolving them. Only six years elapsed between his accession and the emancipation of the serfs. It is easy to make him look personally responsible for setting the process in train and bringing it to fruition. In a speech to representatives of the Moscow gentry in March 1856 he announced that it was better to abolish serfdom from above than to wait until it began to abolish itself from below. In January 1857 he set up a 'Secret Committee on the Peasant Question' to discuss ways in which the abolition of serfdom might be achieved. In November 1857 he instructed V. I. Nazimov, the Governor of Vil'na, Kovno and Grodno, to let the gentry of the three north-western provinces establish local committees for the purpose of determining how their serfs were to be emancipated. By decreeing that the order to Nazimov (the 'Nazimov Rescript') be copied to other governors, Alexander more or less forced the rest of the empire to follow the example of the north-west. By publishing the rescript the tsar brought the government's reformist intentions into the public domain. Since the Secret Committee on the Peasant Question no longer had to be secret it was renamed the 'Main' Committee in January 1858. In the same month journalists were permitted to discuss emancipation freely. In the course of 1858 the many local committees which resulted from the circulation and publication of the Nazimov Rescript began sending their views on emancipation to St Petersburg. To collate their statements Alexander appointed 'Editing Commissions' in 1859. In two waves, one in late 1859, the other in early 1860, representatives of the various provincial committees which had come into being as a result of the Nazimov Rescript came to St Petersburg to discuss their ideas with the Editing Commissions. The Editing Commissions reported to the Main Committee, the Main Committee to the State Council, and the tsar signed the completed legislation on 19 February 1861.

When the course of the emancipation of the serfs is described in this way, the importance of the tsar looks overwhelming. Not only did he embark upon freeing the serfs as soon as foreign affairs ceased to occupy the bulk of his attention, but also he intervened repeatedly in the process to galvanize his officials and overcome the mistrust of conservatives. Jerome Blum assigns the tsar pride of place in the list of factors which contributed to the serfs' emancipation.[32] His view finds support in the memoirs of Iakov Solov'ev, one of the major participants in the process of reform, who asserted that 'Only the will of the autocrat could have sustained the numerically small and socially ill placed progressive party, which without it could have been destroyed'.[33] Norman Pereira has drawn attention to four points between 1856 and 1861 at which, but for the tsar, forward movement might have come to an end. First, the publication of the Nazimov Rescript at the end of 1857 cut short the year-long procrastination of the Secret Committee. Second, on a tour of the provinces in the summer of 1858 Alexander made plain to backwoodsmen that their committees should take a positive view of the reformist enterprise. Third, when the provincial gentry still did not take up the cause of reform with alacrity the tsar bypassed them by appointing a majority of keen reformers to the Editing Commissions. Fourth, when draft legislation came before the Main Committee in 1860 Alexander stood firm for change in the face of obdurate resistance from aristocrats. 'On at least four occasions,' therefore, 'the emperor either personally turned things around or used one of his lieutenants to do so'.[34]

The determination Alexander demonstrated as a war-leader undoubtedly resurfaced on a number of occasions after Russia made peace, but explaining the emancipation of the serfs by depicting him as a latter-day Peter the Great oversimplifies Russian politics between 1855 and 1861 and says almost nothing about the shape of the emancipation settlement. Although Alexander lent his authority to domestic reforms, it is unwise to think of him as a daring pilot in extremity. When, as tutor to the heir to the throne, Chicherin saw a good deal of the royal family in 1864, the tsar put him in mind of a major in the army. 'Where did all those great actions come from,' Chicherin wondered, 'which transformed the Russian land and changed its direction overnight?'[35] Not really from the sovereign. Chapter Five argued that the main problem in discussing the peasant question in the reign of Nicholas I is explaining why he addressed himself to it at all, not why he did relatively little. The main problem in discussing the emancipation may be explaining why Alexander addressed himself to it half-heartedly rather than why he addressed himself to it at all. The discussion in Chapter Five pointed out that although Nicholas and his officials accepted that serfdom was immoral, believed that it was unprofitable, could see advantages in reducing the authority of the gentry, and realized that the country's competitors were abandoning landlord–serf relations, they did not feel under any obligation to take immediate and far-reaching action. Nor did Alexander. The relative speed with which emancipation came about after he ascended the throne gives the impression that he addressed himself to it with enthusiasm, but even in Russian politics six years was a long time. In reality, the tsar proceeded with extreme caution. In view of the extent of domestic disquiet in the last year of the Crimean War Alexander had every reason to adopt a policy of radical reform, but it was some time before he did so. His speech to representatives of the Moscow gentry in March 1856 was tame, his creation of a secret committee in 1857 was the traditional way to sweep calls for change under the carpet, the Nazimov Rescript envisaged a form of emancipation which would have severely damaged the peasantry, the relaxation of censorship in January 1858 was short-lived and the provincial tour of 1858 represented yet another futile attempt to persuade nobles to accept a measure they were bent on resisting. It was 1859 before Alexander gave reformers their head by granting them control of the Editing Commissions, and by then the prestige of the throne would have suffered far more from the abandonment of emancipation than from allowing a version of it to go through. The version of emancipation which became law made many concessions to the interests of the gentry. With great trepidation and much backsliding the tsar eventually granted the serfs a sort of freedom, but if their interests had been dear to his heart he could have committed himself earlier and pressed harder for a settlement which gave them an economically viable future. Alexander possessed no blueprint for change in 1855 or 1856. Legislation in the nineteenth-century Russian Empire looks like a series of royal fiats, but the laws whch freed the serfs emerged from a process which the tsar barely understood and over which he had only partial control. The complicated narrative of the emancipation cannot be reduced to the proposition that Alexander sensed he was facing a crisis and believed that attack was the best form of defence.

THE CONTRADICTORY SIGNALS OF 1855 AND 1856

As chairman of the 1848 committee on the peasant question Alexander had presided over the cancellation of the one statute enacted between 1825 and 1855 which allowed serfs to buy their freedom irrespective of the wishes of serf-owners. For a number of years after he ascended the throne he remained highly deferential to gentry concerns. Although his caution sprang largely from natural inclination, it coincided, up to a point, with the dictates of common sense. The election of Ermolov as head of the militia in Moscow (and subsequently in St Petersburg) showed that, even when the country was at war, nobles would respond with displeasure to decrees which took their serfs away from them. The Crimean disaster failed to persuade the majority of the gentry that serfdom was an anachronism. Although the country's economy suffered intolerable strains as a result of the war, hardship was much greater in the public domain than the private. 'It was the state which suffered most'.[36] The government's budgetary deficit went up six- or seven-fold, its ability to back paper money with gold went down by more than 50 per cent, and in 1856 it spent 84 per cent of its income on debt repayments and the armed forces,[37] but the private sector suffered less severely than the Treasury and people who engaged in industry or commerce positively benefited. The authorities' ability to pay for reforms was diminishing at a time when the gentry's lack of enthusiasm for restructuring their finances was as great as ever.

Thus even if he had wanted to introduce a programme of radical social reform, Alexander had to tread carefully. He gave few signs that radical social reform was his long-term objective. One of his first actions was to tell the St Petersburg gentry assembly that its devotion to the throne had sweetened his father's last moments.[38] Nicholas had probably devoted those last moments, in part, to regretting that he had failed to do more for the peasantry,[39] but if Alexander understood the late tsar to mean that he should introduce changes he was slow to take the injunction to heart. In the summer of 1855 he dismissed a Minister of Internal Affairs who as Governor of the south-western provinces had worked hard, in the 1840s, to regulate the way in which Polish landlords treated their Ukrainian serfs. Bibikov was no liberal, but neither were some of those who eventually made major contributions to the emancipation of 1861. Given firm instructions the dismissed minister would probably have made a better reformer than his successor, S. S. Lanskoi, who in August 1855 'proclaimed the rights of the nobility to be inviolable'.[40] Since the principal advantage of being a noble was the right to exploit peasant labour, serfdom looked set to continue.

After making peace Alexander appeared to move in the direction of reform, but his celebrated speech to marshals of the Moscow gentry needs to be set in context. When, on 19 March 1856, the tsar issued a manifesto which spoke of the blessings which were to descend upon the empire as a result of the peace treaty, he envisaged 'equal justice and equal protection for everyone, so that each can enjoy in peace the fruits of his own righteous labours'.[41] The egalitarian implications of this announcement led the Governor-General of Moscow to ask the tsar for clarification, with the result that on 30 March Alexander made the oral remarks which are usually taken to represent the beginning of the emancipation process. He had learned, he told his audience,

that rumours have spread among you of my intention to abolish serfdom. To refute any groundless gossip on so important a subject I consider it necessary to inform you that I have no intention of doing so immediately. But, of course, and you yourselves realise it, the existing system of serf owning cannot remain unchanged. It is better to begin abolishing serfdom from above than to wait for it to begin to abolish itself from below. I ask you, gentlemen, to think of ways of doing this. Pass on my words to the nobles for consideration.[42]

The language of Alexander's speech was no more radical than that which Nicholas I had used in 1842 when defending the ineffectual Law on Obligated Peasants.[43] Admitting that 'the existing system of serf owning' had to change was so commonplace in mid-nineteenth-century Russia that its capacity to shock was minimal. Although, in referring to the possibility that serfdom might 'abolish itself from below', the tsar seemed to be responding to the rural disturbances which had resulted from Nicholas's militia creations, in all probability he simply lifted the phrase from a Third Department report of 1839 whose purpose, though reformist, had hardly been the complete transformation of government policy.[44] Alexander raised none of the questions which would have to be answered if emancipation were to take place: whether serfs were to be granted land as well as liberty, whether and how they were to pay for them, and how local government was to be conducted if the jurisdiction of serf-owners came to an end. Above all, the tsar knew perfectly well that the gentry were unlikely to help him. Almost all attempts to improve the lot of the serfs in the previous two or three generations had failed because they depended on the gentry's goodwill. In 1856 Alexander was very far from accepting that emancipation meant compulsion. Only a faint line can be drawn from his speech in Moscow to the statutes of February 1861.

In the short term the speech not only failed to accelerate the coming of reform, but even postponed it. Although the tsar's reflections lacked substance and realism, they caused a flurry among the gentry which alarmed the authorities and led the Minister of Internal Affairs to despatch an emollient circular to provincial governors. The government abandoned public references to the possibility of emancipation and 'groped for a means of resolving the peasant question by turning to the experience of the past'.[45] The process of information-gathering which ensued was certainly no more radical than that sanctioned by Nicholas I when he set up the Committee of 6 December 1826. Just after the despatch of the circular to provincial governors A. I. Levshin, the Deputy Minister of Internal Affairs, began compiling a historical memorandum on serfdom which reviewed 200 years of legislation on the subject and drew on the documents generated by Nicholas I's secret committees. Lanskoi presented the completed memorandum to the tsar in December 1856 and recommended the establishment of various bodies to act on it. Alexander took only part of the advice. He appointed a single, secret committee, whereas Lanskoi had sought to involve a relatively wide range of people in the emancipation process and had made no reference to secrecy. Nor did Alexander accept Lanskoi's opinion that members of the new committee ought to be 'convinced of the need to move towards a new order'.[46] The Secret Committee on the Peasant Question, which convened for the first time on 3 January 1857, consisted entirely of Nicholaevan grandees. Since Lanskoi was the only appointee who could have been described as a reformer, the new body augured ill for the cause of reform.

Even Lanskoi's opinions were distinctly moderate. He and Levshin, his deputy, knew that they had to do something, but in 1856 their ideas were unambitious. On the one hand they doubted whether peasants should receive land as well as personal freedom; on the other they felt that emancipation had to be introduced gradually, at different times in different places. Their philosophy amounted to introducing other parts of the empire to the relationship between landlords and peasants which obtained in the Baltic provinces. By leaving landowners in possession of the land, the Baltic emancipation of 1816–19 had perpetuated peasant dependency. Its drawbacks were obvious, but so long as the tsar sought noble acquiescence in reform it probably represented the only sort of emancipation which had a chance of reaching the statute book. It was certainly the only sort acceptable to the small number of landowners who were prepared to embark upon change. These were mainly to be found in Kovno, Grodno and Vil'na, the three north-western provinces to the south of the Baltic littoral.

Proximity to a region in which the peasants were already free was not the only reason why the gentry of the north-western provinces were prepared to countenance emancipation. As Poles they had been subject to St Petersburg's longstanding attempts to interfere in relations between Polish nobles and non-Polish peasants. For nearly a generation they had been resisting the introduction of written inventories of peasant obligations, whose purpose was to prevent noblemen treating serfs in the arbitrary manner to which they were accustomed. By comparison with inventories, emancipation on the Baltic model was an attractive proposition. In 1855 Alexander had appointed his friend General V. I. Nazimov (the reactionary who had clamped down on Moscow University in the last years of Nicholas I) to the Governor-Generalship of the three provinces at issue. In May 1856, two months after his speech in Moscow, the tsar met Nazimov at Brest and discovered that, in the north-west, his words had fallen on fruitful soil. At the coronation, which took place in Moscow at the end of August 1856, Levshin, the Deputy Minister of Internal Affairs, quizzed gentry representatives from many parts of the empire on the question of emancipation and found sympathy for the idea only among the north-westerners whose feelings on the matter had already been communicated to the tsar. On 26 October 1856 Alexander gave written instructions to Nazimov to collect the ideas of the north-western gentry more systematically.

This was the second of the two main developments in the emancipation process which took place in 1856. Neither the creation of the Secret Committee on the Peasant Question, however, nor the orders to Nazimov promised to be significant milestones. By setting up the Secret Committee Alexander acted in the style of his father; by ordering Nazimov to delve more deeply into the views of the north-westerners he showed sympathy for a landless concept of emancipation which belonged to the reign of Alexander I. The regime seemed to be moving in the direction not so much of freeing the serfs as of turning a blind eye to them (by consigning their future to yet another assembly of antediluvian officials) or making their condition worse (by opting for a form of emancipation which would blight their future). If the government had executed the plans it came up with in 1856, peasants would have been justified in thinking that the devil of serfdom was preferable to the deep blue sea of reform.

Even in 1856, however, there were signs that the ideas of Lanskoi, Levshin, and the north-western gentry might eventually be upstaged. More generous approaches to the question of emancipation were to be found not only in the many unofficial memoranda which were passing from hand to hand, but also in the minds of a few well-placed individuals whose views could hardly be ignored. The Grand Duchess Elena Pavlovna made her first practical contribution to the improvement of conditions in the countryside when she asked Nikolai Miliutin to tell her how to free the serfs on her Ukrainian estate of Karlovka. Miliutin, architect of the St Petersburg municipal reform of 1846, was head of the Economic Department of the Ministry of Internal Affairs and potentially the most influential of the 'enlightened bureaucrats' who had been consolidating their links with each other since the end of the 1830s.[47] 'He had a practical outlook on life, the ability to understand things quickly (even things about which he knew little), and an understanding of people'.[48] His brother Dmitrii had been making a good case for emancipation at the War Ministry, but his own importance, in the long run, was to be greater. Although he was by no means a radical, he felt that the government's best chance of maintaining its authority was to give more ground – literally – than it was promising to do. In his memorandum for Elena Pavlovna he did not concern himself just with her estate in Ukraine. 'The preface and to a still greater degree the text of the memorandum evince the author's hidden intention to provide general ideas for the transformation of the whole of Russia'.[49] Miliutin either said or implied that the time had passed for half-measures like the Law on Free Agriculturalists of 1803, the Baltic emancipation of 1816–19 and the Law on Obligated Peasants of 1842. Serfs had to receive not only personal freedom and title to their dwelling-places and kitchen gardens, but also allocations of land which would enable them to survive and prosper. Since land allotments would be carved out of land that belonged to the gentry, serfs would have to pay for them. Since they lacked the necessary cash, the government would be obliged to furnish them with credit. Liberated serfs would then redeem their debts over a period of years. Miliutin realized that landowners would not take kindly to his plan of campaign, but he felt that the government could win their support by setting up gentry committees to work out local details and by sanctioning a debate on peasant affairs in the press.

The tsar turned down Miliutin's general principles on the same day he instructed Nazimov to continue canvassing opinion in the north-western provinces. In so far as the idea of emancipation moved forward in government circles in 1856, the landless variety prevailed over the landed. Of the two broad social groups between which the tsar had to mediate, he clearly set greater store by the gentry than the peasantry. Mindful, perhaps, of the events of 1801 and 1825, he feared aristocratic recalcitrance more than a peasant rebellion. His conservative sympathies were clear. He not only handed control of the new Secret Committee to grandees but in the same month, December 1856, raised the qualification for promotion to the hereditary nobility from the achievement of rank five on the Table of Ranks to the achievement of rank four. Rank four could be conferred on civil servants only by royal patent. Henceforward, at least in theory, the highest echelons of society were less likely to be permeated by gifted but landless bureaucrats than they had been in the past. The proportion of highly placed advisers who had nothing to lose if serfs were emancipated would accordingly diminish. Alexander seemed not so much to be moving in the direction of reform as to be making the achievement of emancipation more difficult. In 1856 the one sign he gave that peasants might be freed sooner rather than later was the suspension, in July, of the existing rules for recruitment into the army. Since the existing rules applied to a serf-based society, suspending them implied that the social order on which they depended was to be altered. Perhaps Dmitrii Miliutin's explanation of the Russian army's deficiencies had struck home. The other Miliutin, however, had been less successful. Despite the backing of the Grand Duchess Elena Pavlovna, he had been unable to undo the work of Lanskoi and Levshin. The peasants' chances of acquiring personal freedom were very much alive, but their chances of acquiring land remained small.

Yet if Russians had known how the process of emancipation was to develop and what its terms were to be, they might have thought that Nikolai Miliutin possessed a crystal ball. Ideas very similar to his proposals for Karlovka eventually prevailed over those of the tsar, the gentry and his own ministerial superiors. One reason for their long-term viability derived from the extent to which they reflected the ideas of the non-governmental intelligentsia. Russian policy-makers could usually ignore the views of non-bureaucrats, but the abolition of the Committee of 2 April 1848 (Nicholas I's hard-line censorship agency) made it harder for the authorities to prevent reformist sentiments from appearing in print. The tsar probably dissolved the committee in December 1855 on the grounds of inefficiency rather than because he planned to treat writers more liberally,[50] but while he planned a suitable alternative censorship became less stringent. The open discussion of serfdom was still forbidden, but Westernizers and Slavophiles both set up flagship journals. Chicherin stopped writing private memoranda and started a debate on the peasant commune. Only four works on the subject had appeared in Russia before 1850, but ninety-nine came out between 1856 and 1860.[51] It was to be 1858 before the government explicitly extended freedom of speech, but inadvertently it was beginning to relax as early as 1856. It also revealed one or two clearer signs of generosity. Passports for foreign travel became freely available, with the result that 6,000 were issued in 1856 and 26,000 in 1859.[52] At his coronation in August 1856 Alexander amnestied the surviving Decembrists, the Polish rebels of 1830–1, and most of the Petrashevtsy. Signs like these were enough to convince educated contemporaries that it was worth trying to maintain the pressure on the authorities which they had already begun to generate. Herzen observed a 'sharp and remarkable' difference between essays he received from Russia in 1856 and those that had arrived in 1855.[53] His response was to urge the tsarist regime 'Onward! Onward!' in the second issue of *The Polar Star*.[54] Tolstoy went so far as to say that 'He who was not alive in the Russia of 1856 does not know what life is'.[55] Not even bureaucrats could wholly ignore the prevailing atmosphere of intellectual excitement. If it continued, radical proposals like those of Nikolai Miliutin stood a chance of more serious consideration.

THE DECISION OF 1857 TO GRANT THE SERFS THEIR FREEDOM

Radicalism, however, was very far from the thoughts of the Secret Committee on the Peasant Question. At its second meeting, on 17 January 1857, a majority of the members tried to persuade the tsar that he should allay suspicion and dampen expectations by pretending, in an edict, that he was planning no changes in the condition of the serfs. When this proposal was rejected the committee detailed three of its members to work out how emancipation might be achieved. They failed to reach a consensus and in April and May submitted separate reports. Predictably, in view of the fact that he was a major landowner, P. P. Gagarin recommended landless emancipation on the Baltic model. Neither Baron Korf nor Iakov Rostovtsev owned serfs, but the one was faint-hearted and the other unimaginative. The best Korf could think of was leaving everything to the provincial gentry, which Alexander had tried without success in his Moscow speech of March 1856. Rostovtsev proposed reform in three stages: legislating to prevent landowners from abusing their current powers; turning serfs into Free Agriculturalists or Obligated Peasants; and completely emancipating the peasants at some point in the distant future. At least he had read the available documents, but his memorandum 'differed not at all, in essence, from decisions taken by secret committees in the reign of Nicholas I'.[56] None of the three papers was going to set the world on fire.

While the triumvirate was at work, moreover, Orlov, the senior member of the Secret Committee, completed a manoeuvre which rendered peasant reform even less likely than it was already. At the end of the Crimean War he had convinced Alexander that if peace were to last Russia needed a major figure as her ambassador in Paris. His candidate for the post was the long-serving and reform-orientated Minister of State Properties, P. D. Kiselev, who in 1856 was the only Russian official with the desire, the knowledge and the power to promote the idea of peasant reform in the midst of a hostile bureaucracy. In accepting Orlov's suggestion and transferring Kiselev to Paris, Alexander damaged the prospects of reform to a much greater extent than he had by replacing Bibikov with Lanskoi at the Ministry of Internal Affairs. The damage was two-fold, for within months of Kiselev's departure a reactionary took his place. Orlov and others engineered factional strife in the Ministry of State Properties which in April 1857 led to the appointment as minister of M. N. Murav'ev, a man who believed that 'the question [of emancipation] had been dreamed up by ... academics, theoreticians, [and] sons of priests' and who planned to treat state-owned peasants as harshly as serfs. The addition of Murav'ev to the Secret Committee, which took place on the recommendation of Orlov immediately after his appointment as minister, was probably the low point of the emancipation story.[57]

Shortly afterwards the tide seemed to turn. En route to taking the waters in western Europe, the tsar met General Nazimov at Vil'na and learned that the gentry of the north-western provinces remained keen on freeing their serfs. At the spa town of Kissingen in Bavaria he fell under the influence of his aunt, the Grand Duchess Elena Pavlovna. With the assistance of various experts the Grand Duchess had been developing Miliutin's Karlovka proposals at Wildbad in the Black Forest. One scholar claims that 'the Wildbad group was delving deeper into the emancipation issue than had any governmental or gentry body in Russia before'.[58] Elena Pavlovna and her principal advisers, Kiselev and August von Haxthausen, were waiting for Alexander when he arrived at Kissingen. Elena reminded her nephew that Nicholas I had regretted his failure to do more for Russia's well-being. Haxthausen deluged Alexander with memoranda. Relieved, perhaps, to have escaped the obstructionism of his officials in St Petersburg, the tsar responded favourably. He gave Kiselev the chance to comment on the Secret Committee's recent papers and expressed particular approval of Haxthausen's opinion that the serfs had to be emancipated before their dissatisfaction expressed itself in revolt. Alexander appeared to have shifted his ground. From Kissingen he ordered the head of the Secret Committee to abandon his delaying tactics, and almost immediately after his return to St Petersburg, in July 1857, he offset the appointment of Murav'ev to the Secret Committee by adding his brother, the Grand Duke Konstantin Nikolaevich.

Even now, however, no decisions had been taken on the speed of emancipation or the form it should take. One of the lesser members of the Wildbad group, Konstantin Kavelin, was credited by a contemporary with 'primacy in establishing the principle of the landed rather than the landless emancipation of the peasants',[59] but neither he nor his friend Nikolai Miliutin had secured the adoption of their views as official policy. After Kissingen Alexander made Kavelin tutor to the heir to the throne, but he may not have realized the extent of the tutor's radicalism. In July 1857 even Kiselev believed that because emancipation with land was for the time being impossible, freeing the serfs ought to be postponed for the foreseeable future.[60] Alexander probably agreed with him. In August he calmly accepted the Secret Committee's decision to adopt the slow-moving approach to reform laid down by Iakov Rostovtsev. The tsar had been enthusiastic about change so long as he remained in the orbit of Elena Pavlovna, but in St Petersburg his convictions or his courage deserted him.

Few people outside the government knew that the regime was even considering emancipation. In the first number of *The Bell*, in July 1857, Herzen reported a rumour that the Secret Committee had been established. He added, however, that it was said to have broken up without achieving anything. The non-achievement of the Russian authorities remained the keynote of Herzen's journalism. In the August number of *The Bell* he published an anonymous letter from St Petersburg which pointed out that two years of the new reign had elapsed to no purpose. In September he used recent edicts to illustrate the government's indecision and halfheartedness. In October he invented the celebrated image of 'Chinghis-Khan with telegraphs' to buttress the argument that Russia might be turning into a sort of latter-day oriental despotism.[61] Negative evidence confirms the impression that educated Russians had no notion they were approaching a watershed. Intellectuals had begun reading Alexis de Tocqueville's *The Old Regime and the Revolution*, a seminal study of eighteenth-century France which came out in Paris in 1856. The book's first Russian readers seem not to have taken up its principal insight, that the most dangerous moment for an authoritarian government arrives when it tries to reform itself. The reactions of Lev Tolstoy, who sympathized with Tocqueville's admiration of paternalism in the French countryside, and Chicherin, who admired the French centralization which Tocqueville found distasteful, said much about the two men's very different attitudes towards the quandary in which Russia found herself, but turned on the second rather than the third part of Tocqueville's study.[62] It was the third part of the book that spoke about the danger of making changes; in the summer of 1857 Part Three may have seemed less important than Part Two because the tsarist authorities had yet to give an unequivocal sign of their commitment to reform.

At last, however, they did so. If the Grand Duchess Elena lost ground with the tsar after his return to St Petersburg, General Nazimov could be put off no longer. In late September 1857 he reported to the Ministry of Internal Affairs that the north-western gentry had expressed formal approval of landless emancipation. To convert the principle into practice he needed detailed instructions from the centre. In October he came to St Petersburg to press for them, and by 20 November, after intense activity in the Ministry of Internal Affairs and the Secret Committee, the instructions were ready. The document which embodied them, the Nazimov Rescript, marked the real beginning of the peasants' emancipation. It is true that, at first sight, the rescript left a great deal to be desired. The government decreed that land was to remain the property of the landlords, that peasants were to remain subject to communal organizations (which reduced the likelihood that they might turn into entrepreneurs), that the gentry would continue to exercise police duties in the countryside, and that state and local taxes were to be paid as before. Peasants were to be given their household plots, but had to pay for them. They were to be allowed to use some of the gentry's farmland, but not necessarily in perpetuity and only in return for labour services or cash. The authorities also gave themselves the most important voice on the gentry committees which were to decide on land boundaries and the size of the peasants' payments.

On the face of it, this plan of campaign did not seem very innovative. Instead of speaking of 'the emancipation of the peasants', the rescript referred only to 'the improvement of the peasants' way of life'. It related, moreover, only to a small and atypical part of the empire. Yet all those involved in Nazimov's instructions sensed the importance of the step they were taking. The tsar thought he had found a model for ameliorating the condition of the peasants which the gentry would accept. The Minister of Internal Affairs was becoming increasingly sympathetic to the views of

Nikolai Miliutin and saw the rescript (which was drafted by Levshin, his deputy), as a means of wresting the initiative in peasant affairs from the Secret Committee. Even the Secret Committee had a reason for allowing the Rescript to be promulgated: by committing itself to a relatively modest programme of reform, the government seemed to be discouraging radicals from pressing their case. If conservatives could hold the line, they stood a chance of enacting a settlement that suited them.

The main importance of the rescript, however, lay not in its relatively modest provisions or acceptability to the various policy-makers in central government, but in the rapidity with which it was circulated and published. 'The government's open acknowledgement that preparation of a peasant reform was under way ... marked a dividing line in the political behaviour of the absolute monarchy'.[63] Whereas neither the statutes of 1816–19 which freed the peasants of the Baltic provinces nor the south-western 'inventory reform' of the 1840s had been included in the Complete Collection of the Laws, in late 1857 the government went public with major plans before they had even been finalized. In effect, the tsar involved the educated community in the making of law. To use the vogue word of the hour, he ran the risk of glasnost.[64] This was the really startling feature of the official policy adopted in late 1857. It is harder to explain why the government involved the public in its actions than it is to explain why the various parties involved in the preparation of the rescript thought it could be turned to their advantage. Although the Secret Committee formally agreed to publication of Nazimov's instructions, many contemporaries recorded the attempts of committee members to prevent it. According to Aleksandr Koshelev, Orlov warned the tsar that he risked destroying the gentry and losing his throne.[65] Alexander seemed to have become a decisive proponent of reform. He seemed, indeed, to have become much more decisive altogether, for at exactly the same time as he signed the rescript, he created a new governmental body under his own chairmanship, the Council of Ministers, whose purpose was apparently to strengthen his grip on the central administration.[66]

Even at the end of 1857, however, depicting the tsar as a committed reformer is unwise. The picture sits ill with his behaviour in general. Though he could be determined, he was rarely incisive. In all probability he failed to understand the consequences of his actions. The summer conversations in Kissingen, the presence in St Petersburg of the Grand Duke Konstantin Nikolaevich, the greater enthusiasm for reform of Lanskoi at the Ministry of Internal Affairs – all these undoubtedly altered the balance of opinion to which he was exposed and made him more susceptible to reformist sentiments; but he may also have been naive enough to believe that the gentry at large would follow the example of the north-westerners and welcome the measure he was putting to them. In this he was to be disappointed. Far from having run its course, the struggle for the emancipation of the serfs was about to enter an even more heated phase than the one it had just been going through.

THE DECISION OF 1858 TO FREE THE SERFS WITH LAND

The principal question, whether the serfs were to be emancipated at all, had been answered, for after the circulation of the Nazimov Rescript to provincial governors and its publication in the journal of the Ministry of Internal Affairs there was no doubt that the relationship between landowners and privately owned peasants was going to be put on a new footing. Discussion turned from the question of principle to questions of practice: how change was to be effected and what post-emancipation society was to look like. Resolving these issues without generating revolts on the part of the gentry or the peasantry required a balancing act which tested the regime to the limits. Broadly speaking, 1858 witnessed commitment to emancipation with land, 1859 the preparation of statutes to bring it about, 1860 and 1861 the modification of the draft legislation and 1861 its implementation. The first of these stages was much the most important, for despite the promulgation of the Nazimov Rescript a betting man would not have laid money, at the end of 1857, on the proposition that peasants were going to acquire both freedom from manorial jurisdiction and some of the landlords' property.

In the first half of 1858 gentry committees like those which the Nazimov Rescript set up in the north-western provinces came into being throughout the European part of the empire. Legitimately confused about the sort of emancipation they were expected to recommend, provincial nobles bombarded the central authorities with requests for a fuller statement of their intentions. The Secret Committee – now called the Main Committee – produced two very different policy statements in the course of the year. In April it inclined to the view that, apart from personal freedom, serfs should acquire no more than their dwelling-places and kitchen gardens. In December it decided that they were also to acquire farmland. Explaining why the authorities changed their mind and committed themselves to the transfer of land is a prime difficulty in the history of the emancipation. Five considerations, three of them long-standing, two novel, seem to have been particularly important: pressure from reform-minded people outside the ranks of the government; the growing influence of enlightened bureaucrats in the Ministry of Internal Affairs; unrest in the countryside; chaos within and among the provincial gentry committees; and the unpredictable swing to the left of Iakov Rostovtsev, one of the key traditionalists on the Main Committee. Even the longstanding considerations (the first three) took forms in 1858 which increased their weight, but it was probably the last two that tipped the balance in favour of the radical solution.

One of the reasons why pressure from reform-minded people outside the ranks of the government intensified in 1858 derived from the fact that, up to a point, the authorities gave it their blessing. In December 1857 the new head of the Third Department, V. A. Dolgorukov, revealed an unlikely enthusiasm for cooperating with the liberal intelligentsia when he asked the Slavophile Aleksandr Koshelev to send him his hard-hitting 'Memoranda on the Dissolution of the Enserfed Estate in Russia'.[67] The following month the government relaxed its rules on censorship. In February and April 1858 *The Contemporary* took advantage of the relaxation to publish an article entitled 'On the New Conditions of Peasant Life', the second part of which asserted uncompromisingly that 'the government cannot agree on any pretext to emancipating the serfs without land'.[68] Since, in April 1858, the Main Committee was adopting a landless rather than a landed approach to emancipation, this second instalment of the essay caused a storm. It appeared anonymously, but the author, Konstantin Kavelin, had been circulating his views in manuscript since 1855 and was readily identifiable. When someone who was a protégé of the Grand Duchess Elena Pavlovna, a close friend of Nikolai Miliutin, and the tutor to the heir to the throne decided to run the risk of going into print, conservatives realized that they were being subjected to a deliberate attempt on the part of reformers to prevent them from treating serfs harshly. Kavelin lost his position as tutor and the government reinstated its ban on discussions of serfdom.[69]

The press, however, remained lively. The second half of the year witnessed a superficially arcane debate on vodka which touched on the whole question of government finances (because more than one-third of the state's revenue derived from its involvement in the vodka trade).[70] The newly founded *Military Miscellany* acquired a readership of 6,000 in a few months by adopting an openly reformist position *vis-à-vis* the army.[71] One of this periodical's editors, the radical journalist Nikolai Chernyshevskii, had been behind the publication of Kavelin's work in *The Contemporary* and was finding many subtle and not so subtle ways to advance reform in the St Petersburg press. Everyone, moreover, seemed to be reading *The Bell*. Kavelin had caught the empress with the second number in her hands as early as August 1857, and by the end of 1858 the head of the Third Department was passing copies from the tsar to Prince Menshikov.[72] Lanskoi and Rostovtsev read the magazine avidly. Although the first issue for 1858 welcomed the Nazimov Rescript with a banner headline, and although Herzen freely acknowledged that Alexander II had earned his place in history by setting the process of emancipation in train, by May 1858 *The Bell* had restarted its pressure for emancipation with land and soon it was insisting that much remained to be done before the process of reform bore fruit.[73] Thus Herzen, in London, filled the gap created by the government's response to the appearance of Kavelin's essay in April.

Meanwhile, reformers within the bureaucracy were coming into their own because they were concentrated in the ministry whose expertise was now at a premium. Since large serf-owners tended not to live on their estates or to know much about rural conditions, few of the people whom the tsar had charged with thinking about emancipation had any idea of the complexities of the task. So long as the possibility remained that nothing would happen they felt no compulsion to educate themselves. After the

Nazimov Rescript they had to start wrestling with details. The best source of information was the Ministry of Internal Affairs, but the ministry's leading figures were virtually unanimous in their support for a version of emancipation which provided peasants with land. Lanskoi, the minister, had moved into the reformist camp and become reliant on Nikolai Miliutin. Miliutin understood the need for landed emancipation as a result of his collaboration with Elena Pavlovna on the plans for Karlovka. When, in March 1858, the need to cope with the technical questions to which emancipation gave rise led to the creation of two new sections within the ministry – the Land Department and the Statistical Department – it was hardly surprising that Lanskoi and Miliutin staffed them with people who combined specialist knowledge with liberal sympathies. An emancipation settlement that turned on the advice of the Ministry of Internal Affairs was likely to treat serfs generously.

The precise part played by peasant unrest in the genesis and character of the reform has long been hotly disputed. Daniel Field wrote in 1976 that 'The fear of peasant unrest ... cannot be shown to have been decisive in the decision to emancipate', but Larisa Zakharova took him to task eight years later for failing to explain the emancipation in terms of 'the fear of a peasant rising or the moods and struggle of the peasantry'.[74] So far as the early history of the emancipation process is concerned Field's position is probably stronger than Zakharova's, for although Nicholas I's call for a militia gave rise to disturbances among the peasantry in 1855, although almost all the memoranda which circulated in private during the Crimean War referred to the possibility of peasant risings, and although Alexander II alluded to the prospect of rural uprisings both in his speech to the Moscow gentry and in his comments on the papers submitted to him by Haxthausen, it is hard to prove that rural developments took pride of place among the reasons for setting reform in train. It is not hard, however, to make a strong case for the view that unrest in a particular part of the empire in 1858 loomed large in the regime's decision to opt for the version of emancipation which gave peasants land. The 'Baltic path' to emancipation – the landless variant – was discredited at the very time disagreements over the way forward were at their height. The year 1858 witnessed about 100 peasant disturbances in Estonia, almost as many as the 123 which, according to one estimate, took place in all the Russian provinces of the empire put together.[75] If the free but landless peasants of Estonia were dissatisfied with their lot, replicating their experience in the empire as a whole looked unwise. Not only the intelligentsia but also conservative officials and the tsar appear to have recognized the fact.[76]

It seemed unlikely, however, that the committees of provincial gentry which sprang up in the wake of the Nazimov Rescript would welcome any form of emancipation, let alone emancipation with land. The Poles of the north-western provinces who responded enthusiastically to the tsar's entreaties were untypical. Nobles in other parts of the empire were likely to prove obdurate. Predictably, most of the new gentry committees did indeed reveal hostility to emancipation, but they also revealed two other things. First, although the majority of the provincial gentry were determined 'anti-abolitionists', not quite all of them were. Aleksandr Koshelev, whose memoranda on emancipation Dolgorukov had been keen to acquire at the end of 1857, served on the provincial committee in Riazan'. The Kaluga committee included three one-time Decembrists and a member of the Petrashevskii circle, none of whom had abjured the political opinions of his youth. Aleksei Unkovskii's enlightened activities on the Tver' committee occupy pride of place in one of the best-known English-language books on the emancipation of the serfs.[77] When, therefore, the government obliged the gentry to put their views on paper, chinks began to appear in the armour of gentry intransigence. Second, and more important, even nobles who were determined to be recalcitrant expressed their recalcitrance in many different ways. The central authorities were not in the habit of seeking advice on legislation, and did so in 1858 only because of the importance of the issue. When provincial committees produced two or even three sets of recommendations, the centre's longstanding inclination to act as it saw fit returned in full measure. On his six-week tour of the provinces in August and September 1858, the tsar encountered a spectrum of opinions which ranged from Tver' on the left, where Unkovskii was at least as radical as Nikolai Miliutin, to Nizhnii Novgorod on the right, where the local gentry wanted serfs to pay not only for any property which they received in the event of emancipation, but even for the freedom of their bodies (which the gentry did not own). The range of opinions expressed by nobles on the provincial committees made plain to St Petersburg that it had to act alone. It had to do something, because uncertainty had to be brought to an end; but only enlightened bureaucrats at the centre could cut through the diversity of opinion in the provinces. The provincial gentry's disunity reduced their capacity to obstruct the work of the Ministry of Internal Affairs.

The Ministry benefited to an even greater extent from a remarkable shift in the opinions of Iakov Rostovtsev. As a member of the Secret Committee of 1857 Rostovtsev had given no indication that he might turn into a keen reformer. In the first half of 1858 his inclinations seemed to be as conservative as ever. Because of his betrayal of the Decembrists in 1825 and his long identification with the regime of Nicholas I, he had few friends on the left of the political spectrum who could advise him on the way in which emancipation should proceed. He knew so little about the serf question that at first he thought it involved no more than granting the peasants their personal freedom. After realizing that it also involved reordering agrarian relations he proceeded to fall under the spell of Mikhail Pozen, a large landowner from Poltava who was determined to prevent emancipation from damaging the interests of the gentry. Via Rostovtsev, Pozen's conservative opinions became enshrined in the Main Committee's unimaginative April programme. Rostovtsev had committed what one enthusiastic reformer called 'a grave political mistake'.[78] Anonymously, Miliutin launched a campaign against him in *The Bell.*[79] Yet in August and September 1858, when on holiday in Germany, Rostovtsev wrote the tsar four letters in which it became apparent that he had changed his ground. He admitted in the first of the series that providing serfs with land seemed to pose insuperable practical difficulties, but in the last he argued 'that the acquisition of landed property on the part of the peasants can be accomplished durably and even quickly'.[80] What occasioned these letters is unclear. Rostovtsev always took assignments seriously and tended to work hard at informing himself. Perhaps the conservatism of his views in 1857 derived from the fact that he had spent too much time studying the narrow-minded documents bequeathed by Nicholas I. In 1858 he was certainly impressed by *The Bell*, by reports of the disturbances in Estonia, and by his correspondence with Evgenii Obolenskii (one of the three Decembrists of Kaluga). Perhaps he sensed an opportunity to make amends for his behaviour in 1825. Whatever the cause, there can be no doubt that the effects of his conversion were far-reaching. Of the many reasons for adopting the concept of emancipation with land, none weighed more strongly with the tsar than the advice of a proven traditionalist and long-term friend. In mid-October 1858 Alexander lent his imprimatur to Rostovtsev's letters by putting them to the Main Committee. Emancipation with land had found its way on to the agenda.

GETTING PRINCIPLES ON TO THE STATUTE BOOK

By December 1858 St Petersburg had taken two of the three decisions which led to the statutes of 1861: the decision to emancipate and the decision to emancipate with land. The last two years of the emancipation process were devoted to the third decision: how to turn statements of intent into workable laws. In February 1859 the tsar put the conservatively inclined Main Committee into cold storage and created 'Editing Commissions' under Rostovtsev for the purpose of drawing up legislation. Originally there were to be two of these, one for the preparation of a general statute and one to deal with local variations, but the arrangement proved unworkable and by the end of April 1859 there were four, each with responsibility for both the general and the particular aspects of its field. Since a number of key personnel served in more than one section and since the new body had plenary as well as sectional meetings, it makes better sense to speak of a single 'Commission' than to use the plural terminology of contemporaries.

The creation of the Editing Commission marked the apogee of the reform drive. With the zeal of a convert, Rostovtsev rigged the membership. Iakov Solov'ev calculated that of the thirty-nine appointees only thirteen could be called opponents of reform, and three of those withdrew when they realized their helplessness.[81] The Commission was supposed to be guided in its deliberations by the Nazimov Rescript, the programme adopted by the Main Committee in December 1858, and the schemes devised by the provincial gentry committees, but the first and third of these were too conservative for its taste and in the first year of its life it gave them short shrift. When delegates from various provincial committees came to St Petersburg for consultations in August 1859, Nikolai Miliutin cut the ground from under their feet by presenting them with an outline of the Commission's views which went far beyond what they had in mind. In 1859 the terms of the emancipation settlement looked likely to benefit the peasantry at the expense of the gentry.

In February 1860, however, Rostovtsev died. Conservatives were delighted by the appointment as his successor of Count Viktor Panin, a reactionary whose lack of enthusiasm for discussion was reflected in the fact that he kept parrots because they said what he told them to.[82] Petr Semenov, a liberally inclined participant in the emancipation process, believed that in appointing Panin the tsar had in fact 'revealed a greater degree of far-sightedness than any of those active in the peasant question'. By choosing a non-reformer, Semenov argued, Alexander allayed the fears of the gentry without jeopardizing the work which had already been completed.[83] There are grounds for doubting this opinion. Rostovtsev's last memorandum and Panin's first differed significantly. Whereas the former emphasized that the whole point of emancipation was to provide serfs with land (not just to grant them freedom), the latter spoke of enabling peasants to acquire land only 'when feasible and necessary'.[84] If Panin had had his way, peasants would have waited for land indefinitely. A second group of provincial delegates arrived in St Petersburg just after his appointment and provided him with a sympathetic audience for his opinions. The tide of reform began to ebb. When the Commission completed its work in October 1860 (after 409 meetings in a little over eighteen months), conservative bodies, the Main Committee and the State Council, made further inroads into the legislation which had been drafted under Rostovtsev. The principle of emancipation with land survived, but the statutes of 19 February 1861 fell a long way short of the dreams entertained by radicals. The tsar was well aware that the legislation left much to be desired and delayed publishing it until 5 March, the first day of Lent: 'alarmed by the prospect of riot,' wrote an admittedly hostile contemporary, 'he hesitated a long time before choosing a day for promulgating the sham freedom and eventually chose the day when it was least of all expected'.[85] A soldier involved in the extensive security operation which attended the publication of the statutes regretted the need to quarter troops in villages but admitted the force of the Latin tag *Si vis pacem, para bellum*: 'If you want peace, prepare for war'.[86] If peasants could get out of hand when the government was trying to raise a militia, it was not unreasonable to suppose that they would run amok on learning what the government meant by freedom.

What exactly the government did mean by freedom was hard to discern in the nineteen legislative Acts which together constituted the emancipation. The General Statute was perplexing enough, but the local statutes not only divided the empire west of the Urals into four broad areas – Russia, Ukraine east of the Dnieper, Ukraine west of the Dnieper, and the north-western provinces (although even this is an over-simplification) – but also subdivided the four areas into zones (by type and profitability of economic activity). A summary can hardly do justice to the corpus as a whole, but it is easy enough to point to the settlement's principal weaknesses. In apparent contravention of everything for which committed reformers had striven, the statutes stated explicitly that all land remained the property of the gentry. Admittedly, nobles had to grant serfs 'perpetual use of their do-micile' and the use of 'a portion of arable', but serfs had to 'fulfill obliga-tions to the noblemen' in return for them.[87] Lords and peasants were given two years to prepare charters which would map out the peasants' 'portions of arable land' and define the extent of their 'obligations'. While the char-ters were being drawn up, the existing relations between landlords and serfs were to remain in place.

If the statutes had gone no further, it might have been said that the regime was simply trying to turn all serfs into 'obligated peasants' (in line with Nicholas I's statute of 1842). In reality, the tsarist authorities sub-stituted for the Nicholaevan concept of 'obligated' peasants the slightly more beneficent concept of 'temporarily' obligated peasants. The new charters were to be a staging post. Once they were in place, not only could peasants buy (rather than just occupy) their dwelling-places, but also in certain circumstances they could 'acquire in full ownership' the land which the charters assigned them.[88] If they bought both – the dwelling-places and the land – they ceased to be 'temporarily obligated' and became inde-pendent smallholders. Theoretically, therefore, the statutes made possible the social transformation for which liberals had been striving. The snag lay in the circumstances under which a peasant could move from permanent use to 'full ownership' of the land which he worked. Although he could buy his dwelling-place whether his former owner wanted him to or not, he could acquire farmland only if the owner chose to sell it. Thus nobles who decided to be obstreperous could perpetuate 'temporary obligation' indefi-nitely.

Remarkably, nobles chose to be accommodating. 'At the beginning of 1881 no less than 84.7 per cent of former serfs had become owners of their allotments'.[89] The gentry permitted their former serfs to become smallhol-ders because the legislation of 1861 enabled them to part with land on ex-tremely advantageous terms. The statutes laid down the maximum size of peasant land allotments. Where peasants were already working areas larger than the maximum, landowners were allowed to trim their holdings. Predictably, they took the parts from which they could make money. Since, in the last stage of the reform's passage, the State Council reduced the maximum size of peasant allotments to a point where many existing peasant holdings exceeded it, the provision for 'trimming' came into operation very frequently. Provided, furthermore, that peasants were not reduced to possessing less than one-third of the maximum allotments, landlords were entitled to at least one-third of any land under discussion. On estates where the nobleman had not been engaged in farming, this was a second provision that had the effect of reducing the quantity of land which peasants received. Miliutin and other committed reformers had hoped to assign peasants the areas they were working already, but in the event they lost about 20 per cent of the land they had been using.[90] By the time the gentry had increased the quantity of land over which they exercised direct control (and improved its average quality), most of them were keen to sell off the rest. With cash in their pockets they could pay off their debts and plough money into their restructured estates.

The sums they received, moreover, usually exceeded the value of the land they gave up. The peasants' 'redemption dues' were calculated not on the basis of the land which came into their possession but on the basis of the rents and services that they owed under serfdom. Since no detailed register of these existed at the point of emancipation, one of the main purposes of the post-1861 charters was to set them down on paper. Landlords usually managed to inflate the levels of the peasants' obligations, as the arbitrators who supervised the preparation of the charters belonged to the gentry estate and tended to take the landlords' side. Once high levels had been set, nobles who chose not to turn rents into cash were acting to the detriment of their own best interests. Admittedly, they received rather less than the capitalized value of the rents if they decided to move from 'temporary obligation' to redemption without the consent of their peasants. Even the smaller sum, however, was large enough to encourage them to proceed. They would have been less well advised to move from temporary obligation to redemption if they had had to wait for the money which the peasants owed them, but the government realized that peasants were in no position to redeem their obligations overnight and advanced most of the money to which nobles were entitled in the form of interest-bearing bonds.

Thus although the laws of 1861 succeeded in turning serfs into smallholders, the methods they employed were heavily biased in the gentry's favour. Because peasants had to pay back the sums of money which the government advanced on their behalf at 6 per cent interest over forty-nine years, it was to be a long time before their freedom was complete. The formulae employed to calculate their annual payments produced figures no higher than the rents laid down in the charters, but as we have already seen, and as Alexander Gerschenkron stresses, the rents laid down in the charters were excessively high.[91] Prosperous peasants, furthermore, were unable to become independent agents by paying off their debts quickly. The statutes made peasant communes rather than individuals responsible for redemption payments, with the result that an economically successful peasant was prevented from bettering himself quickly by peasants whose entrepreneurial inclinations were less well developed than his own.

It looks, then, as if the reformers had laboured in vain. A severe critic of the statutes of 1861 might respond to the question 'Why did Alexander II free the serfs?' by saying that he failed to do so. Without going quite so far, historians have indeed been critical. Academician Druzhinin held that the object of the framers of the statutes was 'to retain in the hands of the gentry estate the maximum quantity of land and to facilitate the gentry's transition to more profitable farming based on free labour by providing them with the essential capital and reserves of the necessary manpower'.[92] In two closely argued and provocative essays Alfred Rieber claimed that the object of the emancipation was not even to benefit the gentry (let alone the peasantry), but rather to put the principal institutions of the autocracy, the treasury and the army, in a position to recover from the ravages of the Crimean War.[93]

Whether the emancipation was as limited or reactionary in its effects as these analyses imply is the subject of Chapter Nine, but it is certainly unwise to imply, as does Rieber, that ill effects derived from malign intentions. The enlightened bureaucrats who were primarily responsible for drawing up the legislation of 1861 may not have achieved everything for which they were striving, but they were undoubtedly trying to achieve more than the modernization of the gentry's sources of income or the revivification of the state machine. We have already noted Miliutin's desire to maintain the size of the peasants' landholdings. Reformers knew that the peasant commune stood in the way of economic diversification in the countryside, but felt that it had to be retained because it served to protect the interests of peasants against those of outsiders.[94] Rieber's view that the purpose of the emancipation was to fill the state's coffers with the peasants' redemption payments does not square with the background to the reform's financial arrangements. At the beginning of the emancipation process reformers had hoped to transfer land from the gentry to the serfs by drawing on the resources of the exchequer. In 1857, however, the state had started encouraging the creation of private joint-stock companies for the construction of railways, with the result that investors had taken their money out of state banks and put it into railway-building. By the end of the emancipation process, the authorities lacked the wherewithal to pay for the transference of land. As a result, the framers of the statutes of 1861 had to saddle serfs with mortgages, which was very far from their original intention.[95] Since historians who confuse effects and intentions may be mistaken in other regards, the question whether the emancipators had laboured in vain is one which should be handled with care. The legislation of 1861 was undoubtedly flawed, but it also set in train changes which affected most levels of Russian government and all levels of Russian society. The consequences of the emancipation were to be even more remarkable than the political process from which the statutes emerged.

NOTES

1. B. N. Chicherin, *Vospominaniia: Zemstvo i Moskovskaia Duma* (Moscow, 1934), p. 117.
2. S. M. Solov'ev, *Izbrannye trudy; Zapiski* (Moscow, 1983), p. 336.
3. Marquis de Custine, *Letters from Russia*, ed. and tr. Robin Buss (Harmondsworth, 1991), p. 7.
4. Sir Donald Mackenzie Wallace, *Russia* (2 vols, London, 1905), ii. 100.
5. B. N. Chicherin, *Vospominaniia: Moskovskii universitet* (Moscow, 1929), p. 131.
6. Peter Kropotkin, *Memoirs of a Revolutionist* (Boston, Mass. and New York, 1899), p. 244.
7. Nicolas Sollohub, 'The Death of Nicholas I: From the Memoirs of Countess Sollohub', OSP 16 (1983), 181.
8. E. M. Feoktistov, *Za kulisami politiki i literatury 1848–1896* (Leningrad, 1929), p. 348.
9. Sollohub, 'The Death of Nicholas I' (above, n. 7), p. 178.
10. Leo Tolstoy, *The Sebastopol Sketches*, tr. David McDuff (Harmondsworth, 1986), p. 56 (with the correct spelling 'Sevastopol'' substituted for 'Sebastopol').
11. Ibid., p. 184.
12. Winfried Baumgart, *The Peace of Paris 1856: Studies in War, Diplomacy, and Peacemaking*, tr. Ann Pottinger Saab (Santa Barbara, Calif. and Oxford, 1981), p. 58.
13. N. I. Tsimmer, 'O sud'be Sevastopolia na zakliuchitel'nom etape voiny 1853–1856 godov', VI, 1970 no. 9, p. 199.
14. I. V. Bestuzhev, 'Iz istorii krymskoi voiny 1853–1856 gg.', IA, 1959 no. 1, pp. 204–8.
15. B. H. Sumner, *Peter the Great and the Ottoman Empire* (Oxford, 1949), p. 40.
16. S. M. Solov'ev, *Izbrannye trudy* (above, n. 2), p. 336.
17. A. A. Sergeev, 'III otdelenie i Krymskaia voina', KA 3 (1923), 294.
18. See p. 132.
19. A. P. Pogrebinskii, 'Gosudarstvennye finansy Rossii nakanune reformy 1861 goda', IA, 1956 no. 2, p. 120.
20. Alfred J. Rieber, ed., *The Politics of Autocracy: Letters of Alexander II to Prince A. I. Bariatinskii 1857–1864* (Paris and The Hague, 1966), pp 24–5.
21. W. Bruce Lincoln, 'The Circle of the Grand Duchess Yelena Pavlovna, 1847–1861', SEER 48 (1970), 381; L. G. Zakharova, *Samoderzhavie i otmena krepostnogo prava v Rossii* (Moscow, 1984), p. 39.
22. P. A. Valuev, 'Duma russkogo vo vtoroi polovine 1855 goda', RS 79 (1893), 503–14.
23. Anon (B. N. Chicherin), 'O krepostnom sostoianii', *Golosa iz Rossii* 2 (1856), 131.
24. N. M. Druzhinin, *Izbrannye trudy: Vneshniaia politika Rossii, Istoriia Moskvy, Muzeinoe delo* (Moscow, 1988), p. 152.
25. I. N. Kovaleva, 'Slavianofily i zapadniki v period Krymskoi voiny (1853–1856 gg.)', IZ 80 (1967), 191.
26. Anon (B. N. Chicherin), 'Sovremennye zadachi russkoi zhizni', *Golosa iz Rossii* 4 (1857), 99.
27. Iskander (Herzen), 'Pis'mo k imperatoru Aleksandru vtoromu', *Poliarnaia zvezda* 1 (1855), 13.

28. Druzhinin, *Izbrannye trudy* (above, n. 24), p. 165.
29. John Shelton Curtiss, *Russia's Crimean War* (Durham, NC, 1979), pp. 535–6.
30. Anon (B. N. Chicherin), 'O krepostnom sostoianii' (above, n. 23), p. 171.
31. Chicherin, *Zemstvo* (above, n. 1), p. 117.
32. Jerome Blum, *Lord and Peasant in Russia from the Ninth to the Nineteenth Century* (Princeton, NJ, 1961), p. 576, and Blum, *The End of the Old Order in Rural Europe* (Princeton, NJ, 1978), pp. 357–76, esp. p. 373.
33. Ia. A. Solov'ev, 'Krest'ianskoe delo v 1856–1859 gg.', RS 27 (1880), 320.
34. N. G. O. Pereira, 'Alexander II and the Decision to Emancipate the Russian Serfs, 1855–61', CSP 22 (1980), 114.
35. Chicherin, *Moskovskii universitet* (above, n. 5), p. 131.
36. William L. Blackwell, *The Beginnings of Russian Industrialization 1800–1860* (Princeton, NJ, 1968), p. 186.
37. L. G. Zakharova, 'Samoderzhavie, biurokratiia i reformy 60–kh godov XIX v. v Rossii', VI, 1989 no. 10, p. 6; W. Bruce Lincoln, 'The Daily Life of St. Petersburg Officials in the Mid Nineteenth Century', OSP 8 (1975), 97.
38. Sollohub, 'The Death of Nicholas I' (above, n. 7), p. 179.
39. Iskander, 'Pis'mo' (above, n. 27), p. 13.
40. Pereira, 'Alexander II' (above, n. 34), p. 103.
41. Ibid., p. 104.
42. George Vernadsky et al., eds, *A Source Book for Russian History from Early Times to 1917* (3 vols, New Haven, Conn. and London, 1972), iii. 589.
43. For a Russian text of the 1856 speech which may be more authoritative than that employed for the translation cited in n. 42, but which makes the speech seem even more cautious, see Zakharova, *Samoderzhavie i otmena* (above, n. 21), pp. 41–2.
44. For the likelihood that Alexander II was echoing the 1839 report (which was quoted on pp. 139–40) see S. V. Mironenko, *Stranitsy tainoi istorii samoderzhaviia: Politicheskaia istoriia Rossii pervoi poloviny XIX stoletiia* (Moscow, 1990), p. 115.
45. Zakharova, *Samoderzhavie i otmena* (above, n. 21), p. 43.
46. Mironenko, *Stranitsy* (above, n. 44), p. 198.
47. See pp. 168–9 above, and W. Bruce Lincoln, *Nikolai Miliutin: An Enlightened Russian Bureaucrat* (Newtonville, Mass., 1977).
48. B. N. Chicherin, *Vospominaniia: Moskva sorokovykh godov* (Moscow, 1929), p. 130.
49. Zakharova, *Samoderzhavie i otmena* (above, n. 21), p. 47.
50. V. G. Chernukha, *Pravitel'stvennaia politika v otnoshenii pechati 60 – 70-e gody XIX veka* (Leningrad, 1989), p. 63.
51. V. A. Aleksandrov, *Sel'skaia obshchina v Rossii (XVII – nachalo XIX v.)* (Moscow, 1976), p. 3.
52. Zakharova, 'Samoderzhavie, biurokratiia i reformy' (above, n. 37), p. 6.
53. Iskander (Herzen), 'Ot izdatelia', *Golosa iz Rossii* 2 (1856), 3.
54. I-r (Herzen), 'Vpered! Vpered! (31 Marta 1856 goda)', *Poliarnaia zvezda* 2 (1856), iii–x.
55. N. Ia. Eidel'man, *Tainye korrespondenty 'Poliarnoi zvezdy'* (Moscow, 1966), p. 8.
56. Zakharova, *Samoderzhavie i otmena* (above, n. 21), p. 63.
57. N. M. Druzhinin, *Gosudarstvennye krest'iane i reforma P. D. Kiseleva* (2 vols, Moscow, 1946–58), ii. 536–42; Gavriil Popov, 'Fasad i kukhnia "velikoi" reformy', EKO, 1987 no. 1, p. 149 (for the quotation); Zakharova, *Samoderzhavie i otmena* (above, n. 21), p. 55; Daniel Field, *The End of Serfdom: Nobility and Bureaucracy in Russia, 1855–1861*, p. 389, n. 52.

58. August von Haxthausen, *Studies on the Interior of Russia*, ed. S. Frederick Starr (Chicago, 1972), p. xxxviii. Daniel Field disagrees: *End of Serfdom* (above, n. 57), p. 391, n. 77.

59. P. P. Semenov-Tian-Shanskii, *Memuary, t. 3–4: Epokha osvobozhdeniia krest'ian v Rossii (1857–1861 gg.)* (Petrograd, 1915–16), iii. 19.

60. Zakharova, *Samoderzhavie i otmena* (above, n. 21), p. 65.

61. *Kolokol*, 1 July, 1 August, 1 September, 1 October 1857, pp. 3, 14–15, 19, 28; for the context in which Herzen employed the Chinghis-Khan image see the end of Chapter Four and the beginning of Chapter Five.

62. Kathryn B. Feuer, 'Alexis de Tocqueville and the Genesis of War and Peace', *California Slavic Studies* 4 (1967), 92–118; B. Chicherin, 'Staraia frantsuzskaia monarkhiia i revoliutsiia', in Chicherin, *Ocherki Anglii i Frantsii* (Moscow, 1858), pp. 152–275 (and Chicherin, *Moskva* [above, n. 48], pp. 278–86).

63. Zakharova, *Samoderzhavie i otmena* (above, n. 21), p. 81.

64. See W. Bruce Lincoln, 'The Problem of *Glasnost'* in Mid-Nineteenth Century Russian Politics', ESR 11 (1981), 171–88.

65. A. I. Koshelev, *Zapiski* (Berlin, 1884), p. 91.

66. V. G. Chernukha, *Vnutrenniaia politika tsarizma s serediny 50–kh do nachala 80–kh gg. XIX v.* (Leningrad, 1978), pp. 136–55.

67. Koshelev, *Zapiski* (above, n. 65), p. 92 (and pp. 55–166 of the second pagination for the memoranda themselves).

68. Anon, 'O novykh usloviiakh sel'skogo byta', *Sovremennik* 68 (1858), first pagination, p. 505.

69. Charles A. Ruud, *Fighting Words: Imperial Censorship and the Russian Press, 1804–1906* (Toronto, 1982), p. 108; V. N. Rozental', 'Ideinye tsentry liberal'nogo dvizheniia v Rossii nakanune revolutsionnoi situatsii', in M. V. Nechkina, ed., *Revoliutsionnaia situatsiia v Rossii v 1859–1861gg.* (Moscow, 1963), pp. 383–97; Daniel Field, 'Kavelin and Russian Liberalism', SR 32 (1973), 59–78; Semenov, *Memuary* (above, n. 59), iii. 66; Zakharova, *Samoderzhavie i otmena* (above, n. 21), p. 98.

70. David Christian, *'Living Water': Vodka and Russian Society on the Eve of Emancipation* (Oxford, 1990), p. 260.

71. W. Bruce Lincoln, *The Great Reforms: Autocracy, Bureaucracy, and the Politics of Change in Imperial Russia* (DeKalb, Ill., 1990), p. 148.

72. Zakharova, *Samoderzhavie i otmena* (above, n. 21), pp. 66, 109.

73. *Kolokol*, 1 January, 15 February, 1 May 1858, pp. 51, 67, 110–15; for one of the many essays on the contemporary reception of *The Bell* in Russia see B. S. Ginzburg, 'Otnoshenie chitatel'skikh krugov Rossii k stat'iam "Kolokola" (1857–1861 gg.)', in Nechkina, *Revoliutsionnaia situatsiia* (above, n. 69), pp. 306–37.

74. Field, *End of Serfdom* (above, n. 57), p. 52; Zakharova, *Samoderzhavie i otmena* (above, n. 21), p. 16.

75. Iu. Iu. Kakhk, 'Krest'ianskie volneniia v Estonii', *Istoriia SSSR*, 1958 no. 3, p. 143.

76. Iu. Iu. Kakhk, *'Ostzeiskii put'' perekhoda ot feodalizma k kapitalizmu: Krest'iane i pomeshchiki Estliandii i Lifliandii v XVIII – pervoi polovine XIX veka* (Tallin, 1988), pp. 309–20.

77. Terence Emmons, *The Russian Landed Gentry and the Peasant Emancipation of 1861* (Cambridge, 1968).

78. Semenov, *Memuary* (above, n. 59), iii. 66.

79. *Kolokol*, 1 September 1858 (pp. 181–2); Lincoln, *Miliutin* (above, n. 47), p. 44.

80. Anon, *Materialy dlia istorii uprazdneniia krepostnogo sostoianiia pomesh-chich'ikh krest'ian v Rossii v tsarstvovanie Imperatora Aleksandra II* (3 vols, Berlin, 1860–2), i. 381–2, 395.
81. Ia. A. Solov'ev, 'Krest'ianskoe delo' (above, n. 33), p. 342.
82. Popov, 'Fasad i kukhnia' (above, n. 57), p. 165.
83. Semenov, *Memuary* (above, n. 59), iii. 442–3.
84. Ia. Rostovtsev, 'Doklad, ili tak nazyvaemoe: politicheskoe zaveshchanie', *Golosa iz Rossii* 8 (1860), 138–9; Zakharova, *Samoderzhavie i otmena* (above, n. 21), 204–5, as translated by Gary M. Hamburg in Larisa Georgievna Zakharova, 'Autocracy and the Abolition of Serfdom in Russia, 1856–1861', *Soviet Studies in History: A Journal of Translations* 26, no. 2 (Fall 1987), p. 73 (a publication which summarizes the first four chapters of Zakharova's book and gives Chapter Five and the Conclusion in full).
85. E. P. Pertsov, 'Zapiski sovremennika o 1861 g.', KA 16 (1926), 150.
86. P. A. Zaionchkovskii, ed., 'O pravitel'stvennykh merakh dlia podavleniia narodnykh volnenii v period otmeny krepostnogo prava', IA, 1957 no. 1, p. 166.
87. 'The Emancipation Manifesto', in Basil Dmytryshyn, ed., *Imperial Russia: A Source Book, 1700–1917* (3rd edn, Fort Worth, Texas, 1990), p. 308.
88. Ibid.
89. A. Gerschenkron, 'Agrarian Policies and Industrialization: Russia 1861–1917', in *The Cambridge Economic History of Europe*, vol. 6, ed. H. J. Habakkuk and M. M. Postan (Cambridge, 1965), p. 738.
90. Zakharova, *Samoderzhavie i otmena* (above, n. 21), p. 235 (and Zakharova, 'Autocracy and the Abolition of Serfdom' [above, n. 84], p. 107).
91. Gerschenkron, 'Agrarian Policies' (above, n. 89), p. 740.
92. N. M. Druzhinin, *Russkaia derevnia na perelome 1861–1880 gg.* (Moscow, 1978), p. 24.
93. Rieber, *Politics* (above, n. 20), pp. 15–97; Rieber, 'Alexander II: A Revisionist View', JMH 43 (1971), 42–58.
94. L. G. Zakharova, 'Krest'ianskaia obshchina v reforme 1861 g.', *Vestnik Moskovskogo universiteta, Seriia 8: Istoriia*, 1986 no. 5, pp. 36–42.
95. Steven L. Hoch, 'The Banking Crisis, Peasant Reform, and Economic Development in Russia, 1857–1861', AHR 96 (1991), 795–820.

CHAPTER NINE

In the Wake of Emancipation

RESPONSES TO THE LEGISLATION OF 1861

Immediate reactions to the emancipation were hostile. 'On reading the [General] Statute,' wrote Herzen's collaborator Nikolai Ogarev, 'the first question you involuntarily ask yourself is: for whom is it written?' 'Least of all', he believed, 'for the peasants'. The length and complexity of the document were such that 'not a single literate peasant will master it and not a single illiterate peasant will listen to it. A statute for peasants has to be written on a single sheet of paper'.[1] The one thing the serfs did understand was that they were not yet free. Because their relations with the landlords were to remain unaltered for at least two years (while charters were drawn up describing the obligations they were supposed to redeem), they believed that the government had cheated them. Disturbances occurred in forty-two of the forty-three provinces to which the legislation applied. According to the Ministry of Internal Affairs (which admitted that its statistics were highly approximate), 647 incidents took place between April and July 1861. The sharpest clash occurred in the village of Bezdna in the eastern province of Kazan', where a certain Anton Petrov began claiming that the statutes really did grant wholesale freedom. Thousands flocked to him, soldiers fired on the crowd, dozens died, and Petrov was executed.

The gentry were almost as dissatisfied as the peasantry. On the right of the spectrum, nobles in the province of Tula lamented the effect of emancipation on their economic interests and sought a way of preventing the central administration from overriding their interests in the future. To this end they proposed that gentry representatives be summoned from all parts of the empire to a national commission which 'should have the right to present its drafts of proposed laws directly for consideration' by the tsar. The equally conservative nobles of Smolensk echoed Tula's belief in the need for joint discussions with 'representatives from other provinces', while the nobles of Tver', one of the few gentry groups to espouse the cause of immediate emancipation rather than the conversion of serfs into temporarily obligated peasants, argued that the new laws had been botched, that 'the reforms so urgently required cannot be achieved by a bureaucratic order', and that the 'convocation of elected representatives from all the Russian land represents the only means for a satisfactory solution'.[2]

Radical intellectuals were the most disenchanted of all. The Bezdna affair evoked an indignant response from Afanasii Shchapov, a graduate of Kazan' Ecclesiastical Academy who began teaching Russian history at Kazan' University in November 1860. 'I enter the university department of history,' Shchapov declared in his inaugural lecture, 'not with the thought of statehood, not with the idea of centralization, but with the idea of nationality (*narodnost'*) and of regionality'.[3] Five days later he illustrated his radicalism by lecturing sympathetically on the Decembrists. At the Kazan' requiem for the victims of Bezdna (which took place in the emotionally charged atmosphere of Palm Sunday) he stepped forward at the end of the service with a commemorative address in which he referred to the dead peasants as 'friends, killed for the people'.[4] 'The history of the Russian people', wrote Shchapov from prison a month later, 'fills our heart with the belief and the hope that sooner or later a time must come for the Russian people when it acquires political self-consciousness and, as a result, political self-government'.[5]

If opinions like those of Shchapov could emerge in remote Kazan' – they were partly generated, it seems, by members of the local ecclesiastical hierarchy[6] – it was hardly surprising that the more sophisticated radicals to be found in other places expressed even greater disillusionment with the government's performance. In London Herzen pointed out that not even the eighteenth-century rebel Emel'ian Pugachev had been shot 'on the sly' like Petrov.[7] All but one of the five parts of Ogarev's provocatively entitled 'Analysis of the New Serfdom' concluded with the ringing declaration that 'The people have been deceived by the tsar'.[8] Anonymous writers began calling for action. 'A Great Russian' put out a flysheet in St Petersburg in July 1861 which argued that 'The educated classes must take the conduct of affairs out of the hands of the incapable government and into their own'; otherwise, 'patriots will be compelled to call upon the people to do what the educated classes refuse to do'.[9] A long letter to *The Bell* argued that expecting Russia's 'educated classes' to solve the country's problems was futile. What Russia needed was revolutionary cells with roots among the people and contempt for abstract theory.[10]

The so-called 'Great Russian' – by this time a committee – put out two more pamphlets in September 1861, only to be upstaged by the simultaneous appearance of a much more forthright proclamation. *To the Young Generation* averred that 'We do not need a tsar, or an emperor, or the Lord's anointed, or a robe of ermine covering up hereditary incompetence'. The authors wanted an 'elective and limited' executive, the abolition of censorship, 'the development of the principle of self-government', equal rights, and the collective ownership of the land. If necessary, they were prepared to 'call for a revolution to help the people'.[11] *The Bell* had asked in July, 'What do the people need?', and had answered its own question by saying 'It is very simple, the people need land and liberty'.[12] 'Land and Liberty' became the name of an amorphous political movement which operated in various parts of the Russian Empire between 1861 and 1863 and strove to convert the radicalism engendered by the emancipation into action. In March 1862 the novelist Ivan Turgenev satirized Russia's revolutionary youth in *Fathers and Sons*, but the fires that devastated St Petersburg two months later led many to suppose that radicals were tough enough to engage in arson. At the moment the fires began, Petr Zaichnevskii, a twenty-year-old Moscow University student who had been in prison since the previous year, managed to publish *Young Russia*, 'the most bloodcurdling and extreme' of all the calls to action which circulated in the wake of the emancipation.[13] Unlike the 'Great Russian' and the authors of *To the Young Generation*, Zaichnevskii made no bones whatever about using violence. Rather, he looked forward to the day when those who sympathized with him would 'kill the men of the imperial party without pity'.[14] As the summer of 1862 began, the regime seemed to be under serious threat.

The authorities had compounded their unpopularity among radicals by appearing to draw back from reform after publishing the emancipation statutes. Without conceding that the gentry of Tula, Smolensk, and elsewhere were justified in calling for an assembly which would give them a chance to vent their spleen, Alexander II seemed to be no less frightened than they by the enormity of the changes he had sanctioned. At the end of April 1861 he dismissed two of his brightest stars – Sergei Lanskoi and Nikolai Miliutin, the Minister and Acting Deputy Minister of Internal Affairs. In June he replaced an enlightened Minister of Education with an admiral who had conducted the Russian mission to Japan during the Crimean War and was identified in the public mind with oriental despotism. The incoming Minister of Internal Affairs, Petr Valuev, had been accounted a liberal when he criticized the state of the empire at the time of the Crimean War, but had apparently become less enthusiastic about change with the passage of time. In 1858 he had moved from the Governorship of Kurland to a position in the Ministry of State Properties, an institution which had forsaken the sympathy for reform which it had displayed under Kiselev. By 1861 observers considered Valuev to be the creature of M. N. Murav'ev, his benighted Minister, and of Viktor Panin, Rostovtsev's conservative successor as chairman of the Editing Commission. When Valuev became Minister of Internal Affairs Dmitrii Miliutin wrote that 'The landowning party had every justification for counting on [him] for the realization of their views'.[15] At the end of June 1862, not long after *Young Russia* and the fires in St Petersburg – and immediately after an attempt on the life of the Grand Duke Konstantin Nikolaevich – Valuev produced a paper on the internal condition of the empire in which he admitted the many difficulties under which the government was labouring but proposed no more than converting the State Council into a somewhat more representative body and bypassing the judicial system to deal with radicals more speedily.[16] The government's main concern now seemed to be stifling dissent before it became intractable. Enacting further reform was apparently far from its thoughts. A historically inclined contemporary might have been tempted to compare Alexander II's outlook in mid-1862 with that of Alexander I in 1805 or Nicholas I at the end of 1830. In different degrees, both the earlier tsars had devoted their first years on the throne to improving the condition of the empire, but one of them had been distracted by Napoleon and the other by foreign war and a rebellion in Poland. Neither had succeeded, to any great extent, in returning to the path of reform. By legislating for the emancipation of the serfs Alexander II had achieved more than either of his immediate forebears, but he had also upset peasants, nobles and intellectuals. He had revealed a capacity for giving with one hand and taking away with the other. Many indicators suggested that reform was too dangerous to be allowed to continue and that the tsar's capacity for embracing change had been exhausted.

The regime recovered, however, from the immediate aftermath of the emancipation, and continued to work on modernizing the empire's institutional and social structure. It is doubtful, indeed, whether the difficulties it faced in 1861 and 1862 were as great as they look, and it is highly unlikely that the tsar decided in 1861 to substitute conservatives for reformers at the heart of the imperial administration.

Peasant disturbances were numerous in the spring and early summer of 1861, but declined sharply thereafter. P. A. Zaionchkovskii calculated for the period June 1861 to December 1863 that even if the number of incidents in which troops were used against peasants is doubled or tripled (which may be a legitimate procedure in view of the possibility of underreporting), no more than 4 per cent of the places where peasants lived were affected.[17] It is sometimes thought paradoxical that, when part of the rationale for emancipating the serfs was the elimination of disorder in the countryside, the legislation of 1861 increased it.[18] In fact, violence soon diminished. Once serfs began paying redemption dues they discovered that their new taskmaster, the state, was less efficient and less demanding than the gentry. Even if the authorities had wanted to rule the countryside with a rod of iron they were in no position to do so. The regime did not employ the equivalent of the landlords' bailiffs. As the peasants put it, 'God is high and the tsar is far away'. More to the point, the pre-emancipation budgets of the gentry were less well able to sustain a deficit than the post-emancipation budget of the regime. Both were unbalanced, but the former reached breaking point sooner than the latter. Peasants under serfdom tended to be forced to fulfil their obligations. When pressed too hard, they rioted. After 1861 (or rather, after they started making redemption payments), 'Peasants could and did accumulate huge arrears without any definitive confrontation with the authorities'.[19] Alexander II was well advised, at the point of emancipation, to plan an elaborate security operation, but he did not have to maintain it indefinitely.

Nor did he have to worry for long about hostility on the part of the gentry. A combination of minor adjustments to the statutes of February 1861 and a show of determination enabled the tsar to scotch aristocratic demands for participation in government. In April 1861 even the head of the Third Department thought that the regime would be forced to grant a constitution, but he added that 'not only would the emperor not make up his mind to assent to the gradual introduction of constitutional forms, but he had even spoken out firmly against it very recently and had evidently not changed his mind on the question'.[20] Alexander's resolution led on the one hand to the arrest of liberally orientated nobles in Tver' and on the other to the last of his propaganda campaigns in the countryside. 'Just as his 1858 trips had made known his commitment to emancipation, those of 1862 showed his determination to preserve the prerogatives of the auto-crat'.[21] In September 1862, for example, Alexander ran a risk when he visited Novgorod to celebrate the thousandth anniversary of the putative foundation of the Russian state. Since the province was a hotbed of gentry resistance to the emancipation, confrontation looked a real possibility. As the royal ship tied up on the river Volkhov, however, the courage of the assembled nobles deserted them. When Alexander addressed the nobles the next day they were practically eating out of his hand.

The regime was less keen to placate intellectuals than it was to calm the gentry, but despite the alarming pronouncements of 'the Great Russian' and the authors of *To the Young Generation* and *Young Russia*, it had less need to do so. Thinking people agreed on the need for a radical liberaliza-tion of the empire's social and political structure, but disagreed about the means of achieving it. Relatively few intellectuals took the view that the regime should be kept under constant pressure. The perceptive Boris Chi-cherin spotted as early as 1858 that *The Bell* was 'better at throwing govern-ment and society into confusion than at suggesting the precise path they should follow'.[22] After visiting Herzen in London he accused him of substi-tuting passion for reason. 'By moderation, caution, and the rational discus-sion of social questions', he wrote, 'you could make the authorities trust you; at the present time you are merely frightening them'.[23] At the end of 1862 Chicherin gave his letter to Herzen a wider currency by assigning it pride of place in a book of essays on the principal political questions of the day. By then other intellectuals had come out against the radicals. In the autumn of 1861 the Slavophile Ivan Aksakov tried to dissuade students from engaging in disturbances by urging them to return to their books and to 'study Russia and the Russian nationality (*narodnost'*), in order to fill the gulf which still separates us from the people'.[24] The writer Nikolai Leskov, who at the time of the emancipation was far from hostile to the cause of change, launched a virulent attack on contemporary 'liberals' in May 1862. 'Alarmist and badly educated people', he wrote, 'do not understand that it is possible to be an outright enemy of the entire contemporary order with-out being a liberal'. Leskov was prepared to accept the utility of the term 'liberal', but only if it referred to advocates of moderation. 'For people who take a sober view of life,' he said, 'a person is liberal who is prepared not to take thought for his personal interests but to expend all his energy on standing up for the juridical independence of every citizen and the freedom of every action which does not undermine the well-being and the tranquillity of society'.[25] The key words were the last. Leskov believed that 'undermining the well-being and tranquillity of society' was the principal object of the intellectuals whom he sought to put in their place. In the case of his *bête-noire*, the literary critic Nikolai Chernyshevskii, he was right. The two men's inability to make common cause illustrated one of the main reasons why the government had less to fear from oppositionists than the radical manifestos of 1861–2 appeared to suggest.

Even if intellectuals outside the government had been agreed on the way forward, it is unlikely that they would have been successful in generating widespread enthusiasm for their opinions. The authorities were quite prepared to intervene against radicals, and radicals were inexperienced in the ways of conspiracy. In June 1862 the government imposed an eight-month ban on *The Contemporary*, the journal which published Chernyshevskii. Herzen's suggestion that it continue in the West created more problems than it solved. His circle had been penetrated by an informer. An emissary from London to St Petersburg was picked up at the imperial frontier and a large number of compromising letters fell into the hands of tsarist investigators. Not only Chernyshevskii but also the leading light in the St Petersburg branch of 'Land and Liberty' were arrested. Although Chernyshevskii lived another twenty-seven years, he never again walked the streets of the capital. The key figure in 'Land and Liberty', Nikolai Serno-Solov'evich, died in Siberia in 1866. Until radicals grasped the need to conduct their affairs in absolute secrecy, their chances of conspiring effectively were remote.

Their views might have attracted wider sympathy if the regime had been engaging in repression across the board, but although the tsar appeared to move to the right when he appointed Valuev to the Ministry of Internal Affairs and Admiral Putiatin to the Ministry of Education, he was very far from abandoning the cause of reform. He was determined to restore order in the countryside, to avoid giving the impression that nobles could force him into concessions, and to silence the most determined of his critics, but he neither abandoned the task of implementing the emancipation statutes nor fought shy of enacting the additional measures to which freeing the serfs gave rise. The appointment of Valuev was not quite the retrograde step that some contemporaries thought it to be. The worst that can be said of the new minister is that he 'undoubtedly possessed a definite political programme, but he was too cautious and too indecisive to carry it out'.[26] It is true, as Sergei Solov'ev pointed out, that 'Fate did not send [Alexander II] a Richelieu or a Bismarck',[27] but neither did it send him a Metternich. In September 1861 Valuev wrote a long paper on the progress of emancipation which concluded by acknowledging that 'Sometimes the need arises to legitimize things which have not been and could not have been envisaged by a law'.[28] The paper contained many suggestions for streamlining the way in which change was taking place in the countryside. It implied, furthermore, that the regime had to approach the reform of local government and the law courts with a much greater sense of urgency. Although most of the adjustments Valuev proposed to the statutes of emancipation appeared to favour the gentry at the expense of the peasantry, one of them, the abolition of the peasant commune, might have had the opposite effect, and none of them was designed to turn the clock back.

State agencies other then the Ministry of Internal Affairs, furthermore, either had become convinced that the government would run more risks by abandoning reform than it would by continuing with it, or were acquiring ministers whose commitment to change was actually greater than that of their predecessors. The Third Department recommended in an official memorandum of 1861 that the government strive 'to retain in its own hands the standard of the progressive movement which it itself has started'.[29] When Putiatin rapidly proved a dismal failure at the Ministry of Education, the tsar replaced him with the much more enlightened Aleksandr Golovnin. Viktor Panin gave way at the Ministry of Justice to Dmitrii Zamiatnin. Murav'ev lost the Ministry of State Properties. Nikolai Miliutin's brother Dmitrii became Minister of War and Mikhail Reitern Minister of Finances. The new appointments, all made at the end of 1861 or the beginning of 1862, bespoke a regime that was about to make further changes. The emancipation of the serfs had been drawn up at a time when most of the tsar's principal advisers belonged to the age of Nicholas I. Within a year of the promulgation of the statutes, most of the chief posts in the empire were held by people whose sympathy with the new social order was greater than that of the emancipators. The chances of further liberalization were considerable.

MILITARY AND FISCAL REFORM

Slowly, the rate of change began to accelerate. In 1862 the regime was hesitant about addressing itself to the broad governmental and social implications of the emancipation of the serfs, but new developments in the military and fiscal spheres signalled that its enthusiasm for reform was returning.

In respect of the army, something had been achieved already. Although Dmitrii Miliutin's predecessor as War Minister, General Sukhozanet, had been considered an unimaginative choice for the position at the time of his appointment in 1856, he had instigated or been obliged to accept 'Literally hundreds of changes' in the conduct of military affairs.[30] Most of them were paltry, but a few made plain that Alexander II's attitude to the army differed from that of his father. Large numbers of soldiers were demobilized.

245

The draft was suspended between 1856 and 1859. Military colonies which supplied infantry (but not those that supplied cavalry) were dissolved in 1858. In the same year, the tsar involved himself personally in the foundation of the reformist journal *Military Miscellany*. In 1859 he formalized Nicholas I's reduction of military service from twenty-five years to fifteen. Above all, Alexander overrode his cautious War Minister in the one region of the empire where troops were still on active service. By making his close friend Prince Aleksandr Bariatinskii Viceroy of the Caucasus and ordering him to take all necessary steps to bring the campaign against Shamil to a successful conclusion, the tsar gave an innovator scope for the exercise of his talents. Bariatinskii captured Shamil in 1859 after introducing 'greater independence for local commanders, more practical training for officers and men, and more stringent criteria for promotions'.[31] He had shown what a little flair might do for the army as a whole. Since, in the year of Shamil's capture, a partial mobilization of Russian troops on the empire's Galician frontier took five months, the regime had every reason to extend the lessons it learned in the Caucasus to the rest of the military machine.

Well placed at the time of Alexander II's accession, Dmitrii Miliutin had been a penetrating analyst of the empire's military weaknesses at the beginning of 1856. The appointment of Sukhozanet distressed him, but he served as Bariatinskii's chief of staff in the Caucasus and was the real architect of his triumph. Success in the Caucasian war and the friendship between Bariatinskii and the tsar restored him to favour at the centre and gave him the chance of putting his ideas into practice. Though committed to reform, he was no radical. His political opinions were probably more right-wing than those of his brother Nikolai. 'Reform', he wrote, 'can be undertaken here only in an authoritarian manner (*vlast'iu*)'. Popular initiative was to be deplored: 'any revolution which smacks of fanaticism, a violent revolution, a people's revolution ... merely destroys without creating anything new'. Within clearly defined limits, however, Miliutin believed in change. On 15 January 1862 he submitted proposals to the tsar which became 'the basic blueprint' for his multifarious activities at the War Ministry.[32]

The new minister had long known why Russia's military outgoings were larger than those of her competitors. 'The main reason for the size of the [military] budget', Miliutin wrote in 1862, 'is the number of troops'.[33] Before the emancipation of the serfs the government had been reluctant to return peasants to the countryside after they had served in the army, for fear that they would use their training to promote discontent. In effect, soldiers in the pre-reform army served for life. After emancipation the state could transform recruitment by enlisting more people each year but putting them on the reserve list much sooner. Miliutin pointed out that if 125,000 men were enlisted annually but required to serve for no more than seven or eight years, in seven years the country would possess a trained reserve of 750,000 men. If annual recruitment were higher still, recruits could be released earlier and the reserve would be larger. The War Minister was already thinking in terms of extending the obligation to serve in the army from the peasant estate to the community as a whole.

He also had strong views on the way in which the army was organized. As things stood when he became minister, the empire created wholly new regiments and divisions when it expanded its forces in wartime. Miliutin rightly believed that this practice gave rise to major administrative complications. His alternative was to increase the army's number of permanent divisions from thirty-one to forty-seven, to maintain them at a relatively low level in peacetime, but to triple them in size on the outbreak of war. Summoning troops from the reserve would be easier if the formations in which they were to be deployed existed already. Suddenly creating new formations was a recipe for administrative chaos.

These were only the most important of Miliutin's ideas, some of which took effect very quickly. Between 1862 and 1870 the size of the reserve went up from 210,000 men to 553,000. The division of the empire into fifteen military districts in August 1864 made possible the more efficient call-up of reservists in wartime and the partial transfer of decision-making to local commanders. The induction of recruits became a more civilized process in September 1862 when Miliutin declared that their heads need not be shaved and that they ought to be conducted to the barracks in everyday clothing rather than clothes that made them look like convicts. Military education ceased to be a sort of 'royal secret' and became the preserve of the War Ministry. A commission established in October 1862 created gymnasia for aspiring officers in which the curriculum hardly differed from that of secondary schools for civilians. In future, officers received specialist military training only after they had been educated in the round. Miliutin had begun not only to reduce expenditure, but also to introduce military personnel to the spirit of post-emancipation society.

Like the War Minister, Reitern at the Ministry of Finances accelerated the introduction of changes which had been in the air since 1855. A committed member of the circle of reformers which centred on the Grand Duke Konstantin Nikolaevich, he spent four years in the second half of the 1850s investigating the financial procedures of various west European countries and the United States. Before he returned home, another economist with experience of foreign practices, V. A. Tatarinov, set in train the changes which came to a head in 1862. Tatarinov argued that all ministries and other governmental institutions should be obliged to produce detailed estimates for the year ahead at the time they submitted their annual accounts. In this way the centre could compare past and future. He advocated a unified central approach to budgeting and recommended above all that the State Control, the regime's auditing body, be given access to the accounts of all government agencies. The tsar had good reason to listen to the advice of his financial experts, for not only were his finances in a desperate state but also he could not easily borrow on western markets so long as the empire's accounting procedures remained inadequate.[34]

Many of the contemporary suggestions for improving the management of the empire's finances bore fruit during Reitern's first year as minister. The state began publishing its accounts. The government tried to drive out inflation by announcing that it was prepared to exchange paper money for specie. The tsar improved the Ministry of Finances' chances of introducing economies by ordering that state agencies would have to prepare detailed estimates of their future expenditure. A decision was taken in principle to require agencies with independent sources of income to transfer them to the central treasury. The rights of the State Control to check accounts began to increase. Above all, Reitern presided over the abolition of tax farming. Only one farm remained, for vodka, but abolishing it was a major step in view of the fact that it was the source of about two-fifths of the state's total revenue. Because merchants paid enormous sums for the right to sell vodka, the imperial government had long been prepared to over-look their chicanery at the point of sale. St Petersburg had become increas-ingly aware, however, of the corruption to which imperial officials fell prey as a result of their involvement in the merchants' activities. The authorities were particularly anxious, moreover, to prevent the recurrence of rural dis-turbances like those of 1858 and 1859, when peasants had boycotted the taverns and rioted because vodka had become too expensive for them. As early as 1860 'it could be said that the abolition of tax farming was ... offi-cial Imperial policy'.[35] Two years later, under Reitern, the decision was taken to replace the vodka farm with an excise tax. When the tax came in at the beginning of 1863, vodka became cheaper and more readily avail-able, state revenues held up, and the former monopolists of the retail trade began to invest their accumulated capital in railways, banks and mines. In financial and administrative terms the reform proved to be one of the grea-test successes of the 1860s. Indirectly it also constituted the biggest single indication, in the immediate aftermath of the emancipation, that the im-perial authorities were still interested in altering the relations between so-cial classes. Although the War Minister had considered imposing conscription on members of the privileged estates, he had not yet dared to recommend it. Centralizing revenue collection and publishing the empire's accounts had won Reitern the respect of financial experts, but had not done much to earn him the applause of the community at large. The ex-cise, on the other hand, benefited the poor. Although the government changed its way of profiting from the sale of drink mainly for negative rea-sons – to stave off rural unrest and reduce under-the-counter payments to civil servants – the abolition of the vodka farm looked like a victory for the common man.

THE CHURCH

The work of Miliutin and Reitern made plain that the Russian government retained its commitment to reform even in the immediate aftermath of the emancipation. Having addressed themselves to the army and the treasury, the authorities turned to the Orthodox Church. Ecclesiastical dignitaries had been contemplating certain reforms of their own, but pressure for a radical approach to the church's problems had been generated by a rank-and-file priest and by laymen. The priest, Ivan Belliustin, devoted a lengthy manuscript to the wretched lives of the non-monastic clergy. Their education, he said, was irrelevant to their duties, their poverty such that they had to spend most of their time keeping body and soul together. Bishops were unlikely to help them, for 'Whatever the cost, even if it means the destruction of the church, [bishops] try to preserve that power and significance which prelates possessed in the fifteenth to the seventeenth centuries'.[36] Belliustin called upon the tsar to circumvent the ecclesiastical hierarchy and breathe life into the clerical estate.

A minor clergyman from the province of Tver' appeared to have little chance of influencing the government, but Belliustin was in touch with Mikhail Pogodin, the longstanding apologist for Nicholas I who had discovered a capacity for criticizing the regime in the course of the Crimean War. Via Pogodin, Belliustin's diatribe was published in Paris in 1858. Under the title *A Description of the Rural Clergy*, the book circulated widely in Russia and impressed important people. Even the highly conservative Procurator of the Holy Synod, A. P. Tolstoi, thought many of its arguments justifiable. In 1859 the tsar intervened personally to prevent church leaders from consigning Belliustin to a monastery in the White Sea. The *Description* alarmed the regime because of its implications for the maintenance of order in the countryside. If the condition of the rural clergy was as bad as the book claimed, who was to speak for the government in the provinces? The secular authorities needed priests who could attract the loyalty of their parishioners. Valuev had been critical of the ecclesiastical hierarchy since at least 1855, when he asked why the church needed the physical force of the state to prevent schism and re-convert dissenters.[37] By the end of the 1850s the state had an additional reason for addressing itself to the fate of priests. In the western provinces, where the Christian population was overwhelmingly Catholic or in communion with Rome, peasants were refusing to fulfil the economic obligations which they owed to the Orthodox clergy. Ever sensitive to the possibility of internecine strife among the nationalities of the empire, the tsar compelled the Holy Synod to consider ways of resolving the matter. It reported in mid-1861, but suggested only that the peasantry of the western provinces fulfil their obligations in cash rather than labour. By this time the government was of the opinion that difficulties which arose in relations between clergy and peasants sprang not merely from the economic arrangements on which the livelihood of priests depended, but from the priests' character. Only better priests could achieve satisfactory relations with their parishioners, and producing better priests meant giving thought to the clerical estate as a whole.

As Minister of Internal Affairs, Valuev was by this time in a position to act. In August 1861 he made clear that he wanted to move beyond the problem of the western provinces to the problem of priests in general. 'The Orthodox clergy and Church in the western area', he said, 'will not assume the status appropriate to their rank so long as this same clergy at the very centre of the state remain in their present condition and on their present level'.[38] Though the tsar remained principally interested in solving the riddle of the western provinces, he allowed his minister to broaden the debate. Nikolai Pomialovskii's fictional *Seminary Sketches*, which began to appear in *The Contemporary* in mid-1862, put part of the case for church reform to a wider public. Despite resistance from successive heads of the Holy Synod (who resented the intrusion into their business of the Ministry of Internal Affairs), Valuev secured the establishment in December 1862 of a commission to investigate the life of the church: 'the "emancipation of the clergy" had begun'.[39]

HIGHER EDUCATION

While the ecclesiastical commission was deliberating, the government put its mind to resolving the complex set of problems which had arisen in the universities. Soon after ascending the throne Alexander had relaxed the constraints on higher education which his father had introduced in the wake of the European revolutions of 1848. In the second half of the 1850s the Ministry of Education abolished enrolment quotas, exempted the badly off from the payment of fees, readopted the principle of despatching promising scholars to western Europe for postgraduate training, allowed women to attend lectures, ended the practice of monitoring students' off-campus behaviour, reintroduced contentious subjects like west European law and the history of philosophy, and appointed broad-minded officials to the headships of the empire's educational districts. Above all, the ministry effected a radical transformation of the professoriate. Of the staff employed in universities at the beginning of 1854 50 per cent had left their posts by the end of 1862.[40] Afanasii Shchapov of Kazan' University was perhaps the most radical of the new appointees, but most of the newcomers differed sharply from their predecessors. Quondam dissidents joined the establishment. The Ukrainian federalist Mykola (Nikolai) Kostomarov, who had been banished to Saratov after the exposure of the Kirillo-Methodian Society in 1847, became a Professor of History at St Petersburg University in 1859. Boris Chicherin joined him as a Professor of Law in 1861. Since St

Petersburg University also employed Konstantin Kavelin (the prime advocate of conferring land as well as liberty on the peasants), Vladimir Spasovich (an enthusiastic Polish nationalist), Aleksandr Pypin (a cousin of the trenchant journalist Nikolai Chernyshevskii) and Boris Utin (a former associate of Mikhail Petrashevskii), it could have been said to represent almost all the forward-looking opinions of the day. At Moscow University, where the political economist I. V. Vernadskii found ways of advocating the emancipation of the serfs even before discussion of the subject was officially permitted, the staff changed so much that the liberally inclined Sergei Solov'ev began to look like a conservative. At Kiev the historian P. V. Pavlov captivated students by dwelling on the putative democracy and federalism of pre-Petrine Russia. The appointment of the famous doctor and educational theorist Nikolai Pirogov to the headship of the Odessa educational district in 1856 demonstrated that under Alexander II enlightened academics could not only serve in educational institutions, but also run them. Only at the University of Dorpat, in Estonia, did the intellectual atmosphere change rather slowly.

From the point of view of the authorities, revitalizing the universities was a policy fraught with danger. Politically motivated intellectuals tended not to fall silent on receiving official positions but to capitalize on their prominence. Shchapov was only one of the newly appointed professors whose inaugural lecture hinted at a political programme. Kostomarov expressed an almost identical antipathy to the state in his inaugural lecture of November 1859. Boris Chicherin's (very different) political opinions found equally clear expression in his inaugural of October 1861. Students, meanwhile, grew in number and changed in character. The student body was still tiny (just under 3,000 in 1854, just under 5,000 in 1860), but the rate of growth outfaced administrators. The removal of entry quotas encouraged young people who had been denied access to universities in the last years of Nicholas to enter them under Alexander, with the result that students tended to be older and more politically engaged than they had been in the past. Because undergraduates could engage in off-campus activities without being supervised by the university authorities, they began to play a more significant part in society at large. Although about two-thirds of students still came from the gentry estate, an increasing proportion of them seem to have been poor. Many took advantage of the new regime's financial generosity. 'By 1859,' for example, 'two-thirds of all registered students at Moscow University were exempt from fees'.[41] In short, the government's liberality turned universities into a powder-keg. Staff spoke out and students began to organize. The lectures of the former and the associations of the latter appeared to be serving not only academic and economic purposes but also the promotion of political instability.

Which of the many recent changes played the major part in the university disturbances of the early 1860s is unclear. Patrick Alston emphasizes the students' poverty, Regina Eimontova their political opinions, Daniel Brower the interaction of the two.[42] Incompetence at the Ministry of Education certainly lit the touch-paper. Before leaving the ministry in mid-1861 the sensible Evgraf Kovalevskii came up with a programme for reducing the volatility of the universities which might have been effective if it had been introduced gradually. The new minister, Admiral Putiatin, acted on the programme forthwith. Abolishing the remission of fees, prohibiting student meetings, taking over student loan banks and closing student-run libraries alienated not only the students but also their professors. Even Chicherin, whose inaugural lecture recommended deference to the state, called the ban on student associations 'a preposterous thought' and the non-remission of fees 'impolitic'.[43] Most of the leading professors at St Petersburg University resigned their posts. By the end of 1861 the university had been closed. With the professors' backing, disaffected St Petersburg students tried to set up a 'free university' at the beginning of 1862, but they gave up the attempt after a month when the government arrested a professor for lecturing in a supposedly provocative manner on the upcoming national millennium. The fires of May 1862 only confirmed the authorities in their antipathy to students. Since the St Petersburg pattern was repeated at universities elsewhere in the empire (except at Dorpat), the higher education system appeared to have fallen apart. In June 1862 a four-hour session of the Council of Ministers which suspended *The Contemporary* and decided to open only one section of St Petersburg University in the coming academic year left the liberal Grand Duke Konstantin Nikolaevich 'deeply sad'.[44]

In view of the way in which the government treated universities in 1861 and 1862, the law of June 1863 which redesigned their *modus operandi* preserved a remarkable degree of the generosity towards them which had been evident in the second half of the 1850s. If there was a sphere in which the authorities had a certain justification for retreating from the policy of reform (and in which they could have afforded to act without alienating a numerically significant part of the population), it was that of higher education. Yet the tsar replaced Putiatin with Golovnin, appointed a commission which 'conducted the most extensive investigation into the idea of a Russian university ever undertaken by the old regime',[45] took advice even from the liberal Professor Kavelin, and introduced a law which improved the funding of universities, gave professors a large degree of control over university affairs, maintained the principle that universities were open to all classes of the community, and allowed universities to go on dedicating themselves, first and foremost, to the study of the liberal arts. As James Flynn says, this was 'in most important respects a faithful return to the statute of 1835',[46] which sounds like a dubious compliment until one remembers that Nicholas I's supposedly restrictive statute on universities actually preserved most of the enlightened principles of the statute of 1804.

LOCAL GOVERNMENT

By mid-1863, therefore, the regime had given several indications that its interest in remodelling the state's institutions had survived the shock of emancipating the serfs. Its confidence appeared to be growing, for in 1864 the tsar enacted three measures that were second in importance only to the emancipation itself.

The first of these dealt with local government. As we saw in Chapter Five, even in the reign of Nicholas contradictory principles had informed the autocracy's attitude towards administration. The growth of the tsar's chancery had embodied a 'personal' principle, whereas the abolition of the majority of governors-general had implied adherence to a 'ministerial' principle and the reform of the municipal government of St Petersburg had intimated sympathy for a 'representative' principle. In Nicholas's lifetime the personal principle prevailed over the others, but once his successor embarked on emancipation the other two had to be considered more seriously. Severing the umbilical cord between landlords and peasants vastly increased the proportion of the population for which the centre was directly responsible. Before 1861 the state had left most rural tasks to the gentry, but nobles who had been deprived of their serfs had no reason to think of themselves as agents of the government. How could the centre 'maintain its administrative ties with the masses to ensure adequate national defense and tax collection?'.[47] It was unreasonable to suppose that an enlargement of Nicholas I's 'personal' principle could fill the vacuum in the countryside, for when the serfs were free they were even more likely to misinterpret dictates from the centre than they had been as bondmen. The logical alternative was to promote the 'ministerial' principle by strengthening the chain of command which led from the Ministry of Internal Affairs to the provincial governors. But although the imperial bureaucracy was growing in size, it was too small to take over all the duties for which landlords had been responsible. Nor was it well enough coordinated to give the Ministry of Internal Affairs a clear run. The third and least well developed principle, the 'representative' principle, began to come into its own. Frederick Starr calls the second and third principles 'decentralization' (which involved giving local officials more power but preserved the notion of bureaucratic or 'ministerial' hegemony) and 'self-government' (which meant introducing representative organs and giving non-bureaucrats in the provinces a larger say in the management of their affairs).[48] These were Alexander II's only real choices, but before he decided between them the notion of tying the provinces more closely to the centre had to be ruled out of court.

At the beginning of the reign the tsar seemed to favour decentralization (the 'ministerial' principle). In a decree of October 1856 he strengthened the hand of provincial governors. They and the Ministry of Internal Affairs were delighted, but other ministries with outposts in the countryside objected to the new constraints on their freedom of action. In the first months of 1858 conservatives at the centre proposed the reinstatement of Nicholas I's 'personal' principle. They believed that, instead of conferring greater powers on provincial governors, the regime should create an additional network of provincial administrators who would owe their allegiance to the tsar and whose prime purpose would be the maintenance of order rather than the fostering of local initiative. Military governors-general were to be put in charge of groups of provinces throughout the empire, not just in the imperial borderlands and in St Petersburg and Moscow. At the district level new officials, 'district captains' (*uezdnye nachal'niki*), were to be introduced to enact the decrees of the governors-general. In accepting Murav'ev's proposals the regime made plain that, although it had just committed itself firmly to the emancipation of the serfs (in the Nazimov Rescript), it was not yet prepared to adopt the principle of decentralization or to move towards provincial self-government.

Nikolai Miliutin was appalled. The vitriolic anonymous letter he despatched to *The Bell* in the summer of 1858 had much less to do with the half-hearted way in which the government was handling the question of emancipation than with the way in which the regime proposed to run the empire after emancipation had been achieved. Military rule, he believed, would wreck the country. If the proposals of early 1858 reached the statute book, 'The whole of Russia will turn into nothing more than a military colony (*obratitsia v odno voennoe poselenie*), and who will save it from the new Arakcheev who is emerging in the person of Iakov Ivanovich Rostovtsev?'[49] Fortunately, from Miliutin's point of view, the 1858 project aroused extreme dissatisfaction among the gentry.[50] If it had been implemented they would have lost not only their control over the peasantry but also virtually all authority in provincial affairs. In view of the emergence of an unlikely alliance between reform-minded bureaucrats and provincial noblemen, the government abandoned the idea of running the countryside autocratically. When, on 25 March 1859, the tsar announced the principles on which Russian local government was to be based in the future, he acknowledged that provision had to be made for involving the public. The representative principle had superseded the ministerial and the personal. Two days after changing tack, Alexander set up a Commission on the Reorganization of Provincial and District Institutions to work out how the new principle was to be embodied in legislation. Plans for the reform of local government were now in step with those for the emancipation of the serfs. Just as the regime had decided, by 1859, to make land available to serfs (not merely to emancipate them), so now it grasped that strengthening the centre's authority in the countryside ran counter to the policy of increasing the freedom of its subjects.

From March 1859 it was clear that, when the empire's local government was put on a new footing, people other than bureaucrats would be participating in it. What was not clear was the manner or the extent of their involvement. In view of the fact that Miliutin was made chairman of the new local government commission the prospects for a generous solution looked good, but the commission made little progress in the first year of its life. Miliutin himself was at fault. However strongly he objected to military governors-general, he also believed strongly in the maintenance of law and order. As a result, he devoted more attention to the question of policing the countryside than to the creation of local representative institutions. 'In 1857, in [Iaroslavl',] a province that covered almost 14,000 square miles and sheltered more than 950,000 people, the Ministry of Internal Affairs had at its disposal only 244 policemen'.[51] Since other provinces were no better off, policing was a major issue; but spending time on it impeded the development of representative institutions. In April 1860 the Minister of Internal Affairs presented 'Temporary Rules on District Land Offices' to the State Council, but in June the tsar returned them to the ministry to await the preparation of a Statute on Provincial Institutions. The reconstruction of local government was to take place only after the serfs had been liberated, by which time Miliutin's days at the Ministry of Internal Affairs were numbered.

Inadvertently, Miliutin not only impeded but positively retarded the coming of local representative institutions, since the Commission on the Reorganization of Provincial and District Institutions proposed the introduction of 'peace arbitrators'. The idea behind these was beneficent. They were to be elected by peasants from among the ranks of the gentry in order to defend peasant interests in the wake of the emancipation. In due course, after the ties that bound nobles and peasants had been finally severed, they were to become elective Justices of the Peace with jurisdiction over all estates of the realm. In conception they were a 'first step toward further reforms in the field of local administration and the courts'.[52] In the event, however, they were appointed rather than elected and usually served the interests of the gentry estate. Charged in 1861 with supervising the charters of peasant obligations which had to be drawn up immediately after the emancipation, in most cases they sanctioned charters from which the gentry profited. Peace arbitrators thus came to epitomize not the 'representative' but the 'personal' or the 'ministerial' approach to the management of the countryside.

Another part of the emancipation legislation appeared to do more for the cause of local representation, but proved to create as many problems as it solved. Legislators believed that although peasant communes were well qualified to take decisions about the planting and harvesting of crops and the repartition of peasant landholdings, they were imperfect instruments for the conduct of administrative and judicial affairs in the countryside. The emancipators thought a commune could serve administrative and judicial purposes only if it embraced a coherent area of peasant settlement. Since the gentry had tended to buy and sell land without reference to the administrative cohesion of the parcels they exchanged, two or more communes often existed side by side in a single centre of rural population. From the point of view of the emancipators, 'where a settlement consisted of various estates and more than one commune, there, evidently, two units had to exist ...: one economic (the land commune), the other administrative'.[53] To bring the second of these into being, the authors of the 1861 legislation created a level of local administration below the levels which existed already. Small peasant communes were grouped for administrative and judicial purposes into cantons or 'volosti'. The office-holders and agencies which ran the new units – the elder, the clerk, the executive board, the assembly, the court – were elected by the peasants whom they served, but it is only with considerable reservation that volosti can be said to have increased the representative character of the imperial polity. The ancient word 'volost'' meant 'authority' (in modern Russian, *vlast*'). Introducing a new source of authority in the countryside was the principal reason why the emancipators believed volosti had to be created. Although the new level of provincial administration gave peasants an additional form of self-government, its real purpose was the improvement of St Petersburg's line-management. Because there were fewer volosti than communes, the former could be pressurized more easily than the latter.

Even in so far as volosti marked a victory for the principle of representation, they did so without improving relations between the different estates of the realm. Indeed, because they were exclusively peasant institutions they actually widened the gap between peasants and privileged. To make the principle of representation effective, the regime had to create institutions in which the various social orders interacted with each other. Ironically, it was the cautious Valuev rather than the enlightened Miliutin who brought such institutions nearer. In Valuev's opinion new local assemblies would reward the gentry for parting with their serfs and enable the government to buy off liberals. Neither of these reasons for creating assemblies at the district and provincial levels implied a desire to make them broadly representative or to give them much clout, but as the draft legislation passed through the upper reaches of the government keen reformers got their hands on it. When, on 1 January 1864, the tsar legislated for the creation of the new assemblies – 'zemstva' (or, if the plural is anglicized, 'zemstvos') – they seemed not only to represent provincial society as a whole but also to possess considerable authority. Delegates to the district zemstva were elected for a period of three years by three categories of voter voting separately: landowners, property-owners in the towns, and delegates from the volosti. Delegates to the higher assemblies were elected by the lower. Assemblies met only once a year but set up permanent executive boards. Zemstva could raise taxes and had the right to make representations to the central government. They were explicitly instructed to involve themselves in local economic affairs, education, medical care, prisons and road maintenance. They were supposed to 'function independently within the sphere of activity entrusted to them'.[54] On paper, they were the most significant addition to the structure of Russian local government since Catherine the Great's reconstruction of provincial administration in 1775. Their creation appeared to mark a clear victory for the 'representative' approach to administration at the expense of the 'personal' and the 'ministerial'.

PRIMARY SCHOOLS

Zemstva made an immediate difference to the prospects of Russian primary education. Neither Catherine the Great's Commission on Popular Schools of 1782 nor the education statutes of 1804 and 1828 nor the foundation of elementary schools by the Ministry of State Properties and the Holy Synod had succeeded to any great extent in promoting the cause of peasant literacy. The empire contained many more primary schools in 1850 than in 1780, but fewer, relatively speaking, than the countries with which the Russian Empire was competing. When, in 1856, Nikolai Pirogov began to write about educational matters in the press, the government responded by re-establishing the long-dead Academic Committee of the Ministry of Education. In 1858 the committee started preparing a primary education statute, but between 1859 and 1862 the most striking development in respect of primary schools owed its origins to private individuals. First in Kiev, then in St Petersburg and elsewhere, Sunday schools appeared like mushrooms. 'Within three years there were 500 literary clinics in operation without a ruble's expense to the state'.[55] In theory, the Ministry of Education welcomed schools which it did not have to pay for and in which the instructors – student volunteers – confined themselves to teaching adult illiterates how to read and write. In practice, however, the authorities viewed Sunday schools with considerable suspicion. By the end of 1860 the education minister was reflecting darkly on the fact that one of the Kiev schools was teaching history and one of the Moscow schools both French and German. Since the Third Department had convinced itself that Sunday schools were hotbeds of sedition, it was hardly surprising that in June 1862 the government closed them down.[56]

The rate at which Sunday schools sprang up nevertheless strengthened the authorities' conviction that they would have to make better provision for the education of the masses. Between 1860 and 1863 the Academic Committee of the Ministry of Education produced three versions of a statute. Although it sought to make schools accessible, it also held that attendance at them should be voluntary, that pupils should pay for the instruction they received, that public education should be developed gradually rather than immediately, and that, although schools would still be run by different agencies, societies and private individuals, they should teach the same things and be managed identically. The main weakness of the programme was that schooling could hardly be called accessible when those who were supposed to benefit from it had to pay for tuition. The proposed legislation also failed to commit the authorities to a definite programme of school-building and put forward an extremely unambitious curriculum. Primary education was to cover only religion, reading, writing and arithmetic. The full course of study was to last only a year. Admittedly, the draft legislation made provision for a more demanding sort of primary education in parts of the country which expressed a desire for it, but the likelihood of this superior version taking root was small in view of the poverty of the peasants who would have to pay for it.

Despite its highly unambitious character, the version of the statute which reached the State Council was toned down still further. References to a 'higher' form of primary education were cut out. Instruction in languages other than Russian was prohibited. Sunday schools were legitimized, but required to teach boys and girls separately (with the result that they needed extra buildings and instructors). Advocates of the view that primary education should be placed in the hands of the clergy failed to win their case, but priests were given entire control of religious instruction and assigned a major role in the new provincial schools councils.

One scholar holds that the many 'changes and corrections [to which the statute on schools was subjected] confirm that the government had no serious intention of promoting even the most elementary primary education among the people'.[57] This conclusion needs to be modified in the light of the changes in local government. Late in the genesis of the law on zemstva, the new assemblies were permitted to use their resources for schools. They were not supposed to play a part in managing them, but it soon became clear that they would do so. When the final version of the law on schools was enacted in July 1864, zemstva representatives received two places on the newly created school boards. Other agencies received only one. Although the extra representation for zemstva did not arise out of St Petersburg's enthusiasm for local government (but out of the determination of central agencies to prevent any one of their number dominating the rest), it nevertheless ensured 'a large dose of decentralization' in primary education and gave primary schools a better chance than they would have had otherwise.[58] A law on secondary schools which followed in November 1864 gave further evidence of the government's preparedness to devolve certain sorts of power from the centre to the provinces. Since universities had become relatively autonomous in 1863, the authorities' general attitude towards education seemed to indicate a readiness on their part to give up some of the prerogatives of the central bureaucracy.

COURTS

The reform of the courts in November 1864 reduced the power of the centre much further, but the origins of this striking development were even more remarkable than its outcome. What turned out to be the most far-reaching of all the post-emancipation measures of Alexander II derived, ironically, from the government's concern for the gentry. The court reform is sometimes thought to have originated in concern for the peasantry. One scholar writes that whereas before 1861 'a Russian serf had been a legal nullity', afterwards he received 'entirely new legal entitlements and obligations extending into every basic transaction of everyday life',[59] with the result that the government had to redesign the empire's judicial system in order to integrate the peasantry into the community at large. Another scholar claims that since the government was trying to create a class of peasant smallholders, it had to safeguard the peasant's person, his property and his entrepreneurial activity; 'Securing these conditions without an apparatus of justice was impossible'.[60] Though logical, these arguments are inaccurate. The government did indeed make new judicial arrangements for the peasantry, but it made them in 1861. The statutes which brought serfdom to an end introduced new courts at the level of the volost' which dealt solely with the affairs of the peasantry. The authorities did not intend to give peasants legal parity with the other estates of the realm, but to continue treating them as a separate estate. Although 'the designers of the [volost'] court viewed it as a transitional form of rural justice',[61] volost' courts remained outside the general judicial system of the empire until 1912.

Why then, if the government dealt with the problem of peasant justice at the time of the emancipation, did it reconstruct the empire's legal system in 1864? It is true that enlightened officials and liberal members of the intelligentsia were pressing for change. It is true, too, that reform was necessary. Nicholas I had put some order into 200 years of imperial legislation by publishing the Complete Collection and Digest of the Laws, but he had done nothing to alter judicial procedure. Herzen believed that the reputation of the courts suffered more from the way in which they transacted their business than from the verdicts at which they arrived. '[A] man of the humble class who falls into the hands of law', he wrote, 'is more afraid of the process of law itself than of any punishment. He looks forward with impatience to the time when he will be sent to Siberia; his martyrdom ends with the beginning of his punishment'.[62] The unreformed legal system was both slow and malign. In civil cases it was designed to protect the interests of debtors (the gentry). In criminal cases the accused was guilty until proved innocent. There were no juries or lawyers. Judges sat behind closed doors and took only written evidence, basing their decisions on the records of preliminary investigations conducted by the police. The executive arm of the administration interfered constantly.

In view of these deficiencies, it was hardly surprising that the reformers who centred on the Grand Duke Konstantin Nikolaevich addressed themselves to transforming the courts very soon after Alexander II ascended the throne. Unil 1861, however, their victories were few. Viktor Panin, the longstanding Minister of Justice, and Dmitrii Bludov, the equally well-established head of the Second Department (the body which codified Russian law in the 1830s), resisted the thought of root-and-branch change. Bludov was prepared to adjust the existing system, but not to substitute adversarial for inquisitorial justice or to introduce barristers, juries, open courts and elected Justices of the Peace. Dmitrii Zamiatnin, the deputy Minister of Justice, and Sergei Zarudnyi, Bludov's assistant at the Second

Department, were juridical radicals, but although they registered a few successes in their quest for change (notably the foundation of the enlightened *Journal of the Ministry of Justice* in 1859), they needed more than idealism to convert their superiors.

Discontented gentry unlocked the door which legal reformers had been unable to unlock for themselves. In the immediate aftermath of the emancipation most landowners felt even less warmly towards the imperial bureaucracy than they had felt in the past. Having relied on the administration to perpetrate abuses on their behalf, they now believed that it was abandoning them. They thought a redesigned legal system might constrain the civil service and protect their economic interests. Having lost their serfs, they realized that they would have to alter not only the basis on which they conducted their money-raising activities, but also perhaps the activities themselves. Some of them were likely to become entrepreneurs and to start taking risks. They needed a dependable legal environment for the conduct of their business. The judicial system now had to protect creditors instead of debtors. The arbitrary judicial procedures of the Nicholaevan age could not fulfil the economic purposes which, in the view of the gentry, courts now had to serve.

Valuev put the gentry's case to the tsar. In his first memorandum as Minister of Internal Affairs he argued that nobles were justified in saying that the emancipation threatened their economic interests. He believed that the threat was temporary and held that, if nobles took a broad view, their prospects were good, but he also sensed the extreme urgency of the state's need to foster entrepreneurial activity. 'Material obstacles to this', he told the tsar, 'have long been discerned in the inadequacies of your judicial structure and judicial procedure'. Although projects for the reform of the courts were being drawn up and had in some cases been completed, 'the date of their publication cannot yet be predicted with any certainty'.[63] 'This report', says the major student of the nineteenth-century Russian legal system, 'determined the fate of the judicial reform'.[64] The tsar responded immediately to Valuev's call for the acceleration of the reform of the courts. In October 1861 he took the matter out of the hands of the old guard and transferred it to keen reformers. Before the end of the year he went on to make P. P. Gagarin head of the Department of Laws of the State Council. Gagarin epitomized both the pre- and the post-emancipation interests of the gentry. Having been a diehard opponent of freeing the serfs, he was very interested indeed in continuing the fight for noble rights through the medium of the courts. In respect of the law he became a radical. In January 1862 he convinced the tsar of the need to permit Russian jurists to derive their reform plans from the examples of west European states. Within a year his civil servants produced a document called 'The Basic Principles for the Reform of the Courts', which recommended all the steps Panin and Bludov had resisted for twenty years.

Most of the 'Basic Principles' found expression in the statutes of November 1864. The stated aim of the legislation was 'to establish in Russia courts of justice that are swift, equitable, merciful, and equal for all our subjects, to elevate the authority of the judiciary, to give it the independence that befits it, and in general to strengthen among our people ... respect for the law'.[65] The statutes established a five-tier system. District zemstvo assemblies elected Justices of the Peace (JPs) to deal with minor offences. They had to be twenty-five years old, to have received at least secondary education, and to be substantial property-owners. Joint sessions of JPs constituted the second tier of the new judicial administration. Although judges were appointed by the authorities at the remaining levels (circuit courts, judicial tribunals, and the Senate, which acted as a court of appeal), they could be dismissed only if they broke the law themselves. Because they were well paid, they were disinclined to take bribes. Their independence reduced the executive's capacity for interfering in the legal process. Elements of the old inquisitorial system of justice survived in the appointment of examining magistrates to collect pre-trial evidence (a practice sanctioned by French judicial procedure), but the creation of the profession of barrister turned trials into open adversarial contests on the pattern of judicial procedure in Britain. The most startling innovation was the introduction of juries. The framers of the 'Basic Principles' sought above all to generate a sense of law in the mind of the public. The involvement of the executive in the unreformed courts had led people to believe that the law was their enemy. Juries tended to dissipate this feeling. Although conservatives believed that juries were appropriate only in societies whose population had already achieved a degree of sophistication, reformers argued that they could promote the social responsibility from which they were supposed to emerge. Time was to prove the reformers right.

THE PRESS

Unlike the movement for judicial reform, which owed much to the right of the political spectrum but finished on the left, the government's attitude towards freedom of the press began by reflecting the views of the left of the political spectrum but finished on the right. The 'Temporary Rules on Censorship and the Press' of April 1865 plumped for constraint at the expense of glasnost. When, in December 1855, the tsar abolished the notorious Committee of 2 April 1848, he implied that he would be treating the press with a new generosity. His first Minister of Education, Avraam Norov, began contemplating censorship reform in March 1857. Briefly, in the first half of 1858, the government seemed to lift press restrictions altogether (with the result that Kavelin was able to publish his plea for emancipation with land). In January 1859, however, the cause of press reform took a turn for the worse when the tsar appointed a Committee on Press Affairs which smacked of the committee of 1848. The following month Alexander complained to his brother of 'the unbridled character of our reckless literature, which ought to have been reined in long ago'.[66] The 1859 committee was dissolved a year later, but only because the government had decided to treat the press with greater subtlety. No one in authority thought of abolishing censorship altogether. Enlightened bureaucrats sought to put it in the hands of a newly created ministry; conservatives proposed transferring it from the liberal Ministry of Education to the Ministry of Internal Affairs. An influential official argued in January 1860 that although glasnost was laudable, 'it must always have an indissoluble link ... with the bases and forms of the State and civic structure'.[67] In 1861 the benighted Admiral Putiatin, Minister of Education, not only supported the idea of transferring censorship to the Ministry of Internal Affairs but also proposed the approach to the press that eventually found its way into law. Offending works, he thought, should be suppressed after they had been published rather than when they were in manuscript. This sounded like an improvement on the status quo, but it turned out to be a two-edged sword.

Between 1861 and the beginning of 1863 the Ministry of Education and the Ministry of Internal Affairs ran censorship jointly. Gradually, the latter prevailed over the former. Even a sympathizer conceded that Aleksandr Golovnin possessed few qualifications for heading the education ministry.[68] He enjoyed a number of successes in respect of the new statutes for universities and for primary and secondary schools, but where the press was concerned he was unable to turn his liberal inclinations into workable edicts. He tried to persuade editors of journals to back the government, but made clear that he would prosecute them if they refused. This was 'a difficult and devious policy to implement'.[69] Some of the problems he faced were not of his own making. Censors were having to deal with an unmanageable number of publications. In the past they had reported to the tsar every month, but by the end of 1861 newspapers had complicated their task to such an extent that they were reporting daily.[70] The press seemed to be full of stories about the fractious behaviour of students, the circulation of revolutionary appeals to the population, the degeneration of relations between Russians and Poles, and the fires in St Petersburg. In the view of the government, discussing such matters in print made resolving them harder. In May 1862 the authorities issued a set of press rules which enabled them to suspend *The Contemporary* and a number of other journals. In July 1862 Valuev persuaded the tsar to inaugurate a campaign of press management. State publications were to be instructed and private publications 'stimulated' to present the activities of the authorities in a favourable light.[71] In January 1863 Golovnin acquiesced in the outright transfer of responsibility for censorship to the Ministry of Internal Affairs.

After the usual lengthy period of gestation, the government produced the 'Temporary Rules' of 1865 (which remained in place until 1905). Superficially, they made publishing easier, for editors of the country's leading periodicals received permission to print their material without seeking prior approval. What the government gave away with one hand, however, it took back with the other. Under the old system editors, writers and printers were technically free from the threat of punishment if, by hook or by crook, they managed to defeat the censor. Under the rules of 1865 they remained responsible for their publications after they had seen them into print. Editors still had to submit their material for inspection (after it had been printed, but before it was distributed); they could be penalized both by indictment in the courts and by direct action on the part of the Minister of Internal Affairs; and they had to lodge monetary bonds with the authorities to facilitate the payment of fines if the government moved against them. Nikolai Ogarev correctly divined that 'the censorship reform constrains the press more than it liberates it'.[72] Some editors believed they would be better off if they refused to take advantage of the new rules and continued to let the censor see their material in manuscript. Valuev foresaw this possibility and let it be known that, in so far as preliminary censorship continued to be available, it would be harsh. Aleksandr Nikitenko believed that Valuev had embarked on 'an enormous plan ... to destroy any tendencies in literature which he considers harmful'.[73] In 1868 Valuev admitted as much. He had been trying, he said, to arm the government with 'preventative, defensive, and repressive measures which were no longer to be found in the earlier legislation on censorship'.[74] The minister's one regret was that he had not been able to implement his scheme in full.

THE WEAKNESSES AND STRENGTHS OF THE REFORMS OF THE 1860S

It did not take sophisticated powers of analysis to deduce from the new rules on the press that the government's reform drive was at an end. Although the tsar emancipated the state peasants in 1866, increased the representative element in the administration of the empire's cities in 1870, and introduced universal military service in 1874, he was much less willing to countenance innovation in the last sixteen years of his reign than he had been in the first ten. None of the later reforms implied that he was seeking fresh fields to conquer. The emancipation of the state peasants was an extension of the emancipation of the serfs, the reform of municipal government a corollary of the introduction of zemstva, the introduction of universal military service a logical consequence of Miliutin's desire to reduce the size of the active army and increase the size of the reserve. Having acquiesced in radical change in the first half of the 1860s, Alexander appeared to confine himself, in the later part of his reign, to tying up loose ends. The death of his eldest son in 1865 probably sapped his morale; an attempt on his life in April 1866 certainly inclined him to view further reform with disfavour; and Prussia's startling victory over Austria at the battle of Sadowa on 21 June / 3 July 1866 required him to devote more time to the changing balance of power in Europe. With the exception of Reitern at the Ministry of Finances and Dmitrii Miliutin at the War Ministry, most of the reform-minded officials who attained senior positions in 1861 and 1862 gave way to conservatives in the second half of the decade. Dmitrii Tolstoi replaced Golovnin at the Ministry of Education, K. I. Pahlen succeeded Zamiatnin at the Ministry of Justice, Aleksandr Timashev replaced Valuev at the Ministry of Internal Affairs, and the Third Department became even more oppressive under Petr Shuvalov than it had been under Dolgorukov.

Alexander may have felt by 1865 that he had completed his programme, but the sudden end of the reform drive also supports the hypothesis that he was not much of an innovator in the first place. Since, in the build-up to the emancipation, he had been slow to accept the need for letting peasants acquire land, and since, after the emancipation, his enthusiasm for change lasted a mere four years, it may be that his reputation as the 'Tsar-Liberator' is ill deserved. Even his victories can be made to look like defeats. The flaws in the emancipation of the serfs mentioned at the end of Chapter Eight can be explained in terms of the constraints on the emancipators' freedom of action, but peasants nevertheless remained the poorest and the most heavily exploited section of the population. Those who engaged in agriculture were not only short of land but also saddled with redemption payments. Those whose principal activities were non-agricultural hardly benefited at all. Communes were supposed to protect the former serfs against their former landlords, but they proved unequal to the machinations of the gentry arbitrators and tended to prevent energetic peasants from striking out on their own. After collating the evidence for the emergence of peasant individualism in the immediate aftermath of the emancipation, Boris Mironov concluded that 'for the time being' collectivism remained the predominant characteristic of the peasants' mentality.[75] By retaining the poll tax and introducing volost' courts the government made plain that it had no intention of granting the peasantry fiscal or juridical parity with the other estates of the realm. The question of abolishing the poll tax cropped up in 1870 and the volost' courts were subjected to detailed scrutiny between 1871 and 1874, but the regime fought shy of additional legislation. The fact that by 1881 the overwhelming majority of peasants had moved from 'temporary obligation' to redeeming their land was not a measure of their enthusiasm for the statutes of 1861 but the result of pressure on the part of the gentry. From the point of view of the peasants, it could be said that the world which the emancipation brought into being barely improved on the world that it brought to an end.

It is also possible to level damning criticisms at most of the reforms that ensued. The government waited a decade before rendering the gentry liable to military service because it feared the consequences of another attack on their interests. When Reitern tried to stabilize the currency he depleted the state's metal reserves so rapidly that the attempt was soon abandoned. The authorities succeeded in changing the way in which the state raised money from vodka but experienced enormous difficulty in persuading the former monopolists of the retail trade to pay off the mammoth credits they had been granted under the system of vodka auctions. Reitern took six years to reorganize the state's revenue-gathering activities and failed to extend his more rigorous accounting procedures either to the state's management of its investment in railways or to the management of financial relations with foreign powers (two of the most significant areas of financial activity). Direct taxation remained inequitable. The poll tax, from which the gentry were exempt, not only survived but was 80 per cent higher in 1870 than it had been when the reforms began. Although it expired a few years after Alexander II's death, the imperial regime legislated for the introduction of an income tax only in 1916.

Church reform took place long after Valuev initiated it in 1862 and hardly embodied the goals for which he had been striving. Between 1867 and 1869 a series of measures on seminaries, ecclesiastical academies, the overpopulation of the clerical estate and the overmanning of churches seemed to reflect a desire on the part of the authorities to rescue clerics from the conditions described by Belliustin; but in reality the state was trying to modernize the church without troubling itself about the majority of the church's servants. The ultra-conservative Dmitrii Tolstoi (who combined the post of Minister of Education with that of Procurator of the Holy Synod) saw merit in rendering the church better able to promote the interests of the state, but cared little for the clerical rank-and-file. His purpose was to create circumstances in which talented priests would prosper but the weakest go to the wall. Even if the measures of the late 1860s had achieved their purpose, they would have brought misery in their train. In the event they 'slightly ameliorated the material condition of a few clergymen', but 'left the Church little better – if not worse – than it was in 1825'.[76]

Wearing his other hat, Tolstoi was hardly the man to breathe life into the universities statute of 1863 or the statutes on primary and secondary education of 1864. He recognized the importance of primary schools and encouraged their growth by creating teacher training colleges and a government inspectorate, but he failed to press for mandatory primary education, he spent only about 6 per cent of the Ministry of Education's budget on the schools themselves, and he stifled local initiatives by intervening more vigorously than his predecessors in the management of the primary network. Admittedly, the decisions he had to make about allocating the funds at his disposal were painful, in view of the fact that the state devoted less than 1 per cent of its total outgoings to the needs of the educational system. He was obliged, furthermore, to pay special attention to secondary and tertiary education, because the government depended on the upper levels of the educational system to produce the requisite number of civil servants. At the secondary and tertiary levels, however, Tolstoi allowed his political prejudices to prevail over the country's need for a highly trained workforce. In 1871 he secured imperial confirmation of the principle that aspiring beneficiaries of tertiary-level education had to complete the course of study on offer at the empire's classical gymnasia. Hitherto it had sometimes been possible to enter university after attending a secondary school which concentrated on modern disciplines. In Tolstoi's opinion, such disciplines bred 'egotism and the formation of the most erroneous concepts'.[77] To be certain that the classical gymnasia were politically inoffensive he increased the number of hours they devoted to Latin and Greek and reduced the time they spent on all other subjects apart from mathematics. Although a student who could read Demosthenes on Philip of Macedon or Cicero on corruption in Sicily was just as likely as a chemist to take an interest in the world around him, at secondary level he was far too beset by declensions and conjugations to imagine the speculative delights which awaited him. At university level Tolstoi improved the supply of professors but prevented a significant increase in the size of the student body by tightening up entrance requirements. Although universities were teaching 60 per cent more students in 1880 than they had taught in 1859, the population as a whole had been growing almost as rapidly; a disproportionate rise in the number of Russian university students was not to take place until the turn of the century.[78]

The zemstva became nests of gentry. Remarkably, Valuev claimed in the mid-1860s that 'In the zemstvo assemblies ... preponderance has been granted to the peasants'.[79] Nothing could have been further from the truth. If the government had indeed created local representative assemblies with the object of including the newly emancipated peasants in the political nation, it would have established them in the western provinces as well as in the imperial heartland. Because it knew perfectly well that they were a means of compensating the gentry for the influence they had lost in 1861, it waited nearly fifty years before bestowing them on a region where the peasants were manageable but the gentry were recalcitrant Poles. Boris Chicherin (who was moving to the right) admired zemstva precisely because they were socially exclusive. His longstanding involvement in the district and provincial assemblies of Tambov left him with 'nothing but happy memories' because 'The zemstvo is the flower of the gentry'.[80] Theoretically, of course, peasants could have played a larger part in the activities of zemstva if they had chosen to do so (which is perhaps what Valuev had in mind when he represented the new assemblies as a concession to the peasants' interests), but in state-designed talking-shops the former serfs were unable to rid themselves of the habit of deference to their former masters. If zemstva had existed at the level of the volost' as well as at the levels of the district and the province, peasants might have considered that they were worth taking seriously on the grounds that they stood a chance of penetrating to the grassroots of society. At the level of the district and the province, however, the new assemblies were too remote from the peasants' concerns to justify the risk of throwing caution to the winds.

If altruistic gentry had taken the zemstva in hand, they might have turned them into constructive devices for the amelioration of local conditions. Only a few gentry were noted for their altruism, however, and the government had been careful to ensure that their chances of exploiting the zemstva were minimal. In the eyes of the government, zemstva were fundraising bodies rather than forums for political discussion. The word 'self-government' (*samoupravlenie*) found no place in the legislation of 1864 (though it appeared in the parallel statute of 1870 which increased the involvement of the public in the running of cities). Although the chairmen of zemstvo executive boards were elected by zemstvo assemblies, they had to be approved by the Ministry of Internal Affairs. The authorities forbade zemstva to collaborate with each other. Because zemstva lacked the power of enforcement they found it difficult even to collect local taxes. In *Anna Karenina*, which came out in the 1870s, Lev Tolstoy's liberally inclined hero Konstantin Levin called his zemstvo 'nothing but a plaything' and 'a means for the local *coterie* to make a little money'.[81] These criticisms were nearer the mark than the impression created by Chicherin's enthusiasm.

If the government's commitment to local assemblies was less than wholehearted, its reconstruction of the judicial system probably erred on the side of utopianism. In respect of the courts the empire's plight was so parlous that reformers more or less started from scratch. Neither the administration nor the public was ready for the ultra-sophisticated blueprint which resulted. The attempt on the tsar's life of 1866 took place at the very time the new courts were opening. Although 'elements of adversarial procedure' figured in the prosecution of the culprits, the commission which dealt with the affair 'acted quite independently of the judicial statutes'. The case was heard behind closed doors in the Peter and Paul Fortress and the press was forbidden to discuss the matter.[82] Even if the authorities had accepted the new constraints on their freedom of judicial action, they faced the enormous problem of convincing a mistrustful citizenry of the value of judicial procedure. Jeffrey Brooks points out that although bandits figure prominently in Russian popular ficton of the period 1861–1917, the Russian bandit was no Robin Hood. His 'realm is not that of justice and equality', for Russian peasants were keener on freedom than order.[83] Persuading them to look for redress in the courts was not something that could be achieved at the stroke of a pen. The government might have had greater success in fostering respect for the law if it had dovetailed peasant courts with the rest of the new judicial system, if it had withdrawn the stipulation that officials could be indicted in the courts only with the consent of their superiors, if it had been committed to forsaking the swingeing punishments at its disposal,[84] and if it had remained true to the principle of jury trials when political violence began to mount in the 1870s, but a society whose legal consciousness was minimal in the 1860s needed decades of tranquillity to digest the unfamiliar notion of abandoning direct action for reliance on lawyers and judges.

Although the zemstva and the transformation of the courts left much to be desired, they were significant enough innovations to render the administration of the Russian countryside yet more complicated than it was already. In view of the fact that many central government ministries had rural offices, provincial governors (who represented the Ministry of Internal Affairs) had always found it difficult to impose themselves on the regions committed to their charge. After 1864 their task became still harder, for they had to vie not only with the employees of other state agencies but also with the new local assemblies and the reconstructed courts. They were still in charge of the rural police, but the police were too few in number to enable them to assert themselves. In times of crisis such as the assassination attempt of 1866 the centre increased the governors' powers, but in the normal course of events they often seemed to belong to the dignified rather than the efficient part of the constitution. Governors, says Richard Robbins, had been 'transformed into general supervisors of a [provincial] administration that they could no longer fully control'.[85] Yet the centre had no thought of abolishing them, for abolition would have meant giving representative bodies more power than the regime was prepared to concede. By preserving the 'ministerial' principle in the countryside while introducing the principle of popular representation St Petersburg probably believed that it was keeping its options open, but its two-faced policy succeeded only in making the confusion of rural administration worse confounded.

The major drawback of the reforms of the 1860s, however, was not the inadequacy of particular edicts or the juxtaposition of old and new, but the tsar's refusal to establish a central representative organ in which the problems attendant upon reform might have been subjected to public scrutiny. For Hugh Seton-Watson, 'The decision against a national assembly in the early 1860's was a turning-point in Russia's history'.[86] There can be no doubt that the decision was taken by the tsar himself, for his own brother and a number of very highly placed officials recognized the advantages to be derived for establishing some sort of central representative body. The Grand Duke Konstantin Nikolaevich returned to the subject constantly.[87] Valuev wrote of the possibility throughout his tenure of the Ministry of Internal Affairs.[88] Aleksandr Golovnin wrote shortly after his dismissal from the Ministry of Education that 'the central government ... ought to transfer part of its activities to local society and ... should summon representatives of society to take part in deciding important affairs of the central power'.[89] The liberally inclined Russian ambassador to Belgium, N. A. Orlov, objected to a pan-imperial parliament on the grounds that the gentry would turn it to their advantage, but in startling letters of 1865 advocated the introduction of local parliaments and the conversion of the state into a federation.[90] Valentina Chernukha almost understates the case when she begins her essay on the parliamentary question under Alexander II by saying that 'the circle of those who advocated the adoption of representative principles was wider than used to be thought'.[91]

The tsar, however, was not to be persuaded. He was keen to run a tight ship but determined not to leave the wheel-house. Two of the major students of his reforms observe that despite the many changes he set in train, 'the concept of state embodied in the person of the autocrat as mediator between various groups in the Russian polity was in no way altered'.[92] Although, in November 1861, Alexander gave formal status to the Council of Ministers he had established in 1857 (thus hinting that he might be prepared to work with a cabinet, if not with a parliament), and although he allowed the notion of a central representative body to be aired in public in 1865, it was not until the very end of his reign, when he was under severe pressure from terrorists, that he broke up the imperial chancery which Nicholas I had made the linchpin of royal authority and accepted modest proposals for involving society in the activities of the central government. Perhaps Valuev was right to complain, in an unguarded moment, that 'our government rests on no moral foundations and acts with no moral authority'.[93] Since the tsar still made law on his own, it may be that the reforms of the 1860s were a grand illusion. In theory, they could have been reversed at any time.

Conceptually limited, poorly executed, incomplete, unsustained and insecure, the measures enacted by Alexander II nevertheless transformed the Russian Empire. The tsar wrought better than he knew. Alfred Rieber, who believes that Alexander's objectives were narrowly military and fiscal, admits that 'the emancipation undermined the whole legal and institutional structure which had existed in Russia since the seventeenth century'.[94] Alexander Gerschenkron, who makes much of the difficulty of tracing a direct link between the abolition of serfdom and the industrial awakening of the Russian Empire (on the grounds that the latter took place twenty years after the former), admits that after 1861 the country possessed a larger 'reservoir from which entrepreneurial talent could emerge', that agricultural output improved on large estates, that 'through the mechanism of redemption payments the role of the money economy was greatly increased', that gentry whose fortunes declined were those whose outlook was 'traditionally averse to industrial development', and that 'Above all, the psychological impact of the abolition of serfdom was immense'.[95] It is not possible here to trace in detail the many respects in which, despite their obvious failings, the new laws of the 1860s improved the empire's prospects. To do so would necessitate going way beyond 1881. By way of concluding the chapter, however, it is perhaps worth considering two of the major criticisms levelled at the 'Great Reforms' and seeing whether they can be countered: first, the proposition that peasants were no better off after the 1860s than they had been before, and second, the view that the prime beneficiaries of the reforms were the gentry.

Most authorities have stressed the respects in which the peasants' economic fortunes declined as a result of the emancipation, but James Y. Simms, Heinz-Dietrich Löwe and Stephen Wheatcroft have begun to put a different view.[96] In a study of the province of Orel between 1861 and 1890 Christine Worobec asks whether the maintenance of the peasant commune damaged the economic fortunes of the peasantry to the extent that it is customary to argue.[97] The population explosion of late imperial Russia, usually included on the negative side of the peasants' ledger, may have been a paradoxical indicator that their lot was improving. Peter Gatrell's explanation of the rise in population turns mainly on the fact that Russian peasants traditionally married young and had large numbers of children.[98] This fails to explain why the rate of increase was much more rapid in the last half-century of the old regime than it had been in the last half-century of serfdom. Without comparing rates of population increase in the pre- and post-emancipation periods it is difficult to grasp that the later rate may have reflected the success of the reform. Gatrell acknowledges that in certain parts of the empire land was available to peasants in the aftermath of the emancipation. He concedes that improved nutrition (though not an improvement in medical services) reduced the perinatal mortality rates of the peasants' children. He discusses the greater ease with which emancipated peasants could leave the land to find work in the cities. But he does not look hard enough for the difference between the pre- and the post-emancipation worlds. As we saw in Chapter Five, enlightened Russians sometimes argued prior to 1861 that serfdom ought to be abolished because serfs were dying out. The argument was probably ill founded, but the fact that it could be put indicated contemporary uncertainty about the population's rate of increase. No such uncertainty was possible in the decades after 1861. Something other than peasant traditions had intervened to make the imperial peasantry one of the fastest-growing communities in the world. The accelerated rise in the peasants' numbers created many difficulties for them, but also testified to improvements in their circumstances and to the fact that they were taking a new view of their opportunities.

After the reforms of the 1860s the peasants' opportunities included the chance to receive an education. Between 1856 and 1878 the number of Russian primary schools increased from just over 8,000 (with 450,000 pupils) to nearly 25,000 (with more than 1 million pupils). Although it failed to make primary education compulsory, the tsarist regime seems to have remained true to the educational commitment it expressed in the statute on universities of 1863 and the statutes on primary and secondary schools of 1864. Admittedly, the number of primary schoolchildren in the imperial population as a whole rose only from seven per thousand in 1856 to twelve per thousand in 1878 (when full enrolment would probably have meant achieving the figure of ninety per thousand), but despite the fact that Dmitrii Tolstoi invested little money in primary schools he appears to have brought significant numbers of schools into being.

In reality the state was not the prime mover in the growth of primary education. In a magisterial book, conveniently summarized in a hard-hitting article, Ben Eklof has demonstrated conclusively that in the generation immediately after the reforms of the 1860s the peasants themselves, not the authorities, took the initiative in developing the lower reaches of the Russian educational network.[99] In the light of Eklof's work it seems unreasonable to relate the growth of Russian primary education to the reforms of the 1860s. The two developments appear to have happened at the same time but not to have been causally linked. It certainly cannot be argued that the government was responsible for the growth of primary schools by virtue of the fact that it created zemstva, for one of Eklof's main points is that the zemstva did not act energetically in the sphere of education until the 1890s. If primary education took off after the emancipation, it took off because of pressure from below rather than in the wake of imperial legislation. In a sense the growth of primary education can even be said to reflect the failure of the reforms, for another of Eklof's points is that peasants sought the ability to read and write in order to prevent themselves being duped by official decrees. They were not interested in education as an abstract good. 'Overwhelmingly, they adopted a survival rather than a profit-maximization approach to schooling'.[100]

It is wrong, however, to make too sharp a distinction between the growth of rural education and the activities of the government, and it is unwise to exaggerate the utilitarianism with which peasants looked upon schools. The first tendency overlooks the fact that, although Alexander II's bureaucrats did little to promote popular schooling, they rarely tried to stand in its way. Not only the community at large but also the government experienced the 'psychological impact of the abolition of serfdom'. The regime was too strapped for cash to increase the peasants' well-being, but it passed facultative legislation and permitted a wider range of social developments than it had been prepared to tolerate earlier in the nineteenth century. In the Russian context, toleration amounted to encouragement. The second tendency (exaggerating the utilitarianism of the peasants' attitude to education) needs to be set in the context of the work of Jeffrey Brooks, who has made clear that between 1861 and 1917 peasants developed an enormous appetite for reading fiction. Brooks's work implies that some of the peasants who learnt how to read in order to protect their traditional interests moved on to higher things, a development which, even without further support, bespeaks a people whose instincts were far from wholly defensive. What peasants read, moreover, strengthens the impression that in the wake of emancipation their aspirations were changing. They tended, for example, to think of 'Success' as something to be achieved in the city. Brooks goes so far as to claim that analysis of the common people's reading matter shows their 'values ... were more consistent with the growth of a market economy in Russia ... than were those of their more educated compatriots'.[101] Literacy remained low in the nineteenth-century Russian Empire – it stood at 21 per cent in the census of 1897 – but after 1861 it was growing rapidly among the young, in the cities, and in the rural as well as the urban parts of the central provinces. Contemporary entrepreneurs were quick to perceive that enlightenment might be profitable. The number of bookshops in the empire went up from 63 in 1864 to 611 ten years later. Book production went up 400 per cent between 1855 and 1881 and was accelerating four times more rapidly in the provinces than in Moscow and St Petersburg.[102] The newly emancipated may not have read Tolstoy and Dostoevsky, but their interest in literacy seems to have gone well beyond the desire to scrutinize official edicts.

Population growth and the peasants' interest in education were signs that, whatever privations the common people suffered in the wake of the emancipation, they believed life had more to offer than it had offered in the past. Neither of these products of the legislation of the 1860s constituted a stated objective of the government, but both owed something to the administration's activities. In some ways, therefore, peasants can be said to have benefited from the regime's innovations. Nobles, meanwhile, may not have been the reforms' main beneficiaries. At first sight, of course, their gains were considerable. They retained the lion's share of agriculturally profitable land; they were well paid for the land they lost; and they quickly came to dominate the zemstva. By 1905, however, they owned 40 per cent less land than they had owned in 1861.[103] Some of those who sold up did so because they had found better ways of investing their wealth, but most had discovered that they were unable to run their estates when they had to pay for labour. The civil service, furthermore, became even less of a noble preserve in the second half of the nineteenth century than it had been in the first. 'The rapid expansion of the bureaucracy in the post-Emancipation decades created a demand for educated manpower which the classes legally eligible for enrollment in the civil service [predominantly the gentry] were unable to satisfy'.[104] Just as non-nobles bought land, so non-nobles continued the process, already well under way, of undermining the gentry's hold on the empire's administration. Non-nobles, moreover, continued to penetrate the gentry estate and to water it down. The edicts of December 1856 which prevented civil servants from achieving ennoblement until they had reached rank four on the Table of Ranks were designed to please the traditional nobility, but failed to prevent entryism. Because, in 1857, there were only 857 civil servants in ranks one to four, it looked as if there were not going to be many opportunities for people to achieve nobility by promotion within the civil service. By 1903, however, there were 3,765 holders of the first four ranks.[105] The government had simply increased the number of offices which carried entitlement to nobility.

If, despite appearances, the reforms of the 1860s can be said to have improved the prospects of the peasantry and reduced the authority of nobles, there can be little doubt that they marked a radical break with the past. There can be little doubt either that improving the prospects of the peasantry and reducing the authority of the gentry was the subtext of the principal reformers' activity. None of the enlightened bureaucrats of the reign of Alexander II was a social revolutionary, but all of them sought greater social fluidity. Like the tsar, they were determined to maintain order, but they were also anxious to discover new sources of energy. If the authorities had been able to forget about rehabilitating the empire in international affairs, and if they had been able to prevent the radical intelligentsia from believing that they could be pressurized into making further concessions, they might have been more obviously successful in their domestic endeavours. As we shall see in Chapters Ten and Eleven, however, these were respects in which their record was poor.

NOTES

1. *Kolokol*, 15 June 1861, p. 846.
2. Gregory L. Freeze, *From Supplication to Revolution: A Documentary Social History of Imperial Russia* (New York and Oxford, 1988), pp. 110, 112, 105.
3. Roger Bartlett, 'A. P. Shchapov, the Commune, and Chernyshevskii', in Bartlett, ed., *Russian Thought and Society 1800–1917: Essays in Honour of Eugene Lampert* (Keele, 1984), p. 70.
4. A. P. Shchapov, 'Rech' vo vremia panikhidy po ubitym krest'ianam v s. Bezdne', in F. F. Kuznetsov, ed., *Shestidesiatniki* (Moscow, 1984), p. 355.
5. A. Sidorov, ed., 'Pis'mo A. P. Shchapova Aleksandru II v 1861 g.', KA 19 (1926), 158.
6. See Gregory L. Freeze, 'A Social Mission for Russian Orthodoxy: *The Kazan Requiem of 1861 for the Peasants in Bezdna*', in Ezra Mendelsohn and Marshall S. Shatz, eds, *Imperial Russia 1700–1917: State, Society, Opposition: Essays in Honor of Marc Raeff* (DeKalb, Ill., 1988), pp. 115–35.
7. *Kolokol*, 15 June 1861, p. 849.
8. Ibid., 15 June – 1 September 1861, pp. 848, 866, 874, 888.
9. Mikh. Lemke, *Ocherki osvoboditel'nogo dvizheniia "shestidesiatykh godov"* (St Petersburg, 1908), p. 359.
10. *Kolokol*, 15 September 1861, pp. 895–7.
11. George Vernadsky et al., eds, *A Source Book for Russian History from Early Times to 1917* (3 vols, New Haven, Conn. and London, 1972), iii. 639.
12. *Kolokol*, 1 July 1861, p. 853.
13. Abbott Gleason, *Young Russia: The Genesis of Russian Radicalism in the 1860s* (Chicago and London, 1983), p. 170.
14. Vernadsky, *Source Book* (above, n. 11), iii. 641.
15. P. A. Zaionchkovskii, 'P. A. Valuev (Biograficheskii ocherk)', in P. A. Valuev, *Dnevnik* (2 vols, Moscow, 1961), i. 28.
16. V. V. Garmiza, ed., 'Predlozheniia i proekty P. A. Valueva po voprosam vnutrennei politiki (1862–1866 gg.)', IA, 1958 no. 1, pp. 141–4.
17. P. A. Zaionchkovskii, *Provedenie v zhizn' krest'ianskoi reformy 1861g.* (Moscow, 1958), p. 131.
18. See, for example, Daniel Field, *The End of Serfdom: Nobility and Bureaucracy in Russia, 1855–1861* (Cambridge, Mass., 1976), p. 52.
19. Terence Emmons, 'The Peasant and the Emancipation', in Wayne S. Vucinich, ed., *The Peasant in Nineteenth-Century Russia* (Stanford, Calif., 1968), p. 71.
20. Valuev, *Dnevnik* (above, n. 15), i. 101.
21. Richard Wortman, 'Rule by Sentiment: Alexander II's Journeys through the Russian Empire', AHR 95 (1990), 765.
22. B. N. Chicherin, *Vospominaniia: Puteshestvie za granitsu* (Moscow, 1932), p. 50.
23. *Kolokol*, 1 December 1858, p. 238.
24. N. I. Tsimbaev, *Slavianofil'stvo: Iz istorii russkoi obshchestvenno-politicheskoi mysli XIX veka* (Moscow, 1986), pp. 134–5.
25. N. Leskov, 'Despotizm liberalov', in Leskov, *Chestnoe slovo* (Moscow, 1988), p. 84.
26. Garmiza, 'Predlozheniia' (above, n. 16), p. 139 (from the editor's introduction).
27. S. M. Solov'ev, *Izbrannye trudy; Zapiski* (Moscow, 1983), p. 345.
28. O. N. Shepeleva, ed., 'Zapiska P. A. Valueva Aleksandru II o provedenii reformy 1861 g.', IA, 1961 no. 1, p. 81.

29. D. C. B. Lieven, 'The Security Police, Civil Rights, and the Fate of the Russian Empire', in Olga Crisp and Linda Edmondson, eds, *Civil Rights in Imperial Russia* (Oxford, 1989), p. 250.

30. E. Willis Brooks, 'Reform in the Russian Army, 1856–1861', SR 43 (1984), 68.

31. Ibid., p. 77.

32. Quotations from P. A. Zaionchkovskii, 'D. A. Miliutin (Biograficheskii ocherk)', in D. A. Miliutin, *Dnevnik* (4 vols, Moscow, 1947–50), i. 31, 21, and, on the proposals of January 1862, from Forrestt A. Miller, *Dmitrii Miliutin and the Reform Era in Russia* (Nashville, Tenn., 1968), p. 33.

33. Martin McCauley and Peter Waldron, *The Emergence of the Modern Russian State, 1855–81* (Basingstoke and London, 1988), p. 83.

34. A. P. Pogrebinskii, *Ocherki istorii finansov dorevoliutsionnoi Rossii (XIX–XX vv.)* (Moscow, 1954), p. 56.

35. David Christian, *Living Water: Vodka and Russian Society on the Eve of Emancipation* (Oxford, 1990), p. 359.

36. I. S. Belliustin, *Description of the Clergy in Rural Russia: The Memoir of a Nineteenth-Century Parish Priest*, ed. and tr. Gregory L. Freeze (Ithaca, NY and London, 1985), p. 159.

37. P. A. Valuev, 'Duma russkogo vo vtoroi polovine 1855 goda', RS 79 (1893), 512.

38. Gregory L. Freeze, *The Parish Clergy in Nineteenth-Century Russia: Crisis, Reform, Counter-Reform* (Princeton, NJ, 1983), p. 239.

39. Gregory L. Freeze, 'P. A. Valuyev and the Politics of Church Reform', SEER 56 (1978), 86.

40. R. G. Eimontova, *Russkie universitety na grani dvukh epokh: Ot Rossii krepostnoi k Rossii kapitalisticheskoi* (Moscow, 1985), p. 108.

41. William L. Mathes, 'The Origins of Confrontation Politics in Russian Universities: Student Activism, 1855–1861', CSS 2 (1968), 32.

42. Patrick L. Alston, *Education and the State in Tsarist Russia* (Stanford, Calif., 1969), p. 48; Eimontova, *Russkie universitety* (above, n. 40), pp. 229, 304; Daniel R. Brower, *Training the Nihilists: Education and Radicalism in Tsarist Russia* (Ithaca, NY and London, 1975), p. 127.

43. B. N. Chicherin, *Vospominaniia: Moskovskii universitet* (Moscow, 1929), pp. 32–3.

44. D. Gorbov, ed., 'Iz dnevnika V. K. Konstantina Nikolaevicha', KA 10 (1925), 227.

45. Alston, *Education and the State* (above, n. 42), p. 51.

46. James T. Flynn, 'Russia's "University Question": Origins to Great Reforms 1802–1863', *History of Universities* 7 (1988), 25.

47. W. Bruce Lincoln, *The Great Reforms: Autocracy, Bureaucracy, and the Politics of Change in Imperial Russia* (DeKalb, Ill., 1990), p. 91.

48. S. Frederick Starr, *Decentralization and Self-Government in Russia, 1830–1870* (Princeton, NJ, 1972).

49. *Kolokol*, 1 September 1858, p. 181; for a slightly more temperate outburst on the same subject from the Governor of Tobol'sk, see Lemke, *Ocherki osvoboditel'nogo dvizheniia* (above, n. 9), pp. 456–67.

50. V. V. Garmiza, *Podgotovka zemskoi reformy 1864 goda* (Moscow, 1957), p. 131.

51. Robert J. Abbott, 'Police Reform in the Russian Province of Iaroslavl, 1856–1876', SR 32 (1973), 293.

52. L. G. Zakharova, *Samoderzhavie i otmena krepostnogo prava v Rossii* (Moscow, 1984), p. 214, as translated in Zakharova, 'Autocracy and the Abolition of Serfdom in Russia, 1856–1861', *Soviet Studies in History : A Journal of Translations* 26, no. 2 (Fall 1987), p. 84.

53. P. P. Semenov-Tian-Shanskii, *Memuary, t. 3–4: Epokha osvobozhdeniia krest'ian v Rossii (1857–1861 gg.)* (Petrograd, 1915–16), iii. 243–4.

54. Vernadsky, *Source Book* (above, n. 11), iii. 613.

55. Alston, *Education and the State* (above, n. 42), p. 58.

56. For the education minister's dark reflections see *Kolokol*, 1 April 1861, p. 801; on the Sunday school movement in general see Lemke, *Ocherki osvoboditel'nogo dvizheniia* (above, n. 9), pp. 399–438; Reginald E. Zelnik, 'The Sunday-School Movement in Russia, 1859–1862', JMH 37 (1965), 151–70; and I. T. Dronov, 'Pervye voskresnye shkoly v Rossii', VI, 1970 no. 6, pp. 198–202.

57. V. Z. Smirnov, *Reforma nachal'noi i srednei shkoly v 60–kh godakh XIX v.* (Moscow, 1954), p. 142.

58. Ben Eklof, *Russian Peasant Schools: Officialdom, Village Culture, and Popular Pedagogy, 1861–1914* (Berkeley, Calif., 1986), p. 64.

59. H. McCoubrey, 'The Reform of the Russian Legal System under Alexander II', *Renaissance and Modern Studies* 24 (1980), 122.

60. M. G. Korotkikh, 'Sudebnaia reforma 1864 g. v Rossii', VI, 1987 no. 12, p. 32.

61. C. A. Frierson, 'Rural Justice in Public Opinion: The Volost' Court Debate 1861–1912', SEER 64 (1986), 529.

62. Alexander Herzen, *My Past and Thoughts*, tr. Constance Garnett (rev. edn, 4 vols, London, 1968), i. 180.

63. Shepeleva, 'Zapiska P. A. Valueva' (above, n. 28), p. 79.

64. Richard S. Wortman, *The Development of a Russian Legal Consciousness* (Chicago and London, 1976), p. 258; for a less subtle interpretation of the importance of Valuev's memorandum in the genesis of the judicial reform see B. V. Vilenskii, *Sudebnaia reforma i kontrreforma v Rossii* (Saratov, 1969), p. 123.

65. Vernadsky, *Source Book* (above, n. 11), iii. 614.

66. 'Dnevnik Velikogo kniazia Konstantina Nikolaevicha', VI, 1990 no. 8, pp. 145–6.

67. W. Bruce Lincoln, 'The Problem of *Glasnost'* in Mid-Nineteenth Century Russian Politics', ESR 11 (1981), 181.

68. E. M. Feoktistov, *Za kulisami politiki i literatury 1848–1896* (Leningrad, 1929), p. 132.

69. Daniel Balmuth, 'Origins of the Russian Press Reform of 1865', SEER 47 (1969), 375.

70. V. G. Chernukha, *Pravitel'stvennaia politika v otnoshenii pechati 60 – 70-e gody XIX veka* (Leningrad, 1989), p. 32.

71. Valuev, *Dnevnik* (above, n. 15), i. 183, 391.

72. *Kolokol*, 17 August 1865, p. 1656.

73. Aleksandr Nikitenko, *The Diary of a Russian Censor*, abr., ed. and tr. Helen Saltz Jacobson (Amherst, Mass., 1975), pp. 297–8.

74. Valuev, *Dnevnik* (above, n. 15), ii. 446.

75. Boris Mironov, 'The Russian Peasant Commune after the Reforms of the 1860s', SR 44 (1985), 463.

76. Freeze, *Parish Clergy* (above, n. 38), p. 459.

77. Allen Sinel, *The Classroom and the Chancellery: State Educational Reform in Russia under Count Dmitry Tolstoy* (Cambridge, Mass., 1973), p. 145.

78. Samuel D. Kassow, *Students, Professors, and the State in Tsarist Russia* (Berkeley, Calif., 1989), table on p. 16.

79. Garmiza, 'Predlozheniia' (above, n. 16), p. 148.

80. B. N. Chicherin, *Vospominaniia: Zemstvo i Moskovskaia Duma* (Moscow, 1934), p. 20.

81. L. N. Tolstoy, *Anna Karenin*, tr. Rosemary Edmonds (Harmondsworth, 1954), p. 31 (pt I, ch. 5).

82. N. A. Troitskii, *Bezumstvo khrabrykh: Russkie revoliutsionery i karatel'naia politika tsarizma 1866–1882gg.* (Moscow, 1978), pp. 71–2.

83. Jeffrey Brooks, *When Russia Learned to Read: Literacy and Popular Literature, 1861–1917* (Princeton, NJ, 1985), p. 186.

84. For the one edict of the 1860s which did significantly modify the penalties to which criminals were subjected, see Bruce F. Adams, 'Progress of an Idea: The Mitigation of Corporal Punishment in Russia to 1863', *The Maryland Historian* 17 (1986), 57–74.

85. Richard G. Robbins, Jr., 'His Excellency the Governor: The Style of Russian Provincial Governance at the Beginning of the Twentieth Century', in Mendelsohn and Shatz, *Imperial Russia 1700–1917* (above, n. 6), p. 77.

86. Hugh Seton-Watson, *The Russian Empire 1801–1917* (Oxford, 1967), p. 352.

87. As L. G. Zakharova reiterates in her introduction to the recent publication of part of his diary: VI, 1990 no. 5, p. 112.

88. Valuev, *Dnevnik* (above, n. 15), i. 101, 119, 181, 209, 324–5; ii. 14–15, 19.

89. W. Bruce Lincoln, 'Reform and Reaction in Russia: A. V. Golovnin's Critique of the 1860's', CMRS 16 (1975), 171.

90. A. S. Nifontov, 'Pis'ma russkogo posla N. A. Orlova 1859–1865 gg.', in B. S. Itenberg et al., eds, *Revoliutsionery i liberaly Rossii* (Moscow, 1990), p. 233; and Feoktistov, *Za kulisami* (above, n. 68), pp. 57–9.

91. V. G. Chernukha, *Vnutrenniaia politika tsarizma s serediny 50-kh do nachala 80-kh gg. XIX v.* (Leningrad, 1978), p. 15.

92. Jacob W. Kipp and W. Bruce Lincoln, 'Autocracy and Reform: Bureaucratic Absolutism and Political Modernization in Nineteenth-Century Russia', RH 6 (1979), 16.

93. Valuev, *Dnevnik* (above, n. 15), ii. 155.

94. Alfred J. Rieber, 'Alexander II: A Revisionist View', JMH 43 (1971), 48.

95. A. Gerschenkron, 'Agrarian Policies and Industrialization: Russia 1861–1917', in *The Cambridge Economic History of Europe*, vol. 6, ed. H. J. Habakkuk and M. M. Postan (Cambridge, 1965), pp. 764–5.

96. James Y. Simms, Jr., 'The Crisis in Russian Agriculture at the End of the Nineteenth Century: A Different View', SR 36 (1977), 377–98; Heinz-Dietrich Löwe, *Die Lage der Bauern in Russland 1880–1905* (Sankt Katharinen, 1987); Stephen G. Wheatcroft, 'Crises and the Condition of the Peasantry in Late Imperial Russia', in Esther Kingston-Mann and Timothy Mixter, eds, *Peasant Economy, Culture, and Politics of European Russia, 1800–1921* (Princeton, NJ, 1991), pp. 128–72.

97. Christine D. Worobec, 'The Post-Emancipation Russian Peasant Commune in Orel Province, 1861–90', in Roger Bartlett, ed., *Land Commune and Peasant Community in Russia: Communal Forms in Imperial and Early Soviet Society* (Basingstoke and London, 1990), pp. 86–105.

98. Peter Gatrell, *The Tsarist Economy 1850–1917* (London, 1986), pp. 49–61.

99. Eklof, *Russian Peasant Schools* (above, n. 58), and Eklof, 'Peasants and Schools', in Eklof and Stephen Frank, eds, *The World of the Russian Peasant: Post-Emancipation Culture and Society* (Boston, Mass., 1990), pp. 115–32. The figures in the previous paragraph are taken from p. 116 of Eklof's article.

100. Eklof, 'Peasants and Schools' (above, n. 99), p. 118.
101. Brooks, *When Russia Learned to Read* (above, n. 83), p. 296. 'Success' is the title of Brooks's ch. 8 (pp. 269– 94).
102. Brooks, *When Russia Learned to Read* (above, n. 83), p. 110; I. I. Frolova et al., eds, *Kniga v Rossii 1861–1881* (3 vols, Moscow, 1988–91), i. 20.
103. A. P. Korelin, *Dvorianstvo v poreformennoi Rossii 1861–1904gg.: Sostav, chislennost', korporativnaia organizatsiia* (Moscow, 1979), p. 286.
104. Jerry Lee Floyd, 'State Service, Social Mobility, and the Imperial Russian Nobility, 1801–1856', unpublished PhD dissertation, Yale University, 1981, p. 297.
105. Ibid., p. 295.

CHAPTER TEN

Russia and Europe

RUSSIAN FOREIGN POLICY IN THE POST-CRIMEAN ERA

At the start of *Russia and Europe*, which first appeared in a St Petersburg journal in 1869, the scientist and philosopher Nikolai Danilevskii pointed out that although Britain and France had come to the defence of the Ottoman Empire in 1854, they had done nothing to resist the Austro-Prussian attack on Denmark ten years later. He explained this inconsistency by arguing that the Great Powers of central and western Europe were hypocritical in their attitude to international relations. Quite prepared to sanction aggression when they undertook it themselves, they objected to forward moves on the part of anybody else. Russia, Danilevskii concluded, should refuse to work with them; she should reject conventional diplomacy and develop the resources of Slavonic culture.[1]

In part, Danilevskii was responding to Russia's humiliation in the Crimean War. In so far as he grasped the extent to which the war left Russia isolated, his argument was sensible. If he had gone on to recommend neutrality and pacifism – which, as we shall see, he did not – *Russia and Europe* might have been a force for good. In the immediate aftermath of the Crimean disaster the Russian Empire was in no position to play a significant part in international affairs. The military and naval operations of the war had been relatively minor, but the diplomatic effects had been considerable. The war, says David Wetzel, had been fought 'to remake the European order'.[2] From the point of view of the victors it appeared to have been a success, for the reduction of Russian power certainly brought the old order to an end. From the point of view of St Petersburg, long-term reliance on Austria and Prussia had turned out to be a mistake. The various officials who had urged Alexander II's predecessors to adopt a British orientation – Kochubei at the beginning of the century, Capodistria after the Congress of Vienna, Nesselrode under Nicholas I – had been right to point out the dangerous consequences of taking a different course. Good relations with Britain now looked impossible. Russia had so little to bargain with that it was difficult for her to make friends with anyone. The clauses

of the Peace of Paris which demilitarized the Black Sea were 'more puni-
tive than any terms presented to a Great Power in the whole of the nineteenth century'.[3] In international relations, adopting a low profile seemed
to be the Russian government's only option.

Aleksandr Gorchakov, who succeeded Nesselrode at the Ministry of
Foreign Affairs in 1856, appeared to accept the empire's fate. In a widely
publicized circular of 21 August / 2 September he announced that Russia
forswore interventionism. He seemed almost to anticipate Trotsky's off-the-
cuff remark about publishing a few proclamations and shutting up shop.[4]
The tsar, he said, not only would abandon all thought of assisting his fellow autocrats, but also for the time being would abandon international
affairs altogether; Russia had to concentrate on domestic reconstruction.
Gorchakov often returned to the theme of the 1856 circular in the twenty-
six years he held office. In 1865 he told the tsar that 'In the present circumstances of our state and of Europe as a whole, Russia's main attention must
be unrelentingly focused on the realization of the business of our domestic
development; all external relations must be subordinated to this fundamental task'.[5] In late 1876 the foreign minister was exasperated to learn that
'some people in England' still thought St Petersburg had designs on the
Ottoman Empire. 'What proof', he asked rhetorically, 'must be given to the
English ministry of a disinterestedness based not on political virtue but on
reason and common sense?'.[6]

Yet Gorchakov was less pacific than he pretended to be. Even the 1856
circular had ominous undertones. Its most famous sentences, 'Russia is not
sulking. Russia is thinking' (*La Russie ne boude pas. La Russie se
recueille*),[7] combined the resignation of Job with the wrath of Achilles.
Gorchakov had no intention of consigning his ministry to inactivity. He
told Kiselev, the new Russian ambassador to France, that he was 'looking
for a man who would help him annul the clauses of the treaty of Paris concerning the Black Sea fleet and the borders of Bessarabia, that he was looking for him and he would find him'.[8] These apparently modest ambitions
implied the entire rejection of the Crimean settlement. Gorchakov was cautious, but he was much less cautious than Nesselrode.

Even if his inclinations had been entirely peaceable, he did not make
foreign policy on his own. Less temperate souls played a part. The Ministry
of Finances stood for peace, but the Ministry of War was prepared to take
chances. The ever inscrutable Alexander II was 'ready enough to listen to
warnings that the moment was not ripe for a forward policy', but 'consist-
ently backed the expansionists' when he thought that they had a chance of
success.[9] The diplomat Nikolai Ignat'ev disagreed fundamentally with
Gorchakov on the need for proceeding with care, yet managed to retain
the crucial post of ambassador to Constantinople for the greater part of the
1860s and 1870s. Sometimes – in another anticipation of Soviet developments – Ignat'ev differed from the head of the foreign ministry in St Petersburg as much as the Comintern differed from the Commissariat of Foreign
Affairs in the first half of the 1920s.[10]

279

Ignat'ev kept his job not only because certain members of the government supported him, but also because he spoke for significant elements in the community at large. The latter consideration was more important than it had been in the first half of the century. The days had passed when a tsar could change the course of the empire's foreign policy in an audience with a foreign ruler on a raft in the Niemen. Foreign affairs were becoming public property. The Ministry of Internal Affairs possessed draconian powers over the press, but it had to use them with care. The trenchant letters of Mikhail Pogodin had failed to persuade Nicholas I to raise the banner of Slavonic confederation at the time of the Crimean War, but only a few years later the right-wing journalist Mikhail Katkov had to be taken more seriously. The government came under intolerable pressure from the public in the Balkan crisis of 1875–8. Between April and September 1876, when Turks were slaughtering Bulgarians, more than a thousand articles appeared on Bulgaria in the sixteen most widely distributed Russian newspapers.[11] By that time even Russian peasants seemed to be taking an interest in the Slavs of the Ottoman Empire. Of the fifteen thousand rubles collected on the Bulgarians' behalf in the province of Pskov, twelve thousand came from the countryside.[12] The letter of 22 October / 3 November 1876 in which Gorchakov expressed indignation at British mistrust of Russia's intentions also acknowledged that 'national and Christian sentiment in Russia ... imposes on the Emperor duties which His Majesty cannot disregard'.[13]

But the tsar did not send his troops into the Balkans in 1877 simply because the public was baying for blood. He was also the victim of a shifting diplomatic environment and a newly minted interventionist ideology.

Inadvertently, Nikolai Danilevskii's *Russia and Europe* illustrated the novelty of the post-Crimean diplomatic environment when it criticized the difference between the way in which Britain and France reacted to conflict between Russia and Turkey in 1854 and the way in which they reacted to conflict between the Germanic powers and Denmark ten years later. The first of these conflicts had a lengthy pedigree, but the second heralded the start of something new. In the period between the Congress of Vienna and the Crimean War the Germanic powers had rarely fought wars. Prussia had even avoided most of the fighting which took place between 1792 and 1815. After attacking Denmark, however, Prussia went on to fight Austria in 1866 and France in 1870. In 1871 Bismarck brought much of German-speaking Europe into a Prussian-led German Empire. Many considerations played a part in the transformation of Prussia from the least to the most important of the continental Great Powers, but one of them was certainly the fact that although the Crimean War had destroyed the Concert of Europe, it had failed to put anything in its place. All European diplomats understood the fluidity of the post-Crimean context. In 1856 France appeared to be the principal beneficiary of the change in the balance of power, but Napoleon III appreciated that he would have to take additional risks if he were to become the linchpin of a new European order. His considerable prestige was of too recent origin to pass unchallenged. Prussia shortly discovered in Bismarck the outstanding diplomat of the age and exploited the fault-lines in the Crimean settlement more effectively than her continental rivals. In the exciting times that resulted, an already weakened Russia ran the risk of being weakened further unless she maintained a high level of diplomatic activity. Even if he had wanted to do so, Gorchakov could not easily have distanced the Russian Empire from international affairs. He was bound to take a view on the many issues to which the Crimean settlement gave rise or which it failed to resolve. Russia could neither maintain the reduced international role she had been assigned in 1856 nor pursue domestic reform unless the external environment promised a certain predictability. Because the dismissal of the Russian Empire from European affairs threw the international environment into disarray, Russians had to involve themselves in diplomacy whether they chose to or not.

The transformation in the fortunes of Prussia reflected not only the power vacuum created by the outcome of the Crimean War but also the material importance, in mid-nineteenth-century Europe, of the ideology of nationalism. That a relationship existed between nationalist ideology and the creation of the German Empire is undeniable, though how it operated in practice has been a subject of much controversy. Russia's intellectual frontiers were permeable and she had been developing a sense of her national identity since at least the turn of the century. Despite appearances to the contrary, neither of the two principal manifestations of Russian nationalism under Nicholas I, the regime's policy of 'Official Nationality' and the Slavophiles' emphasis on the virtue of immemorial Russian customs, had had the effect of greatly altering the Russian view of the outside world. Under Alexander II, however, Russian nationalism mutated. Broadly speaking, it followed the path that nationalism was taking elsewhere. Although, at the time of the central and west European revolutions of 1848, nationalists had tended to form alliances with liberals in the cause of change, after 1848 nationalism became identified ever more closely with the right of the political spectrum. A few nationalists went on trying to persuade subjugated peoples to break with their masters, but most tended to be conservatives who sought to bolster existing regimes or militants who sought to impress on foreigners the superior merit of their ethnic group.

Alexander II's empire contained nationalists of all the contemporary types. Subversives, the Poles who started the rebellion of 1863, seemed not to pose the authorities undue problems, if only because the one thing on which the vast majority of Russians agreed was that Poles had to be kept in their place. Even Polish nationalism, however, involved the empire in international complications. The tsar insisted that his Polish subjects were his own affair, but Napoleon III (whose nationalism was of the militant variety) chose to believe otherwise. By the time the Russians had put down the Polish rebellion of 1863–4 they had been so vigorously condemned in Europe that their international standing was probably lower than it had been in 1856. Since, however strongly they believed in devoting themselves to reform at home, the tsarist authorities could not allow their credibility in the world at large to disappear altogether, the effect of the Polish revolt was to increase their desire for diplomatic rehabilitation.

The bolstering and acquisitive varieties of nationalism, which were closely related, found their respective outlets under Alexander II in Russian attitudes towards Asia and the Balkans. Their importance for the course of Russian foreign policy was greater than that of the subversive variety, for Asia and the Balkans affected the vital interests of the other Great Powers. Although, under Alexander II, Russian activity in Asia resulted in the acquisition of a great deal of territory, whereas Russian activity in the Balkans did not, it was still the case that the former sprang mainly from a desire to enhance the Russian Empire's prestige whereas the latter issued from a preconceived desire to alter international boundaries. Despite the extensive arguments of N. A. Khalfin and others, it does not seem likely that Russia sought additonal territory in central Asia because she thought it would benefit her. Historians divide more or less equally on the question whether economic considerations or enhanced prestige were the predominant factor in Russia's central Asian policy, but those who place the emphasis on enhanced prestige seem to be having the better of the argument.[14] With respect to the Balkans, on the other hand, Russians who urged a forward policy usually did so out of a desire for acquisition. The foreign minister was not of their number (except in respect of southern Bessarabia, the small strip of land between the Russian Empire and the Danube delta which St Petersburg had lost in 1856), but the foreign minister was far from being master in his own house. Ignat'ev at Constantinople pressed constantly for aggressive action, and behind Ignat'ev stood ideologues whose voice grew louder by the day.

These were the proponents of panslavism, a doctrine which in its extreme form spoke of liberating the Slavs of the Ottoman and Habsburg Empires and uniting them under the Russian banner. Panslavism could be made to look noble. In so far as it drew attention to the virtue of indigenous Slavonic cultures, it was an international variant of Slavophilism, whose emphasis on religion and tradition had been quietist. In so far as it dealt in movements of national liberation, it belonged to the subversive branch of nationalism which sometimes made common cause with liberalism. But at heart it was acquisitive. Most Russian panslavs were really pan-Russianists. Their main reason for promoting Slavonic culture was to increase Russian power. Having begun by pointing out the two-faced response of the principal European countries towards active foreign policies in different parts of the continent, Danilevskii's *Russia and Europe* did not go on to argue that the hypocrisy of the West required Russia to retreat into her shell. On the contrary, the book's thesis was that attack was the best form of defence. Russia should establish a Slavonic Union with its capital in Constantinople. 'Both Turkey and Austria', Danilevskii said, 'have lost all reason for existing'. They were dead on their feet, 'insanitary like all corpses, the source of peculiar illnesses and infections'.[15] What kept them in being was the fact that they were useful pawns in the hands of diplomats who believed in maintaining a European balance of power. The concept of the balance of power, in Danilevskii's view, had to be abandoned. 'Sooner or later,' he believed, 'a [Russian] struggle with Europe (or at least with the greater part of Europe) is inevitable on account of the Eastern Question, on account of the freedom and independence of the Slavs, on account of control over Constantinople, on account of everything that in the eyes of Europe is the focus of Russia's illegal ambition, but in the eyes of every Russian worthy of the name is the inescapable requirement of her historical calling'.[16] *Russia and Europe* left its readers in no doubt that if Danilevskii had his way conflict would arise in the immediate future.

Panslavists were unpopular with the Russian foreign ministry. Gorchakov used distinctly undiplomatic language when he ridiculed one of them by saying that she would not be happy until she was sitting on the dome of Saint Sophia in Constantinople. Behind Danilevskii's ponderous tract lay a racism that in other hands (and in other countries) was to bring Europe to its knees. *Russia and Europe* contained a theory of the 'Slavonic cultural-historical type' that reeked of ill-digested Darwinism. Yet in the sense that Danilevskii epitomized the feeling of humiliation to which many educated Russians fell victim in the wake of the Crimean War, he was not alone. Gorchakov knew only too well that the Russian Empire would be unwise to risk another war, but he was not averse to using the tool Danilevskii excoriated – traditional diplomacy – to make up the ground the country had lost. Ignat'ev at Constantinople, Dmitrii Miliutin at the Ministry of War, Russian generals in Asia, and probably the tsar were prepared to go further. If they had been capable of taking a broad view of the needs of their country, they would have been pacific to the point of inertia. After a generation of international predominance, however, they had difficulty in reconciling themselves to marginalization. They had even less reason for doing so at a time when rivalries among European countries were intensifying and the chances of profiting from Europe's disarray were considerable.

In view of the range of opinion and the number of influences which acted on Russian foreign policy under Alexander II, it is hardly surprising that the narrative of Russian foreign affairs between 1856 and 1881 reveals considerable confusion. Russia might be said to have pursued three tactics, the western, the eastern and the southern. The first took the form of forging new ties with the principal states of central and western Europe; the second meant enlarging the scope of Russian activity in Asia; the third involved returning to the general area of the 1850s defeat. All three tactics were discernible throughout the reign, but their relative importance changed repeatedly. Foreign policy seemed to take a new turn every seven years. The first tactic, looking for allies among the Great Powers, prevailed over the other two between the end of the Crimean War in 1856 and the Polish rebellion of 1863. The second tactic, Asian expansion, predominated in the seven years between 1863 and the Franco-Prussian War of 1870. The third tactic, a return to the south (or what from a western perspective was the 'Eastern Question'), took over in 1870 and culminated in Russia's attack on Turkey in 1877. Continuing to think in terms of a Concert of Europe (the western tactic) while acquiring additional territory (the eastern tactic) and trying to claw back the losses of 1856 (the southern tactic) was a recipe for confusion and disappointment. The inability to settle on a single tactic, however, reflected the empire's fundamental difficulty: its powerlessness. By the end of the reign the western and southern tactics had been found wanting and the potential of the eastern tactic had been almost exhausted.

COURTING FRANCE (1856–63)

At the time of the Polish rebellion of 1863 the Russian ambassador to Belgium said that 'apart from internal reforms a great power must have alliances, which ... would give it the chance to devote itself to the improvement of its internal way of life in peace and quiet. We devoted ourselves to the latter but forgot about the former. It has turned out that at the first sign of a problem everyone is against us'.[17] This was an unduly negative account of the way in which Russia had been conducting her foreign affairs since 1856. She had indeed been seeking allies, but her endeavours had failed to generate beneficial relationships. The one significant country with which St Petersburg was on good terms in 1856 was the United States, but America was of little value as an ally in Europe. Prussia had barely harmed the Russians in the course of the Crimean War, but was not a maritime power and could play no part (in the 1850s) in the reopening of the Black Sea to Russian warships. Russia needed to deal with countries whose interest lay in adjustments to the European order. Two of the Crimean victors, Piedmont and France, fell into this category. The Piedmontese had sent troops to the Black Sea in the hope of gaining support from the Great Powers in their quest for territorial gains in northern Italy. The French supported the notion of change in Italy because Piedmontese gains would be made at the expense of Austria, whose defeat would undermine the anti-French diplomatic arrangements of 1815.

Like Piedmont and France, Russia was anti-Austrian. After the way in which Vienna had repaid her during the Crimean War for her assistance in Hungary in 1849, she sought revenge. Various individually trivial manoeuvres signalled her rapprochement with the north Italians. In October 1856 the tsar's mother took up winter residence at the Piedmontese resort of Villafranca near Nice. Victor Emmanuel II called on her in January 1857. Russian ships began arriving from the Baltic. In February 1857 the Grand Duke Konstantin Nikolaevich, brother of the tsar and head of the Russian Naval Ministry, received the highest Piedmontese decoration at a ceremony in Turin. 'Nice, for a time, appeared to have become almost a Russian city'.[18]

From the point of view of St Petersburg, however, France was potentially much more useful than Piedmont. The Crimean War had been only the first of Napoleon III's attempts to disrupt the balance of power. In 1854 he was anti-Russian, but his real *bête-noire* was the Concert of Europe. In September 1857 the tsar met Napoleon III at Stuttgart. The Grand Duke of nearby Baden thought the meeting presaged French intervention in southern Germany,[19] but Napoleon's ambitions lay elsewhere. At Stuttgart Alexander promised not to come to the Austrians' assistance if France joined Piedmont in an attack on the Habsburg provinces of Lombardy and Venetia. In September 1858, when Napoleon sent his cousin to meet the tsar in Warsaw, Alexander agreed not only to remain neutral in the event of a French war with Austria, but also to move a Russian corps to the Austrian border. The French, in their turn, promised to assist the Russians in their endeavour to escape from the restrictive clauses of the post-Crimean peace treaty.

Napoleon had not yet revealed the full extent of his plans. In December 1858 a French naval officer brought draft written agreements from Paris to St Petersburg. France now proposed that Russia take Vienna's eastern province of Galicia in return for permitting the French acquisition (from Piedmont) of Savoy and Nice. If Austria fell prey to internal disorder as a result of the forthcoming war, Russia was to sanction the emergence of an independent Hungary. France, in her turn, would support Russian abrogation of the demilitarization of the Black Sea. Napoleon was to give St Petersburg a month's notice of the outbreak of war; St Petersburg was to sever diplomatic ties with Vienna a few weeks after the commencement of hostilities.

Gorchakov thought these proposals benefited France to a much greater extent than they benefited Russia. The Grand Duke Konstantin Nikolaevich agreed with him. After meeting Napoleon III in Paris at more or less the same time as the French naval officer was negotiating in St Petersburg, he reported to the tsar that France was seeking not just Russian neutrality but 'our active assistance'. Napoleon understood, the Grand Duke said, that Russia's finances and her preoccupation with emancipating the serfs prevented her from attacking Austria herself, but Paris nevertheless sought Russian collusion in the reconstruction of Europe. According to Konstantin, Napoleon's vision extended far beyond the Lombard plain. He sought to turn the continent against Great Britain by strengthening France and Russia, weakening Prussia and the lesser German states, and destroying the power of Austria. In other words, he sought to renew the Tilsit alliance of 1807. For the first time, Konstantin believed, the French Emperor had shown his hand.[20]

Russia's interest lay only in the abrogation of the Black Sea clauses of the Peace of Paris. Even if she had been convinced that France would support her in the achievement of this goal (which she was not), she had no intention of encouraging plans that would lead to a general conflagration. Whereas a short war in north Italy might give rise to diplomatic exchanges from which the Russian Empire could profit, Napoleon's grand design threatened to engulf the continent. Russia agreed a treaty with France on 19 February / 3 March 1859, but promised no more than 'benevolent neutrality' in the event of a Franco-Piedmontese attack on Austria. The treaty also stated that if war broke out in north Italy other countries were to be informed 'that this struggle cannot endanger the interests of great mutual powers, whose balance of power will not be affected'.[21] Having signed the treaty, Russia went on trying to solve the Italian problem through diplomatic channels. Some scholars have argued that the point of her diplomatic activity in March and April 1859 was to clear the way for France's onslaught, but a recent student has demonstrated that its purpose was rather different: 'the cardinal problem, from the point of view of Russian diplomacy' was no longer the intensification but the 'localization' of the Italian crisis.[22]

French and Piedmontese forces duly invaded Austria's possessions in north Italy, but the French pulled out of the war after about two months without facilitating the extension of Piedmont to the Adriatic. Napoleon III was aware that without the wholehearted support of Russia he stood no chance of bringing Austria to her knees. Russia mobilized very slowly on Austria's eastern flank. Napoleon contented himself, in 1859 and 1860, with sponsoring the transfer of various Habsburg-ruled lands to Piedmont in return for the cession of Savoy and Nice. The idea of supporting St Petersburg in a public call for the remilitarization of the Black Sea went by the board. The Russian colony at Villafranca, still centred on the Dowager Empress, objected almost as loudly as Garibaldi to the transfer of Piedmontese territory to France. Russia's first attempt at finding an associate in central or western Europe had been a failure. Gorchakov vented his spleen in a letter to Kiselev: 'the Emperor of the French', he wrote, 'will always find us on his side in all questions in which our collaboration will benefit France and not harm Russia, but he should not count on us as a weapon in combinations designed to further his personal vainglory'.[23]

Thus the western dimension of Russian foreign policy bore little fruit in the years immediately after the Crimean defeat. Asian developments were more encouraging. It would be naive to argue that because the Russians were stymied in Europe they turned automatically to the opposite end of their domains, but it was convenient for them that N. N. Murav'ev had been urging expansion in the Far East since his appointment as Governor of Eastern Siberia in 1847. In 1849–50 Murav'ev argued the case for moving the empire's frontier to the river Amur. Britain, he said, would take the mouth of the river unless the Russians got there first. Kamchatka could be supplied more easily by river than by land. Trade with China had been in decline since Britain's victory in the Opium War of 1839–42 and would improve only if the Amur were in Russian hands. Control of the Amur would enable Russia to compete with Britain as the principal foreign influence within the Chinese Empire as a whole.[24] Murav'ev began acting on his own advice in the early 1850s, but it was not until the first years of Alexander II that he carried his policy to its logical conclusion. As a result of the Russo-Chinese Treaties of Aigun and Tientsin, which were signed in 1858, and the Treaty of Peking, signed in 1860, Russia acquired not only the left or northern bank of the Amur but also the land between the river Ussuri and the Sea of Japan.[25] In effect, she revised in her favour the entire basis on which Russo-Chinese relations had been conducted since the Treaty of Nerchinsk of 1689. She acquired an enormous if sparsely populated tract of territory, a common frontier with Korea, much greater proximity to Japan, and the potential for greatly improved access to the Pacific. In 1858 she founded the city of Khabarovsk and in 1860 Vladivostok. The question of annexing the strategically important island of Sakhalin was next on her agenda. The maritime powers of western Europe looked upon these gains with envy, but if Russia maintained good relations with the United States she stood a good chance of containing their animosity. Murav'ev recognized that sooner or later Russia would have to cede Alaska to the Americans, and recommended as early as 1853 that St Petersburg surrender the province with a good grace in order to cement her friendship with Washington.[26]

The late 1850s also witnessed Russian successes elsewhere in Asia, in the Caucasus and the vast Muslim region between the western edge of China and the Caspian. By capturing Shamil in 1859, Prince Bariatinskii eliminated the last real pocket of Caucasian resistance to Russian rule. When Ignat'ev, the future ambassador to Constantinople, undertook a diplomatic mission to the central Asian khanates of Khiva and Bukhara in 1858, he revived the debate among Russians about how best to secure the region from northward penetration on the part of the British. Article Six of the Treaty of Peking of 1860 gave Russia the right to trade at Kashgar in Sinkiang, which abutted on Afghanistan and was in some ways the gateway to India. Yet Russia behaved much more cautiously in the Caucasus and central Asia than she behaved in the Far East. In one of his many statements of the need for restraint Gorchakov impressed upon the head of the Asiatic Department of the Ministry of Foreign Affairs that 'the immutable rule underlying our policy [is] not to rush ahead lest we go backwards later'.[27] Not only the foreign ministry and the Ministry of Finances but even the Ministry of War resisted the notion of taking risks. British interests in central Asia were too great to make risk-taking advisable. Ignat'ev's mission to Khiva and Bukhara took place at the invitation of the local khans and was entirely an exercise in information-gathering. The khans were more or less permanently at odds with each other and sought to involve the Russian Empire in their quarrels, but St Petersburg was not to be tempted. Even in the Caucasus the tsar had to proceed with care. On a visit to Tiflis in September 1861 he sought to reconcile the Georgian nobility to the loss of their serfs, but the subsequent resolution of the land question left Georgian ex-serf-owners in a much better position than their counterparts in other parts of the empire.[28] Since Murav'ev's activities in the Far

East required the foreign ministry to keep a close watch on the responses of Britain and France, neither Alexander nor his advisers were prepared to take on other Asian problems.

In the Balkans, paradoxically, St Petersburg behaved with some confidence. In 1856 Gorchakov agitated for the right to take back an island in the Black Sea where Russia had maintained a lighthouse before the Crimean War. He then provoked dissension between Britain and France on the matter of the new Danubian frontier between the tsarist and Ottoman empires.[29] Whereas Nicholas I had rarely shown much interest in Balkan minorities, Alexander viewed them as a possible resource. In 1856 Gorchakov expressed disapproval of the French idea that Montenegro should acknowledge Turkish suzerainty. In 1858 he proposed an international conference on the question of constitutional instability in Serbia. When the almost independent principalities of Moldavia and Wallachia both elected Alexander Cuza as their sovereign in 1859 (in contravention of rules laid down by the Great Powers), Russia backed them and managed 'to counteract to some degree the unpopularity left from the period of the [Russian] protectorate'.[30] When Mikhail Obrenović ascended the Serbian throne in 1860 and began working for the full independence of his country, St Petersburg showed signs of a readiness to support him. When, in the same year, Bulgarians set out on the long road which led to the separation of their branch of the Orthodox Church from the Greek Patriarchate of Constantinople, Russia offered them a certain degree of encouragement.[31]

But the Russian government had by no means committed itself to the doctrine of panslavism. Gorchakov took fright when the Turks bombarded Belgrade in 1861. The tsarist regime's need for peace took precedence, for the time being, over its desire for revenge. Russian intellectuals were bolder than the authorities. Almost every issue of *Russian Colloquy*, the Slavophile journal which came out in Moscow from 1856 to 1860, found room for work on the Slavs of the Habsburg and Ottoman Empires.[32] The first of a number of 'Slavonic Benevolent Committees' came into being in Moscow in 1858. Turgenev included a Bulgarian revolutionary in his novel *On the Eve* of 1859. Aleksei Khomiakov wrote a celebrated open letter to the Serbs in 1860 in which he asserted that Russians 'could never be as sympathetic toward any other peoples as toward you and the other Slavs, particularly those of the Orthodox faith'.[33] Although some of these expressions of solidarity with the Slavs of the Balkans went too far for the taste of St Petersburg, and although very few of them received a wide circulation, a climate of opinion was gradually emerging in which Danilevskii and other thinkers of the late 1860s would find themselves at home.

THE CONSEQUENCES OF THE POLISH REBELLION
(1863–70)

One of the effects of the Polish rebellion of 1863 was to require advocates of Slavonic solidarity to focus exclusively on the Balkans or to give up pan-slavism for pan-Russianism. But the effects of the rebellion were numerous. It reminded Russians that relations with nations at home could be as problematical as relations with nations abroad; it further reduced the tsar's chances of finding a worthwhile ally among the Great Powers; and it probably inclined the imperial regime to take bigger risks in Asia. At home, it made clear that Nicholas I's 'Official Nationality' had failed to knit the empire into a coherent whole; abroad, it necessitated the realignment of the western, southern and eastern strands in Russian foreign policy.

The immediate causes of the rebellion lay in Alexander II's abandonment of his father's vigilance. Mikhail Gorchakov, cousin of the imperial foreign minister, succeeded Ivan Paskevich as Viceroy of the Congress Kingdom in 1856 and relaxed the regime's authoritarian policies. Warsaw received an archbishop and a medical school. Progressive Polish landowners were permitted to set up an Agricultural Society which they quickly turned into a surrogate parliament. For many reasons – not only concessions on the part of the Russians, but also propaganda on the part of Polish *émigrés* in western Europe, movements for national liberation among Romanians and Italians, the beginnings of constitutional reform in adjacent Austria, the Polish sympathies of Napoleon III, the activities of radical students, the patriotism of junior army officers, and the tsar's concern for social reform in the empire at large – the Poles of the Congress Kingdom fell prey to a crisis of rising expectations. Their excitement reached fever pitch in early 1861. In January they demonstrated on the thirtieth anniversary of the battle of Grochów (one of their successes in the rising of 1830–1). When a second demonstration in the middle of the following month led to five deaths, 'mass indignation swept Warsaw'.[34] The tsar needed calm to enact the emancipation of the serfs. In the hope of assuaging Polish unrest he included in the administration of the Congress Kingdom the Marquis Wielopolski, a realist who sought to further the interests of the Polish gentry without promoting confrontation with Russia. Wielopolski's fellow gentry regarded him as a collaborator and obliged him to withdraw to St Petersburg. In May 1862 he returned as prime minister under a new Viceroy, the Grand Duke Konstantin Nikolaevich. Reforms ensued in education, in the condition of Polish Jewry, in the relations between landlords and peasants, and in the ethnic complexion of the Kingdom's administration, but the tide of unrest continued to swell. 'Polish magnates ... wished to make it clear that they would never voluntarily endorse Poland's partitions';[35] Polish radicals wished to undo the partitions altogether. Battle commenced in January 1863.

The 'January Insurrection' proved harder to put down than the 'November Uprising' of 1830 because it took the form of an insurgency rather than a war between regular armies. The Russians defeated most of the rebels in 1863 but were still mopping up resistance in October 1864. They failed to prevent unrest from penetrating the western region of the empire proper. Although the inhabitants of the three southernmost of the western provinces took little part in the rising because the social engineering of Nicholas I had emasculated the local Polish nobles,[36] the central and northern borders of the Congress Kingdom posed many difficulties. Alexander II was particularly resistant to the idea of permitting links between the Kingdom and the eastern lands of the former Polish-Lithuanian Commonwealth. Soon after the insurrection broke out he put the die-hard M. N. Murav'ev in charge of the northern part of the western region, where he earned the nickname 'hangman of Vil'na'.

In one respect, however, St Petersburg responded to the Polish rebellion with a reluctant subtlety. After Wielopolski and the Grand Duke Konstantin gave up their positions in the Congress Kingdom in the summer of 1863, the principal figure in the Russian administration became the rehabilitated Nikolai Miliutin. By calling out of retirement one of the principal architects of the emancipation of the serfs, the tsar declared an interest in tackling the social as well as the national causes of Polish unrest. The Agricultural Society founded in Warsaw in 1857 had devoted much of its attention to the relationship between landlords and peasants. Whoever succeeded in converting the peasants' labour dues into cash rents – or better still, into freeholds – stood a chance of winning their gratitude. Although the insurgents proclaimed a land reform on the day they launched the revolt, they needed time to convince the peasants of their sincerity. Before Miliutin's arrival in Warsaw, St Petersburg had already come close to matching the rebels' agrarian policy in the western provinces. As a result of Miliutin's labours it matched them in the Congress Kingdom too. Valuev, the Minister of Internal Affairs, was mistaken when he complained, in December 1863, that the Russian authorities had failed to come up with 'an idea which at least one Pole could adopt as his own'.[37] Polish peasants (who were not the people Valuev had in mind) stood to gain almost as much from the Russians as they would have gained if victory had gone to the rebels. More peasants joined the insurgents of 1863 than had joined the Polish rebellions of 1794 and 1830, but not enough to give the revolt a chance of success.

The Russians, however, lost as much in victory as the Polish gentry lost in defeat. Perceptive Russian officials knew that reinstating the anti-Polish policy of Nicholas I would get St Petersburg nowhere. Nikolai Orlov, the Russian ambassador to Belgium, went further than most of his fellow-countrymen when he recommended making the tsar's brother King of Poland and granting the country a much larger degree of independence, but Valuev spoke for many contemporaries when he acknowledged in private that Russian political culture was simply too unattractive to persuade the Poles of its merits.[38] Introducing policies designed to turn future generations of Poles into Russians also constrained the regime in its handling of the lesser imperial minorities. Like the Poles, the lesser minorities had derived certain advantages from the change of reign. The tsar revived the Finnish Diet when the January Insurrection was still in progress.[39] He lifted many of the restrictions on Jews.[40] The three major Ukrainians whom his father had prosecuted in 1847, Shevchenko, Kulish and Kostomarov, inaugurated an influential phase in the definition of the Ukrainian identity at the end of the 1850s which culminated in the publication in St Petersburg in 1861 and 1862 of the journal *The Foundation* (*Osnova*). After 1863, the regime thought twice about allowing national minorities to go their own way. Whether or not Kostomarov was right to say that before the Polish revolt Russians tended to welcome the enthusiasm of Ukrainians for the development of their language and literature, in July 1863 Valuev instructed the Minister of Education to act as if 'there was not, is not, and cannot be any special Little Russian [i.e. Ukrainian] language'.[41] The post-1863 backlash affected Finns and Jews less severely than Ukrainians, but only because Finns were too few in number to constitute a threat to the empire and certain Jews welcomed Russian culture as a means of escaping from their own. Non-Russians suffered much less severely at the hands of Alexander II than they did at the hands of his father, son and grandson, but after the Polish rebellion St Petersburg no longer felt able to permit them untrammelled development. Russian policy towards the lesser minorities of the empire was in disarray.

Foreign policy, meanwhile, had to be wholly restructured. St Petersburg had maintained an uneasy friendship with France after the Italian events of 1859, but the French response to the Polish rebellion brought the relationship to an end. France had been pro-Polish since the end of the eighteenth century. Napoleon III had sought to raise the Polish question both at the Paris negotiations which put an end to the Crimean War and at his meeting with Alexander II in Stuttgart in 1857. When his cousin visited Warsaw in 1858, Poles began to believe that French influence lay behind the more liberal treatment they were receiving at the hands of the Russians. Napoleon was acting out of self-interest. Like the campaigns in the Crimea and north Italy, unrest in Russian Poland gave him a chance of upsetting the European order which the Great Powers had established at the end of the Napoleonic Wars. If he had been able to unite the continent behind a policy which obliged St Petersburg to grant the Poles further concessions, he might have made France the arbiter of European affairs. At first he enjoyed a measure of success. Early in 1863 not only the British Foreign Office but certain unusual elements in British society seemed ready to join a campaign on the Poles' behalf.[42] Austria had occasion to feel dissatisfied with Russia because of Russia's mobilization on her Galician frontier in 1859. The combination of France, Britain and Austria was reminiscent of the coalition which had defeated the tsar in 1856. If an anti-Russian coalition had been reassembled, it would have started to look permanent. The French seemed to be determining the course of international relations.

In the event, St Petersburg stood up for itself and Napoleon's plans evaporated. In November 1863 the Emperor of the French admitted that his attempts to put pressure on the Russian Empire had come to nothing.[43] His alternative was a pan-European Congress to discuss the entire settlement of 1815, but this was a non-starter because Britain feared French aggrandizement and Austria could only lose from a reconstruction of Europe. Napoleon's diplomatic activity during the Polish crisis failed to promote French interests. No one else, however, seemed to profit from his embarrassment. Russia, after all, lost the one foreign associate with whom she had established a tentative friendship, while Austria antagonized everyone by trying to plot a middle course between conciliation and aggression.[44]

The principal beneficiary of the Polish crisis of 1863 turned out to be Prussia. Soon after the Polish rebels raised their banner the authorities in Berlin despatched General Alvensleben to St Petersburg to promise the return of Polish fugitives who fled to their territory. The agreement to which the mission gave rise, the Alvensleben Convention, marked the beginning of a collaboration with Russia which lasted twenty-seven years. It is very unlikely that Bismarck knew where the convention might lead.[45] He probably sought an agreement with the Russians merely in order to increase the tsar's determination to put down the Poles, for Prussia had to prevent the rebellion in the Congress Kingdom from infecting her own Polish subjects. Since Russia was well disposed towards Prussia anyway because of the family ties between the Romanovs and the Hohenzollerns, and since the convention lapsed in just over a month because Gorchakov 'regarded [it] as unnecessary and rather humiliating',[46] Alvensleben's mission hardly seemed to change anything. But it predisposed St Petersburg to support Berlin in the years ahead, at a time when good relations between the two capitals benefited the latter much more than the former. Bismarck's wars of 1864, 1866 and 1870 changed the map of Europe to Russia's detriment. One of Russia's traditional foreign policy concerns was to perpetuate the existence of two Germanic powers. When Prussia outdistanced Austria, St Petersburg's chances of coping with central Europe diminished. A generation after the creation of the German Empire in 1871 Russia had to go to war to prevent German control of the continent. Had the tsar not moved closer to Berlin as a result of the crisis of 1863 he might have understood more clearly that the startling European events of the later 1860s were threatening his long-term interests. Although he seemed, as a result of the Polish crisis, merely to replace one western associate with another, in reality the western dimension of his foreign policy was becoming harder to handle than ever.

The eastern dimension offered better prospects. Having acquired large tracts of territory on the Pacific seaboard in the late 1850s, Russia spent the 1860s investigating their resources and improving her chances of defending them. Nikolai Przheval'skii, the greatest of nineteenth-century Russian explorers, won his spurs in the vicinity of the Ussuri in 1867. The tsar strengthened the empire's diplomatic position in the Far East by currying favour with the United States. When tension was at its height in Europe in

1863 he put himself in the Americans' debt by seeking shelter for his warships in New York and San Francisco. At the same time St Petersburg deferred to American commercial interests by signing an agreement under which Americans were to lay telegraph cables across the Bering Straits and Siberia. The construction of the telegraph link was abandoned when a cheaper link across the Atlantic was completed in 1866, but Russia still earned respect for her willingness to cooperate. In 1867 St Petersburg parted with Alaska. Some Americans doubted the wisdom of buying it in view of the fact that the territory appeared to be worthless, but there could be no doubt that by surrendering its foothold on the eastern coast of the Pacific the Russian Empire was making plain its deference to Washington. By the end of the 1860s Russia had acquired a valuable eastern counterweight to Britain and France, both of whom viewed her Pacific gains with disquiet.

The Polish rebellion not only played a part in encouraging St Petersburg to seek closer relations with Washington but also upset the ever-fragile balance within the tsarist administration on the subject of the central Asian khanates. Russian policy towards Muslim Asia in the 1850s had consisted mainly of information-gathering, but in the middle of the Polish crisis the tsar lent his name to a change of course. Although Reitern, the Minister of Finances, secured official endorsement in February 1863 of his long-held opinion that attacking the khanates was unwise, Dmitrii Miliutin, the Minister of War, began pressing for an eastern adventure when tension over Poland reached its peak in July. Miliutin believed that if Russia dominated the khanate of Kokand, 'we can constantly threaten England's East Indian possessions. This is especially important since only there can we be dangerous to this enemy of ours'.[47] For once, the Ministry of Foreign Affairs accepted that a diversion in central Asia might be advantageous. The tsar took the hawks' advice and issued an order to 'close the lines' – to bridge the gap between the lines of Russian forts that were already encroaching on Kokanese territory from Siberia and the Aral Sea. The closure of the lines by Colonels Cherniaev and Verevkin in June 1864 turned out to be the beginning of a twenty-year campaign of conquest. Cherniaev exceeded his brief. After trying and failing to take Tashkent in October 1864 he succeeded in June 1865 and brought Russian forces to the central Asian oases. Forts had been enough to keep watch on Muslim nomads, but dealing with the settled population of the oases required the introduction of day-to-day administration. In July 1867 the tsar created the Governor-Generalship of Turkestan and ended the regime's longstanding practice of running its central Asian affairs from the faraway cities of Omsk and Orenburg. Although Bukhara, Kokand's western neighbour, had awoken to the Russian threat, it could not prevent the first Russian Governor-General, Kaufman, from capturing Samarkand in 1868 and dictating a commercial convention which gave St Petersburg 'everything that for almost three centuries Russia's envoys had been unable to obtain'.[48] By the end of the 1860s Russia seemed to have as much reason for congratulating herself on the success of her central Asian policy as she had for taking pride in the Far Eastern gains of the late 1850s.

Few senior bureaucrats, however, were prepared to acknowledge in public that the conquest of central Asia was an unmixed blessing. Cherniaev earned no praise for exceeding his orders. He lost his command in 1866 and was not to return to the land he had conquered until Alexander III appointed him Governor-General of Turkestan in 1882. The near-unanimity which emerged among the makers of Russia's central Asian policy in 1863 broke down almost as soon as it materialized. Reitern still objected to expansion for financial reasons. Valuev thought expansion bizarre. On learning that Cherniaev had taken Tashkent he confided to his diary that 'No one knows why or for what' and that 'There is something erotic [sic] in everything we do on the far-flung periphery of the empire'.[49] Gorchakov feared the reaction of the outside world. In a circular of November 1864 designed for communication to foreign governments he tried to allay suspicion by saying that Russia's position in central Asia was 'the same as the position of any civilized state which comes into contact with a semi-barbarous people'. Either St Petersburg had to 'condemn its frontiers to endless disturbances' or it had to 'move further and further forward'. In choosing the latter course it was 'motivated less by ambition than by extreme necessity'. Russia was merely responding to circumstances in the way Americans responded to them in the West, the French in Africa, the Dutch in South-East Asia, and the British in India.[50]

If Gorchakov meant what he said, Russia acquired her central Asian empire more by accident than design. She certainly does not appear to have been motivated by the prospect of material gain. The major study of trade relations between Russia and central Asia in the generation before the military take-over concludes that although the tsarist government had a natural interest in improving its economic standing, its principal reason for becoming ever more deeply involved in the affairs of the khanates was to prevent Britain taking control of them from the south.[51] David Mackenzie propounds the even simpler explanation that St Petersburg lost control of the army. The emollient tone of Gorchakov's circular may have been genuine, he says, but 'pious statements were powerless to halt ambitious generals'.[52]

These arguments are dubious. One should be careful about attributing Russian imperialism to wayward soldiers, domino theory, or the fit of absence of mind. The tsar approved of Cherniaev's triumphs. Gorchakov may not have sought the capture of Tashkent, but at the beginning of 1865 he also told the Governor of Orenburg not to allow it to be captured by Bukhara. Dmitrii Miliutin participated in the drawing-up of Gorchakov's circular, but privately regretted that the Ministry of Foreign Affairs was tying the government's hands.[53] Although the aggressively inclined Nikolai Ignat'ev had to give up the directorship of the Asiatic Department of the foreign ministry in 1864, he was immediately appointed Russian minister in Constantinople, a position which gave him at least as many opportunities for promoting a forward policy as he had had in St Petersburg. In other words, it is risky to argue that the central government was committed to a policy of minimal involvement in central Asian affairs. Although nineteenth-century Russians often 'manifested a striking degree of unease about their place in European civilization', they seem to have been unanimous in the view that 'Russia was the bearer of the fruits of civilization in Asia'.[54] Gorchakov and Miliutin had to tread softly when explaining Russia's central Asian policy to foreigners, but it is unreasonable to suppose that they could not have brought the generals' activities to an end if they had wanted to do so.

After Ignat'ev took up residence at Constantinople, St Petersburg's policy on the southern frontier of the empire became almost as hard to pin down as its reasons for annexing territory in central Asia. Unabashed by the loss of the directorship of the Asiatic Department, Ignat'ev elaborated a view of Russia's objectives in the south which appeared to differ dramatically from the views of his superiors. He agreed with Gorchakov that the primary objective of southern policy ought to be the remilitarization of the Black Sea, but he also advocated Russian domination of Ottoman policy-making and a Russian-led Slavonic union to subvert the Habsburgs and challenge Bismarck. Since the second and third of these goals meant war, and since Gorchakov, in Ignat'ev's opinion, 'preferred fine-sounding phrases and brilliant diplomatic fictions to real practical action',[55] severe disagreement between the ambassador and his minister looked inevitable. It duly surfaced in 1866, when a German prince became King of Romania and Crete rebelled against Turkey. On the one hand, the installation of a Hohenzollern on the Romanian throne looked to Russians like the eastward march of German power; on the other, an Orthodox rebellion against the Sultan gave St Petersburg an opportunity to counterbalance the Romanian developments by cultivating support for the rebels.

Ignat'ev used the Cretan rebellion to build castles in the air. In an official memorandum of late 1866 he insisted that 'events do not wait for our military and economic preparedness. They arise independently of our will, and force us to adapt ourselves to them'.[56] In Ignat'ev's view, Russia ought to be provoking unrest throughout the domains of the Sultan. She should pressurize the Kingdom of Greece to support both the rebels in Crete and all other disaffected Greeks who remained in Ottoman hands. To make further difficulties for Constantinople, St Petersburg should promote the idea of an alliance between Greece and Serbia. Since the prince of Serbia had been attempting to unite the Slavs of the Balkans from the moment he ascended the throne, he would enter into a Greek alliance in the hope of rallying Bulgarians, Montenegrins and Bosnians to the cause. The result would be a rising of Christians from the Bosphorus to the Adriatic and from Belgrade to the southern Aegean. Russia, Ignat'ev believed, should remain on the sidelines but 'reserve her right to raise her voice when the unavoidable antagonism should appear between Greeks and Slavs'.[57]

What was remarkable about this plan of campaign was not that it failed to win support in St Petersburg but that it failed to get Ignat'ev the sack.

Although Ignat'ev acknowledged that Russia was not yet in a position to press for the dissolution of the Ottoman Empire, his policy spelt danger. There was never any chance of its adoption by the tsar. The only tangible indication of official sympathy for the cause of the Greeks might be said to have been the marriage of the King of Greece to the daughter of the Grand Duke Konstantin Nikolaevich in 1867. After the death of the Serbian prince who dreamed of Balkan union, Serbia became Austrophil. The Cretan question was resolved at a conference in Paris in 1869 at which advocates of the status quo won a total victory. In view of Russia's material weakness, these developments were predictable. The mystery of Russia's official policy in the south in the 1860s was not that it was cautious, but that the man principally charged with its implementation seemed to be wholly at odds with it. Why did St Petersburg allow Ignat'ev to remain at his post?

The answer seems to be two-fold: public opinion supported him and Gorchakov was less pacific than he seemed to be. In the 1860s educated Russians were much more inclined to take an interest in the fortunes of their Slavonic cousins than they had been in the 1850s. More than 200 articles on the Slavs of the Balkans appeared in the journal *The Voice* between 1863 and 1869.[58] Chernyshevskii's cousin, the academically inclined but politically motivated Aleksandr Pypin, published a two-volume *Survey of Slavonic Literatures* in 1865. The Moscow Slav Congress of 1867, which attracted twelve Serbs, two Montenegrins, one Bulgarian and sixty-three representatives of the Slavonic minorities of the Habsburg Empire, evoked a 'public display of sympathy' in Russia which 'would have been unthinkable only a decade before'.[59] Slavonic Benevolent Committees like that founded in Moscow in 1858 sprang up in St Petersburg in 1868, in Kiev in 1869, and in Odessa in 1870. Although hardly anyone seems to have read Danilevskii's *Russia and Europe* when it first appeared in 1869, General Rostislav Fadeev's contemporaneous, like-minded and much briefer *Opinion on the Eastern Question* became a best-seller.

The rise of Russian panslavism in the 1860s probably owed most to an intellectual who was not really a panslav at all. Mikhail Katkov, who became editor of the semi-official *Moscow News* in 1863, responded to the Polish rebellion with a fearsome Russian nationalism. He spoke so strongly in favour of the maintenance of an absolutely unitary imperial state that even the government believed he should express himself more tactfully.[60] His nationalism was also the principal determinant of the way in which he looked at the world beyond the empire's borders. His interest lay not in panslavism but in pan-Russianism – in upsetting a European order which prevented Russia from exercising the authority she had enjoyed in the first half of the century. He was completely devoid of mystical leanings and possessed none of the Slavophile commitment to Orthodoxy and rusticity. Nevertheless, his view of international relations put him in the panslav camp. Although his vision of Russian domination differed sharply from the panslav dream of a community of free Slavonic nations in which even Poles had equal status with their cousins, both conceptions entailed the subversion of the Ottoman and Habsburg Empires and the promotion of the Slavonic communities of south-eastern Europe. Until Europe was reconstructed there was little to choose between Katkov's pan-Russianism and the activities of the various Slavonic Benevolent Committees. If Gorchakov had tried to dismiss Ignat'ev from the Russian Embassy at Constantinople, he would have had to reckon not only with a climate of opinion in which Russians were becoming gradually more sympathetic to Slavs in other countries, but also with *Moscow News*, the most influential of contemporary Russian newspapers.

Gorchakov's views, however, were not quite as far removed from those of Ignat'ev as they appeared to be. The two men differed on means rather than ends. When Prince Carol of Hohenzollern-Sigmaringen became King of Romania in 1866, the Russian Ministry of Foreign Affairs argued that his election was illegal because the peace treaty which ended the Crimean War prohibited the installation of a non-Romanian on the throne of Moldavia or Wallachia. Since Russia's general hostility to the Peace of Paris was well known, her attempt to rely on it in a matter of detail made her look not only hypocritical but also short of diplomatic resources. Yet Gorchakov was shrewder than his critics. If the international community had supported him Prince Carol would have been deposed, Romania weakened, and Russia's position on her south-western frontier strengthened; if, on the other hand, the new king remained on the throne – which he did – Russia could argue that the framers of the Peace of Paris were disregarding it and that the tsar, in his turn, could disregard the part of the treaty which prevented Russia from constructing a fleet in the Black Sea.

In other words, Gorchakov was no less determined than Ignat'ev to upset the international order and return the Russian Empire to its rightful position of power. His methods were different, but his goals were similar. He was careful, but not inert. His assessment of Russia's international situation at the end of 1866 revealed the subtlety of his position. On the one hand, he advised caution. Russia had little material power at her disposal. Domestic reforms would eventually put the country in a position to engage in political and cultural struggle and reassume the mantle of protector of the Balkan Slavs, but for the time being St Petersburg had to avoid violence, concentrate on moral leadership, negotiate international agreements and use what influence it possessed to avoid complications. On the other hand, a crisis was approaching. Many considerations supported the view that the Crimean settlement was breaking down: the north Italian war of 1859 and the subsequent emergence of the Kingdom of Italy; the Austro-Prussian attack on Denmark in 1864; the recent war between Prussia and Austria; Italy's acquisition of Venice and her hunt for allies on the eastern side of the Adriatic; intrigues on the part of the French; the activities of Polish emigrants in French service; the economic penetration of the Ottoman Empire by both France and Britain; the likelihood that Austria would attempt to make up the ground she had lost in Germany by turning her attention south-eastwards; the increasingly evident frustration of the Balkan

Slavs and their probably justified belief that Russia would be obliged to fight on their behalf if they rose against their Turkish masters.[61] By listing these developments, Gorchakov implied that a time was coming when Russia would have to take action. In a way he relished the prospect. He was certain that Russia would not have to take on two European powers simultaneously.[62] He disagreed with Ignat'ev about tactics, but not about strategy.

ATTEMPTING TO PROFIT FROM THE FRANCO-PRUSSIAN WAR (1870–5)

Gorchakov struck in 1870. A brief period of cooperation with France and Austria in 1866 and 1867 persuaded him that attempts to reverse the outcome of the Austro-Prussian War might have the unfortunate effect of reviving the Polish question. In 1868 he turned back to Prussia.[63] On 19/31 October 1870, in the middle of the Franco-Prussian War, he announced that Russia would no longer observe the clauses of the 1856 settlement which prevented her from constructing a Black Sea fleet. Gorchakov argued that the peace of 1856 had been infringed many times. The Great Powers had allowed the Romanian principalities to join forces with each other in 1859 and to elect a foreign prince as their ruler in 1866, but had done nothing to assist the other Christian inhabitants of the Ottoman Empire. Whole squadrons of foreign warships had violated the Black Sea's neutrality. The invention of ironclads made foreign navies more threatening than they were in the 1850s. In these circumstances, the tsar could no longer consider himself bound by the peace of 1856 in so far as it limited his 'sovereign rights' in the Black Sea.[64]

St Petersburg appeared to have broken its bonds. Gorchakov had achieved the goal which he set himself on becoming foreign minister. The policy of close association with Prussia seemed to have proved its worth. Just after the abrogation of the Black Sea clauses the tsar gave another indication of his new-found self-confidence. On 5 November 1870 he announced major changes in the army. The war minister was to draw up recommendations on 'the extension of direct involvement in military service ... to all estates of the realm'.[65] Nine years after coming into office, Dmitrii Miliutin had received permission to introduce universal conscription.

These measures, the abrogation of the Black Sea clauses and the commitment to universal conscription, give the impression that in the autumn of 1870 the tsarist regime abandoned conciliation for militancy. Up to a point, the impression is correct. There had been straws in the wind even before 1870, for the foundation of the Putilov Works in St Petersburg in

1868 and the mining town of Iuzovka in the south-eastern Ukraine in 1869 both implied concern for the sinews of war. For three years after November 1870 Miliutin concentrated on turning the principle of universal conscription into reality. Discussion turned on the length of time recruits were to serve, on whether they could buy themselves out, whether higher education should confer immunity, whether exemptions should be granted to the inhabitants of certain parts of the empire, and how the government was to select the 30 per cent of the relevant age agroup that it needed at any one time. The press took a lively interest in the government's proceedings. *The Voice*, for example, approved of conferring exemption from the draft on educational grounds and of the idea that no one should be allowed to buy himself out, but sought special treatment for clerics of various creeds and for artists. Heated discussions took place in 1873 in a commission of the State Council chaired by the Grand Duke Konstantin Nikolaevich. Gorchakov, at this stage, wanted to move more slowly than Miliutin. In the final debates, which took place in the general assembly of the State Council, participants were treated to the engaging spectacle of the minister of education arguing the case against educational exemptions while the minister of war argued the case in favour. But on 1 January 1874 universal conscription became law. In theory, all males over the age of twenty-one were to be liable for military service irrespective of their social origins. One of the major distinctions between the gentry and the other estates of the realm had been abolished. Strictly speaking, the regime had gone back on Peter III's decree of 1762 which freed Russian nobles from the obligation to serve the state. The universality of conscription marked an important stage in the development of the concept that subjects of the tsar were equal before the law. In practice, of course, the law of 1874 worked imperfectly. Gentry who were determined to escape their military duty usually succeeded in finding a part of the law which enabled them to do so. Although the government obtained more recruits, between 1874 and 1880 about half of those subject to the draft escaped it by invoking the statute's clauses on the number of males in a household.[66] The numbers of those who secured exemption on educational grounds were few but went up steadily (which at least meant that the introduction of the new law persuaded elements in the community whose commitment to education had not been very great to take it more seriously). The loopholes, however, were less important than the fact that the new rules on military recruitment succeeded in frightening foreign countries. *The Times* of London said that Russia had 'never yet sent more than 150,000 men across her frontiers', whereas in future she would 'dispose of at least 500,000 for a foreign war'.[67] The Russian bear seemed to be sharpening its claws.

The notion that the tsar had moved on to the offensive can be supported by the way in which he conducted the eastern dimension of his foreign policy. In 1875 Japan was obliged to accept that Russia had established its control over the island of Sakhalin. In central Asia, meanwhile, the Emir of Bukhara had been trying to play off his enemies against each other. While seeking the Russian Governor-General's assistance in the pacification of rebels in the eastern part of his domain, he had tempted the rebels with a promise of independence if they could drive the Russians out. The short-term consequences of this policy were less damaging than they might have been, but drawing the Russians ever more deeply into the affairs of the region was to ensure that eventually they controlled it completely. In the course of putting down the rebels of Bukhara, the Russian Governor-General engaged in military activity in all three of the Muslim khanates. To restore order he obliterated Kokand and tied Khiva to Russia's apron strings. Bukhara retained a suprising degree of independence, but only because Kaufman chose to be generous.[68] Meanwhile, Russia was developing the second of her routes into the central Asian heartland. Whereas in 1865 she had reached Tashkent from the north, in 1869 she founded Krasnovodsk on the eastern shore of the Caspian and put herself in a better position to threaten Khiva and Bukhara from the west. By the middle of the 1880s she had conquered what was to become the Soviet republic of Turkmenia and established her writ from the Kara Kum to the Pamirs. After 1985 even Soviet historians abandoned the vain attempt to claim that central Asia became Russian because the natives of the area for some reason welcomed annexation.[69] Alexander II's policy towards the region was one of barely controlled aggression.

In abrogating the Black Sea clauses, introducing universal military service and continuing to extend the empire's authority in the Far East and central Asia, Russia appeared to have thrown caution to the winds. In reality, however, she hedged her bets. The circular on the remilitarization of the Black Sea went less far than it might have done. It made no reference to Russia's second biggest cause for complaint about the settlement of 1856, the fact that it cut her off from the Danube.[70] It declared the tsar's readiness to observe all aspects of the 1856 settlement other than the one he repudiated. It said that he was prepared to confirm, to renew or to alter the general provisions of the 1856 settlement in accordance with the wishes of the other Great Powers. After promulgating the circular, Russia accepted Bismarck's suggestion that her unilateral action of October 1870 be ratified by a European conference. Representatives of the tsar and of Prussia, Austria, France, Britain, Italy and the Sultan met in London for nearly two months at the beginning of 1871 and issued the 'London Convention' of 1/13 March, which rubber-stamped Russia's action and made sure that she continued to play a full part in international relations.[71] Despite asserting her right to build warships in the Black Sea, Russia did not actually start building them for another decade.

Thus it became clear that Gorchakov's abandonment of patient diplomacy had been exceptional. His dealings with the European powers in the early 1870s were conservative even by the standards of his breed. A radical diplomatic policy in 1871 would have taken the form of approaches to France. Russia had benefited from her close association with Prussia in the 1860s, but after the creation of the German Empire she ran the risk of becoming Bismarck's poodle. Gorchakov realized that France ought to be spared complete humiliation in the wake of the Franco-Prussian War and achieved a minor diplomatic success when he persuaded Berlin to reduce her post-war indemnity from six to five milliard francs, but he felt much safer with the devil he knew than with the emergent French Third Republic. Within about two years of France's defeat he seemed to be settling back into the diplomatic pattern of the pre-Crimean era, when St Petersburg colluded with Berlin and Vienna to preserve the status quo. The 'League of the Three Emperors', which came into being as a result of agreements between the tsar and the Emperors of Germany and Austria-Hungary in May and June 1873, called to mind the age of Metternich.[72] Gorchakov's capacity for risk-taking seemed to disappear as soon as it surfaced. The notion that in 1875 he somehow compelled the Germans to give up plans for a second attack on France is a myth.[73]

Not surprisingly, panslavs believed that St Petersburg's deference to Berlin derogated from the Russian Empire's dignity. In Constantinople, Ignat'ev deplored the League of the Three Emperors. Katkov fulminated against the rise of Prussia even before the proclamation of the German Empire and subsequently put himself at the head of those who advocated a rapprochement with France. St Petersburg's dependence on Berlin had become so great, he believed, that the tsar no longer possessed a 'Russian Ministry of Foreign Affairs' but a 'Foreign Ministry of Russian Affairs'.[74] The uxorious heir to the Russian throne (the future Alexander III) felt dislike for Prussians because his wife came from Denmark. When the heir to the German throne visited St Petersburg at the end of 1871, the tsarevich refused to receive him. The Slavophiles Vladimir Cherkasskii and Ivan Aksakov created a minor incident when, in congratulating the tsar on the abrogation of the Black Sea clauses, they took the opportunity to give him unwelcome advice on the future direction of government policy.[75]

Although the government deplored these manifestations of what Valuev's successor at the Ministry of Internal Affairs called 'ultra-patriotism',[76] it could overlook them so long as the Balkans remained at peace. The eastern and western dimensions of Russian foreign policy were manageable. Britain disliked Russian expansion in the east, but needed greater provocation before she would take up the cudgels. Unless trouble arose to the south of the Russian Empire, Gorchakov had little to fear. Russian panslavs could hardly exert much influence on the authorities without a Balkan focus for the promotion of the Slavonic cause. At the beginning of the 1870s the Slavonic minorities of the Ottoman Empire seemed to be getting their way without help from their northern cousins. In February 1870 the Turks allowed the creation of an independent Bulgarian Orthodox Church in a decree which made 'the first official use of the word Bulgarian for five centuries'.[77]

VICTORY AND DEFEAT IN THE BALKANS (1875–8)

It was only a matter of time, however, before relations between the Turks and their Slavonic subjects again became fraught. A rising in Hercegovina in July 1875 marked the start of a complex chain of events which in April 1877 gave rise to the fourth Russo-Turkish war of the nineteenth century. The delicate balance between assertiveness and accommodation which had been the hallmark of Russian foreign policy at the beginning of the 1870s foundered on the interaction of South Slav nationalism and Russian panslavism. By the time the Balkan crisis of the mid-1870s had been re-solved, St Petersburg's diplomatic options were as few in number as they had been in 1856. The First World War lay a generation ahead, but the Austro-German alliance which made it possible came into being in 1879. Gorchakov said in 1856 that Russia was 'thinking', but Russians never thought hard enough to grasp that only by abstaining completely from military activity on their southern frontier could they avoid catastrophe.

The reasons why the local difficulty of 1875 occasioned a Russian inva-sion of the Ottoman Empire in 1877 included (in a rough attempt at ascending order of importance) the impact of the rising in Hercegovina on the more northerly Turkish province of Bosnia; the ambitions of Serbia to the east and Montenegro to the south; the likelihood that disorder in the western Balkans would be matched in the east (which it was when the Bulgarians rebelled in April 1876); a *coup d'état* in Constantinople in 1876 which substituted Russophobes for temporizers; the inevitable involvement of the Habsburg Empire in unrest on its southern frontier; the freewheeling activity of ambassador Ignat'ev at Constantinople; the Russian public's im-mense enthusiasm for war on behalf of the Balkan Slavs; and to speak more loosely, the strain which any crisis in Europe was bound to put on an international order which was still adapting to the changes wrought by Bismarck in the wars of 1864, 1866 and 1870.

No diplomat could have dealt successfully with all these challenges. The cautious Gorchakov chose to concentrate on squaring Austria. He was probably right to believe that Austro-Russian rivalry had become the fun-damental reason why Balkan crises were hard to localize, but he was wrong to think that the interests of St Petersburg and Vienna could be rec-onciled. Squaring Austria was about as easy as squaring the circle. Whereas even the Russian government (let alone the Russian public) thought that the way to solve Balkan crises was gradually to strengthen the hand of Balkan Christians, Austria thought discontent in the Balkans required her to annex more territory. Austrians believed that if the Slavs of the Balkans became stronger, they would act like a magnet on the Slavs of the Habsburg Empire. If, then, Austria chose to support Slavonic causes, her reason for doing so was not to increase the Balkan Slavs' freedom of action but to make them dependent on Vienna rather than Constantinople. In June 1876 the Slavonic principalities of Serbia and Montenegro went to war

302

with the Sultan on behalf of Bosnia and Hercegovina. The following month, at Reichstadt in Bohemia, Gorchakov and the Austrian foreign minister tried to coordinate their response. They agreed not to intervene and not to allow the Turks to impose crushing terms in the event of victory, but they took very different views of what ought to happen if the Turks were defeated. Russia envisaged the enlargement of Serbia and Montenegro, whereas Austria envisaged incorporating most of Bosnia and Hercegovina into the Habsburg Empire.[78] Serbia and Montenegro lost the war in a matter of months and new territorial arrangements turned out to be unnecessary, but the end of one Balkan war merely presaged another. Order of a kind had returned to the western half of the Balkan peninsula, but the east was still in ferment. The boundaries of the Sultan's domains still looked likely to change, and Russia still had to face the problem that, so long as she worked closely with Austria, she was unlikely to achieve a settlement that furthered her interests.

In January and March 1877 Gorchakov more or less accepted the Austrian vision of the Balkans' future in the course of preparing the ground for a Russian push into Bulgaria.[79] His concessions made it possible for Russia to invade the Ottoman Empire without fear of Austrian retaliation, but they reduced Russia's chances of achieving a peace that suited her. After winning a short but inglorious war which turned mainly on the difficulty of capturing the fortress of Plevna, the Russians could no longer escape the fact that deference to Austria prevented them from deriving much benefit from their intervention. At this point they became over-ambitious. Under the Treaty of San Stefano of March 1878 the tsar required the Ottoman Empire to return southern Bessarabia, to cede the important cities of Batumi in Transcaucasia and Kars in eastern Anatolia, to acknowledge the complete independence of Serbia, Romania, and Montenegro, and above all to turn Bulgaria into an autonomous but Russian-dominated principality with frontiers far to the west and south of the Bulgarian heartland.[80] Turkey was obliged to accept the terms she was offered, but Austria and the other Great Powers were determined to reverse the Russian diktat. Bismarck convened a congress in Berlin which in July 1878 rendered the Treaty of San Stefano a dead letter.[81] Although Russia retained her territorial gains and although Serbia, Romania, and Montenegro achieved recognition of their independence, the 'big Bulgaria' was whittled down to size, Macedonia was returned to the Ottoman Empire, and Austria acquired control over Bosnia and Hercegovina.

After 1878 the likelihood of cooperation between Austria and Russia was even smaller than it had been when Alexander II ascended the throne. During the Crimean War Vienna had failed to come to the aid of St Petersburg; at San Stefano St Petersburg had shown that it was willing, given the chance, to ride roughshod over the interests of the Habsburgs. When Russia had been put in her place at the Congress of Berlin an Austrian Archduke commented: 'this friendship with Russia is a thing of the past, at least for our lifetime'.[82] The 1879 alliance between Austria and Germany was predicated on the two countries' mistrust of the tsar. Bismarck worked hard in the 1880s to restore Russia to the orbit of the Germanic powers, but after his dismissal in 1890 Berlin abandoned the effort and the Russian Empire formed an alliance with France.

It is true that if Gorchakov had had his way Russia would probably not have gone to war in 1877 and would certainly not have attempted to create the large Bulgarian principality which obliged Austria and the other Great Powers to resist her. The Treaty of San Stefano was not of the foreign minister's making. He rejected the idea of boundary changes both in his official memoranda and in private conversation. In January 1876, for example, when the Balkan crisis was in its early stages, he told one of his subordinates that Russia was 'a great non-power' and ought to eschew expansionism.[83] Yet Gorchakov had demonstrated in October 1870 that he could be aggressive when it suited him, and even in the second half of the 1870s he was keen to take back southern Bessarabia. He would eventually have had to face the fact that the attitudes of Austria and Russia to the future of the Balkans were irreconcilable. Russians who thought the problem should be faced immediately disagreed with their foreign minister only in respect of timing.

The architect of the Treaty of San Stefano was Ignat'ev, who differed from Gorchakov throughout the crisis. Since France's defeat at the hand of the Prussians in 1870–1 he had been so influential at Constantinople that at times he seemed to be running the Ottoman Empire. It was hardly surprising, therefore, that in 1875 his inclination was to make a bilateral deal with Turkey rather than involve the Great Powers. In Ignat'ev's opinion, negotiating with Austria was bound to damage Russia's interests. 'The first blow at our position in Constantinople', he wrote later, 'was struck by the three Emperors in a rather ordinary insurrection of some Hercegovinian districts near the frontiers of Montenegro'.[84] In other words, St Petersburg ought not to have involved itself in a multilateral attempt to give comfort to the rebels of the western Balkans. If the revolt had been a success, the prime beneficiary would have been Austria. When the Serbs went to war with the Ottoman Empire, Ignat'ev recommended assisting in their suppression in order further to enhance the Russian Empire's prestige at Constantinople. Since Russia was too far away from Serbia to support her unilaterally or to turn her into a satellite, she ought not to help her. The eastern Balkans, however, were a different story. They could be liberated by Russian forces and turned into a Russian protectorate. When diplomatic efforts failed to persuade the Sultan that he should treat Bulgarians more generously, Ignat'ev was the first to recommend military action on their behalf and the prime mover in the attempt to create a 'big Bulgaria'.

It would be logical to suppose that the tsar withdrew his favour from Gorchakov and conferred it on Ignat'ev because the foreign minister's policy conceded too much to Austria. It also seems to have been the case, however, that Alexander fell prey to panslavism. Although, in 1875, he adhered firmly to the notion of working for a diplomatic solution through the

League of the Three Emperors, and although in May 1876 he showed a remarkable lack of sympathy for non-Russian Slavs when he banned the use of the Ukrainian language within the Russian Empire,[85] in October 1876 he issued an ultimatum to the Turks which obliged them to halt their successful military action against the Serbs and Montenegrins. Shortly afterwards he stated publicly that, because he did not believe negotiations between the Turks and the Great Powers would succeed, he 'firmly intend[ed] to act independently'.[86] By June 1877, when he joined the Russian forces at Ploesti in Romania, he was ripe for conversion to the cause of Bulgarian liberation.

What determined the tsar's change of heart remains unclear, but Ignat'ev may have been right to say of the 1876 ultimatum that 'The Emperor was driven forward by the idea that the Russian people would enter the war in spite of the Government and without waiting for its decision'.[87] Educated Russians (and perhaps even the peasantry) had taken the Balkan Slavs to their heart. The Slavonic Benevolent Committees founded in the 1850s and 1860s reached the apogee of their influence. Cherniaev, the maverick soldier who captured Tashkent in 1865, found his way to Belgrade in April 1876, took over the Serbian war effort, and became a hero at home.[88] Lev Tolstoy immortalized the many Russians who volunteered for service in Serbia by despatching Vronskii to the war in the last pages of *Anna Karenina*. Russian journalists beat even their British counterparts to the draw in reporting on the atrocities perpetrated by the Turks in Bulgaria.[89] The Slavophile Aleksandr Koshelev claimed that when Russia finally went to war with Turkey in April 1877 'the general joy was boundless'.[90] Interest in news from the front was so great that Russia experienced her first 'commercial newspaper boom'.[91] Critics of the war – Boris Chicherin, the writers Vsevolod Garshin and Mikhail Saltykov-Shchedrin, the Ukrainian *émigré* Mykhailo Drahomanov[92] – were few and far between.

In abandoning Gorchakov for Ignat'ev, therefore, Alexander II may have been trying to improve his standing in the eyes of the public. Since, as we shall see in Chapter Eleven, he was under severe domestic pressure for other reasons, he may have believed that he needed a success. Since the victory over Turkey was less than wholly convincing, however, and since the ensuing diplomacy turned out badly, the regime's reputation suffered. After the poor performance of the army in front of Plevna, only the capture of Constantinople would have been enough to satisfy domestic warmongers. Panslavists fumed when the Great Powers rewrote the Treaty of San Stefano. Moderate intellectuals took comfort from the fact that Russia had been obliged to return to the path of multilateral negotiation, but went on blaming the authorities for deviating from it in the first place.[93]

In other words, foreign affairs remained as problematical at the end of the reign of Alexander II as they had been at the beginning. The regime had abrogated the Black Sea clauses of the Peace of Paris and regained southern Bessarabia, but had failed to bring the empire's diplomatic isolation to an end. Although Gorchakov had spoken frequently of the need to give domestic reform precedence over international relations, not even he, let alone the tsar, Ignat'ev, Dmitrii Miliutin, Cherniaev, Katkov and Nikolai Danilevskii, had been able to accept that Russia needed to give up foreign affairs altogether. Not for the last time, Russians compounded their problems by overestimating the importance of maintaining their position in the world at large.

NOTES

1. N. Ia. Danilevskii, *Rossiia i Evropa* (Moscow, 1991 [reprint of 1871 edn]), pp. 5–22.
2. David Wetzel, *The Crimean War: A Diplomatic History* (Boulder, Colo., 1985), p. 160.
3. Ibid., p. 159.
4. Leon Trotsky, *My Life: An Attempt at an Autobiography* (Harmondsworth, 1975), p. 355.
5. N. S. Kiniapina, *Vneshniaia politika Rossii vtoroi poloviny XIX v.* (Moscow, 1974), p. 13.
6. M. S. Anderson, ed., *The Great Powers and the Near East 1774–1923* (London, 1970), p. 93.
7. S. S. Tatishchev, *Imperator Aleksandr II: ego zhizn' i tsarstvovanie* (2 vols, St Petersburg, 1903), i. 229.
8. L. I. Narochnitskaia, *Rossiia i otmena neitralizatsii Chernogo moria 1856–1871gg.* (Moscow, 1989), p. 28.
9. David Gillard, *The Struggle for Asia 1828–1914* (London, 1977), p. 133.
10. For the duality of Soviet foreign policy in the 1920s see Teddy J. Uldricks, *Diplomacy and Ideology: The Origins of Soviet Foreign Relations 1917–1930* (London and Beverly Hills, Calif., 1979), esp. p. 158.
11. L. I. Rovniakova, *Bor'ba iuzhnykh slavian za svobodu i russkaia periodicheskaia pechat' (50–70-e gody XIX veka): Ocherki* (Leningrad, 1986), p. 235.
12. A. V. Buganov, 'Otnoshenie krest'ianstva k russko-turetskoi voine 1877–1878 godov (Po materialam poslednei chetverti XIX v.)', *Istoriia SSSR*, 1987 no. 5, p. 185.
13. Anderson, *Great Powers* (above, n. 6), p. 93.
14. For the differences among historians on the reasons for Russian expansion in central Asia see David MacKenzie, 'Expansion in Central Asia: St. Petersburg vs. the Turkestan Generals (1863–1866)', CSS 3 (1969), 286, n. 1, and N. S. Kiniapina's review of G. A. Khidoiatov, *Iz istorii anglo-russkikh otnoshenii v Srednei Azii v kontse XIX v. (60–70 gg).* (Tashkent, 1969), in VI, 1971 no. 7, p. 174.
15. Danilevskii, *Rossiia i Evropa* (above, n. 1), p. 362.
16. Ibid., p. 435.
17. A. S. Nifontov, 'Pis'ma russkogo posla N. A. Orlova 1859–1865 gg.', in B. S. Itenberg et al., eds, *Revoliutsionery i liberaly Rossii* (Moscow, 1990), p. 227.
18. W. E. Mosse, *The Rise and Fall of the Crimean System 1855–71: The Story of a Peace Settlement* (London, 1963), p. 107.

19. William Carr, *The Origins of the Wars of German Unification* (London and New York, 1991), p. 114.
20. L. G. Zakharova, 'Velikii kniaz' Konstantin Nikolaevich i ego dnevnik', VI, 1990 no. 5, pp. 113–14, 121–2, 128–9.
21. Basil Dmytryshyn, ed., *Imperial Russia: A Source Book, 1700–1917* (3rd edn, Fort Worth, Tex., 1990), p. 295.
22. M. A. Chepelkin, 'Diplomatiia Rossii nakanune avstro-italo-frantsuzskoi voiny 1859 g.', *Vestnik moskovskogo universiteta, Seriia 8: Istoriia*, 1987 no. 5, pp. 61–72 (quotations from p. 62).
23. F. Rotshtein, ed., 'K istorii franko-russkogo soglasheniia 1859 g.', KA 88 (1938), 246.
24. Dmytryshyn, *Imperial Russia* (above, n. 21), p. 334–5.
25. Ibid., pp. 296–304 (for the texts of the treaties).
26. N. N. Bolkhovitinov, *Russko-amerikanskie otnosheniia i prodazha Aliaski 1834–1867* (Moscow, 1990), p. 92.
27. Kiniapina, *Vneshniaia politika* (above, n. 5), p. 229.
28. Ronald Grigor Suny, ' "The Peasants Have Always Fed Us": The Georgian Nobility and the Peasant Emancipation, 1856–1871', RR 38 (1979), esp. 32, 49–50.
29. Mosse, *Crimean System* (above, n. 18), pp. 55–75.
30. Barbara Jelavich, *Russia and the Formation of the Romanian National State 1821–1878* (Cambridge, 1984), p. 98.
31. For most of the evidence in this paragraph see S. A. Nikitin, 'Russkaia diplomatiia i natsional'noe dvizhenie iuzhnykh slavian v 50 – 70-e gody XIX v.', in Nikitin, *Ocherki po istorii iuzhnykh slavian i russko-balkanskikh sviazei v 50 – 70-e gody XIX v.* (Moscow, 1970), pp. 59–68.
32. Michael Boro Petrovich, *The Emergence of Russian Panslavism 1856–1870* (New York, 1956), p. 112, n. 17; Rovniakova, *Bor'ba iuzhnykh slavian* (above, n. 11), pp. 31–65.
33. Peter K. Christoff, *A. S. Xomjakov* (The Hague, 1961), p. 248.
34. R. F. Leslie, *Reform and Insurrection in Russian Poland 1856–1865* (Westport, Conn., 1969 [1st pub. 1963]), p. 94.
35. Piotr S. Wandycz, *The Lands of Partitioned Poland, 1795–1918* (Seattle, Wash., and London, 1974), p. 169.
36. For this argument see Daniel Beauvois, *Le Noble, le serf et le revizor: la noblesse polonaise entre le tsarisme et les masses ukrainiennes (1831–1863)* (Paris, 1985), passim.
37. P. A. Valuev, *Dnevnik* (2 vols, Moscow, 1961), i. 259.
38. Nifontov, 'Pis'ma Orlova' (above, n. 17), p. 227; Valuev, *Dnevnik* (above, n. 37), i. 338.
39. D. G. Kirby, ed., *Finland and Russia 1808–1920: A Selection of Documents* (London and Basingstoke, 1975), pp. 35, 51–3.
40. John D. Klier, 'The Concept of "Jewish Emancipation" in a Russian Context', in Olga Crisp and Linda Edmondson, eds, *Civil Rights in Imperial Russia* (Oxford, 1989), pp. 133–5.
41. N. I. Kostomarov, *Istoricheskie proizvedeniia; Avtobiografiia* (Kiev, 1989), p. 534; M. K. Lemke, *Epokha tsenzurnykh reform 1859–1865 godov* (St Petersburg, 1904), p. 303.
42. See J. F. Kutolowski, 'Victorian Provincial Businessmen and Foreign Affairs: The Case of the Polish Insurrection, 1863–1864', *Northern History* 21 (1985), 236–58.
43. Stanisław Bóbr-Tylingo, *Napoléon III, L'Europe et La Pologne en 1863–4* (Rome, 1963), pp. 338–9.

44. On Austria see Richard B. Elrod, 'Austria and the Polish Insurrection of 1863: Documents from the Austrian State Archives', IHR 8 (1986), 416–37.
45. Robert H. Lord, 'Bismarck and Russia in 1863', AHR 29 (1923–4), 24–48.
46. Ibid., p. 41.
47. MacKenzie, 'Expansion in Central Asia' (above, n. 14), p. 289, n. 8.
48. Hélène Carrère d'Encausse, *Islam and the Russian Empire: Reform and Revolution in Central Asia* (London, 1988), p. 38; for the text of the convention see Seymour Becker, *Russia's Protectorates in Central Asia: Bukhara and Khiva, 1865–1924* (Cambridge, Mass., 1968), p. 315.
49. Valuev, *Dnevnik* (above, n. 37), ii. 60–1.
50. Martin McCauley and Peter Waldron, *The Emergence of the Modern Russian State, 1855–81* (Basingstoke and London, 1988), p. 176; for the date of Gorchakov's circular see Tatishchev, *Aleksandr II* (above, n. 7), ii. 116.
51. M. K. Rozhkova, *Ekonomicheskie sviazi Rossii so Srednei Aziei: 40 – 60-e gody XIX veka* (Moscow, 1963), p. 236.
52. MacKenzie, 'Expansion in Central Asia' (above, n. 14), p. 310.
53. For the double standards of both Gorchakov and Miliutin see the editorial matter in Valuev, *Dnevnik* (above, n. 37), ii. 452, n. 74.
54. Seymour Becker, 'The Muslim East in Nineteenth-Century Russian Popular Historiography', *Central Asian Survey* 5, nos 3–4 (1986), 44.
55. McCauley and Waldron, *Emergence* (above, n. 50), p. 170.
56. Alexander Onou, 'The Memoirs of Count N. Ignatyev', *The Slavonic Review* 10 (1931–2), 394.
57. Ibid., 396.
58. Rovniakova, *Bor'ba iuzhnykh slavian* (above, n. 11), p. 121.
59. Petrovich, *Emergence of Russian Panslavism* (above, n. 32), p. 201.
60. For the latest account of the complex relationship between Katkov and the authorities see V. G. Chernukha, *Pravitel'stvennaia politika v otnoshenii pechati 60 – 70-e gody XIX veka* (Leningrad, 1989), pp. 151–97.
61. For extensive quotation from Gorchakov's annual report for 1866 see S. A. Nikitin, 'Rossiia i slaviane v 60-e gody XIX v.', in his *Ocherki* (above, n. 31), pp. 149–51.
62. N. S. Kiniapina, 'Bor'ba Rossii za otmenu ogranichitel'nykh uslovii Parizhskogo dogovora 1856 goda', VI, 1972 no. 8, p. 39 (another quotation from the 1866 report).
63. For Russian cooperation with France and Austria and especially for new evidence on the closeness of Russia and Prussia in the period immediately prior to the Franco-Prussian war see Narochnitskaia, *Rossiia i otmena* (above, n. 8), pp. 110–65.
64. For the full text of the announcement of October 1870 see ibid., pp. 218–21; for translated extracts see McCauley and Waldron, *Emergence* (above, n. 50), pp. 164–6.
65. P. A. Zaionchkovskii, *Voennye reformy 1860–1870 godov v Rossii* (Moscow, 1952), p. 261.
66. See the table in ibid., p. 333.
67. *The Times*, 19 January 1874.
68. For the treaties of 1873 between Russia on the one hand and Khiva and Bukhara on the other see Becker, *Russia's Protectorates* (above, n. 48), pp. 316–21.
69. See, for example, M. A. Annanepesov, 'Prisoedinenie Turkmenistana k Rossii: Pravda istorii', VI, 1989 no. 11, pp. 70–86.

70. Kiniapina, 'Bor'ba Rossii za otmenu' (above, n. 62), p. 41.
71. For the full text of the convention see Narochnitskaia, *Rossiia i otmena* (above, n. 8), pp. 221–3; for translated extracts see Anderson, *Great Powers* (above, n. 6), p. 85.
72. For the texts of the agreements see Dmytryshyn, *Imperial Russia* (above, n. 21), pp. 337–9.
73. For a summary of 'the strange events of 1875' see George F. Kennan, *The Decline of Bismarck's European Order: Franco-Russian Relations, 1875–1890* (Princeton, NJ, 1979), pp. 11–23.
74. E. M. Feoktistov, *Za kulisami politiki i literatury 1848–1896* (Leningrad, 1929), p. 112; see also W. E. Mosse, *The European Powers and the German Question 1848–71* (Cambridge, 1958), pp. 389–94 (an appendix entitled 'The Russian National Press and the "German Peril", 1870–1') and Chernukha, *Pravitel'stvennaia politika* (above, n. 60), p. 181.
75. A. Presniakov, ed., 'Moskovskii adres Aleksandru II v 1870 g. (Iz perepiski K. P. Pobedonostseva s I. S. Aksakovym)', KA 31 (1928), 144–54.
76. Feoktistov, *Za kulisami* (above, n. 74), p. 108.
77. B. H. Sumner, 'Ignatyev at Constantinople', *The Slavonic Review* 11 (1932–3), 568.
78. For the difference between the Russian and Austrian positions at Reichstadt see Anderson, *Great Powers* (above, n. 6), pp. 88–92.
79. For extracts from the relevant documents see ibid., pp. 94–6.
80. The extracts from the Treaty of San Stefano in Dmytryshyn, *Imperial Russia* (above, n. 21), pp. 363–72, are fuller than those in Anderson, *Great Powers* (above, n. 6), pp. 98–101.
81. For documents on the Congress of Berlin (including the final act) see Anderson, *Great Powers* (above, n. 6), pp. 101–12, and McCauley and Waldron, *Emergence* (above, n. 50), pp. 173–5.
82. George Hoover Rupp, *A Wavering Friendship: Russia and Austria 1876–1878* (Cambridge, Mass., 1941, repr. Philadelphia, Pa, 1976), p. 535.
83. The subordinate reported his views to Valuev: Valuev, *Dnevnik* (above, n. 37), ii. 326.
84. Onou, 'The Memoirs of Count N. Ignatyev' (above, n. 56), p. 399.
85. See Fedir Savchenko, *Zaborona ukrainstva 1876 r.* (Kiev, 1930), passim, and McCauley and Waldron, *Emergence* (above, n. 50), p. 209.
86. McCauley and Waldron, *Emergence* (above, n. 50), p. 172.
87. Onou, 'The Memoirs of Count N. Ignatyev' (above, n. 56), p. 406.
88. See David MacKenzie, 'Panslavism in Practice: Cherniaev in Serbia (1876)', JMH 36 (1964), 279–97.
89. I. Koz'menko, 'Russkoe obshchestvo i aprel'skoe bolgarskoe vosstanie 1876 goda', VI, 1947 no. 5, p. 98.
90. A. I. Koshelev, *Zapiski* (Berlin, 1884), p. 228.
91. Louise McReynolds, 'Imperial Russia's Newspaper Reporters: Profile of a Society in Transition, 1865–1914', SEER 68 (1990), 278.
92. B. N. Chicherin, *Vospominaniia: Zemstvo i Moskovskaia Duma* (Moscow, 1934), pp. 78–85: Vsevolod Garshin, *From the Reminiscences of Private Ivanov and Other Stories*, tr. Peter Henry et al. (London, 1988), pp. 12, 25–35, 242; S. Makashin, *Saltykov-Shchedrin: Poslednie gody 1875–1889* (Moscow, 1989), pp. 79–85; M. P. Dragomanov (Drahomanov), 'Vnutrennee rabstvo i voina za osvobozhdenie', in Dragomanov, *Sobranie politicheskikh sochinenii*, ed. P. B. Struve and B. Kistiakovskii (2 vols, Paris, 1905–6), ii. 75–109.

93. For both panslav and moderate responses to the outcome of the Balkan crisis see V. I. Ado, 'Berlinskii kongress 1878 g. i pomeshchich'e-burzhuaznoe ob-shchestvennoe mnenie Rossii', IZ 69 (1961), 101–41.

CHAPTER ELEVEN

Populism

TRIALS AND TERRORISTS

While the tsar's soldiers and diplomats were fighting the Turks and negotiating the treaties of San Stefano and Berlin, his judges and lawyers were prosecuting revolutionaries. In January 1877 they tried various malcontents for demonstrating outside St Petersburg's Kazan' Cathedral. In February and March of the same year, in the 'trial of the fifty', they dealt with a Moscow-based 'Pan-Russian Social-Revolutionary Organization'. In May they procured the condemnation of the 'South Russian Union of Workers'. In October they set in train the three-month 'trial of the 193', the largest political trial in Russian history. In March 1878 they sought the conviction of Vera Zasulich for attempting to kill St Petersburg's Governor-General. In July 1878, in Odessa, they condemned to death the terrorist Ivan Koval'skii.

If the trials were designed to frighten the regime's opponents, they were a failure. In April 1879 Aleksandr Solov'ev attempted to shoot the tsar as he finished his walk in the Summer Garden. In February 1880 Stepan Khalturin tried to blow up the Winter Palace. On 1 March 1881 a group of conspirators led by Sof'ia Perovskaia enacted a complex plot to kill the tsar by throwing bombs at him as he made his way back to the Winter Palace after taking exercise at the St Petersburg riding school. The first bomb missed, but Alexander descended from his carriage to inspect the damage and was hit by the bomb that killed him.

Since this book begins and ends with the murder of a tsar, it might be said that not much had changed in Russia between 1801 and 1881. The murders, however, took different forms and had very different causes. It is a minor indication of the difference between Russia in 1801 and Russia in 1881 that whereas Paul was murdered at night in his bedchamber, Alexander was murdered in daylight in the street. More important, the murderers of 1881 thought they were acting on behalf of people other than themselves. They thought, indeed, that they were acting on behalf of the people as a whole. The subversive doctrines which gave rise to the trials of political activists and the attempts on the life of the tsar go by the generic name of populism (*narodnichestvo*), a creed whose many different manifestations all gave the people (*narod*) a higher priority than the political superstructure.

By the 1860s the feeling that the Russian state took little notice of the masses had been developing among educated Russians for at least two generations. The concept of 'people-ness' or 'nationality' (*narodnost*') had been popularized on the left of the political spectrum in the 1820s in the hope that the growth of state power might be arrested. Nicholas I's Minister of Education, S. S. Uvarov, had tried to turn 'people-ness' to the state's advantage by hitching it to 'Orthodoxy' and 'Autocracy' in 1833, but the nonconformist impulse which brought it to life refused to disappear. Whatever the obscurity of the ideas of the Slavophiles, their antipathy towards Peter the Great and their enthusiasm for the peasant commune made clear that they set greater store by the common people than by governmental institutions and bureaucrats. After Alexander Herzen experienced the failure of the 1848 revolutions in western Europe, he too came to feel that the Russian Empire's best way forward lay in building on the communal instincts of the peasantry rather than adopting the unsuccessful philosophies of western liberals. One of the effects of the debate which followed the emancipation of the serfs was to reveal that although enlightened bureaucrats thought the existing order could be put to rights, non-governmental intellectuals disagreed. In the view of the latter, redesigning the empire would merely improve the position of the privileged. Since many educated people outside the government believed that the privileged would leave the poor to their own devices, they promoted the notion that action had to be taken rapidly to prevent the rift between the highest and the lowest orders of society from widening.

POPULISTS AND SOCIAL CHANGE

Disagreements between educated people inside and outside the government were deep-seated, but they were hardly sufficient to explain why radicals turned to violence. Nor, apparently, were the deficiencies of the regime glaring enough to warrant the response which gave rise to the trials of 1877–8 and the murder of the tsar. At first sight, the behaviour of the dissidents of the 1870s was perverse. However flawed the legislation of the early 1860s, subjecting a tsar who had enacted the most far-reaching reforms since the time of Peter the Great to greater pressure than most of his predecessors hardly seemed to be sensible. Yet Russia contained more dissidents in the 1870s than at any earlier point in the century. Why did radical populism take hold when the government had been trying to put its house in order?

Of the many answers to this question, the most logical seems to be that the inadequacy of the reforms of the 1860s became increasingly apparent and that conspiracies and violence sprang from widespread disillusionment. Implicitly, this was the view of Nikolai Bunge, a senior figure at the Ministry of Finances who painted a lurid picture of the empire's economic circumstances in a paper of September 1880.[1] Bunge gave the impression that the emancipation of the serfs and the subsequent legislative changes had done nothing for the empire's material well-being. The immediate cause of his disquiet was the expense of fighting the Turks, but he said enough about structural problems to imply that the country's fundamental difficulties lay deeper. If a senior government official could be so critical, it is easy to imagine the opinions of educated people outside the government who had been reared in a tradition of dissent. If the reforms of the 1860s had failed to improve the country's prospects, the likelihood of public protest was considerable. Perhaps the people who figured in the trials of 1877–8 and who launched a campaign against the life of the tsar in 1879 were simply the public face of widespread social unrest.

The trouble with this argument is that the evidence for mass dissatisfaction with the policies of the regime seems not to have been as great as it ought to have been. If the people who were supposed to be getting poorer gave few signs of enthusiasm for revolt, why did dissidents feel the need to act in their name?

The empire was certainly experiencing significant social change. Towns have not played much part in this book because prior to the reign of Alexander II fewer than 8 per cent of the population lived in them, but around the middle of the century they started growing rapidly. The population of Kiev nearly doubled between 1861 and 1874, that of Moscow roughly tripled between 1846 and 1897. Types of employment changed significantly: 46,000 Muscovites were employed in 'large-scale industry' in 1853, 77,000 in 1890. City life was unhealthy. 'In the 1870s an estimated one-third of all Kievans suffered from venereal disease'. Peasants were leaving their villages for the towns or hunting for land in underpopulated parts of the empire. Official figures on the granting of internal passports suggest that internal migration 'more than tripled between the 1860s and 1880s'. Since many of those who travelled undoubtedly did so without acquiring a passport first, the true figure was certainly higher. Jeffrey Brooks points out, again on the basis of official figures, that 'Approximately 12 million people legally designated as peasants were living outside their native provinces or districts in 1897', and that '300,000 settlers migrated from European Russia to the lands beyond the Urals from 1861 to 1885'. When the South-Western Section of the Imperial Russian Geographical Society conducted a census of the population of Kiev in March 1874, one of the many things it discovered was that more than two-thirds of the inhabitants of the city had been born somewhere else.[2]

An entire social group, women, entered the reckoning of legislators for the first time. In 1858 the government committed itself to providing them with secondary education. In 1859 they were given permission to attend university lectures. Their involvement in the Sunday School movement of 1859–62 inclined the authorities to view them with suspicion, but legislation of January 1871 gave them the right to work in telegraph, railway, postal and business offices, and to teach and become midwives. In 1872 the Ger'e Higher Women's Courses started at Moscow University, with the object of training women to teach in secondary schools. Amazingly, 'In a country where student corporate activity was considered seditious and where the educational system was based on strict centralization, the women directed the courses themselves'. The ultra-conservative Minister of Education, Dmitrii Tolstoi, seems either to have thought that educating women was safer than educating men because women were less likely to turn into dissidents, or that letting women study within the confines of the empire was a lesser evil than obliging them to seek education abroad. Official university-level courses for women, the first of their kind in Europe, opened in Russia in 1878. In Russia proper in 1881 some 45 per cent of the total number of students in secondary schools and some 20 per cent of the total in higher education were female, proportions exceeded only in the United States.[3]

Despite these and other signs of social change, however, it was to be the 1880s and 1890s, if not the turn of the century, before the social and economic consequences of the emancipation of the serfs found expression in mass support for the radical transformation of the tsarist regime. It is not possible to argue, for example, that the beginnings of the emancipation of the female inhabitants of the Russian Empire played much part in the genesis of populism. Although some of the most famous populists were women – Vera Figner, Vera Zasulich, Sof'ia Perovskaia, Ekaterina Breshko-Breshkovskaia – Dmitrii Tolstoi seems to have been right, on the whole, to believe that women would reject the idea of becoming revolutionaries; 'even Soviet sources can only locate about a dozen heroines' among the many women educated in the 1870s. It is true that city-based workers began to pose the regime significant problems. Whereas between 1861 and 1865 the authorities counted 85 strikes and worker disturbances, in the first half of the 1870s there were 175. Some of the strikes, moreover, were large scale. In May 1870 800 textile workers struck at the Nevskii works in St Petersburg. The Governor of Moscow commented that the hands of the clock were approaching the time when the question of the antagonism between labour and capital might make itself heard. In October 1871 the head of the Moscow division of the Third Department informed his superiors that artisans were becoming keen readers of newspapers and taking up questions which in western Europe had given rise to 'the so-called workers' movement'. The following month, after strikes at two local factories, the Governor of Moscow told the Ministry of Internal Affairs that workers were meeting in taverns to discuss the propositions that 'manufacturers lived by the sweat of labourers' and that 'consequently ... it was not a sin to remove the obstacles to the well-being of the working class, and would not be a bad thing to ruin manufacturers by setting light to their factories and machines'. Although, at the end of 1871, the government instituted public readings of improving literature in the hope of offsetting the influence on workers of other sorts of reading matter, the 1870s witnessed not only the first involvement of workers in an overtly political demonstration (that of December 1876 outside the Kazan' Cathedral in St Petersburg), but the foundation of both South and North Russian Workers' Unions and some ringing speeches by workers at political trials. Fifty-three strikes took place in 1878, sixty in 1879. In November 1878 as many as 2,000 workers withdrew their labour at a cotton mill in St Petersburg. Not only textile workers but also metal workers, railway workers, tobacco workers and seasonal port labourers all went on strike in various parts of the country at one time or another.[4]

But although workers felt an inchoate sense of grievance, they rarely shared or even understood the objectives of non-worker propagandists. Most of them retained their roots in the countryside and tended to adhere to the monarchist ideals of the peasantry. Their major concerns were economic rather than political – better rates of pay and the improvement of conditions in the factory. The big issue in the strike of November 1878 at the 'New' cotton mill in St Petersburg was not the overthrow of the autocracy but the exploitation of adolescents. The Kazan' Square demonstration of late 1876 featured not only the flying of the red flag but also support for Serbia, an objective which was anathema to the intellectuals who played a part in proceedings because Serbian success would have redounded to the credit of the tsar. The arrests which followed the demonstration persuaded St Petersburg workers that collaborating with non-workers was detrimental to their interests, with the result that when the Northern Union of Russian Workers was founded three years later it proceeded from 'the cardinal assumption that only workers should be permitted to enter'.[5] Thus revolutionary populism came to a head at a time when its chances of evoking sympathy among the working population of the empire's cities seemed to be diminishing rather than growing.

Nor did the populists of the 1870s find much support among peasants. The atmosphere in the countryside was less febrile in the 1870s than it had been at the time of the emancipation. Indeed, it was much more tranquil than it ought to have been. The fundamental economic problems of the peasantry had not been ameliorated by the change in their legal status. In some ways the peasants' difficulties had intensified. They were still tied to the commune and still locked into the principle of dividing the land into strips rather than fields. They had to continue paying dues to landlords so long as they remained in the state of 'temporary obligation'. Owing to the landlords' manipulation of the statutes of 1861, peasants who had moved from temporary obligation to freedom tended to be working smaller holdings than they had worked under serfdom. They also had to find cash for their redemption payments and could no longer make use of the pastures and woods which had been available to them when they belonged to the gentry. Famine in Samara in 1873 and 1874, cholera on the Volga in 1878 and 1879, the poor harvests of 1879 and 1880, high taxes, the war of 1877, the international economic depression which began in 1873 and the relative shortage of alternative employment in the towns reminded peasants that they were still at the mercy of circumstances beyond their control. They ought to have been ready to rise.

The government, moreover, believed that they might do so. The statutes of 1861 laid down that for nine years peasants would be obliged to accept whatever allocations of land the gentry decided to give them. On 19 February 1870 the nine-year period expired and the authorities expected an increase in peasant assertiveness. No such increase took place. According to figures put together by the Third Department, only 128 peasant disturbances took place in the six years 1870–5, one-sixth of the number which occurred in 1861. Admittedly, some of the disturbances were major. By the mid-1870s, for example, 50,000 former state peasants in the Chigirin district of the province of Kiev were refusing to obey the demands of the authorities. At no point, however, did problems of peasant unrest get out of hand. Between 1876 and 1881 the number of peasant disturbances only slightly exceeded the number for the period between 1870 and 1875. Very few peasants, it seemed, were prepared to ape the activities of Anton Petrov at Bezdna in 1861.[6]

'It is necessary', of course, 'to judge the scope of the peasant movement by more than the number of disturbances'.[7] Peasants rioted less often than they had in the past but were by no means content with their lot. They may have realized that circulating rumours and indulging in gossip served their purposes better than malefaction, for the authorities were better at handling opponents who came out into the open than they were at controlling chatter. Especially in the last years of the reign, peasants showed many signs of believing that the government intended to increase the size of their holdings. The idea of 'black repartition', a general redistribution of land, was not only promoted by city-based intellectuals who took an interest in the fortunes of the peasantry but also existed in the minds of the potential beneficiaries. Peasants interpreted almost any unusual activity on the part of the authorities as a sign of St Petersburg's desire to improve their lot. They took the introduction of universal military service in 1874 as evidence of the tsar's preparedness to move against the gentry. They interpreted the appearance of zemstvo statisticians in the countryside as the prelude to a revision of the emancipation settlement. In the wake of the Russo-Turkish war of 1877–8 they thought that they would receive additional land in return for their contributions to the war effort. A former rector of the St Petersburg Agricultural Institute who had been exiled to his estate in the province of Smolensk in 1870 observed of the years 1878 and 1879 that rural discussion of a revised statute of emancipation was universal. 'This thought', he said, 'is deeply embedded in the consciousness not only of the peasant (*muzhik*), but in that of every ordinary Russian person who is not himself a boss'.[8] When the nobleman Aleksandr Solov'ev attempted to kill the tsar in April 1879 peasants expressed the view that the authorities would punish the gentry for his deed by depriving them of some of their property. On 16 June 1879 the Minister of Internal Affairs, L. S. Makov, felt obliged to quash rumours of land redistribution by publishing an official statement to the effect that it formed no part of the government's plans.

The most interesting thing about disquiet in the countryside in the 1870s, however, was not its prevalence but the fact that peasants looked for relief to the tsar. They were no more interested in revolutionary answers to their problems than were their cousins in the towns. As they revealed in their reaction to Solov'ev's attempt at regicide, they thought of populist revolutionaries as bosses. Iakov Stefanovich, the city-based agitator who played a key part in exacerbating the obstreperousness of the peasants of Chigirin, achieved his objective only by forging documents in the name of the tsar. As we shall see below, students who left the towns for the countryside in the summer of 1874 in the hope of finding sympathy for a radical transformation of the existing order became extremely disillusioned. Later radicals fared no better. Rozaliia Bograd, a medical student who subsequently married Georgii Plekhanov (the organizer of the demonstration outside the Kazan' Cathedral in December 1876), spent the summer of 1877 in the village of Shirokoe in the province of Samara. Unlike many of her peers, she succeeded in establishing good relations with the local community, but she was still obliged to conclude that while 'the population of the village was of an inquisitive bent', it was 'not revolutionary'.[9] If very few peasants listened sympathetically to agitation on the part of outsiders, even fewer went beyond rumour-mongering to the practice of sedition. Petr Mart'ianov, the peasant who published an open letter to Alexander II in *The Bell* and subsequently died at hard labour, might be called the swallow who failed to make a summer.[10] Only 92 of the 662 people who were prosecuted in political trials in Russia between 1871 and 1879 belonged to the peasant estate, and 45 of them appeared in the single, highly unusual affair of the peasants of Chigirin.[11]

POPULISTS, EDUCATION, AND THE ROLE OF IDEAS

If, then, the activities which gave rise to the six great political trials of 1877 and 1878 and the subsequent attempts on the life of the tsar are not to be explained by pointing to massive popular dissatisfaction with the policies of the government, their origins must be sought elsewhere. The best places to look are the Russian educational system and the writings of a few influential ideologists. It was convenient, of course, for Russian students who fell under the influence of would-be opinion-formers to believe that there was a relationship between the world around them and the theories which attracted them, but the notion that such a relationship existed was less a re-flection of Russian reality than a function of their capacity for making the wish father to the thought.

State Secretary A. A. Polovtsov derived the impression from the trial of an obscure peasant in 1878 that 'an entirely goodhearted person who came to St Petersburg with the intention of receiving an education there was bound inevitably to become a nihilist, an enemy of the existing order'.[12] Strictly speaking he was wrong, for the overwhelming majority of those who passed through the Russian educational system in the 1860s and 1870s turned into loyal servants of the state. In a sense, however, he was right. A large proportion of the relatively small number of people who be-came 'enemies of the existing order' were better educated than their con-temporaries. Enrolment in tertiary education was not a sufficient reason for taking up radical ideas, but it came close to being a necessary qualification. Daniel Brower's investigation of radicals active in St Petersburg between 1840 and 1875 reveals that 76 per cent of the 50 who were active between 1840 and 1855, 96 per cent of the 148 who were active between 1855 and 1869, and 87 per cent of the 202 who were active between 1870 and 1875 had studied in higher educational institutions.[13] It also reveals that more radicals were active in St Petersburg in the last and shortest of Brower's three sub-periods than in either of the other two, which seems to imply that the radicalizing effects of higher education were increasing. Since the tertiary educational sector was growing in size, however, speculating on the rate of radicalization is difficult. Not only did the number of students in Russian universities increase by 67 per cent between 1869 and 1882,[14] but tertiary-level education was available in a growing number of technical col-leges. As we shall see, the Petrovskaia Agricultural Academy in Moscow became the principal recruiting ground for a famous dissident almost im-mediately after its foundation in 1865.

Why a minority of Russian students became radicals when the majority did not is a question which has never been answered satisfactorily. Answers couched in terms of social origins founder on the fact that most students still belonged to the ranks of the gentry. It is true that, by more or less banning members of the clerical estate from entering universities in March 1879,[15] the government gave the impression that it thought radicals sprang from the lower orders. It is also true that many gentry were too poor to differ significantly from members of the estates beneath them, that the proportion of non-gentry students was slowly rising, and that more than two-thirds of the St Petersburg activists of the first half of the 1870s at-tended tertiary educational institutions in which the composition of the stu-dent body was less gentry-dominated than it was in the universities. Activists of the 1870s nevertheless included Petr Kropotkin, who came from a long line of princes, and Sofia Perovskaia, whose forebears in-cluded governors, ministers, ambassadors, and the morganatic spouse of a tsar. Explaining why Russian aristocrats became radicals is about as easy as explaining why Patti Hearst joined the Symbionese Liberation Army. Very few populists, however, came from the lowest rungs of society, and hardly any could say with Andrei Zheliabov that by birth they were peasants.

Some of the students who became radicals undoubtedly became dependent on the material and psychological support they received in tight-knit student circles. Under Alexander II a significant proportion of Russian university students attended universities far from their homes. In the academic year 1877–8 991 of the 1,418 students at St Petersburg University had received their secondary education outside the St Petersburg educational district.[16] Equivalent figures for the other universities of the empire were much smaller, but it was not until the reign of Alexander III that the government required people who sought a university education to attend their local institution. It was hardly surprising that students who were effectively migrants looked to each other for support, or that in certain circumstances a student self-help group might turn from the pursuit of comfort and entertainment to political ideas, the desire to convert others, and a belief in the need for action. What effected the transformation, however, is hard to pin down.

A major factor seems to have been reading matter. Chernyshevskii's novel *What is to be Done?*, Vasilii Bervi-Flerovskii's *The Condition of the Working Class in Russia*, Nikolai Mikhailovskii's essay 'What is Progress?', Petr Lavrov's *Historical Letters*, and Mikhail Bakunin's *Statism and Anarchy* notably altered the intellectual environment.

Chernyshevskii wrote *What is to be Done?* in the Peter and Paul Fortress after his arrest in July 1862. Incredibly, in what was 'perhaps the most spectacular example of bureaucratic bungling in the cultural realm during the reign of Alexander II',[17] the censors allowed the novel to appear in print in 1863. Subtitled 'Tales about New People', it centred on Vera Pavlovna Rozal'skaia, the daughter of a St Petersburg apartment block caretaker who escaped the philistinism of her parents. What endeared the novel to readers was its message that ordinary people could take charge of their lives. Chernyshevskii introduced a god-like background figure, Rakhmetov, to emphasize that his major protagonists were unexceptional. If Vera Pavlovna could throw off the ties that bound her, so could others. In an open address to his readers, the novelist put the point bluntly: 'Come up out of your godforsaken underworld, my friends, come up. It's not so difficult'.[18]

The nature of the 'godforsaken underworld' in which most Russians dwelt was the subject of Bervi-Flerovskii's *Condition of the Working Class in Russia*, 'an exhaustive survey of the nation's misery' which appeared in St Petersburg in 1869.[19] Aleksandra Kornilova, who read the book with Sof'ia Perovskaia almost as soon as it came out, spoke for many of her peers when she said that it evoked 'intense sympathy for the sufferings of the people, their unbearable labour and extraordinary ignorance'.[20] A circle of St Petersburg dissidents showed the importance they attached to the book by reprinting it in 1872. When Rozaliia Bograd sought to raise the political consciousness of a Samara shoemaker in 1877, she used Bervi-Flerovskii to broaden his horizons.

319

Thus radicals derived inspiration from empirical literature as well as from fiction. When they read Mikhailovskii, Lavrov and Bakunin, they entered the realm of political and sociological theory. Mikhailovskii's 'What is Progress?' (1869) taught that 'an exclusively objective evaluation cannot give a complete picture of the facts of social life'.[21] Progress, in other words, was spiritual as well as material; people had the power to influence the world around them. Lavrov's *Historical Letters*, which appeared in the form of essays in 1868 and 1869 and as a book in 1870, went beyond Mikhailovskii by arguing that developed individuals not only had the power to make a mark on the world around them, but were under an obligation to do so. In Lavrov's opinion, leading a just life meant not only attending to 'the development of one's personality in physical, intellectual, and moral respects', but also atoning for the selfishness on which personal fulfilment depended by furthering civilization rather than merely acting as its custodian.[22]

Mikhail Bakunin called Lavrov's ideas 'meaningless scholarly twaddle',[23] but not for the obvious reason that they made excessive demands on their adherents. He thought they would prove ineffectual. Even if people took them seriously, he believed, change would be long delayed and slow. The object of Bakunin's *Statism and Anarchy*, which was printed in Switzerland in 1873 but quickly penetrated the Russian countryside, was to effect change quickly. Bakunin did not believe the transformation of the Russian Empire had to be put off until intellectuals had developed their personalities and accumulated disciples. People who adopted this view had got hold of the wrong end of the stick; 'in order to alter thought,' Bakunin said, 'one must first of all change life'.[24] He rejected the notion that 'changing life' was a distant prospect. He thought the conditions for changing Russia were present already. Unlike most theorists of populism, he trusted the people to know their best interests. Their communal traditions, he thought, had prepared them for that 'anarchy' which was infinitely preferable to the growth of the state. Non-peasants who sought the destruction of the state needed only to move into the countryside and light the touch-paper of revolution.

The overwhelming effect of Russian ideological tracts of the 1860s and 1870s was to encourage their readers to believe that the circumstances in which ordinary people lived their lives were unbearable and could and should be altered. Many readers also formed the impression that action had to be taken quickly. The first volume of Karl Marx's *Capital*, which appeared in German in 1867 and in Russian translation in 1872, inveighed against the pernicious effects of capitalism in western Europe. The capitalist mode of production was gaining ground in Russia and threatened to depress the condition of the population still further. That populists feared the coming of capitalism is certain. The title of Bervi-Flerovskii's book was an obvious echo of Engels's *Condition of the Working Class in England in 1844*, and the records of the court which tried most of the populists who were prosecuted in the 1870s showed that many of them had a certain acquaintance with the writings of Marx.[25] Edward Acton has made clear that populists were not averse to industrialization *per se*, but rejected the kind that was taking place in the west.[26] According to populists, Russian industrialization had to rest on the communal traditions of the Russian countryside. Like Marx, populists held that socialism was a laudable goal, but they sought to arrive at it by a different route. They rejected the materialist notion of unavoidable economic stages. The structure of Russian society, they believed, was unique. Whereas western societies could achieve socialism only by experiencing capitalism first, the survival in Russia of the peasant commune gave Russians the chance to generate a socialist order on the back of feudalism. As late as 1885 Lev Tikhomirov argued that the Russian variant of socialism would not be 'the product of the development only of "capitalist production"', but would rather be marked by 'the coming together of the surviving forms of communal Russia with the socializing life of Europe'.[27] By the mid-1880s many populists were changing their views (Tikhomirov himself was to become a monarchist), but in the 1870s their commitment to the possibility of a 'Russian road to socialism' was well-nigh total. Marx (and the emancipation of the serfs) made them feel that the Russian road might shortly be closed. The need for haste was considerable.

KARAKOZOV AND NECHAEV

Because none of the ideological tracts which the educated and the semi-educated devoured in the 1860s and 1870s made clear how the objectives in which populists believed were to be attained, activists had to work out modes of operation for themselves. Violence seemed to be the keynote in the 1860s; propagandistic activities at the beginning of the 1870s; agitation in 1874; a combination of agitation and propaganda between 1875 and 1878; and violence between 1879 and 1881. The swings of the pendulum were so great that, as both Boris Koz'min and Richard Pipes have pointed out,[28] subsuming all the revolutionary activity of the 1860s and 1870s under the single name 'populism' is probably a mistake. It is certainly anachronistic, for in the language of the period the term 'populist' (*narodnik*) referred only to a dissident who took up residence in the countryside with the object of getting to know the peasantry. Nikolai Morozov, who became a leading advocate of the use of terror, said that in the first half of the 1870s the people whom historians have dubbed populists were known simply as 'radicals' (by contrast with 'liberals', who spoke of freedom but did nothing to promote it, and 'nihilists', who were characterized by the eccentricity of their manners).[29] Although virtually all Russian dissidents of the 1860s and 1870s sought to promote the people at the expense of the state, the narrative of their activities reveals extensive tactical differences.

According to Franco Venturi, still the major non-Russian historian of the Russian dissident movements of the 1860s and 1870s, 'the first purely and typically Populist nucleus' was that which produced Dmitrii Karakozov, the man who fired on Alexander II in 1866 and was at least partly responsible for the government's abandonment of reform.[30] Having been expelled from Kazan' University for involvement in the disturbances of 1861, the mentally unstable Karakozov returned to his studies in 1863 but transferred to Moscow University in 1864. There he joined a circle of students led by his cousin, Nikolai Ishutin, who had been recruiting sympathizers for a year. Ostensibly, Ishutin's association was no more than another of the many self-help groups set up by students of non-metropolitan origin, but in reality it was much more dynamic. Even judging by the highly suspect evidence which members of the circle gave to the crown's investigators, Ishutin's coadjutors exemplified the entire range of contemporary dissident ideologies. Some of them believed in putting the existing machinery of state to new uses, some wanted to alter it, some to consign it to oblivion. Karakozov was in the first camp. The point of killing the tsar, he said, was to place on the throne the reform-minded Grand Duke Konstantin Nikolaevich. Ivan Khudiakov, the circle's agent in St Petersburg, portrayed himself as a believer in constitutionalism and gradualism. The government could be pressurized, he thought, into summoning an 'Assembly of the Land' (a representative body employed by Muscovite tsars in the sixteenth and seventeenth centuries). Ishutin went further. The authorities ought to think long and hard, he said, about the socio-economic conditions under which the masses laboured. His own disillusionment arose from witnessing the hardships experienced by ex-serf factory workers in Kaluga in 1865. They were worse off, he thought, than they had been before the emancipation. Better working conditions would obviate the need for actions of the type undertaken by Karakozov. Ishutin envisaged a socialist order in which local communities would be the building blocks of society. Members of a community would work half the land in their own interests, half in the interests of society as a whole. Decisions affecting only a single community would be taken locally. Decisions affecting the population in general would be taken by a gathering of community representatives.

Ishutin claimed not to be an extremist. He denied contemplating the acquisition of funds by robbery and dissociated himself from Karakozov's attempt at regicide. His object, he said, was to form links with the peasantry and the urban working class in order to introduce them to socialism. When his preparations were in order, he planned to propose to the government that it accept his socialist principles. In the event of a refusal he would set in train a popular revolution. According to Khudiakov, revolution was scheduled for a point about five years ahead. Ishutin admitted that the circle had contemplated establishing a subsection called 'Hell' whose members were to be dedicated to violence, but his own view, he said, was that the proposal was unworkable. Karakozov had pressed for creating 'Hell' rapidly, but other members of the circle had demurred. 'You can imagine our horror,' said Ishutin, 'when we learned from Khudiakov that Karakozov was in St Petersburg'. The would-be assassin had been persuaded to return from the capital and go into hospital, but he had then started claiming that he would get better treatment in St Petersburg. The attempt on the tsar had taken place after his second departure for the north. Ishutin insisted that although his circle was guilty of a number of things, it did not espouse violence.[31]

The 'long-haired hulk in the red shirt' was undoubtedly lying.[32] At the point when he began his activities, the violent flysheets of 1861 and 1862 were still in the air. Intellectually, Ishutin was the heir of Petr Zaichnevskii. The evidence of junior members of the circle made it apparent that his imagination was vivid. When recruiting a seventh-grade schoolboy in Penza in 1863 he not only spoke of the need for a revolution to introduce socialism in Russia but also asserted that a 5,000-strong party committed to this objective already existed. Later, he claimed to know of a pan-European committee for organizing bomb plots. On the spectrum of political activity which ran from discussion and propaganda on the right to violence and terror on the left, his group was well to the left of centre.

They were not nearly so far to the left, however, as Sergei Nechaev, the nineteen-year-old son of a house-painter from the textile town of Ivanovo who arrived in St Petersburg just after Karakozov fired on the tsar. Less privileged and less highly educated than most of those with whom he associated, Nechaev outdid all of them in the resolution with which he dedicated himself to toppling the existing order. 'I have lived for forty years and I have met many people', said his associate Ivan Pryzhov, 'but I have never met anyone with Nechaev's energy, nor can I imagine that anyone like him exists'.[33] After coming to the capital Nechaev worked as a schoolteacher and attended lectures at St Petersburg University. Disaffection among students enabled him to form a coterie which, in the winter of 1868–9, produced an elaborate 'Programme of Revolutionary Actions'. After asserting that the condition of the masses was wretched, that the tsarist regime was incapable of undertaking economic reform, and that 'the only way out – is political revolution', the programme laid down a timetable. By May 1869 circles of dissidents were to be set up in St Petersburg and Moscow. Between May and September they were to establish additional organizations in provincial towns and draw up a detailed description of the object and methods of their organization. In October 1869 they were to return from the provinces to the centre, finalize the party rules, and 'begin systematic revolutionary activity embracing all of Russia'. A mass uprising was to take place in the spring of 1870, when, under the statutes of emancipation of 1861, the gentry would lose the right to impose land allocations on their former serfs. At that time peasants would be in a position to express the full extent of their dissatisfaction.[34]

Although disturbances among the students of St Petersburg in March 1869 produced a round of arrests which broke up Nechaev's circle and obliged him to flee abroad, he adhered to his plan of campaign. In Switzerland he gulled Mikhail Bakunin into collaborating with him on the detailed rules of his non-existent organization. Conventionally known as the 'Catechism of a Revolutionary', these rules were one of the most extraordinary products of the nineteenth-century Russian revolutionary movement. From strictly organizational matters (the construction of a network of cells, members of which were to be in touch only with the cells immediately above and below them), the 'Catechism' proceeded to the type of person whom Nechaev and Bakunin admired and the tasks which they expected their acolytes to undertake. 'The revolutionary', Nechaev believed, 'is a doomed man. He has neither his own interests, nor affairs, nor feelings, nor attachments, nor property, nor even name. Everything in him is absorbed by a single, exclusive interest, by a total concept, a total passion – revolution'. The goal of the revolutionary was 'merciless destruction'. Those in authority over society were to be executed or exploited. The people at large were to be provoked into undertaking a 'massive rebellion'.[35]

True to the schedule he had drawn up before fleeing abroad, Nechaev returned to Russia in August 1869. This time he based himself in Moscow. Students of the Petrovskaia Agricultural Academy flocked to his banner, but one of them, Ivan Ivanov, proved less compliant than the others. Nechaev and four associates murdered him. When, on 25 November 1869, Ivanov's weighted corpse was washed up on the bank of a lake in the Academy grounds, the police and the Third Department began rounding up everyone with whom Nechaev had ever been associated. Nechaev himself escaped to western Europe, but seventy-nine people stood trial between July and September 1871. The 'Programme of Revolutionary Actions' and the 'Catechism of a Revolutionary' became public knowledge. Nechaev had not only failed to promote the cause of revolution but had apparently dealt it a mortal blow. The exposure of his methods obliged potential revolutionaries to return to the drawing board. The premise on which he based his activities, moreover, had turned out to be ill founded, for the spring of 1870 went by without occasioning significant unrest in the countryside.

The trial of Nechaev's associates, remarkably enough, did the revolutionary cause some good. Despite the reform of the courts in 1864, Ishutin's circle had been tried in camera. In 1871 the authorities believed that they had such a strong case against the friends of Nechaev that they could afford to try them in public. The plan backfired; Nechaev's associates succeeded in conveying the impression that Nechaev had misled them. The scholarly Petr Tkachev, whom we shall meet again, made a particularly favourable impression on the court. His common-law wife delivered a well-received address on the oppression of Russian women. Only four of the accused, those who had participated in the murder of Ivanov, were condemned to hard labour; forty-two were acquitted. Dostoevsky vilified Nechaev in a novel (*The Devils*), but most educated contemporaries – even the poet Fedor Tiutchev and the novelist Nikolai Leskov, neither of whom was a radical – accepted the view that Nechaev's associates were more sinned against than sinning. Stung by its defeat, the government created a special department of the Senate to try future political cases. Thus Nechaev indirectly demonstrated that the tsarist authorities were less than wholly committed to the observation of legal niceties. They certainly bypassed the law in his own case, for the trial which followed his extradition from Switzerland in 1872 had the distinction of being the most improperly conducted of all the political trials held in Russia between 1871 and 1876.[36]

THE CHAIKOVTSY AND THE GOING TO THE PEOPLE

After Nechaev, Russian dissidents appeared to give up all thought of conspiracy, revolutionary cells, direct action and terror. The effect of Nechaevism on radicals was to give militancy a bad name. Populists dedicated themselves to self-education. 'Lavrovism' (the development of the individual) took precedence over 'Bakuninism' (revolutionary agitation). A seventeen-year-old youth from Astrakhan who arrived in St Petersburg in the autumn of 1869 witnessed a confusing debate among students on the question whether propaganda was preferable to terror. 'I did not know', he said, 'what it was better to start doing: distribute books or engage in murder'.[37] In keeping with most other populists at the beginning of the 1870s, he decided to distribute books. Nechaevism seemed to be a dead letter.

Circulating dissident literature lay at the heart of the activities of a group of students at the St Petersburg Medico-Surgical Academy. Known misleadingly as 'Chaikovtsy' (after N. V. Chaikovskii, an early but uninfluential member), their leader was Mark Natanson, who ran a student library at the Medical Academy from which he dispensed books on the social questions of the day. Natanson made available the radical journalists Dobroliubov and Nekrasov, the west European historians Mignet and Motley, the Russian historians Kostomarov and Shchapov, the naturalists Sechenov and Darwin, the west European socialists Lassalle and Louis Blanc, and selections from the work of Voltaire and Marx. He formed close ties with the capital's booksellers and publishers and procured works that were hard to get hold of (Bervi's *Condition of the Working Class in Russia* and Lavrov's *Historical Letters*). He made arrangements for the printing abroad of proscribed works such as the essays of Chernyshevskii and Marx's *Civil War in France* (which a member of the circle translated into Russian). His fellow 'librarian', V. M. Aleksandrov, went to Switzerland to run the group's printing press. In the summer of 1873 the Chaikovtsy purchased in Vienna everything they needed for the establishment of an underground press in Russia, though developments at home prevented them from setting it up.

The Chaikovtsy were few in number. Even counting their close associates in the women's circle of Sof'ia Perovskaia, there seem to have been only thirty-six of them.[38] Because of their hostility to the dictatorial inclinations of Nechaev, they kept their dealings informal. Between 1869 and 1871 the closest they came to a statement of aims was a document entitled 'A Programme for Circles Devoted to Self-Education and Practical Activity', which rested on the abstractions of Lavrov's *Historical Letters*. Although the authorities suppressed the circle's reprint of Bervi's *The Condition of the Working Class in Russia*, tried to prevent the Chaikovtsy from distributing Bervi's *ABC of the Social Sciences*, and pursued Natanson indefatigably, it was hard to believe that they had much to fear from a coterie whose principal interest, self-improvement, affected no one but the members.

The regime probably sensed, however, that students would be unable to confine themselves for long to the circulation of high-brow literature. Nor did they. Even in 1869 they spent their summer holidays accumulating information on conditions in the countryside. In January 1871 they arranged a meeting in St Petersburg of sympathizers from Moscow, Kiev, Khar'kov, Odessa and Kazan'. At the end of 1871 two members of the circle began making contact with factory workers. However imperfectly expressed, the desire for action was never far from the surface. It gained ground when Prince Petr Kropotkin became a member in May 1872. 'At that time,' Kropotkin said later, 'the circle had nothing revolutionary in it'.[39] In 1872 and 1873 it changed course. Kropotkin differed from the other members not only in background and age (he was thirty), but also in ideological orientation. Three months in Switzerland immediately prior to joining the Chaikovtsy had turned him into a Bakuninist. He had difficulty persuading his new associates to give up work among the educated and replace it with agitation among the common people, but gradually he developed among the Chaikovtsy the inclinations which some of them had voiced already. In late 1873 he wrote what might be called the circle's second manifesto (if the 'Programme for Circles Devoted to Self-Education' can be called the first). Entitled 'Must we concern ourselves with investigating what constitutes a perfect future order?', the essay answered its own question in the affirmative and went on to discuss what 'a perfect future order' would look like and how it was to be achieved. Kropotkin left his readers in no doubt that the future was to be socialist, that state organizations were to be eliminated, and that the present social order was to be toppled by way of popular revolution. The task of the Chaikovtsy was to bring the revolution nearer: 'our goal must be to implement our force so as to hasten this outburst, to clarify those hopes and aspirations which exist in unclear forms among the enormous majority'.[40]

Although Kropotkin by no means dominated the Chaikovtsy, by the end of 1873 intellectual currents within the circle had been running in his favour for almost two years. Members had been increasing their contacts with the factory workers of St Petersburg. Reginald Zelnik and Pamela Sears McKinsey explain this aspect of the group's activity in different ways,[41] but the question whether the Chaikovtsy thought of factory workers as displaced peasants or as proletarians is less important than the fact that their enthusiasm for making contact with non-students was growing. In 1872 Sof'ia Perovskaia investigated conditions among the peasants of Samara. In 1873 Sergei Kravchinskii and Dmitrii Rogachev conducted propaganda in the province of Tver'. The Chaikovtsy were turning from theory to practice. From seeking out the under-privileged to engaging in agitation among them was a short step. It was being given a high priority, moreover, by the 'Dolgushintsy', a rival group whose commitment to action encouraged the Chaikovtsy in the revision of their opinions. The Siberian Aleksandr Dolgushin had founded a circle in St Petersburg at about the same time as Natanson but had been arrested at the beginning of 1870 and prosecuted in the trial of Nechaev's associates in 1871. Although he and his Siberian associates had been cleared, the authorities were right to think that they were dangerous. In 1872 and 1873 they did more than their contemporaries to take the ideas of populist intellectuals to the people at large. Early in 1873 they persuaded Vasilii Bervi, author of *The Condition of the Working Class in Russia*, to put the case for social equality in a pamphlet suitable for distribution among the peasantry. In another such pamphlet the leader of the group called for the abolition of the peasants' remaining obligations to their former landlords, the redistribution of land, the replacement of long-service recruitment into the army by local military training, decent schools, the abolition of internal passports, and above all 'that the government consist not of nobles alone but of people chosen by the masses themselves'.[42] The Dolgushintsy moved to Moscow in the spring of 1873, set up an illegal printing press, began distributing their pamphlets in the countryside, and sought to promote an immediate revolution. Since Kropotkin's arguments and the natural inclinations of certain Chaikovtsy were tending towards activism already, the enthusiasm of Dolgushin's circle made a pacific approach to the need for social change look increasingly faint-hearted.

Official moves against Dolgushin and many of the Chaikovtsy prompted radicals who remained at liberty to throw caution to the winds. In the summer of 1874, rural forays of the kind undertaken by Perovskaia in 1872 and Kravchinskii in 1873 ceased to be experimental and became general. Under the slogan 'To the People!', disaffected city-based intellectuals fanned out along the highways and byways of the empire. Especially from Moscow, but also from St Petersburg, Kiev and other seats of learning, between 1,000 and 2,000 students and former students took their theories into the countryside. Their activities left traces in thirty-seven provinces of the empire.[43] Bakunin wrote in *Statism and Anarchy* in 1873 that 'The chief defect which to this day paralyzes and makes impossible a universal popular insurrection in Russia is the ... isolation and separateness of the local peasant worlds'. The duty of radicals, Bakunin thought, was to 'shatter that isolation' by introducing peasant communities to 'the vital current of revolutionary thought, will, and deed'.[44] By forsaking self-education for action the rural agitators of 1874 made plain their Bakuninism.

Their efforts, however, came to nothing, for the premise on which

Bakunin rested his arguments was mistaken. Peasant communities rejected the idea of attacking the authorities. The main effect of the 'going to the people' was to demonstrate the populists' naivety. Examples abound of the radicals' inability to convince peasants of the need for revolution. In the province of Iaroslavl', a literate peasant asked N. K. Bukh what purpose would be served by introducing elective government. After all, he said, peasants elected the heads of volosti already, but however sober and sensible a candidate appeared to be at the moment he stood for election, he soon became a rogue and a drunkard. In an address to the peasants of Vasil'evka in the province of Samara, Porfirii Voinaral'skii dwelt on his audience's tax burden, the inadequacy of their landholdings, and the frequency of hunger. When, however, he called on the peasants to turn on the upper orders, and when he claimed that if they did so the tsar would be compelled to abdicate and land would be transferred to those who worked it, his words fell on deaf ears. A peasant asked him who would deal with malefactors once the existing authorities had been removed. The reply 'The community' proved unsatisfactory, for the peasant believed that although a community could deal with a single criminal, it was incapable of dealing with ten or twenty at a time. Voinaral'skii lost his temper, called the peasants idiots, spat, and said that although the French had no tsar, they still managed to live and conduct their affairs. This argument, one suspects, carried little weight on the banks of the Volga, though it is true that in the province of Chernigov peasants expressed positive interest in the lives of the ordinary inhabitants of other countries. From the point of view of a city-based agitator, however, the Chernigovites drew strange conclusions from what they were told. On learning that in England the labour force was landless, they deduced that the English gentry had seized the commoners' property, that the same would happen in the Russian Empire unless they backed the tsar in his determination to keep the gentry at bay, that although they possessed insufficient land the tsar would give them more, and that without land it was impossible to pay taxes, fill the treasury, or keep the state in being. The agitators who conducted this exchange might have concluded with some justification that whatever advantages Bakunin discerned in anarchy, peasants were natural statists. To judge by an exchange of 1875, they were certainly not socialists. An agitator was trying to paint a picture of the socialist order which he hoped his audience would help him create. A peasant interrupted with the excited thought that, after the land had been redivided, he would make the most of the additional property which fell into his hands by hiring labour. Putting social relations on an equitable footing was going to be difficult if what peasants really wanted was the replacement of one sort of exploitation with another.[45]

It is still sometimes said that the peasantry not only failed to sympathize with urban agitators, but denounced them to the tsarist authorities. Daniel Field, however, adduces strong evidence to show that the many arrests of 1874 resulted not from denunciations on the part of peasants but from the

antipathy of 'merchants, priests, stewards, and squires'. Field acknowledges that peasants displayed an 'adamantine unresponsiveness to populist ideas' but points out that they were equally unsympathetic to enforcers
of the law. Despite their monarchism, they steered clear of the tsar's officials. Unsympathetic to the urban radicals who appeared in their midst,
they did not turn them in.[46]

The upshot of this argument is that those who 'went to the people'
might have stood a better chance of persuading peasants to see their point
of view if they had approached them with greater circumspection. If, instead of penetrating all parts of the country simultaneously and expecting
quick results, they had infiltrated the villages gradually and put down
roots, they might have seemed unimportant to the non-peasant part of the
rural population and gained the time to find peasant adherents. Some
populists drew this conclusion for themselves. Aleksandr Lukashevich admitted at the end of 1877 that at the time of the 'going to the people' he
had been extremely naive. He had decided that radicals had to acquaint
themselves with the people at large, but he had no idea how to set about
it. Since he was a Pole from the Ukrainian part of the empire, he had never
been in a Russian peasant's hut. He had believed that the only way of
bridging the gap between the peasantry and the intelligentsia was to don
peasant garb and enter the peasant milieu. With benefit of hindsight he
thought that his attitude had been ill conceived. He recommended a person who was thinking of 'going to the people' to associate first with ordinary folk in the towns – in inns, in hostels and in taverns frequented by
migrant peasants. Preparation, in other words – and by implication, gradualism – would serve the radical cause better than haste.[47]

THE RISE AND FALL OF LAND AND LIBERTY

The reaction of Lukashevich to the set-back of 1874 indicated a tendency
on the part of certain populists to turn from Bakuninism to Lavrovism. Having implied the need for preparation in his *Historical Letters* of the late
1860s, Lavrov made his views clearer after slipping out of Russia in early
1870. In the programme of his journal *Forward!* and in the essay 'Knowledge and Revolution', both of which appeared in Zurich in 1873, he emphasized that 'the reconstruction of Russian society must be carried out ...
not only *for the benefit* of the people, but also by the people'. In view of
'the unpreparedness of the majority and its low level of literacy', revolutionaries could not expect 'the reconstruction of Russian society' to take
place in the near future. They should not imagine, therefore, 'that they
have merely to join the ranks of the people'. Rather, they should prepare
themselves for heightening the masses' political consciousness 'when the

time comes'; 'only thorough knowledge provides this preparation'.[48] In these explicit statements of his political creed Lavrov was attempting to combat Bakunin's *Statism and Anarchy*. In theory Bakunin shared the view that revolutions had to be made by the people who were to benefit from them, but since he had convinced himself that the Russian peasantry were ripe for revolution already, he denied the need for time-consuming self-education on the part of revolutionaries. After the populists' failure to provoke a mass upheaval in 1874, Lavrov looked right and Bakunin wrong. The experience of defeat encouraged part of the populist movement to abandon direct action for preparation and gradualism. Thus Rozaliia Bograd spent the summer of 1877 in the province of Samara not to circulate calls for a rising, but to educate herself and the peasants. She already admired her future husband Plekhanov, but as an avowed Lavrovist fought shy of his Bakuninism. Deborah Hardy devotes a chapter of her book on the populists of the second half of the 1870s to showing that Bograd was not the only radical who believed that the correct response to the disappointments of 1874 was to continue 'going to the people', but not to expect immediate results.[49]

After 1874, however, most populists needed to feel that they were getting somewhere. Indeed, the humiliation of the arrests and the government's preparations for a massive trial (the 'trial of the 193') embittered radicals who remained at liberty and heightened their desire for action. Lavrov's plan of campaign was too slow-moving. Even Bakunin's philosophy began to seem moderate. Certain radicals felt that, if they had overestimated the revolutionary potential of the common people, the day was coming when they would have to make revolution on their own. They would have been appalled to think that they were returning to the views of Karakozov and Nechaev, but in contemplating the idea of acting without the support of the masses they were opening the door to violence. Had they but known it, the one-time Nechaevist Petr Tkachev was elaborating a philosophy to suit them. Tkachev had been arrested in 1869 and condemned at the trial of Nechaev's associates in 1871, but in late 1873 he fled to Switzerland. In emigration he enunciated ideas which differed sharply from those of Bakunin and Lavrov. Like Nechaev, but unlike all the populists of the early 1870s, Tkachev denied that the masses had to decide their own fate. On the contrary, he held that change could be effected only by a small group of conspirators. If radicals hoped to transform the Russian Empire, they had to abandon their belief in the revolutionary potential of the peasantry, accept the importance of organization, and conquer the state machine. The revolution was to be made in the name of the people, but was not to be the product of a popular revolt.

In view of the terrorist conspiracies which marked the final stage of populism, it is tempting to argue that the failure of the 'going to the people' turned radicals into supporters of Tkachev. While it can be demonstrated, however, that populists read Chernyshevskii, Bervi, Mikhailovskii, Lavrov and Bakunin, it is not easy to demonstrate that many of them read

Tkachev. Only one complete set of *The Tocsin*, the journal Tkachev published in Switzerland, is to be found in a Soviet library.[50] 'The distribution of *The Tocsin* and its influence in Russia were insignificant'.[51] Evgeniia Rudnitskaia has demonstrated a connection between Tkachevist circles abroad and a circle led by Petr Zaichnevskii in Orel between 1873 and 1877,[52] but by the mid-1870s Zaichnevskii was on the periphery of Russian revolutionary politics. S. S. Volk makes the best case for the influence of Tkachev on the terrorist phase of the populist movement,[53] but the main reason Tkachev seems important today derives from the fact that Lenin spoke highly of him more than a quarter of a century after he had elaborated his theories.[54]

Despite the populists' ignorance of Tkachev's activities, however, they edged towards similar views 'under the pressures of circumstance'.[55] They made plain in 1875 that they did not intend to take the defeat of the 'going to the people' lying down. The 'Pan-Russian Social-Revolutionary Organization', which functioned briefly in Moscow, and the 'South Russian Union of Workers', which functioned briefly in Odessa, showed that one of the ways in which they responded to lack of success in the countryside was to readdress themselves to workers in the towns.[56] In the southern part of the empire, they began to consider a mode of activity among the peasantry which depended neither on the basic assumption of 1874 (that peasants were natural revolutionaries) nor on the Lavrovist assumption that only by long residence in the villages could populists reveal to peasants where their true interests lay. This new mode of activity, the invention of Iakov Stefanovich, turned on the exploitation of the peasants' monarchism. In *Statism and Anarchy* Bakunin had called the peasants' 'faith in the tsar' one of the 'three dark features' that 'cloud the Russian people's ideal, distorting its character and very much impeding and retarding its realization'.[57] Stefanovich found a way of turning the monarchism of the peasants to the advantage of revolutionaries. His activities in the Chigirin district of the province of Kiev between 1875 and 1877 showed that certain populists had abandoned the notion of the peasants' enthusiasm for rebellion and replaced it with a readiness to engage in organization and provocation.

Stefanovich said that he first learned of the complex developments among the peasants of Chigirin from reports in the *émigré* Russian press.[58] Indirectly, he may have been aware of Ekaterina Breshko-Breshkovskaia's activities in the Chigirin district at the time of the 'going to the people'. A Chigirin peasant told Breshkovskaia in 1874 that at the beginning of the 1870s the members of a village community had protested unanimously about the activities of local land surveyors. Nineteen of the complainants had been flogged and six despatched to Siberia. The peasant concluded that nothing could be achieved by a single rural community. 'It is necessary', he said, 'to write a charter and distribute it throughout the country, to bring about a mass uprising. ... It will then be possible to deal with both the government and the army'.[59] Devising a false royal charter and distributing it among the peasants was precisely what Stefanovich did. He first appeared in Chigirin at the end of 1875. His 'primary task', he said later, 'was injecting a revolutionary element into [the peasants'] dumb protest'. He intended 'to try and create a revolutionary organization'; 'The ultimate goal of this secret peasant society was to be an insurrection'.[60] In February 1876 he set off for St Petersburg with a petition from the Chigirin peasants, returning at the end of the year with a fabricated 'Imperial Secret Charter' which called on the peasants to 'rise as one man ... and take possession of all the land'.[61] The upshot, in 1877, was probably the largest set of peasant disorders to take place anywhere in the empire in the reign of Alexander II. Many arrests ensued and forty-five peasants stood trial in Kiev in June 1879, but Stefanovich had shown what could be done by conspiratorial methods. In a heated exchange of 1878 with the ultra-Lavrovist Ukrainian *émigré* Mykhailo Drahomanov, he insisted that what the Ukraine needed was not the gradual raising of its inhabitants' consciousness but 'as many socialist revolutionaries as possible'.[62]

The implication of Stefanovich's activity was that populists would improve their chances of transforming social relations if they abandoned the idea of relying on the masses' capacity for spontaneous action and turned their minds to organization. Largely because of distaste for the strong-arm tactics of Nechaev, the radicals who belonged to the circles of the early 1870s and 'went to the people' in 1874 objected to organization on principle. After 1874, however, they thought again. When they set up a body called 'Land and Liberty' in 1876, they accepted the need for a much higher degree of coordination than had been evident in their earlier activities. The new body (which should not be confused with the organization of the same name which led a shadowy existence for a few years at the beginning of the 1860s) soon began taking steps whose effect was to change the course of Russian political life. Superficially, it lowered the populists' sights. 'We limit our demands', said the organizers, 'to those which can be realistically met in the near future, i.e. to the people's demands and desires as they stand at the moment'.[63] Ostensibly, the founders of Land and Liberty claimed to be continuing in the traditions of their predecessors – not to be leading the peasants, but following them. It was Land and Liberty that developed the practice of settling in villages rather than merely visiting them for short-lived bouts of agitation. The organizers of Land and Liberty claimed not to be interested in changing the political structure of the empire. They conceived political freedoms as by-products of their activity, 'coke in the extraction of lighting-gas, smoke when you heat a stove'.[64] On the other hand, they ruled nothing out. They were not explicitly hostile to purely political activity or even to terrorism. They did not consider state institutions inherently meretricious. Although the state was to disappear after the revolution, it was not to do so immediately. Peasants would not acquire complete control over their lives, for communes would have to give up some of their functions to a central government. Peasants lacked the sophistication to take charge of all their affairs. Land and Liberty thought of itself as the heir of the populists who had 'gone to the people', but in reality it began a shift in the direction of activities which earlier populists would have considered at odds with the social foundations of Russian society. Instead of plumbing the depths of society, the populists of the second half of the 1870s placed greater emphasis on scaling the heights.[65]

The first sign of Land and Liberty's enthusiasm for direct action was the resolution its members displayed in springing Kropotkin from gaol, an event which should have involved a red balloon and actually did involve a violinist and a specially purchased racing trotter.[66] The organization's main undertaking in 1876, however, was the demonstration outside St Petersburg's Kazan' Cathedral in December. Populists had been in contact with the workers of St Petersburg since at least 1871, but this was the first time they tried to bring them out on to the streets. They were uncertain whether the undertaking was legitimate. Lavrovists among them still believed that the common people ought to decide for themselves whether they wanted to demonstrate; Plekhanov felt that it was time to take advantage of urban unemployment and attempt to persuade workers to join forces with non-worker radicals. Since the demonstration was poorly supported and gave rise to some thirty arrests, it was a failure; but in that it taught populists that the lower orders were out of sympathy with them it confirmed the notion that if radicals were to further their objectives they would have to do so without relying on popular support.[67]

The political trials of 1877 made radicals feel that the promotion of their objectives would have to take place quickly. Whatever the government's difficulties in the war with Turkey, it seemed to be winning its battles at home. It is true that, from the government's point of view, the trials were less than satisfactory. The uncompromising speech of the factory worker Petr Alekseev at the trial of the Pan-Russian Social-Revolutionary Organization (the 'trial of the fifty') became 'a permanent fixture on the revolutionary scene during the last forty years of the tsarist regime'.[68] Ninety of those who appeared in the dock at the 'trial of the 193' were acquitted and only twenty-eight were sentenced to hard labour.[69] But although the Ministry of Justice and the Third Department complained about the Senate's leniency,[70] revolutionaries could hardly congratulate themselves on a swingeing victory. Even the defendants who gained their liberty had served years in prison before coming to trial. Meanwhile, an incident in the St Petersburg preliminary detention centre tipped populists over the brink. In July 1877 the Governor-General of St Petersburg ordered the flogging of one of the Kazan' Square demonstrators for failing to show deference towards him. Since it was illegal to subject political prisoners to corporal punishment, radicals were outraged. At a time when populist philosophy was in flux, when radicals were beginning to employ provocative tactics in both town and country, when even Bakuninism had come to seem pacific, and when the government was running an apparently endless series of prosecutions, the flogging of Bogoliubov turned out to be the straw that broke the camel's back. From setting up discussion circles, teaching factory workers to read, seeking mass support in the villages, and attempting to organize demonstrations in St Petersburg, populists moved on – or back – to terrorism. Assassinations required planning, but not the sort of lifelong preparation envisaged by Lavrov. They could be undertaken without the support of the masses. They turned out to be an imperfect tool for the realization of radical goals, but they were the perfect outlet for the populists' mounting frustration.

Paradoxically, neither of the two celebrated terrorists of 1878, Vera Zasulich and Sergei Kravchinskii, thought of terrorism as a major revolutionary tactic. The former eventually became a Marxist and the latter one of the most constitutionally orientated of all Russian *émigrés*. Yet in January 1878 Zasulich tried to kill the Governor-General of St Petersburg and in August 1878 Kravchinskii assassinated the head of the Third Department. Zasulich claimed she was repaying Governor-General Trepov for ordering Bogoliubov to be flogged, but her real reason for attacking him seems to have been personal. Her lover, Lev Deich, had been an associate of Stefanovich at Chigirin and was languishing in a Kiev gaol. Radicals in Petrograd felt they had to put off arranging his release until Trepov had been punished. To expedite matters, Zasulich attacked Trepov herself.[71] Kravchinskii went to great lengths to downplay his attack on General Mezentsev. Immediately after the murder he published *A Death for a Death*, a pamphlet which argued that his goal was the achievement of a socialist society. Political structures, he said – and therefore, political actions – were a matter of indifference to him. Russians were by nature inclined to hold back from political struggle and especially from 'all bloody measures'. Mezentsev's murder had been undertaken simply to give radicals some respite from official pressure. 'The government itself has put the dagger and the revolver in our hands'. Kravchinskii made three demands: complete freedom of speech; a complete end to arbitrary activity on the part of the administration; and a full amnesty for political prisoners. He demanded no more because he did not believe that the government could grant him more. His economic demands could be met only by the bourgeoisie. He did not ask the government to grant a constitution. 'The question whether you share power with the bourgeoisie is not our concern. Whether you grant or do not grant a constitution is a matter of complete indifference to us. Do not violate our human rights – that is all we want of you'.[72] In late October 1878, in the first number of the illegal journal *Land and Liberty*, Kravchinskii made yet plainer that terror was peripheral to the achievement of radical goals. It might bring about the downfall of the government, he said, but it 'has nothing to do with the struggle against the foundations of the existing order'. If the government fell before society had been transformed, 'then, lacking any roots in the people, we shall be unable to take advantage of our victory. It will be a Pyrrhic victory. ... At the cost of a bloody struggle and inevitable heavy sacrifices, we shall gain nothing for our cause'.[73]

To judge by Zasulich's confusion of the political with the personal and Kravchinskii's attempts to assign terrorism a back seat, populists turned to violence with a degree of hesitation. Kravchinskii, however, said one thing in public and another in private. In a letter to Zasulich of July 1878 he doubted whether the peasantry could be persuaded of the need for social transformation. 'Several years' wearisome experience', he wrote, 'is bound to convince any sober individual that "scientific socialism", the socialism of the West, bounces off the Russian masses like a pea off a wall'.[74] If a popular revolution lay far in the future, the temptation to procure change by the use of terror became considerable. Many populists succumbed to it more readily than Kravchinskii. It was ironic that the major terrorist achievements of 1878 were accomplished by doubters, but not remarkable that they happened at all. In the southern part of the empire, in Kiev, Khar'kov and Odessa, terrorist actions became regular occurrences after Zasulich set the ball rolling in St Petersburg.[75] Nikolai Morozov and Aleksandr Mikhailov disliked having to publish Kravchinskii's depreciation of terror in the first issue of *Land and Liberty*.[76] In the winter of 1878–9 populists who supported the use of terror gained the upper hand over those who did not. When Kravchinskii fled abroad to escape the police, his place in the upper echelons of the revolutionary movement was taken by the increasingly militant Lev Tikhomirov. The arrest of Dmitrii Klements early in 1879 further depleted the ranks of the gradualists. Plekhanov remained true to non-violence, but found himself marginalized. In March 1879 Morozov began publishing the fire-breathing *Land and Liberty Leaflet (Listok Zemli i voli)*. The following month Aleksandr Solov'ev tried to kill the tsar. In June 1879 proponents of terror from the southern and northern parts of the empire met at Lipetsk near Voronezh to agree their future strategy. A few days later, at Voronezh itself, populists who believed in terror met those who did not at a general session of Land and Liberty. Superficially, the two wings of the movement patched up their differences, but Plekhanov's early withdrawal from the meeting made plain that advocates of violence were defeating their rivals.[77] In St Petersburg, Plekhanov tried to regain the ground he had lost. The presence in the capital of Deich, Stefanovich and Zasulich, none of whom believed in the primacy of terror, encouraged him to think that he stood a chance of overcoming the effects of the Voronezh meeting. Sof'ia Perovskaia assured him that although she sought the murder of the tsar, she intended subsequently to return to agitation in the countryside. Others, however, proved less amenable. The rift between terrorists and pacifists deepened. By October 1879 Land and Liberty had fallen apart. Two new organizations, The People's Will and Black Repartition, took its place. By emigrating in 1880, the 'Plekhanovites' in Black Repartition implicitly accepted that leadership of the populist movement belonged henceforward to the terrorists of The People's Will.

THE PEOPLE'S WILL

The People's Will differed from its immediate predecessors not only in its commitment to terrorist tactics, but also in structure. Apart from the fact that it centred on a coterie rather than an individual, it bore a certain resemblance to Nechaev's organization of 1869. Although by 1881 it had acquired several thousand sympathizers and some five hundred full members,[78] the twenty or so people who sat on its executive committee determined policy without reference to the rank-and-file. Superficially, the organization seemed to be true to its forerunners in respect of ideology. In a programmatic statement of 1 January 1880 the executive committee proclaimed that they were 'socialists and populists' whose 'immediate task' was 'to bring about a political upheaval that would transfer power to the people'. After the tsarist regime had been overthrown, a constituent assembly was to be summoned to discover the people's wishes. The People's Will would stand for election on the basis of broad local government, freedom of expression, the independence of communes, transferring land to the peasantry, making over factories to the workers, and replacing the standing army with a territorially based militia.[79] These goals reappeared in the programme which The People's Will designed for urban workers in November 1880 and found their most strident expression in the letter which the executive committee despatched to Alexander III nine days after killing his father.[80]

Ideologically speaking, the last generation of populists seemed to be in tune with everything for which their predecessors had striven in the course of the 1870s. Closer analysis, however, tells a different story. The published programmes of The People's Will masked the fact that the movement set greater store by taking over the state machine than by abolishing it. Populists who 'went to the people' in 1874 had been attracted by the second of the two great abstractions which Bakunin discussed in *Statism and Anarchy*. The People's Will had a taste for the first. Members of the executive committee were implacably opposed to the existing government, but not to governments in general. They spoke of 'transferring power to the people', but failed to make plain how the transfer was to be effected. If, in order to organize elections to a constituent assembly, they proposed to hold power themselves, they had abandoned the conviction of earlier populists that all power tends to corrupt. They came close to implying that people could be forced to be free.

They may not have realized the direction in which their policies were tending. One scholar argues that their version of socialism meant 'not the death of statism ... but its dawn'.[81] This is too harsh a criticism if it is taken to mean that The People's Will knew what it was doing. In a letter of 1882 to their critics in the Russian revolutionary emigration, members of the executive committee who had survived the governmental onslaught which followed the assassination of the tsar claimed that 'overturning the state' was their 'to be or not to be'.[82] In the light of this assertion, accusing them of statism seems unfair. They appear not to have drawn a distinction, however, between overturning the state and overturning the government. Their prime concern was the acquisition of force. 'Is terror necessary? Are newspapers necessary? Is a change of programme necessary? Is activity among young people, workers, soldiers, the peasantry, in zemstva, in the intelligentsia and so on necessary? To all these and all similar questions we reply: how much force will this or that tactic deliver?'[83] In the view of revolutionaries who criticized The People's Will, the executive committee's obsession with force was statist. Force was what state machineries used to keep the masses in their place. Putting force before activity at the grassroots was putting the cart before the horse. Once accumulated, force was hard to give up. Revolutionaries with force at their disposal could turn into dictators.

Whether the principal figures in The People's Will would indeed have turned into dictators is a question which was never put to the test, for the murder of the tsar and failed to shake the government's resolve exposed most of the conspirators to capture. On 3 April 1881 Sof'ia Perovskaia, Andrei Zheliabov, Timofei Mikhailov, Nikolai Rysakov and Nikolai Kibal'chich went to the gallows. The authorities' determination to keep power in their hands had been growing rapidly since April 1879, when, three days after Solov'ev's attempt to kill him, Alexander II had introduced 'temporary governors-general'.[84] The regime intensified its efforts to batten down the hatches after Khalturin bombed the Winter Palace in February 1880. One of the temporary Governors-General, Mikhail Loris-Melikov, was put in charge of a 'Supreme Administrative Commission for the Maintenance of State Order and Public Tranquillity'. In an appeal to the inhabitants of St Petersburg he promised 'not to recoil from the most severe measures to punish those who are guilty of the criminal acts that are disgracing our society'.[85] After the dissolution of the Supreme Administrative Commission in August 1880 Loris-Melikov became Minister of Internal Affairs and head of a new Police Department which embarked on infiltrating the revolutionary movement with double agents. The ideology of The People's Will lived on to compete with Marxism,[86] but the organization collapsed in the mid-1880s.

Admittedly, Loris-Melikov combined the iron fist with the velvet glove. Even Russians to whom terrorism was anathema appreciated that concessions on the part of the authorities might allay discontent. When the war with Turkey was going badly in 1877, Valuev told a senior bureaucrat that 'after these military failures the government will undoubtedly want to do something for the people'.[87] Boris Chicherin responded to the terrorism of Zasulich and Kravchinskii in 1878 by recommending that the gentry be given a role in the making of government policy.[88] In the autumn of 1879 Dmitrii Miliutin advocated surrendering half the seats on the State Council to representatives elected by the zemstva.[89] In a sarcastic open letter to the head of the Supreme Administrative Commission the Ukrainian *émigré*

Mykhailo Drahomanov asked Loris-Melikov whether he was powerful enough to convoke an 'Assembly of the Land'.[90] Loris-Melikov gave the impression that he was. In April 1880 he advised the tsar to increase the involvement of the gentry, the zemstva, and municipal administrations in the making of laws which concerned them. On 28 January 1881 he proposed that the many reforms he was contemplating in the financial sphere and in local government be submitted to a consultative body to which zemstva and municipal administrations would each send two delegates.[91]

Since Loris-Melikov was probably more powerful in 1880 and 1881 than any servant of the Russian crown between 1855 and 1905,[92] it is likely that the regime would have embarked on a new round of reforms if the tsar had survived. On the morning of his death, Alexander accepted Loris-Melikov's proposals of 28 January. A week after the assassination, the prospect of reform disappeared. At a meeting of the Council of Ministers the notion of inviting public participation in the activities of the government was subjected to a withering indictment by Konstantin Pobedonostsev, the ultra-conservative Procurator of the Holy Synod. Many contributors to the debate sympathized with the views of Loris-Melikov, but the new tsar, Alexander III, took the side of his Procurator.[93] On 29 April 1881, when Alexander III publicized his belief in safeguarding 'the strength and verity of autocratic power', Loris-Melikov asked to be relieved of his duties.[94]

CONCLUSION

In 1974 Richard Pipes claimed that the decade which followed the murder of Alexander II witnessed the creation in Russia of 'a bureaucratic-police regime which ... has been in power there ever since'.[95] It is not necessary to accept this intemperate judgement to believe that the terrorist wing of the populist movement dramatically reduced Russia's chances of evolving peacefully. The tsarist regime was hardly dynamic at the point of Alexander II's death, but neither was it torpid. Although Loris-Melikov was very far from proposing the transference of power to the people, and although he planned reform under pressure from radicals, many members of the bureaucracy held that the government would have to involve sections of the community in the making of legislation if the empire was to go on competing with its rivals. After 1881 the concept of involvement became indelibly associated with the concept of regicide. If, in the first half of the 1870s, populists had all become Lavrovists instead of Bakuninists, or if, in 1879, they had all joined Black Repartition instead of The People's Will, a compromise might eventually have been effected between the government and its opponents. Terrorism made compromise impossible.

NOTES

1. N. Kh. Bunge, 'O finansovom polozhenii Rossii', in A. P. Pogrebinskii, 'Finansovaia politika tsarizma v 70 – 80- kh godakh XIX v.', IA, 1960 no. 2, pp. 132–43.
2. The quotations in this paragraph come from Michael F. Hamm, 'Continuity and Change in Late Imperial Kiev', in Hamm, ed., *The City in Late Imperial Russia* (Bloomington, Ind., 1986), p. 90 (venereal disease); Daniel R. Brower, *The Russian City between Tradition and Modernity, 1850–1900* (Berkeley, Calif., 1990), p. 87 (internal passports); and Jeffrey Brooks, *When Russia Learned to Read: Literacy and Popular Literature, 1861–1917* (Princeton, NJ, 1985), pp. 11 and 16 (peasant migration). Figures on population growth, the number of industrial workers in Moscow, and the proportion of Kievans who were born outside the city are from Hamm, 'Continuity and Change', p. 83; Robert Gohstand, 'The Shaping of Moscow by Nineteenth-Century Trade', in Hamm, ed., *The City in Russian History* (Lexington, 1976), p. 160; and *Kievskii telegraf*, 30 March 1875.
3. The information in this paragraph is taken from Cynthia H. Whittaker, *The Women's Movement During the Reign of Alexander II: A Case Study in Russian Liberalism*, on-demand supplement to JMH 48, no. 2 (June 1976); quotation from p. 9.
4. The quotations in this paragragh come from Whittaker, *Women's Movement* (above, n. 3), p. 12, and V. Ia. Laverychev, 'O nekotorykh liberal'nykh tendentsiiakh v politike tsarizma po rabochemu voprosu v nachale 70-kh godov XIX v.', IZ 115 (1987), 212–13. The figures on strikes come from B. S. Itenberg, *Dvizhenie revoliutsionnogo narodnichestva: Narodnicheskie kruzhki i 'khozhdenie v narod' v 70-kh godakh XIX v.* (Moscow, 1965), p. 64; M. I. Kheifets, 'Vtoraia revoliutsionnaia situatsiia v Rossii (K voprosu o krizise verkhov v 1879–1881 godakh)', VI, 1962 no. 2, p. 48; and R. M. Plekhanova, 'Iz vospominanii "Moia zhizn"', VI, 1970 no. 12, p. 115, n. 8. On the strike at the Nevskii works in St Petersburg in May 1870 see Reginald E. Zelnik, *Labor and Society in Tsarist Russia: The Factory Workers of St. Petersburg 1855–1870* (Stanford, Calif., 1971), pp. 331–69.
5. Reginald E. Zelnik, 'Populists and Workers: The First Encounter between Populist Students and Industrial Workers in St. Petersburg, 1871–74', SS 24 (1972–3), 269; see also Pamela Sears McKinsey, 'The Kazan Square Demonstration and the Conflict Between Russian Workers and Intelligenty', SR 44 (1985), 83–103.
6. On the lack of significant peasant disturbances around 19 February 1870 see Peter A. Zaionchkovsky, *The Abolition of Serfdom in Russia*, ed. and tr. Susan Wobst (Gulf Breeze, 1978), p. 193; for the figures in this paragraph see Itenberg, *Dvizhenie* (above, n. 4), pp. 60–1, and Peter A. Zaionchkovsky, *The Russian Autocracy in Crisis, 1878–1882*, ed. and tr. Gary M. Hamburg (Gulf Breeze, 1979), p. 32; on Anton Petrov see the opening of Chapter Nine.
7. V. A. Fedorov, 'Ideia 'chernogo peredela' v krest'ianskom dvizhenii v Rossii na rubezhe 70 – 80-kh godov XIX v.', *Vestnik Moskovskogo universiteta, Seriia 8: Istoriia*, 1982 no. 6, p. 35.
8. A. N. Engel'gardt, *Iz derevni: 12 pisem 1872–1887* (Moscow, 1987), p. 534.
9. R. M. Plekhanova, 'Iz vospominanii "Moia zhizn"', VI, 1970 no. 11, p. 109.

10. P. Mart'ianov, 'Pis'mo k Aleksandru II', *Kolokol*, 8 May 1862, pp. 1093–7; A. V. Kleiankin, 'Krest'ianin Petr Mart'ianov – korrespondent "Kolokola"', VI, 1967 no. 1, pp. 212–14.

11. N. A. Troitskii, *Tsarskie sudy protiv revoliutsionnoi Rossii: Politicheskie protsessy 1871–1880 gg.* (Saratov, 1976), pp. 338–90 (my own calculation from the author's biographical appendix).

12. A. A. Polovtsov, 'Iz dnevnika (1877–1878 gg.)', KA 33 (1929), 184.

13. Daniel R. Brower, *Training the Nihilists: Education and Radicalism in Tsarist Russia* (Ithaca, NY and London, 1975), p. 37.

14. G. I. Shchetinina, *Studenchestvo i revoliutsionnoe dvizhenie v Rossii: posledniaia chetvert' XIX v.* (Moscow, 1987), p. 27.

15. Ibid., p. 33.

16. Ibid., p. 24.

17. Joseph Frank, *Dostoevsky: The Stir of Liberation 1860–1865* (London, 1987), p. 285.

18. Nikolai Chernyshevsky, *What is to be done?*, tr. Michael R. Katz (Ithaca, NY and London, 1989), p. 313.

19. See Derek Offord, 'The Contribution of V. V. Bervi-Flerovsky to Russian Populism', SEER 66 (1988), 236–51 (quotation from p. 237).

20. V. N. Ginev, ed., *Revoliutsionery 1870-kh godov: Vospominaniia uchastnikov narodnicheskogo dvizheniia v Peterburge* (Leningrad, 1986), p. 63.

21. W. J. Leatherbarrow and D. C. Offord, eds, *A Documentary History of Russian Thought: From the Enlightenment to Marxism* (Ann Arbor, Mich., 1987), p. 259.

22. B. S. Itenberg, *P. L. Lavrov v russkom revoliutsionnom dvizhenii* (Moscow, 1988), pp. 106–7.

23. Michael Bakunin, *Statism and Anarchy*, ed. and tr. Marshall S. Shatz (Cambridge, 1990), p. 202.

24. Ibid., p. 207.

25. T. V. Antonova, '"Kapital" v revoliutsionnom podpol'e Rossii 1870-kh godov', VI, 1983 no. 3, pp. 180–3.

26. Edward Acton, 'The Russian Revolutionary Intelligentsia and Industrialization', in Roger Bartlett, ed., *Russian Thought and Society 1800–1917: Essays in Honour of Eugene Lampert* (Keele, 1984), pp. 92–113.

27. L. Tikhomirov, 'Zaprosy vremeni', *Vestnik narodnoi voli* 4 (1885), 269.

28. B. Koz'min, '"Narodniki" i "narodnichestvo"', *Voprosy literatury*, 1957 no. 9, pp. 116–35; Richard Pipes, '*Narodnichestvo:* A Semantic Enquiry', SR 23 (1964), 441–58.

29. N. A. Morozov, *Povesti moei zhizni* (2 vols, Moscow, 1962), i. 72–3.

30. Franco Venturi, *Roots of Revolution: A History of the Populist and Socialist Movements in Nineteenth-Century Russia*, tr. Francis Haskell (Chicago and London, 1983 [first published in Italian in 1952]), p. 331; on the government's abandonment of reform see pp. 263–4, above.

31. For the evidence which Ishutin and others gave to the Murav'ev Commission in the wake of Karakozov's assassination attempt see Aleksei Shilov, ed., 'Pokushenie Karakozova 4 aprelia 1866g.', KA 17 (1926), 91–137.

32. The description is that of a hostile contemporary, as quoted in M. V. Nechkina, *Vasilii Osipovich Kliuchevskii: Istoriia zhizni i tvorchestva* (Moscow, 1974), p. 127.

33. Venturi, *Roots of Revolution* (above, n. 30), p. 377.

34. For a translation of Nechaev's 'Programme of Revolutionary Actions' see Philip Pomper, *Sergei Nechaev* (New Brunswick, NJ, 1979), pp. 56–9.
35. For translations of Nechaev's 'Catechism' see Pomper, *Nechaev* (above, n. 34), pp. 90–4, and Michael Confino, ed., *Daughter of a Revolutionary: Natalie Herzen and the Bakunin / Nechayev Circle*, tr. Hilary Sternberg and Lydia Bott (London, 1974), pp. 221–30 (quotations from Pomper).
36. Troitskii, *Tsarskie sudy* (above, n. 11), p. 145. For the remarkable story of Nechaev's imprisonment in the Peter and Paul Fortress in St Petersburg, where he suborned his guards and established contact with a later generation of revolutionaries, see P. Shchegolev, *Alekseevskii ravelin: Kniga o padenii i velichii cheloveka* (Moscow, 1989 [repr. of 1929 edn.]), pp. 171–338. Still in prison, Nechaev died of scurvy in 1882.
37. V. N. Ginev, 'Blestiashchaia pleiada', in Ginev, ed., *Revoliutsionery 1870-kh godov* (above, n. 20), p. 12.
38. Itenberg, *Dvizhenie* (above, n. 4), p. 143.
39. Peter Kropotkin, *Memoirs of a Revolutionist* (Boston, Mass. and New York, 1899), p. 305.
40. Martin A. Miller, *Kropotkin* (Chicago and London, 1976), p. 104.
41. Zelnik, 'Populists and Workers' (above, n. 5); Pamela Sears McKinsey, 'From City Workers to Peasantry: The Beginning of the Russian Movement "To the People"', SR 38 (1979), 629–49.
42. For the pamphlets by Bervi and Dolgushin see V. G. Bazanov and O. B. Alekseeva, eds, *Agitatsionnaia literatura russkikh revoliutsionnykh narodnikov: Potaennye proizvedeniia 1873–1875gg.* (Leningrad, 1970), pp. 74–95 (quotation from p. 85).
43. B. S. Itenberg, 'Nachalo massovogo "khozhdeniia v narod"', IZ 69 (1961), 144.
44. Bakunin, *Statism* (above, n. 23), p. 215.
45. The examples in this paragraph come from Itenberg, *Dvizhenie* (above, n. 4), pp. 305, 314–15, 329, 342.
46. Daniel Field, 'Peasants and Propagandists in the Russian Movement to the People of 1874', JMH 59 (1987), 415–38 (quotations from pp. 437, 435).
47. A. O. Lukashevich, 'Nechto iz popytochnoi praktiki', in V. Nevskii, ed., 'K istorii "khozhdeniia v narod"', KA 15 (1926), esp. pp. 121–2.
48. Extracts from the programme of *Forward!* (third version) and from 'Knowledge and Revolution' are to be found in Leatherbarrow and Offord, *A Documentary History of Russian Thought* (above, n. 21), pp. 269–77 (quotations from pp. 269, 271).
49. Deborah Hardy, *Land and Freedom: The Origins of Russian Terrorism, 1876–1879* (New York, 1987), pp. 29–45.
50. B. M. Shakhmatov, 'Zhurnal i gazeta "Nabat" P. N. Tkacheva (ukazatel' soderzhaniia)', in B. S. Itenberg, ed., *Revoliutsionery i liberaly Rossii* (Moscow, 1990), p. 293.
51. V. A. Tvardovskaia, 'Problema gosudarstva v ideologii narodovol'chestva (1879–1883gg.)', IZ 74 (1963), 153.
52. E. L. Rudnitskaia, '"Obshchestvo narodnogo osvobozhdeniia" i ego russkie sviazi', in Itenberg, *Revoliutsionery i liberaly* (above, n. 50), pp. 140–63.
53. S. S. Volk, *Narodnaia volia 1879–1882* (Moscow and Leningrad, 1966), pp. 238–40.
54. See V. Bonch-Bruevich, 'Biblioteka i arkhiv RSDRP v Zheneve', *Krasnaia letopis'*, 1932 no. 3 (48), p. 113.

55. Deborah Hardy, *Petr Tkachev, the Critic as Jacobin* (Seattle, Wash. and London, 1977), p. 312.
56. On the Pan-Russian Social-Revolutionary Organization see Venturi, *Roots of Revolution* (above, n. 30), pp. 524–35, and Troitskii, *Tsarskie sudy* (above, n. 11), pp. 168–80; on the South Russian Union of Workers see Venturi, p. 560, and Troitskii, pp. 181–7.
57. Bakunin, *Statism* (above, n. 23), p. 206.
58. Daniel Field, *Rebels in the Name of the Tsar* (Boston, Mass., 1989), p. 203, n. 17.
59. Itenberg, *Dvizhenie* (above, n. 4), pp. 325–6.
60. Field, *Rebels* (above, n. 58), p. 137.
61. Ibid., p. 173.
62. M. P. Dragomanov (Drahomanov), 'Ukrainskaia "Gromada" v retsenzii g. Stefanovicha', in Dragomanov, *Sobranie politicheskikh sochinenii*, ed. P. B. Struve and B. Kistiakovskii (2 vols, Paris, 1905–6), ii. 228 (from the reprint of Stefanovich's attack on Drahomanov which is appended to Drahomanov's reply).
63. Koz'min, '"Narodniki" i "narodnichestvo"' (above, n. 28), p. 117.
64. Tvardovskaia, 'Problema gosudarstva' (above, n. 51), p. 154.
65. For a discussion of the ideology of Land and Liberty which makes a number of the points made here see R. V. Filippov, 'K otsenke programmnykh osnov "Zemli i voli" 70–kh godov XIX veka', VI, 1982 no. 5, pp. 16–30.
66. See Kropotkin, *Memoirs* (above, n. 39), pp. 362–77.
67. For the alienation of St Petersburg workers from populists as a result of the demonstration outside the Kazan' Cathedral see V. S. Antonov, '"Severnyi soiuz russkikh rabochikh": nekotorye voprosy istorii ego sozdaniia', VI, 1980 no. 2, esp. p. 37, and McKinsey, 'The Kazan Square Demonstration' (above, n. 5).
68. Robert Otto, 'A Note on the Speech of Peter Alekseev', SR 38 (1979), 654.
69. Troitskii, *Tsarskie sudy* (above, n. 11), p. 197.
70. See Sh. Levin, ed., 'Final protsessa 193', KA 30 (1928), 184–99.
71. For Zasulich's motives see Jay Bergman, 'Vera Zasulich, The Shooting of Trepov and the Growth of Political Terrorism in Russia, 1878–1881', *Terrorism* 4 (1980), 25–51.
72. Anon. (S. M. Kravchinskii), *Ubiistvo shefa zhandarmov general-ad'iutanta Mezentseva: Smert' za smert'!* (St Petersburg, 1878), pp. 2, 12.
73. George Vernadsky et al., eds, *A Source Book for Russian History from Early Times to 1917* (3 vols, New Haven, Conn. and London, 1972), iii. 663.
74. E. Korol'chuk, ed., 'Iz perepiski S. M. Kravchinskogo', KA 19 (1926), 196.
75. For a list of the Ukrainian terrorist actions of 1878 see V. N. Ginev and A. N. Tsamutali, 'V bor'be za svobodu', in their *'Narodnaia volia' i 'Chernyi peredel': Vospominaniia uchastnikov revoliutsionnogo dvizheniia v Peterburge v 1879–1882gg.* (Leningrad, 1989), p. 8.
76. N. A. Morozov, *Povesti* (above, n. 29), ii. 348–9.
77. For a masterly summary of the populists' complex debates in late 1878 and the first half of 1879 see V. A. Tvardovskaia, 'Krizis "Zemli i voli" v kontse 70-kh godov', *Istoriia SSSR*, 1959 no. 4, pp. 60–74.
78. Volk, *Narodnaia volia* (above, n. 53), p. 277.
79. Vernadsky, *Source Book* (above, n. 73), iii. 664.
80. For the programme of November 1880 and the letter to Alexander III see Vera Figner, *Zapechatlennyi trud* (2 vols, Moscow, 1964), i. 401–11.
81. Tvardovskaia, 'Problema gosudarstva' (above, n. 51), p. 185.

82. L. G. Deich, ed., *Gruppa 'Osvobozhdenie truda' (iz arkhivov G. V. Plekhanova, V. I. Zasulich, i L. G. Deicha* (6 vols, Moscow and Leningrad, n.d. and 1924–8), iii. 145.

83. Ibid.

84. Vernadsky, *Source Book* (above, n. 73), iii. 665.

85. Ibid.

86. See, for example, Norman M. Naimark, *Terrorists and Social Democrats: The Russian Revolutionary Movement under Alexander III* (Cambridge, Mass., 1983), and Robert Service, 'Russian Populism and Russian Marxism: Two Skeins Entangled', in Bartlett, *Russian Thought and Society* (above, n. 26), pp. 220–46.

87. Polovtsov, 'Iz dnevnika' (above, n. 12), p. 175.

88. B. N. Chicherin, *Konstitutsionnyi vopros v Rossii: rukopis' 1878 goda* (St Petersburg, 1906).

89. P. Zaionchkovskii, 'D. A. Miliutin: biograficheskii ocherk', in Miliutin, *Dnevnik*, ed. Zaionchkovskii (4 vols, Moscow, 1947–50), i. 57.

90. M. P. Dragomanov (Drahomanov), 'Solov'ia basniami ne kormiat: pis'mo k generalu Loris-Melikovu', in Dragomanov, *Sobranie politicheskikh sochinenii* (above, n. 62), ii. 259.

91. For the advice of April 1880 see Vernadsky, *Source Book* (above, n. 73), iii. 666; for the proposals of January 1881, Marc Raeff, *Plans for Political Reform in Imperial Russia, 1730–1905* (Englewood Cliffs, NJ, 1966), pp. 137–8.

92. As Thomas Pearson points out in *Russian Officialdom in Crisis: Autocracy and Local Self-Government, 1861–1900* (Cambridge, 1989), p. 103.

93. For an eye-witness account of this meeting see A. Sergeev, ed., 'K istorii Loris-Melikovskoi "konstitutsii" (Zasedanie soveta ministrov 8 marta 1881g.)', KA 8 (1925), 132–52; the views of Pobedonostsev appear on pp. 141–4.

94. Vernadsky, *Source Book* (above, n. 73), iii. 680; 'Perepiska Aleksandra III s gr. M. T. Loris-Melikovym (1880–1881gg.)', KA 8 (1925), 127.

95. Richard Pipes, *Russia under the Old Regime* (Harmondsworth, 1977 [first published in 1974]), p. xvii.

Bibliography

The bibliography is confined to work in English. For some of the material in Russian and a few items in other languages see the references at the end of the chapters. Two collections of documents which cover most aspects of nineteenth-century Russian history are B. Dmytryshyn, ed., *Imperial Russia: A Source Book, 1700–1917* (3rd edn, Fort Worth, Tex., 1990) and G. Vernadsky et al., eds, *A Source Book for Russian History from Early Times to 1917* (3 vols, New Haven, Conn. and London, 1972), vols 2–3. Less wide-ranging source books appear below. To save space, I have identified authors only by surname and initials (rather than by surname and first name). The bibliography is organized as follows:

THE STATE

Tsars and reigns
Armed forces and wars
Foreign relations
Bureaucrats and the central administration
Law and the courts
Local government

IDEAS

Education
Censorship
Intellectuals
Revolutionaries

SOCIETY

Social groups in general
Nobles
Priests
Peasants
Merchants
Towns, urban workers, industry
Women
Non-Russian nationalities

THE STATE

Tsars and reigns

Jackman, S. W., ed., *Romanov Relations: The Private Correspondence of Tsars Alexander I, Nicholas I and the Grand Dukes Constantine and Michael with their sister Queen Anna Pavlovna 1817–1855* (London, 1969).

Keep, J. L. H., 'The Military Style of the Romanov Rulers', *War and Society* 1 (1983), 61–84.

Lincoln, W. B., *Nicholas I: Emperor and Autocrat of All the Russias* (London, 1978).

Lincoln, W. B., *The Great Reforms: Autocracy, Bureaucracy, and the Politics of Change in Imperial Russia* (DeKalb, Ill., 1990).

McCauley, M. and Waldron, P., *The Emergence of the Modern Russian State, 1855–81* (Basingstoke and London, 1988) (documents).

McConnell, A., *Tsar Alexander I: Paternalistic Reformer* (New York, 1970).

Mosse, W. E., *Alexander II and the Modernization of Russia* (London, 1958).

Palmer, A., *Alexander I, Tsar of War and Peace* (London, 1974).

Pereira, N. G. O., *Tsar-Liberator: Alexander II of Russia 1818–1881* (Newtonville, Mass.,1983).

Presniakov, A. E., *Emperor Nicholas I of Russia: The Apogee of Autocracy 1825–1855*, ed. and tr. J. C. Zacek (Gulf Breeze, Florida, 1974).

Riasanovsky, N. V., *Nicholas I and Official Nationality in Russia, 1825–1855* (Berkeley, Calif., 1959).

Rieber, A. J., ed., *The Politics of Autocracy: Letters of Alexander II to Prince A. I. Bariatinskii 1857–1864* (Paris and The Hague, 1966).

Rieber, A. J., 'Alexander II: A Revisionist View', JMH 43 (1971), 42–58.

Wortman, R. S., 'Images of Rule and Problems of Gender in the Upbringing of Paul I and Alexander I', in E. Mendelsohn and M. S. Shatz, eds, *Imperial Russia 1700–1917: Essays in Honor of Marc Raeff* (DeKalb, Ill.,1988), 58–75.

Wortman, R. S., 'Rule by Sentiment: Alexander II's Journeys through the Russian Empire', AHR 95 (1990), 745–71.

Armed forces and wars

Bradley, J., *Guns for the Tsar: American Technology and the Small Arms Industry in Nineteenth-Century Russia* (DeKalb, Ill.,1990).

Brooks, E. W., 'Reform in the Russian Army, 1856–1861', SR 43 (1984), 63–82.

Curtiss, J. S., *The Russian Army under Nicholas I* (Durham, NC, 1965).

Curtiss, J. S., *Russia's Crimean War* (Durham, NC, 1979).

Durova, N., *The Cavalry Maiden: Journals of a Female Russian Officer in the Napoleonic Wars*, tr. M. F. Zirin (London, 1988).

Ferguson, A. D., 'The Russian Military Settlements, 1825–1866', in A. D. Ferguson and A. Levin, eds, *Essays in Russian History: A Collection Dedicated to George Vernadsky* (Hamden, Conn., 1964), 107–28.

Garshin, V., *From the Reminiscences of Private Ivanov and other stories*, tr. P. Henry et al. (London, 1988) (fiction).

Hollingsworth, B., 'The Napoleonic Invasion of Russia and Recent Soviet Historical Writing', JMH 38 (1966), 38–52.

Jenkins, M., *Arakcheev: Grand Vizier of the Russian Empire* (London, 1969).

Josselson, M. and Josselson, D., *The Commander: A Life of Barclay de Tolly* (Oxford, 1980).

Keep, J. L. H., *Soldiers of the Tsar: Army and Society in Russia 1462–1874* (Oxford, 1985).

Keep, J. L. H., 'The Case of the Crippled Cadet: Military Justice in Russia under Nicholas I', CSP 28 (1986), 36–51.

Keep, J. L. H., 'Justice for the Troops: A Comparative Study of Nicholas I's Russia and France under Louis-Philippe', CMRS 28 (1987), 31–54.

Keep, J. L. H., 'The Sungurov Affair, 1831: A Curious Conspiracy', in E. Mendelsohn and M. S. Shatz, eds, *Imperial Russia 1700–1917: Essays in Honor of Marc Raeff* (DeKalb, Ill.,1988), 177–97.

Kimerling, E., 'Soldiers' Children, 1719–1856: a Study of Social Engineering in Imperial Russia', FOEG 30 (1982), 61–136.

Kipp, J. W., 'Consequences of Defeat: Modernizing the Russian Navy, 1856–1863', JFGO 20 (1972) 210–25.

Le Donne, J. P., 'The Administration of Military Justice under Nicholas I', CMRS 13 (1972), 180–91.

McNeal, R. H., *Tsar and Cossack, 1855–1914* (Basingstoke and London, 1987).

Miller, F. A., *Dmitrii Miliutin and the Reform Era in Russia* (Nashville, Tenn., 1968).

Pipes, R., 'The Russian Military Colonies, 1810–1831', in Pipes, *Russia Observed: Collected Essays on Russian and Soviet History* (Boulder, Colo., 1989), 83–101.

Screen, J. E. O., 'Russian Officer Training in the 1860–70s: the Helsinki Yunker School', SEER 65 (1987), 201–17.

Shaw, M. E., 'E. V. Tarle's *Krymskaia Voina*: Visions and Revisions', CASS 7 (1973), 188–208.

Stanyukovich, K., *Running to the Shrouds: Russian Sea Stories*, tr. N. Parsons (London and Boston, Mass., 1986) (fiction).

Tolstoy, L. N., *The Sebastopol Sketches*, tr. D. McDuff (Harmondsworth, 1986) (fiction).

Violette, A., 'The Grand Duke Konstantin Nikolayevich and the Reform of Naval Administration, 1855–1870', SEER 52 (1974), 584–601.

Wieczynski, J. L., 'The Mutiny of the Semenovsky Regiment in 1820', RR 29 (1970), 167–80.

Wirtschafter, E. K., *From Serf to Russian Soldier* (Princeton, NJ, 1990).

Foreign relations

Anderson, M. S., *The Eastern Question 1774–1923: A Study in International Relations* (London and Basingstoke, 1966).

Anderson, M. S., ed., *The Great Powers and the Near East 1774–1923* (London, 1970) (documents).

Atkin, M., 'The Pragmatic Diplomacy of Paul I: Russia's Relations with Asia, 1796–1801', SR 38 (1979), 60–74.

Atkin, M., *Russia and Iran, 1780–1828* (Minneapolis, Minn., 1980).

Baumgart, W., *The Peace of Paris 1856: Studies in War, Diplomacy, and Peacemaking*, tr. A. P. Saab (Oxford, 1981).

Bolsover, G. H., 'Nicholas I and the Partition of Turkey', SEER 27 (1948–9), 115–45.

Curtiss, J.S., *Russia's Crimean War* (Durham, NC, 1979).

Davison, R. H. '"Russian Skill and Turkish Imbecility": The Treaty of Kuchuk Kainardji Reconsidered', SR 35 (1976), 463–83.

Feldbaek, O., 'The Foreign Policy of Tsar Paul I, 1800–1: An Interpretation', JFGO 30 (1982), 16–36.

Geyer, D., *Russian Imperialism: The Interaction of Domestic and Foreign Policy 1860–1914*, tr. B. Little (Leamington Spa, 1987).

Gillard, D., *The Struggle for Asia 1828–1914* (London, 1977).

Grimsted, P. K., *The Foreign Ministers of Alexander I: Political Attitudes and the Conduct of Russian Diplomacy, 1801–1825* (Berkeley and Los Angeles, Calif., 1969).

Grimsted, P. K., 'Czartoryski's System for Russian Foreign Policy, 1803: A Memorandum, Edited with Introduction and Analysis', *California Slavic Studies* 5 (1970), 19–91.

Horvath, E., 'Russia and the Hungarian Revolution (1848–1849)', *The Slavonic Review* 12 (1933–34), 628–43.

Ingle, H. N., *Nesselrode and the Russian Rapprochement with Britain, 1836–1844* (Berkeley, Calif., 1976).

Jelavich, B., *Russia and the Formation of the Romanian National State 1821–1878* (Cambridge, 1984).

Jones, R. E., 'Opposition to War and Expansion in Late Eighteenth-Century Russia', JFGO 32 (1984), 34–51.

Kazemzadeh, F., *Russia and Britain in Persia 1864–1914* (New Haven, Conn., 1967).

Kennan, G. F., *The Decline of Bismarck's European Order: Franco-Russian Relations, 1875–1890* (Princeton, NJ, 1979).

Lord, R. H., 'Bismarck and Russia in 1863', AHR 29 (1923–24), 24–48.

MacKenzie, D., 'Panslavism in Practice: Cherniaev in Serbia (1876)', JMH 36 (1964), 279–97.

MacKenzie, D., *The Serbs and Russian Pan-Slavism 1875–1878* (Ithaca, NY, 1967).

Morgan, G., *Anglo-Russian Rivalry in Central Asia 1810–1895* (London, 1981).

Mosse, W. E., *The Rise and Fall of the Crimean System 1855–71* (London, 1963).

Onou, A., 'The Memoirs of Count N. Ignatyev', *The Slavonic Review* 10 (1931–32), 386–407, 627–40; 11 (1932–3), 108–25.

Paxton, R. V., 'Russian Foreign Policy and the First Serbian Uprising: Alliances, Apprehensions, and Autonomy, 1804–1807', in Wayne S. Vucinich, ed., *The First Serbian Uprising 1804–1813* (Boulder, Colo., 1982), pp. 41–70.

Petrovich, M. B., *The Emergence of Russian Panslavism 1856–1870* (New York, 1956).

Puryear, V. J., *England, Russia, and the Straits Question 1844–1856* (Berkeley, Calif., 1931).

Ragsdale, H., *Détente in the Napoleonic Era: Bonaparte and the Russians* (Lawrence, Kan., 1980).

Ragsdale, H., 'Russia, Prussia, and Europe in the Policy of Paul I', JFGO 31 (1983), 81–118.

Rich, N., *Why the Crimean War? A Cautionary Tale* (Hanover, 1985).

Roberts, I. W., *Nicholas I and the Russian Intervention in Hungary* (Basingstoke and London, 1991).

Rupp, G. H., *A Wavering Friendship: Russia and Austria 1876–1878* (Cambridge, Mass., 1941, repr. Philadelphia, Pa., 1976).

Saab, A. P., *The Origins of the Crimean Alliance* (Charlottesville, Va., 1977).

Saul, N. E., *Russia and the Mediterranean 1797–1807* (Chicago and London, 1970).

Saul, N. E., *Distant Friends: The United States and Russia, 1763–1867* (Lawrence, Kan., 1991).

Schroeder, P., *Austria, Great Britain, and the Crimean War* (Ithaca, NY, 1972).

Schroeder, P., 'The Collapse of the Second Coalition', JMH 59 (1987) 244–90.

Strong, J. W., 'Russia's Plans for an Invasion of India in 1801', CSP 7 (1965), 114–26.

Sumner, B. H., 'Ignatyev at Constantinople, 1864–1874', *The Slavonic Review* 11 (1932–33), 341–65, 556–71.

Sumner, B. H., 'The Secret Franco-Russian Treaty of 3 March 1859', EHR 48 (1933), 65–83.

Sumner, B. H., 'Russia and Panslavism in the Eighteen-Seventies', TRHS, 4th series, 18 (1935), 25–52.

Sumner, B. H., *Russia and the Balkans, 1870–1880* (Oxford, 1937).

Wetzel, D., *The Crimean War: A Diplomatic History* (Boulder, Colo., 1985).

Zawadzki, W. H., 'Prince Adam Czartoryski and Napoleonic France, 1801–1805: A Study in Political Attitudes', HJ 18 (1975), 245–77.

Zawadzki, W. H., 'Adam Czartoryski: An Advocate of Slavonic Solidarity at the Congress of Vienna', OSP 10 (1977), 73–97.

Zawadzki, W. H., 'Russia and the Re-opening of the Polish Question, 1801–1814', IHR 7 (1985), 19–44.

Bureaucrats and the central administration

Bennett, H. A., 'Evolution of the Meanings of *Chin*: An Introduction to the Russian Institution of Rank Ordering', *California Slavic Studies* 10 (1977), 1–43.

Christian, D., 'The Political Ideals of Michael Speransky', SEER 54 (1976), 192–213.

Christian, D., 'The Political Views of the Unofficial Committee in 1801: Some New Evidence', CASS 12 (1978), 247–65.

Christian, D., 'The "Senatorial Party" and the Theory of Collegial Government, 1801–1803', RR 38 (1979), 298–322.

Christian, D., 'The Supervisory Function in Russian and Soviet History', SR 41 (1982), 73–90.

Christian, D., 'Vodka and Corruption in Russia on the Eve of Emancipation', SR 46 (1987), 471–88.

Gooding, J., 'The Liberalism of Michael Speransky', SEER 64 (1986), 401–24.

Gooding, J., 'Speransky and Baten'kov', SEER 66 (1988), 400–25.

Heilbronner, H., 'Alexander III and the Reform Plan of Loris-Melikov', JMH 33 (1961), 384–97.

Jenkins, M., *Arakcheev: Grand Vizier of the Russian Empire* (London, 1969).

Kipp, J. W., 'M. Kh. Reutern on the Russian State and Economy: A Liberal Bureaucrat during the Crimean Era, 1854– 60', JMH 47 (1975), 437–59.

Kipp, J. W. and Kipp, M. A., 'The Grand Duke Konstantin Nikolaevič: The Making of a Tsarist Reformer, 1827–1853', JFGO 34 (1986), 3–18.

Kipp, J. W. and Lincoln, W. B., 'Autocracy and Reform: Bureaucratic Absolutism and Political Modernization in Nineteenth-Century Russia', RH 6 (1979), 1–21.

Lincoln, W. B., 'The Circle of the Grand Duchess Yelena Pavlovna, 1847–1861', SEER 48 (1970), 373–87.

Lincoln, W. B., 'Count P. D. Kiselev: A Reformer in Imperial Russia', *Australian Journal of Politics and History* 16 (1970), 177–88.

Lincoln, W. B., 'The Ministers of Nicholas I: A Brief Inquiry Into their Backgrounds and Service Careers', RR 34 (1975), 308–23.

Lincoln, W. B., 'Reform and Reaction in Russia: A. V. Golovnin's Critique of the 1860's', CMRS 16 (1975), 167–79.

Lincoln, W. B., 'The Daily Life of St Petersburg Officials in the Mid-Nineteenth Century', OSP 8 (1975), 82–100.

Lincoln, W. B., 'The Composition of the Imperial Russian State Council under Nicholas I', CASS 10 (1976), 369–81.

Lincoln, W. B., *Nikolai Miliutin: An Enlightened Russian Bureaucrat* (Newtonville, Mass., 1977).

Lincoln, W. B., *In the Vanguard of Reform: Russia's Enlightened Bureaucrats 1825–1861* (DeKalb, Ill., 1982).

Lincoln, W. B., *The Great Reforms: Autocracy, Bureaucracy, and the Politics of Change in Imperial Russia* (De Kalb, Ill., 1990).

McFarlin, H. A., 'The Extension of the Imperial Russian Civil Service to the Lowest Office Workers: The Creation of the Chancery Clerkship, 1827–1833', RH 1 (1974), 1–17.

Narkiewicz, O. A., 'Alexander I and the Senate Reform', SEER 47 (1969), 115–36.

Orlovsky, D. T., 'Recent Studies on the Russian Bureaucracy', RR 35 (1976), 448–67.

Orlovsky, D. T., *The Limits of Reform: The Ministry of Internal Affairs in Imperial Russia, 1802–1881* (Cambridge, Mass., 1981).

Pintner, W. M., 'The Social Characteristics of the Early Nineteenth-Century Russian Bureaucracy', SR 29 (1970), 429– 43.

Pintner, W. M. and Rowney, D. K., *Russian Officialdom: The Bureaucratization of Russian Society from the Seventeenth to the Twentieth Century* (Chapel Hill, NC, 1980), chs 8–10.

Raeff, M., *Michael Speransky: Statesman of Imperial Russia 1772–1839* (2nd edn, The Hague, 1969).

Raeff, M., 'The Bureaucratic Phenomenon of Imperial Russia', AHR 84 (1979), 399–411.

Rieber, A. J., 'Bureaucratic Politics in Imperial Russia', *Social Science History* 2 (1978), 399–413.

Roach, E. E., 'The Origins of Alexander I's Unofficial Committee', RR 28 (1969), 315–26.

Squire, P. S., *The Third Department: The Political Police in the Russia of Nicholas I* (Cambridge, 1968).

Torke, H. J., 'Continuity and Change in the Relations between Bureaucracy and Society in Russia, 1613–1861', CSS 5 (1971), 457–76.

Yaney, G. L., *The Systematization of Russian Government: Social Evolution in the Domestic Administration of Imperial Russia 1711–1905* (Urbana, Ill., 1973).

Law and the courts

Adams, B. F., 'Progress of an Idea: The Mitigation of Corporal Punishment in Russia to 1863', *The Maryland Historian* 17 (1986), 57–74.

Atwell, J. W., 'The Russian Jury', SEER 53 (1975), 44–61.

Crisp, O. and Edmondson, L., eds, *Civil Rights in Imperial Russia* (Oxford, 1989).

Czap, P., 'Peasant-Class Courts and Peasant Customary Justice in Russia, 1861–1912', JSH 1 (1967–8), 149–78.

Engelstein, L., 'Gender and the Juridical Subject: Prostitution and Rape in Nineteenth-Century Russian Criminal Codes', JMH 60 (1988), 458–95.

Frierson, C. A., 'Rural Justice in Public Opinion: The Volost' Court Debate', SEER 64 (1986), 526–45

Kutscheroff, S., 'Administration of Justice under Nicholas I of Russia', *American Slavic and East European Review* 7 (1948), 125–38.

LeDonne, J. P., 'Criminal Investigations Before the Great Reforms', RH 1 (1974), 101–18.

Pearson, T. S., 'Russian Law and Russian Justice: Activity and Problems of the Russian Justices of the Peace, 1865–1889', JFGO 32 (1984), 52–71.

Raeff, M., *Michael Speransky: Statesman of Imperial Russia 1772–1839* (2nd edn, The Hague, 1969), ch. 11.

Wagner, W. G., 'Tsarist Legal Policies at the End of the Nineteenth Century: A Study in Inconsistencies', SEER 54 (1976), 371–94.

Wortman, R. S., 'Judicial Personnel and the Court Reform of 1864', CSS 3 (1969), 224–34.

Wortman, R. S., *The Development of a Russian Legal Consciousness* (Chicago and London, 1976).

Wortman, R. S., 'The Politics of Court Reform', in D. K. Rowney and G. E. Orchard, eds, *Russian and Slavic History* (Columbus, Ohio, 1977), 10–25.

Local government

Abbott, R. J., 'Police Reform in the Russian Province of Iaroslavl, 1856–76', SR 32 (1973), 292–302.

Czap, P., 'P. A. Valuyev's Proposal for a *Vyt* Administration, 1864', SEER 45 (1967), 391–410.

Emmons, T. and Vucinich, W. S., eds, *The Zemstvo in Russia: An Experiment in Local Self-Government* (Cambridge, 1982).

Hanchett, W., 'Tsarist Statutory Regulation of Municipal Government in the Nineteenth Century', in Hamm, M. F., ed., *The City in Russian History* (Lexington, Kent., 1976), 91–114.

Hartley, J., 'Town Government in Saint Petersburg Guberniya after the Charter to the Towns of 1785', SEER 62 (1984), 61– 84.

Jones, R. E., *Provincial Development in Russia: Catherine II and Jacob Sievers* (New Brunswick, NJ, 1984).

Le Donne, J. P., 'The Provincial and Local Police under Catherine the Great, 1775–1796', CSS 4 (1970), 513–28.

Le Donne, J. P., 'Catherine's Governors and Governors-General 1763–1796', CMRS 20 (1979), 15–42.

Lincoln, W. B., 'The Russian State and its Cities: A Search for Effective Municipal Government, 1786–1842', JFGO 17 (1969), 531–41.

Lincoln, W. B., 'N. A. Miliutin and the St. Petersburg Municipal Act of 1846: A Study in Reform under Nicholas I', SR 33 (1974), 55–68.

Pearson, T. S., *Russian Officialdom in Crisis: Autocracy and Local Self-Government, 1861–1900* (Cambridge, 1989).

Robbins, R. G., *The Tsar's Viceroys: Russian Provincial Governors in the Last Years of the Empire* (Ithaca, NY, 1988).

Saltykov-Shchedrin, M. E., *The History of a Town*, tr. I. P. Foote (Oxford, 1980) (fiction).

Saltykov-Shchedrin, M. E., *The Pompadours: A Satire on the Art of Government*, tr. D. Magarshack (Ann Arbor, Mich., 1985) (fiction).

Starr, S. F., *Decentralization and Self-Government in Russia, 1830–1870* (Princeton, NJ, 1972).

Wcislo, F. W., *Reforming Rural Russia: State, Local Society, and National Politics, 1855–1914* (Princeton, NJ, 1990).

IDEAS

Education

Alston, P. L., *Education and the State in Tsarist Russia* (Stanford, Calif., 1969).

Brower, D. R., *Training the Nihilists: Education and Radicalism in Tsarist Russia* (Ithaca, NY and London, 1975).

Edwards, D. W., 'Count Joseph de Maistre and Russian Educational Policy, 1803–1828', SR 36 (1977), 54–75.

Eklof, B., *Russian Peasant Schools: Officialdom, Village Culture, and Popular Pedagogy, 1861–1914* (Berkeley, Calif., 1986).

Flynn, J. T., 'The Role of the Jesuits in the Politics of Russian Education 1801–1820', *Catholic Historical Review* 56 (1970), 249–65.

Flynn, J. T., 'Tuition and Social Class in the Russian Universities: S. S. Uvarov and "Reaction" in the Russia of Nicholas I', SR 35 (1976), 232–48.

Flynn, J. T., 'Russia's "University Question": Origins to Great Reforms 1802–1863', *History of Universities* 7 (1988), 1–35.

Flynn, J. T., *The University Reform of Alexander I 1802–1835* (Washington, DC, 1988).

McClelland, J. C., *Autocrats and Academics: Education, Culture, and Society in Tsarist Russia* (Chicago and London, 1979).

Mathes, W. L., 'The Origins of Confrontation Politics in Russian Universities: Student Activism, 1855–1861', CSS 2 (1968), 28–45.

Mathes, W. L., 'N. I. Pirogov and the Reform of University Government, 1856–1866', SR 31 (1972), 29–51.

Pushkin, M., 'Raznochintsy in the University: Government Policy and Social Change in Nineteenth-Century Russia', IRSH 26 (1981), 25–65.

Sinel, A., *The Classroom and the Chancellery: State Educational Reform in Russia under Count Dmitry Tolstoy* (Cambridge, Mass., 1973).

Walker, F. A., 'Popular Response to Public Education in the Reign of Tsar Alexander I (1801–1825)', *History of Education Quarterly*, Winter 1984, pp. 527–43.

Whittaker, C. H., *The Origins of Modern Russian Education: An Intellectual Biography of Count Sergei Uvarov, 1786–1855* (DeKalb, Ill., 1984).

Zacek, J. C., 'The Lancastrian School Movement in Russia', SEER 45 (1967), 343–67.

Zelnik, R. E., 'The Sunday-School Movement in Russia, 1859–1862', JMH 37 (1965), 151–70.

Censorship

Balmuth, D., 'Origins of the Russian Press Reform of 1865', SEER 47 (1969), 369–88.

Balmuth, D., *Censorship in Russia, 1865–1905* (Washington, DC, 1979).

Choldin, M. T., *A Fence around the Empire: Russian Censorship of Western Ideas under the Tsars* (Durham, NC, 1985).

Foote, I. P., 'Firing a Censor: The Case of N. V. Elagin, 1857', OSP 19 (1986), 116–31.

Lincoln, W. B., 'The Problem of *Glasnost'* in Mid-Nineteenth Century Russian Politics', ESR 11 (1981), 171–88.

Monas, S., *The Third Section: Police and Society in Russia under Nicholas I* (Harvard, Mass., 1961), esp. ch. 4.

Nikitenko, A., *Diary of a Russian Censor*, abridged, ed. and tr. H. S. Jacobson (Amherst, Mass., 1975).

Russo, P. A., '*Golos* and the Censorship, 1879–1883', SEER 61 (1983), 226–37.

Ruud, C. A., 'The Russian Empire's New Censorship Law of 1865', CSS 3 (1969), 235–45.

Ruud, C. A., 'Golovnin and Liberal Russian Censorship, January-June 1862', SEER 50 (1972), 198–219.

Ruud, C. A., *Fighting Words: Imperial Censorship and the Russian Press, 1804–1906* (Toronto, 1982).

Intellectuals

Acton, E., *Alexander Herzen and the Role of the Intellectual Revolutionary* (Cambridge, 1979).

Benson, S., 'The Conservative Liberalism of Boris Chicherin', FOEG 21 (1975), 17–114.

Black, J. L., *Nicholas Karamzin and Russian Society in the Nineteenth Century: A Study in Russian Political and Historical Thought* (Toronto, 1975).

Bowman, H. E., *Vissarion Belinski 1811–1848: A Study in the Origins of Social Criticism in Russia* (Cambridge, Mass., 1954).

Brown, E. J., *Stankevich and his Moscow Circle 1830–1840* (Stanford, Calif., 1966).

Christoff, P. K., *An Introduction to Nineteenth-Century Russian Slavophilism* (4 vols, The Hague, etc, 1961–91) (Studies of A. S. Khomiakov, I. V. Kireevskii, K. S. Aksakov and Iu. F. Samarin).

Field, D., 'Kavelin and Russian Liberalism', SR 32 (1973), 59–78.

Frank, J., *Dostoevsky* (Princeton, NJ, 1976–).

Gleason, A., *European and Muscovite: Ivan Kireevsky and the Origins of Slavophilism* (Cambridge, Mass., 1972).

Herzen, A., *My Past and Thoughts*, tr. C. Garnett, rev. edn. by H. Higgens (4 vols, London, 1968).

Herzen, A., *From the Other Shore and The Russian People and Socialism*, tr. M. Budberg and R. Wollheim (Oxford, 1979).

Herzen, A., *Childhood, Youth and Exile*, tr. J. D. Duff (Oxford, 1980).

Herzen, A., *Who is to Blame?*, tr. M. R. Katz (Ithaca, NY and London, 1984) (fiction).

Herzen, A., *Ends and Beginnings* (Oxford, 1985) (Selections from the Garnett translation, London, 1968).

Katz, M., *Mikhail N. Katkov: A Political Biography 1818–1887* (The Hague and Paris, 1966).

Kelly, A., '"What is real is rational": the political philosophy of B. N. Chicherin', CMRS 18 (1977), 195–222.

Leatherbarrow, W. J. and Offord, D. C., eds, *A Documentary History of Russian Thought: From the Enlightenment to Marxism* (Ann Arbor, Mich., 1987).

Lukashevich, S., *Ivan Aksakov 1823–1886: A Study in Russian Thought and Politics* (Cambridge, Mass., 1965).

McNally, R. T., *Chaadayev and his Friends: An Intellectual History of Peter Chaadayev and his Russian Contemporaries* (Tallahassee, Fla, 1971).

Malia, M., *Alexander Herzen and the Birth of Russian Socialism* (Cambridge, Mass., 1961).

Offord, D., *Portraits of Early Russian Liberals: A Study of the Thought of T. N. Granovsky, V. P. Botkin, P. V. Annenkov, A. V. Druzhinin and K. D. Kavelin* (Cambridge, 1985).

Partridge, M., *Alexander Herzen: Collected Studies* (Nottingham, 1988).

Raeff, M., *Russian Intellectual History: An Anthology* (New York, 1966).

Roosevelt, P. R., *Apostle of Russian Liberalism: Timofei Granovskii* (Newtonville, Mass., 1986).

Schapiro, L., *Rationalism and Nationalism in Russian Nineteenth-Century Political Thought* (New Haven, Conn. and London, 1967).

Schapiro, L., *Turgenev: His Life and Times* (Oxford, 1978).

Walicki, A., *The Slavophile Controversy: History of a Conservative Utopia in Nineteenth-Century Russian Thought* (Oxford, 1975).

Revolutionaries

Acton, E., 'The Russian Revolutionary Intelligentsia and Industrialization', in R. Bartlett, ed., *Russian Thought and Society 1800–1917: Essays in Honour of Eugene Lampert* (Keele, 1984), 92–113.

Bakunin, M., *Statism and Anarchy*, ed. and tr. M. Shatz (Cambridge, 1990).

Barratt, G., *Voices in Exile: The Decembrist Memoirs* (Montreal and London, 1974).

Barratt, G., *The Rebel on the Bridge: A Life of the Decembrist Baron Andrey Rozen 1800–84* (London, 1975).

Bartholomew, F. M., 'V. N. Maykov and the *Karmannyi slovar' inostrannykh slov*', SEER 62 (1984), 85–97.

Bergman, J., 'Vera Zasulich, the Shooting of Trepov, and the Growth of Political Terrorism in Russia, 1878–1881', *Terrorism* 4 (1980), 25–51.

Brower, D. R., 'Fathers, Sons, and Grandfathers: Social Origins of Radical Intellectuals in Nineteenth-Century Russia', JSH 2 (1968–9), 333–55.

Chernyshevsky, N., *What is to be Done?*, ed. and tr. M. R. Katz and W. G. Wagner (Ithaca, NY and London, 1989) (fiction).

Gleason, A., *Young Russia: The Genesis of Russian Radicalism in the 1860s* (Chicago and London, 1983).

Gooding, J., 'The Decembrists in the Soviet Union', SS 40 (1988), 196–209.

Gooding, J., 'Speransky and Baten'kov', SEER 66 (1988), 400–25.

Hardy, D., *Petr Tkachev: The Critic as Jacobin* (Seattle, Wash., and London, 1977).

Hardy, D., *Land and Freedom: The Origins of Russian Terrorism, 1876–1879* (Westport, Conn., 1987).

Kelly, A., *Mikhail Bakunin: A Study in the Psychology and Politics of Utopianism* (New Haven, Conn, and London, 1987).

Knapp, L., ed. and tr., *Dostoevsky as Reformer: The Petrashevsky Case* (Ann Arbor, Mich., 1987).

Kropotkin, P., *Memoirs of a Revolutionist* (Boston, Mass. and New York, 1899).

Lincoln, W. B., 'M. V. Butashevich-Petrashevskii and his Circle: Some Notes on the Intellectual and Social Climate of St. Petersburg in the 1840s', AJPH 19 (1973), 366–76.

Lincoln, W. B., 'A Re-examination of some Historical Stereotypes: An Analysis of the Career Patterns and Backgrounds of the Decembrists', JFGO 24 (1976), 357–68.

McKinsey, P. S., 'From City Workers to Peasantry: The Beginning of the Russian Movement "To the People"', SR 38 (1979), 629–49.

McKinsey, P. S., 'The Kazan Square Demonstration and the Conflict between Russian Workers and *Intelligenty*', SR 44 (1985), 83–103.

Mazour, A. G., *The First Russian Revolution, 1825* (Stanford, Calif., 1961).

Miller, M. A., *Kropotkin* (Chicago and London, 1976).

Naimark, N. M., *Terrorists and Social Democrats: The Russian Revolutionary Movement under Alexander III* (Cambridge, Mass., 1983).

Offord, D., *The Russian Revolutionary Movement in the 1880s* (Cambridge, 1986).

Offord, D., 'The Contribution of V. V. Bervi-Flerovsky to Russian Populism', SEER 66 (1988), 236–51.

O'Meara, P., *K. F. Ryleev: A Political Biography of the Decembrist Poet* (Princeton, NJ, 1984).

Pipes, R., '*Narodnichestvo*: A Semantic Inquiry', in Pipes, *Russia Observed: Collected Essays on Russian and Soviet History* (Boulder, Colo., 1989), 103–21.

Pomper, P., *Peter Lavrov and the Russian Revolutionary Movement* (Chicago and London, 1972).

Pomper, P., *Sergei Nechaev* (New Brunswick, NJ, 1979).

Raeff, M., *The Decembrist Movement* (Englewood Cliffs, NJ, 1966) (documents).

Seddon, J. H., *The Petrashevtsy: A Study of the Russian Revolutionaries of 1848* (Manchester, 1985).

Service, R., 'Russian Populism and Russian Marxism: Two Skeins Entangled', in R. Bartlett, ed., *Russian Thought and Society 1800–1917: Essays in Honour of Eugene Lampert* (Keele, 1984), 220–46.

356

Turgenev, I. S., *Fathers and Sons*, tr. R. Edmonds (Harmondsworth, 1965) (fiction).

Venturi, F., *Roots of Revolution: A History of the Populist and Socialist Movements in Nineteenth-Century Russia*, tr. F. Haskell (Chicago and London, 1983).

Walicki, A., *The Controversy over Capitalism: Studies in the Social Philosophy of the Russian Populists* (Oxford, 1969).

Wortman, R., *The Crisis of Russian Populism* (Cambridge, 1967).

Zelnik, R. E., 'Populists and Workers: The First Encounter between Populist Students and Industrial Workers in St. Petersburg, 1871–74', SS 24 (1972–3), 251–69.

SOCIETY

Social groups in general

Freeze, G. L., 'The *Soslovie* (Estate) Paradigm and Russian Social History', AHR 91 (1986), 11–36.

Freeze, G. L., *From Supplication to Revolution: A Documentary Social History of Imperial Russia* (New York and Oxford, 1988), pt II.

Nobles

Becker, S., *Nobility and Privilege in Late Imperial Russia* (DeKalb, Ill., 1985).

Emmons, T., *The Russian Landed Gentry and the Peasant Emancipation of 1861* (Cambridge, 1968).

Hamburg, G. M., 'Portrait of an Elite: Russian Marshals of the Nobility, 1861–1917', SR 40 (1981), 585–602.

Hamburg, G. M., *Politics of the Russian Nobility 1881–1905* (New Brunswick, NJ, 1984).

Lieven, D., *Russia's Rulers under the Old Regime* (New Haven, Conn. and London, 1989).

Manning, R. T., *The Crisis of the Old Order in Russia: Gentry and Government* (Princeton, NJ, 1982).

Pipes, R., *Karamzin's Memoir on Ancient and Modern Russia: A Translation and Analysis* (Cambridge, Mass., 1959).

Raeff, M., *Origins of the Russian Intelligentsia: The Eighteenth-Century Nobility* (New York, 1966).

Priests

Belliustin, I. S., *Description of the Clergy in Rural Russia: The Memoir of a Nineteenth-Century Parish Priest*, ed. and tr. G. L. Freeze (Ithaca, NY, and London, 1985).

Edwards, D. W., 'The System of Nicholas I in Church-State Relations', in R. L. Nichols and T. G. Stavrou, eds, *Russian Orthodoxy under the Old Regime* (Minneapolis, Minn., 1978), 154–69.

Flynn, J. T., 'The Role of the Jesuits in the Politics of Russian Education 1801–1820', *Catholic Historical Review* 56 (1970), 249–65.

Freeze, G. L., 'P. A. Valuyev and the Politics of Church Reform', SEER 56 (1978), 68–87.

Freeze, G. L., 'A Case of Stunted Anti-clericalism: Clergy and Society in Imperial Russia', ESR 13 (1983), 177–200.

Freeze, G. L., *The Parish Clergy in Nineteenth-Century Russia: Crisis, Reform, Counter-Reform* (Princeton, NJ, 1983).

Freeze, G. L., 'Handmaiden of the State? The Church in Imperial Russia Reconsidered', J Eccl Hist 36 (1985), 82–102.

Freeze, G. L., 'A Social Mission for Russian Orthodoxy: The Kazan Requiem of 1861 for the Peasants in Bezdna', in E. Mendelsohn and M. S. Shatz, eds, *Imperial Russia 1700–1917: Essays in Honor of Marc Raeff* (DeKalb, Ill., 1988), 58–75.

Freeze, G. L., 'The Orthodox Church and Serfdom in Prereform Russia', SR 48 (1989), 361–87.

Wieczynski, J. L., 'Apostle of Obscurantism: the Archimandrite Photius of Russia (1792–1838)', J Eccl Hist 22 (1971), 319–31.

Zacek, J. C., 'The Russian Bible Society and the Russian Orthodox Church', *Church History* 35 (1966), 411–37.

Peasants

Bartlett, R., ed., *Land Commune and Peasant Community in Russia: Communal Forms in Imperial and Early Soviet Society* (Basingstoke and London, 1990).

Blum, J., *Lord and Peasant in Russia from the Ninth to the Nineteenth Century* (Princeton, NJ, 1961).

Brooks, J., *When Russia Learned to Read: Literacy and Popular Literature, 1861–1917* (Princeton, NJ, 1985).

Crisp, O., 'The State Peasants under Nicholas I', in her *Studies in the Russian Economy before 1914* (London and Basingstoke, 1976), 73–95.

Czap, P. 'Peasant-Class Courts and Peasant Customary Justice in Russia, 1861–1912', JSH 1 (1967–8), 149–78.

Davison, R. M., 'Koshelyov and the Emancipation of the Serfs', ESR 3 (1973), 13–37.

Deal, Z. J., *Serf and State Peasant Agriculture: Kharkov Province 1842–1861* (New York, 1981).

Domar, E.D. and Machina, M. J., 'On the Profitability of Russian Serfdom', J Ec Hist 44 (1984), 919–55.

Druzhinin, N. M., 'The Liquidation of the Feudal System in the Russian Manorial Village 1862–1882', *Soviet Studies in History: A Journal of Translations* 21, no. 3 (1982–3), 14– 67.

Eklof, B., *Russian Peasant Schools: Officialdom, Village Culture, and Popular Pedagogy, 1861–1914* (Berkeley, Calif., 1986).

Eklof, B., 'Ways of Seeing: Recent Anglo-American Studies of the Russian Peasant (1861–1914)', JFGO 36 (1988), 57–79.

Eklof, B. and Frank, S. P., eds, *The World of the Russian Peasant: Post-Emancipation Culture and Society* (Boston, Mass., 1990).

Engel, B., 'Peasant Morality and Pre-Marital Relations in Late Nineteenth-Century Russia', JSH 23 (1989–90), 695–715.

Esper, T., 'The Condition of the Serf Workers in Russia's Metallurgical Industry, 1800–1861', JMH 50 (1978), 660–79.

Esper, T., 'The Incomes of Russian Serf Ironworkers in the Nineteenth Century', P & P 93 (1981), 137–59.

Field, D., *The End of Serfdom: Nobility and Bureaucracy in Russia, 1855–1861* (Cambridge, Mass., 1976).

Field, D., 'Peasants and Propagandists in the Russian Movement to the People of 1874', JMH 59 (1987), 415–38.

Field, D., *Rebels in the Name of the Tsar* (Boston, Mass., 1989).

Frierson, C. A., 'Rural Justice in Public Opinion: The Volost' Court Debate', SEER 64 (1986), 526–45.

Gatrell, P., *The Tsarist Economy 1850–1917* (London, 1986), ch. 4.

Gerschenkron, A., 'Agrarian Policies and Industrialization: Russia 1861–1917', in *The Cambridge Economic History of Europe* vol. 6, ed. H. J. Habakkuk and M. M. Postan (Cambridge, 1965), 706–800.

Grant, S. A., '*Obshchina* and *Mir*', SR 35 (1976), 636–51.

Haxthausen, A. von, *Studies on the Interior of Russia*, ed. S. F. Starr (Chicago and London, 1972).

Hoch, S. L., *Serfdom and Social Control in Russia: Petrovskoe, a Village in Tambov* (Chicago and London, 1986).

Hoch, S. L., 'The Banking Crisis, Peasant Reform, and Economic Development in Russia, 1857–1861', AHR 96 (1991), 795–820.

Hoch, S. L. and Augustine, W. R., 'The Tax Censuses and the Decline of the Serf Population in Imperial Russia, 1833–1858', SR 38 (1979), 403–25.

Kolchin, P., *Unfree Labor: American Slavery and Russian Serfdom* (Cambridge, Mass., 1987).

Lincoln, W. B., 'The Karlovka Reform', SR 27 (1969), 463–70.

Melton, E., 'Proto-Industrialization, Serf Agriculture and Agrarian Social Structure: Two Estates in Nineteenth-Century Russia', P & P 115 (1987), 69–106.

Melton, E., 'Enlightened Seignorialism and its Dilemmas in Serf Russia, 1750–1830', JMH 62 (1990), 675–708.

Mironov, B. N., 'The Russian Peasant Commune after the Reforms of the 1860s', SR 44 (1985), 438–67.

Moon, D., *Russian Peasants and Tsarist Legislation on the Eve of Reform: Interaction between Peasants and Officialdom, 1825–1855* (Basingstoke and London, 1992).

Pallot, J. and Shaw, D. J. B., *Landscape and Settlement in Romanov Russia 1613–1917*(Oxford, 1990), chs 4–6, 9.

Pereira, N. G. O., 'Alexander II and the Decision to Emancipate the Russian Serfs, 1855–61', CSP 22 (1980), 99–115.

Perrie, M., *Alexander II: Emancipation and Reform in Russia 1855–1881* (London, 1989: Historical Association, 'New Appreciations in History', no. 17).

Pushkarev, S. G., 'The Russian Peasants' Reaction to the Emancipation of 1861', RR 27 (1968), 199–214.

Rudolph, R. L., 'Agricultural Structure and Proto-Industrialization in Russia: Economic Development with Unfree Labor', J Ec Hist 45 (1985), 47–69.

Simms, J. Y., 'The Crisis in Russian Agriculture at the End of the Nineteenth Century: A Different View', SR 36 (1977), 377–98.

Skerpan, A. A., 'The Russian National Economy and Emancipation', in A. D. Ferguson and A. Levin, eds, *Essays in Russian History: A Collection Dedicated to George Vernadsky* (Hamden, Conn., 1964), 161–230.

Suny, R. G., '"The Peasants have Always Fed Us": The Georgian Nobility and the Peasant Emancipation, 1856–71', RR 38 (1979), 27–51.

Troinitskii, A., *The Serf Population in Russia According to the 10th National Census*, tr. E. Herman (Newtonville, Mass.,1982).

Vucinich, W. S., ed., *The Peasant in Nineteenth-Century Russia* (Stanford, Calif., 1968).

Wheatcroft, S. G., 'Crises and the Condition of the Peasantry in Late Imperial Russia', in E. Kingston-Mann and T. Mixter, eds, *Peasant Economy, Culture, and Politics of European Russia, 1800–1921* (Princeton, NJ, 1991), 128–72.

Worobec, C. D., 'Customary Law and Property Devolution among Russian Peasants in the 1870s', CSP 26 (1984), 220–34.

Worobec, C. D., 'Horse Thieves and Peasant Justice in Post-Emancipation Imperial Russia', JSH 21 (1987–8), 281–93.

Worobec, C. D., *Peasant Russia: Family and Community in the Post-Emancipation Period*(Princeton, NJ, 1991).

Zaionchkovsky, P. A., *The Abolition of Serfdom in Russia*, ed. and tr. S. Wobst (Gulf Breeze, Florida, 1978).

Zakharova, L. G., 'Autocracy and the Abolition of Serfdom in Russia, 1856–1861', *Soviet Studies in History: A Journal of Translations* 26, no. 2 (1987), 12–115.

Merchants

Christian, D., *'Living Water': Vodka and Russian Society on the Eve of Emancipation* (Oxford, 1990), esp. ch. 6.

Dowler, W., 'Merchants and Politics in Russia: The Guild Reform of 1824', SEER 65 (1987), 38–52.

Fitzpatrick, A. L., *The Great Russian Fair: Nizhnii Novgorod, 1840–90* (Basingstoke and London, 1990).

Owen, T. C., *Capitalism and Politics in Russia: A Social History of the Moscow Merchants 1855–1905* (Cambridge, 1981).

Owen, T. C., *The Corporation under Russian Law, 1800–1917* (Cambridge, 1991).

Rieber, A. J., 'The Moscow Entrepreneurial Group: The Emergence of a New Form in Autocratic Politics', JFGO 25 (1977), 1–20, 174–99.

Rieber, A. J., *Merchants and Entrepreneurs in Imperial Russia* (Chapel Hill, NC, 1982).

Towns, urban workers, industry

Bater, J. H., *St Petersburg: Industrialization and Change* (London, 1976).

Blackwell, W. L., *The Beginnings of Russian Industrialization 1800–1860* (Princeton, NJ, 1968).

Bradley, J., *Muzhik and Muscovite: Urbanization in Late Imperial Russia* (Berkeley, Calif., 1985).

Brower, D. R., 'Labor Violence in Russia in the Late Nineteenth Century', SR 41 (1982), 417–31 (with discussion at 432–53).

Brower, D. R., 'Urbanization and Autocracy: Russian Urban Development in the First Half of the Nineteenth Century', RR 42 (1983), 377–402.

Brower, D. R., *The Russian City between Tradition and Modernity, 1850–1900* (Berkeley, Calif., 1990).

Crisp, O., *Studies in the Russian Economy before 1914* (London and Basingstoke, 1976), ch. 1.

Falkus, M. E., *The Industrialisation of Russia 1700–1914* (London and Basingstoke, 1970).

Gatrell, P., *The Tsarist Economy, 1850–1917* (London, 1986), ch. 5.

Hamm, M. F., ed., *The City in Russian History* (Lexington, Kent., 1976).

Hamm, M. F., ed., *The City in Late Imperial Russia* (Bloomington, Ind., 1986).

Haywood, R. M., *The Beginning of Railway Development in Russia in the Reign of Nicholas I, 1835–1842* (Durham, NC, 1969).

Herlihy, P., *Odessa: A History 1794–1914* (Cambridge, Mass., 1986).

Johnson, R. E., *Peasant and Proletarian: The Working Class of Moscow in the Late Nineteenth Century* (Leicester, 1979).

Lincoln, W. B., 'The Russian State and its Cities: A Search for Effective Municipal Government, 1786–1842', JFGO 17 (1969), 531–41.

Lincoln, W. B., 'N. A. Miliutin and the St. Petersburg Municipal Act of 1846: A Study in Reform under Nicholas I', SR 33 (1974), 55–68.

Lindenmeyr, A., 'Raskolnikov's City and the Napoleonic Plan', SR 35 (1976), 37–47.

Pintner, W. M., *Russian Economic Policy under Nicholas I* (Ithaca, NY, 1967), ch. 6.

Schmidt, A. J., 'The Restoration of Moscow after 1812', SR 40 (1981), 37–48.

Zelnik, R. E. 'Populists and Workers: The First Encounter between Populist Students and Industrial Workers in St. Petersburg, 1871–74', SS 24 (1972–3), 251–69.

Women

Durova, N., *The Cavalry Maiden: Journals of a Female Russian Officer in the Napoleonic Wars*, tr. M. F. Zirin (London, 1988).

Engel, B. A., *Mothers and Daughters: Women of the Intelligentsia in Nineteenth-Century Russia* (Cambridge, 1983).

Engel, B. A. and Rosenthal, C. N., ed. and tr., *Five Sisters: Women Against the Tsar* (London, 1975) (memoirs).

Engelstein, L., 'Gender and the Juridical Subject: Prostitution and Rape in Nineteenth-Century Russian Criminal Codes', JMH 60 (1988), 458–95.

Freeze, G. L., 'Bringing Order to the Russian Family: Marriage and Divorce in Imperial Russia, 1760–1860', JMH 62 (1990), 709–46.

McDermid, J., 'The Influence of Western Ideas on the Development of the Woman Question in Nineteenth-Century Russian Thought', *Irish Slavonic Studies* 9 (1988) 21–36.

Maxwell, M., *Narodniki Women: Russian Women who Sacrificed themselves for the Dream of Freedom* (New York, 1990).

Ransel, D. L., ed., *The Family in Imperial Russia: New Lines of Historical Research* (Urbana, Ill. 1978)

Ransel, D. L., *Mothers of Misery: Child Abandonment in Russia* (Princeton, NJ, 1988).

Stites, R., *The Women's Liberation Movement in Russia: Feminism, Nihilism, and Bolshevism, 1860–1930* (Princeton, NJ, 1978).

Whittaker, C. H., *The Women's Movement During the Reign of Alexander II: A Case Study in Russian Liberalism*, on-demand supplement to JMH 48, no. 2 (June 1976).

Non-Russian nationalities

Allworth, E., ed., *Central Asia: 120 Years of Russian Rule* (Durham, NC, 1989).

Aronson, C., *A Jewish Life under the Tsars: Autobiography 1825–1888*, ed. and tr. N. Marsden (Totowa, NJ, 1983).

Aronson, I. M., *Troubled Waters: The Origins of the 1881 Anti-Jewish Pogroms in Russia* (Pittsburgh, Penn., 1990).

Bassin, M., 'Inventing Siberia: Visions of the Russian East in the Early Nineteenth Century', AHR 96 (1991), 763–94.

Becker, S., *Russia's Protectorates in Central Asia: Bukhara and Khiva, 1865–1924* (Cambridge, Mass., 1968).

Becker, S., 'The Muslim East in Nineteenth-Century Russian Popular Historiography', *Central Asian Survey* 5, nos 3–4 (1986), 25–47.

Brooks, E. W., 'Nicholas I as Reformer: Russian Attempts to Conquer the Caucasus, 1825–1855', in I. Banac et al., eds, *Nation and Ideology: Essays in honor of Wayne S. Vucinich* (Boulder, Colo., 1981), 227–63.

Carrère d'Encausse, H., *Islam and the Russian Empire: Reform and Revolution in Central Asia* (London, 1988).

Davies, N., *God's Playground: A History of Poland* (2 vols, Oxford, 1981).

Dmytryshyn, B. et al., ed. and tr., *The Russian American Colonies: A Documentary Record 1798–1867* (Portland, Oregon, 1989).

Flynn, J. T., 'Uvarov and the "Western Provinces": A Study of Russia's Polish Problem', SEER 64 (1986), 212–36.

Gibson, J., *Imperial Russia in Frontier America: The Changing Geography of Supply of Russian America, 1784–1867* (New York, 1976).

Henriksson, A., *The Tsar's Loyal Germans: The Riga German Community; Social Change and the Nationality Question, 1855–1905* (Boulder, Colo., 1983).

Jewsbury, G. F., *The Russian Annexation of Bessarabia, 1774–1828* (Boulder, Colo., 1976).

Jones, S. F., 'Russian Imperial Administration and the Georgian Nobility: The Georgian Conspiracy of 1832', SEER 65 (1987), 53–76.

Khalfin, N. A., *Russia's Policy in Central Asia 1857–1868*, abr. and tr. H. Evans (London, 1964).

Kirby, D. G., *Finland and Russia 1808–1920: From Autonomy to Independence: A Selection of Documents* (London and Basingstoke, 1975).

Klier, J. D., *Russia Gathers her Jews: The Origins of the 'Jewish Question' in Russia, 1772–1825* (DeKalb, Ill., 1986).

Klier, J. D., 'The Concept of "Jewish Emancipation" in a Russian Context', in Crisp, O. and Edmondson, L., eds, *Civil Rights in Imperial Russia* (Oxford, 1989), 122–44.

Koropeckyj, I. S., *Ukrainian Economic History: Interpretive Essays* (Cambridge, Mass., 1991), chs 8–13.

Leskov, N. S., *The Jews in Russia: Some Notes on the Jewish Question*, ed. and tr. H. K. Schefski (Princeton, NJ, 1986).

Leslie, R. F., *Polish Politics and the Revolution of November 1830* (London, 1956).

Leslie, R. F., *Reform and Insurrection in Russian Poland 1856–65* (Westport, Conn., 1969).

Long, J. W., *From Privileged to Dispossessed: The Volga Germans, 1860–1917* (Lincoln, Nebr., 1988).

MacKenzie, D., 'Kaufman of Turkestan: An Assessment of His Administration 1867–1881', SR 26 (1967), 265–85.

MacKenzie, D., 'Expansion in Central Asia: St. Petersburg vs. the Turkestan Generals (1863–1866)', CSS 3 (1969), 286–311.

MacKenzie, D., 'Russia's Expansion in Central Asia (1864–1885): Brutal Conquest or Voluntary Incorporation? A Review Article', CSS 4 (1970), 721–35.

O'Connor, M., 'Czartoryski, Józef Twardowski and the Reform of Vilna University, 1822–1824', SEER 65 (1987), 183–200.

Pienkos, A. T., *The Imperfect Autocrat: Grand Duke Constantine Pavlovich and the Polish Congress Kingdom* (Boulder, Colo., 1987).

Pierce, R. A., *Russian Central Asia, 1867–1917: A Study in Colonial Rule* (Berkeley, Calif., 1960).

Pipes, R., 'Catherine II and the Jews: The Origins of the Pale of Settlement', in Pipes, *Russia Observed: Collected Essays on Russian and Soviet History* (Boulder, Colo., 1989), 59–82.

Pogorelskin, A. E., '*Vestnik Evropy* and the Polish Question in the Reign of Alexander II', SR 46 (1987), 87–105.

Raeff, M., *Siberia and the Reforms of 1822* (Seattle, Wash., 1956).

Rayfield, D., *The Dream of Lhasa: The Life of Nikolay Przhevalsky (1839–88), Explorer of Central Asia* (London, 1976).

Rhinelander, A. L. H., 'The Creation of the Caucasian Vicegerency', SEER 59 (1981), 15–40.

Rhinelander, A. L. H., *Prince Michael Vorontsov: Viceroy to the Tsar* (Montreal, 1990).

Rogger, H., *Jewish Policies and Right-Wing Politics in Imperial Russia* (Basingstoke and London, 1986).

Rudnytsky, I. L., ed., *Rethinking Ukrainian History* (Edmonton, Alberta, 1981).

Rywkin, M., ed., *Russian Colonial Expansion to 1917* (London and New York, 1988).

Saunders, D., *The Ukrainian Impact on Russian Culture 1750–1850* (Edmonton, Alberta, 1985).

Stanislawski, M., *Tsar Nicholas I and the Jews: The Transformation of Jewish Society in Russia 1825–1855* (Philadelphia, 1983).

Subtelny, O., *Ukraine: A History* (Toronto, 1988).

Suny, R. G., '"The Peasants have Always Fed Us": The Georgian Nobility and the Peasant Emancipation, 1856–71', RR 38 (1979), 27–51.

Suny, R. G., 'Russian Rule and Caucasian Society in the First Half of the Nineteenth Century: The Georgian Nobility and the Armenian Bourgeoisie, 1801–1856', *Nationalities Papers* 7 (1979), 53–78.

Suny, R. G., *The Making of the Georgian Nation: From Prehistory to Soviet Rule* (London, 1989).

Thackeray, F. W., *Antecedents of Revolution: Alexander I and the Polish Kingdom, 1815–1825* (Boulder, Colo., 1980).

Thaden, E. C., ed., *Russification in the Baltic Provinces and Finland, 1855–1914* (Princeton, NJ, 1981).

Thaden, E. C., *Russia's Western Borderlands, 1710–1870* (Princeton, NJ, 1984).

Urry, J., *None But Saints: The Transformation of Mennonite Life in Russia 1789–1889* (Winnipeg, Manitoba, 1989).

Wandycz, P. S., *The Lands of Partitioned Poland, 1795–1918* (Seattle, Wash. and London, 1974).

Wood, A., ed., *The History of Siberia: From Russian Conquest to Revolution* (London and New York, 1991).

Zipperstein, S. J., *The Jews of Odessa: A Cultural History, 1794–1881* (Stanford, Calif., 1985).

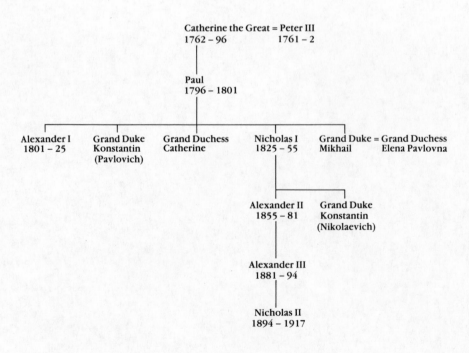

Catherine the Great = Peter III
1762 – 96   1761 – 2

Paul
1796 – 1801

Alexander I	Grand Duke	Grand Duchess	Nicholas I	Grand Duke = Grand Duchess
1801 – 25	Konstantin	Catherine	1825 – 55	Mikhail	Elena Pavlovna
	(Pavlovich)				

Alexander II   Grand Duke
1855 – 81   Konstantin
                (Nikolaevich)

Alexander III
1881 – 94

Nicholas II
1894 – 1917

Table 1. Romanov family tree, 1762–1917

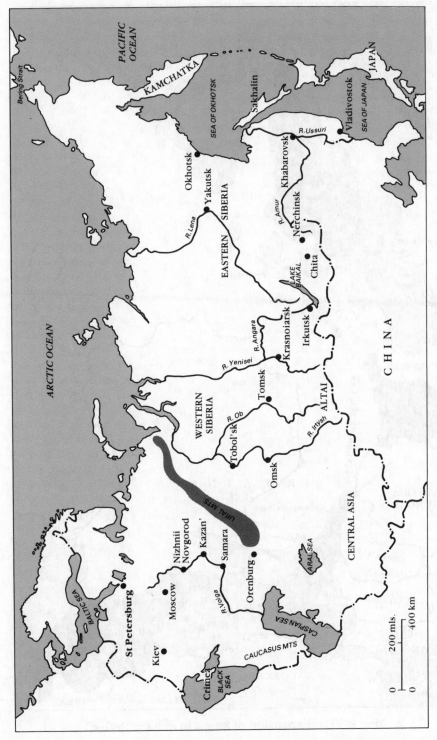

Map 1. The Russian Empire

Map 2. The Expansion of Russia in Europe 1801–81

Map 3.   The Provinces of European Russia

369

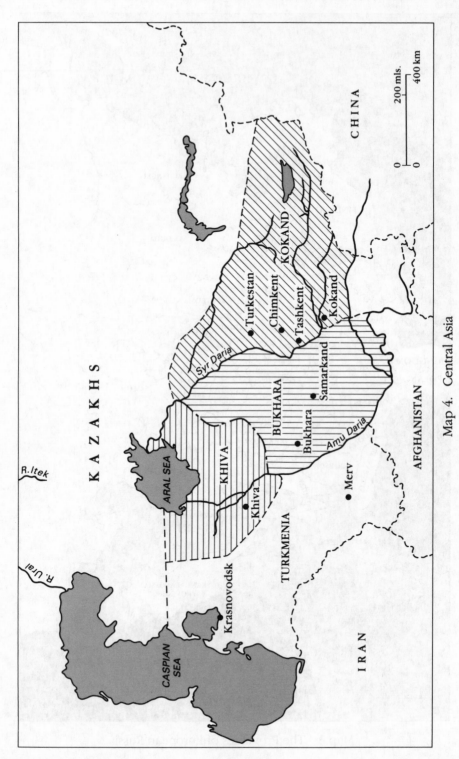

Map 4. Central Asia

Index